Laura Stone began her cycling career in Cambridge, which is as flat as a puncture patch, by speeding to Classics lectures on a £5 bike. She then graduated to the hillier polders of Holland, where she updated the *Rough Guide to the Netherlands*.

After a collision with a bus on Putney Bridge in London she got back on her bike by booking a one-way ticket to the Indian Himalaya where she pedalled around very happily for five (accident-free) months, enough to qualify her to update the mountain chapters of the *Rough Guide to India*. She spent the next two years cycling solo around the entire Himalaya to research this guidebook.

Himalaya by Bike
First edition: August 2008

Publisher
Trailblazer Publications
The Old Manse, Tower Rd, Hindhead, Surrey, GU26 6SU, UK
Fax (+44) 01428-607571
info@trailblazer-guides.com
www.trailblazer-guides.com

British Library Cataloguing in Publication Data
A catalogue record for this book is available from the British Library

ISBN 978-1-905864-04-1

Editors: Françoise Higson, Lucy Ridout, Chris Scott
Series Editor: Patricia Major
Typesetting: Chris Scott
Layout: Chris Scott & Laura Stone
Proofreading: Anna Jacomb-Hood
Cartography: Nick Hill
Index: Jane Thomas

Printed on chlorine-free paper by D2Print (☎ +65-6295 5598), Singapore

Himalaya
BY BIKE

LAURA STONE

with contributions by
EDWARD FOULKES, JACQUI FURNEAUX, JOE MEARNS
VIJAY PARMAR, STEVE PELLS, PETER QUAIFE
ROBIN SEARLE AND ERIKA BIRD

TRAILBLAZER PUBLICATIONS

Acknowledgements

The greatest thanks are to my family and to Joe who have all lived through the writing of this book. Joe and my sister Jennie deserve special mention for cycling with me in Tibet and Ladakh respectively; as do my Mum and Dad for joining me in Leh and being so valiant about altitude sickness, bed bugs and bad food. Over the last five years all my family have put me up and put up with me ricocheting between Europe and Asia; at times it must have been very difficult, especially when I set off alone to Pakistan, so a heartfelt thank you for your support.

I had the idea for *Himalaya by Bike* while eating noodles with Kym McConnell, author of Trailblazer's *Tibet Overland* (thanks, Kym!), but without Trailblazer's publisher, Bryn Thomas, this book wouldn't exist so thank you, Bryn, for your belief in adventurous guidebooks and for taking a chance that more commercial publishers would baulk at. Nick Hill, the cartographer, transformed my spaghetti-like maps into works of art (a Himalayan effort in itself) and Chris Scott, the editor, had to learn to tell his Ghulmets from his Gulmits while moving to France, writing his own book and setting off for Morocco – thanks to Françoise Higson and Lucy Ridout for the extra help. At Trailblazer I'd also like to thank eagle-eyed Anna Jacomb-Hood, the legendary and inspirational Patricia Major, Jane Thomas for her indexing skills and Corinne Sinclair for being lovely and reminding me to dress better.

Throughout the Himalaya I have met some wonderful people: the extended family of Sohail Azar in Islamabad, Kinley Tshering and his Himalayan Adventure gang in Bhutan, Satish Bardewa of Yak & Yeti in Gangtok, Pratap Chatterjee and his wife who took me out on the town in Kolkata, the family in Palchan's Shop 777, Tsunder Namgyal in Leh, Tanzin Negi in Manali, Muzffar Tholla in Srinagar, Yaqoob in Gilgit and the Qureshi family in Murree. Thanks also to fellow travellers for amusing me along the way: Simon Norris (who taught me how to mountain bike – just let go!), Adrian and Astrid, Richard Julian, Yo Giralte, David Anderson, Astrid and Stefan, Jan Elmlinger, Manja Lilek and Gregor Prosen, Chrissi Dietsche, Jim Manthorpe, Millie Perks and Rom, Tescha Beyer and Andy, Yoav Biler, Sarah White and Jean-Michel Kuhry, Kobi Haikun and Thierry Mauraton. Thanks also to my fantastic contributors (see title page) for sharing their knowledge and experience; it's a better book thanks to you!

There have also been memorable strangers: the man on Khardung La who exclaimed 'you are looking like a lady but shaking hands like a he-man!', the ladies of Hunza who gave me tea and piled fresh cherries into my panniers, a Kyrgyz lady in Xinjiang who brought thermoses of hot water, the Chinese truck driver on the Khunjerab who gave me the first orange I'd eaten in weeks, the Rupshu nomads who invited us to their wedding … all acts of hospitality and kindness, sometimes beyond people's means, which made researching this book the incredible experience it was.

A final thanks to Dutch artist Herman van Veen and his family for taking in and entertaining a lost, bedraggled and exhausted girl on a bicycle in March 2002. It was my first night of cycle touring and yet another reminder that the world out there is not to be feared but embraced.

A request

Every effort has been made by the author and the publisher to ensure that the information contained in this book is as up to date and accurate as possible. Nevertheless things will change; even before the ink is dry. If you notice any changes or omissions that you think should be included in the next edition of this book, please write to the author at laura@himalayabybike.com or c/o Trailblazer (address on p.2).

Updated information and a whole lot more at:
www.himalayabybike.com

Cover photo: On Chang La (see box p155), Ladakh, India © Laura Stone

CONTENTS

INTRODUCTION

And the only thing people regret is that they didn't live boldly enough. **Ted Hughes**

There are few places on our planet as spectacular as the Himalaya, where you can encounter everything from desert to glacier, geckos to snow toads, Sufi mystics to Buddhist monks and bamboo huts to impregnable fortresses. And there's no better way to experience this landscape than by bike: the freedom and exhilaration of riding across the world's biggest mountain range is breath-taking in both senses. As many of these rides are also in the further reaches of two emerging world powers – India and China – this is an especially exciting time to be seeing the world from a more eastern perspective.

Many people imagine the Himalaya to look like it does in the famous mountaineering images: snow, sky, not much else. Actually the snow line is usually above 6000m in summer while in winter the roads are impassable which means that most riding on the south side of the Great Himalaya will be done in a landscape of trees, while desert awaits on the Tibetan Plateau. The cycling here is a challenge but the physical effort only heightens the reward: a fantastic pass spread with prayer flags, looking onto the greatest mountain range on earth. Most people rough it on the rides and then splurge at the end on a great hotel room with a hot shower, delicious food and clean sheets; never more memorable than when so well earned! Each ride, however short, will have its ups and downs both physical and mental and, no matter how many people you may be among, this will be your own challenge. Enjoy it!

PLANNING 1

Route options

The **routes** in this book are a mix of Himalayan classics such as Manali to Leh in Ladakh and the Friendship Highway (Lhasa to Kathmandu), as well as rides in lesser-known areas such as Sikkim and Bhutan. Other routes, while legendary, are less pedalled such as the Karakoram Highway which snakes between northern Pakistan and western China. Some routes in this book have no proper name but are nicknamed by their start and end points or by the region that they travel through such as Spiti. Some simply have no label so are named by the state or country they're in, as with Sikkim and Bhutan.

HOW TO USE THE ROUTE GUIDES

The following routes are split up into suggested days representing the distance a fully loaded cycle tourer can expect to cover in good weather conditions in the recommended season. Those travelling substantially faster or slower should plan their days using the cumulative distances, maps and elevation profiles, cross-referenced with the text.

With the exception of natural disasters, the routes rarely alter but towns along them can change by the month, especially in touristy areas or in rapidly developing regions such as western China. The latest editions of mainstream guidebooks from the likes of Lonely Planet or Rough Guides will have more detailed town accounts; this book provides just a couple of recommendations to ensure you can get a meal and a roof over your head. When describing **where to stay** 'dbl' means double room, 'sing' a single room, 'com' is a communal or shared bathroom and 'att' signifies an en suite or attached bathroom (usually just a toilet and tap in budget places).

What the mainstream guidebooks usually miss out is the information between A and B which is vital to a cyclist: places to eat and sleep, the availability of water, are those 90km up- or downhill, is it tarmac or goat trail and so on. This is covered in detail in the route guides with updates posted on the book's website (see below). Don't worry if the spelling of place names differ slightly on the road!

The white-backed **route maps** are presented vertically (rather than north upwards) so that the open book can sit on a handlebar bag without the need for rotation. All the maps have been drawn from a logged GPS track. **Altitudes** and **profiles** were also derived from a GPS with a barometric altimeter, except in Sikkim where altitudes had to be obtained from a cycle computer. Distances are averaged between a GPS and a cycle computer with a discrepancy of about 2km or 3% on a typical 60km day (the GPS distance was usually shorter). As touring cyclists will know, cycle computers can differ by up to 10% from each other.

Please send updates, corrections and feedback to Trailblazer (contact details on p2) or to the website: 💻 **www.himalayabybike.com**. Here you'll also find more photos as well as Google Earth maps with the GPS waypoints and downloadable tracks in KML format.

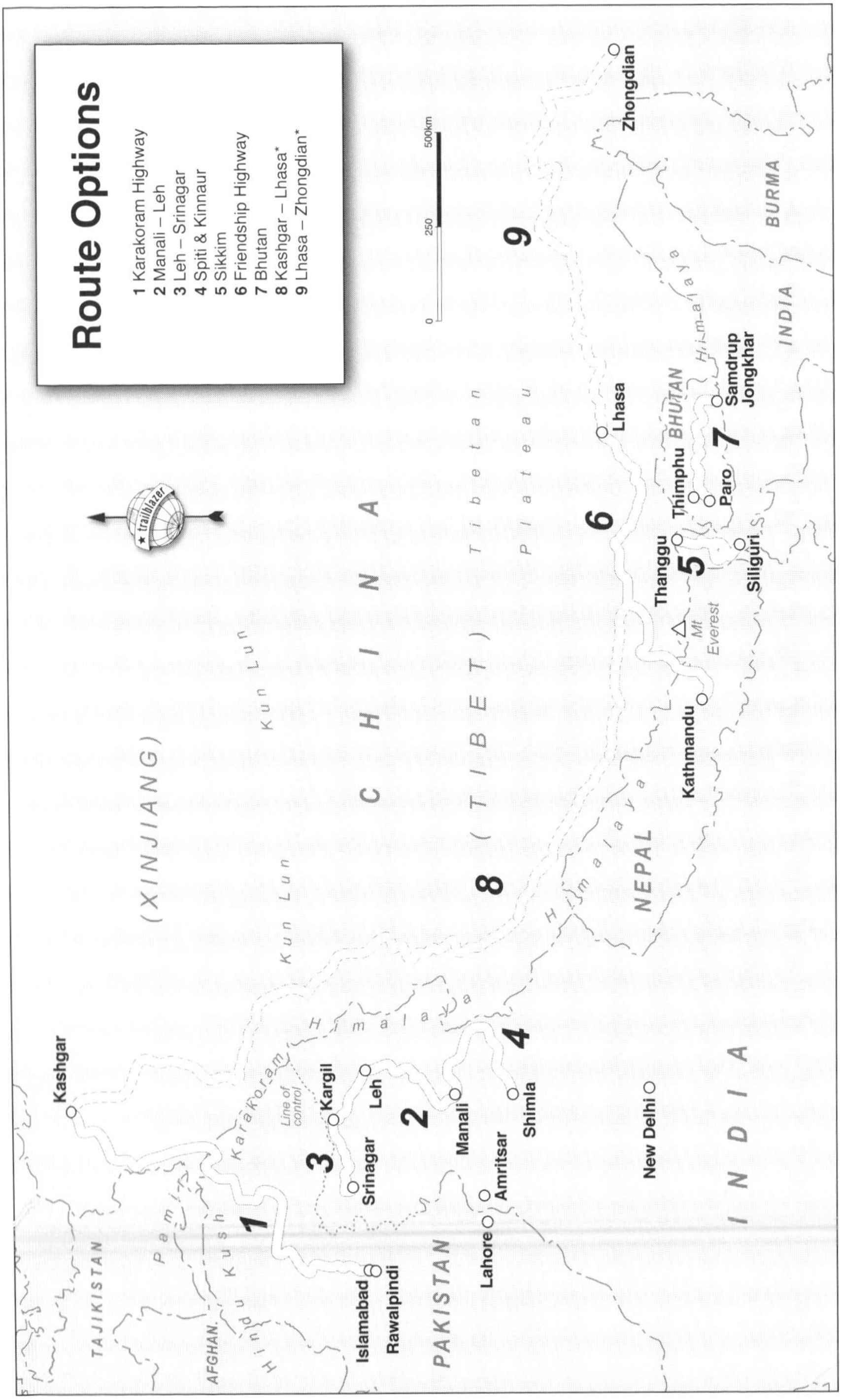
Route Options
1 Karakoram Highway
2 Manali – Leh
3 Leh – Srinagar
4 Spiti & Kinnaur
5 Sikkim
6 Friendship Highway
7 Bhutan
8 Kashgar – Lhasa*
9 Lhasa – Zhongdian*
0
250
500km
trailblazer
(XINJIANG)
CHINA
(TIBET)
Tibetan Plateau
Kun Lun
Karakoram
Himalaya
Hindu Kush
Pamir
TAJIKISTAN
AFGHAN.
PAKISTAN
INDIA
NEPAL
BHUTAN
BURMA
Kashgar
Islamabad
Rawalpindi
Srinagar
Kargil
Leh
Line of control
Manali
Lahore
Amritsar
Shimla
New Delhi
Kathmandu
Mt Everest
Thanggu
Siliguri
Thimphu
Paro
Lhasa
Samdrup Jongkhar
Zhongdian
1
2
3
4
5
6
7
8
9

RIDE NAME COUNTRY	DISTANCE kilometres / miles	DURATION (cycling days)	ALTITUDES Start	 max	 finish	RIDING DIFFICULTY	LODGING OPTIONS	ROAD CONDITIONS	COST
1 Karakoram Highway Pakistan, China	1300 km 807 miles	**1 month** (17 days)	518m (1699ft	**4695m** 15,403ft	1388m 4553ft)	🚲🚲🚲🚲 hills and heat	🏠	***	£
2 Manali–Leh India	500 km 310 miles	**21 days** (7-10 days)	2050m (6725ft	**5350m** 17,552ft	3505m 11,499ft)	🚲🚲🚲🚲 altitude, rough passes	🏕 & 🏠	***	£
3 Leh–Srinagar India	437 km 271 miles	**13 days** (7-9 days)	3505m (11,499ft	**4105m** 13,467ft	1602m 5255ft)	🚲🚲🚲 passes	🏠	****	£
4 Spiti & Kinnaur India	651 km 404 miles	**1 month** (20 days)	2050m (6725ft	**4567m** 14,983ft	2132m 6994ft)	🚲🚲🚲🚲 bad roads	🏠	**	£
5 Sikkim India	745 km 462 miles	**1 month** (20 days)	125m 410ft	**4990m** 16,371ft	1575m 5167ft	🚲🚲🚲🚲 steep	🏠	****	£
6 Friendship Highway Tibet (China), Nepal	956 km 594 miles	**3 weeks** (13 days)	3630m 11,909ft	**5251m** 17,227ft	1298m 4258ft	🚲🚲🚲🚲 winds, high passes	🏕 & 🏠	***	£
7 Bhutan (exit to India)	803 km 499 miles	**3 weeks** (14 days)	2276m 7467ft	**3743m** 12,280ft	183m 600ft	🚲🚲🚲 hilly but good tarmac	🏠	*****	£££
8 Kashgar–Lhasa* China	3000 km 1864 miles	**10 weeks** (63 days)	1310m 4298ft	**5400m** 17,716ft	3630m 11,909ft	🚲🚲🚲🚲🚲	🏕 & 🏠	**	£
9 Lhasa–Zhongdian* China	1609 km 1000 miles	**1 month** (22-26 days)	3630m 11,909ft	**5008m** 16,430ft	3250m 10,662ft	🚲🚲🚲🚲	🏕 & 🏠	**	£

* These routes covered in outline form only – see appendix (p321)

HIMALAYA – ABODE OF THE SNOWS

Between south and central Asia an immense mountain system arcs across the Indian subcontinent from Nanga Parbat in Pakistan to the highlands of Bhutan and the Indian state of Arunachal Pradesh. The entire system is known to the world by its Sanskrit name of Himalaya or 'abode of the snows'. This icy vastness comprises numerous mountain ranges of which the highest and most inhospitable is the Great Himalaya that towers over northern India, Nepal and Sikkim.

On the Great Himalaya's southern side lesser ranges, such as the Shivalik, Pir Pinjal and the Zanskar ripple into the Himalayan foothills. To the north lie the grasslands and lakes of the Tibetan plateau.

Commonly lumped in with the Himalaya, other famous ranges may be adjacent but are in fact distinct and separate geological formations. They include the **Hindu Kush** (Afghanistan, Pakistan), the **Pamirs** (Tajikistan, Kyrgyzstan, Afghanistan and Pakistan), the **Kun Lun** (China) and the **Karakoram** (Pakistan, China, India). Together these ranges (see map p8) hold over a hundred of the world's highest mountains, dominated of course by **Mt Everest** (8848m). Beyond this snowy spine of Asia the next highest peak is Aconcagua (6962m) on the border of Argentina and Chile.

The Himalaya, despite its height, is one of the youngest mountain systems on earth. Roughly 50 million years ago the Indian Plate set off across the Tethys Sea and smashed into the Eurasian Plate; we know the crumple zone as the Himalaya. Fossils of sea creatures can be seen near Kaza in Spiti (see p189) and even just below the summit of Mt Everest, which still rises annually by 5mm as the Indian Plate keep pushing north.

For pure mountain scenery the **Karakoram Highway** ('KKH', see p66) through Pakistan's Northern Areas is unsurpassed. Mountains such as Nanga Parbat (8125m/26,656ft) and Rakaposhi (7788m/25,551ft) seem almost to touch the road while their peaks soar more than six thousand metres above it. From the **Friendship Highway** (see p241) Everest's North Face is not much more than a white pointy peak on the horizon but is an awe-inspiring sight from Base Camp, a five-day detour (see p277). **Sikkim** (see p210) and **Bhutan** (see p293) are both lower in altitude with routes plunging to below 500m but what they lack in sheer altitude they make up for with hills!

Three of the routes above cross the Great Himalaya range: the **Manali–Leh Highway** at Baralacha La (4918m/16,135ft), the **Leh–Srinagar Highway** at Zoji La (3545m/11,630ft) and the **Friendship Highway** at Yarle Shung La (5140m/16,863 ft). The trans-Tibet routes from Kashgar to Lhasa and on to Zhongdian are the two highest routes, offering more **5000m passes** than anywhere else in the world. The Karakoram Highway skirts the westernmost bastion of the Himalaya between Gilgit and Tashkurgan, crossing into China at the 4695m Khunjerab Pass. Sikkim and Bhutan both lie to the south of the Great Himalaya range in the Himalayan foothills.

If **culture and religion** are a factor in choosing where you go the KKH passes through predominantly Islamic areas in both Pakistan and China; routes into and out of Ladakh blend Hinduism (Himachal Pradesh), Buddhism (Ladakh) and Islam (Kashmir). Bhutan and Tibet are both Buddhist; Sikkim is Hindu and Buddhist. Pakistan is the most **conservative** of all these areas while Bhutan is arguably the most relaxed. Safety is as much a concern in Kashmir and Assam (the exit point from eastern Bhutan) as it is in Pakistan, especially for solo women travellers (see p71); keep up to date with the news if you plan to visit.

All these routes can be ridden in their entirety except the KKH. Since 2001 the Chinese authorities have forbidden unescorted travel between the Khunjerab Pass and Tashkurgan. In practical terms this means cyclists are put on a bus between Sost in Pakistan and Tashkurgan, lopping a couple of hundred kilometres off the ride.

The difficulty rating given to the rides on the previous page is relative to the Himalaya: none of these rides can be described as a Sunday afternoon pedal along a towpath but if you're up to the challenge this really is landscape to inspire and enthral you. Because these rides are tough, **training** (see box p55) will ensure you're fit enough to enjoy the experience. The difficulty rating is based on a loaded bicycle with heavy panniers; anyone carrying little or no luggage will find the rides much easier.

If you're **short of time** another factor is how long it takes to reach the start point: see p21 for details on getting to the rides. Obtaining **visas** (see p26) can also have an influence on your itinerary. If you're travelling overland note that it can be difficult to pick up visas for Pakistan (especially in Iran). If you're already in Nepal be warned it's often impossible to enter Tibet except on an organized jeep tour; better to approach Tibet through a mainland Chinese city such as Beijing or Chengdu. It's currently impossible to enter either Tibet or China from India. Similarly, your nationality may restrict where you can travel; for example Israeli citizens cannot enter Pakistan. See the first page of the individual route chapters for overviews of the routes.

ROAD CONDITIONS

No mountain road is ever going to stay in good shape for long but some are definitely worse than others. The **KKH** is generally tarmac but prone to **landslides** from Gilgit northwards in which case you may find yourself carrying your bike over loose rockfalls. The Chinese resurfaced their side in 2005 so once past Tashkurgan the surface is excellent but in 2006 China and Pakistan

A REASSURING WORD ABOUT GRADIENTS

Initially the idea of *cycling* in the Himalaya may seem incongruous if not slightly mad. It certainly has its moments, such as when nightfall and a blizzard descend as you haul your bike over yet another landslide with a pack of Imodium and roll of Andrex not quite close enough to hand. However, one thing which is always on your side is the gradient of the roads.

Himalayan roads are playgrounds for touring cyclists but the primary purpose of most roads is usually to get troops to a border or to supply goods to remote regions. The local trucks and buses are not powered by sophisticated or modern engines though they'll often have an optimistic Mercedes Benz symbol emblazoned somewhere on their livery. Indeed, in many regions more time is spent on beautification than maintenance so the trucks grinding up and down the passes are usually travelling on a wing and a prayer. Like humans, internal combustion engines struggle as atmospheric pressure decreases at altitude. Because of this mountain roads above 3000m or so are graded gently to give the clanking and wheezing trucks and buses a chance to make it to the top (they often don't) and then safely down the other side.

This is good news for cyclists too; the higher you climb the easier the gradient, even if the surface is atrocious. The steep roads lurk at lower altitudes, namely around Murree and in Sikkim.

SAMPLE ITINERARIES

Two weeks is really the minimum time required for any Himalayan trip; three weeks and more allow the bike touring rhythm to work its magic. Routes in italics are not covered in this book but check the website.

Two weeks

India Leh to Srinagar
Pakistan Gilgit to Khunjerab

Three weeks

Pakistan Karakoram Highway, starting in Gilgit
India Manali to Leh or around Leh then Leh to Srinagar
Sikkim Siliguri to Gangtok; west Sikkim
Bhutan Thimphu to Trashigang

One month

Pakistan Karakoram Highway, starting in Islamabad
India Manali to Leh, *Leh and the lakes*
Tibet Friendship Highway
Sikkim Siliguri to Gangtok; west and north Sikkim
Bhutan Paro to Samdrup Jongkhar

Six weeks

Pakistan Karakoram Highway including side valleys and the roads to *Skardu and/or Chitral*
India Manali to Leh, Leh and the lakes, Leh to Srinagar.
India Spiti & Kinnaur (starting from Shimla), Manali to Leh
Tibet Friendship Highway to Lhatse then onwards to Mt Kailash; Lhasa to Zhongdian

Two months

Pakistan Karakoram Highway, return to Gilgit then head west to *Peshawar via Chitral*
India Spiti & Kinnaur (starting from Shimla), Manali to Leh, Leh and the lakes, Leh to Srinagar
Tibet & Nepal
Friendship Highway, *Kathmandu to Pokhara, off-road Annapurna Circuit*

Three months

Pakistan, China and Nepal or Tibet
Karakoram Highway, from Kashgar continue east either to Kathmandu or Lhasa; Kashgar–Lhasa–Zhongdian
India & Pakistan
Spiti (starting from Shimla), Manali–Leh–Srinagar. Cross into Pakistan and ride Karakoram Highway.
India Srinagar–Leh–Manali–Spiti, *explore Uttaranchal*

Four months or more

You could start with the Karakoram Highway in the west and head east, spending the monsoon months in Ladakh, reaching Tibet for Sep/Oct and finishing off with Bhutan in Oct/Nov. Or from Kashgar you could strike east past Mt Kailash to Lhasa; from there you could either head south on the Friendship Highway to Kathmandu or continue east to Zhongdian. Your itinerary will also be dictated by political considerations; for example Tibet was closed to all foreigners in early 2008. But where one door closes, another one opens... be flexible and have fun joining the dots!

agreed to upgrade the KKH by trebling its width: if this work goes ahead road conditions will become unpleasant during construction.

Manali–Leh is generally tarmac too but with seasonally bad sections on the passes; Baralacha La is often a trouble spot and streams can wash out bridges after heavy rain. **Leh–Srinagar** is mostly excellent tarmac as this is a vital military route. **Spiti** is awful for the first 100km; after that it's good tarmac until Kinnaur which should have excellent tarmac but is prone to landslides as well as flooding from the river Sutlej. Such landslides can usually be crossed on foot and washed away bridges will sometimes be replaced by a pulley system on which people and bicycles can be winched across.

Sikkim has good tarmac roads except in the restricted area around Gurudongmar Lake in the far north. Chinese road crews have been resurfacing the **Friendship Highway** since 2003; at the time of writing the only section left to tarmac is between Tingri and the Nepali border. The worst section of this is the massive 1300m descent from Nyalam to Dram on loose stones churned up with mud if it's been raining. **Bhutan** has the best roads in the Himalaya – perfect tarmac and little traffic east of Thimphu.

BORDER CROSSINGS

There are no border crossings open to foreigners travelling independently between India and China and the only Pakistan/India border crossing currently open to foreigners is on the plains of Punjab between Lahore (Pakistan) and Amritsar (India), a long way from the mountains. Where there are two names below they refer to the towns on either side of the border.

Pakistan (Northern Areas)–**China** (Xinjiang)	Khunjerab Pass
Pakistan (Punjab)–**India** (Punjab)	Atari–Wagah
India (Uttar Pradesh)–**Nepal** (west)	Banbassa–Mahendranagar
India (Uttar Pradesh)–**Nepal** (centre)	Sonauli–Bhairawa
India (Bihar)–**Nepal** (centre)	Raxaul–Birganj
India (West Bengal)–**Nepal** (east)	Panitanki–Kakarbitta
Nepal–**China** (Tibet)	Kodari–Zhangmu Restrictions on the Nepali side (see p249)
India (West Bengal)–**Bhutan** (west)	Jaigaon–Phuentsoling
India (Assam)–**Bhutan** (east)	Darranga–Samdrup Jongkhar

Border crossings which might open to foreign tourists in the next few years are listed below and biking in the Himalaya would be transformed if this happens. For the first time in centuries it would be possible to traverse the Himalaya from Pakistan all the way to Sikkim: from the KKH across to Srinagar, on to Leh and then beyond to Tibet in the east from where you could head south from Gyantse to Gangtok.

Pakistan (Azad Kashmir)–**India** (Kashmir):	Muzaffarabad–Srinagar This is currently only open to locals after security screening.
India (Ladakh)–**China** (Tibet):	Demchok–Tashigong
India (Sikkim)–**China** (Tibet):	Gangtok–Yardong via Nathu La. Currently only open to Indian and Chinese traders.

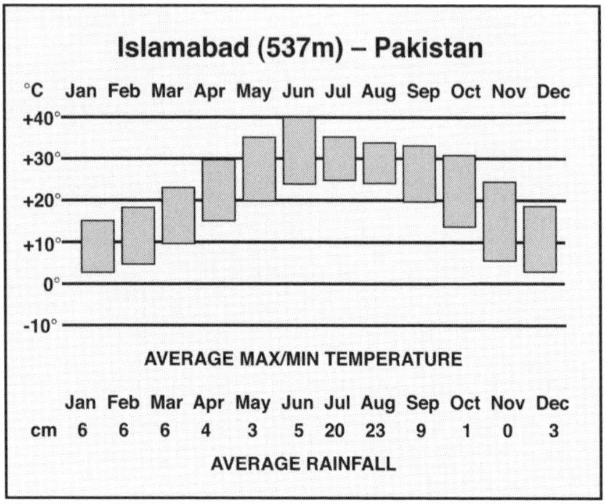

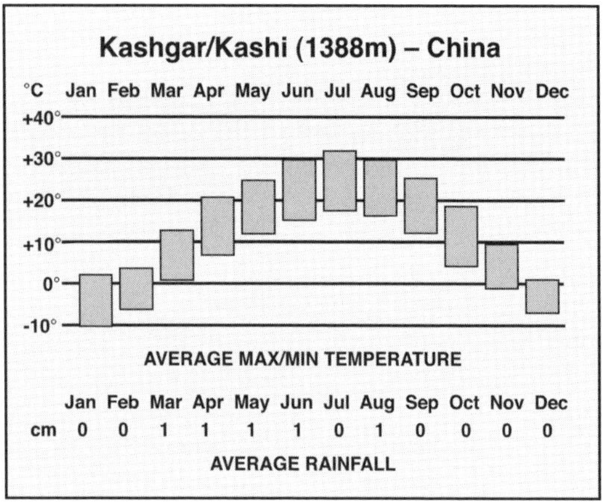

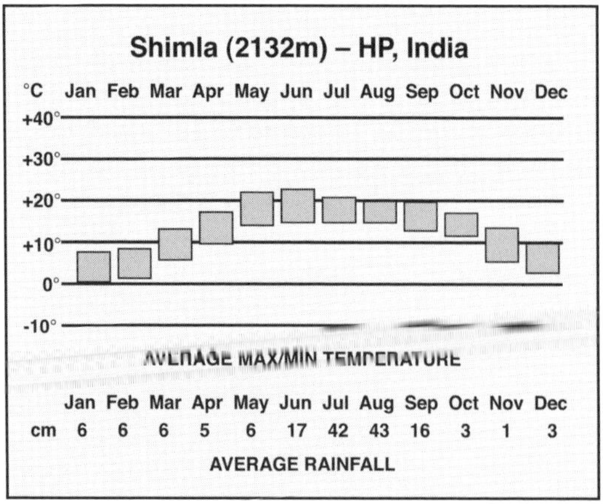

When to go

Spring (April–May) and **autumn** (mid-Sept–Oct) are the best times to visit the lower Himalaya as summer brings ferocious heat followed by the breaking of the monsoon. On the other hand the **higher routes** are only open for a few late summer months each year. As you might expect **winter** in Tibet and Ladakh is bitterly cold – the average temperature in Leh is below freezing for more than half the year. Whatever the season, **mountain weather is always unpredictable** so it's best to be prepared for blistering sunshine and frost-biting cold.

The monsoon

Arab sailors were the first to name a seasonal wind sweeping over the Arabian Sea trailing downpours in its wake; they called it the *mausim*. Today the monsoon, as it is now known, is more closely associated with the Indian subcontinent and its unchanging cycle of drought and flood.

The monsoon season usually starts in mid-June as the first rains hit the coast of South India. Over the next few weeks clouds trundle steadily northwards towards the Himalaya, dousing everything along their way. The rains reach Islamabad and Delhi in **early July**; the leaden monsoon clouds and enormous thunderstorms that announce their arrival make for an ecstatic release from weeks of white-hot skies and deadening heat. The rains are generally spent by **mid-September**. During the monsoon season humidity is very high though the rain itself usually only falls for a couple of hours during the afternoon, followed by bright sunshine which sets the earth steaming.

While fungus might grow on your clothes, monsoon season in the Indian subcontinent is an interesting time to visit, if not necessarily to travel. But in remote areas dirt roads turn into mud baths and where glacial streams flow across metalled roads (Spiti, Manali–Leh, Friendship Highway) they can rip away the tarmac leaving a bed of loose rocks. Usually the Indian Himalaya block the monsoon clouds but in recent years even Ladakh and Spiti have seen heavy rainfall and floods in July and August.

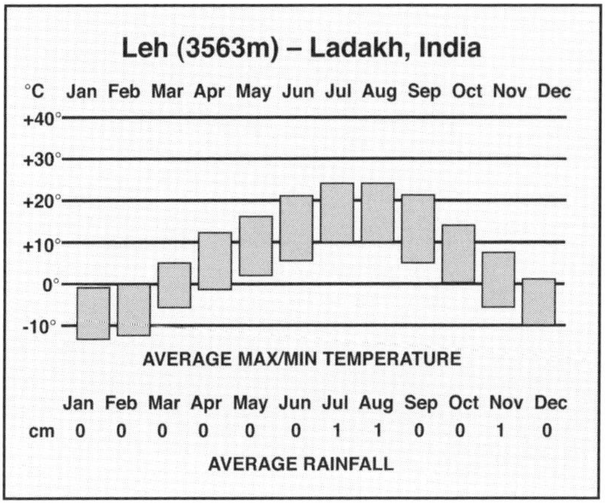

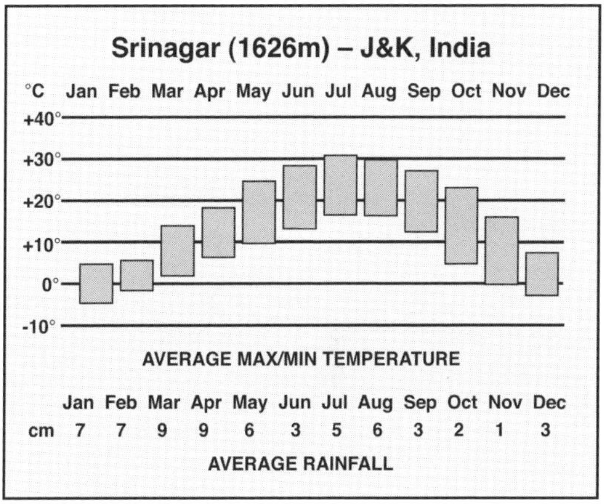

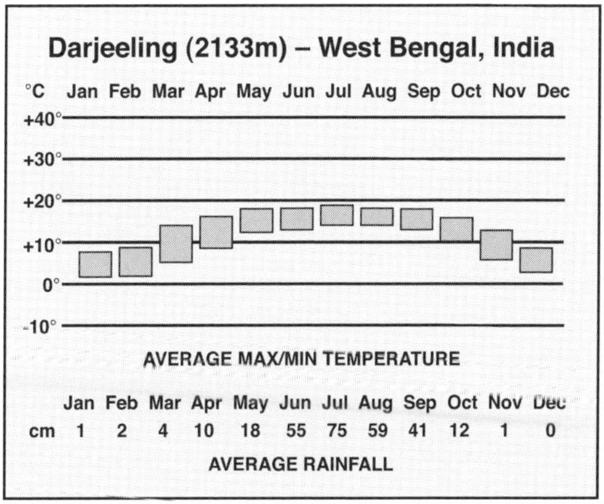

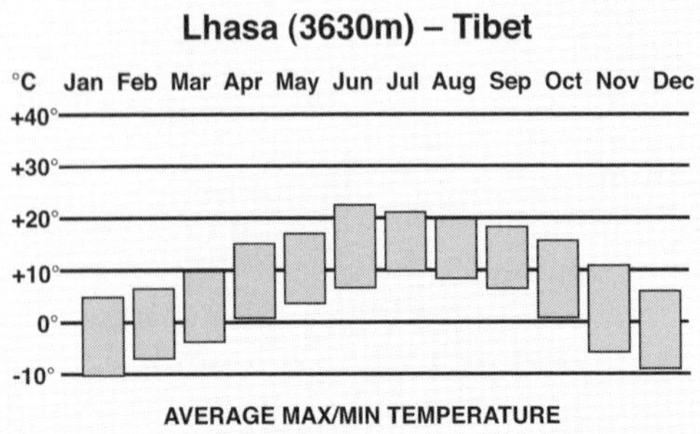

	Jan	Feb	Mar	Apr	May	Jun	Jul	Aug	Sep	Oct	Nov	Dec
cm	0	1	0	0	2	6	12	8	6	1	0	0

AVERAGE RAINFALL

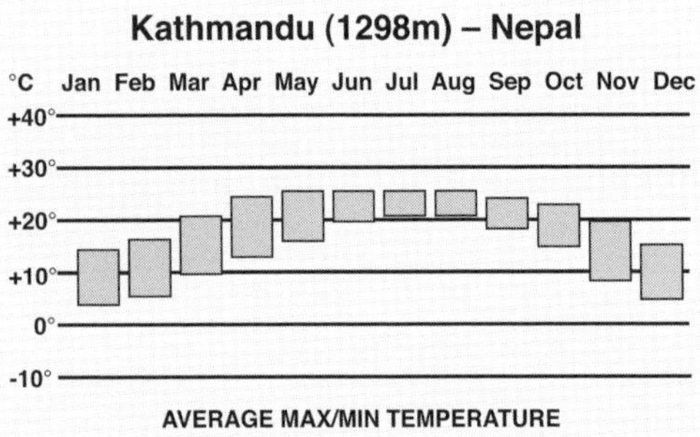

	Jan	Feb	Mar	Apr	May	Jun	Jul	Aug	Sep	Oct	Nov	Dec
cm	1	1	3	3	10	20	37	32	18	5	0	1

AVERAGE RAINFALL

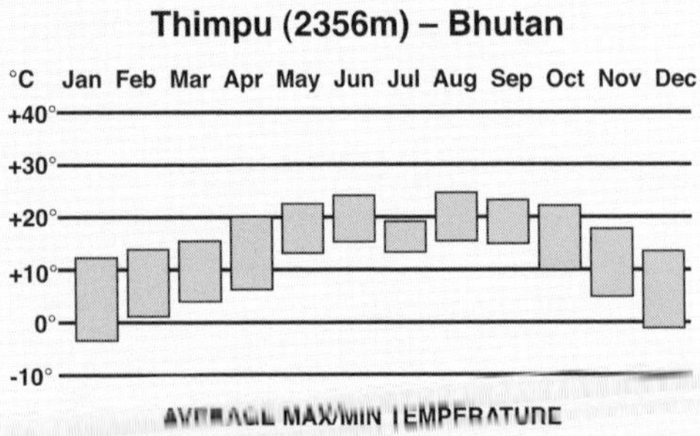

	Jan	Feb	Mar	Apr	May	Jun	Jul	Aug	Sep	Oct	Nov	Dec
cm	1	4	2	6	12	25	37	35	15	4	1	0

AVERAGE RAINFALL

Best times

Among other meteorological factors all these timings are dependent on **snowfall**; both the thaw and the return of winter which can vary by up to a **fortnight** from one year to the next.

Karakoram Highway: April to May and October to November

Depending on the **snowfall**, spring and autumn are the best times to set off from Islamabad as between May and July temperatures exceed 40°C/104°F; for most people this is just too hot when the first week is so hilly. After the heat come the monsoon rains from July to mid-September. In high summer Indus Kohistan as far as Gilgit can get dangerously hot with temperatures rising above 50°C/122°F; avoid cycling at this time if you can and if you can't be sure to carry enough water (see p72 for more on cycling in extreme heat). Even at night the temperature only drops to around 35°C/95°F and as few hotel have air-conditioning it's often difficult to sleep properly.

From Gilgit northwards the climate is cooler and depending on snowfall the Khunjerab Pass can be blocked until early May. Spring (April–May) in northern Pakistan is especially pretty as the cherry trees burst into blossom, painting valleys such as Hunza a delicate wash of pink. However, the weather can still be unsettled with cloudy days of rain or snow. Post-monsoon, the skies in autumn (October–November) are clear and blue with perfect mountain views and pleasant temperatures.

Manali–Leh: mid-June to mid-October

The Indian army does its best to keep the Manali–Leh Highway open between 15 June and 15 September. Sometimes nature does its best to keep them busy by snowing out of season, swelling rivers which wash away bridges and smothering the roads in landslides. The state buses and 4WD jeeps will run as

BEST TIMES FOR HIMALAYAN BIKING

	KKH	Manali to Leh	Leh to Srinagar	Spiti and Kinnaur	Sikkim	Tibet	Bhutan
JAN	Roads closed	Roads closed	Roads closed	Roads closed	Below 0°C	Below 0°C	Below 0°C
FEB	Roads closed	Roads closed	Roads closed	Roads closed	Best time	Below 0°C	Below 0°C
MAR	Roads closed	Roads closed	Roads closed	Roads closed	Best time	Windy	Best time
APR	Best time	Roads closed	Roads closed	Roads closed	Best time	Windy	Best time
MAY	Above 35°C	Roads closed	Roads closed	Roads closed	Best time	Windy	Best time
JUN	Above 35°C	Best time	Best time	Roads closed	Rain	Rain	Rain
JUL	Above 35°C	Best time	Best time	Best time	Rain	Rain	Rain
AUG	Above 35°C	Best time	Best time	Best time	Rain	Rain	Rain
SEP	Best time	Best time	Best time	Best time	Best time	Best time	Best time
OCT	Best time	Best time	Best time	Best time	Best time	Best time	Best time
NOV	Roads closed	Roads closed	Roads closed	Roads closed	Best time	Below 0°C	Below 0°C
DEC	Roads closed	Roads closed	Roads closed	Roads closed	Below 0°C	Below 0°C	Below 0°C

Best time	Roads closed	Below 0°C	Above 35°C	Windy	Rain
(bicycle)	×	(snowflake)	(chilli)	(bicycle with arrow)	(bicycle, shaded)

late into October as they can (usually mid-October) before snow blocks the highest passes until next summer.

Leh–Srinagar: May-June and October-November

The Indian army also maintains the Leh–Srinagar Highway which, although much lower than the Manali–Leh Highway, experiences higher snowfall. The road usually opens in May though late snows can block it until June. Likewise, it should officially close at the beginning of October but in some years has stayed open until mid-November.

Spiti and Kinnaur: July to mid-October

Kunzam La (4550m) is the only pass into Spiti and is usually free of snow by July but snowbound once more by the end of October. Kunzam La is at the western end of the Spiti valley; to the east there are no passes at all which means that Kinnaur and Spiti (as far west as Losar) should be reachable year-round from Shimla. However, during summer the entire region is prone to landslides that can close the road for days and cut off entire valleys.

Sikkim: January to April and October to December

Sikkim's elevation leaps about from a hot and sticky 315m (Rangpo, the entry point to Sikkim) to an arid and breathtaking 4996m (Gurudongmar Lake) so the climate varies wildly even within one riding day. From January to April you can expect cold (but not freezing) weather with some sun during the day and clear views of the mountains. In April there are occasional showers and by May the showers have increased and the mountains are often hidden in haze. June and September have showers mixed with good weather but views are hazy. The monsoon drenches Gangtok throughout July and August but by October the rains are done and the weather is crystal clear with mountain views that just get better as temperatures drop into November and December.

Friendship Highway: mid-September to November

Winter (December–February) in Tibet is extremely cold and dry with correspondingly great views. But the high passes are often blocked by snow and unless you have proper equipment and experience in sub-zero temperatures it's just too risky. Spring (March–May) is exceedingly windy with sandstorms so unpleasant that cyclists have resorted to riding at night when the winds drop. By summer (June–August) the winds ease, the thermometer climbs above freezing but now the rains begin, flooding the rivers which in turn make some roads impossible to ford even for 4WDs. By far the best season is autumn (September–November) as the rains have usually retreated by mid-September

DAYLIGHT HOURS

With the routes in this book covering a range of latitudes from around **N40°** (Kashgar; also Madrid and New York) to just below N20° (Kathmandu; also Canary Islands and Orlando, FL) **daylight hours** in the the Himalaya throughout the year are not particularly extreme.

Should you find yourself in Kashgar around Christmas there'll be 9 hours 20 minutes of daylight doing little to thaw the sub-freezing temperatures. Down in Kathmandu there'll be another hour or so. In **high summer** you'll get 14 hours of daylight around Kathmandu and 17 hours in Kashgar.

RAMADAN

It's best to avoid Pakistan during Ramadan, the ninth Muslim month that is marked by prayer and fasting. Between dawn and dusk, all Muslims must abstain from food, water, cigarettes and sex.

Although non-Muslims are exempt from these rules, you still shouldn't eat or drink anything in public during daylight hours. Not that it's easy to as nearly all restaurants are closed until dusk. Eid-ul-Fitr is a day of festivity to celebrate the end of Ramadan. Since the Islamic calendar starts each new month with the sighting of the new moon, its months are noticeably different from those of the Gregorian calendar and the dates for Ramadan vary each year. The provisional dates for the next few years are:

2009	22 August–21 September
2010	11 August–9 September
2011	1 August–30 August

but you still have the advantage of long daylight hours. October is the best month for views, temperature and daylight; by the end of November the daylight hours are short and the nights and passes are extremely cold.

Bhutan: February to June or September to December

Bhutan has a reputation for cloudy weather for which it can blame neighbouring Assam, the wettest place on the planet. Like Sikkim, the weather isn't extreme but passes can be cold. A Bhutanese visa is cheaper (by $35 per day) during the monsoon months of July and August but for the best chance of clear skies and beautiful views visit in November or December.

FESTIVALS AND ANNUAL EVENTS

The people of the Himalaya are, on the whole, extremely devout and love a party so as well as celebrating festivals in their respective Islamic, Hindu or Buddhist calendars there are also festivals marking the changing of the seasons. There are also plenty of smaller, local festivals throughout the year which can add an unexpected highlight to your travels.

Pakistan

Pakistan's festivals mostly celebrate important dates in the Islamic calendar. The three main ones are: **Eid-ul-Fitr** which marks the end of Ramadan (see above); **Eid-ul-Azha** ten weeks later which commemorates the Prophet Ibrahim's ('Abraham' in The Bible) sacrifice of a lamb instead of his son Ismail; and finally **Muharram**, the anniversary of the martyrdom of Imam Hussein, the grandson of the Prophet Mohammed, who was killed in the Battle of Karbala. The death of Hussain nearly 1300 years ago marks the schism between Sunnis and Shia sects and young Shia men take to the streets and flay their backs with nail-studded whips. Religious feeling runs dangerously high and this is a bad time to be anywhere like Gilgit which has a history of violence between the two sects.

North India

India's Hindu festivals are among the most boisterous in the world and are an experience that shouldn't be missed. The best celebration of **Dussehra** (see p20) is at Kullu, 40km south of Manali. Many Indians travel to the family home to celebrate major religious festivals, so all public transport (including

At the Ladakh Festival (September)

flights) can get booked up weeks in advance. Similarly many businesses are closed during the major Hindu festivals which can last as long as ten days. Don't expect any office work – such as the processing of visas – to get done during this time.

The Buddhist calendar is full of monastic festivals that are usually celebrated with a *chaam* (masked dance). Cultural festivals, such as the **Ladakh** festival (see below) are often the work of state tourist boards and can feature more tourists than culture. When not celebrated throughout India the location of the festival is in brackets.

January/February	**Dotor chaam** (Enchey gompa, Sikkim)
February/March	**Losar** (New Year), celebrated by Tibetans (Sikkim)
March	**Holi**, Hindu festival marking the coming of spring by dousing everyone in reach with water and coloured powder.
March 10	**Anniversary of the 1959 Tibetan uprising in Lhasa**, commemorated in Dharamsala.
March/April	**Eid-ul-Azha** (see Pakistan p19)
Mid-March/May	**International Flower Festival** (Gangtok, Sikkim)
Late May/early June	**Saga Dawa** (aka **Buddha Jayanti**), the holiest of Buddhist festivals, celebrating the birth of Lord Buddha, then in later years his attainment of Buddhahood and then ultimately of Nirvana; also **Tse-Chu chaam**, masked dance depicting the life of Guru Padmasambhava (Rumtek gompa, Sikkim)
August 15	**Independence Day** (public holiday)
August / September	**Phang Lhabsol**, Sikkimese festival celebrating Mt Kanchendzonga and the Treaty of Brotherhood between the Lepchas and the Bhutias.
September 1-15	**Ladakh Festival**, a showcase of polo, archery, dancing and music.
September/October	**Dasain** (aka **Durga Puja** in West Bengal or **Dussehra** in Himachal Pradesh) is a 10-day festival which celebrates the victory of Durga over the demon Mahishasura, Rama's victory over Ravana and more generally the triumph of good over evil. **Diwali** (aka **Deepwali** or **Tihaar** in Sikkim) is celebrated 15 days after Dasain and is a five-day festival which starts with a thorough house-cleaning and ends with thousands of lit oil lamps and the noisiest night of fireworks in the year.
December	**Kagyat Chaam** (Sikkim)
December/January	**Losar** (New Year), celebrated in Ladakh.

Tibet

Although most of the festivals in the Buddhist calendar, such as **Losar** (New Year) and **Saga Dawa** (see above), are still celebrated in Tibet, others such as **Monlam** (the prayer festival) and the current **Dalai Lama's birthday** (6 July) are not. For these you need to travel to Dharamsala, North India, home of the

Dalai Lama's Tibetan Government in Exile. Tibet's best-known festivals, such as the impromptu **horse festivals** occur in the summer.

Bhutan

Each of Bhutan's *dzongs* (religious fortresses) holds its own *tsechu*, a festival to honour Guru Rinpoche for bringing Buddhism to Bhutan. The larger tsechus of Punakha and Thimphu are heavily promoted and especially popular with tourists; try to time your visit with one of the smaller tsechus if you prefer a more intimate experience.

January	**Trongsa Tsechu** (Trongsa), **Lhuntshe Tsechu** (Lhuntse)
February	**Punakha Dromche** (Punakha)
March	**Chorten Kora** (Trashi Yangtse)
June	**Nimalung Tsechu** and **Kurjey Tsechu** (both in Bumthang)
September	**Thimphu Drubchen** and **Thimphu Tsechu** (both in Thimphu), **Tangbi Mani** (Bumthang)
October	**Jambay Lakhang Drup** and **Prakhar Duchoe** (both in Bumthang)
December	**Mongar Tsechu** (Mongar), **Trashigang Tsechu** (Trashigang)

Getting there

The **Karakoram Highway** and **Bhutan** routes both start at international airports (Islamabad and Paro respectively), whereas the nearest international air hub for the North India rides is Delhi; allow a day to reach Manali by bus (**Manali–Leh**), a day to reach Shimla by bus (**Spiti**) or a day in Delhi to connect with the early morning flight to Leh (**Leh–Srinagar**).

Kolkata (Calcutta) is the nearest international air hub for **Sikkim**; allow a day for the internal flight to Bagdogra which is only 16km from the start of the ride at Siliguri. Tibet and the **Friendship Highway** is complicated by the permit issue: if you're not travelling overland fly to Beijing or Chengdu and pick up a Tibet permit and flight to Lhasa (see p248). There are more details on getting to the start of the rides at the beginning of each route chapter.

BY AIR

Within Asia, **Delhi** is the most practical hub for northern India and for onward flights to Nepal and Bhutan although there are few facilities for passengers in transit at the airport.

For those bringing bicycles, the **luggage allowance** and charge for excess luggage is just as important as the airfare when choosing a ticket. If the airline is strict be warned: the excess charge for the bicycle and luggage can exceed the price of the ticket. Ensure before booking that the bicycle is included as part of your luggage and avoid airlines that count them as freight.

Rides are listed on the next page with their closest international airports, after which the airport code and its full name appear in brackets.

Karakoram Highway

Islamabad (ISB; Islamabad Airport), Pakistan. **Pakistan International Airways** (💻 www.piac.com.pk) flies from North America, Asia and Europe to Pakistan; **British Airways** (💻 www.ba.com) has frequent flights from the UK. Once a week, a **China Southern Airlines** (💻 www.cs-air.com/en) flight connects Islamabad with Kashgar.

Kashgar (KHG; Kashi Airport), China. Kashgar is known by its Chinese name, Kashi. Kashi airport is served by **China Southern Airlines** (💻 www.cs-air.com/en) and **Hainan Airlines** (💻 www.hnair.com). There are daily flights to Urumqi and the weekly flight to Islamabad (see above). Urumqi is the aviation hub for western China and has daily flights to Beijing (see 💻 www.elong.net).

Manali–Leh, Leh–Srinagar and Spiti

Delhi (DEL; Indira Gandhi Airport), India. Airlines such as **Virgin Atlantic** (💻 www.virginatlantic.com) fly direct and offer extremely competitive fares. The new crop of Indian budget airlines, such as **Air Sahara** (💻 www.airsahara.net) and **Jet Airways** (💻 www.jetairways.com) also offer direct international flights. For long-distance flights from the Americas, Asia and Australasia the only direct connections are with **Indian Airlines** (💻 www.indian-airlines.nic.in).

Sikkim

Kolkata (CCU, Netaji Subhas Chandra Airport), India. There are no direct flights from North America or Australasia to Kolkata. **Air India** (💻 www.airindia.com), **Lufthansa** (💻 www.lufthansa.com) and **British Airways** (💻 www.ba.com) fly from Europe. Within India, all the budget Indian airlines fly to Kolkata and many onwards to Bagdogra.

Friendship Highway

Lhasa (LXA; Gongkar airport), Tibet. The only international flight into Lhasa is with **China Southwest Airlines** from Kathmandu. Independent travellers cannot buy tickets for this flight as the airline will only sell tickets through travel agents, who in turn sell the ticket as part of a minimum three-day organized tour including the crucial Tibet permit (see p242). From within China the situation is much easier. The Tibet permit is still necessary but arranging one is faster and cheaper in Beijing or Chengdu. See the Tibet chapter for more details on reaching Lhasa from China and Hong Kong.

Kathmandu (KTM; Tribhuvan Airport), Nepal. Only **Austrian Airlines** (💻 www.aua.com) flies direct from Europe (Vienna) to Kathmandu. With all

TIME ZONES AND INTERNATIONAL DIALLING CODES

Country	Time zone	International dialling code
Pakistan	GMT + 5hrs	+92 (eg 0092 from the UK)
China*	GMT + 8hrs*	+86
India	GMT + 5hrs 30mins	+91
Nepal	GMT + 5hrs 45 mins	+977
Bhutan	GMT + 6hrs	+975

Deduct one hour from the time difference during Daylight Saving Time (DST or 'summer time'). * See p110 for 'local time' in Xinjiang.

ORGANIZED CYCLING TOURS

If you only have a couple of weeks holiday and lack the time or confidence to plan a trip yourself an organized tour could be the answer; an appetite-whetter with a safety net! The only major restriction with organized tours is where they operate: it's hard to find tours outside of northern India or Bhutan.

An organized tour will allow you to enjoy your holiday without a care in the world. In return for your money the tour operator should find the best-value places to stay and to eat, juggle the logistics as well as crisis-manage during the trip. If you're lucky enough to have an **enthusiastic and knowledgeable guide** they will be an unending source of facts and stories about the region affording you a far greater insight than if you were travelling independently. The best of them will have ridden all the routes themselves and may even ride with you – some will allow cyclists to ride at their own pace without piling on the pressure to keep up or, even worse, to get in the back-up vehicle.

This **back-up vehicle**, if there is one, will carry your luggage so you can cover the distance with less effort, have more time to take breaks and be left with enough energy at the end of the day to socialize with your fellow bikers. A back-up team will provide medical and mechanical support and conjure piping-hot mugs of tea, hot meals and even cakes from a kerosene stove.

However, there will be situations such as landslides and blocked roads that even the most organized of tour companies cannot overcome. Where independent cyclists can usually clamber over a landslide, an organized tour's back-up jeep will have to turn around and run the trip somewhere else. This happens every year in the Himalaya.

Check itineraries very carefully for high-altitude tours such as Manali–Leh and Tibet as some tour schedules don't allow enough time for proper **acclimatization**. Likewise, watch out for some surprising omissions: Exodus currently charges over £2000 for a 20-day cycling tour in Tibet but clients have to buy their own lunch and dinner. Others sell their trips as cycling tours but will put you in a jeep for all the uphills! Of course you might think this is a brilliant idea.

Tour Operators

Small travel outfits based in places like Kathmandu or Gangtok are often the ground agents for big overseas operators so can offer an identical package but at local prices. You get what you pay for though. There's likely to be no insurance and no chance of a refund if your trip goes wrong. You'll also miss out on someone to liaise between you and the local ground staff should there be a problem. Here's an idea of what is currently available:

- **Exodus** (💻 www.exodus.co.uk) Lhasa–Kathmandu (20 days) £2099. Includes international flights, excludes visas.
- **Greenrock** (💻 www.greenrock.co.uk) Lhasa–Kathmandu (24 days) £2200. Traverse Bhutan (20 days) £2950. Includes international flights and visas.
- **KE Adventures** (💻 www.keadventure.com) Karakoram Highway (15 days) £945, Leh–Manali (18 days) £1045, Lhasa–Kathmandu (25 days) £1795, Bhutan (15 days) £2295. Excludes international flights and visas.
- **Out There Biking** (💻 www.out-there-biking.com) Manali–Leh (20 days) £795, Spiti & Lahaul (16 days) £750. Excludes international flights and visas.
- **Red Spokes** (💻 www.redspokes.co.uk) Karakoram Highway (17 days) £775, Lhasa–Kathmandu (24 days) £1295, Manali–Leh (17 days) £745. Excludes international flights and visas.
- **Tiger Eye Adventure** (India only, 💻 www.tigereyeadventure.com). Spiti Valley (14 days) $1050. Bicycle 'safari' (including a cook, tent, mattress and food) costs an extra $30 per day.
- **Royal Mountain Travel** (Nepal only, 💻 www.responsibletravel.com) Lhasa–Kathmandu (24 days), £1136. Excludes international flights, hotel meals and visas.
- **Himalayan Adventure** (Bhutan only, 💻 www.himalayan-adventures.com) 'Big Dragon' (a 20-day traverse of Bhutan) $4030. All prices based on three people minimum and exclude international flights and visas.

RIDING ALONE

If no one responds to your call, walk alone, walk alone!

Rabindranath Tagore

For some, travelling solo is the only way to go: total freedom, no arguing over where to stay, how much to spend, when to go or what to do. Just remember it's not easy to be alone in Asia – the locals are curious and friendly! Some cyclists start riding on their own but fall in with bikers heading in the same direction. If the idea of running into other Westerners is unappealing travel out of season on these routes, or use them to reach more remote regions.

Travelling alone offers the best of both worlds. If you want company there are always people to talk to – even when there's no common language – and if you don't solitude is yours.

Alone it's easier for local people to approach you so you'll probably be offered opportunities that others miss. As always, your experience depends on your state of mind. Some people are more cautious on their own and avoid risks they'd take with a friend by their side. Others miss having someone to share the experience with. But don't let this hold you back.

Many people in the Himalaya are protective of foreigners travelling on their own and will go out of their way to help, especially if you're a woman. However, travelling alone does expose you to greater risk. Even in safer regions if you have an accident there's no companion to fetch help or to patch you up. If you're ill there will be no one to go out and get medicine or a doctor or to take you to hospital.

Finally anyone with a serious medical history should think carefully about the risks of travelling alone – in some regions the locals are afraid to take responsibility for a sick foreigner.

the others you have to choose whether you want to transit via the Middle East, Central Europe (Vienna) or India (Delhi). The cheapest option is often to transit via Delhi as there are a number of airlines shuttling between there and Kathmandu.

Bhutan

Paro (PBH; Paro Airport), Bhutan. Paro is Bhutan's only international airport and is used exclusively by Bhutan's national airline, **Druk Air** (💻 www.drukair.com.bt). The flight schedule is straightforward: to the west Paro–Kathmandu–Delhi; to the south Paro–Dhaka, Paro–Gaya and Paro–Kolkata; to the southeast Paro–Bangkok.

BY TRAIN

If time is not an issue **from Europe** there are two train routes into Asia. Starting from London and routing through Paris they include:

London–Moscow–Almaty (Kazakhstan) or Bishkek (Kyrgyzstan) or Urumqi (China)

A chance to travel a thread of the Silk Route. See Trailblazer's *The Silk Roads* for more details. Visas are required for: Russia, Kazakhstan or Kyrgyzstan and China. London to Moscow takes three days, Moscow to Almaty or Bishkek takes five days, or Moscow to Urumqi takes a week via Almaty.

London–Istanbul–Lahore (Pakistan) or Delhi (India)

This is the original hippy trail to Asia albeit on rolling stock rather than wheels. The train timetables are straightforward until Zahedan in eastern Iran from where there's a twice-monthly service to Quetta in Pakistan which includes a ferry crossing of Lake Van and a bus transfer between Bam and Zahedan. From Lahore in Pakistan it's only sixty kilometres to Amritsar in India's Punjab province. Trains to Delhi leave Amritsar throughout the day. Visas are required for: Iran (difficult), Pakistan and India. London–Lahore takes two to three weeks.

By rail from North America or Australasia

There are two options: fly to a hub in Europe from **North America** and take either of the two routes above from there, or fly to Beijing and then travel by train to either Lhasa (direct) or Kashgar (via Urumqi).

From **Australia** or **New Zealand** fly to Singapore, train to Bangkok, bus to Phnom Penh, train to Saigon, train to Hanoi and then a final train to Beijing. Practical advice on booking these various stages is given on websites such as www.seat61.com. China Railway's website at www.tielu.org is only in Chinese; for information in English about popular tourist trains see www.china-train-ticket.com.

BY BIKE

If you have the time why not ride to the Himalaya, like Göran Kropp (see box below)? Many round-the-world bikers starting in **Europe** follow the Danube southeast then once in Turkey either continue east via Iran into Pakistan, or head for the Caucasus and Central Asia, popping out into China via Kyrgyzstan. Trailblazer's *Adventure Cycle-Touring Handbook* details routes between Europe and Asia; Lonely Planet's 'On Your Bike' Thorn Tree branch (www.lonelyplanet.com/thorntree/index.jspa) is full of further information and opinions.

WHEN HIMALAYA BY BIKE JUST ISN'T ENOUGH

In 1996 the Swedish climber Göran Kropp made international headlines when he summited Mt Everest after riding there from Stockholm. He'd pulled his climbing kit (all 65kg of it) on a trailer through Germany, Czechoslovakia, Hungary, Romania, Bulgaria, Turkey, Iran, Pakistan, India and Nepal. The journey took four months and brought him to Kathmandu in the spring of 1996. From there he carried his climbing kit to Namche Bazaar and onwards up to Base Camp. Independent and bloody-minded to the last he then climbed Everest without Sherpas ('an unjustifiable luxury') or oxygen ('like taking steroids for the Olympics'). Apparently he even made fresh tracks through the snow to avoid following the footsteps of others.

The climbing season on Everest in 1996 is infamous, thanks partly to John Krakauer's book *Into Thin Air* and the IMAX film *Everest*. A combination of bad weather, inexperienced climbers and poor judgement resulted in eleven climbers dying in one storm. Despite the furore around him Kropp summited on his third attempt and then pedalled back to Sweden, taking a year in total for the round trip.

There are two accounts of his amazing journey: the book *Ultimate High: My Everest Odyssey* and a TV documentary *I Made It: Göran Kropp's Incredible Journey to the Top of the World*. Kropp went on to climb Shishapangma (8013m) and Everest once again, this time with his girlfriend Renata Chlumska. Together they ran a travel adventure company and were planning a 18,000km circumnavigation of America by kayak when Kropp was killed in a climbing accident in Washington State, USA, aged just 35.

From Australia and New Zealand the overland journey starts at Singapore from where you use the following as the basis of a route:

Malaysia	Quiet coastal road via Muar to Kuala Lumpur–Kuala Lipis–Dabong–Kuala Kurai–Kota Bharu
Thailand	Narathiwat to Pattani–Songkla–Nakhon Si–Thammarat–Chumphon–Bang-Saphan–Prachuap Khirikan–Cha-am–Phetchaburi–Bangkok
Laos	Savannaket to Muang Phalan–Sopene–Lao Bao
Vietnam	Hue–Hoi An to Hanoi–Bac Ha–Sapa
China	Kunming to Lufeng–Dali–Lijiang–Kangdding–Emeishan–Leshan–Chengdu

Visas, permits and paperwork

All the countries covered in this guide require **visas**. For some, such as China, Pakistan and India, it's quickest to apply for the visa in your **home country** or, if you live abroad, from the country you live in. If you apply in person at the embassy check its website beforehand – firstly to make sure it won't be celebrating a national holiday, and secondly for what you'll need to provide which is usually: **two passport photos**, a **completed application form** (often available to download from an embassy's website), the **visa fee in cash** and a **passport with a minimum six months' validity** left on it. Some nationalities may also need to show their flight tickets, itinerary and sufficient funds.

If you cannot visit an embassy in person **visa agencies** such as CIBT (www.uk.cibt.com) can do the work for you for a fee of around £40. Even if you don't use CIBT's services their website provides more up-to-date advice than those of many embassies.

You can set the date of entry for most visas thereby buying yourself enough time to get there. Many visas differentiate between **validity** and **duration**: for example a Pakistani visa can be valid for six months from the date of issue but allows a maximum stay once in the country of sixty days, in which case you must use those sixty days within the six-month validity of the visa. The exception is the visa for India (see p29) which starts from the date of issue, not date of entry.

If you're on the road already, requests for visas from a third country may require a letter of introduction (LoI) also known as a letter of recommendation (LoR) from your embassy for which they will charge up to £50 if you're British. Add in the time it can take to process a visa – up to ten days in some countries – and then the fact that the embassy might ultimately refuse you (the Indian embassy in Kathmandu is notorious for this) and you may end up wishing you'd sorted it out before leaving home.

The information given in the table opposite is what you can expect for a tourist visa. Issue times refer to applications **in person** (visa agencies may take longer), duration refers to **working** days and **dollar** prices relate to the relevant local currency.

PAKISTAN	UK	USA	CANADA	AUSTRALIA	NZ
Price	£55	$120	$100	$70	$164
Issue time	Same day	5 days	3 days	3 weeks	1 week
Duration		60 days single entry			

CHINA	UK	US	CAN	AU	NZ
Price	£30	$30	$50	$30	$60
Issue time	4 days Same day add £20	4 days Same day add $30	4 days Same day add $50	4 days Same day add $50	7 days Same day add $60
Duration		Usually 30 days single entry			

INDIA	UK	US	CAN	AU	NZ
Price	£30	$60	$62	$75	$90
Issue time	Same day	Same day	Same day	7 days	5 days
Duration		6 months multiple entry			

NEPAL	UK	US	CAN	AU	NZ
Price	£20	$30	$62	$70	$100
Issue time	Next day	7 days	Apply in USA	Same day	3 days
Duration		30 days single entry			

For **Bhutan** visa applications see p30.

PAKISTAN

With a few obscure exceptions including Iceland and Tonga, just about everybody needs a visa to enter Pakistan. The maximum-length **tourist visa** available is for three months with double entry, though when you apply you will more likely be offered a thirty-day single entry visa.

In 2007 Pakistan restarted offering **transit visas** for travellers coming from China over Khunjerab Pass to Sost. The duration is said to range from a week to a month and is extendible for three days to six months in Northern Areas' towns such as Gilgit and Skardu as well as Islamabad. Israeli nationals cannot enter Pakistan.

At home

UK High Commission for Pakistan, 34-36 Lowndes Square, London, SW1X 9JN
☎ 020-7664 9200 (automated), 💻 www.pakmission-uk.gov.pk

USA Embassy of Pakistan, 3517 International Court Avenue, NW, Washington, DC 20008
☎ 202-243 6500, 💻 www.pakistan-embassy.org

Australia High Commission for Pakistan, 4 Timbarra Crescent, O'Malley, Canberra ACT 2606
☎ 02-6290 1676, 💻 www.pakistan.org.au

New Zealand High Commission for Pakistan, 182 Onslow Road, Khandallah, Wellington
☎ 04-479 0026/0027, 💻 pakhcwellington@xtra.co.nz

Canada High Commission for the Islamic Republic of Pakistan, 10 Range Road, Ottawa, Ontario K1N 8J3
☎ 613-238 7881, 💻 www.pakmission.ca

Abroad
If you are entering from China along the KKH you can get a transit visa at Sost. Otherwise Pakistani embassies in Beijing, Iran (Teheran), Nepal (Kathmandu) and India (New Delhi) as well as some Central Asia 'stans (notably Uzbekistan) can issue tourist visas. Some embassies can make difficulties, claiming you should apply in your home country, but travelling overland by bicycle ought to be a good excuse. Some may also require a LoI from your home embassy who in turn may refuse to provide it on safety grounds. The Pakistani Consulate in Hong Kong will only issue tourist visas to Hong Kong nationals; everyone else must go to Beijing where a thirty-day tourist visa takes two working days to issue.

Extending your visa
Once in Pakistan, the best place to extend your visa is Islamabad, although it's also possible in Gilgit and Skardu. The duration and cost of the extension depends on your nationality and where you apply (Gilgit is said to only issue two weeks) – the longest extension possible is three months. Contact the Visa Section Officer of the Ministry of Interior, R Block, Pak Secretariat, Islamabad, (☎ 052-920 7290), for more details.

CHINA
For UK nationals China is the one case where it's better to apply abroad. The Chinese embassy in London will issue, at best, a sixty-day single entry visa for tourists. However, the Chinese embassies in Amsterdam, Paris and Hong Kong issue three-month visas to independent travellers. Do not mention **Tibet or Xinjiang** on your visa application – the Chinese authorities do not like people travelling independently in these regions – open cities such as Beijing or Shanghai will raise no hackles. Nationals of both Australia and New Zealand should apply for their visas at least one month before leaving home.

At home

UK	31 Portland Place, London W1B 1JL ☎ 020-7631 1430 (2-4pm), 🖳 www.chinese-embassy.org.uk
USA	The Visa Office of the Embassy of the People's Republic of China, 2201 Wisconsin Avenue, NW, Suite 110, Washington DC 20007 ☎ 202-338-6688, 🖳 www.china-embassy.org/eng
Canada	Embassy of the People's Republic of China, 515 St. Patrick Street, Ottawa, Ontario, Canada, K1N 5H3 ☎ 613-789-3434 (24hrs), 🖳 www.chinaembassycanada.org/eng
Australia	Embassy of the People's Republic of China in Australia, 15 Coronation Drive, Yarralumla, ACT 2600 ☎ 02-6273 4780, 🖳 http//au.china-embassy.org/eng
New Zealand	Embassy of the People's Republic of China, 2-6 Glenmore Street, Wellington ☎ 04-4749 631, 🖳 www.chinaembassy.org.nz/eng

Abroad
You can get a visa at the Chinese embassy in **Pakistan**: Diplomatic Enclave, Ramna 4, Islamabad (🖳 http://pk.chineseembassy.org/eng).

Very few cyclists turning up at Kodari (the Nepal/Tibet border town) with visas issued outside of Nepal are allowed to cross into Tibet – most are told to return to Kathmandu and join a group tour. If you only want to cycle the Friendship Highway, this option isn't as bad as it sounds – jeeps take as little as two days to reach Lhasa (but see the section on Acute Mountain Sickness on p61) and between Shigatse and Lhasa they take the faster, central route which most cyclists eschew for the prettier, bumpier southern route past Gyantse. The downside is that you will have seen the landscape between Kodari and Shigatse before you cycle it.

Visas issued in Kathmandu are for twenty one days maximum; if you're lucky enough to get this long deduct two days for the jeep ride, and you're left with just enough time to acclimatize and ride back to Kodari; very fit cyclists will be able to squeeze in Everest Base Camp too. You'll need to request an individual visa (approx US$25) in addition to the group visa (approx US$40) – you need the group visa to enter Tibet, and the individual visa to exit it without the rest of the group. State on your application form that you require this extra time to travel onwards to Beijing – don't tell them you'll be riding a bicycle in Tibet.

INDIA

The standard issue is a six-month multiple entry tourist visa (specify six months and multiple entry on your application form), which **starts from the date of issue**, not from the date of entry into India. No visas are issued at India's land borders or international airports.

At home

UK	High Commission of India, India House, Aldwych, London, WC2B 4NA, ☎ 020-7632 3149, 💻 www.hcilondon.net Visas are also available from the Consulate General of India in Birmingham and Edinburgh (for details see the London website).
USA	Embassy of India Consular Wing, 2536 Massachusetts Avenue, NW, Washington, DC 20008 ☎ 202-939-9806, 💻 www.indianembassy.org
Canada	High Commission of India, 10 Springfield Road, Ottawa, Ontario K1M 1C9 ☎ 613-744-3751 (24h) / 3752 / 3753, 💻 www.hciottawa.ca
Australia	High Commission of India, 3-5, Moonah Place, Yarralumla, Canberra, ACT-2600 ☎ 02-6273 3999, 💻 www.hcindia-au.org
New Zealand	High Commission of India, 180 Molesworth Street, PO Box 4045, Wellington 6015 ☎ 04-473 6390, 💻 www.hicomind.org.nz

Abroad

In Pakistan, the High Commission of India (G-5, Diplomatic Enclave, ☎ +92 51 814371) takes ten working days to process a six-month multiple-entry Indian tourist visa. The Embassy of India in China (1, Ritan Dong Lu, Beijing 100600, ☎ +86 10 6532 1908, 💻 www.indianembassy.org.cn) also issues six-month multiple-entry visas in five working days, though it charges an extra Y100 for non-Chinese. Their office in Hong Kong (16 D, United Centre, 95 Queensway, ☎ +85 2 2528 4028) issues the same in three working days. In Nepal (☎ +977 1 444 0653), the visa takes seven working days to process; in Bhutan two days. Check with the embassies for the latest visa fees.

It is not possible to extend an Indian tourist visa. Neighbouring Nepal, Sri Lanka, Bangladesh and Pakistan all issue new six-month tourist visas.

NEPAL

Getting into Nepal is easy as you can buy a thirty-day single entry tourist visa (US$30 but payable in Nepali rupees, Chinese RMB or Indian rupees) at land borders as well as Kathmandu airport. Nepali visas run from the January to the December. Validity is six months from the date of issue.

At home

UK	Embassy of Nepal, 12a Kensington Palace Gardens, London W8 4QU ☎ 020-7229 1594, 💻 www.nepembassy.org.uk
USA	Embassy of Nepal, 2131 Leroy Place NW, Washington, DC 20008 ☎ 202-667-4550, 💻 www.nepalembassyusa.org
Canada	Honorary Consulate General of Nepal, 120 Eglinton Ave East, Suite 707, Toronto, ON M4P 1E2 ☎ 416-975-0910, 📠 416-322-2928 CAN$45 for single entry 60-day tourist visa.
Australia	See 💻 www.dfat.gov.au for your nearest Consulate General.
New Zealand	Contact Quest, 721 Cameron Road (PO Box 15171), Tauranga, ☎ 02-7439 2312, 💻 pgibbs@xtra.co.nz

Abroad

Tourist visas can be bought for US$30 or equivalent at all India/Nepal and China/Nepal land borders and also at Tribhuvan International Airport, Kathmandu.

It costs US$30 to **extend** a tourist visa for thirty days at the Department of Immigration (Kathmandu) or the Immigration Office (Pokhara); your visa can be extended for a total of 120 days.

BHUTAN

Bhutan is closed to independent tourists; anyone who wishes to visit must arrange a visa through a government-approved travel agent. The daily tariff is a sobering US$200 per person per day for a group of three or more. If you want to travel alone, there is a US$40 surcharge per day. The tariff during July and August – the monsoon season – is cheaper at US$165. See 💻 www.tourism.gov.bt for further information.

REGIONAL PERMITS

Karakoram Highway

Only one permit is required along the KKH: the Khunjerab National Park beyond Sost which charges **$4 for an entry permit** at the checkpoint on the KKH. No permits are required for Xinjiang (China), although the stretch of the KKH between Khunjerab and Tashkurgan (the Chinese customs post) is a restricted area and all cyclists have to take the bus (see p106).

India

The proximity of Ladakh, Spiti and Sikkim to China means that foreigners require **Inner Line Permits** to access regions within 40km of the Chinese border. All permits require passport photos so be sure to carry at least four as photo booths are not a common sight up here.

In practice most of Ladakh is permit-free unless you want to climb Khardung La into Nubra, explore Dha Hanu or cycle to the lakes adjoining the border. All foreign visitors to Spiti require an Inner Line Permit to travel along the western edge of Tibet between Sumdo and Jangi. Inner Line Permits can be obtained from local travel agents or, failing that, from the government officials themselves (usually the District Commissioner or 'DC'); the standard deal is Rs100 for a seven-day permit. For years there has been talk of abolishing the Inner Line Permit but there are no signs this will happen in the near future. All visitors to Sikkim require an entry permit which is also called an Inner Line Permit; this is easily picked up for free in Rangpo and Darjeeling. It's valid for fifteen days and can easily be extended twice at the Foreigners' Registration Office (FRO) in Gangtok, making for a total possible 45 days in Sikkim.

Friendship Highway, Kashgar–Lhasa and Lhasa–Zhongdian

All travellers to Tibet require a '**Tibet permit**' – a piece of paper that you will almost certainly never see because the travel agent booking your flight/jeep/tour will deal with it. Without this you cannot legally enter Tibet . The status of closed/open areas and towns can change rapidly especially in times of political unrest; check international news and ask other travellers for the latest information. Restricted areas, if accessible, will require an Alien's Travel Permit (ATP) for which you will need to contact the local Public Security Bureau (PSB) and probably pay a fee. On the Friendship Highway ATPs are required in theory but have not been checked since 2005.

Bhutan

There are permits required to enter some parts of Bhutan but your travel agent will take care of all of them.

Costs and money

The true **cost** of a Himalayan cycling adventure obviously adds up to a lot more than the flight and daily expenses on the road. The plus side is that hopefully you've already spent money on the following:

- a serviced bike in good shape
- clothing
- panniers and racks
- camping gear including tent, stove and sleeping bag
- guidebooks and maps
- cycle computer and maybe a GPS
- immunizations
- travel insurance
- visas
- travel arrangements

The cost of the trip also depends on how you like to travel. India and Pakistan are the cheapest countries to travel in where a few hardy individuals can ride

EXCHANGE RATES

	Pakistan Rupee	India Rupee	Nepal Rupee	China Renminbi (RMB) or Yuan (Y)	Bhutan Ngultrum (Ngu)*
UK £1	Rs130	Rs83	Rs133	Y13	Ngu83
€1	Rs101	Rs65	Rs105	Y10	Ngu65
US $1	Rs66	Rs43	Rs68	Y7	Ngu43
Can $1	Rs64	Rs41	Rs66	Y6	Ngu41
Aus $1	Rs62	Rs40	Rs64	Y6	Ngu40
NZ $1	Rs49	Rs32	Rs51	Y5	Ngu32

For the latest rates check online at www.xe.com
* The Bhutanese Ngultrum is linked to the Indian rupee; both can be used in Bhutan.

around India and Pakistan on US$5 a day but this means sleeping rough or with a family and eating the staple diet of *dahl baaht* (lentils and rice). Most budget travellers expect to spend around US$10 a day which in India will buy a cheap room for the night and simple but varied meals and snacks. Nepal has tourist resorts at European prices – tempting after a rough fortnight in Tibet – and in Tibet prices are high anyway. By regional standards Bhutan is off the scale: an all-inclusive package here costs US$200 a day.

Budget-breakers include sightseeing, tours, expensive bike repairs and emergency jeeps or flights if you get ill. Some days camping in the middle of nowhere you'll spend nothing; other days, especially when you've reached your destination, deserve a real splurge on a good hotel and great food.

All of these countries operate a **two-tiered** system for tourist attractions: one price for nationals and another, much higher price for foreigners: Rs20 jumps up to Rs750 in the case of India's Taj Mahal.

MONEY

For trips over a month it's worth thinking about how you're going to manage what money you have left at home. Internet banking is useful for keeping track and saves someone at home from having to deal with your finances. As for cash, the **US dollar** is the best foreign currency to carry in Asia.

If you don't have a **credit card** consider getting one. Some airlines will only accept credit cards, not debit cards. A credit card also offers protection against online fraud but note that any banks now slap on a charge if you withdraw cash from a foreign ATM; better to use a debit card for this.

Visa has got the best presence in Asia (see http://visa.via.infonow.net for an ATM locator), followed at a distance by MasterCard and then American Express. Debit cards with any symbol other than Visa (eg any of MasterCard's offshoots such as Maestro, Switch, Solo or Cirrus) are often refused. Installed in 2007, **Bhutan's ATMs** do not yet accept foreign cards. Even if you have no intention of using it, a credit card is invaluable in an emergency.

Debit cards are good for ATMs and more convenient than **travellers' cheques**, though without doubt travellers' cheques are the safest way to carry large amounts of money. Thomas Cook and American Express travellers' cheques are accepted throughout Asia although money-changers prefer

CLASSIC SCAMS OF INDIA

Everyone knows the expression 'If something seems too good to be true, it probably is', and on your first visit to India it's worth keeping this at the back of your mind.

Confidence tricksters abound and they usually target lone foreigners in their early 20s. The psychology relies on the traveller either being naïve or greedy and letting the con artist pressure them into doing something they aren't comfortable with but can't put their finger on why. Trust your **gut instincts**! Most people eventually wake up and walk away unscathed but con artists can be extremely persuasive; they are professionals after all.

Sometimes your newfound 'friend' turns nasty with a threat of physical violence, and in the worst cases (in Rajasthan and Kashmir) travellers have found themselves under house arrest. Those who are 'had' often admit they felt under pressure and didn't want to appear rude. Quite a few also say that they *knew of the scam before they fell for it* – that is how good the tricksters are.

If someone is selling you a story, question it and watch the reaction. If they react badly walk away. Don't let yourself be bullied. The worst scam is the Agra gem scam and its variants.

The Agra gem scam

This originated in Agra but has been used in Manali and Delhi. You are befriended and told about your new friend's gem/gold/carpet business. They suggest you post the gems/gold/carpet back to your country thereby saving them having to pay duty. You get a cut of the deal when the gems/gold/carpets are sold and everyone makes money. You will be shown folders full of travellers' details: see, lots of people do this, and you will be encouraged to sign a contract. All they need is a copy of your credit card as insurance. Should you fall for this scam cancel the payment and block your credit card immediately. Explain the situation to your bank and go to the police.

The pre-paid taxi at Delhi airport

Sadly a pre-paid taxi (avoiding the need to haggle with the driver) doesn't always mean hassle-free and late-night Delhi taxi drivers can sense a gullible greenhorn. Usually around Connaught Circus they'll tell you they don't where your hotel is and will pull over to ask at the 'tourist office'. Ask yourself what kind of tourist office is open in the middle of the night. Should you find yourself in the 'office' a phone call (to the room next door) will establish that your hotel is either full or closed. They will then suggest a hotel of their own/trip to Kashmir and so on. Cut this one short by telling the taxi driver to drop you at New Delhi Railway Station forthwith. Hold onto the pre-paid receipt until the end – without it the driver will not be paid.

Baby hungry, need milk

This one occurs in Delhi. Foreigners are approached by a woman holding a baby but instead of begging for money she asks only for milk – 'no money, only milk'. She will steer you to a shop to buy the milk (either fresh in cartons or in powdered form) at which point the shopkeeper may ask for an outrageous sum – one tourist paid Rs2500 ($60) for two cartons because he felt too embarrassed to refuse. The woman later returns the milk to the shopkeeper, keeps a percentage of the profits and goes back to find another soft-touch. Like professional child beggars, this one is hard to say no to.

Thanks to the India Mike travel forum (💻 www.indiamike.com)

cheques issued in US dollars to Euros and might well refuse sterling. When buying travellers' cheques look for somewhere you can cash in any unused cheques on your return. Once abroad some money-changers offer a good exchange rate but sting you on commission charges and others do the reverse. As with everything shop around for the best rates. Note that the rate for travellers' cheques is nearly always worse than that for hard cash. In India keep hold of some **ATM and foreign exchange receipts** as these 'encashment receipts' may be requested when booking flights and trains.

CARRYING YOUR MONEY

You'll often have to carry enough cash to last at least a fortnight so many cyclists carry a small amount in a zipped pocket or handlebar bag, and stash travellers' cheques and credit cards in something they **always carry with them**. Ortlieb handlebar bags have space under the plastic liner for a Ziploc bag of cash, cards and photocopied documents.

Some people like to use a **money belt** (the kind that is actually a trouser belt), and keep an emergency $100 hidden somewhere crafty like within the frame of the bike. In unsafe areas, some travellers also carry a **fake wallet** containing expired cards and valueless notes which can be handed over quickly in the event of a mugging (highly unlikely in the Himalaya).

What to take

Most people new to cycle touring make the mistake of taking too much gear and spending too much money on unnecessary stuff. For anyone who loves outdoor shops and clothing the temptation to buy lots of kit before a big trip is hard to resist but only a few things are really worth spending good money on and most items are available cheaply in Asia. The section below details what would work best in the Himalaya and also serves as a checklist for anyone wanting to hire a bike whether independently or on an organized tour.

A BICYCLE FOR THE HIMALAYA

All sorts of bikes have crossed the Himalaya from recumbents and tandems to folding bikes and hand-cranked trikes. Take what works for you but new or used, take a well-tested machine that you've owned (and ideally trained on) for a few months so there are no nasty surprises when you set off on your first route.

Key features

If you're new to bike touring it's best to be conservative in your choice. Above all you want a simple, tough, trouble-free machine as there will be enough other challenges to deal with. You want a bike that can survive being slung on the roof of a bus or in a plane's hold, bounced off the side of a jeep and dropped regularly on rough trails without ending up like pretzel.

One thing all Himayalan bikes will need is a good range of **gears** to crawl up the passes: aim at three chain rings the smallest with **22 teeth** and a rear cassette with a range of around 11 to 32 teeth. You'll also want **brakes** on which you can rely during descents lasting several hours. Remember that besides the gradients, the extra **weight** you'll be carrying will put added stress on both these components.

You'll also need a cycle frame with threaded mounting points or **braze-ons** for water bottles and more importantly, a **rear pannier rack**. Cycling with a full backpack is a short-cut to sweaty misery. One key feature of touring and expedition bike frames, which mountain bikes lack, are **longer chain stays** to provide foot clearance when panniers are mounted on a rear rack.

Less evident at a glance, the **frame**, **wheels** and **tyres** need to be up to the rigours of potholed roads and rough tracks. And with weeks of riding ahead, you must also consider day-long **comfort**. On a bike this may seem limited to fat tyres, a decent saddle and possibly suspension, but acquiring a bike that's the **right size** and with a riding position that **suits you** is a time consuming endeavour. You'll know it when you find it but that can take some experimentation and has little to do with a snazzy paint job or a cool brand.

With the daunting prospect of pedalling uphill for days it's easy to obsess over a bike's weight when cruising online catalogues. It's worth remembering that the typical 5kg weight difference between a capable steel or aluminium-framed steed and a slick machine hand forged by gnomes from unobtanium in the forests of Lichtenstein will actually add up to a pair of full water bottles and whether you've been to the toilet recently. As a rule, compared to a decent city hybrid a typical high end tourer or 'expedition bike' is not that light: up to 14kg or around 31lbs but with the added material intelligently focused in critical areas of the frame as well as on essential components like tough racks, rims and tyres. Lightness is for racers or high-income cycling dilettantes; what you need in the Himalaya is toughness and dependability partly derived from the bike's components but also down to the quality and construction of the frame.

A Himalayan heffalump at 14kg but strong as an ox and bomb-proof

Frame material

> *I cycled with two English guys in Iran on Thorn Ravens – the fact that they had steel bikes helped them to fly down some bumpy dirt tracks that I'd never be able to do so happily with an alu frame...* Peter Gostelow; 45,000 trouble-free kms across Asia on a Cannondale hybrid.

Chances are if you own a bike these days it's made of **aluminium** alloy. Aluminium has become the most popular frame material not because it's light (strength for strength there's not much in it compared to steel) but because automated factory robots find the thick tubes easy to weld. This in turn has reduced production costs and price and so increased popularity.

Unlike more supple steel frames, aluminium can **fatigue**; cracks slowly develop and grow as the frame is flexed or repeatedly stressed (something which suspension alleviates). This can take many years of riding and up to a point aluminium frames are over-engineered to cope with this, but when it happens the frame's integrity is finished and so is your bike ride. A ride across the Himalaya on a loaded bike will stress a frame for sure.

Even if repair was possible, aluminium welding gear is not the sort of thing you can find on a Ladakhi backstreet; steel-welding facilities are. However, as Peter Gostelow has proved, how you treat your bike has a lot to do with it. For adventure cycling choose a new or not too old aluminium-framed bike with a solid frame fitted with chunky braze-ons for your racks (and note that it's easy to accidentally cross thread braze-ons on the relatively soft aluminium frames). Many high-end European expedition bike builders like Koga and VSF produce touring models in aluminium but even away from this exotica, by settling for aluminium you simply have a much greater choice at a lower price.

Though highly unfashionable outside cult circles, among trans-continental cognoscenti chrome molybdenum **steel** is regarded as the best frame material for touring in remote locations and developing countries – and the Himalaya ticks both these boxes.

'Cro moly' designated '**4130**' (such as Reynolds' famous '531' brand) is well suited to light-weight tubing in high stress applications. Even over many years compliant cro-moly steel does not suffer from fatigue as readily as stiffer aluminium alloys, but if you do have any problems with your frame there is a good chance a friendly local welder can fix it. No other frame material offers this practicality. This isn't to say that they're inferior, but it's confidence inspiring to know that your frame was designed to take the weight of your loaded panniers and that it will cope with rough roads when hurtling downhill at 45mph carrying all that weight, year after year.

On quality cro-moly frames **braze-on** mounting points are the norm; not the case on other types of frame. Check your bike has them. If not, there are rack systems that utilize clamps but they won't all offer anywhere near the same security and rigidity over rough terrain as racks screwed to braze-ons. A feebly mounted rack flexing under its load can create a dangerous shimmy or weave when hitting a bump on a fast downhill (more on p47).

Good touring steel frames are expensive as the tubes' thinness requires them to be built by loving human hands; cheap steel frames built by unfeeling robots are crude and heavy. This small diameter tubing can give a steel bike a puny look to onlookers used to a typical fat-tubed aluminium bike. In fact steel is only beaten by titanium for strength and has a further advantage in responding less harshly to jarring surface shocks than stiff aluminium.

This **comfort factor** is another reason why traditional steel-framed bikes without the complication or weight of suspension or the need for fat mountain bike tyres are more suited to adventure touring.

It has to be said that advances in frame building technology have much reduced aluminium's harshness since its advent twenty-odd years ago. And of course the now common suspension forks (see opposite) fitted to most mass market bikes successfully dampen any perceived harshness.

The only suspension here is in the seatpost.

While light, strong and responsive, both **titanium** and **carbon fibre** frames are expensive exotic materials that are irreparable in the field. Unless you know better they are really more suited to high-performance racing than high-altitude Himalayan touring.

Suspension

These days you can buy a garish no-brand MTB in a supermarket with full-suspension for around £100; they look great if you happen to be nine years old or until you try and pick one up. Just about all quality-brand MTBs also come with suspension forks, as do many city/leisure or hybrid bikes. To all but a few drop-bar die-hards this is a great thing for the obvious reasons: riding becomes more comfortable if not safer. The difference between continuing or crashing after hitting a bump on a downhill bend could come down to having a front fork or not. Only two types of bikes have ignored the trend towards suspension: road racing bikes and until recently most touring or expedition bikes.

You don't need the typical 100mm or more of travel that mountain bike suspension forks come with these days; just half of that will do. The problem is today the technology and therefore the quality units are found in the cross-country (XC) or downhill racing sector; shorter travel forks which end up on hybrid or city bikes are not as sophisticated or robust.

The better mountain bike forks come with the ability to vary the spring (compression) as well as the damping (rebound) response but one feature you will really want in the mountains is the ability to '**lock out**' a suspension fork, effectively making it rigid. Without it, when climbing hard the fork springs bob up and down absorbing energy from each pedal stroke instead of transmitting it directly to the ground. It's why you'll never see suspension on a road racing bike where speed and efficiency are paramount. Rigid forks are what you want for the long Himalayan road ascents and suspension is what you might like on the rough flat or downhill stages which follow.

Again, the problem is these days there are few quality forks which come with modest suspension travel and lock out. Avoid forks which rely purely on air springing; the heavier **coil and oil** versions require less maintenance and will work OK even when leaking. When air seals go it's probably a job for a bike shop. For **rack systems** designed specifically for front suspension bikes see p46. Good fork brands to look for are Rock Shox, Marzocchi, Fox and Pace.

Rear suspension is not necessary for Himalayan road touring, partly because even if your bike is getting a beating you can stand up and absorb the hits on bended legs (more on p60). Furthermore, suspension designs vary considerably among manufacturers which means the solid racking a Himalayan bike must have becomes much more complicated. A few companies out there offer solutions, such as 💻 www.axiomgear.com or 💻 www.oldmanmountain.com, or you may find it easier to fabricate your own rear rack with a local welder.

If you can crack this nut and carry your luggage securely a very pleasing

Tout Terrain's full suspension Panamericana touring bike with an integrated rack and available with Rohloff Speedhub: that will be around £3000 please. © Tout-Terrain.de

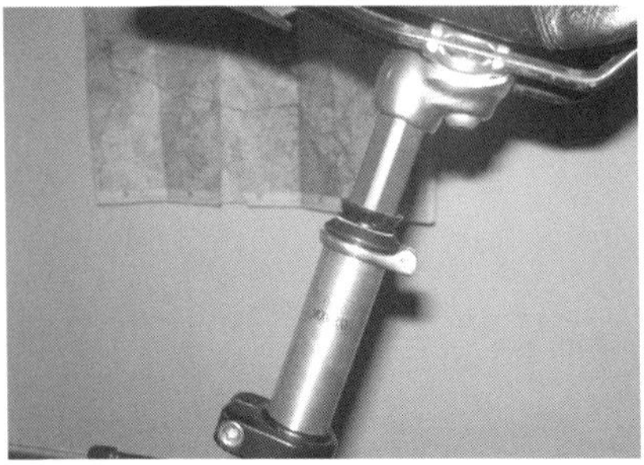

Take the sting out of your tail with a suspension seatpost. Up to a point it can make saddle choice less critical.

ride awaits on **rough descents** as you cruise comfortably past other cyclists whose eyeballs are beginning to froth. Elsewhere though, you'll want to lock the forks out in an effort to regain pedalling efficiency.

An inexpensive way of insulating your backside from moderate but persistent road shocks is to fit a **suspension seatpost**. Travel will typically be no more than an pre-tensionable inch or two; enough to transform a firm saddle into something you don't mind sitting on all day.

Bike styles

What was once just simply a 'pushbike' is now divided into many categories and sub-categories. Some don't have the frame geometry, stability or carrying ability needed for Himalayan touring but four styles fit the bill: mountain bikes, hybrids or trekking bikes, tourers and, not surprisingly, 'expedition' bikes.

Mountain bikes

It's the Himalaya so it's got to be a mountain bike, right? Indeed MTBs have many of the desirable features listed earlier and can be easily adapted for touring depending on the route and road conditions. Starting with a mountain bike certainly opens up the options for suspension set up, frame materials and choice of brands. The gear ratios will also be suited to the sort of gruelling climbs you can expect and the 'relaxed' frame geometry will be fairly comfortable. Any example from the well-known brands costing around £500 will be more than up to the job with a solid frame and good components (see p41). All you need to do is change excessively knobbly tyres for something smoother to create less drag and wear on long tarmac stages.

As already mentioned, the bike's rear triangle must have **braze-ons** to solidly mount rear racks as well as the strength to take fully loaded panniers. It's well worth confirming this with your bike shop or some clever dick on the

LOCAL BIKES

It's always a relief to see local people on bikes in the Himalaya as it usually means that the road ahead is vaguely flat. In cities on the Indian plains bicycles are true beasts of burden and can be seen weaving through the maelstrom of traffic, festooned with aluminium milk churns or half hidden under piles of mattresses.

While the strength of these metal mules is beyond question, they do not take to the mountains easily. For that you'll need a mountain bike which is available locally such as a Hero in India, a Giant in Tibet (see p253) or a Trek in Nepal (see p291). Hero bikes are the cheapest and least reliable with things most likely to fall apart in this order: gears then brakes then pedals, cranks and seat posts. Sounds like fun? Then Delhi is the place to buy one. It's easy and cheap to accessorize the bike in a cycle market with a bell, a front-basket and racks (but not panniers).

internet before you buy. As a rule the more expensive an MTB the more specialized it is for off-road racing and, quality components apart, the less suitable it is for Himalayan touring. One example will be **short chain stays** placing the rear wheel as far forward as possible to aid traction on loose or muddy climbs. Your greater need is to be able to pedal without your heel hitting your pannier on every stroke. If you have large feet make sure that the rack and pannier combination you use on your Himalaya-bound MTB gives you clearance to spin the pedals.

If you can find a good **steel-framed** MTB so much the better. In the 1980s chunky steel frames from Specialized, Marin and Trek were the norm. Today a few models, among them Kona's Explosif and Orange's P7 series, stick with cro-moly but in a sophisticated, thinner-walled incarnation that is more suited to lightweight racing than heavily loaded touring. If you're looking for a steel-framed mountain bike to convert to a tourer you're best off tracking down an example at least ten years old. Just remember a lot of other tourers are thinking along the same lines so the eBay bargain you may be expecting is unlikely. But if you do find a good steel frame and equip it with quality components and tough touring accessories you will have essentially made yourself what these days is called an Expedition bike.

Expedition bikes

Designed specifically for the sort of routes that appear in this book, these are the bikes you buy if money is no object. They are commonly built from cro-moly **steel** with plenty of braze-ons and a relaxed, stable geometry suited to long days in the saddle with a full load. Both rims will be tough and heavy and back wheels will feature 36-spokes when used with derailleur gears to add further strength ('symmetric' Rohloff hubs require only 32). More often than not they offer the gear ratios of a mountain bike providing the range you need to pedal over a 5000m pass.

HOW TO LOVE YOUR BICYCLE (AND NOT WANT TO THROW IT OFF A CLIFF)

The relationship between a long-distance tourer and their bike can be the stuff of love stories. The bond between rider and trusty steed is forged over thousands of hours in the saddle and thousands of kilometres on the road. It's no wonder that Hong Kong-bound cyclist Edward Genochio, whose bicycle was famously stolen in the dead of night by a Mongolian horseman, met with such an overwhelmingly sympathetic response from fellow cyclists when his story hit the papers.

Take the time to perfect your bike set up so that spending long hours in the saddle will be a joy, not a chore. This is where your choice of bike is crucial: some breeds like road bikes sacrifice comfort for speed, some frame materials are comfier than others (aluminium is the harshest) and other bikes may look OK but are more hassle than they're worth (really cheap bikes).

Once you have your frame think about tyre and saddle choice (see pp43-4). Then there are comfort-specific components to consider such as suspension seat posts, multi-adjustable handlebar stems and multi-position handlebars with gel grips. Further tweaks can be made to the height and position of the saddle and handlebars. But just as importantly your skeleton needs time to adapt to the unnatural position of riding a bicycle. Long bike rides are the key here and will expose problems that may go unnoticed on shorter rides. Once these tweaks are finalized all you need are the bonding trials and tribulations of an adventure and bike love will be yours!

BMC Cargo ready for the road.
© bmc-racing.com

The technology is usually conservative, relying on proven materials and systems which are unlikely to break or which can be fixed or maintained in the field. Examples include Brooks saddles (which can be reshod in yak hide), Rohloff's 14-speed internal hub, 'cup and cone' as opposed to cartridge bearings, and at present usually no suspension or disc brakes.

These are specialized, often handmade machines catering for a niche market and therefore cost from £1000 or more. But they are fully equipped (or are specifiable) with the sort of racks, tyres and other components you'd probably end up buying anyway and with chainstays long enough to accommodate panniers without fouling your feet.

It would be a mistake to buy such a bike for your first tour, but if you're already sure you have a taste for it then an expedition bike is the ultimate machine. Major bike manufacturers don't really serve this category seriously: examples will come from non-household-name marques like the British Thorn **Raven Tour**, the Dutch **Koga Miyata**, the Swiss **BMC Cargo**, the German-made Tout Terrain **Silk Route** or Germans Cycles' **Acid** series, and the American Surly **Long Haul Trucker**.

Hybrid bikes

This is the type of bike that people new to cycling take to most easily and is ideal if you're certain your chosen route is not going to be too rough. With a more upright seating position and an accent on comfort, they evolved from early mountain bikes which many riders, attracted by the flat handlebars, powerful brakes and convenient shifters, adapted for commuting or light recreational riding.

The gear range on a hybrid is wider than an MTB – more road oriented – and wheels are often **700c**: larger diameter and narrower and which roll with less effort than fat, 26-inch MTB wheels (at the price of less cushioning and less grip on the dirt). Frames are nearly all aluminium so, as with mountain bikes, check the rear frame triangle's strength for carrying luggage and the presence of chunky braze-ons. Frame fatigue should not be such a problem as, compared to MTBs, hybrids lead easy lives (until pointed at the Himalaya!). Many hybrid bikes come with plush saddles, adjustable stems, suspension seat posts and suspension forks with the moderate range travel ideal for touring (but not necessarily with lock-out).

A sub-category of hybrids is rather grandly called trekking bikes, basically a hybrid with all the accessories a regular rider is likely to buy: mudguards, lights, a stand and racks. They are common in the more bike-savvy Europe than in the UK for example, where a bare bike is seen as 'lighter' (if less functional as a daily ride). In fact if you're from the UK it's well worth seeing what a given manufacturer sells in Holland or Germany under the same model name; chances are you'll be envious. Don't get too excited about trekking bikes; they're better described as 'fully equipped commuting bikes' and the accessories you get won't all be necessary or up to Himalayan touring.

Every major bike manufacturer produces a range of hybrids these days. Choose carefully and aim for a top of the range model with tough rims and other components; anything cheap is strictly for popping out to the shops, not exploring the Tibetan plateau.

Touring bikes

Touring bikes are a mix of the elements that make a road bike so quick on good surfaces: a committed but more relaxed frame geometry, 700c wheels with narrower tyres, useful gear ratios and dropped handlebars for a powerful and aerodynamic stance. This last factor is what puts off many novice riders and almost certainly contributed to the flat-barred mountain bike boom in the 1980s. They can certainly cover the miles efficiently but even old touring stalwarts complain of back, neck and wrist aches while staring at the front wheel all day. Tourers are great for domestic or continental touring but you need to consider whether this type of bike with its drop bars and thin tyres will be easy to handle on rough tracks.

These bikes nearly always feature full sets of braze-ons so are very practical when it comes to mounting racks and panniers. They're also very conventional which means you're unlikely to find new-fangled features like disc brakes or front suspension, instead you'll almost certainly get mudguards and maybe even a bell.

Gearing on these bikes is usually a triple front chainring which should be fine if you're fit, but if you're in any doubt you may want to talk to your bike shop about extending the gear range for the long climbs ahead. The frames come in either steel or aluminium which gives you the flexibility to go for the practicalities of steel if you're going on a long trip. Examples include Cannondale's Touring Classic and the legendary old-school range of Dawes's cro-mo Galaxy models.

BICYCLE COMPONENTS AND ACCESSORIES

When you look beyond the paint job and a good price it's actually the **components** of a bike that separate one near identical model from another. Hubs spin round, derailleurs pivot, V-brakes grip and shifters click readily, but some examples perform more smoothly, reliably and for longer than others. And then there are the elite category of components which do all that and weigh next to nothing.

Bike manufacturers buy in these components from outside companies like Suntour, SRAM and Shimano, all of which produce ranges or 'groupsets' (hubs, derailleurs, shifters, brakes, etc) varying in quality as well as intended use. When it comes to buying a bike you will do well to acquaint yourself with the groupset hierarchy. For example, the commonly specified range of Shimano groupsets run up from Alivio and Acera to LX, Deore, XT and XTR. Alivio and Acera will feature on low end hybrids and mountain bikes while Deore and XT components will come on bikes in £500-1000 price range. Unfortunately canny bike manufacturers commonly mix Alivio hubs with Deore shifters for example. Scrutinize the specifications of a bike carefully so you know what you're getting.

INCHING UP THE HILLS

Because Himalayan climbs can go on for over 50km and exceed 5000m (16,400ft) in altitude, **low gears** are important, especially when hauling luggage over bad roads.

The number of gears a bicycle has is not as important as their **range**. For the Himalaya a generous MTB derailleur set-up adds up to chainrings at 42/32/20 and sprockets from 13 to 28 which gives a gear range of 18- to 84 'gear inches'. 'Gear inches' is a way of quantifying your gear range, see the Sheldon Brown website below for more gear talk. For the Himalaya your lowest gear should work out no higher than **21 inches**.

Further discussion on the significance and terminology of gears can be found at 💻 www.kenkifer.com/bikepages/touring/gears.htm while the late Sheldon Brown's handy **gear inch calculator** resides at 💻 www.sheldonbrown.com/gears.

Riding a bike with low-end components will get you to work, but the brakes will be mushy, the shifting less than effortless and the attention to detail only average. Load this bike up and ride it at the Himalaya and soon things will unravel as bearings and bolts loosen no matter how much you adjust them, cranks bend, wheels go out of true and cheap suspension forks pop their corks. You get what you pay for and in the Himalaya, where your LBS will be a chap with a hammer, you'll get a lot less aggravation riding a bike fitted with quality components.

Brakes

Brakes can be important when riding down the side of the world's biggest mountain range. These days there are two main systems: **V-brakes** and disc brakes, and which one you use will influence the choice of pannier racks. V-brakes are most commonly seen on mid-range bicycles and work on the well-proven cable pulley and brake pad system. They're cheap, light, reliable and easy to maintain; spare parts are easily carried. V-brakes also work with almost every type of rack. Their drawbacks are they require the rims to be perfectly straight and in wet and muddy conditions they don't brake as well. Pads wear out quickly in these conditions and the wheel rims wear through heavy braking too at which point you will appreciate Shimano's XT V-brakes: an excellent cartridge system which takes just seconds to replace worn pads.

On a bicycle **disc brakes** work on the same principle as on a car or motorbike. The calliper houses one or more pistons which push the break pads on the disc attached to the wheel hub. They operate either hydraulically or are levered by a cable. This latter, fluid-free system may be more suitable for remote touring as leaking or spongy hydraulics are not so field repairable.

Do as the rock suggests; slow down and enjoy looking at the other rocks.

Disc braking enables excellent braking in all conditions with very little pressure needed. There are no soft rubber pads to wear out or rim degradation. And best of all you can ride and brake fine with your rims out of true which means less time spent fiddling with a spoke key. Disc-brake technology is now commonplace and is seen even on inexpensive bikes. The drawbacks are that disc brakes are heavier than V-brakes and require special wheels that can accommodate the disc and calliper and can handle the torque at the hub instead of the rim. You will also need to look for disc brake specific racks.

Derailleur gears or hub gears

Rear **derailleurs** are the norm on almost all bicycles but it only takes one clumsy baggage handler, one pothole when loaded on a bus roof or one crash to damage beyond repair the rear derailleur hanger (the small metal tab which attaches your rear derailleur to the bike frame). One solution is to fit the bike with a **replaceable derailleur hanger** and carry a spare.

For the mountains you can't beat 22-32-44 up front with an 11-34 cassette on the back. The lowest gear is no faster than walking but the huge 11-34 range is ideal and the 11T gives a lot more welly than 13T which is still quite common. Even if the lowest nine-speed gear is so slow you'd be liable to fall off unless you could pedal uphill at 100rpm, you can never have too low a gear. It's not just the gradient, it's also the out-of-breath feeling and sometimes dust that slows you down. With a 22T in front, you can stay in that granny ring and deal with it. There's also a psychological advantage to having very low gears: no matter how tough a climb is you can take heart that you always have a couple more speeds in reserve. Running out of gears and *still* panting like a spaniel is demoralizing.

Derailleurs are the norm but many specialist touring bike manufacturers like Thorn, Koga and German touring marques now offer the 14-speed **Rohloff Speedhub**; an enclosed hub that requires very little maintenance and should last for years (and as yet unmatched by Shimano and the like). The near-perfect linear spacing of each of the fourteen speeds translates to a typical 24-speed derailleur set up on which many gears overlap. The drag of the gears inside the oil-filled hub means a Rohloff is slightly less efficient than a derailleur set up in good conditions, but in the Himalaya derailleurs rarely stay in good condition for long. The bad news is you can buy and equip an entire Himalaya-ready bike with quality derailleurs for just the price of a Speedhub and fitting. Either used or new these hubs are by far the best value when fitted on a bike frame designed for them, such as the Thorn Raven Tour.

Rohloff Speedhub gets a clean in Gilgit, Pakistan.

Tyres

The width of the tyres, tread pattern, weight and the pressure they run at can all have an impact on comfort and pedalling ease on rough roads. Their resistance to punctures is also a crucial factor.

The best sort of tyre for the Himalaya is a mountain bike tyre with a road-oriented tread pattern that can be run at a high-pressure. Schwalbe's virtually puncture-proof Marathon XR or the Specialized Hemisphere both fit the bill. These tyres come in various widths but 1.95″ is fat enough for most routes. Just make sure your bike frame is wide enough to accommodate this tyre size. The route descriptions at the start of each chapter detail the road conditions so choose your tyres' knobbliness accordingly. Those without suspension could run Schwalbe Marathon XRs half flat on dirt roads to soak up the worst of the bumps. Finally, though about as far from Schwalbes in quality as you can get, 26″ tyres and inner tubes are easy to find in Asia but outside of Kathmandu, **there are no 700c tyres or inner tubes in the Himalaya**.

Saddle

This is the most personal of choices and might demand a lot of trial and error to get right. Be sure to do so **before you go**! Bum injuries are not only unpleasant but are also difficult to monitor if travelling alone. The most important consideration when buying a saddle is where your weight lies: you need it to rest on your sitting bones. Anywhere forward of them will guarantee pain.

There's now an amazing assortment of saddles featuring the latest technologies and ergonomic designs. Newer styles are often gel-filled and male-specific ones are split down the middle to take weight off the perineum. Female-specific saddles are wider and shorter to suit the hips and pelvis and "specific soft tissue relief areas".

These modern saddle designs can seem very comfortable from first use but they're not as hard wearing as more traditional leather saddles like the legendary **Brooks** range. A few people find the typical 1000km breaking in period for a Brooks more agony than it's worth (avoid 'quick fix' leather softening agents which will ruin a Brooks) but like a good shoe, this 100-year-old design eventually moulds to your anterior profile resulting in a personalized saddle.

Despite what you might think avoid squidgy gel-filled saddles: they're designed for short runs to the shops, and all that soft gel is waiting to chafe your bottom to bits. For touring saddles (and touring in general) less is more.

Water bottles

Three bottles gives a useful range and autonomy. While researching this book I relied on one regular 750ml cycling bottle and two one-litre Nalgenes as well as a folded four-litre water bag which gave a capacity of nearly seven litres; on the Karakoram Highway in summer that didn't even last a day. A transparent water bag makes it easy to see when it needs a clean (keeping it out of sunlight slows down algae growth), you can then filter untreated river water out of this bag into your bottles. For water filtration see p60.

Two water bottles and a tea jar: going local in western China.

Easy to clean Nalgene wide mouth bottles are touring bikers' stalwarts. They're tough, never leak and best of all they can be filled with boiling water to warm your sleeping bag at bedtime and then drunk in the morning. They fit into plastic Profile bottle cages but, as with all plastic bottle cages, treat them gently in very cold weather as they can become brittle.

Bottle cages with a non-standard wide mouth such as Profile's Aqua Rack or a long cage with a strap like Modula's XL will take locally bought one-litre and even 1.5L mineral water bottles. Expect these bottles to last about a fortnight before eventually puncturing; one which held a carbonated drink like Coke will be a bit stronger. Making a hole in the top cap turns them into a squeezy-style bike bottle, making lots of pinprick holes creates a nifty shower head and a thread tied around the neck means it can be refilled in glacial streams without freezing your hand off.

Other useful items

Many touring cyclists are fans of Shimano's M324 pedals which are SPD on one side and flat on the other (great for crossing rivers in flip flops). Non-essential but useful accessories include **bungees** (available in Asia but much better quality in the West), a **cycle computer** (bring a spare magnet and battery), a **bell** (best bought locally for colour and timbre) and a **kickstand** to save your panniers grating against walls and rocks. The most fun accessory is an **air horn** so you can honk your way around the Himalaya like everyone else. What Pakistani bike shops lack in useful bike parts they more than make up for in accessories like plastic handlebar flowers and leopard print saddles.

Tools and spares

Dawn Till Dusk in Kathmandu (see p291) and Spinn Café in Lhasa (see p253) are the only places in the Himalaya that stock quality components so you'll need some spares. India and Pakistan do not import foreign bicycle parts. Should you have a serious problem such as a broken derailleur then either get yourself to Kathmandu or Lhasa, or order one from home and find somewhere pleasant to wait while the part is couriered to you. Another option on popular routes is to offer to buy the part from a fellow touring cyclist about to return home. At the very least you will need:

- puncture patches
- tyre levers and inner tubes (check the valve is the right type!)
- brake pads
- brake and gear cables
- chain links
- spokes
- bolts of all necessary sizes, especially for racks
- chain oil (eg Finish Line)
- small 35mm film canister of lithium grease
- cable ties
- duck tape and WD40
- mini pump and a good multi-tool (eg Topeak Alien)

THE ZEN OF BIKE MAINTENANCE

"If it doesn't move and it should, use WD40. If it moves and it shouldn't, use duck tape"
Alistair Humphreys

A 55kg cyclist on a 60kg bike. Note the hand warmers! Bar Khun, Pakistan

You could also include a spare **folding tyre** since local 26" tyres cost about $1 but won't last more than 500km. Handy under-saddle tool bags hold patches, Allen keys and tubes perfectly but have been known to disappear from unattended bikes. In choosing a lock go for a **cable** not a D-lock. It doesn't have to be fancy but does need the length. Don't forget the spare key.

CARRYING THE LOAD

The **pannier** of choice for most tourers is the Ortlieb Classic. They're justifiably popular as they last for years and are not the most expensive panniers on the market. The roll-over closing system is extremely straightforward and waterproof. The attachment system is strong and simple – just grab the handles and pull upwards – but not obvious to others, which is a bonus. Both the closing and attachment systems are easy to use with frozen hands. Some people prefer panniers that have interior compartments but the stitching for these compromises the panniers' waterproofing. When choosing panniers look for a strong, waterproof fabric. Over the years PVC fares better than proofed cordura.

Racks

The best touring racks are made from **steel** with a simple design that any pannier system can fit on securely. Tubus and Old Man Mountain are leading brands and both also offer racks for front-suspension bikes: the Swing and Sherpa respectively. Thorn's steel Expedition series racks are very solid with a maximum load of 12kg at the front and an impressive 60kg on the rear. Just be sure your back wheel can take this weight too. Chunky **aluminium** racks like the Tortec Expedition rack cost half the price of a steel version but will probably only survive a short trip on smooth roads with a modest payload.

PACKING TO STAY SANE

With their black holes of space Ortlieb panniers (see above) are perfect for odd-shaped items that would never fit in pockets but, to make the most of them, it's important to have a packing system. The use for each pannier changes with every trip but the following rules might be helpful:

- keep the things you use most at the top of a pannier, in your handlebar bag or bungeed on the back (but see below)
- put the heaviest, least-used things (like bike spares) at the bottom to maintain a low centre of gravity
- if you have front panniers, keep them light to help steering – bulky but light items like sleeping bags, down jackets and tent fabric are best placed here.
- use bags inside the panniers: a cloth bag for clothes, plastic bag for books etc; different colours help identification, as do different fabrics when trying to find things in the dark.
- use different panniers for different jobs: for example a day-time pannier for food and clothes and a night-time pannier with thermarest, cooker, pots and pans, sleeping bag, etc.
- don't bungee anything of value on the rear rack – little hands might help themselves.

STOP IT! YOU'RE GIVING ME THE SHIMMIES

No, it's not a ghastly skin disease or some neo-Thuggee cult, but the consequences can be just as alarming. A shimmey is a steering wobble that a bike can suddenly develop, usually when going downhill fast. It can be triggered by a surface defect, a gust of wind or an involuntary movement from the rider.

Like any vibration it has, to paraphrase an expert from the CTC, 'a natural frequency that depends on the characteristics of the vibrating system.' The key factors on a bicycle are the stiffness of the frame, steering geometry and weight distribution.

At a critical moment (which may never occur on your bike) the wheel speed and the frame wobble frequency meet and are harmonized. At this point the slightest input produces a violent shaking sensation that gets worse as it's fed by your speed.

Narrow tyres at high pressures travelling fast on smooth roads (not a typical Himalayan biking scenario) are shimmey-prone situations, but so are cheap racks swaying in the breeze. Fit a solid rack and make sure it's tight. One Himalayan rider switched from a stock Dawes alloy rack to a steel Tubus and never shimmied again. Also balancing the weight right and left and making sure it's not mounted too far behind the rear axle makes a difference. And of course make sure your headset is correctly adjusted.

When mounting **front panniers** it's common to experience a slight wander as you set off but should a wobble develop at more dangerous speeds do not attempt to fight it. Instead resist clenching the handlebars too tight and hold the top tube between your legs to further dampen the vibration while gently applying the brakes from the rear. Even one leg resting against the top tube can calm the wobble.

By Chris Scott, based on an article on the CTC website: 🖳 www.ctc.org.uk

Be careful with front pannier racks – too much weight on weak racks can cause them to flex inwards and jam in the spokes with predictably nasty consequences.

CAMPING KIT

Camping kit isn't essential on most of these rides but is still recommended for the freedom and flexibility it gives, except in Sikkim which has plenty of guesthouses but little level ground to camp on; the hills out there are hard enough without having to carry unnecessary kilos.

Tents are freedom. However, if camping really isn't your thing then in most of India, Nepal and Pakistan it's not necessary to bring a tent and stove. Roadside restaurants and hotels however basic will keep you going. That said, the string beds (*charpoys*) outside roadside restaurants in Pakistan and India should be avoided by single women. Camping is necessary for cyclists on the Manali–Leh Highway and in Tibet and China, especially for the long trans-Tibet routes. When plotting a route on a map don't forget the importance of acclimatization – sometimes camping is necessary to avoid altitude sickness (see p61).

Sleeping bags, liners and mats

You'll spend a third of your time asleep in the Himalaya so it's worth spending good money on a sleeping bag. A bag is essential whether you intend to camp or not as bedding in some basic hotels can contain more wildlife than a national park. **Down** bags (make sure it's nearly 100% and not a feather mix) are cosy and pack down small but must not get wet as they take days to dry. Synthetic bags dry quickly but don't feel quite as comfy and are slightly more

GPS UNITS, ALTITUDE AND THE WEATHER

No GPS maps exist for Pakistan, India, Nepal, China and Bhutan so a GPS unit is useless for route planning in the Himalaya. However, a GPS will tell you your current location, distance travelled and your route so far. Download each track onto a PC with mapping software and you can relive your entire trip in metre-by-metre detail.

The better GPS units also have barometric altimeters which record your ascents and descents; as they use atmospheric pressure to gauge elevation they are also good at predicting the weather. When standing still, dropping elevation means high pressure (usually a good thing); conversely when the elevation goes up, you should go down. For this reason no altitude is ever truly fixed by GPS and readings can be out by as much as 50 vertical metres. Cycle computers and watches featuring altimeters are even less accurate. Add to this the fact that the Himalaya are growing each year and altitudes definitely shouldn't be taken too seriously.

All the routes in this guide were mapped using a Garmin eTrex Summit with Garmin's Trip and Waypoint Manager and Mapsource software. Mapsource files can also be downloaded into Google Earth; to see the routes in this book in 3D detail visit 🖳 www.himalayabybike.com.

bulky warmth for warmth. A well looked after down bag will last many years after a synthetic bag has lost its loft.

Choose your bag according to the expected climate: for camping in summer months you could get away with a three-season bag but for late autumn at altitude you'll need a bag rated to at least -15ºC depending on how much you feel the cold. Some manufacturers, such as Marmot, design bags especially for women with toe boxes for cold feet, wider hip space and shorter length.

Silk **liners** take up no space, are extremely light and boost the sleeping bag's performance. Choose the shape that matches your sleeping bag – probably 'mummy'. In Asia a tailor can make a silk or cotton bed sheet bag for you locally if you provide about 1.5m of material. Where better to do it than in Kashgar on the old Silk Route!

Compact **inflatable mats** such as those from Thermarest or Expeds are by far the warmest and most comfortable option but some may prefer the original closed cell foam mats which are far cheaper and are of course puncture proof. For all-round warmth, **full length** is best though ultra-lite cyclists insist the three-quarter length mattresses are enough.

Tent

You'll need a good quality three- to four-season tent that's both light and compact. Weight is important but so is specific suitability to the weather you expect to encounter. The ideal tent has a freestanding inner with a waterproof outer flysheet and a mosquito-proof door on each side. The inner part is also useful in hotel rooms infested with creepy crawlies and mosquitoes – put it on the floor and move in with your hopefully bug-free bed mattress for an undisturbed night's sleep.

Avoid tents with a completely mesh inner if it's going to be cold as you will freeze. In prolonged bad weather – which is unusual in the Himalaya – a tent becomes your home and it's more pleasant to be holed up if you can sit up straight inside and cook in the porch. While light, a tarpaulin or a **bivvy**

ELECTRICAL SOCKETS IN ASIA

All electrical sockets in the countries covered by this book are 220V. Most are triple round-pin but will take two-prong plugs, such as those used in Europe. Everyone else will need a universal converter or a transformer if from North America.

bag does not fit in this category and you'll have zero privacy from curious locals who always pop up in the middle of nowhere.

Stove

The choice of stove will be subject to what fuel is available, how high you're going and how cold it may be expected to become. **Multi-fuel** stoves are the best all round choice as they operate well at altitude and can burn anything from alcohol to kerosene to helicopter fuel. However, most need regular maintenance and all are subject to flaring up and depriving campers of their facial hair. If the stove starts really misbehaving the fault might lie with dirty fuel rather than a useless stove. For speed, ease and weight a **gas cartridge** stove is the least fuss but only viable in Tibet where the canisters are available in Lhasa and Shigatse. However, the butane and propane mix cannot condense when temperatures are near freezing so sleep with the canisters in your bag. Stove heads are OK but, not surprisingly, most airlines refuse to carry any form of gas so buy them in Lhasa.

Kerosene is used as fuel throughout Asia and multi-fuel stoves such as MSR's Whisperlite Internationale have a special kerosene jet as well as the standard petrol one. This stove is also self-cleaning and easy to maintain. If you plan to cook a lot upgrade the fuel bottle to a one-litre bottle from MSR (other brands tend to leak).

White gas, commonplace in North America, is non-existent in the Himalaya. Local stoves bought in India are huge and leak terribly (you'll have to drain the stove of kerosene before moving on); they're also unreliable and you'll need to carry spare o-rings and gaskets as these perish quickly.

Forget matches (even waterproof ones); instead bring a couple of good quality disposable **lighters** from home or make do with local cheapies but be warned; they don't last very long so carry a spare.

COOKING AT HIGH ALTITUDE

The low air pressure at altitude also lowers the boiling temperature of water. Water boils at 100°C at sea-level; at 2000m it's 93°C, 3000m 90°C, 4000m 86°C and 5000m just 83°C. The lower the temperature the longer food takes to cook so staple carbohydrate dishes such as pasta, rice and potatoes take forever at high altitude.

Enter the **pressure cooker**: the stalwart of every Himalayan kitchen. Heavy, unpredictable and eager to burn your dinner, these work by raising the pressure inside the pot thereby reducing cooking time. You can buy them in any town for around Rs350.

Cyclists who don't want to carry the extra weight should buy food like noodles, cous cous or dehydrated meals from home that cooks fast, or buy double portions in restaurants; one to eat in, one to take away to reheat later.

Pots, pans and cutlery

Two pots are plenty and a lid can double up as a plate and frying pan. Space can be saved by storing the stove inside the smallest pot which will also protect it. Lifeventure make a handy knife, fork and spoon set which clips together and has an integral bottle and tin opener.

Tough plastic such as **Lexan** makes for cheap and durable bowls, cutlery and mugs. Tin or enamel mugs can be bought in a local bazaar and used for super-sized cups of tea at roadside cafés; secondary uses are for eating cereal, noodles and soups. Pots, pans and cutlery can be bought locally, but they won't be as light as the pretty titanium ones at home. Ziploc bags, tupperware and old camera film canisters are useful for storing food, seasoning and spices.

MEDICAL KIT

A basic first aid kit is essential. You can either assemble it yourself or save money and time by buying a ready-made one from camping stores and refilling it as necessary in Asia. At the very least bring plasters, antiseptic skin cream, bandages, scissors and sterile dressings. Learn some basic first-aid before you leave so you know what to do in an accident; there are no rescue or emergency services in the Himalaya. Consider carrying sterile syringes and needles (with a doctor's letter stating their purpose to avoid any misunderstandings).

The following might also come in useful: eye drops (for dust), nasal decongestant (for blocked sinuses), painkillers such as paracetamol, insect repellent, a 'click' zapper or cream for treating insect bites, Imodium (for diarrhoea), antifungal powder (for athlete's foot), a thermometer, tubigrips, muscle gel or cream, tweezers and water purification tablets (see p60).

Bike vibrations will reduce tablets in pots to a powder: they'll survive longer if repacked in old film canisters then topped and tailed with cotton wool. Don't forget to tuck the label inside so you can identify them later on.

It's cheaper to wait until Asia to buy oral rehydration salts (ORS), cough sweets (good for the dry, dusty air at altitude) and contact lens solution (in the major cities). Contact lens and glasses-wearers should carry a spare set of glasses.

TOILETRIES AND OTHER ITEMS

All the basics – toothbrush, toothpaste, soap/shampoo, moisturizer, dental floss (the unwaxed kind doubles as sewing thread) and lipsalve – are available in Asia; only high factor sun cream (SPF 30+) is hard to find but you'll need it

BED BUGS

Many of Asia's cheaper hotels are home to a particularly blood-thirsty traveller: the bed bug. Although visible to the naked eye they are hard to spot as they usually only crawl out at night to feed on their favourite dish: the blood of a warm human. They spend the rest of the time in mattress seams or the frame of the bed, digesting their meal.

Bed bug bites are typically in a cluster or a line. You won't feel them straightaway but if you do react to them they will really itch for days. The good news is that there's no danger from the bites as long as you leave them alone and resist scratching them till they bleed, tempting though that is.

at high altitudes. Blistex make a 7ml pot of lip balm called 'MedPlus' which works wonders on wind-dried, cracked and bleeding lips.

The **Himalaya** brand of toiletries available in India and Nepal is cheap and comes in good cycle-friendly sizes. Insect repellent is essential at lower altitudes as there are malaria-carrying mosquitoes in Pakistan and India. A sponge makes washing easier when there's limited water and dries quickly. When there's no water Wetwipes and the like are good for a quick wash of zits, pits and bits. If you think you'll need condoms best bring them from home.

Sundries

Besides the items outlined below you will need a universal sink plug (or a slice of tennis ball), clothes line, mosquito net, padlock (a lock and key is easier in the dark than the combination type), wall plug adapter, alarm clock for early flights, a travel wallet, a manual compass (handy for navigating out of cities if you don't have a GPS) and a folding water carrier.

An **MP3 player** or something similar is nice for when you'd rather listen to music than headwinds or an audiobook while recovering from diarrhoea. Cheap **duffel bags** big enough to hold four panniers and a tent can be bought in any Asian city for a couple of pounds and make travelling on public transport much less hassle.

Batteries	Battery-hungry gadgets such as a GPS will devour weak Asian batteries in under an hour. If battery power is important bring a solar panel or wall charger and rechargeable batteries from home (minimum 2300MhaZ). A recharger such as the Uniross Sprint (💻 www.uniross.com) is compact and charges AAs in under two hours.
Camera	Bring a spare battery and memory cards and work out the best way to protect them all from dust and vibration. Ortlieb sell a foam insert for their handlebar bags which is perfect for SLRs. Internet cafés and camera shops in travellers' hubs can download memory cards and burn the images onto a CD.
Penknife	Or a multitool. Stainless steel with one strong, wide blade, a can opener, tweezers, scissors and pliers will be all useful. Don't lose it to an airline!
Sewing kit	Needles, light and dark nylon thread, safety pins. Or just pay a visit to the local tailor.
Tampons	Hard to find in local bazaars so bring a supply from home. You must dispose of them properly.
Torch	Essential for successfully navigating your way to the loo in the dark and not falling down it if you're in Ladakh. Head torches are the most practical as they leave your hands free and can also be used as an emergency front light in tunnels and at night. Petzl's Zipka is tiny, weighs next to nothing and has an amazing battery life. It's just about powerful enough to find things in the dark, but not to ride by.
Towel / sarong	Some travellers love travel towels but sarongs are larger, lighter, cost a tenth of the price and dry in a tenth of the time. Nor do they smell.

CLOTHING

The people of the Himalaya dress extremely modestly; doing likewise is always appreciated and will make an enormous difference to how you're treated; in some places (see p75) it can go as far as being a matter of personal safety. Local people who possess very little still dress immaculately and find it hard to understand why tourists from rich countries wear dirty or ragged clothes.

PARCELS FROM HOME

On a long trip you might need to have spare parts or something similar sent out from home. Don't have it sent by standard mail. Once the parcel has cleared customs in Asia it can't be tracked and you can waste days, weeks and even months at the post office endlessly to be told to 'come back tomorrow'. Customs are also notoriously light-fingered. A courier service such as DHL is well worth the expense because they deal with customs themselves and your parcel will arrive intact and on time.

Summer days in the high Himalaya are usually warm, dry and bright; at nights the temperature drops and a fleece and warmer trousers will be necessary. On the plains high summer is relentlessly hot: light cottons will protect your skin from the sun and rapid dehydration. High altitude in spring and autumn is cold: bring thermals and windproof outers.

Trousers or a jacket with zipped pockets are a good deterrent against pickpockets: have a system where you know what should be in each pocket so you know immediately if something is missing. Pockets in hard-to-reach places (eg down by the knee or on the chest) will be passed over by a thief in favour of someone else's wallet or passport poking out the back of their trousers. Warm clothes are great for morale at the end of a long day: a fleece with a high zip-up neck is cosy and for cold weather a snug **hat** and full-length thermals made from merino wool or similar are essential. Cyclists riding and camping at altitude very late or early in the year will find a **down jacket** invaluable, even on ascents. Apart from your riding shoes, **flip flops** or Tevas are handy for bathrooms, sunny days and river crossings; in India and Nepal you'll find colourful woolly 'lobster socks' (the ones with a separate toe) for that lovely sock-'n'flip flop look. In cold winds and dust a scarf or snood covers your lower face, ears and throat keeping them warm and dust-free.

Cycling clothing

Road cycling has yet to take off in the Himalaya so people look at rainbow-coloured lycra-clad cyclists sporting swooshy helmets and funny-coloured sunglasses as if they're aliens.

Helmet	A personal choice though recommended against Pakistani stone-throwers or for extended hammering around off-road. A visor or locally bought baseball cap will shield your eyes from the sun.
Sunglasses	100% UV protection will be essential for high altitude and need not be expensive.They will also protect your eyes from dust, gravel and insects. Polarized lenses make the scenery and cobalt skies even more impressive.
Gloves	Fingerless gloves are recommended for padding the ulnar nerve, protection in event of a fall and for lugging heavy panniers without flaying your skin.
Shoes	One pair of SPD shoes you can walk in. For cold weather Shimano's comfy Gore-Tex SPD boots are highly recommended. Bring spare cleats and bolts. Both the Karakoram and Ladakh offer spectacular trekking; if this appeals consider wearing walking boots and using toe clips on the bike.
Jacket	Windproof is more useful day-to-day than waterproof and will keep you warm on the descents.
Tops	Himalayan air is so dry that cotton tops don't get sweaty, and dry quickly in the strong sun too. Wicking tops dry faster but the synthetic fabrics can smell awful after just one day's riding and even worse once marinaded in panniers.

Trousers	Loose three-quarter length trousers are the most practical for cycling. Trekking trousers which unzip to become three-quarter lengths seem useful though the two sections fade at different rates which looks odd. Any woman wearing skin-hugging Lycra can expect hassle in India and worse in Pakistan.
Waterproofs	Waterproof trousers, gloves and a jacket are necessary on the high passes as the weather can turn quickly and you'll be in trouble if you're unprepared. Gloves with a waterproof outer and warm inner fleece (bought cheaply in Lhasa) will be essential in Tibet from September onwards.

MAPS AND GUIDEBOOKS

The **maps** in this book are designed to be used alongside road maps of the Himalaya but roads in Asia can change without warning so don't expect any map to ever be entirely accurate for long. Online at 💻 www.himalayabybike.com there are Google Earth maps with tracks and waypoints for each of the routes in this book: a virtual tour before you leave!

The best overall paper map to help you plan your route is **Nelles'** *Himalaya* 1:1.5m. Its only downside is that it's double-sided so you can't spread it all out at once unless you buy two. Second choice is Gecko Maps' one sided *Himalaya Tibet* at 1:1.6m. It has an index but does not cover the Karakoram Highway.

Map lovers might be interested in two military topographic series which cover the entire Himalaya: the American Army Map Service (AMS) U502 Topographic Survey Maps at 1:250,000 (compiled in the 1950s) and the US Defence Mapping Agency Operational Navigation Chart (ONC) and Tactical Pilotage Chart (TPC) at 1:1m and 1:500,000 respectively and last revised in the

PACKING YOUR BIKE AND CHECKING IN

When you're researching flights be sure to ask about their policy for carrying bikes. Some charge a fixed fee (about £60), some include them as part of the luggage allowance. Some demand your bike travels taped up in a box, others don't mind if you ride it fully loaded to the check-out queue.

If a bike travels in a box it's usually treated badly. Pakistan International Airlines on the other hand accepted my bike with only the pedals removed, handlebars turned and the tyres mostly deflated, and it arrived in Islamabad without a scratch.

If the airline insists on a box, ask your local bike shop for a large one so the racks fit. Start by taking off the pedals. Release the front brake and detach the front wheel. If the box is small, you may have to remove the rear wheel as well. Loosen the headset and turn the handlebars so they are parallel to the top tube. Protect your derailleur by tucking it between the stays and wrapping it up in newspaper. Most importantly secure a bit of wood between the front and rear drop outs to stop them getting bent together. Lower the saddle or remove it from the seat post and tape the wheels alongside the bike. It's tempting to stuff the box with soft items like sleeping bags to save space in the panniers and protect the bike: don't! If the airline rips the box apart they will all get 'lost in transit'.

On returning you'll have to make your own bike box. Shops selling large electrical items like fridges are the best bet. Next stop is a general store for a reel or two of parcel tape, a marker pen and some newspapers. If there is some rope around so much the better. Find somewhere shady, take your bike apart and then fold the box around your bike and wheels. If you're doing this in a public place people will almost certainly help without you asking. Tape up the cardboard-wrapped bike and finish it off with rope. Some security-conscious airports might ask you to open the box but a compromise can be found in the 'dog-wallah' whose sniffer dog can give you the all clear.

1980s and 1990s. These are visual reference charts for pilots so road detail can be inconsistent, but for topographical detail they are unmatched.

Karakoram Highway

John Callahan's *Karakoram Highway* map (1:1m) has very clear mapping with hill shading and insets of major towns; the only thing missing is an elevation profile. Nelles' *Pakistan* (1:1.5m) is not as good as the above but features Nelles' clear cartography with distance markers between towns. As for guidebooks, Footprint's *Northern Pakistan* (2004) is now out of print but is more detailed than Lonely Planet's *Pakistan and the Karakoram Highway* (2008). Insight Guides' *Pakistan* (2007) is great for photos and Moon Publications' *Pakistan Handbook* (1996) may be very old but its author, Isobel Shaw, is the best guidebook writer on Pakistan.

Indian Himalaya

Nelles' *Northern India* map (1:1.5m) includes an 1:650,000 inset for the Manali–Leh Highway and city maps of Delhi and Srinagar. The Nest & Wings' *Himachal Pradesh* map which is sold by most bookshops in Shimla and Manali is more detailed than the Nelles and has kilometre markings between towns as well as spot heights. Nest & Wings' also produce a *Baspa, Kinnaur, Spiti & Lahaul Valleys* map. Also available locally, anyone considering riding off-road in Ladakh should buy Sonam Tsetan's *Trekking Map of Ladakh*. Editions Olizane's *India: Ladakh and Zanskar Trekking Maps* 1:150,000 is a set of three maps featuring very clear cartography; again very useful for anyone planning to ride off-road in that region.

Lonely Planet (LP), Footprint and Rough Guides publish a new *India* title every other year. The Himalayan chapters (Himachal Pradesh, Ladakh, Sikkim) will be more up to date than the older regional titles such as *North India* and *Indian Himalaya* (both LP). The most insightful guidebook to Ladakh is Trailblazer's *Trekking in Ladakh*.

Indus Publishing Company's Exploring Kinnaur & Spiti in the Trans-Himalaya offers most detailed information on the area and is available in Shimla and Manali.

Friendship Highway

Plenty of **mapping** is available, starting with the Tibet Map Institute (www.tibetmap.com) who have published a series of 1:310,000 topographic maps covering the Friendship Highway and routes out to Kailash all online. The Himalayan Map House's *Lhasa–Kathmandu Biking Map* 1:400,000 is available in Kathmandu or through Stanfords Map Shop in London; Nepal Map do a *Kathmandu to Lhasa* road map at 1:700,000 and Reise Know-How's 1:1.5m *Tibet* is a waterproof, double-sided road map with extensive index, longitude and latitude lines and 1:50,000 inset of Lhasa. Gecko Maps' *Kathmandu* 1:25,000 has a 1:10,000 inset of Kathmandu. Finally the International Campaign for Tibet's *On This Spot Lhasa* is a practical city map which also reveals where prisoners of conscience are being held and key locations in the political struggle against the Chinese. Available from the online store at www.savetibet.org or in Kathmandu, do not show this map in public in China.

For guidebooks you can choose between Lonely Planet's *Tibet* (2008), Footprint's *Tibet* (2004), Bradt's *Tibet* (2006) and Trailblazer's *Tibet Overland*

(2002). The author Kym McConnell researched Tibet by mountain bike and details many routes on the Tibetan plateau. The book is also especially strong on Buddhism.

Kotan Publishing's *Mapping the Tibetan World* (2000) spans from Ladakh to Bhutan and is an astonishingly detailed guidebook for independent travellers. The International Campaign for Tibet's *Paradox Lost: How not to be a tourist in Tibet* is a 27-page document written to inform tourists of the reality behind China's gloss of tourism. It can be downloaded for free from www.savetibet.org/documents/pdfs/ParadoxLost.pdf. There are Nepal titles from Lonely Planet (2006), Rough Guides (due 2009) and Footprint (1999).

Sikkim

Schweizerische Stiftung für Alpine Forschung's (SSfAF) *Sikkim* 1:150,000 is the best map available; total overkill for biking but it covers from Darjeeling to Kanchenjunga. ITMB's *Sikkim* 1:140,000 is detailed but inaccurate and Good Earth's *Sikkim: Land of Mystique* (2002) sold in Sikkim or from Stanfords is a pocket-sized guide to the state. Otherwise all the main travel publishers have a Sikkim chapter in their *India* guidebooks.

Bhutan

Himalayan Maphouse's *Bhutan Himalaya* 1:390,000 is general road map with index plus latitude and longitude. ITMB's *Bhutan* 1:389,000 is the same style as their Sikkim title and SSfAF's *Bhutan Himalaya* 1:500,000 is a topographical map of Bhutan marking up main settlements and roads. Odyssey's *Bhutan: Himalayan Mountain Kingdom* (2005) is written by the highly knowledgeable Françoise Pommaret and of course there is a Lonely Planet *Bhutan* (2007).

Phrasebooks

Lonely Planet and Rough Guides both publish a Hindi & Urdu phrasebook which covers the Karakoram Highway. Local dialects from Wakhi to

GETTING READY FOR THE RIDE

While nothing can quite prepare you for hauling 40kg of bike up an oxygen-deprived Himalayan pass, some basic fitness is important if you're only cycling for three weeks or so. Not because being unfit will make you ill – it won't – but because it will be very hard mentally and physically if you're struggling and you'll not enjoy yourself. See www.himalayabybike.com for a training plan before you go.

Any exercise that gets your heart and lungs working is good; better still is commuting by bike or spinning classes in the gym. Best of all is spending hours cycling your fully loaded bike. This will build up the cycling-specific muscles in your legs, get your body used to endurance riding rather than racing and your mind used to mulling for hours. It will really help if – especially if riding solo – you're confident in your ability to ride up hills for hours before you set off for the Himalaya.

Whatever you do don't come out with a new bike, new kit and no experience with either. Go for a tour at home, adjust your bike so it's a good fit and get used to the weight and slower steering.

Finally, make sure you're in good health and well-rested before you leave. Once you land in Asia your body will have a lot of adjustments to make: time zone, humidity, temperature, germs, food and altitude – and not least the culture.

Take it easy, have a wander around and let your mind adjust, especially if it's your first time. Start the cycling once you feel ready for it but don't let initial nerves hold you back.

Burushaski in Pakistan and then Tajik, Kyrgyz and Uighur in China are covered by LP's *Central Asia Phrasebook*. Hindi will cover much of India except for Nepali-speaking Sikkim where Lonely Planet's *Nepali Phrasebook* will be useful. Rebecca Norman's *Getting Started in Ladakhi* is the best book for progressing beyond 'julley' and 'momo'. Lonely Planet's *Tibet Phrasebook* will cover the Friendship Highway; English is widely spoken for those final few days in Nepal so it's only really worth buying Lonely Planet's Nepali phrasebook if you plan to stay longer. A glossary appears on p354.

Health and safety

Biking in the Himalaya will be an experience of a lifetime but it's important to have a realistic idea of what can go wrong. **Altitude sickness** and contaminated **water** and **food** are the most likely causes of illness in the Himalaya. The former is avoidable by taking the time to acclimatize properly and not overnighting at height if you can help it (more on p61) and the second can be minimized by thinking twice about what you eat and drink (see p59).

In terms of **personal security**, most people feel safer on the streets of Asia than they do at home. However, regions such as Kashmir, central Pakistan and India's North Eastern states have a history of violence and political instability. And best not forget that the entire Himalayan chain is prone to natural disasters on an immense scale, from Pakistan's earthquake in 2005 which killed over 70,000 people to the deadly 2006 floods in Ladakh and China's devastating earthquake in Sichuan in 2008. Despite the apparent prosperity of Bhutan and the new wealth in India and China it's important to remember that most people live in poverty where hygiene is poor and education a privilege. Street crime is extremely low in Asia but all Westerners are perceived as rich.

Biking independently in the Himalaya it's important to realize that you'll probably have to treat yourself if you fall ill or have an accident. Good medical facilities are few and far between, there's often a language barrier, and even if you find someone with medical knowledge they might not have the appropriate medicine. There are no emergency services in the remote regions of these countries and no fully equipped hospitals at all in Tibet or Bhutan. If you have a serious accident you will have to be either repatriated or evacuated to somewhere like Hong Kong. Do not accept blood transfusions except in private hospitals. The nearest Western-standard hospitals in case of an emergency are listed on p353. Good travel insurance that will cover the cost of repatriation or evacuation is essential.

BEFORE YOU GO

A couple of months before departure it's worth visiting the dentist as cavities can become troublesome at altitude especially after a few hundred glasses of sugary tea. At altitude air pockets expand forcing out fillings or cracking teeth. Some vaccines like hepatitis require a series of shots over the course of six weeks so ask your doctor or Travel Clinic which ones you need at least two months before you leave. Don't get jabs just before you go as some vaccines might leave you feeling ill and sore for a few days. In the UK it pays to shop around as there are no standard charges, even at GPs. Finally, do not forget **travel insurance** – it's essential in event of an accident or medical emergency.

Everyone travelling out to the Himalaya should discuss how to manage diarrhoea and general infections with their doctor and which antibiotics and

UPHILL STRATEGIES: THE BATTLE FOR HEART AND LUNGS

Many people new to touring in the Himalaya worry about how they'll cope with the immensely long climbs. Here are a few things to bear in mind but with a bit of experience you might find yourself preferring climbing passes to descending them.

At low altitudes the hills are steeper (see box p11) and in summer the weather is usually hot and humid which makes climbing hard work. However, there are also roadside cold drinks shops or restaurants where you can sit in the shade and rehydrate (these are detailed in the route guides). Keeping up your **fluid intake** is crucial. To make a DIY rehydration solution empty a carton of fruit juice into your bottle, top it up with water and add a **big pinch of salt**. Where the road gets rough and technical it helps to pick a line and then focus on something in the distance and aim for that – not looking directly at obstacles often makes them smaller.

At high altitude different factors come into play. Dehydration is still a risk but **altitude sickness** is a real danger. Until you are acclimatized then above 3000m once you decide to climb a high pass you must reach it, get over the top and **come back down** to a safe height. Sometimes it can feel like a race against time: is there still enough daylight to cross the pass and descend to a safe sleeping height on the other side; can I keep up this pace or will I need to take longer rests as I get higher and become more tired; why aren't the kilometre markers going past quicker?!

Once acclimatized only cyclists with camping kit can stop where they like and even then they need flat ground and ideally water. Long high ascents are the one time where even the most relaxed cyclists have to pull themselves together and knuckle down.

Everyone approaches big climbs in their own way: some cycle hard with their heads down then rest and repeat until they reach the top. Others spin away at a steady pace, absorbing their surroundings and finding a meditative rhythm in the pedals. The tortoise rarely beats the hare but the hare often burns out and leaves the tortoise to put up the tent and cook supper. If you can't find your rhythm listening to music helps. Others find themselves counting up to a thousand, swearing or making up rhymes to amuse themselves.

As long as you are **well-fed** and **watered** climbing passes is about detachment from your mind if it, and your body, start wailing 'I can't!'. With a bit of experience your fitness will improve dramatically giving you the confidence to actually look forward to the next mountain pass. Unlike many things in life a pass is a fixed and tangible goal, often with spectacular views and cheerful prayer flags – but to reach each one you must face trepidation, doubt and agony. It's overcoming these fears which makes climbing big passes so rewarding and why cycling in the Himalaya is such a powerful and, in many cases, life-changing experience.

Downhill strategies are another thing altogether. More on them on p60.

RECOMMENDED INOCULATIONS

Vaccination or prophylactic	Pakistan	China	India	Tibet	Nepal	Bhutan
Hepatitis A	√	√	√	√	√	√
Hepatitis B	√	√	√	√	√	√
Typhoid	√	√	√	√	√	√
Polio	√1	√	√	√	√	√
Yellow fever	√2	√	√	√	√	√
Japanese encephalitis	√3	√	√	√	√	√
Rabies	√4	√	√	√	√	√
MMR*	√	√	√	√	√	√
Tetanus-diphtheria	√5	√	√	√	√	√
Malaria	√	x	x	x	x	√

Vaccinations are required if you:
1. have not had the one-off booster as an adult
2. are coming from a yellow-fever infected area (ie Africa, Americas)
3. are staying longer than one month in rural areas
4. will be in direct contact with animals (dogs, cats, monkeys) with no access to medical care
5. are staying longer than six months

* Measles, mumps and rubella

dosages may be needed. Antibiotics can be bought over the counter in China, India, Pakistan and Nepal but fake drugs are rife and you should always check the expiry dates.

If you require a particular medication take along enough supplies unless you're sure it's available locally. Find out the generic name as this will make finding replacements much easier and, in order to avoid any problems at customs, carry a letter from your doctor stating that you need the medication.

Anyone thinking of biking in the Himalaya who has a complicated medical history must discuss the trip with their doctor – the high altitude (over 5000m in India and Tibet), and endurance required puts the body under more stress than you might realize and can be life-threatening when coupled with the lack of medical facilities in the region. Likewise if you have a history of medical problems (eg asthma, diabetes, epilepsy, severe allergies) you must tell your travelling companions (or tour guide) so they know what to expect and what to do in a crisis.

ON THE ROAD: PACING YOURSELF

Listen to your body if you're on the road for a long time. Don't keep pushing yourself if you need to rest. General fatigue, loss of humour and low-level infections that won't clear up are all signs that you're overdoing it. Take it easy and replenish your energy stores with lots of carbohydrates. If you need to, take a break from your bike or even from your travelling companions.

Traditional medicine is still much used in the Himalaya and has a more holistic approach. Ayurveda, Tibetan medicine and Chinese acupuncture might heal the ailments that allopathic Western medicine cannot reach.

Diarrhoea

Diarrhoea is the Indian subcontinent's rite of passage; fortunately for most people an upset stomach will be the only health problem they encounter in the region.

According to the WHO 80% of all travel diseases are due to contaminated drinking water; before you bite into that Kinnauri apple remember that the most common fertilizer in the Himalaya is human faeces. Drinking rancid butter, snacking on streetfood and scoffing fresh cherries is all part of the Himalayan experience but might cause trouble later. Sensible people can avoid stomach problems by doing the following:

- Wash your hands with hot water and soap or an antibacterial dry wash after going to the loo and before preparing or eating food
- Ask for drinks without ice (not that it's likely to be available!)
- Only drink from industrially bottled beverages and check the seals (see 'water' below)
- Ask food to be well-cooked: avoid raw or partly cooked food, fresh seafood (not a common sight), butter and ice cream
- Avoid the temptation of streetside snacks
- Only eat fruit, raw vegetables or salad if they've been washed in disinfected water
- Avoid raw milk, drink only pasteurized milk
- Drink fruit juices from cartons; if mixing fruit juice with water in cycling bottles clean them properly every day (the high sugar content is bacteria heaven)
- Don't use tap water to brush your teeth or take medicines – one sip of contaminated water is enough to pass on amoebas
- Tea, coffee, bottled beer and wine are fine.

Most diarrhoea, as unpleasant as it is, will resolve itself within a few days. Find a room with an en suite bathroom and sit it out, so to speak. Rest, sleep and drink plenty of fluids. Your stomach might feel cold and may cramp and you might feel exceptionally tired. This is normal but if these symptoms persist for more than three days go to the doctor. They're so used to foreigners complaining of diarrhoea and stomach cramps that you could present a broken arm and they'd still prescribe treatment for diarrhoea. If antibiotics are prescribed take the full course and recover properly before heading back out on the road.

You'll probably ignore this if you're on a tight time schedule but anyone with time to spare should invest in getting better. The longer you're ill, the longer it will take to recover. Look on it as training for your stomach: the longer you spend out in Asia the more resilient you will become.

Water purification

In India many of the cheaper bottled water brands are not safe to drink. It's essential for cyclists to carry some means of purifying water as they travel, mainly to avoid dehydration but also to be able to take water from natural sources and avoid carrying extra kilos. Although bottled water is cheap and readily available in towns and some villages, the plastic bottles are dumped as

DOWNHILL STRATEGIES

Now comes the chance to rest those tired legs. While you're still warm, have a **snack** and put on **extra layers** – the wind chill will soon numb you especially in the shade or at each end of the day, and once cold it's hard for a tired, under-nourished body to warm up. Protect your **eyes** from stone chips, flies and dust with eyewear of some sort and wear cycling gloves to save your palms should you fall off.

While merrily gathering speed on a descent take a moment to consider there are no emergency services and few hospitals in the Himalaya. **Concentrate** wholly on the road ahead because potholes, gravel, sand, fords, goats, sharp bends and impromptu games of cricket can appear without warning. This is not a good time to rummage in your handlebar bag or reset the cycle computer to record your top speed. Keep your fingers on the brakes; like ABS on a car, **pumping the brakes** works better than hanging onto them for dear life.

Suspension forks make long, bumpy descents a treat; rigid forks will hammer your wrists and liquify your brains (agony if you have an altitude headache). Lessen the jolts by sliding back on the saddle or even better, **half-stand** off it and 'sit' lightly on the back of your thighs with most of the weight on your feet while keeping your bum low. Keeping part of your body attached even loosely to the saddle, so maintaining 'triangulated contact' (hands, feet, bum / legs) is vital for stability. Let your **bent arms and legs** absorb the bumps, not your saddle-bound backside; any seasoned mountain biker will know the drill. Finally letting some air out of the tyres (but not enough to risk pinch flats) will also help on bad roads.

In **sub-zero** temperatures you may find yourself curled up like a foetus trying to conserve heat and wondering how to tell your numb fingers to brake. Anticipate this scenario at the top of the pass or try to keep descending as the air will eventually warm up. Tearing through fords looks fun but if your shoes get wet your feet will freeze. In cold weather there's no way to get circulation back into them short of getting off the bike and stamping around.

The risk of a **shimmey** (see p47) is low as Himalayan bikes usually run fat tyres and road surfaces are too rough, but should your bike start to wobble copy Bond bad girl Xenia Onatopp and clamp the top tube between your thighs until the bike stops twitching.

rubbish. In tourist hubs such as Leh where thousands of tourists dutifully drink litres of bottled water daily the bottles are a pollutant in themselves.

The most common methods for purifying water are either to use a portable water filter or to add **iodine**. Iodine comes either in tablets or in droplets and is something of an acquired taste (Potable Aqua neutralizing tablets or powder work well). Some iodine tablets take longer than others to work: buy ones that take twenty minutes (it will say on the label).

Methods of purifying water

- Boiling for one minute or three minutes if above 2000m
- Chemical sterilization such as iodine or chlorine
- A portable water filter

If you're travelling for a while it is well worth investing in a quality water filter; the better ones of these pump water through either a ceramic membrane or carbon and glass fibres; cheaper filters with plastic arms can snap and also require more frequent and expensive cartridge replacement. You can drink from most sources of water with these filters but if possible try and find fast moving water upstream of any outlets, habitation or grazing animals.

Among the many types available the Aquapure Traveller (💻 www.bwtechnologies.com) is a bottle-cage sized bottle with a water filter fitted into the cap. It's ideal for short trips as water purification takes just a little shaking and fifteen minutes. The purifying element is limited to 350 litres and replacement cartridges cost just less than a new bottle. The same company also produces a 1.5 or 5 litre Thirst Aid bag for the same price and with the same filtration capacity. The well-known and sturdy Katadyn Pocket filter (💻 www.katadyn.ch) uses a cleanable ceramic core, lasts for an astonishing 50,000 litres and is easy to maintain.

If you're cycling with a water filter in sub-zero temperatures sleep with it in your bag as water freezing in the filter overnight can crack the ceramic core. Note also that some streams in the Himalaya are used by local people for washing only; check before drinking the water.

Altitude sickness

Many travellers in the Himalaya suffer slightly from **Acute Mountain Sickness** (AMS). This is caused by ascending too fast for the body to acclimatize to the decrease in oxygen above 3000m. Long ascents such as the 2000m vertical climb from Manali to Rohtang La and the extremely high altitude of some of the roads (the Khardung La climbs above 5350m) require you to be properly acclimatized.

Acclimatization is a physiological process where over a couple of days the body manufactures more oxygen-carrying red blood cells to make the most of what is available in the thin air. The only way to avoid suffering AMS is to **spend enough time** acclimatizing and the good news is that riding a bike from the lowlands is an ideal way to do it. Drinking plenty of fluids will aid the process and care should be taken to sleep no more than **300m** higher each night, no matter what altitude you peaked at during the day. Anyone arriving in the Himalaya from sea-level (including Delhi) should spend a day or two acclimatizing above 2000m, and at least two days in Leh or Lhasa (both above 3500m) if arriving by plane. While some people are more susceptible than others, no one is exempt: even famous Everest summiteers have suffered from AMS on return to the Himalaya.

Wherever you camp, have a plan for descending if there's an onset of symptoms. If you're travelling solo be doubly cautious. AMS can develop quickly and beyond mild AMS you will not be capable of making good decisions. **People have died from underestimating AMS**.

Symptoms

Normal symptoms include a slightly higher heart rate, slight breathlessness on exertion and unusually vivid dreams. When you have **mild AMS** you will feel off-colour with a headache, mild nausea, a loss of appetite, difficulty sleeping and maybe dizziness. Don't pass off these symptoms as fatigue and don't ascend further – even better descend at least 150m until the symptoms have cleared.

AMS – A DOCTOR'S PERSPECTIVE

At altitudes above 2000 metres altitude sickness can occur and above 3000m it's almost guaranteed without proper acclimatization. It's caused by the thinner air at altitude and comprises a spectrum of conditions from acute mountain sickness (AMS) to life threatening high altitude pulmonary oedema and high altitude cerebral oedema. The initial treatment for all these is immediate DESCENT.

Acute mountain sickness occurs in everyone if their ascent above 3000m is too rapid, although its onset varies from person to person. The general rule of thumb is once above 3000m do not sleep more than 300m higher than the previous night. If you do climb higher during the day, make sure you descend to sleep ('Climb high, Sleep low').

Symptoms of AMS vary from one person to the next, but typically include headaches, nausea, dizziness, loss of appetite, difficulty sleeping, and breathlessness on minimal exertion. Once symptoms of AMS occur, if mild, additional time for acclimatization before further ascent is all that is needed, but if symptoms worsen descent is essential. Ensure that you drink at least three litres a day and use simple analgesics like paracetamol for the headache. Usually a descent of 300-900 metres is all that is needed to improve symptoms. If available, oxygen will help relieve symptoms till lower altitudes are reached.

Diamox (acetazolamide) is often used by climbers to prevent and treat AMS. However, this is a dangerous practice as it hides the early signs of AMS thereby allowing you to climb higher before realizing how sick you really are. If you're thinking about taking Diamox, talk it through with your doctor first. Current recommendations are to take 250mg twice daily from one day before you reach altitude until you are at or below the altitude you started at.

High Altitude Pulmonary Oedema (HAPE) is a life-threatening condition involving the collection of water in your lungs. It usually occurs a couple of days after arriving at altitude and includes shortness of breath, cough (if severe then with pink frothy phlegm), chest tightness and fatigue, along with the symptoms of AMS. Early diagnosis and immediate descent are the only treatments. Oxygen can be used to reduce symptoms but does not treat the underlying problem: descent is vital.

High Altitude Cerebral Oedema (HACE) is similarly lethal: the brain swells in response to low oxygen levels. It's often considered as the end stage of AMS. Its onset at altitude can be rapid but more usually it evolves over days. Symptoms of AMS are often but not always present before the onset of loss of coordination, visual impairment, confusion, and ultimately coma and death. Again early recognition and immediate descent are the only treatments. If available, oxygen and 4mg dexamethasone should be given as soon as possible. In both HAPE and HACE, medical advice should be sought as hospitalization will probably be required.

Dr Edward Foulkes

Severe AMS will give an intense headache which painkillers cannot relieve, loss of coordination and balance, severe fatigue, nausea and vomiting, shortness of breath, rapid breathing and pulse, blue lips and fingers and a dry or blood-producing cough. The danger now is of HAPE (high altitude pulmonary oedema) or HACE (high altitude cerebral oedema) both of which can be fatal. Descend immediately and seek medical attention.

Malaria

The malaria-carrying anopheles mosquito hates the cold so although all these countries are in warm latitudes, the colder air at altitude lowers the risk of contracting the disease. However, there is malaria in the hot lowlands (below 2000m) of the Karakoram Highway in Pakistan and the Samdrup Jongkhar district in Bhutan. Nepal is malaria-free on the Friendship Highway to Kathmandu and around Pokhara. Rainfall creates breeding sites for mosquitoes so the risk of contracting the disease is seasonal and highest after the monsoon rains (July–August). If you plan to spend weeks in malarial areas then discuss the appropriate anti-malarial course with your doctor. Most riders passing through don't take tablets but you should take the following steps to avoid getting bitten:

- Spray clothing and exposed skin with insect repellent containing 20-35% DEET.
- Wear thick clothing that mosquitoes can't puncture.
- Use a mosquito net sprayed with repellent for maximum effectiveness and with mesh size under 1.5mm.
- Splash out on a room with air-conditioning for a night without the whine of wheeling mosquitoes.

Rabies

The rabies virus is transmitted by the saliva of an infected animal either through a bite or by licking broken skin and once symptoms develop it is fatal. Dogs, cats, monkeys and bats can carry rabies and India has one of the worst incidence rates of the virus in the world. The rabies vaccination is recommended for all of the countries in this book but it is expensive. The rabies shot is no longer in the stomach and there is now a pre-exposure vaccine which is a series of three injections into the shoulder over the course of a month. Once vaccinated against rabies if bitten you must still have two more doses of the vaccine within fourteen days.

Despite doctors' recommendations most visitors do not get the rabies jab, reasoning that it's cheaper to avoid contact with animals. Since additional injections are required whether vaccinated or not, getting bitten means the end of a trip anyway. But rabies is a more serious issue for cyclists because of the well-known antipathy between dogs and bicycles.

It's highly unlikely that you'll get bitten in the Himalaya especially since the notorious mastiffs of Tibet seem to have vanished (into a Chinese hot pot?). Most Indian dogs are solar-powered and snooze in the sun to bark at night. Very few are interested in chasing bicycles. If you are chased, stop the bike. Put it between you and the dog(s) and shout, throw rocks or squirt water from your cycling bottle. Make them back off before you get back on the bike. Some long-term tourers invest in a dog deterrent such as the Dog Dazer (💻 www.dogdazer.com). If you're extremely unlucky and get bitten by an animal you suspect to be rabid, immediate evacuation or repatriation is necessary to get the best care possible.

Hazards and traffic

> *Every year, road accidents in India claim more than 120,000 lives. One of every ten people who die in road accidents worldwide is from India, according to the World Health Organization.*
>
> *India Today*, November 2004

The Himalaya is prone to headline-grabbing natural disasters, from local landslides and floods to cataclysmic earthquakes. These are infrequent but one hazard that you will face on a daily basis is **Asian traffic**. In all these countries

Big is Boss and as a mere cyclist you're among the lowest of the low. Only puny pedestrians are less important.

In India and Nepal cows and bullocks are sacrosanct and enjoy this right to the full by chewing the cud in the middle of motorways. Ride defensively, give trucks enough space (they're usually extremely courteous) and keep an eye out for jeeps and army convoys which are less accommodating. In towns the swirl of sauntering pedestrians, stationary cows, nippy scooters and behemoth trucks is mesmerizing and it's here that you truly realize there is no concept of personal space.

People often think that riding a bike on Himalayan roads is dangerous but it's a lot safer than taking the bus. These regions have the highest road accident statistics in the world so it's good to be in control. If you need to, build up confidence at home before tackling Asian cities and mountain roads and once there know that Sundays are the best days to leave capital cities – the traffic and therefore smog is relatively light.

Political unrest

The Himalayan range lies at the edge of ancient empires and modern superpowers. Nearly all of the ancient Himalayan kingdoms have become the states or provinces of much larger nations but the struggle for independence continues in some areas and others are wracked by sectarian violence and terrorism.

Particular flashpoints are: Pakistan, Kashmir (in both India and Pakistan) and India's north east states. In Pakistan suicide bombers have been targeting both the authorities and locations frequented by foreigners such as diplomatic enclaves and Western-run hotels like the Marriott in Islamabad. Nepal and Tibet also have their own troubles but foreigners are not deliberately targeted.

If you are interested in travelling in these areas, follow the news so you can make an informed decision on whether to travel. Bear in mind that if your government advises against travel to a particular region a travel insurance company will probably not cover you. The following websites may be useful:

British Foreign and Commonwealth Office	💻 www.fco.gov.uk
US Department of State	💻 www.travel.state.gov
Australian Department of Foreign Affairs	💻 www.dfat.gov.au/geo
BBC News online	💻 www.bbc.co.uk/worldnews
Horizons Unlimited Bulletin Board	💻 www.horizonsunlimited.com/hubb
Lonely Planet Thorn Tree	💻 www.lonelyplanet.com/thorntree

Nutrition

The local diet is fine for all these routes but make a conscious effort to **eat enough** as it's very common to lose your appetite at high altitude. Fruit and vegetables can be bought along the road (except on the trans-Tibet routes) so it's not necessary to carry multivitamins. The Pakistani, Indian and Nepali staples of rice and dahl are great for energy. How seriously you should take nutrition depends on how long you'll be cycling in Asia: somebody visiting for three weeks doesn't have to worry about it at all since they'll be strong from a Western diet.

I HONK THEREFORE I AM

One of the most loving and frequently consummated relationships in India is that between a driver and his vehicle's horn. Cyclists in particular, unshielded as their eardrums are from the onslaught, can get particularly irritated by this form of address.

When you're the only two vehicles on the road that day, there's plenty of space in the dust and the vehicle is a Tata truck, it defies belief to think that you haven't noticed them. This is missing the point. As well as meaning 'I'm a Tata you puny sykel! Shift your scrawny butt!', the horn functions as a 'Hello!' and as a brake – a cheeky blast will hopefully send lesser vehicles careering to the side, thus clearing the road for the Tata's uninterrupted passage.

It's a very hopeful sort of address. Only in the case of goats, which are impervious to honking and just as possessive of their tarmac as any self-respecting Tata, is the horn used for its traditional purpose. At all other times a lengthy honk is a deeply self-gratifying act to remind everyone in the vicinity of your whereabouts and maybe to remind yourself too, if you've been driving for 36 hours without a break. Do not fear the blast; at least you know they've seen you.

Anyone spending months in Asia should endeavour to eat a balanced diet as far as possible, comprising of protein, carbohydrates, fats, vegetables and fruits. Touring cyclists will inevitably lose weight and inches as pedalling steadily for hours burns away more fat than all-out sporty effort. Once the body has exhausted its fat and glucose reserves, it turns to muscle. The symptoms of this are fatigue, weakness and a low immunity system.

High pesticide use in India may well put you off buying vegetables and fruits in the market but some guesthouses grow their own without chemicals. Always **wash fruit and vegetables** before eating them raw. Bottles and cans of Coke and Pepsi have been found to have 'unacceptably high' (up to 24 times the legal limit) levels of pesticide residue which is ironic given that many Indian farmers actually use Coke as a cheap pesticide. The multinationals fiercely deny the findings but public anger reached such heights that some states, such as Kerala, banned the drinks companies' products altogether.

Drinking enough is just as important as food at high altitude. Exercising in the arid climate and intense sun causes rapid dehydration and drinking plenty will help reduce the symptoms of altitude sickness.

After you get back

Some subcontinental parasites and viruses can cause long-term complications unless you deal with them quickly. If you have any chronic symptoms, or are asymptomatic but worried that you have been exposed to a particular disease tell your doctor you've been travelling in Asia and if necessary ask for a referral to a hospital specializing in tropical diseases. If biking in the Himalaya was a long-held dream you may feel low on your return. There is only one cure: go back!

2 KARAKORAM HWY

ROUTE INFORMATION

- **Start / finish** Islamabad (Pakistan) / Kashgar (Xinjiang province, China)
- **Distance** 1300km (1176km excluding bus transfer from Khunjerab to Tashkurgan)
- **Altitude min / max** 518m/4695m
- **High passes** Two (Khunjerab, Pakistan; Ulugh Rabat, China)
- **Suggested duration** 17 cycling days, excluding Sost/Tashkurgan transfer, rests and excursions. To make the most of the KKH allow at least a month for off-highway exploration
- **Road conditions** 70% tarmac, 30% track
- **Hazards and dangers** Hostile tribal areas between Besham and Chilas, landslides
- **When to go** 1 May–15 November, but avoid the monsoon (July–August)
- **Visas** Required for both Pakistan and China (see p26).

This is the story of those intrepid souls who braved the icy coldness, lack of oxygen and the devilish weather to wreak a miracle called Karakoram Highway…
Plaque to the KKH builders on Khunjerab Pass

For mountain-lovers the Karakoram Highway, or 'KKH' as it's often abbreviated, offers the **best roadside scenery** in Asia. Other rides in the Himalaya are higher but mountains are less of an eye-ful when you're already two-thirds of the way up them. Not so in northern Pakistan. Here lies the highest concentration of 8000m peaks in the world and seen from a lowly 2000m in the Hunza Valley they fill the sky.

Officially the Karakoram Highway starts in Havelian, 100km north of Islamabad, but it is such an insignificant plains town that cyclists either start from **Islamabad** or from **Gilgit**, nearly 500km north.

Setting off from Islamabad means climbing from an altitude of 500 metres which is great for acclimatization but leads through some **hostile** regions like Indus Kohistan which are not. Starting from Gilgit halves the route and presents just the highlights of Hunza and Pakistan's mountain scenery without the slog through the foothills.

If **heading south** from China, at Gilgit you have the option to take the high road via the Shandur Pass in the **Hindu Kush** over to Chitral and Peshawar. There's no guarantee you won't get stoned by kids there either but as it's a rough stony track at times at least there will be plenty of ammo to return. Another interesting option just south of Gilgit is the narrow road leading along the Indus to **Skardu** in Baltistan.

From Islamabad the road to Havelian is mostly hot, dusty, dry and flat. Beyond Havelian the KKH climbs up into the hills of

Hazara to the north of which lies the Indus River. Through Indus Kohistan the KKH and the Indus snake alongside each other past the base of Nanga Parbat (8125m), the westernmost peak in the Himalaya range. North of Nanga Parbat the KKH leaves the Indus to follow the Gilgit and Hunza rivers through the Karakoram range to the foot of the 4695m **Khunjerab Pass**, the world's highest paved international frontier. On the Pakistani side mountains dwarf the KKH as it roller-coasters along narrow valley floors but once the Khunjerab Pass is crossed the landscape changes utterly and the road scrolls through a wide glacial valley to Tashkurgan, China's border town. Only one pass remains, the low ridge of Ulugh Rabat (3955m), before the KKH skirts Karakul Lake and the peaks of Muztagh Ata and Kongur then plunges through the Ghez canyon and spills out onto the desert sands for an easy 80km spin to the oasis town of **Kashgar**.

Ubiquitous along the KKH are the bulbous domes and tapering minarets of mosques; yet fifteen centuries ago this branch of the Silk Route introduced Buddhism to China and Tibet. Despite its Buddhist heritage and unlike all the other Himalayan rides in this book, the KKH is Islamic (see p73) with strong cultural and ethnic ties to next-door Afghanistan and, once in Xinjiang province in China, its Central Asian neighbours of Tajikistan and Kyrgyzstan.

The male-dominated society and religious fervour in some regions make this ride more exciting than relaxing. As a foreigner you may encounter some **hostility** between Islamabad and Gilgit, especially on uphills where you become an easy target; check embassy advisories and the current political situation before leaving. In the event of unrest consider bussing or flying directly to Gilgit; the Hunza Valley nearby manages to be wonderfully laid-back and friendly and its main town, Karimabad, is the tourist hotspot of northern Pakistan.

The Karakoram Highway is not the three-lane motorway its name suggests, at times being a single carriageway track clinging to arid mountainsides. Neither is it nose-to-tail with lorries. For a road that demanded such engineering expertise and cost so many lives in the building it is relatively little-used. The only time I had to stop for traffic was for a herd of goats frantically nibbling at the sparse roadside grass!

Jacqui Furneaux, UK

FACTS ABOUT THE REGION

In Pakistan the KKH travels through Punjab, the North West Frontier Province (NWFP) and the Northern Areas. Though Pakistan is an Islamic state this alone is not enough to hold the nation together. Religious differences persist, especially between the Sunni and Shia sects, and tribal tensions also affect some regions. This is especially so in the North West Frontier Province, a predominantly Pashtun (Pathan) area over which the government has little control. The influx of over two-and-a-half million Afghan refugees to NWFP in recent years as well as the implementation of Sharia law there has led some to claim it's now Taliban-controlled.

South of Gilgit, British and American citizens may encounter some hostility. North of Gilgit many people are Ismaeli Muslim, an altogether more tolerant branch of Islam led by the progressive Aga Khan. The Hunza, Nagar and Gojal regions are the highlight of Pakistan not only for the scenery, which is spectacular, but also for their friendly people.

The construction of the KKH and subsequent initiatives by the Aga Khan Foundation and local NGOs have brought substantial improvements to much

KKH Overview

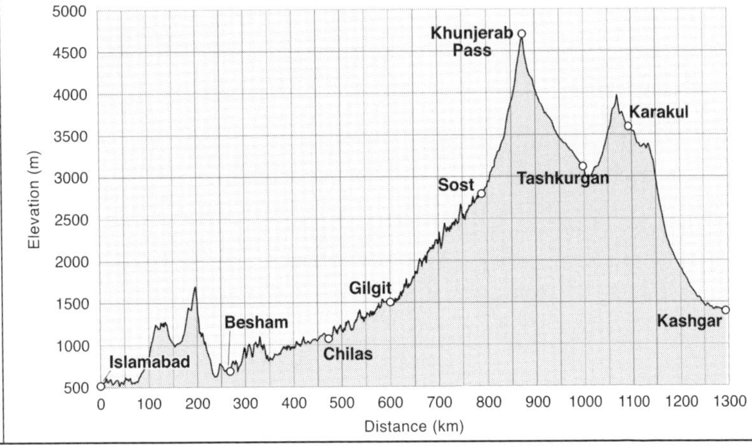

of Pakistan's Northern Areas. While Ismaeli regions such as Hunza have progressed rapidly the more conservative, mullah-led regions such as Nagar have fiercely obstructed development. As the Director of the Nounehal NGO in Nagar put it: "It is often the most backwards areas of Pakistan which are most resistant to change and the most hostile to outsiders."

At the Chinese end of the KKH lies the province of the Xinjiang Uighur Autonomous Region. Xinjiang means 'New Territory' in Mandarin and the long arm of Beijing can be seen in the People's Park in the form of a giant statue of Chairman Mao, apparently one of only three still standing in China. During the so-called 'Great Game' of the nineteenth century when British and Russian interests collided over supremacy of Central Asia, Xinjiang was better known as Chinese Turkestan. Russian blandishments won over the khanates of Khiva, Bokhara and Khokand (present-day Uzbekistan) and those Central Asian states were referred to as Russian Turkestan. Today's curiously slender Wakhan Corridor in Afghanistan (see map opposite) is a relic of political expediency from that era. Throughout the twentieth century the Turkic-speaking Uighur, Tajiks, Wakhis and Kyrgyz Muslims of Xinjiang agitated for an 'East Turkestan Islamic Republic' but in 1949 Xinjiang was absorbed by the communist People's Republic of China much as Tibet was in 1951. The struggle continues among the ethnically-Turkic groups, fuelled on the one hand by the rise of Islamic fundamentalism in Central Asia and on the other by Beijing's policy of transferring more than a million Han Chinese into the province.

Approaching Sost

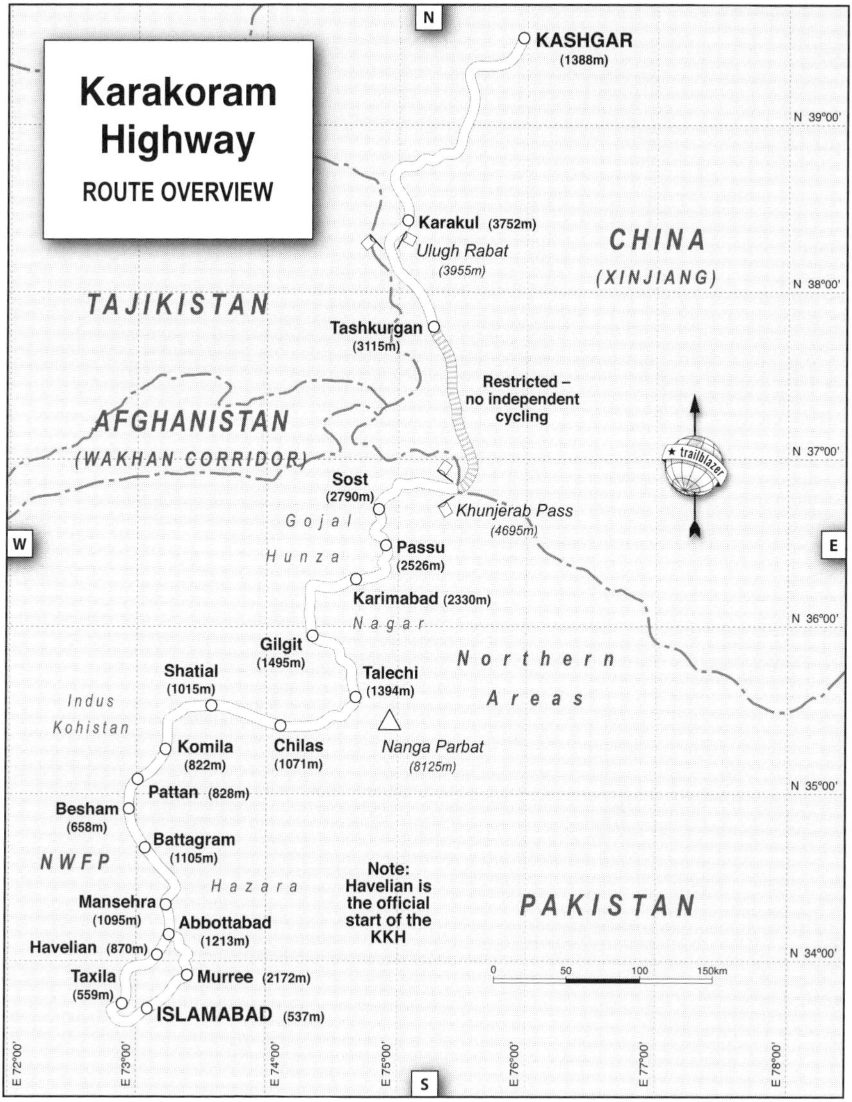

History of the road

Today, with the building of a new two-way highway across the Karakoram, the era of hiring mules and ponies, cooks and coolies, of clinging dizzily to mountain ledges, dodging rockfall and bullets – the very stuff of Central Asian travel – is finally at an end.
Peter Hopkirk, *Foreign Devils on the Silk Road*

Thousands of years before Islam and Christianity, Buddhist monks and traders crossed the Karakoram ranges between Kashgar and Taxila (near Islamabad). The present course of the KKH follows this branch of the Silk Route along which trade flourished during China's Han and Tang dynasties

Don't take spelling seriously on the KKH

(100BC–700AD). It linked the plains of India to the river of ideas and merchandise which flowed between Xi'an in eastern China and the seaports of the Mediterranean. Travellers faced just one pass on the Karakoram route rather than the five passes north of Leh. Along the way they made thousands of rock carvings, including depictions of the life of the Buddha, his first sermon and the Tree of Enlightenment. Some of these extraordinary engravings can still be seen between Shatial and Chilas on the KKH, though if the construction of Basha dam in Indus Kohistan goes ahead, many will be submerged forever.

The Khunjerab Pass was not always the traditional crossing place for the Karakoram. Historically the crossing was made over the Mintaka and Kilik passes about 70km to the northwest, close to Afghanistan and former Russian Turkestan. During the construction of the KKH the Pakistani army deliberately chose the pass furthest from those borders to protect their new military link to China. The road's purpose is as much geopolitical as commercial, aligning China and Pakistan against Russia and India. Both China and Pakistan have annexed territory that was declared India's after Partition.

The Karakoram Highway was the first of the modern trans-Himalayan roads. India responded by building the Manali–Leh Highway and upgrading the Leh–Srinagar Highway. China then helped Nepal to build the Friendship Highway between Lhasa and Kathmandu: another road which makes India nervous but which along with all these highways has opened up great touring opportunities for the likes of us!

Surveying and construction of the KKH started in 1965 and the road was opened to traffic in 1978. In that year an enterprising Norwegian pulled a few diplomatic strings and rode his bicycle up the KKH, though the road was only declared fully open in 1986. Hundreds of Pakistani and Chinese labourers lost their lives constructing the road and it still demands constant attention from the Frontier Works Organization (FWO) based along its length in Pakistan. A significant factor is that the KKH traverses one of the most seismically active regions in the world, for it's here that the Asian and Indian subcontinental plates grate against each other (see p10). In December 2005 an earthquake with an epicentre just 35km east of Mansehra on the KKH killed nearly 75,000 people.

NOT EVERYONE LIKES TO GET STONED

It is a strange fact of the Himalaya that only children in Muslim regions throw stones at cyclists. What is stranger is that adults condone this behaviour. After running a gauntlet of stone-throwers, tripwire setters and one-pen bandits I stopped to ask some adults what it was all about. "They are only wanting attention from you!" was the reply. Young boys throw stones and maybe it is merely attention seeking because they rarely hit their mark. Grown men very occasionally throw stones but if they do they aim to hit and they don't use pebbles.

On the Chinese side, the KKH is more prosaically known as Highway 314 which runs for 1784km from the Khunjerab Pass via Kashgar to Urumchi, capital of Xinjiang. In June 2006 the Chinese and Pakistani governments agreed to rebuild and widen the KKH to triple its transport capacity. The KKH is always subject to road works but these – from Raikot Bridge to Khunjerab and due to last until 2011 – will be almighty!

Restrictions and safety

Both Pakistan and China require **visas** which in the latter case must be obtained in advance. In Pakistan the Chinese embassy is in Islamabad (see p28). Coming south it's now possible to get an extendable Pakistani transit visa at Sost below the Khunjerab border although acquiring a visa in advance means one less thing to worry about.

Since 2001 the Chinese have forbidden independent travellers to ride between Khunjerab and Tashkurgan. Everyone must travel by either bus or jeep from Sost to Tashkurgan, the Chinese customs post 208km away. However, the Pakistan army do allow independent cyclists to ride up to Khunjerab and back before hopping dutifully on the bus. From Tashkurgan to Kashgar the route is open and no permits are required. Pakistan drives on the left, China on the right but animals and children on the road obey no rules. Watch out for impromptu games of road cricket in Pakistan.

Anyone riding through Hazara, North West Frontier Province and Indus Kohistan will find some locals unfriendly if not downright **menacing**. The police often escort foreigners through these regions though not in Indus Kohistan where they too find it safer to keep a low profile. It's strongly recommended that you **don't camp or travel at night in Indus Kohistan**. Between dusk and dawn even Pakistani vehicles travel in a police convoy here.

For women there are a few things to be aware of. Most of Pakistan is still extremely conservative and from Islamabad until Chalt the few women you'll see out in public will either be in groups or escorted by a male relative. To

WOMEN BIKING ALONE IN PAKISTAN

Pakistan and the plains of India are notorious for the hassle foreign women travelling solo suffer there. In many ways this reputation is deserved so the most important thing to realize is that you can't behave in these countries as you would at home. Women in rural Pakistan and India lead much more restricted lives than their Western counterparts. In Pakistan a Western woman is the object of unwanted scrutiny even when covered from top to toe so the best attitude is to expect to be stared at and just get over it. The national dress of **shalwar kameez** and dupatta (see box p75) is very useful for going undercover (literally) and the dupatta blinkers you from the staring.

It takes some time to find the right balance between being friendly and polite and being perceived as 'available'. Western women should think twice before beaming away at strangers because in Pakistan smiles are often interpreted in another sense entirely. The rise of the internet has brought Western porn to the smallest towns in what is an extremely conservative and sexually repressed part of the world. Groups of guys can be a pain, especially south of Gilgit, so it's best to cut inane conversations short. Things that you wouldn't think twice about at home – such as being alone with a man in an office – can also be misunderstood. The old trick of wearing a **wedding ring** counts for little if you're on your own. The one consolation in Pakistan is that, unlike you, male cyclists are expected to spend time with the boys and are just as likely to be propositioned.

CYCLING THE LOWER KKH IN HIGH SUMMER

When the thermometer rises above 45°C most cyclists find an air-conditioned hotel and wait for the mercury to cool or head north to Gilgit and the mountains. But if you're determined to ride here are a few tactics to help prevent heat exhaustion.

Drink a litre of water when you wake up and set off at first light (around 4am); by 8am the skies will be white and the deadening heat will begin to parch your body of water and salts. Take on as much water as you can (it's easy to drink up to **twelve litres a day**), as well as soft drinks and salty TUC biscuits. Watermelons are a good source of hydration if you can't get drinkable water. Drink constantly, douse your clothes and **cover your head**. Avoid cycling between 10am and 4pm.

Sleep in this sort of heat is difficult, few hotels on the KKH have air-con and most travellers (especially women) will not want to sleep on the roof as Pakistanis do in summer. As rooms remain stiflingly hot at night it helps to soak yourself fully clothed under the cold tap; when it's really hot it will only take about fifteen minutes before everything is dry again. Throwing buckets of water on the bed will help cool the sheets. When the ambient temperature exceeds body heat (a mere 37°C) room fans start acting like oven fans so turn them off.

It takes at least a week to acclimatize to heat and humidity; if you push yourself too hard **heatstroke** becomes a real risk. If you feel unwell, tired and dizzy stop, bathe yourself in tepid water and rest in the shade. If your temperature exceeds 39.5°C, your skin is flushed red and you cease sweating seek medical attention immediately.

some Pakistani men a foreign woman travelling on her own is a provocation and fair game and the relentless staring can be infuriating (see box p71). **Women should not cycle through Indus Kohistan alone**.

A hazard that takes everyone by surprise is the **heat** and in the early days of the KKH a few cyclists died from heat exhaustion. Summer temperatures on the plains can exceed 50°C and in the gorges south of Gilgit there's little shade or water. More notorious hazards are the **rock-throwers** south of Gilgit – often bored small boys and a good reason to wear a helmet and eyewear. North of Gilgit well-meaning tourists and NGOs have spawned a generation of children who see all foreigners as a source of pens and money. These 'one-pen' bandits will also throw stones (see box p70) if denied their tribute.

Before travelling to Pakistan check the foreign office websites (see p64). Many people choose to skip the section between Islamabad and Gilgit as the road passes through the North West Frontier Province (usually the subject of a foreign office advisory) and Indus Kohistan, which no one enjoys riding through (see p88). The mountain scenery for which Pakistan should be more famous lies north of Gilgit.

There is occasional **sectarian violence** between Sunnis and Shias in Gilgit and graffiti such as 'kill the USA' is hardly welcoming. It's not unusual for American or British citizens, whose countries are held accountable for the wars in Afghanistan and Iraq, to claim citizenship of a totally inoffensive nation such as New Zealand while travelling through Pakistan. In China there are no safety issues for foreigners.

The KKH is built through geologically unstable terrain. **Rockfalls** and **landslides** occur at any time but are more likely after heavy rain. Don't ride the KKH during the monsoon (July–August) and always look up when you stop at the side of the road.

Malaria is a risk below 2000m in Pakistan and there are plenty of hungry mosquitoes between Islamabad and Karimabad.

Language and religion

Marmot. Love it or hate it.

The national language of Pakistan is Urdu even though it's the first language of less than a tenth of the population. As in India, speaking in English confers status: lessons at private schools are in English and English is the language used by the Pakistani government. Along the KKH there's usually someone around who can speak some English – beardless men wearing spectacles are often a good bet. Local languages include Pashtun in NWFP, Shina near Chilas, Burushaski in Hunza, Wakhi in Gojal and in Xinjiang Uighur, Tajik, Kyrgyz and Mandarin.

Road signs in Pakistan are usually in Urdu and English, and occasionally in Urdu, English, Chinese and Russian. In Xinjiang they are usually only in Chinese.

Some 97% of Pakistanis are Muslim, most of them adherents of one of the country's three main Islamic sects: Sunni, Shia and Ismaeli. Sunni Indus Kohistan and NWFP are quite radical; Ismaeli Hunza is more tolerant and relaxed. South of Gilgit one of the first questions people will ask is 'Are you Muslim?'. Answer how you like but the most shocking response is to say that you're atheist. Officially China has no religion, but Xinjiang Province comprises mostly Sunni Uighurs and a few Ismaeli Tajiks in Kashgar.

Most Pakistanis are extremely courteous and friendly; **hospitality** is taken seriously. Theft is uncommon but people see nothing wrong in playing with your bike's brakes and gears or even lifting it up. This can be infuriating but think twice before you react: our concepts of **property and privacy** are different.

Pakistan is a man's world and this can be very trying for foreign **women travellers** (see box on p71). It can be harder for women to travel as one half of a couple than to travel alone because as the 'other half' a foreign woman can expect to be excluded from conversation and referred to in the third person, such as 'This is your madam?' or even 'Is it yours?'. Women travelling alone are treated as honorary men and, in my experience, have a far less frustrating time.

CULTURAL SENSIBILITIES AND TABOOS

- **Clothing** Both men and women should dress modestly and avoid figure-hugging clothing, even if it is full length. For women this means covering the torso, head, shoulders, arms, legs and ankles. For men it means covering the torso, shoulders, arms and legs. In major cities such as Lahore and Islamabad dress rules are more relaxed.
- **Photographs** Men should not photograph local women and both sexes should ask permission before photographing religious sites.
- **Hospitality** As elsewhere in the Muslim world, in Pakistan it's an Islamic duty to extend hospitality to a stranger. It's therefore rude to refuse hospitality especially if it's something as small as a glass of *chai* (tea). It can take some time to acquire the balance between accepting hospitality and withdrawing gracefully. Many Pakistani people are extremely generous and offer more than they can afford to give so think twice before accepting something and always offer something in return.

Visitors will quickly realize that many Pakistani men are obsessed with **sex**: foreign women are stared at although it's the men who are quizzed endlessly about their intimate relationships. The internet and satellite TV have further skewed conservative Pakistan's view of the West as morally corrupt; private booths in internet cafés allow customers to enjoy observing just how corrupt.

PRACTICAL INFORMATION

Which direction?

Most cyclists who ride the KKH as a stand-alone trip will start in Islamabad to take advantage of the tailwinds up the KKH and to make the most of cycling up into the mountains. Between Gilgit and Sost there's always a guesthouse to stay in at the end of the day: not so in Xinjiang where slow cyclists riding up through the Pamirs from Kashgar will need camping equipment. Those coming from Kashgar are usually on a longer trip – either from Central Asia or Tibet – but don't think that heading south means downhills all the way. Quite apart from the two passes, from Sost onwards the KKH is a rollercoaster ride which often piles up more than 1000m of climbing for little difference in altitude between the start and finish of the day.

Equipment, guidebooks and maps

Hygiene along the KKH is poor and few visitors manage to keep their bowels intact so you'll need some means of **purifying water** as well as treatments for the inevitable stomach upsets. Although the KKH follows the Indus River it's usually inaccessible from the road so don't rely on it for topping up. Tributary streams (known as *nalahs*) are frequent enough to make filtering water a better option than lugging bottled water. Fragile items will need protection from vibration, dust and dirt.

Not all of Pakistan's best scenery can be seen from the KKH: it takes some **walking** to reach the alpine meadows and glaciers of the Northern Areas. Consider using hiking boots (possibly with toe-clips) instead of SPD pedals.

The only Pakistan **guidebook** that gets updated is the Lonely Planet (latest edition 2008); although Footprint's 2004 *Northern Pakistan & Karakoram Highway* has more detailed coverage. By far the best **map** is John Callahan's *Karakoram Highway* (💻 www.johnthemap.co.uk), a labour of love that details the entire route with insets of every town.

Accommodation

Most hotels and guesthouses along the KKH are basic. On the Pakistani side there's a hotel or **guesthouse** every 60kms or so, except north of Sost and in Indus Kohistan. Bicycles can always be kept in your room. Since 2001 tourism in Pakistan has been in crisis so most hotel owners have slashed their prices to try and encourage business, those that haven't can probably be encouraged to do so. Where there are no hotels, roadside restaurants rent out their **charpoys** (wooden bed frames strung with ropes) for the night, effec-

THE SHALWAR KAMEEZ

This is the traditional dress worn by both men and women in Afghanistan, Pakistan, India and Bangladesh. *Shalwars* or *salwars* are baggy, pyjama-like trousers with a loose drawstring waist; the *kameez* is a thigh-length tunic whose side seams are open to the hips. Women wearing the shalwar kameez often drape a long scarf called a *dupatta* around their shoulders and over their head and chest.

In Pakistan the shalwar kameez is the national dress. Men mostly settle for dull shades of pale blue, grey and brown but women in the cities go all out for colour, favouring kameezes in acid yellow, hot pink and rampant scarlet, although in the more conservative regions women's outfits are concealed under all-enveloping *burqas*.

Like being able to speak some Urdu, wearing a shalwar kameez makes an enormous difference to how you are received, especially for women. It might feel like fancy dress but is actually an immensely comfortable garment and a good excuse to wear pyjamas all day long. Markets throughout Islamabad, Rawalpindi and, if you're coming from China, Gilgit sell shalwar kameezes. Two pairs are enough: one in thin cotton and another in a thicker weave or warmer fabric. Avoid synthetic fabrics, choose darker colours so the dirt doesn't show so fast and pick out ones with tapered ankles so the chainrings don't tear into the cloth. An unexpected bonus for women is that it's easier to pee outdoors discreetly in a shalwar kameez than in Western clothes. For the same reason don't approach men dressed in shalwar kameezes if they are crouching.

tively becoming open-air truckers' travel lodges. These are cheap (Rs50) but for men only. Women may be found a room nearby in a home.

In Pakistan (as in India) many restaurants call themselves 'hotels' but only serve food. In **Xinjiang** there are very few settlements and the only hotels are in Tashkurgan, Karakul and Kashgar. In between these places you'll have to either ask local families for a room or camp. If you're lucky and get invited to someone's home take the opportunity but do set a price first (eg Y25 for simple dinner, bed and breakfast) to avoid any misunderstandings. Chinese hotels are notorious for looking flash and offering facilities (hot shower, en suite toilet) that do not work.

Camping equipment is not necessary unless you cycle very slowly, in which case you might need it for Xinjiang. As ever camping is cheaper as many guesthouses and even swanky hotels in Pakistan will let you camp in their garden for free or a nominal sum (eg Rs50). It is not safe to camp by the road in Indus Kohistan.

Food and drink

Both the Chinese and the Pakistanis love their meat, especially when it's gristly and fatty. Mutton is popular in Pakistan though the most common dish comprises rice, *dahl* (lentils) and *sabze* (vegetables fried in oil and spices). Delicate western stomachs tend to find Pakistani food quite oily though the widespread and delicious *naan* bread soaks much of this up.

Fruit and vegetables are in plentiful supply until the far north of Pakistan and Gilgit, Karimabad and Kashgar all have Westerner-friendly food. TUC Salty biscuits and Prince Lu chocolate biscuits are ubiquitous and particularly recommended. Many travellers get sick from contaminated food or water so take the usual precautions (see p59). *Chai* (tea) is completely safe to drink, available everywhere and cooling even in scorching temperatures.

Money

Pakistan uses the **rupee** (Rs), like India. For the KKH the best exchange rate is in Islamabad and the next best in Gilgit; the further you travel north the worse the rate becomes. Travellers' cheques (preferably American Express or Thomas Cook) and cash (preferably dollars) are accepted at the National Bank of Pakistan along the KKH; the only **ATMs** are in Islamabad and Kashgar.

China's currency is the Renmimbi ('people's money') or RMB. Each unit is called a **yuan** (Y), which is often referred to as kuai (kwai) in speech. For each yuan there are ten jiao (often called mao). There's no foreign exchange in Tashkurgan so you'll have to ask around; shopkeepers are usually a good bet. Banks in Kashgar offer foreign exchange (travellers' cheques and cash) and ATMs.

See p32 or www.himalayabybike.com for the latest rates of exchange.

Getting to the ride

By air, British Airways (www.ba.com) and Pakistan International Airlines (PIA, www.piac.com.pk) are the most frequent carriers to **Islamabad**. For **Gilgit** PIA flies twice daily from Islamabad (Rs2600 one-way). The flight is an exhilarating experience as the tiny plane skims the flanks of Nanga Parbat but flights are subject to the mountain's unpredictable weather, are chronically overbooked and so are not a reliable option for those short on time.

Kashgar is known by its Chinese name of **Kashi**; China Southern Airlines (www.csair.com/en) flies to and fro once a week between Islamabad, Kashi and Urumchi; the Kashi/Islamabad leg costs around $260. Within China, Kashgar is reached via Urumchi; flights from Beijing to Urumchi cost from Y1690 and from Shenzen (for Hong Kong) from Y1850. Urumchi to Kashgar currently costs from Y490. Air China's official policy is that bicycles are included in the luggage allowance but on the ground they may insist on charging commercial freight prices which are around Y23/kg.

From Amritsar in India it's just 60km via the Atari/Wagah border to Lahore in Pakistan. The excellent Daewoo Express **bus** service connects Lahore and Rawalpindi (Rs470) departing from 231-A Ferozepur Road near Kalma Chowk in **Lahore**, and from Kohinoor Textile Mills, Fazalabad, Peshawar Road in **Rawalpindi**. Daewoo buses run across central Pakistan and are well worth the extra money as they are well-maintained, air-conditioned, direct and you even get a newspaper, mineral water and snacks on board; see www.sammi.com.pk for routes and fares.

Buses run frequently between Rawalpindi's Pir Wadhai bus station and **Gilgit**, taking 14–16 hours. Northern Areas Transport Corporation (NATCO) and Silk Route are recommended companies with air-con buses and seats costing from Rs500. Buses run daily between Kashgar and Urumchi (journey time 23hrs).

Trains run to Islamabad across the border from Amritsar in India but the bus is quicker. For other routes see www.pakrail.com. A train runs daily in each direction between Urumchi and Kashgar taking 23 hours.

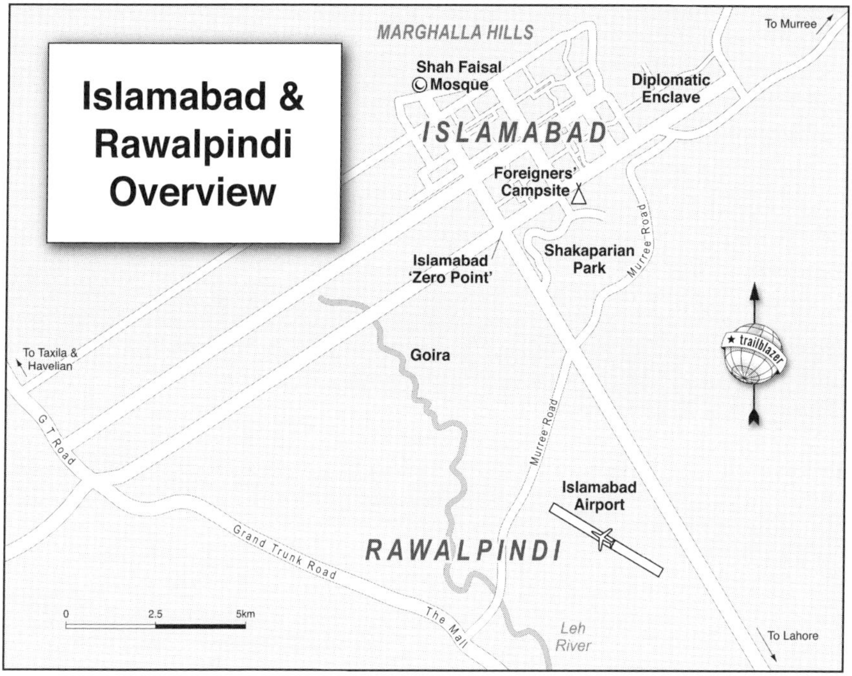

ISLAMABAD and RAWALPINDI (518m)

These two cities are Siamese twins who couldn't look more different. Murree Road connects the two, running from the old military camp of Rawalpindi (Pindi) to Pakistan's 1960s-built capital, Islamabad. Between them they share the vital transport hubs of the international airport and the bus and railway stations.

Rawalpindi is raucous with its narrow side streets and the slap and sizzle of roadside eateries. The lanes are crammed with honking traffic, cheap hotels and covered bazaars selling sacks of spices, goldfish, knock-off Western products and pirate CDs. Juice-sellers and bakers wafting fresh naan provide a respite from the frenzy while its sun-bleached main roads are a fug of diesel fumes and dust.

Conversely, Islamabad is a sterile, purpose-built capital which is relatively cosmopolitan and forward-looking, albeit still a culture shock if arriving from the West. Both Islamabad and Rawalpindi are prone to demonstrations which are best avoided; foreign women might find walking around them alone more hassle than it's worth.

History

Archaeological evidence shows that 2000 years ago Rawalpindi was a Buddhist village. Its strategic position on the Grand Trunk Road (see box p81), attracted Sikh merchants from the Punjab who developed it in the early nineteenth century as a trading centre. The British arrived in the mid-nineteenth century and sited their army camp to the south of the town and today Rawalpindi is the headquarters of the Pakistani army.

By contrast, Islamabad is less than fifty years old. When Pakistan was created in 1947 Karachi was its capital, but the sultry seaport was ill-positioned to govern what were then West and East Pakistan (the latter now Bangladesh). Islamabad, 'place of Islam', was dreamt up in 1958, designed by foreign architects and declared the seat of Pakistan's central government in 1962.

Orientation

The international airport lies just to the east of Murree Road, making it easy to ride in to either Islamabad or Rawalpindi once you've reassembled your bike. Turn left as you exit the airport building and at the traffic lights turn right. After about a kilometre turn right onto Rawal Road, go straight over the roundabout and continue until the T-junction with Murree Road. For Islamabad turn right onto Murree Road, for Rawalpindi turn left.

Though it's just the junction of Shahrah-e-Islamabad and Khayaban-e-Suhrawardy, **Zero Point** is the hypothetical centre of Islamabad. The city is made up of sectors (see city map opposite) and each sector is subdivided into quarters numbered 1–4 in a clockwise direction from the southwest corner. Thus a typical address might read Pitras Bukhari Road, H-8/4 Islamabad. At the centre of each sector is a market.

Rawalpindi is split into halves: the old town lies on the north bank of the Leh River, while on the south side are Saddar Bazaar, the railway station and the cantonment (military camp). Murree Road connects the two halves and is crossed east–west by The Mall which is a stretch of the Grand Trunk Road.

Where to stay

Hotels in Islamabad are generally pricier than in Rawalpindi, though there are some places costing Rs200–500 around Aapbara and Sitara Markets. Most overlanders head for the ***Foreigners' Campsite*** in Shakaparian Park, where a plain furniture-less room or tent pitch costs Rs50. There is a bathroom block and sink for washing dishes (which the armed guards also use for washing their feet), but no left luggage facility. Aapbara Market opposite has cheap restaurants, fresh juice sellers, internet cafés and shops.

In Rawalpindi there are cheap hotels along College Road which leads northwest from Liaqut ('Likkut') Bagh on Murree Road. There are more on Liaqut Road, which is one of the spokes of Forwara Chowk in the old town as well as Kashmir and Adamjee roads on the south side of the river.

Where to eat

All the hotels have either a restaurant or a boy who will run to one. In Islamabad the markets in each sector have cheap food stalls. There are some fancy restaurants too but chefs change often so ask around for the best places. Self-catering is easy from Islamabad's markets; anyone craving one last steak before India should visit the butchers at **Jinnah Super Market**. Fast-food places such as ***Subway*** on Jinnah Avenue are a refuge for those who need time to acclimatize to Pakistan's oily rice, chicken, mutton, eggs and naan. Jinnah Super Market has a 24hr food stand which does good grilled chicken.

Bike shops

There are a few basic bike shops scattered around Aapbara Market in Islamabad but forget about finding Shimano components or 26" inner tubes.

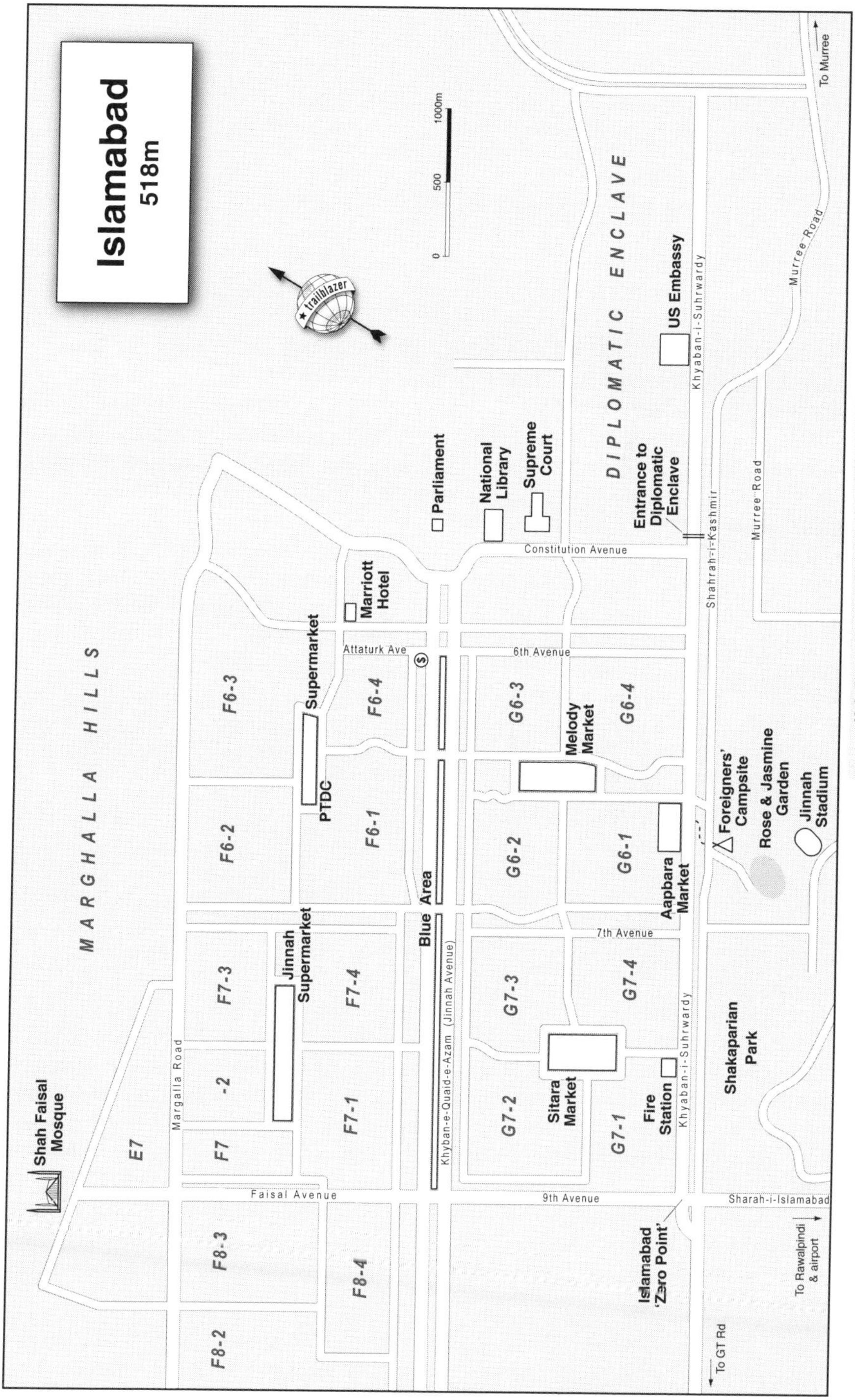
Islamabad
518m
trailblazer
0
500
1000m
MARGHALLA HILLS
DIPLOMATIC ENCLAVE
Shah Faisal Mosque
E7
Margalla Road
F7
-2
F7-1
F7-3
F7-4
Jinnah Supermarket
F6-1
F6-2
F6-3
F6-4
PTDC
Supermarket
Attaturk Ave
Marriott Hotel
Parliament
National Library
Supreme Court
Constitution Avenue
Blue Area
Khyban-e-Quaid-e-Azam (Jinnah Avenue)
6th Avenue
G6-1
G6-2
G6-3
G6-4
Melody Market
Aapbara Market
7th Avenue
G7-1
G7-2
G7-3
G7-4
Sitara Market
Fire Station
Khyaban-i-Suhrwardy
Faisal Avenue
9th Avenue
F8-2
F8-3
F8-4
Islamabad 'Zero Point'
To GT Rd
To Rawalpindi & airport
Sharah-i-Islamabad
Shakaparian Park
Foreigners' Campsite
Rose & Jasmine Garden
Jinnah Stadium
Shahrah-i-Kashmir
Entrance to Diplomatic Enclave
US Embassy
Murree Road
To Murree

BEAUTY AND THE BIKE

Pakistan is the best country in Asia to source bicycle trinkets such as leopard-skin saddle covers, plastic flowers for the handlebars or curly-wurly hub cleaners. But if you really love your bike, the lanes near Liaqut Chowk off Murree Road are full of truck, motorcycle and bike frame painters who can re-spray a bicycle with any design you give them. Why let the trucks have all the fun?

Bike repairs in Pakistan require lateral thinking as no foreign parts are available and therefore few bike mechanics have any experience of them. Anyone who takes one look at your bike and declares 'no problem!' while reaching for a hammer will probably do more harm than good.

Buying a bike locally Pakistani bicycles are clunking beasts of burden and are not designed for nimble mountain climbing. Traders in Gilgit sell cheap Chinese bikes; a better option is to buy the bike in Kashgar (see box p118) then ride it down the KKH where it can be sold for its original value in Gilgit or Islamabad.

Services

• **Banks** There's a 24hr ATM (Visa, Cirrus and Maestro) at the Islamabad Citibank on the corner of Faisal Avenue and Jinnah Avenue, Blue Area (Mon–Thurs 9am–5pm, Fri 9am–12.30pm, Sat 9am–1.30pm). American Express (Mon–Thurs 9am–noon, Fri & Sat 9–11am) is on the corner of Jinnah Avenue and Attaturk Avenue. In Rawalpindi there are several banks in Saddar Bazaar.

• **Bookshops and newsagents** London Book Company in Kohsar Market, F-6/3 Islamabad has guidebooks and a huge selection of books on the region. Mr Books in Super Market (F-6) sells guidebooks, magazines and newspapers.

• **Embassies** Most embassies (including China, UK, US, Canada and Australia) are grouped together in the Diplomatic Enclave to the east of Islamabad. Cyclists may be able to ride up to the embassy's doors; others will be put on a shuttle bus. As you'd imagine, security is tight so carry ID. There's a map of the enclave at the entrance on Khyaban-e-Suhrwardy.

• **Hospital** Shifa International, Pitras Bukhari Road, H-8/4 Islamabad.

• **Information** The Pakistan Tourism Development Corporation (PTDC; Mon–Sat 9am–6pm) on Aga Khan Road in Islamabad's Super Market (F6) hands out a free map of Rawalpindi and Islamabad though Lonely Planet's town maps are better. For current safety information ask your embassy.

• **Internet** There are internet cafés throughout Rawalpindi and Islamabad, including Dandy's in Islamabad's Super Market (upstairs, between Mr Books and Mr Books Two), which has fast connections and a pleasant environment (Rs25/hr).

• **Laundry** All hotels can arrange laundry either in-house or with a *dhobi wallah* (local washerman).

• **Post** Rawalpindi's General Post Office (Mon–Sat 9am–1pm & 1.30–9pm) is on Kashmir Road.

Route guide – Islamabad to Kashgar

From Islamabad there are two ways to the KKH: via the Grand Trunk Road, Taxila and Havelian to the northwest, or to the northeast via Murree on a hilly and scenic route (see box pp84-5) which joins the KKH at Abbottabad. Purists, those interested in the ancient Indus Culture and the as-yet unfit might prefer to stick to the main KKH.

DAY 1 ISLAMABAD (518m) to HARIPUR (562m) 77KM

ISLAMABAD – TAXILA 36.2KM
TAXILA – HARIPUR 41KM

Islamabad (518m) 0/1300km

What better place to start a long journey from than **Zero Point**? Following signs for Peshawar will lead you onto one of Asia's great highways: the Grand Trunk Road (aka 'GT Road'; see box below). You'll pass a reservoir on the right and shortly afterwards the Rawalpindi–Peshawar railway draws parallel to GT Road. At a large junction where the railway turns northwest away from the road, turn right to Taxila. You'll cross railway tracks almost immediately; Taxila Museum is about 3.5km up the road, past the Youth Hostel.

Taxila (559m) 36/1264km

Taxila hosts a UNESCO World Heritage Site of crucial significance to the Silk Route and so is well worth exploring. During the Gandhara civilization (600BC–500AD) it was a major centre of Buddhist and Hindu learning and a ride around the outskirts will reveal several archaeological sites, the most impressive of which are Sirkap (active between 200BC–200AD) and Dharmarajika (300BC–500AD). **Taxila Museum** on the main road (daily 8.30am–5.30pm, Rs200) displays a map of all the sites along with hundreds of artefacts ranging from surgical instruments and farmers' tools to children's toys and women's ivory combs, all of them at least two thousand years old.

THE HISTORY OF THE GRAND TRUNK ROAD

Many people assume today's Grand Trunk Road originates from the 2400km Grand Trunk Road of the British Raj which ran from Kolkata (Calcutta) to Kabul. In fact the road dates back to the little-known Mauryan empire (322-185BC), when it linked the Mauryan capital near present-day Patna in Bihar to Taxila (see above), when the latter lay on the troublesome Mauryan frontier and was an important centre of Buddhist teaching.

During the sixteenth century Sher Shah Suri, the Pashtun ruler of the Indian subcontinent, upgraded this route and it became known as the *Sadak-e-Azam* or Great Road. It was further improved and extended from Kolkata to Kabul during the British era 300 years later; Rudyard Kipling in *Kim* described it as "... a wonderful spectacle. It runs straight, bearing without crowding India's traffic for fifteen hundred miles – such a river of life as nowhere else exists in the world". Nowadays the same road is known popularly as 'GT Road' but more prosaically as NH2 and NH9 on maps. Buddhist monks, bullock carts and armies still travel along it though, as well as the odd BMW and even touring bicycle.

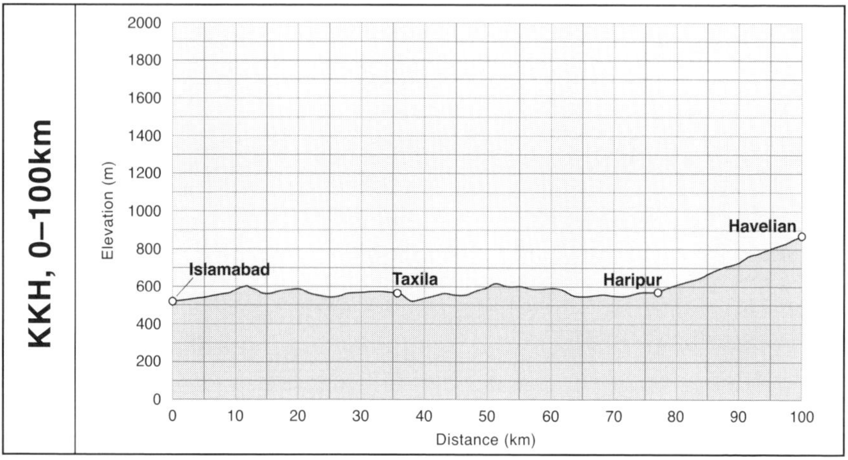

There is even a Hellenic Aphrodite and numerous serene Buddhas, illustrating the extraordinary fusion of East–West culture which occurred here.

If you're stopping over to have a look around the pricey ***Shahyar's Motel*** (en-suite doubles Rs800, a/c Rs1500) is right opposite the Taxila Museum. Nearby the basic ***Youth Hostel*** charges Rs175 (IYHA discount) for a room or pitch. The budget ***Asia Hotel*** a few hundred metres north of the museum was closed at the time of writing. The Shahyar has a restaurant and there are cheap *dhabas* (roadside restaurants) in Taxila bazaar.

Jaulian (563m) Just before Jaulian, 5km after Taxila, the road crosses from Punjab into the much more exotic-sounding North West Frontier Province; your adventure is underway! Jaulian also has several important Buddhist sites and a small bike shop.

Khanpur Dam (591m) You might see camels at the lakeshore here. It's a popular picnic spot and Pakistan's elite have snapped up shorefront properties as holiday homes.

After the dam the road continues along the Potwar plateau past numerous brick works. Low hills rise on both sides of the road and donkeys, cows and chickens wander across it. There are occasional small restaurants until Haripur. After crossing the railway tracks turn right at the fork.

Haripur (562m) 77/1223km
Haripur is a small plains town of little interest. At a crossroads with a stone marker in the middle turn right for the main town. Opposite the United Bank the ***Afaq Hotel*** (doubles Rs250 att) with a restaurant and small, parched garden is a friendly place to overnight.

DAY 2 HARIPUR (562m) to MANSEHRA (1095m) 64.5KM

HARIPUR – HAVELIAN 23.5KM
HAVELIAN – ABBOTTABAD 15KM
ABBOTTABAD – MANSEHRA 26KM

From Haripur the road climbs steadily past the small town of Bhalder to Havelian. The large cantonment to the east just before Havelian is the Pakistan Ordnance Depot.

Havelian (870m) 101/1199km
Though there's not so much as a plaque or amusing road sign the KKH officially starts here and swings northwest of Havelian to cross the Dor River. To reach the town, take the right fork uphill before the Dor Bridge, pass the bus stand on your right and follow the road around. About 500m after the bus stand is the

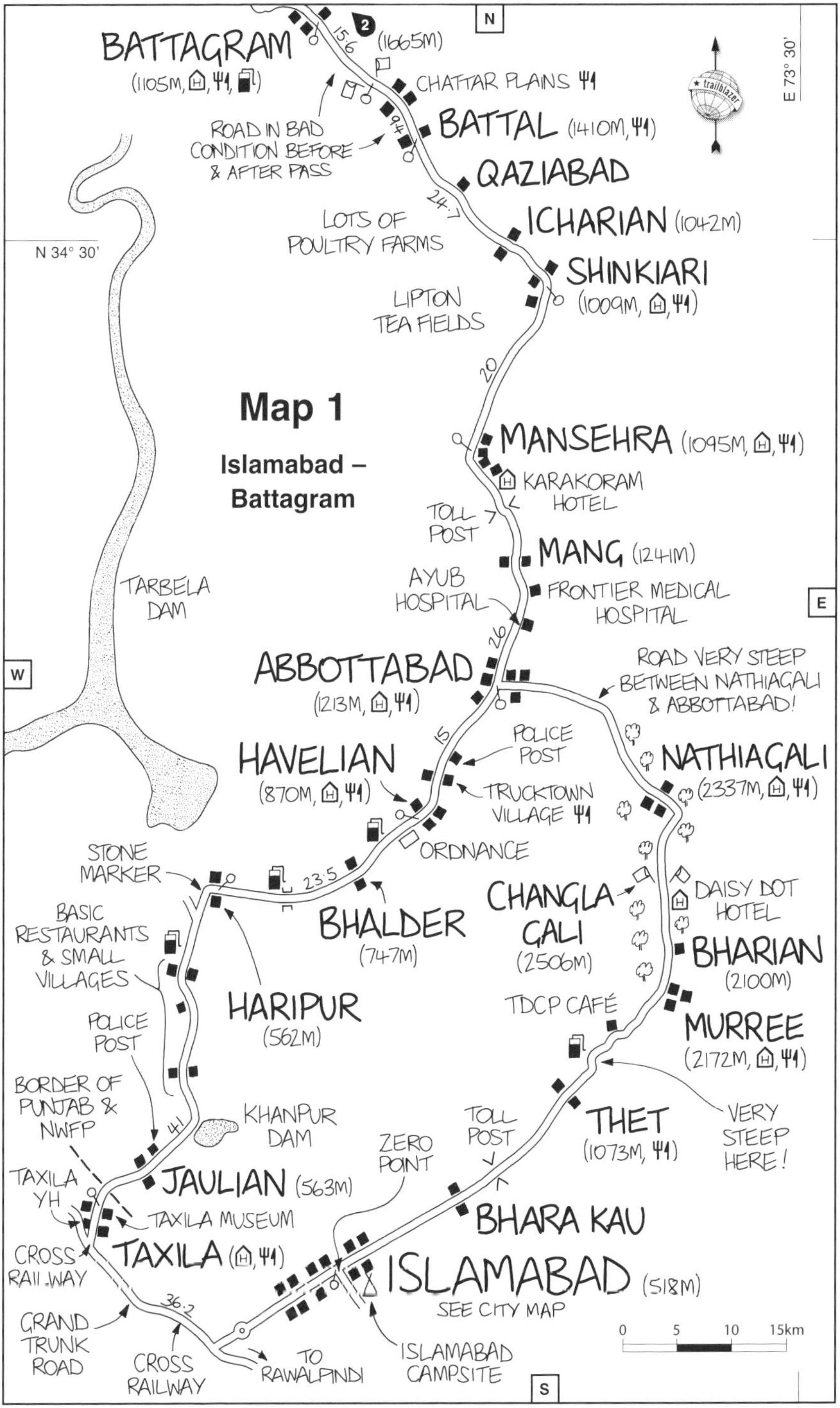

KARAKORAM HIGHWAY

basic ***Zaman Hotel and Restaurant*** (Rs300 negotiable; com); the best rooms are on the third floor and have TVs with BBC World.

The train station is 300m past the Zaman to the southeast. Since 2006 China and Pakistan have been discussing the feasibility of constructing a railway along the KKH, an engineering feat of such mind-boggling complexity it hardly bears thinking about. If the project ever reaches completion the railway will start here.

For the moment though Havelian is where the hills start. After crossing the Dor River the KKH winds its way up to Abbottabad past a couple of small townships and a police checkpoint.

Abbottabad (1213m) 116/1184km
The KKH approaches Abbottabad from the south, past the bus stand and Fokhara Chowk, striking north past the leafy cantonment and the road to Murree (a hilly way back to Islamabad; see box below). Restaurants and hotels line the road though the ***Bolan*** and ***Al-Zahra*** hotels near noisy Fokhara Chowk are cheaper at around Rs350 (att). The road is very busy

ISLAMABAD TO ABBOTTABAD – THE HILLY ROUTE

Distance 122km **Max alt** 2506m **Days** 2½

An **alternative route** which misses Taxila and the KKH's starting point at Havelian but is far quieter and more scenic is the steep route via Pakistan's most famous hill station, Murree. This is the old high road towards Kashmir and Srinagar and in clear weather there are beautiful views across the Jhelum river valley to the snowy peaks of the Pir Pinjal. For fully loaded cyclists these steep roads are a brutal way to start the trip but most of the ride is in cool and shady pine forests with terraced fields spilling down the ridge sides – a great contrast to the hot and dusty Taxila route – and it finishes with an exhilarating descent to Abbottabad and the KKH.

Day 1 Islamabad (518m) – Murree (2172m) 52km
Zero Point–Bhara Kau 11.6km
Bhara Kau–Thet 20.2km
Thet–Murree Chowk 17.2km
Murree Chowk–Murree 3km

On a clear day in Islamabad the hills around Murree are clearly visible from Zero Point. It's best to set off early to avoid cycling the steepest section (the final 20km) in the hottest part of the day and avoid riding on Sundays when the narrow road is crammed with day-tripper traffic.

Zero Point (518m) Head out east on Khayaban-i-Suhrwardy, past the Fire Brigade HQ, the Pakistan Manpower building and the sign misinforming you that Murree is 72km away. At the Aapbara Market traffic lights turn right then immediately left onto Shahrah-i-Kashmir. After 2km bear left to join the main Murree Road (clearly signposted). The first 15km is fairly flat dual carriageway on excellent tarmac, speeding away from the city towards the hills.

Bhara Kau (588m) Shortly after Bhara Kau the dual carriageway ends at a toll post (free for cyclists); the climbing starts immediately after. There are several cafés en route: the overpriced TDCP (Tourism Development Corporation of Punjab) Stopover Cafés (at 28km and 36km), or basic roadside chai shops.

Thet (1073m) There are some particularly steep hairpins at this village.

Charrapani (1558m) There's a TDCP restaurant and washroom here.

Chitta More (1886m) The *White House Hotel* charges Rs1000 for a double room.

Murree Chowk (1942m) Murree Chowk (Murree junction) is at a bend in the road known as Sunny Bank. From here the town is a 3km climb on Cart Road past the Daewoo bus stand and the Punjab Tourism Development office.

Murree (2172m) This town is Pakistan's most popular hill resort and accommodation is at a premium on summer weekends. The between Abbottabad and the Ayub Hospital, 5km north up the KKH.

Ayub Hospital (1201m) If you're already poorly this hospital has English-speaking doctors and there are plenty of pharmacies opposite. From here the traffic lessens and the road rises and falls for 10km before settling into a steady downhill run to Mansehra.

Mansehra (1095m) 142/1158km
The KKH bypasses Mansehra; from the south the town is 3km from the turn-off by the ***Karakoram Hotel***, from the north it's about 1km from Ashoka's Edicts (see box on p86), inscribed on boulders protected by a small corrugated iron roof. Mansehra's centre offers a choice of hotels from the cheap and cheerful (albeit bordello-like) ***Zam Zam*** where titchy doubles are Rs100 (com) or Rs150 (att) to the ***Errum Hotel*** (Rs500–750) and ***Karakoram Inn*** (Rs300–650); the latter also has a garden at the rear for camping. Cyberzone above the Royal Bakery near the Errum Hotel has **internet** access. All the hotels offer food, otherwise head for the streets.

ISLAMABAD TO ABBOTTABAD – THE HILLY ROUTE

cheapest hotels are around the noisy bus stand where there are also plenty of touts; in the town itself the ***Sargodha Guesthouse*** on Imtiaz Shaheed Road is as budget as it gets at Rs500 (triple, att). Most hotels charge a minimum of Rs1000 per night. The British explorer Sir Francis Younghusband was born in Murree in 1863; its Englishness extends to rain in the summer and Marmite at M/SA Rauf & Sons in the bazaar.

Day 2 Murree (2172m) – Nathiagali (2337m) 35km
Murree – Murree Chowk 3km
Murree Chowk – Bharian 8.8km
Bharian – Changla Gali 6km
Changla Gali – Nathiagali 17.2km

Head back to Murree Chowk and follow the signs to Nathiagali. After about one kilometre the road reaches an unsigned T-junction at the Army School. Turn left for Nathiagali and enjoy the brief downhill before a very steep climb to Bharian. The road winds along a ridge with views to Azad Kashmir to the east and, nearing Bharian, the Pir Pinjal peaks which belong to Indian Kashmir.

Bharian (2100m) There are fruit and veg stalls and roadside cafés here. After this mainly Pashtun village you leave Punjab and enter the North West Frontier Province (NWFP) where the road climbs even more steeply uphill to Changla Gali.

Changla Gali (2506m) Just before the ***Daisy Dot Hotel*** (double room Rs1500) there's a small chai stall with great views of the Murree Road snaking far below through the pine and fir trees. Changla Gali is the highest point on this road, after which it rises and falls through a series of valleys to Nathiagali.

Nathiagali (2337m) This hill resort is less developed than Murree but still popular with domestic tourists. The police may allow you to camp near their checkpoint in the grounds of the ***New Pines Hotel***, to the left after the post office. A room at the hotel itself costs Rs3000. All the hotels offer food: ***Skyways Hotel***, towards the end of the village, is a cut above (but not by much).

Day 3 Nathiagali (2337m) – Abbottabad (1213m) 34.5km
From Nathiagali there's a steady climb to the Pakistan Air Force Camp followed by a 20km descent through pine and fir forest which drops over 1000m with corners as steep as 15% – the only reason not to come this way from Abbottabad. The descent ends at a police post on the Dor River, which the road follows into Abbottabad, joining the KKH at a set of traffic lights and a Balochi memorial where Mansehra is clearly signed to the right. After a couple of days in the cool hills, Abbottabad signals the return to small-town plains Pakistan: heat, auto works, dhabas, madcap Suzukis and dust. To continue on the KKH see above.

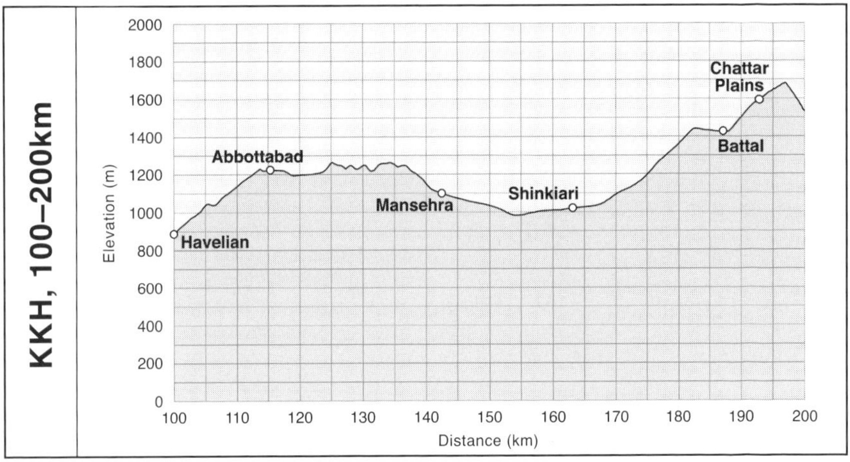

DAY 3 MANSEHRA (1095m) to BATTAGRAM (1105m) 69.7km

Mansehra – Shinkiari 20km
Shinkiari – Battal 24.7km
Battal – Unnamed pass 9.4km
Unnamed pass – Battagram 15.6km

Another hilly day but at least there's plenty of oxygen. From Mansehra onwards the climate becomes less arid and emerald green rice paddies, corn fields and pines fill the landscape. Just before Shinkiari the KKH enters the scenic Pakhli Valley; after Shinkiari bazaar the road turns west alongside the Siran River and then climbs up the valley to create the impression of finally moving into the mountains.

Shinkiari (1009m) 162/1138km

Shinkiari bazaar is a kilometre after the police and army posts (neither will allow you to camp). There's a cheap and dingy ***hotel*** (name in Urdu, doubles Rs100) above the Rainbow Hairdressers on the right after the Suzuki stand. The food is basic and the naan bread is kept warm in a duvet. Fruit and veg stalls opposite the hotel can supplement the meals. Shinkiari is a mainly Pashtun town so there are few women on the streets. Brains Net Café in the bazaar was closed at the time of research but connection was Rs30/hr.

ASHOKA'S EDICTS

Credited with being the first ruler to make Buddhism a state religion, the Mauryan Emperor Ashoka (304–232BC) governed a huge area that stretched from Afghanistan to Assam and from the Pamirs to south India. He had numerous Buddhist edicts inscribed on boulders, cave walls and stone memorials across his realm, many of which still exist today including one near Mansehra.

His edicts reveal a tolerant and progressive leader but Ashoka was not always a man of peace. In his days as a military commander he murdered his brothers and waged many bloodthirsty wars to build his empire. It was after a particularly devastating war with the Kalinga republic in central-eastern India, in which 100,000 men were killed, that he lost his taste for battle. Full of remorse, he converted to Buddhism and became a vegetarian. Many of his edicts are especially pertinent today: 'All religions should reside everywhere, for all of them desire self-control and purity of heart ... contact [between religions] is good. One should listen to and respect the doctrines professed by others.'

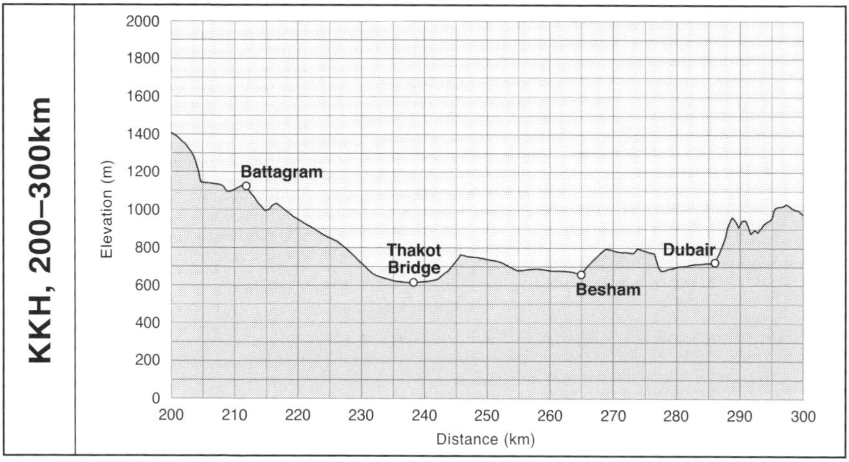

Icharian (1042m) is a small village and the sign declaring that it gets hilly ahead is no joke. Poultry farming is popular here and you'll pass huge hatcheries stuffed full of squawking chickens and the odd cockerel. The road twists and turns around a series of bluffs, always giving the impression that the climb is nearly over and tormenting you with a false descent 16km after Icharian before squiggling further up into a pine forest past Mr Javed's noisy chicken farm.

Qaziabad (1498m) has some small shops and a café.

Battal (1410m) 186/1114km
Some fruit and veg shops and more dhabas line the road. After the short descent into Battal the road continues climbing to the Chattar Plains.

Chattar Plains (1573m) The *Chattar Plains Motel* is friendly but pricey (meat dishes from Rs200) though the portions are big and there's a pleasant garden. You can **camp** here for free or stay in one of the 'cottages' for Rs600. From Chattar Plains onwards women in particular will notice the unnerving change in atmosphere: men often hiss, especially in Battagram.

Unnamed pass (1685m) 196/1104km
This small pass is marked by a derelict police post and the road is in bad condition either side for 3km. From here it's nearly all downhill to Battagram past paddy fields; the final kilometre runs alongside the Nandihar River.

Battagram (1105m) 211/1089km
Because of sporadic sectarian violence the police and even hotel owners might tell you that this town is not a safe place to stay. It certainly felt tense but then the people were also the most hospitable so far. The best hotel is the clearly-signed ***Thai Hotel & Food Mella Restaurant*** (doubles Rs300). If this is out of budget, the basic ***Al Fakhar*** on the left after the MoonTel PCO is cheaper (doubles Rs100) and has a veranda overlooking the bazaar but also vicious bed bugs. A local street snack is sautéed potatoes sprinkled with masala and twisted into a newspaper cone. The ***Food Mella*** restaurant serves Thai soup, trout (Rs110) and Pakistani and Chinese dishes such as dahl and sweet and sour chicken.

Friend or foe?

DAY 4 BATTAGRAM (1105m) to BESHAM (658m) 54km

Battagram – Thakot bridge 27km
Thakot bridge – Besham 27km

From Battagram it's mostly downhill to Thakot Bridge through the lush Nandihar River valley which narrows to a shady, verdant gorge. Once over the bridge the steep-sided Indus Valley can become extremely hot (over 40ºC even in April) and riding here can feel oppressive.

Police Post (815m) The following section is prone to landslides while kids throw stones and the police just laugh. Welcome to Indus Kohistan! Up ahead the road is mostly downhill and shaded by trees and ferns. Terraced fields pile down to the green-grey Nandihar river.

Thakot Bridge (619m) 238/1062km
The Nandihar River joins the brown Indus River a kilometre before Thakot bazaar (there's a small gazebo from where to appreciate the view). Thakot bazaar is poor and dusty with a couple of really cheap charpoy hotels and basic roadside restaurants. There are friendly police posts both sides of Thakot (or Youyi as it was renamed in 2004) Bridge; you can camp on the near side and register your passport details on the far side.

From Thakot the road climbs and falls along the Indus passing a few small villages, slate-grey sandy river banks and a monument to the Chinese and Pakistani workers who 'laid down their lives for the construction of this highway'. Kilometre distances are also given: only 360km to Gilgit, 625km to Khunjerab but a thought-provoking 5425km to Beijing. Indus Kohistan has the reputation of being a bleak gorge thronged by gun-toting fundamentalists but this section at least is leafy and children are friendly.

Besham (658m) 265/1035km
The high valley walls rise either side of the first town of Indus Kohistan with its string of shacks and hotels along a bazaar. A little searching will unearth anything and everything for sale so check you're OK for ammo, hash and cocaine.

With its caravanserai layout including charpoys outside the rooms for socializing the ***Al Safina*** (doubles Rs100; att) is cheap and the ***Paris***, a little further down on the left, is also recommended. Some cyclists have also recommended the ***International*** (Rs100) as being very clean.

The best food is served at the fairy-lit ***Besham Continental*** (double att Rs1000) on the right as you enter the town. Although much cheaper and grubbier, the Al Safina also offers remarkably tasty food.

LIFE IN INDUS KOHISTAN

'Everyone is having guns here. You will see in my restaurant tonight. Money buys you everything. If you have a police escort, people will see. But a bullet ...' (here he put his fingers to his temples and pulled an imaginary trigger) '... a bullet has no eyes.'

Restaurant owner, Besham

DAY 5 BESHAM (658m) to KOMILA (822m) 86km

Besham – Dubair 21km
Dubair – Pattan 19km
Pattan – Komila / Dassu 46km

From Besham onwards the KKH in Indus Kohistan climbs, falls and detours up side valleys which, combined with the heat, lack of shade and unfriendliness makes this section very tiring. Indus Kohistan is Sunni and throughout recent centuries the Kohistanis have, as the historian John Keay put it, 'made up for their lack of numbers with a well-deserved reputation for fanatical Mohammedanism'. **Foreign women should not ride the section between Besham and Chilas alone.** Catch a bus or minivan from Besham up to Chilas, if not to Gilgit (around Rs350).

From Besham a narrow road leads west over the Shangla Pass to Minghora

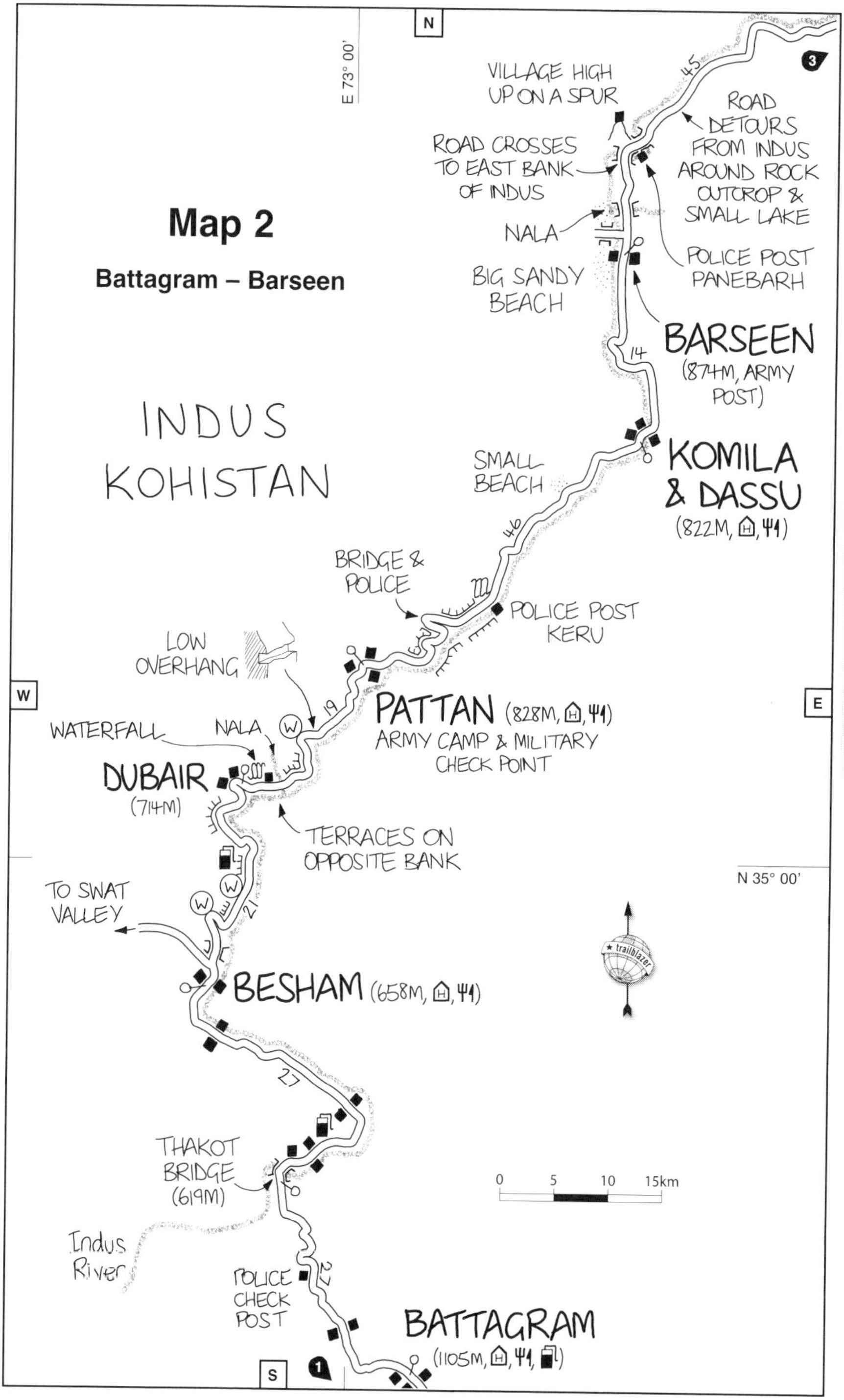
N
S
W
E
E 73° 00'
N 35° 00'
Map 2
Battagram – Barseen
INDUS KOHISTAN
VILLAGE HIGH UP ON A SPUR
ROAD CROSSES TO EAST BANK OF INDUS
ROAD DETOURS FROM INDUS AROUND ROCK OUTCROP & SMALL LAKE
NALA
BIG SANDY BEACH
POLICE POST PANEBARH
BARSEEN
(874M, ARMY POST)
SMALL BEACH
KOMILA & DASSU
(822M)
BRIDGE & POLICE
POLICE POST KERU
LOW OVERHANG
PATTAN (828M)
ARMY CAMP & MILITARY CHECK POINT
WATERFALL
NALA
DUBAIR
(714M)
TERRACES ON OPPOSITE BANK
TO SWAT VALLEY
BESHAM (658M)
THAKOT BRIDGE (619M)
Indus River
POLICE CHECK POST
BATTAGRAM
(1105M)
45
14
46
19
21
27
0 5 10 15km
trailblazer

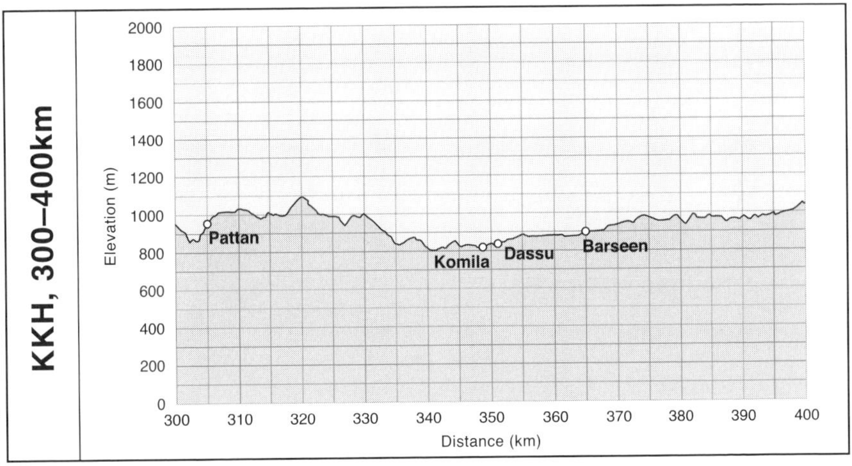

and the notorious Upper Swat Valley. The Indus River continues north with the KKH climbing above it. Slender terraces have been cut from the valley walls but these disappear as the valley narrows and you enter the dark heart of Indus Kohistan. During the British Raj Indus Kohistan was known as 'Yaghistan' or Land of the Ungovernables; not much has changed since then.

At times the road is nothing but a narrow ledge blasted out of the valley walls 500m above the river; a section which claimed the most lives during construction and is still dangerous now.

Dubair (714m) 286/1014km
Precarious concrete buildings teeter on the edge of the Indus and wooden shacks and fruit and veg stalls line the bazaar. Beyond Dubair there's a steady climb though several slide areas with crumbling overhangs. Around **Jajial (828m)** the road is in a bad condition. Terraces on the opposite side of the valley rise for hundreds of meters.

Pattan (828m) 305/995km
This is Kohistan's administrative capital; a town with a bad reputation. Along the KKH there are some grubby hotels like the ***Pattan Tourist Inn*** and the ***Kohistan Inn*** but the safest place is the ***Pattan Rest House*** in Pattan's bazaar which lies below the KKH on the banks of the Indus. Dhabas and veg stalls can also be found in the bazaar.

A military checkpost and army camp lie a kilometre after Pattan. Between Pattan and Dassu the road clings to the steep brown valley wall above the Indus, occasionally detouring up side valleys to cross nalahs.

Komila / Dassu (822m) 351/949km
Set amidst pockets of trees, Komila bazaar is thronged by men and police. Recommended hotels include the ***Arafat*** and ***Greenhills***; cycle-friendly and with good food. Across the bridge Dassu has a couple of basic hotels strung out along the highway: take your pick from the ***Khyber***, the ***Afghan Afridi***, the ***Pakistan Hotel*** and the ***Yasir Restaurant***.

DAY 6 KOMILA (822m) to CHILAS (1071m) 115KM

KOMILA / DASSU – BARSEEN 14KM
BARSEEN – SHATIAL 45KM
SHATIAL – CHILAS 56KM

This stretch of the KKH is even bleaker than the last and the meagre fields scratched into the valley walls help explain why this region is so poor. Between Barseen and Shatial the road can be in a bad condition and there are police

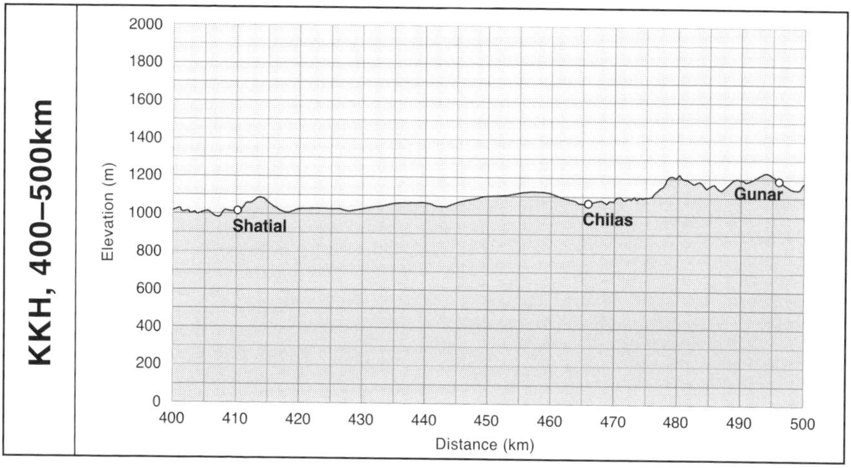

posts at least every 20km. Accommodation is unreliable and most cyclists want to finish this stage of Indus Kohistan as quickly as possible which explains the high mileage.

Barseen (874m) **365/935km**
There's a PTDC motel in the village and an army post just after it. Beyond Barseen the KKH crosses a bridge over the Indus near the Kandia Valley. This detour was forced by local tribesmen who repeatedly attacked KKH labourers in an effort to divert the new road away from their land. It worked and the road was re-routed to the south bank.

Sumer nalah (957km) is a truck-stop with charpoys where the roar of the river drowns out even the kerosene stoves. Kids sell fish on strings and the valley becomes ever bleaker: just rock and sand. After Sumer nalah the north bank of the Indus crosses the border of NWFP into the Northern Areas; the south bank and the KKH remain in NWFP for another 15km or so until the checkpoint at Basha. The narrow Indus gorge opens out and the sheer walls start to tilt back; the small oasis of green up ahead is **Sazin** village and the valley to the north of the Indus is Tangir. Just after Sazin is a large Frontier Constabulary Post; if you need accommodation here you'll have to appeal to their hospitality as they can be reluctant to shelter foreigners.

Shatial (1015m) **410/890km**
Shatial is little more than a collection of shacks before a bridge but try to avoid spending the night here. The track on the opposite bank of the Indus leads to the Gayal, Darel and Tangir Valleys which the British never subjugated and even other Pakistanis can't enter without a permit. They are said to contain a wealth of old forts, tombs and beautifully carved mosques as well as murderous vendettas dating back centuries. More recently they are also said to harbour members of Al Qaeda and the Taliban who fled the invasion of Afghanistan following 9/11.

One drawback of improving the access to these remote valleys is that the blood feuds are no longer confined to them but have spilled out onto the KKH. By the roadside in Shatial is a fifth-century Buddhist rock carving of a stupa and its worshippers.

Basha (1020m) Passport details are requested at the Frontier Registration Post here and again 7km later. Transferring between the police posts of NWFP and the Northern Areas feels like moving across an international border, especially since the Northern Areas has a National Bank of Pakistan right next to the checkpoint. In fact this almost did become an international frontier as the Northern Areas were part of Jammu & Kashmir whose Maharaja acceded to India at Partition in 1947 (see box p97).

AL QAEDA AND TALIBANISTAN

Between Afghanistan and Pakistan's North West Frontier Province (NWFP) lies a border territory known as the Federally Administered Tribal Areas, or FATAs. Its inhabitants are mainly Pashtun and have always been fiercely resistant to outside interference. The British learnt not to meddle with them in the early nineteenth century and when Pakistan inherited them in 1947 it too left well alone, keeping the tribal elders in place as the administration, a paramilitary army drawn from local tribesmen to keep order and exercising only nominal control from the capital.

This changed after 9/11 when it became obvious that members of Al Qaeda and the Taliban were crossing into Pakistan via the FATAs to escape the US-led invasion of Afghanistan. The Pakistan government now found itself in a very difficult position: pressure from the West to crack down on the Taliban and Al Qaeda meant having to send the army into difficult terrain it had no experience in, and which has always been hostile to outsiders.

Meanwhile the Taliban became entrenched in North and South Waziristan along the Afghan border, building training camps, establishing Sharia courts and earning the region a new name: Talibanistan. The local population, trapped between the Taliban and what became 80,000 Pakistani troops, turned on the troops. Initial military success was followed by brutal reprisal with more then 700 soldiers killed, some by decapitation.

To the world President Musharraf pledged a crackdown against the militants but at home his political survival depended on parties that resented his subservience to America. Pakistan's intelligence agency, the ISI, was also widely suspected of being pro-Taliban. So in 2004 the government changed tactics: peace deals were signed with the tribal leaders and the soldiers dismantled the roadblocks, stopped the patrols and remained in their barracks. The fight went out of the army and the Taliban won. Since then jihadists have been pressing further into Pakistan, from the FATAs via NWFP into Gilgit and up to training camps in the Darel and Tangir Valleys, beyond US intelligence and beyond the reach of US-led cross-border punitive strikes. Locals say that there is also an especially large training camp just outside Mansehra for jihadists fighting in Afghanistan and Indian Kashmir, and that the Northern Areas are now acting as a conduit between the two.

Muruski (1044m) After the police post and petrol station there's a small collection of shacks and a dhaba. Beyond Muruski the valley opens further to become quite wide and flat and sand dunes drift alongside the road as it swings around to Chilas. A road sign 2km before the town in Urdu, Russian, Chinese and English is a reminder of the strategic importance of this region.

Chilas (1071m) 466/834km
This is the capital of Diamar district and the biggest town between Besham and Gilgit. Though the centre is only 3km off the highway Chilasis are known for their unfriendliness so most visitors stay at the hotels along the KKH, such as the ***Karakoram Inn*** which is welcoming (double Rs300) and has a small garden at the back. Tell the manager if you're interested in seeing the nearby Buddhist engravings for which Chilas is famous and he'll lend you books and possibly take you there himself. If you'd rather go independently, the Chilas I site is the clump of rocks 150m down a sandy jeep track on the north side of Thalpan suspension bridge, 2.5km east of Chilas. Between Chilas and Thalpan rock carvings of cross-legged Boddhisatvas and stupas line the KKH itself though Islamic zealots have defaced some with political and religious slogans. In *Rockcarvings & Inscriptions in the Northern Areas of Pakistan* Dr Karl Jettmar notes more than 30,000 such drawings and inscriptions in this region, evidence over millennia of the pilgrims, merchants and invaders who travelled along the upper Indus and recorded their names, fears and beliefs along the way.

To stay at Talechi (see p91) you will need to reserve a room with the Northern Areas Public Works Department; the office is on the left of the road from the KKH into Chilas Bazaar.

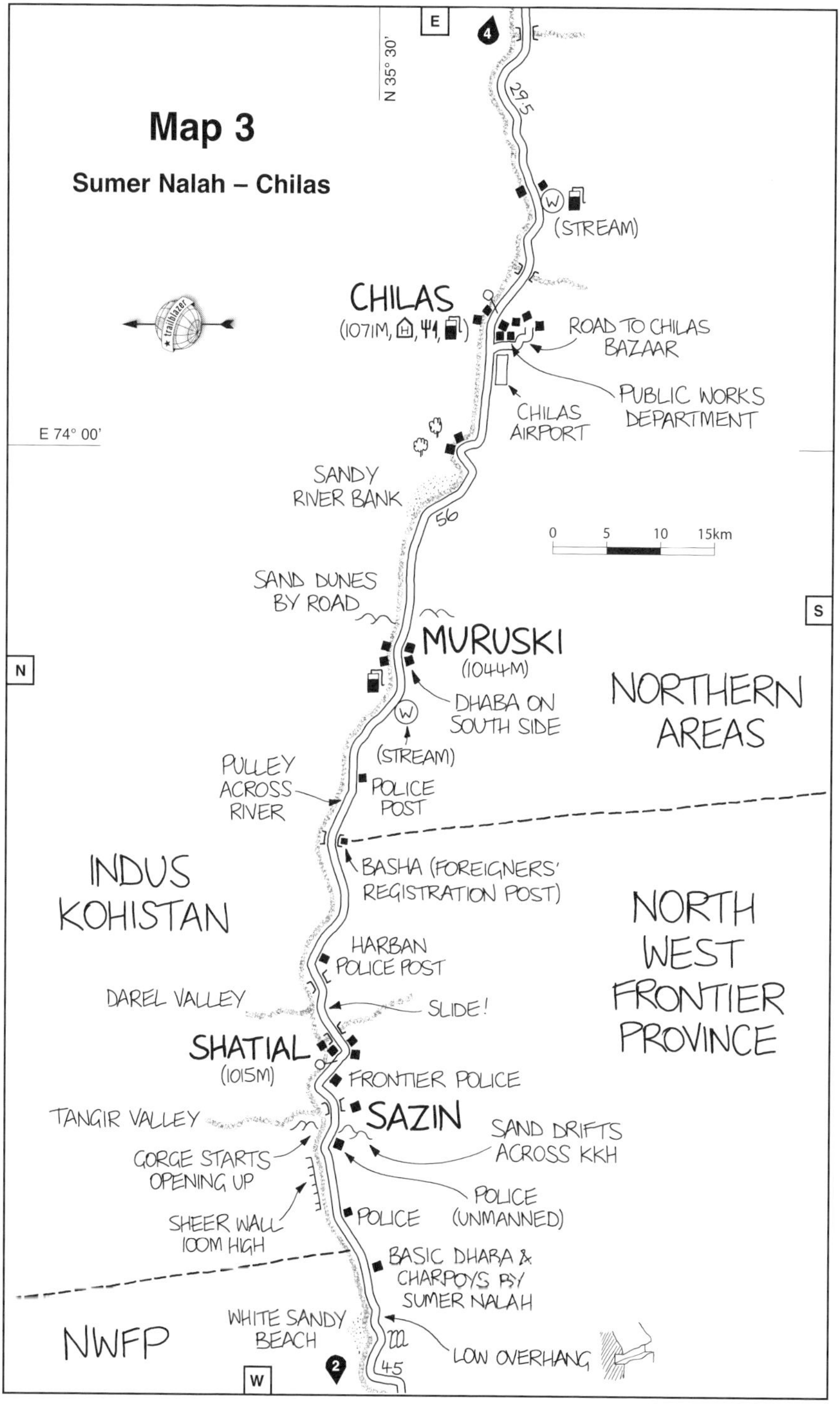

KARAKORAM HIGHWAY

ONE PEN ONE PEN ONE PEN!

This is, as Hugh Swift put it, a 'modern mantra' now shouted at tourists across the Himalaya. In northern Pakistan not handing over fistfuls of pens, money, sweets or chocolate – as NGOs and well-meaning visitors have clearly done before – can provoke stone-throwing. The children's parents may not intervene: foreigners have created this problem for themselves.

DAY 7 CHILAS (1071m) to TALECHI (1394m) 66.6KM

CHILAS – GUNAR FARM 29.5KM
GUNAR FARM – RAIKOT BRIDGE 24.5KM
RAIKOT BRIDGE – TALECHI 12.6KM

From Chilas the KKH climbs erratically up to Talechi through a landslide-prone area between Raikot Bridge and Talechi. There are few villages along the way and very little shade. Nearing Talechi the white bulk of Nanga Parbat looms to the south although clouds usually wreathe the summit. In case you've missed the ninth highest mountain in the world there's a large road sign pointing it out.

Gunar Farm (1167m) 496/804km

A small shop sells cold drinks and snacks and there's even a basic bicycle repair shop nearby. Watch out for Tato Pani ('Hot Water'), a stream between Tatto police post and Raikot Bridge which trickles over the retaining wall – it's hot!

Raikot Bridge (1194m) 520/780km

Here the KKH crosses to the north side of the Indus; just before the bridge a steep 14km jeep track (signed to Nanga Parbat) leads off to Tato village and Fairy Meadows (six hours on foot or Rs1000 in a jeep). The ***Shangri La Motel*** is signed at Raikot Bridge but is closed more often than not. Between Raikot Bridge and Talechi this deep valley can become oven-like which would be bearable if it wasn't for the tantalizing snowfields lying high above.

Talechi (1394m) 533/767km

At last, a friendly village and one which seems to be populated by a huge extended family. The ***NAPWD*** (Northern Areas Public Works Department) ***Inspection Bungalow*** is the only place to stay with rooms for Rs300 or a tent pitch for Rs50. Rooms must be booked in advance at either Gilgit (see p98) or Chilas (see p92). There's also the ***Nanga Parbat Hotel*** (actually a restaurant but with charpoys for Rs50) and a shop. Just before the village a tarmac road leads off to Astor and the Deosai Plains. In perfect weather you can see both Rakaposhi and Nanga Parbat mountains from the village.

NANGA PARBAT, THE KILLER MOUNTAIN

Nanga Parbat, 'Naked Mountain' in Kashmiri, is the last mountain in the Himalayan range. From Talechi the north face looks impressive but is stunted in comparison to the Rupal face on the south side which is an ice-wall four-and-a-half kilometres high: the greatest vertical rock face on the planet. Clouds permitting, some of the best views of Nanga Parbat are from Fairy Meadows, base camp for Nanga Parbat and just 14km off the KKH. At 8125m Nanga Parbat is the westernmost 8000m+ peak and is second in Pakistan only to K2 (8611m). The mountain earned its macabre nickname 'Killer Mountain' because of the many fatalities among its earliest summiteers. Hermann Buhl's mountaineering classic, *Nanga Parbat Pilgrimage* describes his solo ascent of the mountain in 1953 – something thought at the time to be at the very limit of human endeavour. He would have scaled a smaller mountain back then: Nanga Parbat lies on the edge of two tectonic plates which constantly push the peak further skywards.

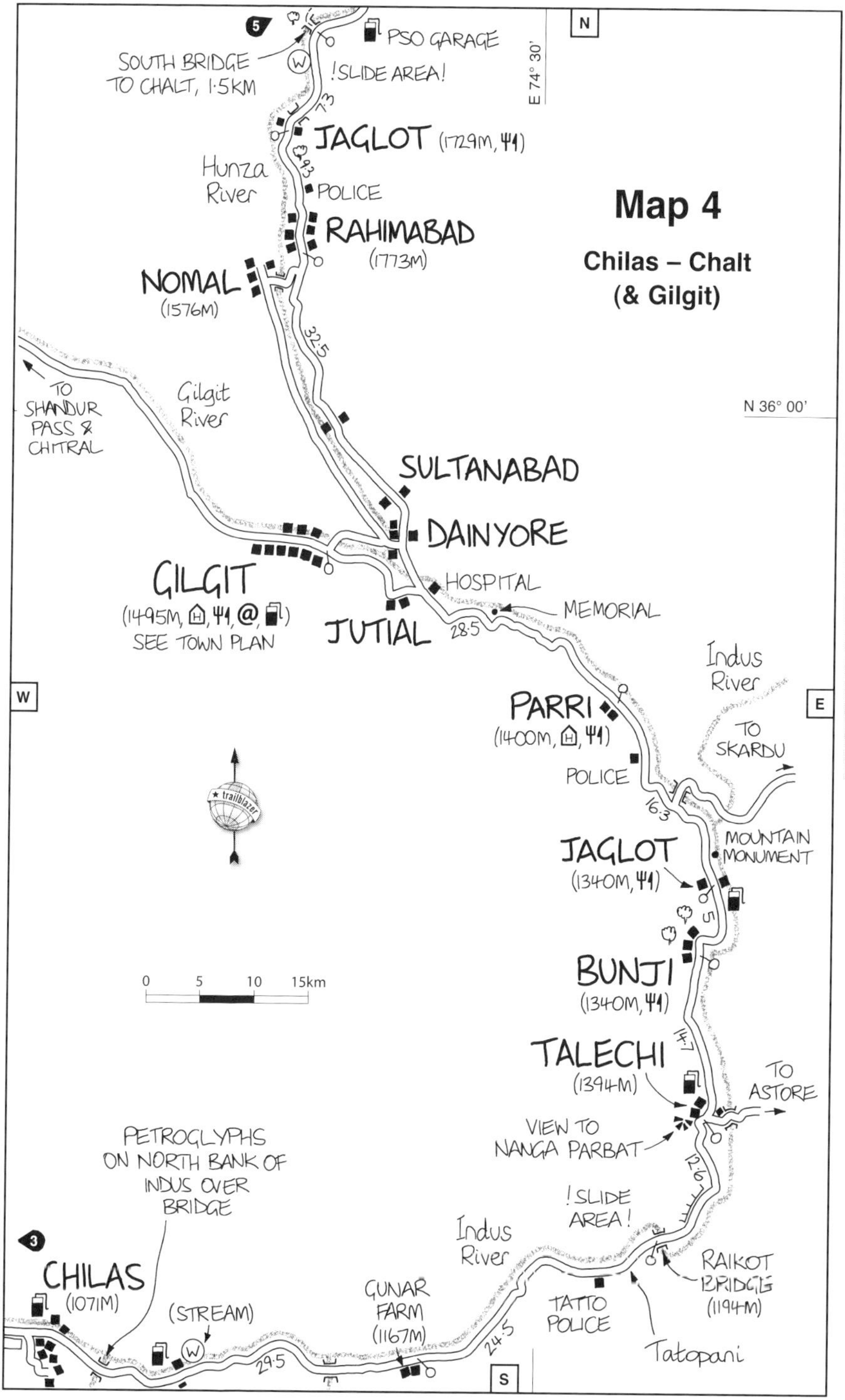
Map 4
Chilas – Chalt
(& Gilgit)
N
W
E
S
E 74° 30'
N 36° 00'
5
SOUTH BRIDGE TO CHALT, 1.5KM
PSO GARAGE
!SLIDE AREA!
7.3
JAGLOT (1729M)
9.3
Hunza River
POLICE
RAHIMABAD
(1773M)
NOMAL
(1576M)
32.5
TO SHANDUR PASS & CHITRAL
Gilgit River
SULTANABAD
DAINYORE
GILGIT
(1495M, @)
SEE TOWN PLAN
HOSPITAL
MEMORIAL
JUTIAL
28.5
Indus River
PARRI
(1400M)
TO SKARDU
POLICE
16.3
JAGLOT
(1340M)
MOUNTAIN MONUMENT
5
BUNJI
(1340M)
14.7
TALECHI
(1394M)
TO ASTORE
VIEW TO NANGA PARBAT
12.6
!SLIDE AREA!
0 5 10 15km
PETROGLYPHS ON NORTH BANK OF INDUS OVER BRIDGE
3
CHILAS
(1071M)
(STREAM)
Indus River
GUNAR FARM
(1167M)
29.5
24.5
TATTO POLICE
Tatopani
RAIKOT BRIDGE
(1194M)

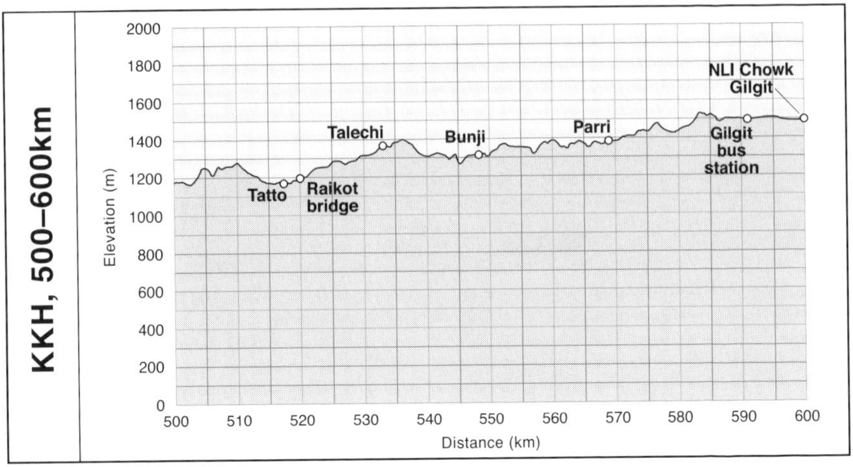

DAY 8 TALECHI (1394m) to GILGIT (1495m) 64.5KM

TALECHI – BUNJI 14.7KM
BUNJI – JAGLOT 5KM
JAGLOT – PARRI 16.3KM
PARRI – GILGIT 28.5KM

Not much happens between Talechi and Gilgit except for the turn-off to Skardu, a few army posts and some tree-shaded villages. Other than these it's a shadeless and hot ride along the Indus then up its tributary the Gilgit River into Gilgit. The highlight of the day is the viewpoint at the meeting of the Hindu Kush, Karakoram and Himalaya ranges.

Bunji (1340m) 548/752km
There's an army post and a couple of dhabas here and then the same again at Jaglot (1340m) 5km down the road.

Mountain Monument (1375m) A sign here proclaims this to be the 'junction point of three mightiest mountain ranges of the world': the Hindu Kush, Karakoram and the Himalaya, though the scenery is surprisingly brown. A couple of kilometres later, near the confluence of the Indus and Gilgit rivers, a tarmac road leads east

PARTITION: THE GILGIT SCOUTS AND THE FIRST KASHMIR WAR

When Sir Cyril Radcliffe sat down with his maps to sever Pakistan from India for Partition, he left the Maharaja of Jammu & Kashmir to choose his state's own destiny: Pakistan, India or independence. While the Hindu Maharaja procrastinated the Gilgit scouts, originally a paramilitary force created by the British but led at the time by the Scot Major William Brown, invaded to claim Srinagar for Pakistan. The Maharaja panicked and appealed to India to help repulse the scouts. India agreed, but for a price – that Kashmir accede to India. The Maharaja agreed and the Gilgit scouts were prevented from reaching Srinagar. This incident became known as the First Kashmiri War and subsequent skirmishes between India and Pakistan have seen Pakistani forces occupying Zoji La and besieging Leh and Indian forces occupying Skardu. Today's Line of Control follows the ceasefire line set in 1949 and the Gilgit scouts still wear kilts of Macdonald tartan and play the bagpipes.

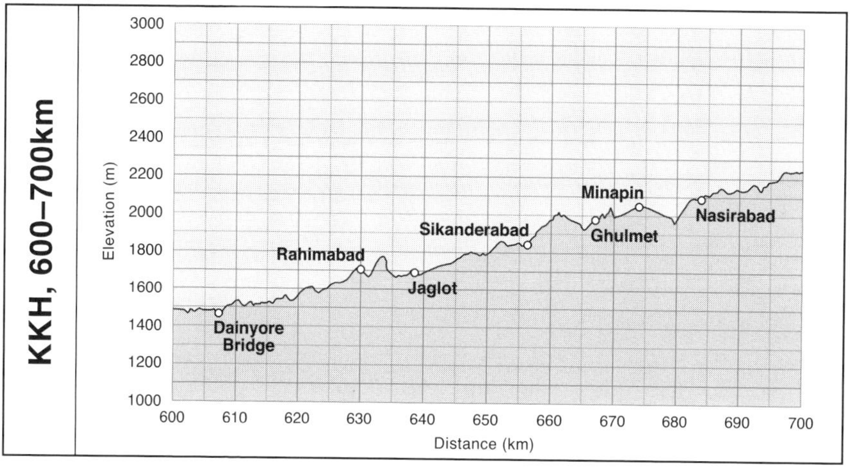

along the Indus to Skardu past Haramosh ('Land of Diamonds') Mountain.

Parri (1400m) **569/731km**

The ***Azam Hotel*** in this small shady village has food, cold drinks and constellations of flies wheeling over the chai glasses. A very basic room costs Rs100. After the hospital the road forks: go left for Gilgit. The KKH continues on the right fork, crossing the river to Dainyore.

PAKISTAN'S NORTHERN AREAS

Pakistan's Northern Areas (NAs) consist of Gilgit and the former states of Hunza, Nagar and Baltistan. Baltistan was once the western edge of Tibet and its capital, Skardu, was the winter capital of Ladakh for over a hundred years. Today the Northern Areas stretch from Skardu in the east to Pakistan's northern borders with China and Afghanistan. Both Pakistan and India consider the Northern Areas as technically part of Kashmir which is why both of them include Gilgit, Skardu and the peak of K2 on their country maps.

The status of the 1.5 million inhabitants of the Northern Areas is ambiguous: they have been administered by Pakistan since Independence in 1947 but they have no legal rights nor elected representation in the Pakistani government. The only plus is that they pay no taxes. The irony and hypocrisy of the Kashmir situation is that while Pakistan argues to the world that Indian Kashmir should belong Pakistan on the basis of its Muslim majority, it has never enfranchised the Northern Areas which are 100% Muslim and which, for the most part, want to belong fully to Pakistan. The construction of the KKH, the current development of Sost as Pakistan's largest inland port and a movement for independence in Indian Kashmir (see p176) has led to some calls for independence: either for the entire state of Jammu & Kashmir or for just the Northern Areas or Balawaristan, to use its historical name.

But the Pakistani government, like its Indian counterpart, will never grant independence to Kashmiris. This region at the meeting points of India, China, Russia, Afghanistan and Pakistan is strategically crucial. Nor will the government commit to the Northern Areas, at least not until the issue of Kashmir is resolved – and it has been in dispute for over fifty years. To do so would be tantamount to accepting the current Line of Control as an international boundary. While Pakistan holds out for the two-thirds of Kashmir still under Indian jurisdiction, it is leaving the one-third it does possess out in the cold.

GILGIT (1495m) 598/703KM

The capital of the Northern Areas is set in a dusty bowl of rocky brown hills and in summer can be extremely hot. At any time the town can be under curfew due to sectarian violence. Its significance on today's Silk Road is obvious in its bazaars where you'll find Chinese goods from bicycles to flowery thermoses. If you get the chance don't miss watching a polo match here. The most famous match of all is held annually on Shandur Pass between the teams of Chitral and Gilgit, but local teams often hold practice matches on Gilgit's polo ground. Many claim that this region is the home of polo, and it's certainly in a rawer, wilder form here than on the prim turf of England's Home Counties.

Where to stay and eat

By far the best-value place to stay in Gilgit is the ***Madina Guesthouse*** just off NLI Chowk. After running the gauntlet through NWFP and Indus Kohistan its oasis-like atmosphere is hard to leave. The simple rooms for Rs100/200/300 are set amongst a garden of roses, hollyhocks and sunflowers and the manager Yaqoob is an ex-bike mechanic. Mirza Baig, who runs a trekking agency from the guesthouse, is also a good source of information and stories. The guesthouse has a pleasant outdoors restaurant and an **internet** café. Those in need of conventional luxury should head for ***Serena Lodge*** in Jutial (💻 www.serenahotels.com/pakistan/gilgit/home.asp, doubles from $117 including breakfast) which holds a legendary High Tea from 3pm on Sundays (Rs150, all you can eat).

Services

• **Banks** The National Bank of Pakistan (Mon–Thur 9am–1pm, Fri & Sat 9am–12.30pm) just off Khazana Road will cash travellers' cheques.

• **Booking PWD bungalows** Anyone cycling southwards should visit the NAPWD Administrative Officer at the Northern Areas Public Works Department on Khazana Road to reserve a room in the NAPWD inspection bungalow at Talechi.

DAY 9 GILGIT (1495m) to MINAPIN (2049m) 76.8KM

GILGIT – RAHIMABAD 32.5KM
RAHIMABAD – JAGLOT 9.3KM
JAGLOT – CHALT TURN-OFF 7.3KM
CHALT TURN-OFF – MINAPIN TURN-OFF 23.4KM
MINAPIN TURN-OFF – MINAPIN 4.3KM

Gilgit (1495m) 598/703km

The quietest route out of Gilgit runs along the west bank of the Gilgit River to Nomal; turn right at the 'Nomal Decent Computer Centre' sign to reach the bridge and the KKH. However, the Nomal route is no shorter and it misses the fun suspension bridge at Dainyore and the unlit tunnel which does a dog-leg through a rock face. Whichever way you reach the KKH from Gilgit it then heads north through a series of 'one pen' villages. The best bazaar is at Jaglot, which has watermelons and roadside restaurants. It's a long day up to Minapin but absolutely worth it for the fantastic views. After a climb from Chalt to Jaffarabad, the road levels and then twists and turns giving fantastic glimpses up to the glaciers and peaks of Rakaposhi and Diran.

Getting out of Gilgit From the NLI bazaar head east along Airport Road until the left turn next to the Park Hotel. Follow the road down to the river, cross the Jinnah Bridge and at the top of the short hill next to the police station turn right. The road winds for 3km until a fork next

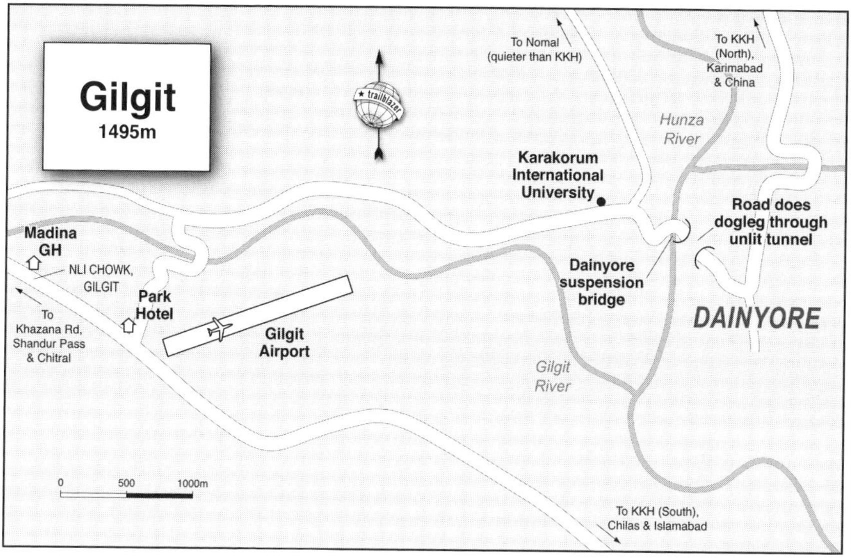

to the Karakoram International University (KIU); turn left for Nomal (20km, KKH 23km) or right to Dainyore and the KKH (1.7km). There are good views from here back to Gilgit.

Rahimabad (1773m) 630/670km
There's a cold drinks stand here.

Jaglot (1729m) 639/661km
Near the friendly FWO Army post is a bazaar and a few cheap roadside restaurants. Between Jaglot and Chalt the road is prone to landslides.

Chalt turn-off (1865m) 647/653km
Immediately left of the 'Welcome to Nagar Valley' sign a jeep track over a wooden suspension bridge leads to Chalt on the far bank of the Hunza River. The jeep track climbs steadily through the fields to this friendly Shia village situated 1.5km from the bridge. From Chalt a concrete bridge crosses the Hunza River further north but this road is much steeper.

As the KKH loops around a spine of rock it swings around to face the sheer western flank of Rakaposhi (7788m), one of the most beautiful mountains in the world. In good weather the peak floats six thousand metres above the KKH, trailing snowdrift and garlanded with clouds. This gorgeous view of Rakaposhi is the exception to the local saying: 'the best views are in Nagar, but you've got to go to Hunza to see them'.

CHALT VILLAGE

From the KKH it's a small detour to the lovely Shia village of Chalt **(1875m)** on the west bank of the Hunza River. In contrast to the dusty KKH, Chalt is cool and shady as it's surrounded by poplars, fruit trees and terraced fields of rice. The only places to stay are the ***Rest House*** and the ***Chalt Tourist Inn*** both of which charge Rs400 (negotiable) for slightly neglected double rooms.

Coming from the south, the jeep road passes alongside the fields, leads through the old bazaar and then crosses a very steep nalah; from here the Rest House is off the first lane to the right, and the Chalt Tourist Inn is to the left after the crossroads (its garden is opposite the Al Hussain Health Care Centre). After the surly villages further south, Chalt is highly sociable and you might be offered two local specialities to snack on: salty tea and the nuts from inside apricot kernels.

Sikanderabad (2003m) Here you'll find a couple of cheap doss houses, restaurants and a post office. Jaffarabad (1.5km further on) has a cold drinks shop. Just after Sikanderabad on the south bank of the Hunza River are the ruins of Nilt Fort, stormed by the British in 1891. After **Thole (1968m)** village is a nalah and a tiny restaurant called ***Rakaposhi Echo Hotel***. The shady garden enjoys a fantastic view up the south face of the mountain.

Ghulmet (2009m) Here clusters of hotels with outdoor restaurants gaze up the Ghulmet Glacier to Rakaposhi. ***Rakaposhi View*** has the best terrace and ***Rakaposhi Paradise*** over the road has better food.

Minapin turn-off (2020m) 670/630KM
The ***Diran Guesthouse*** in Minapin is legendary along the KKH for its good food, gorgeous garden and nearby trek to Rakaposhi Base Camp. Minapin (2049m) is just over 4km off the KKH up a rough up-and-down jeep track and the guesthouse has a price for everyone from Rs50 to camp or a dorm and doubles for Rs300–1000. The trek to Base Camp is highly recommended; British rider Kevin Swain rode it in 2004, taking nine and a half hours to go up and less than an hour to freewheel back.

DAY 10 MINAPIN (2049m) to KARIMABAD (2330m) 34.3KM

MINAPIN – MINAPIN TURN-OFF 4.3KM
MINAPIN TURN-OFF – NASIRABAD 5.1KM
NASIRABAD – ALIABAD 17.3KM
ALIABAD – KARIMABAD TURN-OFF 5.7KM
KARIMABAD TURN-OFF – KARIMABAD 1.9KM

From the Minapin turn-off onwards the road twists and turns giving fantastic glimpses up to the glaciers and peaks of Rakaposhi, Diran, and finally, near Karimabad, Ultar Peak and Bulbulmating.

Nagar/Hunza bridge (1916m) Here the KKH enters the fabled district of Hunza, a wide valley filled with terraced fields and fruit orchards all surrounded by a constellation of snow covered peaks. Spring (April/May) is a particularly beautiful time as the cherry trees blossom. The people of Hunza are as appealing as its scenery: hospitable and open Ismaeli Muslims who speak Burushaski, a unique language that seems to have no relation to any other. According to myth, Hunzakuts are the descendants of Alexander the Great's soldiers and live for over a hundred years in perfect health. In the nineteenth century the British knew them better as Kanjuti, wily raiders who preyed on the trading caravans that ventured along Hunza's precipitous tracks. Today those tracks are the KKH and in summer Hunzakuts usually only stop cyclists to give them kilos of juicy cherries.

Nasirabad (2092m) 684/616KM
This shady village is set directly opposite Rakaposhi with perfect views of the peak towering over Pisan Glacier. It's followed by a bleak canyon prone to landslides until Murtazabad, the next village.

Approaching Karimabad a noticeable side effect of female literacy here is that now both boys *and* girls chant the 'one pen' mantra. Occasionally it's 'Please give me one pen' but mostly it's 'One pen one pen one pen' or even 'Give me one pen'; 'Why?' 'Give me one pen PLEASE.'

The 'FWO Rest Stop and tucshop' (2102m) by the glacial Hasanabad nalah has a shady picnic table and toilet. The road climbs from here into Aliabad.

Aliabad (2238m) 701/599KM
Unlike Karimabad this is a working town with some large **food shops** so it's a better place to stock up on supplies before heading north. The 10km Aliabad link road to Karimabad turns left off the KKH at the Swat Hotel sign, but it's quicker to follow the KKH past the Golden Peak Hotel then tackle the steep 1.9km New Ganesh Road signed to Karimabad.

KARIMABAD (2330m) 709/591KM

This spectacularly situated town is the tourist capital of northern Pakistan and a magnet for travellers, some of whom spend entire summers smoking hash while gazing over the Hunza Valley. Karimabad is surrounded by an amphitheatre of mountains, several of which are over 7000m and whose snowmelt trickles into the village's terraced fields through a series of irrigation channels flanked by poplars. New Ganesh Road brings you in to Karimabad past Kado **Internet** Services (Rs40/hr, 10am–10pm); the Old Hunza Inn is down the first road to your left. Up a steep lane at the top of the village is Baltit fort, pressed hard against the mountains and commanding a panoramic view over the Hunza Valley. It has been immaculately restored and now features a library which is particularly strong on literature of the 'Great Game' era, known more poetically by Britain's nineteenth-century Russian adversaries as 'The Tournament of Shadows'.

Where to stay

Karimabad lacks Gilgit's friendly Madina Guesthouse but the ***Old Hunza Inn*** is popular with cyclists and motorbikers. The doubles for Rs150 (att) below the restaurant are the least shabby and have the best views. You can pitch your tent under the fruit trees for Rs50 although the nearest toilet is across the road and up two flights of stairs – worth knowing if your insides are in freefall. The 3-bed dorms (Rs50 per bed, unlockable door) have an attached bathroom and the dining room (with TV) serves a filling and tasty communal dinner at 7pm for Rs50 for all-you-can-eat soup and main course washed down with pots of green tea. The ***Haider Inn*** next door offers much the same.

Where to eat

It may be a bit commercialized but Karimabad at least has some good food. The ***Café de Hunza*** tempts tourists in with brownies, bowls of cornflakes ('muesli') drenched with yoghurt and honey and even lattes and cappuccinos.

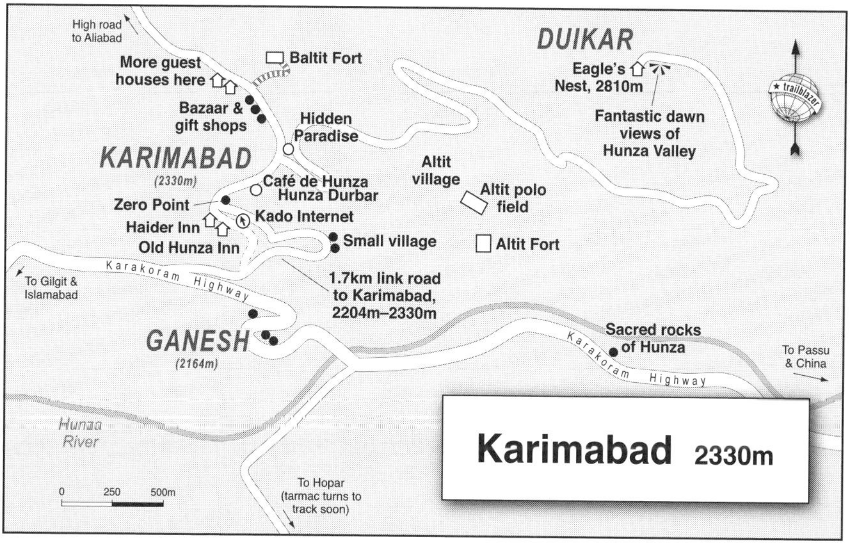

DAWN FROM DUIKAR

Karimabad makes a great base for exploring the nearby valleys and peaks of Hunza and Nagar. To reach Duikar with its gorgeous dawn view over Hunza, take the upper road from Altit and at the crossroads at the shops in Sultanabad turn left up the rough jeep track. The sandy road steepens and deteriorates the further you go but the 500m climb would be possible on an unloaded bike.

Camping is possible at ***Sky Camping*** (Rs50) and the ***Eagle's Nest Hotel*** (Rs50) next door. Eagle's Nest also has dorm rooms (Rs100 per bed) for rent when no tour groups are staying. The dawn views from the rock outcrop above Eagle's Nest (2850m) are a highlight of northern Pakistan: golden peaks and glaciers to the southeast, Diran to the south, Rakaposhi to the southwest, spires to the west, Bulbulmating and Hon to the northwest and another crest to the north. Far below these icy peaks the KKH is a mere scribble.

It also has a small bookshop with some of the best maps in Pakistan. The ***Karimabad Hotel*** sounds grander than it is; this cheap local restaurant is at the top of the shortcut stairs between Sher Gift Shop (on the main road) and the Old Hunza Inn. Just after the junction to Altit the ***Hidden Paradise*** restaurant serves tasty local food at not-very-local prices in a grove of fruit trees with views down to Altit village and fort. Dishes not to be missed include *chapsuro* (nicknamed Hunza Pizza) and *burus berikutz* (local soft cheese flavoured with herbs and sandwiched between chapattis brushed with apricot oil).

Many guesthouses have mulberry, cherry and apricot trees in the garden which are worth raiding in season (summer onwards). Hunzakuts swear that their apricots cure diarrhoea (among other things): many visitors would say they cause it! General stores between Zero Point (see map p101) and the fort sell basic items such as biscuits, cheese and smuggled Chinese beer (Rs200/can). For a proper shop go to Aliabad where the selection is greater and the prices lower.

DAY 11 KARIMABAD (2330m) to PASSU (2526m) 48.9KM

KARIMABAD – KARIMABAD TURN-OFF 1.9KM
KARIMABAD TURN-OFF – GULMIT 34KM
GULMIT – HUSSAINI 5KM
HUSSAINI – PASSU 8KM

After the swoop down from Karimabad, the KKH carves a lazy chicane through the Shia village of Ganesh (pronounced 'GUNesh', not like the pot-bellied Hindu elephant god) before crossing the Hunza River. After the bridge, a jeep track off to the right leads to the villages of Hopar and Hispar, both of which overlook glaciers and offer good trekking opportunities. The KKH climbs for 11km from here.

'The Sacred Rocks of Hunza' (2185m)
Scratched into these rocks are hundreds of engravings, inscriptions and drawings made by travellers on this route since 200AD, when this gorge connected the ancient kingdom of Gandhara (northern Pakistan and eastern Afghanistan) and the Tarim Basin (Xinjiang); similar engravings are found near Chilas (see p92). The curly-horned ibex is a particular favourite – locals say they are the pets of mountain fairies. The rocks are on the north side of the KKH, opposite a brick kiln, and are protected by barbed wire. On the other side of the river Altit Fort, high up on its bluff, glowers up the valley. From here the KKH travels through an arid and rocky ravine with a few slide areas and sandy river banks. Hidden from view are the stupendous mountains and

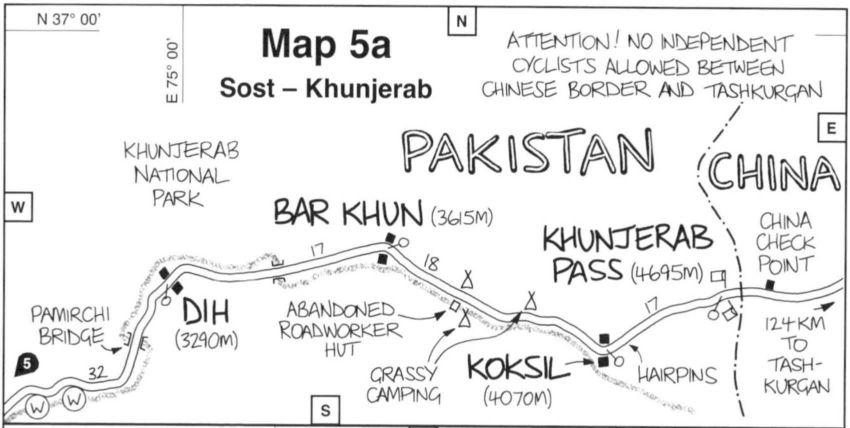

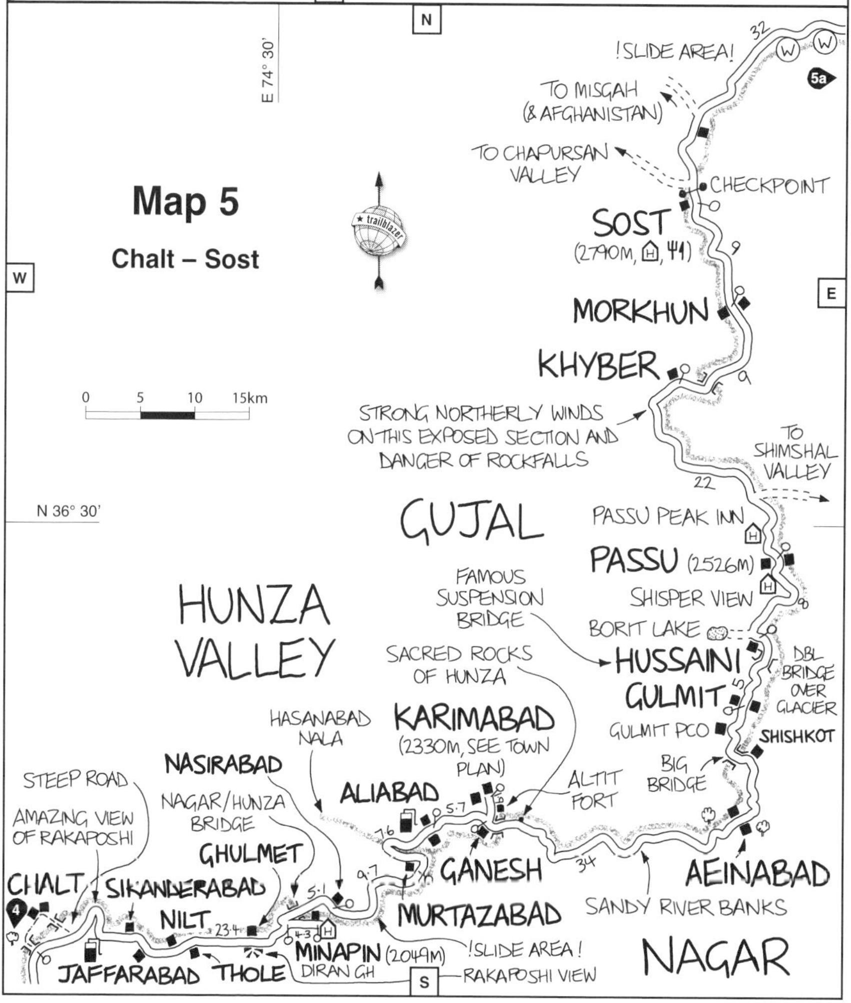

KARAKORAM HIGHWAY

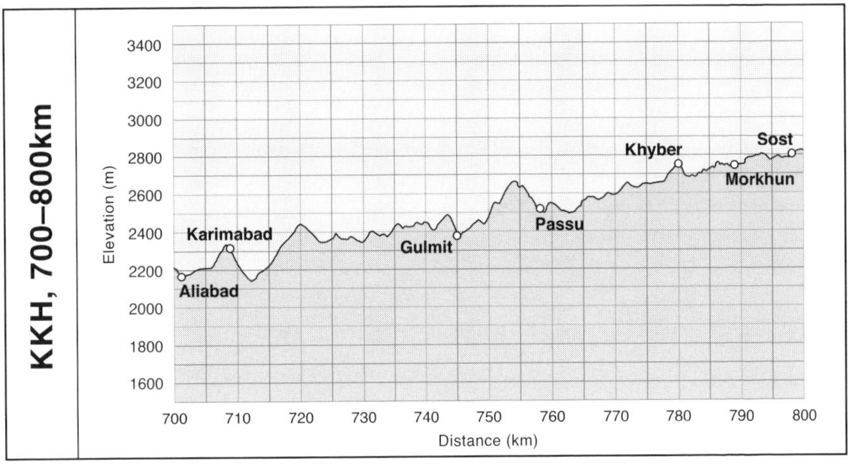

glaciers of the Karakoram which cradle this section of road.

Aeinabad (2329m) A small village in a pocket of trees.

Shishkot (2374m) The bridge to the west of this village marks the border between Hunza and the next district north, Gojal. From here until Tashkurgan the local language is Wakhi. Just after the bridge there's an ice corridor and further on the ***Paradise Hotel***, though it doesn't look too paradisiacal.

Gulmit (2374m) **745/556KM**

This small and friendly farming village has a couple of roadside hotels; the ***Silk Route Lodge*** charges Rs1500 for a double (att) or Rs50 to pitch a tent in the garden. At the junction of the jeep track to the village proper and the KKH is the grubby ***Evershine*** restaurant and some general stores selling pasta, biscuits, batteries and soft drinks.

After Gulmit two bridges cross the dirty Ghulkin glacier which blasts unsuspecting travellers with its icy breath. The KKH then climbs past the village of Hussaini and its famous suspension bridge and onto the glacier's lateral moraine. Ahead, on the far side of the Hunza River, is Tupopdan, a quiver of peaks known locally as the 'Passu Cathedrals'. To the left just before Passu a rough jeep track leads a kilometre to the small glacial Borit Lake where there is a basic hotel.

Passu (2526m) **758/543KM**

After climbing up some dry side-valleys, the KKH swoops down to the village of Passu spread out at the foot of its eponymous glacier. All is green – poplars, fields, even the tin roofs. Guesthouses such as the Shishper View and the Passu Peak Inn are on the KKH, while the village itself is down the jeep track after the bridge.

The people of Passu are friendly and this is a great base for some excellent trekking. The homes are mostly built of stone with tiny wooden doors and windows that give an inkling of the long, cold winters that Passu endures. Apparently sturdy woollens have always been traditional dress in the Gojal region and even today few men wear the shalwar kameez, preferring Western-style clothes instead.

The Shishper View and Passu Peak Inn are the best budget **places to stay**, and many guesthouses will allow you to camp for Rs50 or less. The fancier-looking hotels such as the concrete ***Passu Tourist Lodge*** cater to tour groups and are overpriced. Akbar of the ***Passu Peak Inn*** is quite a character, a retired soldier who runs his guesthouse with military cleanliness and relaxed hospitality. Campers can pitch in his rose-filled garden and gorge themselves on his fruit trees. Dorm beds are Rs100 (6-bed dorm) while rooms are Rs200/300 (att) or Rs400 (deluxe) with hot

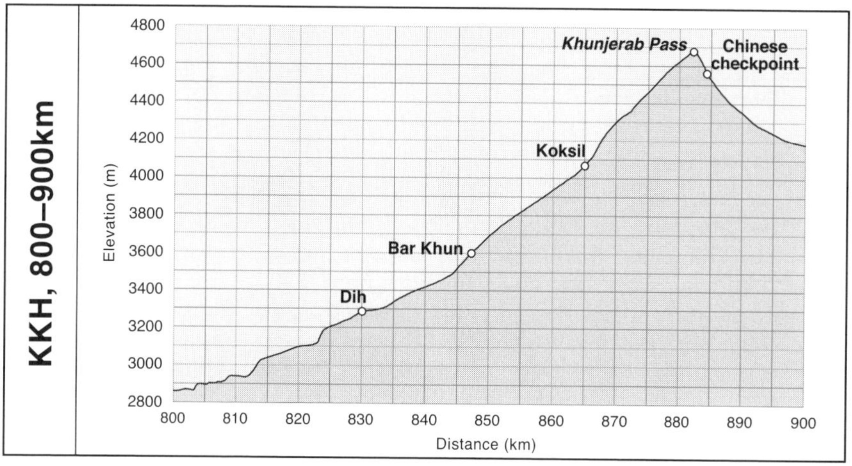

showers. Rooms at the equally friendly ***Shishper View*** range from Rs60 (bed in 3-bed dorm) to Rs150–300 (att) depending on the size and view. The best food is at the strangely formal ***Glacier Breeze*** restaurant (daily 7am–10pm) up the steps by the bridge, whose delicious apricot juice and apricot cake are renowned up and down the KKH. The general store halfway along the jeep track to the village proper sells an odd assortment of things including 'Absolutely World Class Computerised Socks' and 'Elbow Macaroni' but not cigarettes which are banned in Passu.

DAY 12 PASSU (2526m) to SOST (2790m) 40KM

PASSU – KHYBER 22KM
KHYBER – MORKHUN 9KM
MORKHUN – SOST 9KM

The valley between Passu and Sost is prone to strong headwinds and the only shops are in Morkhun. From Passu onwards snow flurries are not unusual even in May.

Beyond Passu's broad bowl the KKH swings back on itself past a few small ponds then crosses the Hunza River near the turn-off to Shimshal. From Morkhun to Sost the mountains rear up around the road which follows the Hunza River to Sost.

Shimshal turn-off (2567m) is 2km after Passu where a jeep track signed 'Welcome to Shimshal Roof of the World' leads over a bridge and east to the Shimshal valley. The scenery here is fantastic: shattered snow-capped peaks to the northeast and the black and white Ghujerab mountains looming to the southeast. To the west is the dirty snout of the mighty Batura glacier which at 57km is one of the longest glaciers outside of the polar caps.

Between the Shimshal turn-off and Khyber the road passes through a dry and dusty gorge whose grit-laden headwinds can be severe. Several caves in the rock face can provide shelter, though the rock face itself can collapse onto the road in high winds.

Khyber (2732m) 780/521km

On top of a hillock with bare rock valleys before and after it is Khyber, a small, friendly oasis of poplars, vegetable patches and burbling water channels. There are lots of development projects but no restaurant or hotel, though apparently the Conservation & Development Centre (CDC) has a simple guesthouse.

Between here and Morkhun is another small village and a FWO post near the ***Greenland Hotel***.

Morkhun (2745m) **89/512km**
There is a general store here. After Morkhun, about 8km before Sost, the valley widens out to become particularly photogenic with jagged peaks stabbing the sky and the Hunza River a greenish-blue (see black and white photo on p68).

SOST (2790m) 798/503km

Officially Sost (or Sust) refers to the lower village, 2km south along the KKH, but most people mean Afitayabad, the ramshackle border town which has sprung up along the KKH between the dry port and the customs post. The two are also known as Old Sost and New Sost. New Sost isn't really a town – it's more a collection of chancers loitering around the customs post and some basic hotels and restaurants catering to them. A few general stores sell basic items and smuggled Chinese goods. While it's not a place you'd want to stay, its frontier feel is quite appealing as Pakistani and Central Asian traders haggle while sitting cross-legged on carpets; tractors trundle through town and sleazy-looking characters conduct shady deals.

Before 2001 you could pedal all the way from Islamabad to Kashgar but the Chinese now insist that all China-bound cyclists use the NATCO or PTDC bus service (see below) to cover the 208km stretch of no man's land between Sost and Tashkurgan. However, the Pakistani army let cyclists pedal up to the Khunjerab Pass and back. There are rumours of cyclists who have succeeded in persuading the Chinese army on the pass to let them through by claiming altitude sickness. Most just take a photo, return to Sost and resign themselves to a bumpy bus or jeep ride back up with gun-toting Chinese soldiers the next day.

Where to stay and eat

The ***Sky Bridge Inn*** on the west side of the KKH offers clean, carpeted double rooms with TV and hot shower for Rs350, a rear garden (camping Rs50) and the best restaurant in town (ginger chicken Rs90). The shack with the satellite dishes opposite the hotel plays VCDs you can watch on your hotel TV. Cheaper, grubbier accommodation choices are the ***Asia Star*** (Rs150) and the ***Badakshan*** (Rs200). The new dry port, up a side road near the Sky Bridge Inn, is reported to have a snazzy Chinese hotel with karaoke.

Services

- **The bus to China** The NATCO office is at the north end of the long customs building. A ticket to Tashkurgan costs Rs1380 ($20) plus Rs690 for a bicycle though this can be negotiated. Cyclists can import their bikes into China but the bicycle must be declared on the paperwork. Officially when you leave China you should export the bike at the same customs post you entered by (ie Tashkurgan) but in practice this is not necessary.
- **Changing money** The National Bank of Pakistan in the car park of the Badakshan (Mon–Sat 9am–1.30pm) offers a bad rate for cash and a worse rate for travellers' cheques. Better to use the black market (ask around in the 'money changer' shops). Better still to find a Pakistani trader heading for China.
- **Doctor** The Aga Khan Foundation runs a good health clinic down in Old Sost, 400m up the signed jeep track from the KKH.

DAY 13 SOST (2790m) to BAR KHUN (3615m) 49KM

SOST – DIH 32KM
DIH – BAR KHUN 17KM

Many cyclists take two and a half days to ride the 168km from Sost to the Khunjerab Pass and back. On paper two days looks manageable: reaching Koksil (67km from Sost) the first night then climbing the pass and returning to Sost on the second day but this only accounts for distance, not **altitude**. Koksil is at 4070m and unless you have been trekking along the KKH you will not be sufficiently acclimatized. Bar Khun, at 3615m, is a better choice for a headache-free night and can be reached in just three hours from Sost. This gives time on the second day to enjoy the ride up to the pass then a long descent to Dih, returning to Sost by lunchtime on the third day. Another option is to **camp** between Dih and Bar Khun, leave the tent standing while you climb the pass and then return to Sost on the third day. Border police (the KSF) and forestry officials at Dih, Bar Khun and Koksil are friendly and hospitable. A smart tailwind whisks up the Khunjerab River valley which is good news for the climb but means some pedalling on the descent.

After the two checkpoints at Sost, there are no more villages until you reach China and beyond the Pamirchi bridge this region is a national park (see box below). This section of road is through a rocky, landslide-prone gorge alongside the icy blue Khunjerab River and has very little traffic. It's a quiet ride: just the rush of the river and the regular scrape and clatter of rocks tumbling down onto the road. The tarmac of the KKH is ruptured in places where huge slabs have fallen off the mountainside, and a crashed Chinese lorry lies abandoned in the river. Another challenge arises where the road ploughs through banks of shale and ice. Just 1.5km from Sost is the turn-off to the Chapursan Valley which abuts Afghanistan's Wakhan Corridor and sounds fascinating, if hard work to reach; see Matthieu Paley's excellent photographs (💻 www.paleyphoto.com and also 💻 www.macp-pk.org/brochure/chapursan.pdf) for a taster.

Another 5.5km further, past the solitary petrol station, is the turn-off to the restricted Misgah Valley. Trekking is possible with a permit but a soldier is posted in the small building opposite to ensure you stay on the KKH.

Pamirchi Bridge (3190m) over the Khunjerab River marks the start of the Khunjerab National Park.

Dih (3290m) 830/471km
Rooms in the ***government rest house*** at Dih cost Rs200 (att) and become available if no officials are staying. **Campers** can pitch for free in the grounds. Also at Dih is a Khunjerab National Park **checkpoint** where every foreigner has to pay $4 or the equivalent in yuan or rupees. For 5km beyond Dih there are a few camping

KHUNJERAB NATIONAL PARK

Local villagers used to graze their yaks and sheep between Dih and Khunjerab but this region is also the natural habitat of several endangered species including snow leopards, Marco Polo sheep and Himalayan ibex. Construction of the KKH took a toll on these species and the area between Dih and Khunjerab was designated the 'Khunjerab National Park' in conjunction with the World Wildlife Fund in 1975. Locals, who have now lost their traditional grazing grounds, say it is not their livestock but hungry and trigger-happy soldiers who necessitated the creation of the park. Either way, tourists expecting to spot wildlife larger than a marmot for their $4 entry fee will probably be disappointed. So will the few who believe the KNP wardens who say there are pandas up here – they're only on the WWF signs. In China, where locals wear marmots as headgear, the far side of the Khunjerab is also supposedly protected as part of the Taxgorgan Natural Reserve.

spots in the stands of trees by the river.

Bar Khun (3615m) 847/454km
The Khunjerab Security Force (KSF) and Khunjerab National Park (KNP) have a hut each at an idyllic spot next to the river and beneath a shining white pyramid of snow and rock. **Camping** is possible next to the river though the winds can be strong here and the higher elevation makes for a cold night. These are lonely postings: women travelling alone should avoid these places and camp elsewhere such as the abandoned road worker building by the river, 8km on from Bar Khun.

DAY 14 BAR KHUN (3615m) to KHUNJERAB PASS (4695m) 35KM

BAR KHUN – KOKSIL 18KM
KOKSIL – KHUNJERAB PASS 17KM

From Bar Khun it's a steady uphill along the Khunjerab River to Koksil ('Cooksill') through several slide areas and ice corridors. The total distance from Bar Khun to Khunjerab Pass and back to Dih is 87km.

Koksil (4070m) 865/436KM
Fill up water bottles here as this is the last stream before the pass. Soldiers at the KSF post are friendly and cyclists can leave extra luggage here for the last 17km climb to the pass.

Switchbacks to the pass start at Koksil, lifting the road out of the river valley onto the saddle where the pass lies. The landscape changes to green and purple glinting rock, with rusty orange boulders perfect for camouflaging the chubby, noisy marmots that live here. Many people start feeling the altitude above Koksil.

Khunjerab Pass (4695m) 882/419KM
Congratulations! In clear weather the pass is beautiful – an expanse of snow with glimpses of the shapely Pamirs beyond. There isn't much up here except a memorial to the KKH workers, a friendly KSF hut and, on the far side of the fence, the impassive Chinese border post. If you're very lucky you may spot grazing ibex goats or Marco Polo sheep. After two days of riding a narrow road in solitude, the sign before the pass 'N35 Kashgar 438, Tashkurgan 143, Alam Ata 1320', in Roman, Chinese and Cyrillic script is an odd reminder of the trans-Asian crossroads you've reached.

It is currently illegal to ride between the Khunjerab Pass and Tashkurgan.

KHUNJERAB (4695M) – TASHKURGAN (3115M), 124KM

Signs on the pass remind drivers to now keep right. Beyond the Chinese army post the road drops steeply off the pass into the Tashkurgan Valley. The police post at Pirali (3975m) has been abandoned apparently because soldiers struggled with the altitude. The scenery is stunning: cloud shadows race over a high-altitude grassy plateau sliced by the Tashkurgan river and flanked by the snowy Tagdumbash Pamirs. The jagged peaks to the northwest look like the Karakorams but are actually outriders of the Kun Lun ('Mountains of Darkness'). Rather than the tight twists and turns on the Pakistani side, here the KKH scrolls ahead giving the first long-distance views in weeks and the feeling of being on top of the world. The villages are simple and agricultural; the women wear brightly coloured jackets, headscarves and trousers and families clop along on donkey carts. Bactrian camels, yaks and donkeys share the road. Towards Tashkurgan the landscape becomes drier and vehicles raise plumes of dust.

0km	4695m	Khunjerab Pass sign
3km	4585m	Chinese checkpost
31km	3975m	Pirali (abandoned Chinese checkpost)
48km	3750m	Fork: LH Afghanistan, RH Tashkurgan
70km	3505m	Scattered buildings
75km	3475m	Village of whitewashed mud houses
105–117km	3255m	Village
124km	3115m	Tashkurgan

TASHKURGAN (3115M) 1006/295KM

The cultural difference between Sost and Tashkurgan is dramatic especially since your first contact will be with Han Customs and police who speak little Urdu, less English and have faces that belong a thousand miles from Central Asia.

The town architecture echoes this: high-rise blue glass buildings line the two-lane highway but despite the traffic lights there's no traffic. Strident exhortations from the tannoy echo across wide, empty avenues. The women of Tashkurgan provide the colour, which is especially striking after Pakistan. Entire flocks of boisterous Tajik women totter around in high heels, pencil skirts and red fitted jackets, giving the impression that this is a resort for 1960s' air stewardesses. The Han girls on the other hand usually wear cheap sports clothes. Many older Uighur men sport wispy beards and wonderful, curly-wurly shoes.

In the Uighur language Tashkurgan means 'stone fortress' and the crumbling mud walls of its fort still stand on the western edge of town. In the second century Ptolemy described it as being 'on the road to Seres, the Land of Silk' (ie China). Whether travellers and invaders used the Mintaka, Kilik or Khunjerab passes they would have descended through the Tashkurgan Valley; the fort's views are so panoramic that they would have been seen from miles away. Once here they would have taken the track to Yarkand alongside the Tashkurgan River or headed north to Kashgar. Today you can see yurts by the river and Tajik and Kyrgyz horsemen herding their sheep along the water meadows.

Where to stay and eat

China's hotels look more glitzy than Pakistan's but it's all façade. Pakistani traders from the bus may be able to point you to a cheap hotel: apparently there's one called the ***Khunjerab Inn*** (sign in Chinese) near the Customs post with double rooms for Y20 (att).

Follow the road north for about a kilometre from the customs post and turn right at the third crossroads for the bus stand and the ***Traffic Hotel*** (Jiatong Binguan in Chinese) which charges Y80/100/120 (att) or Y10 for a dorm bed; if you ask they will keep the dorm single-sex. The common toilets are literally filthy holes. ***Gong De Hotel*** opposite is cheaper and cleaner (en-suite doubles Y60) and come with hot running water, a thermos of hot water, slippers and toilet roll. Another option is the ***Crown Inn*** on Pamir Road (💻 www.crowninntash korgan.com) which looks good and charges Y420/860 (double/deluxe).

The menu at the Traffic Hotel restaurant (through the plastic abattoir flaps) is the stuff of dreams: pages upon pages of soups, noodles, beef, chicken, peanuts, chips, beer – even gin and tonic. Fruit and veg stalls in the bazaar sell

ADJUSTING TO CHINA

Compared to the warm and extrovert society of Pakistan, China feels colder. Very few people come up and start a conversation here whereas in Pakistan travellers face a daily barrage of questions and invitations to take chai, or a cold drink, or to stay in someone's home. This is partly due to language difficulties since few people in Xinjiang can speak English but there's also a different mindset. The people of Xinjiang are just as hospitable as their Pakistani neighbours but if you need help with water, food or accommodation you have to ask. Once you've taken the initiative, most people will gladly help.

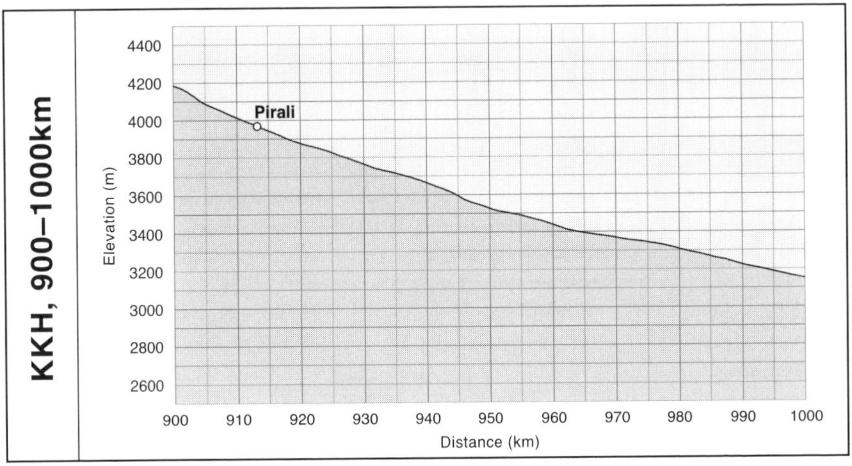

bananas, peaches, watermelons and apples. Street food is good too: skewer men charge 5 mao (Y0.5) per skewer of aubergine, beans, mushroom, tofu discs or chicken claws. The food is pasted with soy sauce and sesame marinade then grilled over hot coals and sprinkled with dried spices.

Services

• **The bus to Pakistan** A bus (or jeep, if the road over the pass is bad) leaves in the morning from outside the Traffic Hotel; tickets to Sost cost around Y140 ($24) and half again for a bicycle. Get tickets early in summer as this is the popular Kashgar–Sost bus and it's often full by the time it reaches Tashkurgan.

• **Changing money** There's nowhere to officially change money until Kashgar. The ticket office in the bus station will change cash (dollars) but not travellers' cheques though the small Xin Yi Shop opposite the bus station ticket counter offers a better black market rate. The Traffic Hotel will also cash dollars and any hotel will accept rupees as room payment – handing over a Rs1000 note will get some pocket money in yuan.

• **Post Office** There are **telephones** for international calls here but no internet.

• **Shopping** It's only when confronted with Tashkurgan's supermarkets full of opaque and indecipherable packets that you appreciate how much English there was in Pakistan. The few English translations – such as 'crispy cowpeas' – generally shed little light, making Tashkurgan a lucky dip when it comes to stocking up for the ride to Kashgar. On the same street as the Traffic Hotel the Shining Light supermarket at least has more price labels than the Smile supermarket further down the road.

TIME AND MONEY IN XINJIANG

Officially Tashkurgan is on Beijing time (GMT+8), which is three hours ahead of Pakistan. Unofficially it's on Xinjiang time ('local time'), which is one hour ahead of Pakistan (ie GMT+6). Banks use Beijing time whereas buses use both so confirm the time zone when you book a ticket.

Throughout Xinjiang, fix the price before agreeing to anything, whether it's tea and naan in a local home or hotel rooms in a town.

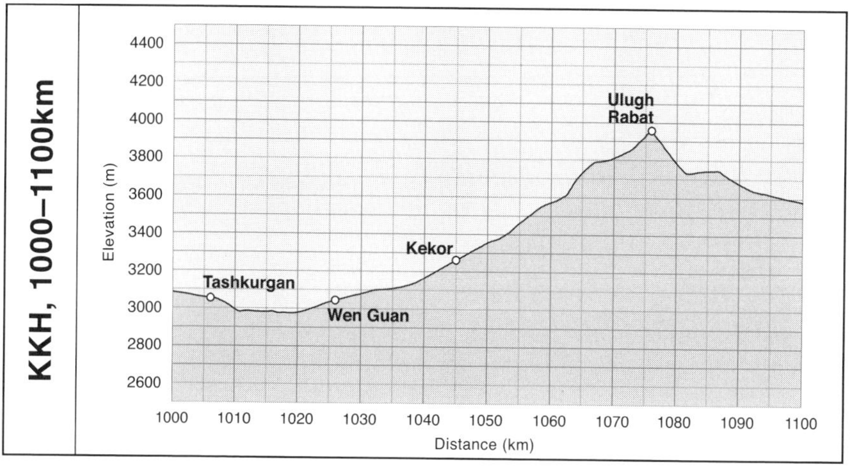

DAY 15 TASHKURGAN (3115m) to KARAKUL (3752m) over Ulugh Rabat (3955m) 95KM

TASHKURGAN – KEKOR 39KM
KEKOR – ULUGH RABAT PASS 31KM
ULUGH RABAT PASS – KARAKUL LAKE 25KM

There are no restaurants or hotels between Tashkurgan and Karakul. Though the climb to the pass is not steep, ferocious northerly winds make this a long, tough day if you don't camp en route.

North of Tashkurgan the highway follows the river whose banks are a popular fishing spot for families, and then heads for some mottled hills that punch through the valley floor like the knuckles of a giant's fist. Scattered houses line the road for the first 10km. The road emerges through these gateway hills onto the grassy Tagh Arma basin dotted with sheep and goats. A few identikit mud brick settlements such as Wen Guan have been built here but the predominant sound is the wind soughing across the plateau. From Wen Guan the road starts its long, gradual ascent to the Ulugh Rabat pass, against the headwinds.

Kekor (3266m) 1045/256KM

This small settlement is marked by an avenue of poplars along the road. There's a police station here and after Kekor the wind funnels through a shallow canyon. About 7km beyond the police station there's an excellent campsite in a small grove of trees next to a Tajik family. The road continues rising almost in a straight line up to the pass.

Ulugh Rabat Pass (3955m) 1076/225KM

The blue archway with Chinese characters is 1km before the actual pass. On the north side the road descends in switchbacks into yak pasture bounded by low hills and, to the east, the bulk of Muztagh Ata (7546m) on whose flanks in 2000 Martin Adserballe (see p157) claimed a Guinness world record for 'cycling' at 7008m. Down below the highway flattens out, passing the vil-

FOOD AND DRINK IN XINJIANG

Uighur *naan* is a dense, bagel-like creation with a soft onion topping. Another great local dish is *laghman*: noodles in a onion, garlic, tomato, green pepper, beef, tomato and courgette sauce – the long-lost relation of spaghetti Bolognese. Every meal in Xinjiang is washed down with green tea; a kettle will be brought to your table and your cup refilled for free.

VERY BASIC MANDARIN CHINESE

Hello	*Ni hao ('nee how')*
Where is the ...?	*... Zai nar?*
Hotel	*Ping yuan*
Bathroom	*Xi shou jian (she show jian)*
Room	*Fangjian*
How much?	*Duoshao qian (doeshow chee-en)?*
Good/not good	*Hao/bu hao (how/boo how)*
Too expensive	*Tai guile (tie gway ler)*
Water	*Shui (shway)*
Restaurant	*Fanguan*
One bottle of cold beer, please	*Qing, yi ping bingda pijou (Ching, ee ping bingda peejoe)*
Meat/no meat	*Ro/mayo ro*
Cheers!	*Ganbei! (lit 'empty glass' so bottoms up!)*
Thank you	*Xie xie (shay shay)*
Road	*Lu*
Goodbye	*Zaijian (tseye jien)*

lage of Edara (2km east of the KKH), a gravel manufacturing plant, and the village of Subaxun before curving around the western shore of Karakul lake.

Karakul lake (3752m) 1101/200KM
Karakul means 'Black Lake' in Turkic and it's a popular tourist stopover, the Kyrgyz yurts on the shore 2km north of the village being a particularly overpriced draw. In sunny weather the lake reflects perfectly the peaks of Muztagh Ata ('Father of Ice Mountains') and Kongur (7649m), the highest mountain in the Kun Lun Range. In low cloud though the lake can be a disappointment.

Local legend tells of a beautiful princess who lived on the mountain and was in love with a prince who lived on a nearby peak. But the princess's father disapproved and was so determined to thwart their love that he split Muztagh Ata in two with his stick, thereby separating the couple forever. The princess, consumed by grief, wept and wept until her tears turned into the glaciers that now feed Lake Karakul.

The ***Karakol Lake Resort*** offers overpriced accommodation in fake shared yurts (Y40 for a bed). A better option is to ask around in the village; set a price beforehand (eg Y25 for a simple supper and a bed). Most people are from Kyrgyz stock and are friendly, though hospitality

THE KYRGYZ OF KARAKUL

Around Karakul you will meet plenty of Kyrgyz, easily identified by their embroidered tall white hats. The layout of many Kyrgyz houses is the same: a large central room with a dung-burning stove, brick floor and brightly-coloured felts and carpets covering the walls. A raised platform takes up most of the room, at the back of which an enormous pile of bedrolls and blankets is hidden by a carpet. Meals are eaten sitting cross-legged on the platform; at bedtime the bedding is unrolled and everyone sleeps side by side. Green or salty (Tibetan-style) tea and disc-shaped naan are always available.

For many families their livelihood depends on their animals: camels, yaks and sheep and everyone takes turns looking after them. Selling handicrafts to tourists is a common sideline: you'll probably be shown jewellery, felts or hats such as the lampshade-like *kalpak*, or 'wild animal' (marmot) hats. As an ethnic minority in China, the Kyrgyz and Uighurs are exempt from the Han Chinese 'one child' policy and are allowed up to three children.

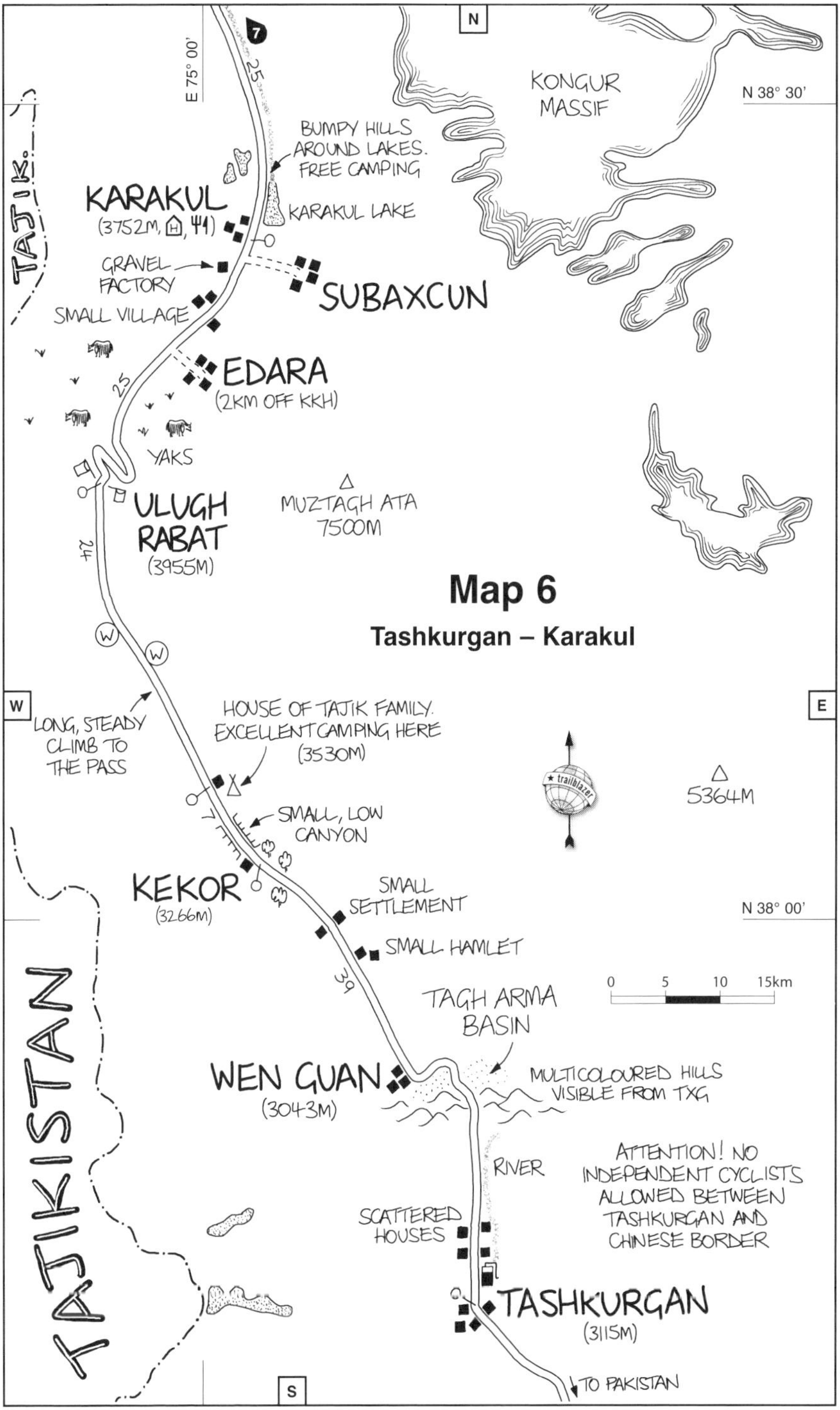
N
E 75° 00'
N 38° 30'
KONGUR MASSIF
TAJIK.
BUMPY HILLS AROUND LAKES. FREE CAMPING
KARAKUL
(3752M, ⌂, Ψ1)
KARAKUL LAKE
GRAVEL FACTORY
SUBAXCUN
SMALL VILLAGE
EDARA
(2KM OFF KKH)
25
YAKS
ULUGH RABAT
(3955M)
MUZTAGH ATA 7500M
24
Map 6
Tashkurgan – Karakul
W
E
LONG, STEADY CLIMB TO THE PASS
HOUSE OF TAJIK FAMILY. EXCELLENT CAMPING HERE (3530M)
SMALL, LOW CANYON
5364M
KEKOR
(3266M)
SMALL SETTLEMENT
N 38° 00'
SMALL HAMLET
39
0 5 10 15km
TAGH ARMA BASIN
WEN GUAN
(3043M)
MULTICOLOURED HILLS VISIBLE FROM TXG
TAJIKISTAN
RIVER
ATTENTION! NO INDEPENDENT CYCLISTS ALLOWED BETWEEN TASHKURGAN AND CHINESE BORDER
SCATTERED HOUSES
TASHKURGAN
(3115M)
TO PAKISTAN
S

here does not come for free. The hills around the lake and its sister lake 5km to the north are large enough to conceal a tent; be discreet to avoid having to pay because as elsewhere in China there is money to be made from natural beauty; 'fees' vary from Y20 to be in the 'scenic area' (ie near the lake) to Y120 for an 'environmental permit' for the half-day trek to Muztagh Ata Base Camp. Another possible excursion is to Kongur Base Camp, for which a guide is recommended.

DAY 16 KARAKUL (3752m) to GHEZCUN (2398m) 71KM

KARAKUL – BULUN KUL 25KM
BULUN KUL – GHEZCUN 46KM

After a gentle climb up from Karakul village, the road starts its descent towards the village of Bulun Kul. The descent proper through the Ghez canyon starts beyond Bulun Kul, past some enormous sand dunes. In poor weather with low cloud this section is almost entirely monochrome and the dunes appear frozen and ghostly. Wild camels can sometimes be seen grazing on the scrub next to the road.

Bulun Kul (3345m) 1126/175KM
A strip of pastureland alongside the river and grazing yaks herald the small village of Bulun Kul. There's no longer a restaurant or hotel here but you may be able to buy some green tea, naan and hard-boiled eggs from the villagers. After the village the road crosses the river and swings around to the northeast.

Ghez canyon (3148m) Wind turbines in the gorge confirm what cyclists already know: the wind roars through here giving those coming from Kashgar a push while slowing down those from Tashkurgan. Eventually the tarmac tilts enough for a free-wheeling descent which can top 60kph. The gorge is about 50km long and is too narrow to camp in except between 7km and 9km after Ghezcun.

Ghezcun (2398m) 1172/129KM
About 16km into the canyon and squeezed in tight between its walls is the small settlement of Ghezcun which has a passport checkpoint and two basic restaurants: the ***Happy Chef*** and the smaller, family-run ***Gunsa*** opposite, which serves bowls of *laghman* (Y4) and also has a basic room next door (Y10). A small general shop sells the four staples of outback Xinjiang; hard-boiled eggs, beer, instant noodles and sweets. Truck brakes screeching at all hours for the checkpoint barrier make this a noisy place to try and sleep.

DAY 17 GHEZCUN (2398m) to KASHGAR (1388m) 128KM

GHEZCUN – UPAL 78KM
UPAL – SHUFUXIAN 31KM
SHUFUXIAN – KASHGAR 19KM

Finally the KKH plunges out of the mountains and into the desert. At Ghezcun the river is fast flowing but then broadens into a lazy sweep dappled by gravel beds towards the mouth of the canyon. Occasional clusters of houses are dotted between manufacturing plants. Within 50km from Ghez the feel of the landscape changes totally from the chill of the mountains to the flat horizons, irrigation channels and the dun tones of desert. Dotted along the road are mud-brick compounds often with trellises of grapes and large mulberry trees in their courtyards. Poplars and willows line the Highway either side of the small villages en route.

From the mouth of the Ghez canyon it's around 30km to Upal and just 80km to Kashgar. Barring an abduction by aliens you're very probably going to make it!

Upal (1496m) 1250/51KM
This small town has a lively bazaar of bakers, yoghurt shops-cum-video dens, laundrettes and street food – but no hotel. A restaurant next to the white academy (name in Chinese) on the left as you approach from the south, has **charpoys**

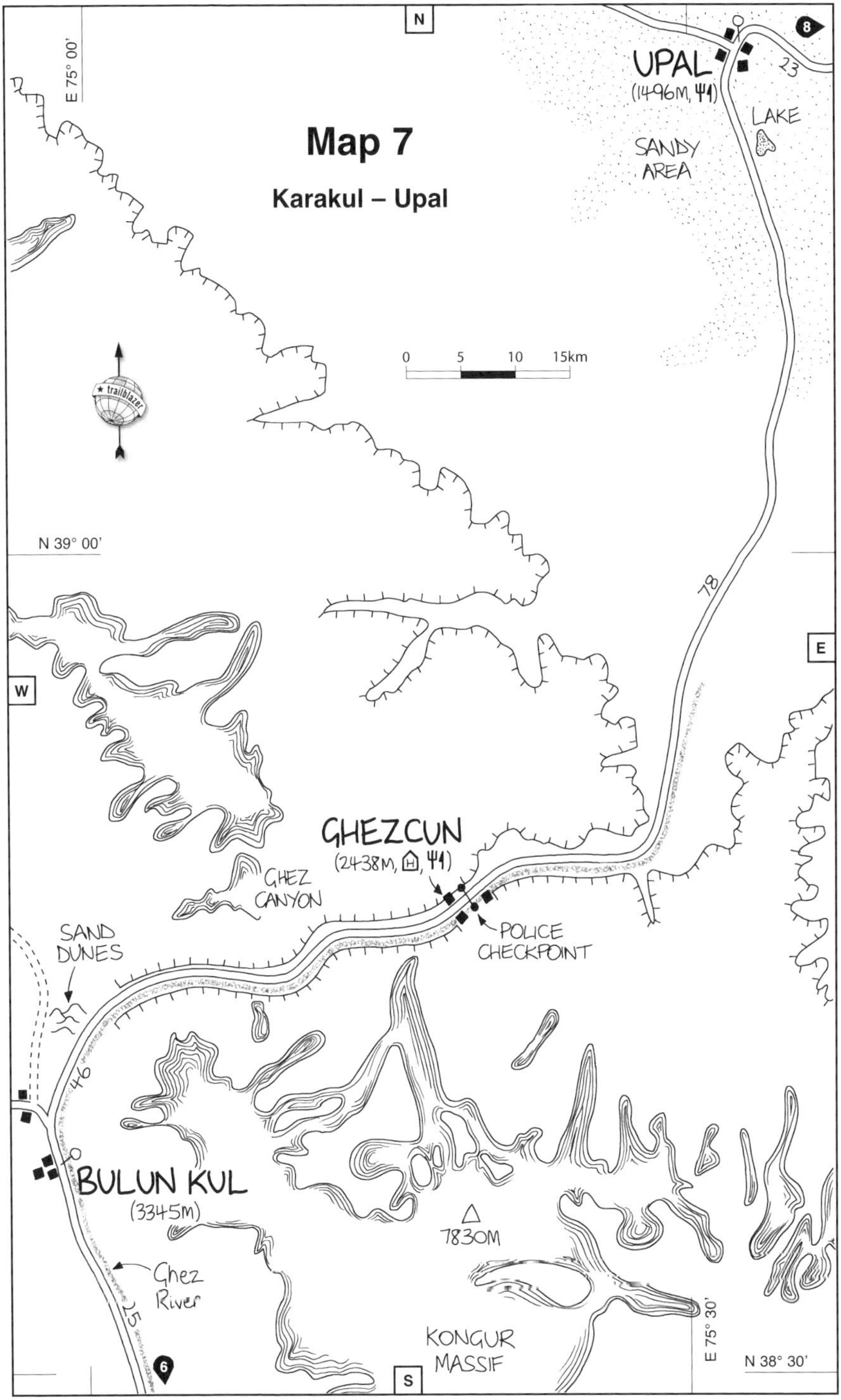
Map 7
Karakul – Upal
N
S
E
W
E 75° 00'
E 75° 30'
N 39° 00'
N 38° 30'
0 5 10 15km
UPAL
(1496M, Ψ1)
23
8
LAKE
SANDY AREA
78
GHEZCUN
(2438M, H, Ψ1)
GHEZ CANYON
POLICE CHECKPOINT
SAND DUNES
46
BULUN KUL
(3345M)
7830M
Ghez River
25
6
KONGUR MASSIF

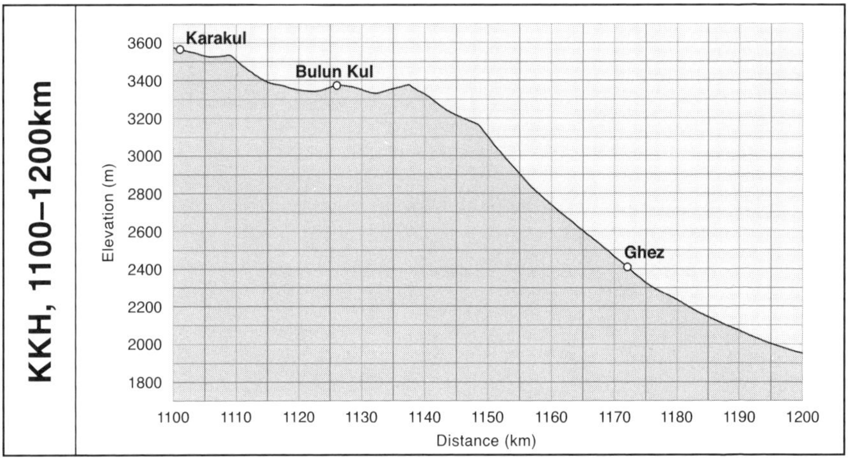

VERY BASIC KYRGYZ

Hello	*Hosh hosh*	Room	*Bolmo*
Tea	*Char*	Thank you	*Rakhmat*
Bread	*Naan*	Goodbye	*Jakshy kalynyz*
Water	*Tsu*		

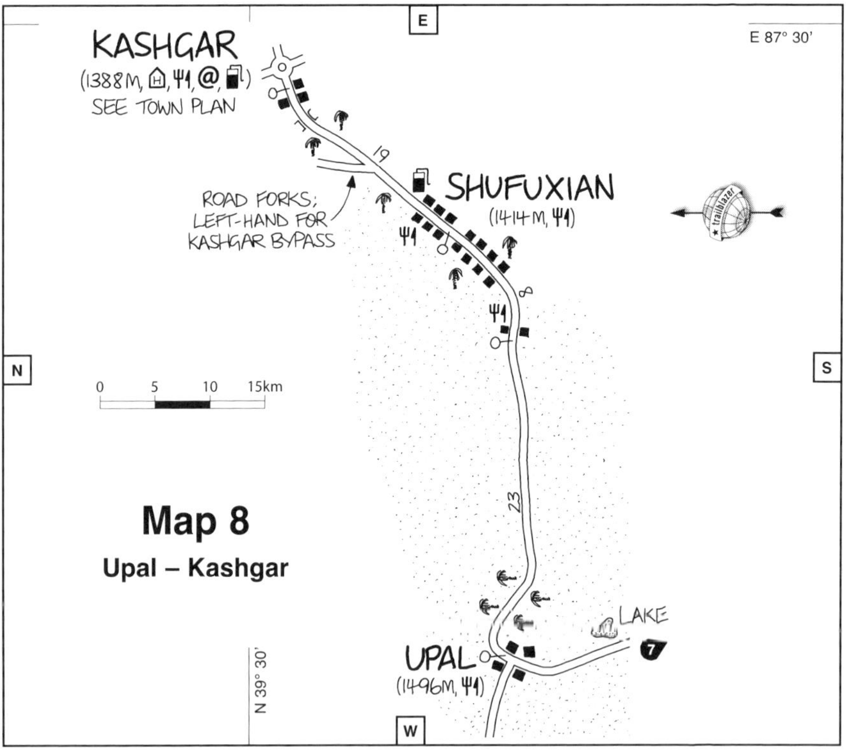

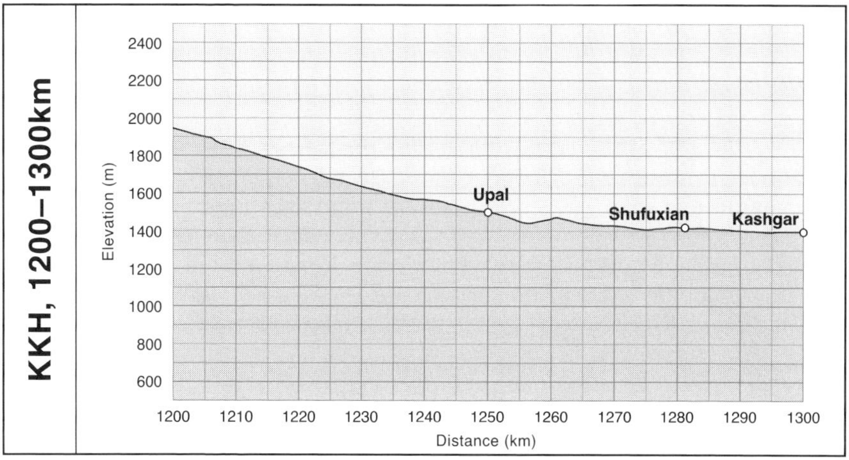

outside (Y5). As it's a flat run from Kashgar, anyone travelling south to Islamabad could end the first day here.

From Upal the sand stretches away, broken only by lines of poplar trees to the snowy Pamirs and, further to the east, the Tien Shan shimmering above in the heat haze. The contrast of scenery at 1500m either side of the Khunjerab frontier is extraordinary: on the Chinese side there's featureless and sparsely populated desert; on the Pakistani side there's 7000m peaks, capricious weather, tricked-out trucks and thousands of friendly Hunzakuts.

It's a flat 51km on good tarmac from Upal to Kashgar; the KKH runs straight, striking out across the desert. About 26km north of Upal there's a small town with restaurants, fruit stalls and general shops.

Shufuxian (1414m) 1281/19km

This sizeable and surprisingly modern town is 31km from Upal. From 40km onwards Kashgar is in your sights.

KASHGAR (1388m) 1300/0km

The KKH enters Kashgar ('Kashi' in Chinese) at a roundabout to the southwest of the city. This city, which is more than two thousand years old, lies on the very edge of the Taklamakan Desert and is hot from June to August when dust clouds from the desert can settle here for days, obscuring the sun and disrupting the flights to Urumchi or Islamabad. To the north lie the Tien Shan ('Celestial Mountains') and to the south the Pamirs. But despite its formidable position, the oasis of Kashgar is lush and green thanks to its rich and fertile loess soil.

These days green-and-white taxis, motorbikes and scooters zoom around the town and its Uighur population is increasingly diluted by immigrating Han Chinese. The Chinese girls are often quite scantily dressed but Kashgar is still predominantly a conservative Muslim town and foreigners dressed immodestly will sense the disapproval.

Kashgar is famed for its **Sunday market** which sells everything from cats and dogs to fruit and veg, knives and pitchforks. By contrast the livestock market is quite small and can get swamped by tour groups but it's still worth seeing for the donkey test-drives, the odd double-bottomed Xinjiang sheep, and negotiations being done Uighur-style. Stalls at the fringes of the market cook up chunks of meat, tasty bowls of laghman noodles, naan and green tea.

Xinjiang runs on two time zones which can surprise those starting their journey in Kashgar. Officially the time zone is Beijing Time, GMT+8; unofficially Kashgar runs on Xinjiang Time which is GMT+6. Banks and government offices always quote Beijing Time; bus companies will quote either so watch out.

Where to stay

The dorms of the Seman and Chini Bagh hotels offer the best-value accommodation. A bed in the 3-bed dorm at the ***Chini Bagh*** costs Y50 (att) but the ***Seman Hotel*** is slightly better at Y25 per bed for a clean 5-bed dorm (att) with TV plus daily supplies of soap, shampoo, foam bath and even toothbrushes. Doubles at the Seman cost Y80 (com) but aren't as clean or such good value, while those at the Chini Bagh cost Y80–Y380. The ***Seman Road Hotel*** is a little tatty but friendlier than the Seman Hotel; rooms are Y80/100 (att) with hot water and TV. The ***Tuman River Hotel*** is next to the bus station; rooms cost Y50/60 (com).

Where to eat

John's Café in the grounds of the Seman Hotel has pleasant shady outdoor seating; it's expensive (coffee Y8) but also offers Western food such as fried eggs on toast, banana pancakes and salads. The proprietor, the self-styled 'John' is a good source of information (see 💻 www.johncafe.net) but he's said to be close to the Chinese authorities so don't openly discuss trans-Tibet plans here. The Caravan Café at 120 Seman Road has now sadly closed. ***Silas***, on the roundabout by the Seman Hotel grills a tasty *junggal kawap* (mutton kebab) and Y3 buys a large skewer of meat. The Uighur way of life is a man's world: the tea houses scattered throughout Kashgar welcome foreign males with great hospitality but even modestly dressed women do not belong.

For street food the **skewer men** roll into town in the evening with their sticks of mushrooms, tofu discs, aubergines and various animal parts. Along Seman Road this meal can be topped off with a Xinjiang Beer (Y3) from the off-licence and ice creams (Y1.5) from the shops. The centrepiece of the yoghurt shops in People's Park is an enormous slab of ice which is chipped at to give ice shavings in the yoghurt; it's delicious but not for delicate stomachs. Carts sell twists of sugary dough, seeds, and fruits such as watermelons, melons, bananas, apricots and tart red berries.

Services

- **Banks** The Bank of China on Renmin Lu (Mon–Fri 9.30am–1.30pm & 4–7.30pm, Sat 11am–3pm, Beijing Time) has an ATM and will exchange cash and travellers' cheques. There are usually some Uighur men hanging around the Seman Hotel's car park offering to change money.

BUYING A BIKE IN KASHGAR

The best place for idle bike shopping in Kashgar is along N Jiafeng Road opposite the Idkah Mosque where an 18-speed, front-suspension Giant bicycle with rear rack and knobbly tyres costs around Y1200. These bikes make it down to Gilgit and even Islamabad though lanky foreigners will not find the frame sizes they need off the shelf. Note also that you cannot buy Western-style bike pumps (ie for Presta as well as Schrader valves) or front racks here.

More serious shoppers should head to to the Giant and Merida shops (see p120) on Kashgar's southern outskirts. The ultimate challenge would be to tackle the KKH on China's classic bicycle: a Flying Pigeon (Fei Ge).

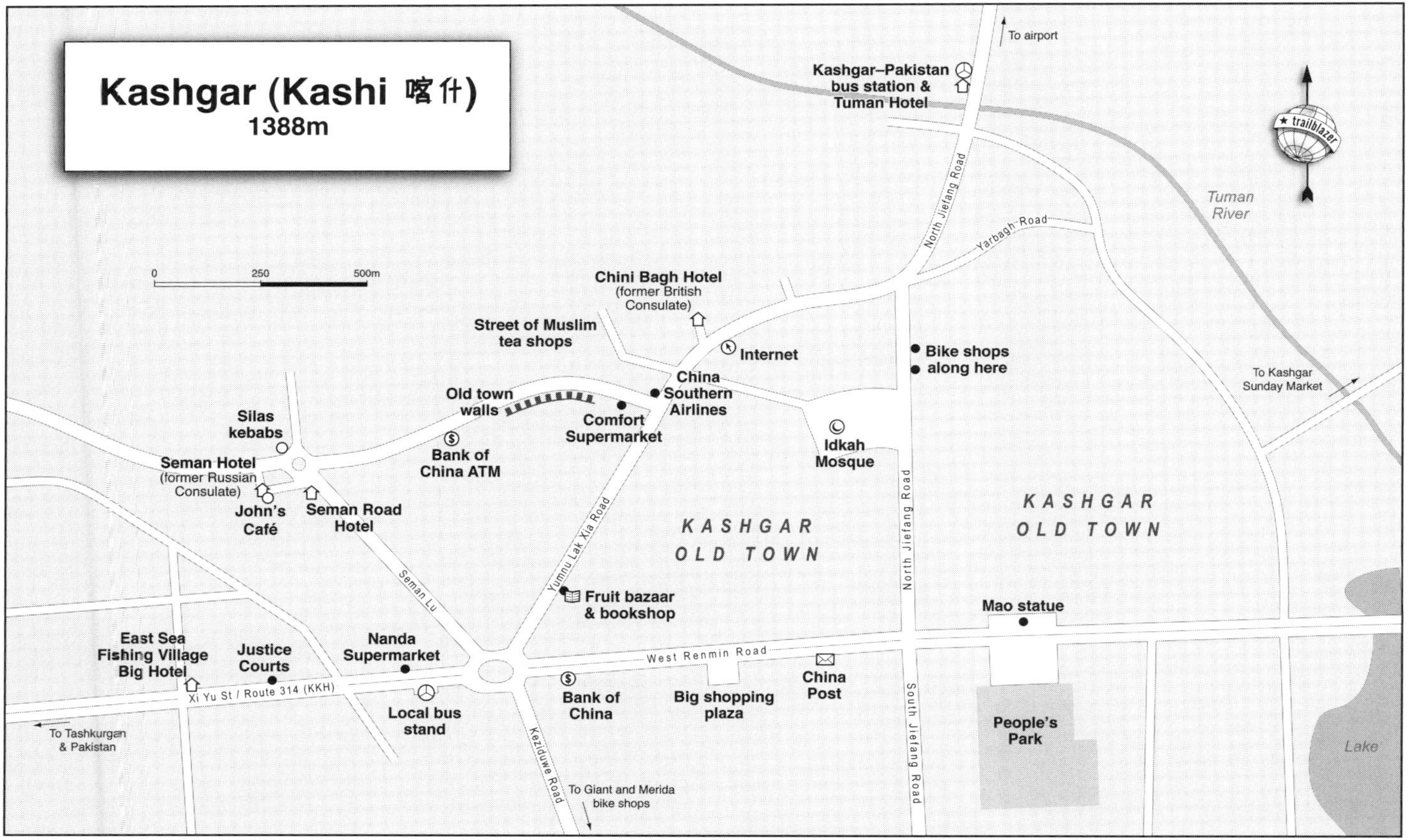
Kashgar (Kashi 喀什)
1388m
0
250
500m
To airport
Kashgar–Pakistan bus station & Tuman Hotel
trailblazer
Tuman River
North Jiefang Road
Yarbagh Road
Chini Bagh Hotel (former British Consulate)
Street of Muslim tea shops
Internet
Bike shops along here
To Kashgar Sunday Market
China Southern Airlines
Old town walls
Comfort Supermarket
Idkah Mosque
Silas kebabs
Bank of China ATM
Seman Hotel (former Russian Consulate)
John's Café
Seman Road Hotel
KASHGAR OLD TOWN
KASHGAR OLD TOWN
Yumnu Lak Xia Road
Seman Lu
Fruit bazaar & bookshop
Mao statue
East Sea Fishing Village Big Hotel
Justice Courts
Nanda Supermarket
West Renmin Road
China Post
Xi Yu St / Route 314 (KKH)
Local bus stand
Bank of China
Big shopping plaza
People's Park
South Jiefang Road
Lake
To Tashkurgan & Pakistan
Keziduwe Road
To Giant and Merida bike shops

• **Bike repair** Kashgar's central bike shops are opposite the Idkah Mosque. There's also a Giant bicycle shop with a broad range of Shimano spares and competent mechanics (though little English) at 37 Tian Kang Rd and a Merida bike shop on Xiaba Rd about 800m further on. Both Tian Kang and Xiaba roads are continuations of Kezigeduwe Road, one spoke off the KKH roundabout.
• **Hospital** The best hospital is not surprisingly the No 1 Hospital north of Kashgar towards the airport. There is a No 2 Hospital south of People's Park.
• **Internet** All the hotels have internet for around Y3/30mins; a basement internet café almost opposite the Chini Bagh hotel (see map) charges Y2/hr.
• **Post office** (Mon–Fri 7.30–11am & 2–4pm, Sat 7.30–11am Xinjiang time) on West Renmin Road. Go upstairs to send letters or parcels.
• **Supermarkets** There are enormous supermarkets by the KKH roundabout.
• **Transport** Green-and-white taxis ply the streets. The international bus station is on the north side of the river; tickets to Tashkurgan: Y44. A bus ticket to Sost in Pakistan is Y290 plus Y50 for a bike on the roof. Check whether the bus runs on Xinjiang or Beijing Time. Taxis and minivans also travel to Sost and are easily booked through John's Café. Taxis (4 people, Y700 each) won't take bikes but minivans will (6 people, Y633 each).

KASHGAR AND THE SILK ROUTE

Kashgar was the last major eastbound staging post on the Silk Route before it forked at the Taklamakan Desert. The north route struck out along the foothills of the Tien Shan; the south along the fringe of the Taklamakan Desert and past the Tibetan bandits of the Kun Lun mountains. To the west of Kashgar the Silk Route threaded through the khanates of Khokand, Samarkhand, Bokhara and Merv in Central Asia towards the Mediterranean coast and onwards to the ports of Rome and Alexandria. In its eighth century heyday during the Tang dynasty this remarkable route spanned half the known world, from Changan the Tang capital (present-day Xi'an) to the Mediterranean.

There was no one definitive Silk Route, rather a tangle of threads that somehow crossed scorching deserts, immense mountain ranges and hostile territories. Traders would not have traversed the route in its entirety unlike famous Silk Road travellers such as Marco Polo, but specialized in certain sections of it. One of the most demanding sections was the feeder route from Leh and Srinagar which crossed the Karakoram pass, now closed, to Yarkand (now known as Yarkant, see p323). It was so gruelling that every trader packed his own shroud; no wonder judging from this contemporary description: "*never once until we reached the plains were we out of sight of skeletons. The continuous line of bones and bodies acted as a gruesome guide whenever we were uncertain of the route.*'

A huge range of commodities other than silk was traded along the Silk Route; it could equally have been known as the 'Cinnamon Corridor', the 'Porcelain Path' or the 'Rhubarb Road'. From China came ceramics, furs, iron, lacquer ware, cinnamon, rhubarb, bronze and of course silk; from Europe came gold, woollen and linen textiles, ivory, coral, amber, precious stones, asbestos and glass. Most significant and enduring of all was the movement of religious ideas: Kushan traders from India using the Silk Route in the first century AD introduced Buddhism to Xinjiang and from there it travelled onwards through Tibet, China and as far east as Japan. Buddhism is the best-known example but during Mongol rule in China there was even a Roman Catholic diocese in Beijing, established in 1307.

Warlords, rapacious middlemen, the collapse of the Mongol empire and the subsequent isolationist policy of the Ming dynasty signalled the demise of the Silk Route 600 years ago. The Chinese took to the high seas instead; a story best told by Gavin Menzies in *1421: the Year China Discovered the World*. But today the Silk Road is in the ascendant once again: modern road and rail links now bind the huge markets of China and the West and electrical goods, heavy metals and tourists are the new cinnamon, amber and silk.

MANALI-LEH HWY 3

ROUTE INFORMATION

- **Start / finish** Manali (Himachal Pradesh) / Leh (Ladakh), India
- **Distance** 500km (including Tso Kar lake excursion)
- **Altitude min / max** 1900m/5300m
- **High passes** Five
- **Suggested duration** Minimum seven days riding; allow three weeks with flights + acclimatization
- **Road conditions** 75% tarmac, 25% mud-packed road
- **Hazards and dangers** Floods and landslides after heavy rain
- **When to go** Mid-June to mid-September
- **Visas** Required for India

Ever since the Manali–Leh Highway was opened to foreigners in 1989 cyclists have revered it as one of the most spectacular rides in the world. It's also the second highest and half of its 475 kilometres traverse a landscape so high and barren that there's no permanent human habitation at all. The scenery is epic and hard-won over a series of 5000m passes which lead from the lush Kullu Valley over high altitude desert to the remote and starkly beautiful region of Ladakh.

But to call it a 'highway' is misleading – in places the road is barely wide enough for two buses to pass and the climate is so extreme that it's only open for three months each year. Leh, the atmospheric capital of Ladakh, is tucked up a side valley of the Indus River, and used to be the starting point for yak caravans crossing the Karakoram to Central Asia and China. From here the traders' first major obstacle was the pass of Khardung La (5359m) which has long claimed to be the highest motorable road in the world; it's just a day's ride north from Leh. Back on the valley floor are the famous Tibetan monasteries of Hemis, Thikse and Matho, which have colourful festivals throughout the summer.

FACTS ABOUT THE REGION

Himachal Pradesh and Jammu & Kashmir are India's northernmost states, closed in from the west by Pakistan and to the north and east by China and Tibet. Both the Pakistani and Chinese borders are contentious: modern Indian maps still include Gilgit and Baltistan in their territory – territory that has belonged to Pakistan since Partition in 1947. Progress towards an official Pakistan–India border in Kashmir stalled at the UN-enforced 'Line of Control' demarcated in the 1970s. The territorial dispute with China in the east is less controversial only because political wrangling has killed fewer civilians and past military action has been decisive: China occupied the uninhabited Aksai Chin plateau in the 1960s and built a road

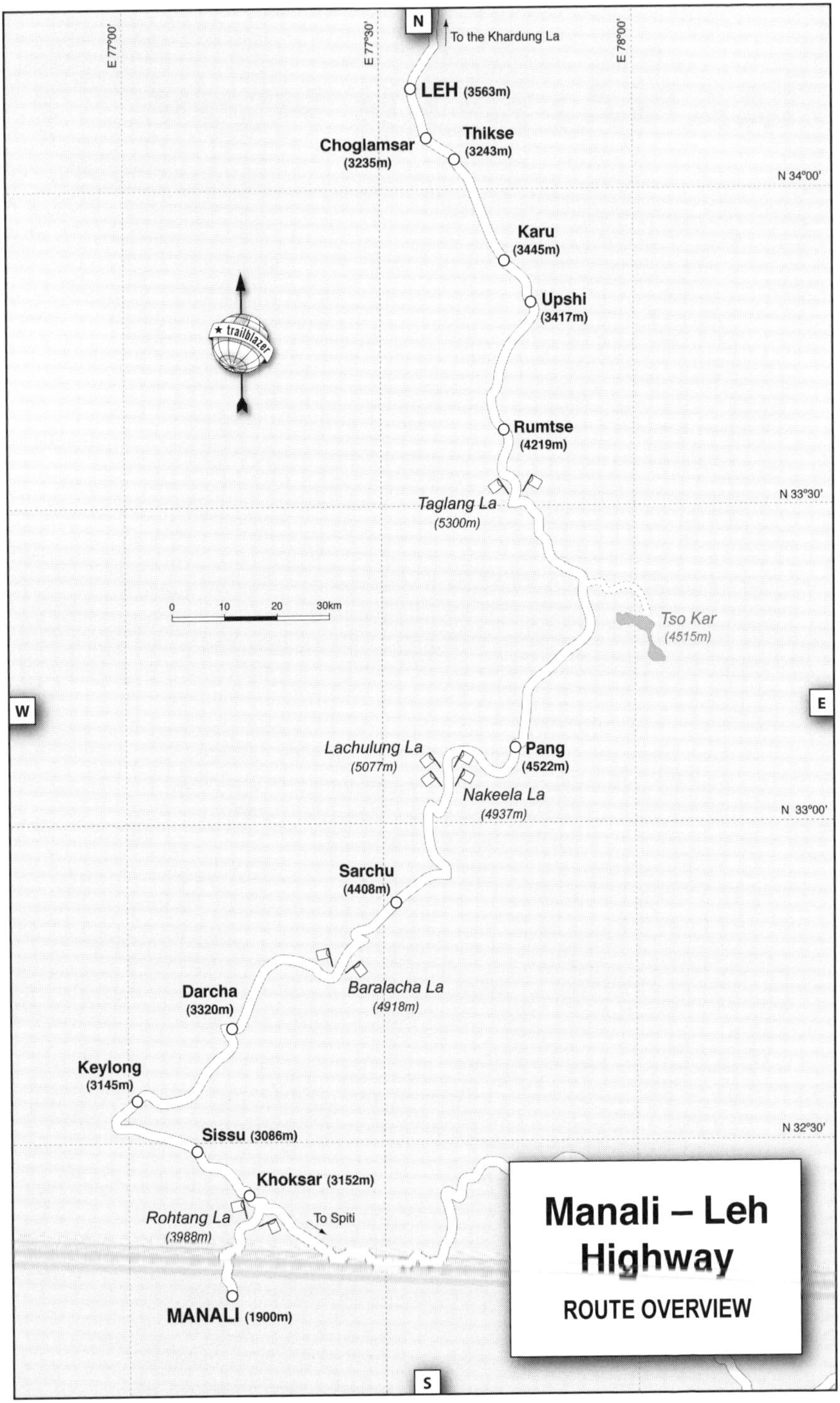
N
To the Khardung La
E 77°00'
E 77°30'
E 78°00'
LEH (3563m)
Choglamsar (3235m)
Thikse (3243m)
N 34°00'
Karu (3445m)
Upshi (3417m)
trailblazer
Rumtse (4219m)
Taglang La (5300m)
N 33°30'
0 10 20 30km
Tso Kar (4515m)
W
E
Lachulung La (5077m)
Pang (4522m)
Nakeela La (4937m)
N 33°00'
Sarchu (4408m)
Baralacha La (4918m)
Darcha (3320m)
Keylong (3145m)
N 32°30'
Sissu (3086m)
Khoksar (3152m)
Rohtang La (3988m)
To Spiti
MANALI (1900m)
Manali – Leh Highway
ROUTE OVERVIEW
S

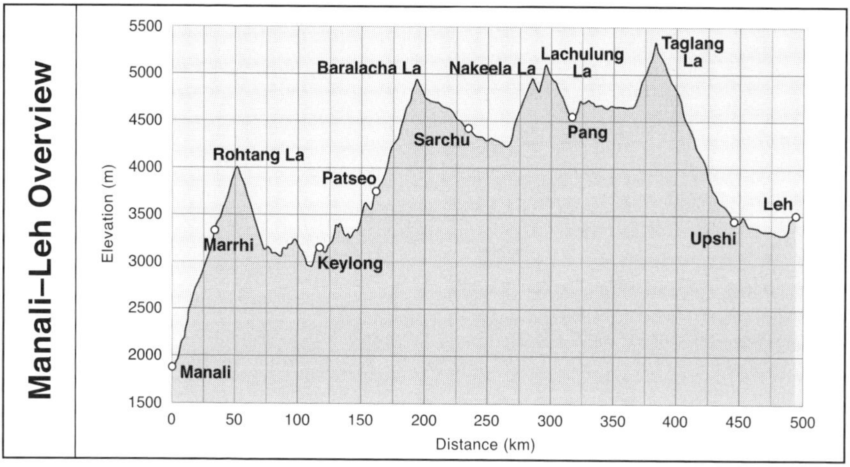

through it before India noticed. India declared war, China won. India remains deeply suspicious of China's intentions and for this reason Inner Line Permits (see p125) are still required within 40km of the border. Some regions are restricted altogether, even to Indian nationals.

Himachal Pradesh ('State of the Himalaya') is where the plains of Haryana and Punjab rise up and fold into the foothills and valleys of the lower Himalaya. The diversity of landscape is enormous: from dusty plain through river valley up to the crossing of the Great Himalaya range at Baralacha La. Beyond this pass and the Sarchu plains the scenery and culture feels Tibetan: here lies Ladakh. This is the easternmost third of Jammu & Kashmir state; the other parts are the Kashmir Valley and Jammu. Zoji La pass divides Kashmir and Ladakh in almost every respect: religion, dress, custom, language – even national allegiance. It's for this reason that foreign travel advisories warning against travel in Jammu & Kashmir usually exempt Ladakh, which has not suffered as Kashmir has.

Ladakh was only opened up to tourism in 1974 when about 500 foreign tourists took the two-day bus journey from Srinagar. Since then, except during the Kargil War in 1999, Ladakh has been considered a safe place for foreigners to travel, unlike Kashmir, Tibet and Nepal. Accordingly it has gained tourists that might otherwise have gone elsewhere in the Himalaya. The opening of the Manali–Leh Highway in the 1980s and the onset of direct flights from Delhi have buoyed tourism figures further to a record-breaking 43,000 in 2006. Leh remains the tourist hub of Ladakh with a summer-long

LADAKHI HOMES

Traditional Ladakhi houses are very cosy, made from mud brick painted gleaming white with tiny wooden doors and windows. The ceilings are fashioned from poplar beams and twigs, and in autumn the roofs usually sport a bouffant hairdo of hay which is used to feed the animals in winter. The kitchen, crammed with pots, teacups and low Tibetan tables (chogtse) is the heart of the home. Modern guesthouses are built of concrete but still follow the same traditional exterior.

'Learn and Repeat' traffic sign in Leh's Main Bazaar

scene of budget travellers, trekkers and cultural tourists.

Life in this part of the Himalaya has always been based on agriculture, but the arrival of developers with large sums of cash has tempted many locals to sell off their land. The enormous success of apple growing in Lahaul, which as a 'tribal area' is heavily subsidized by the government, has led to monoculture in Kullu too – with disastrous results when the entire apple crop was destroyed by disease.

History of the road

Like many routes in the Himalaya, the Manali–Leh Highway follows an old trading route from the Indian plains to Central Asia and Chinese Turkestan. In a reversal of today's situation, the Manali–Leh route was little used in comparison to the 'Treaty Road' between Srinagar and Leh. But during the 1980s, when militancy in Kashmir was at its worst, the Indian government instructed the Border Roads Organization (BRO) to build a new road into Ladakh, and the Highway was opened in 1987. Today the BRO's famous 'Project Himank' (see box below) maintains the highway as well as all the roads in the districts of Ladakh and Kargil, managing to inform and entertain passers by with their renowned road signs.

The Manali–Leh Highway as we know it will cease to exist within a decade. A tunnel (see box opposite) under the Rohtang La is already under construction as is a road through the beautiful valley of Zanskar. The snow-covered passes that block the Manali–Leh Highway for more than half the year will be traffic-free once again.

BRO AND PROJECT HIMANK

As there are always sections of the Manali–Leh Highway under repair or improvement you are certain to meet Himank's road workers, mostly economic migrants from Bihar and Nepal. Their work takes them to some extraordinary locations: the second-coldest place in the world (Drass), the highest tarmac roads in the world (Khardung La and Taglang La) and even the highest battlefield in the world (Siachen Glacier).

Travellers from China, accustomed to compounds for road workers and machinery, might be shocked to see the conditions for labourers in India. Women and children crack rocks by hammer with babies slung on their backs; men boil up drums of tar in wheelbarrows half-hidden by billows of noxious black smoke and flames. Their accommodation is as temporary as a plastic sheet pinned to a rock face. As Himalayan cyclist Steve Pells observed: "In a country which offers a wide selection of crap ways of making a living, being a Himank road builder must be up there with the crappiest". The good news is that their pay is high by Indian standards at Rs120 ($3) per day. This in a country where the vast majority of the population survives on less than Rs80 per day and nearly half make do on less than Rs40.

THE ROHTANG TUNNEL

In 2003 the then Prime Minister Vajpayee laid the foundation stone for a tunnel which will burrow under Rohtang La from the Solang Valley on the south side to Sissu on the north. When the Rohtang Tunnel opens in 2014 it will shorten the current distance between Manali and Khoksar in the Lahaul valley by 46km and, more importantly, keep the road into Lahaul open for most of the year. The Himachal Pradesh government opposed the tunnel for environmental reasons but these objections have been overridden by the need for a secure military supply route to Ladakh and Kashmir. During the Kargil War of 1999, as Pakistani shells rained down on Drass, it became apparent that the Leh–Srinagar Highway which skirts within metres of the Pakistani border was far too dangerous. The tunnel is the first phase of a road into Zanskar which will ultimately cut out both the Rohtang and Baralacha La passes and change the Manali–Leh Highway forever.

Indian newspapers trumpet the 8.8km Rohtang Tunnel project as the 'longest in a mountainous region in the world'. In June 2007 the Swiss opened the world's longest: the 34.5km Loetschberg Tunnel under the Alps, and are already constructing the record-breaking 57km Gotthard Tunnel, due to open in 2017.

Possible future roads include: **Kaza–Leh** via Kibber and Parang La (20km from the Chinese border) and **Manali–Kargil** via Tandi, Udaipur and Padum (Zanskar Valley).

Language and religion

English is widely spoken as is **Hindi**. **Ladakhi** is similar to Tibetan (with the same script) and has the brilliantly foreigner-friendly word '*jullay*' which means just about everything from 'hello' to 'goodbye' and 'thank you'. Road signs are in English or Hindi and distances are usually in Roman numerals.

The people of the Kullu Valley are mostly **Hindu** and their valley is known throughout India as 'the Valley of the Gods'. Local deities are just as important here as the main characters of Hindu mythology. On Manali's Mall (main street) near Himcoop, look out for the tiny Durga temple: her tiger stands roaring outside.

Buddhism is the predominant religion in Lahaul and Ladakh. Leh has a small **Muslim** population, mostly traders whose families have lived there for centuries and who worship at the Jama Masjid mosque just off Main Bazaar.

PRACTICAL INFORMATION

There are **no restrictions** or permits required for the Manali–Leh Highway but if you want to cycle the side route from the Morei Plains to Tso Kar lake then onwards to Puga, Chungmathang and Mahe Bridge to Upshi you must have an **Inner Line Permit**. This can be arranged in Manali and faxed ahead. See p133 for a list of travel agents in Manali who will do this. Likewise many riders like to finish the ride by climbing Khardung La above Leh, for which you must also arrange an Inner Line Permit in Leh (see p156).

Manali–Leh is not dangerous or busy but road conditions can be poor, especially on descents and what traffic there is obeys one rule: Big is Boss. Army convoys are the biggest so be sure to let them through.

Manali has a somewhat dark reputation, as does the nearby Parvati Valley, for the occasional disappearance and in some cases murder of foreign tourists who go trekking without a guide. *Charas* (hashish) is an important

STOCKING UP FOR THE RIDE

The popularity of trekking in Kullu and Ladakh means that the local shops are well stocked for trips. You can find dried noodles, instant noodles, pasta, rice, orange dahl (mansur), chickpeas, flour, salt, cashew nuts, chilli, black pepper, garam masala (a blend of ground spices), green peas, cheese (both sliced cheddar and paneer, an Indian cheese), biscuits (Hide & Seek are tasty), packet soups, dried fruit, nuts, porridge, muesli, chocolate bars (avoid Indian-made Cadbury's Dairy Milk – something disgusting is added to make it melt-proof), tea bags, hot chocolate, milk powder, sugar, Nescafé, Coca Cola, tomato sauce, custard powder, tinned fish, peanut butter, honey, cream in cartons, fruit and veg.

The German bakeries in Manali and Leh sell loaves of brown bread for trekking parties which last for days; other local specialities are apple (in Manali) and apricot (in Leh) jam. Almost all food supplies can be found in or around Superbake near the Durga Temple in New Manali. For dried fruits and nuts there is a shop just to the north of the roundabout in Manali selling everything from figs on strings to pine nuts.

The chemist on The Mall in Manali and also Het Ram on Main Bazaar in Leh offer good advice for medical problems and sell antibiotics and ORS sachets which cyclists would do well to stock up on. Try different brands before you leave: some are less revolting than others.

cash crop here; don't get involved with it. Women should take care not to walk alone between New and Old Manali or between Leh and Changspa late at night.

Which direction?

Cyclists usually like to do things the hard way, so most ride from Manali up to Leh to enjoy the 2500m climb between the two towns.

Since this is one of the highest roads in the world (and certainly the highest tarmac in the world, see p157), proper **acclimatization** is vital. Anyone flying into Leh (3563m) from sea-level must spend at least three days acclimatizing before tackling the 5300m Taglang La. Altitude sickness (see p61) can be fatal so don't underestimate it. On the first day out of Manali there's an even longer climb of 51km but it is at an easy-breathing altitude and tops out at a mere 3978m. Cyclists starting from Manali are usually properly acclimatized before reaching the high passes and more importantly the high sleeping places. Finally, it just feels right to ride up into the mountains and to feel with every sense (as only cycling allows) the transformation from India to the otherworldliness of Ladakh.

Equipment

Wet weather clothing will protect you on the passes and SPF30+ **sunscreen** and UV-proof **sunglasses** are essential. A **tent and stove** are well worth the weight: there are some spectacular places to camp under equally spectacular

TIFFINS

Tiffins are India's answer to Tupperware. The word is an old English one meaning 'luncheon'. In India tiffins are stackable tin containers for carrying meals in: one layer for the rice, another for dahl, a third for pickles or vegetables. Commuters in cities usually dangle their tiffins from their bicycle handlebars. They're a practical way for cyclists to carry double portions (see p49), though some might prefer plastic containers.

night skies, and hot food and drink will keep you energized and warm. There are no bicycle shops en route.

Accommodation

From Manali to Darcha and Upshi to Leh there are plenty of small villages where you can find accommodation. Beyond Darcha there's a 300km stretch where seasonal (July–September) tea tents provide basic food and a (literally) rock-hard bed to sleep on. Road workers' camps and army posts along the way can provide accommodation in an emergency, though women on their own should avoid them.

Food and drink

Bikers should have no complaints in Manali or Leh – it's the stretch in between when food might get monotonous. The ubiquitous breakfast is chai, *chapatti* (flat pancake-like bread) and an omelette flecked with fiery chillies that will have you squatting behind a rock within the hour. 'No chillies, please' in Hindi is *'bina mirch, ji'*. Even those on organized tours would do well to avoid this breakfast. Lunch and dinner staples are dahl and rice with *sabze* (vegetables fried in oil and spices) and maybe dishes of *rajma* (kidney beans) or *channa masala* (chickpeas). This is great food with far more energy packed into it than the instant noodles so beloved of the parachute tent cafés en route.

If you don't like your food swimming in cooking oil then Ladakhi food is even better. *Thukpa* is a broth of fresh diced vegetables floating around hand-made noodles, and *momos* (*mok mok* in rural Ladakh) are small flour dumplings filled with finely chopped vegetables or meat then steamed or fried. Some cooks get creative with their momo fillings: potatoes and peas or ginger and potato (delicious). Campers can load up in the markets of either town with all sorts of staples and delicacies though you won't find dehydrated food: bring that from home. If you start each day with three litres of drinking water getting more water is only an issue on the Morei Plains between Pang and halfway up the climb to Taglang La.

Money

India's currency is the **rupee**, which divides into 10 paise. Make sure to change Rs1000 bills in towns; no one in the villages will have change. Rs100 notes on the road make life easier for everyone. There are ATMs, and banks for cashing travellers' cheques, in both Manali and Leh but nothing in between. Most travellers get by on $10 a day. See p32 for exchange rate information.

Getting to the ride

The quickest way to **Manali** from Delhi by bike is to head north on the N1 to Ambala (215km), then the N21 to Mandi via Chandigarh. From Mandi the N22 leads you direct to Manali. While cyclists do ride this route it's more to say that they've done it rather than because it is enjoyable (it isn't). Most would rather spend their days in the hills so **book a bus seat from Delhi**. This costs anywhere between Rs200 and Rs800 depending on the travel agent not the quality of the bus. The journey is often billed as 14 hours so be prepared for 18 hours or more. Talk to the driver about putting a bicycle on the roof: some demand money, some let you put it up there for free (though you should tip the bus boys if they help you put it up there). Don't put your bike on the roof of a sleeper (ie double-decker) bus: overhanging trees on the avenues out of Delhi have finished some journeys before they've even started – use the lockers underneath instead. There is no railhead near Manali. Jagson Airlines and Deccan Air fly to the tiny Bhuntar airport, just south of Kullu, but **flights are unreliable** and the luggage allowance is only 10kg.

If you start in **Leh**, there are daily flights from Delhi though they're often cancelled due to bad weather. Jet Airways (🖳 www.jetairways.com), Indian Airlines (🖳 www.indian-airlines.nic.in) and Air Deccan (🖳 www.flyairdeccan.net) all fly this route early in the morning for anything between $90 and $200.

MANALI 1900m

The tourist hub of Manali climbs up the west bank of the River Beas at the foot of Rohtang La. Its scenery is typically Himachali: a deep and cool river valley backed by mountains and covered in pines and apple orchards with occasional waterfalls, all of which make it a wonderful respite from the torrid Indian plains. Manali is the northernmost town of the Kullu Valley before the road crosses the Pir Pinjal range and drops into Buddhist Lahaul.

Over time Manali has evolved into two distinct areas: Old and New. **New Manali** is a typical Indian town with a busy bus stand, swarms of auto rickshaws and shops opening out onto narrow pavements. This is the practical end of Manali with welders, hardware stores, fruit and veg markets, dry food stores and a fuel station. Still, it's a crush so most foreigners prefer **Old Manali**, 3km up the hill, which is more laid-back with outdoor cafés, German bakeries and less concrete. Locals have nicknamed the area around the Dragon Guesthouse "Little Tel Aviv" as this is the haunt of the Israeli party crowd. From here there are pleasant walks up the valley through the apple orchards as well as yoga classes in town; great for limbering up for the task ahead.

In season (April–September) the town is a hotchpotch of people: locals speaking Kullu, Kinnauris in their distinctive pill-box caps, Tibetan traders, noisy Punjabi boys on holiday and honeymooners. New Manali is one of India's top honeymoon destinations, Rohtang being something of a Bollywood star as it's often the backdrop for romantic song and dance scenes.

Then there are the foreigners: North Face-clad trekkers, grizzled ancient hippies, gap-year students trying not to get ripped off, bikers chugging around on Enfields and budget travellers zoning out with a *chillum* (hash pipe). Tracking them across the subcontinent come the shoeshine boys of Rajasthan, gem-dealers from Kashmir, Nepali kitchen boys and tailors rat-a-tatting at their gleaming Singer sewing machines.

The world-famous *charas* (hashish) of Manali and its surrounds is draw enough for some but the town also has a growing outdoors scene of rafting, trekking, mountain biking and skiing. For some Indian tourists the highlight is the 'snowpoint' on Rohtang – their first experience of snow. Every year the national Indian papers run a story headlined 'The highest traffic jam in the world?' with a photo of the traffic jam of tourists halfway up Rohtang La.

History

In myth, Manali is 'the home of Manu', a Noah-like figure whose ark rested here after the gods sent a flood to purge mankind. A temple to Manu stands at the top of Old Manali, and it's in this area that you'll find the old village of narrow dung-spattered paths twisting past byres and large pahari-style homes with intricate wooden carvings. In summer you'll often pass women wearing *kiltas* (a conical basket worn on the back) which they use to collect grass for their cows.

The British Raj brought apple trees and trout to Kullu and the hippy trail brought smokers in the 1960s and 70s, but it was militancy in Kashmir in the

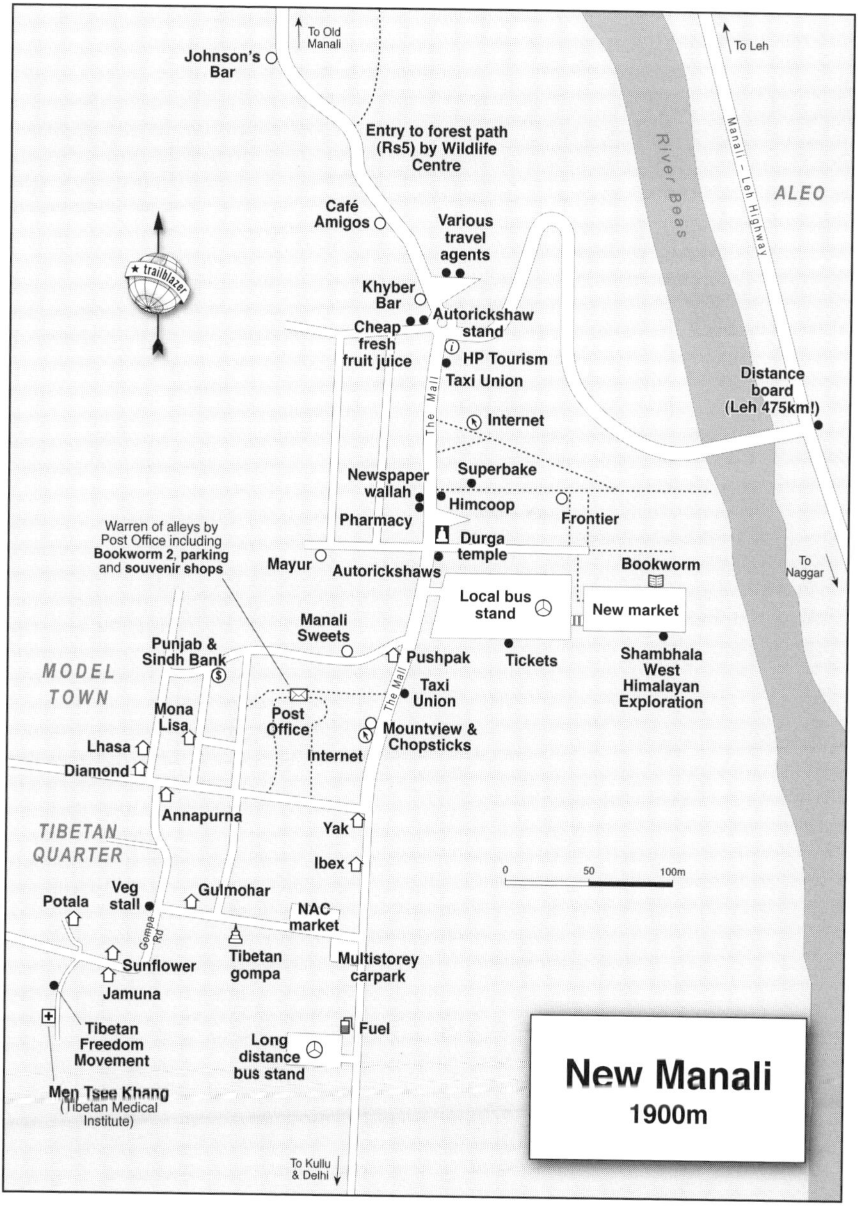

late 1980s which was the making (or spoiling) of Manali. At just 550km from Delhi the resort is easily reached by those wanting to escape the summer heat for snow and mountain air. As India becomes richer more tourists arrive. Soaring land prices made tourism more profitable than agriculture so locals sold their land to developers and New Manali, in all its concrete brashness, was born.

Orientation

The NH22 highway from Kullu tapers as it enters Manali and becomes The Mall, New Manali's main street. To the west of The Mall is 'Model Town' which is a few streets of concrete hotels. The long-distance bus station lies at the south end of The Mall and the roundabout to Leh at the top. From the roundabout a road leads uphill to Old Manali, which starts at the bridge over the Manalsu Nalah. The road climbs more steeply through Old Manali with an especially steep incline between the Ish Café and Pizza Olive – if you can ride this fully loaded you have nothing to fear from the Himalaya. Towards the top of Old Manali and the Manu Temple the guesthouses thin out again until finally Manali feels like a local village.

Where to stay

Outside the 'Indian season' (May–June) the hotels of **New Manali** can compete with Old Manali's guesthouse prices but will include additional facilities such as a TV, phone and en suite bathroom. Model Town is cramped and dark so other areas worth nosing around are down by the Tibetan gompa, giving the benefit of a New Manali location without the noise, and in the lanes to the west of the roundabout.

Along the road to Old Manali try the comfortable ***Mayflower*** (☎ 01902 252 104; 💻 www.negismayflower.com) which has spacious wooden-floored rooms with TV (dbl att Rs1980). For Raj-era décor, an exuberant garden and fewer lackeys the nearby ***Sunshine Guesthouse*** (☎ 01902 252 320) at Rs350 (dbl com) can't be beaten.

Accommodation in **Old Manali** is simple and starts at Rs50 for dives to about Rs150 for a room you'd want to spend time in. Shared bathrooms with hot water that comes in a bucket is the norm. The centre of Old Manali is no quieter than New Manali although here the noise is techno and rattling Enfields. If that's OK the ***Dragon Guesthouse*** complex is the epicentre; the nearby ***Veer Guesthouse*** is friendly and has double rooms for Rs300 (com). At the top of Old Manali, down a narrow lane where the road swings left up to the Manu Temple, are a couple more guesthouses one of which is ***Tiger Eye*** (☎ 01902 252 718, 💻 www.tigereyeadventure.com), run by a helpful Indian–Dutch couple. It's the cleanest guesthouse in Manali and the marble-floored double rooms have en-suite bathrooms with hot showers ($9).

Cheaper places abound, especially if you turn right after the Manalsu Bridge and head past the Tibet Kitchen (see p132). The friendly ***Apple View Guesthouse*** (💻 www.appleviewmanali.com) has only four double rooms which are simple and spacious at Rs150 (com) but other guesthouses nearby are seedy. Near the Ish Café a narrow footpath leads 500m to the peaceful ***Rockaway Cottage*** (dbl Rs200).

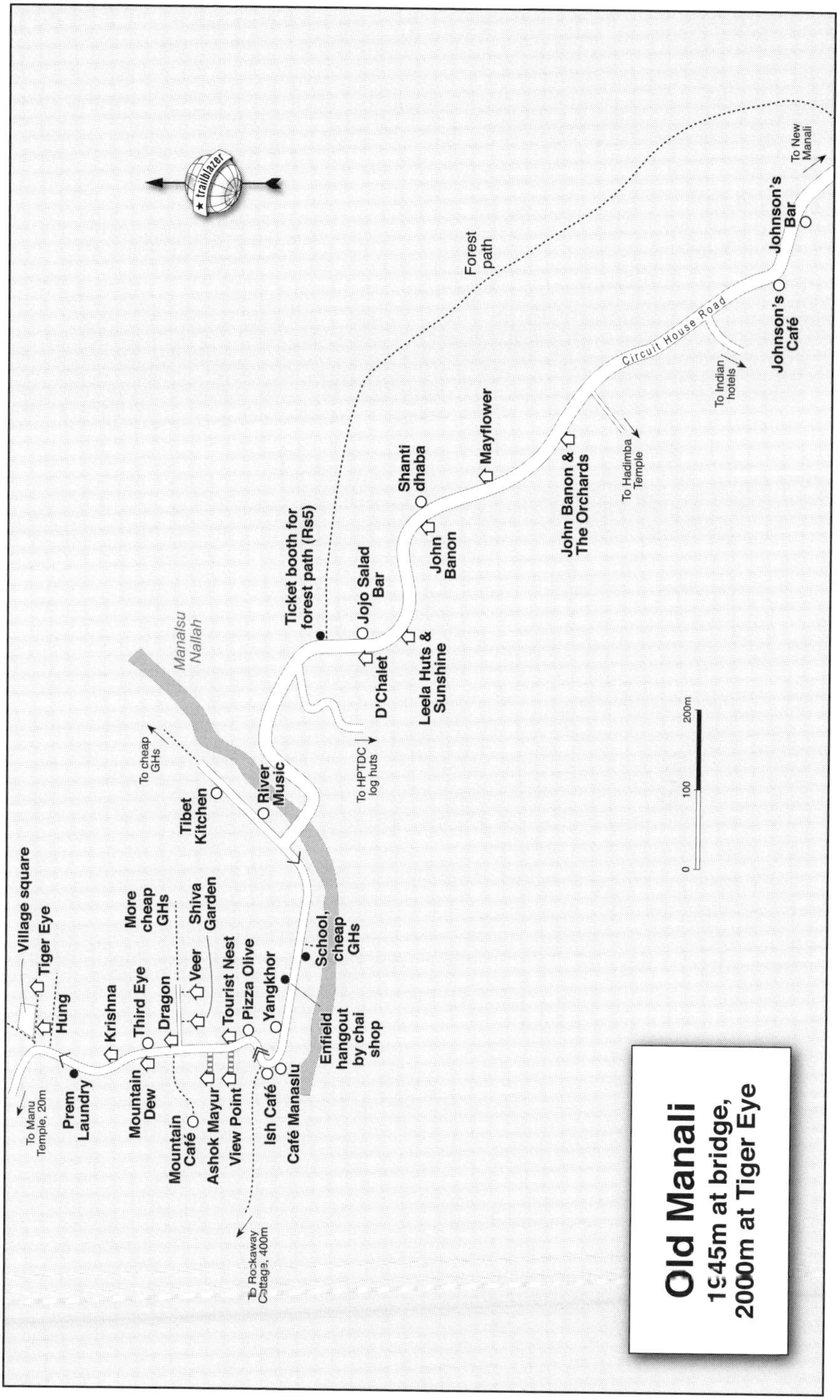

Old Manali
1945m at bridge,
2000m at Tiger Eye
trailblazer
Forest path
To New Manali
Johnson's Bar
Johnson's Café
Circuit House Road
To Indian hotels
To Hadimba Temple
Mayflower
John Banon & The Orchards
Shanti dhaba
John Banon
Ticket booth for forest path (Rs5)
Jojo Salad Bar
Leela Huts & Sunshine
D'Chalet
Manalsu Nallah
To HPTDC log huts
0
100
200m
To cheap GHs
River Music
Tibet Kitchen
Village square
Tiger Eye
Hung
Krishna
More cheap GHs
Third Eye
Dragon
Veer
Shiva Garden
Tourist Nest
Pizza Olive
Yangkhor
School, cheap GHs
Enfield hangout by chai shop
Prem Laundry
Mountain Dew
Mountain Café
Ashok Mayur
View Point
Ish Café
Café Manaslu
To Manu Temple, 20m
To Rockaway Cottage, 400m

Where to eat

All guesthouses have a simple menu and can rustle up tea, toast and probably *lassis* (a yoghurt based drink) and pancakes any time of day. Nearly all of Manali's restaurants try their hand at most dishes: to avoid disappointment (and diarrhoea) give any 'continental' ones a miss.

For a mighty breakfast, Old Manali's open-air ***Mountain Café*** does a splendid plate of toast, eggs, fried potatoes, jam and tea or coffee. Down in New Manali, ***Chopsticks*** have a healthier option of muesli with curd and fresh fruit. For snacks on the hoof the German bakeries throughout Old Manali sell croissants, cinnamon rolls and the like. There's also a counter at ***Café Amigos*** near the roundabout in New Manali selling brownies and other gooey delights. The long-running and simple ***Manu Café*** up at the Temple cooks up cheap local food. For more complex Indian dishes the ***Mayur*** in New Manali is unrivalled. Nearby, the famous ***Manali Sweets*** is the best spot for hot, cavity-inducing *gulab jamun* (dough balls) and *rasmallai* (paneer balls). The simple ***Frontier*** in the Manu Market does a legendary tandoor chicken (Rs100) and fresh coriander relish.

Tibetan food (especially thukpa) is a speciality at the dimly lit ***Chopsticks*** on The Mall, and also at the ***Tibet Kitchen*** by the bridge at Old Manali. Italian dishes are best at ***Il Forno*** on the way to the Hadimba Temple although ***Pizza Olive*** in Old Manali is a fine runner-up. There's even excellent Korean food at the ***Hong Guesthouse*** down the lanes past the Krishna Guesthouse in Old Manali. Those on really tight budgets should follow the schoolchildren in the lanes near the local bus stand to the first-floor Tibetan restaurant tucked in here. The shack-like ***Gaddi*** tea stall just by the bridge in Old Manali also dishes up a cheap plate of momos and refreshing chai. It's very near the **HPMC** shop which sells local apple and plum wine – worth trying. Those who'd like a splurge should order the delicious fresh trout at ***Johnson's Café*** just down the hill from ***Johnson's Bar*** which serves beer in pint glasses and has a big screen for televised sports events.

It's easy to while away an afternoon in ***Café Manaslu*** down by the creek, with its stack of magazines, large pine tables, tasty dishes and a genuinely hospitable owner. Another scenic riverside restaurant is the ***Phuentsok Café*** (see Map 9, p135) down by the River Beas opposite the turn-off to Vashist (2km from Manali), which has wonderful cakes, hearty thukpa and a troupe of Lhasa Apso dogs (not for eating!).

EXCURSIONS FROM MANALI

On the opposite bank of the River Beas perches the village of Vashist whose hot springs are the centre of a long-term traveller scene. There are some good walks around here, particularly up to a waterfall favoured by chillum-puffing saddhus (ascetics), but women should not go alone. Heading southwards along the Aleo (true left bank) is Naggar (30km) with its historical castle which is also a hotel and an interesting Roerich museum. Among other things Nicholas Roerich (1874-1947) was a Russian painter and spiritualist who travelled extensively throughout the Himalaya painting some particularly ethereal landscapes. If you can't wait there's a virtual museum at 🖳 www.roerich.ru.

Services

Is it a coincidence this can be sung to the tune of 'Welcome to the Hotel California'?

• **Bank and post office** The State Bank of India on The Mall has an ATM; any of the money-changers will cash travellers' cheques. If you're cycling through Spiti be sure to get enough money because the next bank is 517km away in Rampur. Likewise, the next ATM to the north is 500km away in Leh. The post office is in Model Town (Mon–Sat 9am–1pm & 1.30–5pm).

• **Bookshops and newsagents** Bookworm has two outlets: one in the New Market run by the effervescent BB and another by the post office in Model Town. You can pick up new travel guides here as well as Western classics, books on the Himalaya and whatever else has taken BB's fancy. A newspaper wallah selling English-language papers sets up shop daily next to the chemist on The Mall.

• **Internet** There are first-floor internet cafés along The Mall (the one above Chopsticks is good), and many more along the road in Old Manali. Internet rates are around Rs30/hr and internet telephone calls around Rs4/min.

• **Laundry** Most budget travellers wash their own clothes in their guesthouses buckets (you can buy plastic brushes cheaply and sachets of Surf for Rs2 on The Mall). For professional help, use Prem Laundry at the top of Old Manali or the A1 Laundry on the corner by Dragon Guesthouse.

• **Left luggage** All guesthouses will let you leave some luggage with them and few will charge.

• **Medical help** Manali's best hospital is the charity-run Lady Willingdon Hospital (☎ 01902 252 379; 💻 www.manalihospital.com).

• **Travel agents** The HPTDC (Himachal Pradesh Tourism Development Corporation) booth near the Hotel Kunzam has a list of travel agents in Manali. Recommended ones are Tanzin Negi at Shambhala West Himalayan Exploration in New Market (☎ 01902 252 690; 💻 www.shambhalatreks.com) and Kuram and Astrid Dutt at Tiger Eye Adventure near the Yangkhor Café in Old Manali (☎ 01902 252 718; 💻 www.tigereyeadventure.com) who also run bicycle and motorbike tours in Ladakh and Spiti.

MTB HIMACHAL

This nine-day mountain bike event starts in Shimla and finishes in Manali. It's as off-road as possible with campsites arranged every night. See 💻 www.mtbhimachal.com for more details, including a detailed route guide if you're looking for an off-road route to do independently. The Nest & Wings guidebooks (available in Manali's bookshops for Rs70–120) have an inset 'Himachal Pradesh' map that should offer just enough detail.

Route guide – Manali to Leh

DAY 1 MANALI (1900m) to MARRHI (3303m) 36.2KM

MANALI–PALCHAN 10KM
PALCHAN–RAHALLA FALLS 18.5KM
RAHALLA FALLS–MARRHI 7.7KM

The road to Leh starts on the left bank of the River Beas and follows it upstream past the auto workshops, the Tibetan colony and the turn-off to Vashist. A sign at the bridge over the Beas details distances until Leh: only 475km to go! For the first few kilometres the road can be quite busy with trucks and jeeps and also wandering children and dogs. The Pir Pinjal range is visible in the distance and around the road are apple orchards, small villages and high up, waterfalls clinging to the rock faces. After 5km the road turns away from the Beas and starts to climb hairpins. This lower section can be hot but the trickling of streams offer some relief.

Palchan (2323m) 10/490KM
The road which crosses a bridge just before Palchan leads to Solang Nalah, Manali's tiny ski piste and the head of the Rohtang Tunnel (see p125). Just beyond the bridge at 10km the tiny ***Shop 777*** on the left sells soft drinks, simple food and fruit and veg. The road switchbacks through Palchan and in summer is often covered in wheat – the villagers use the passing traffic as a threshing machine.

As the road climbs it offers fantastic views back down the valley to the glinting tin roofs of Manali and across to the snow-tipped peaks above Solang. 'Himalayan snowdress' shacks line the road to rent out furry dressing gowns and Wellington boots to visitors from the plains, who are usually very excited by the prospect of their first encounter with snow. This strange garb looks silly but the weather on this pass can turn nasty fast – Rohtang La means 'Piles of Corpses Pass'. The jeep ride up Rohtang is a big deal for many Indian tourists so cyclists may find themselves the object of enthusiastic attention.

Kothi (2440m) The road enters a small shady gorge with rocky outcrops carpeted in brilliant green grass and water trickling down the rock faces. You have reached Kothi, probable site of the planned Himalayan Ski Village resort.

Beyond Kothi the road crosses a small nalah and spirals up past a restaurant into woods of pine and deodar (a Himalayan cedar). The air is noticeably cooler and some sections of the road can be a bit rough. If you look up along the pylons, Marrhi is visible high above. At 25km from Manali the ***Sunny Tea Shop*** brews up chai and Maggi noodles, another shack on the next bend does the same.

Rahalla Falls (2692m) 28.5/471.5KM
Here stretches out the only vaguely flat piece of road between Manali and Rohtang. It lasts about fifty metres so enjoy the breather! There's usually a snack shack by the waterfall. From here on the road switchbacks upwards beyond the treeline, squeezing past huge black and white boulders which look like Himalayan humbugs. The road is very narrow and often in bad condition: nerve-wracking for drivers so give them space. The landscape is still very lush, with thick shrubs and grasses poking out of the shattered rock faces. Pylons march up the slope and you follow them to the pass. At the top of this field of hairpins the road crosses a bridge over the Beas where there are a few basic restaurants, before a final switchback to Marrhi.

Marrhi (3303m) 36.2/463.8KM
Marrhi is a motley collection of souvenir stalls and roadside restaurants (boasting the altitude on their menus) with cheap rooms above. It's often swathed in a mist, shrouding the donkeys and horses and

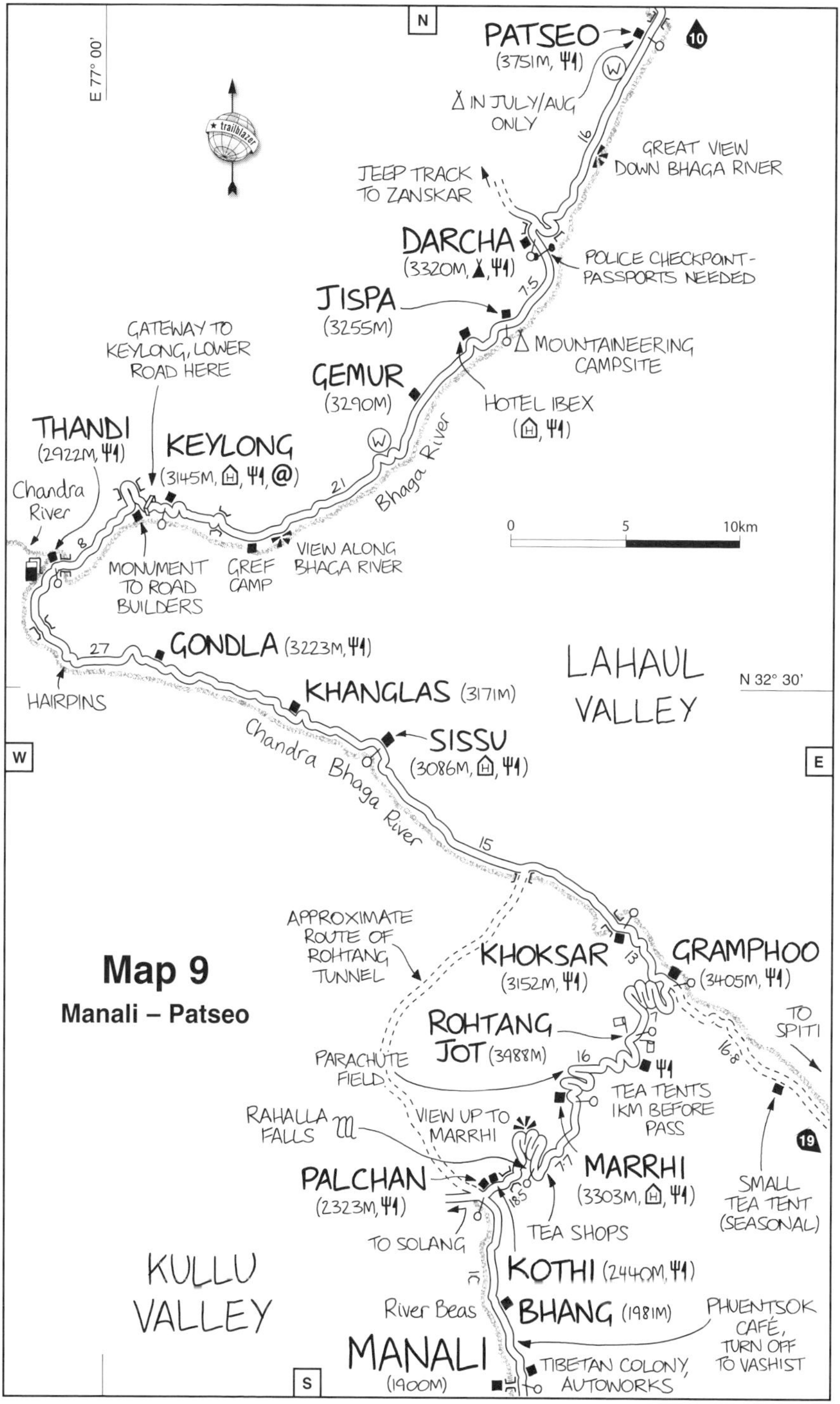
N
E 77° 00'
PATSEO
(3751M, ΨΙ)
IN JULY/AUG ONLY
GREAT VIEW DOWN BHAGA RIVER
JEEP TRACK TO ZANSKAR
DARCHA
(3320M, ▲, ΨΙ)
POLICE CHECKPOINT - PASSPORTS NEEDED
JISPA
(3255M)
MOUNTAINEERING CAMPSITE
GATEWAY TO KEYLONG, LOWER ROAD HERE
GEMUR
(3290M)
HOTEL IBEX
THANDI
(2922M, ΨΙ)
KEYLONG
(3145M, H, ΨΙ, @)
Chandra River
Bhaga River
0 5 10km
MONUMENT TO ROAD BUILDERS
GREF CAMP
VIEW ALONG BHAGA RIVER
GONDLA (3223M, ΨΙ)
LAHAUL VALLEY
N 32° 30'
HAIRPINS
KHANGLAS (3171M)
SISSU
(3086M, H, ΨΙ)
W
E
Chandra Bhaga River
APPROXIMATE ROUTE OF ROHTANG TUNNEL
KHOKSAR
(3152M, ΨΙ)
GRAMPHOO
(3405M, ΨΙ)
Map 9
Manali – Patseo
ROHTANG JOT (3488M)
TO SPITI
PARACHUTE FIELD
TEA TENTS 1KM BEFORE PASS
RAHALLA FALLS
VIEW UP TO MARRHI
PALCHAN
(2323M, ΨΙ)
MARRHI
(3303M, H, ΨΙ)
SMALL TEA TENT (SEASONAL)
TO SOLANG
TEA SHOPS
KULLU VALLEY
KOTHI (2440M, ΨΙ)
River Beas
BHANG (1981M)
PHUENTSOK CAFÉ, TURN OFF TO VASHIST
MANALI
(1900M)
TIBETAN COLONY, AUTOWORKS
S

Manali–Leh, 0–100km

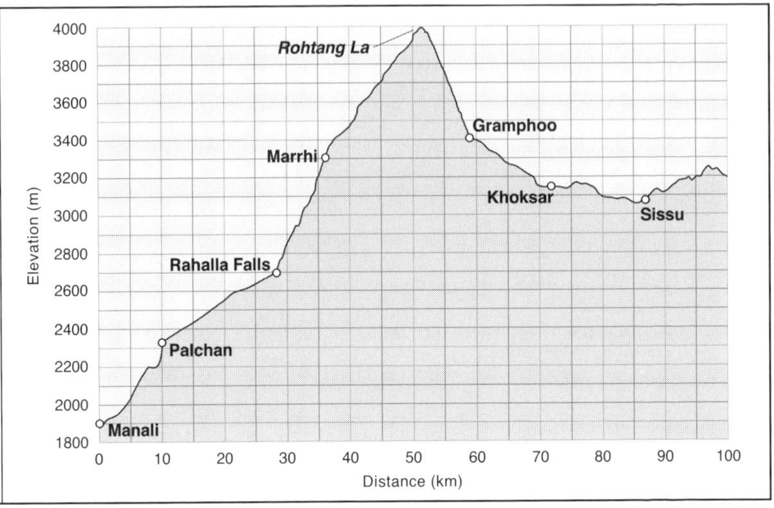

swallowing the toll of the temple bell.

If you've arrived early there may still be time to cross Rohtang La and spend the night in either Gramphoo or Khoksar on the far side of the pass, about another three to four hours riding. Those who stay in Marrhi can enjoy 'the highest altitude wood-fired pizza in the world' at the ***Sagur Valley*** dhaba. The ***Government Rest House*** is quiet and if empty of officials you might be able to negotiate a substantial discount on a Rs1000 double room (att); it's the neat-looking building down a path to the left before the temple. The field on the left as you arrive is good for camping (Rs100, negotiable).

It's at Marrhi that cyclists worry they may have bitten off too much: 36km from Manali sounds easy but you've **climbed over 1400m** and many arrive shattered. Don't worry! Keep warm, eat well, go to bed early. It always takes legs and lungs a couple of days to get into it and few people can train for climbs this big at home.

DAY 2 MARRHI (3303m) to KEYLONG (3145m) over ROHTANG LA (3988m) 86KM

MARRHI–ROHTANG LA 16KM
ROHTANG LA–GRAMPHOO 7KM
GRAMPHOO–KHOKSAR 13KM
KHOKSAR–SISSU 15KM
SISSU–THANDI 27KM
THANDI–KEYLONG 8KM

From Marrhi up to Rohtang kilometre markers count you down to the pass. Once you get above Marrhi the landscape becomes bleaker as the views become more dramatic. A popular sport in Northern India is paragliding and you'll see a jump-off point a kilometre above Marrhi's huts. The weather up on Rohtang is often moody: rolling clouds which then rend apart to reveal a dazzling blue sky behind and high valleys sliced by rivers and waterfalls. Cow parsley, wildflowers in pinks, blues and reds and shrubs dot the fields and there are often horses and donkeys grazing up here.

Every year the snowline is celebrated with a snow figure or two: sometimes a snowman, sometimes a king and his queen perched on their own snowy thrones. Once you reach the snow drifts there's usually someone selling snacks or even hot corn-on-the-cob.

Rohtang La (3988m) 2.2/447.0KM

The pass is often desolate and shrouded in mist. Tea stalls a kilometre before the pass marker sell hot noodles, biscuits, soups and chai. On a clear day the views are spectacular: the gentle and verdant

Kullu Valley lies behind while ahead lies Lahaul – rugged, dramatic and elemental. *"Surely the gods live here, this is no place for men"* observes Kim in Kipling's classic adventure of that name. This is one of the most extreme climate changes in the world: monsoonal India to the southern face of the Great Himalaya range.

Gramphoo (3405m) 59.2/440.8KM

Seven kilometres below the pass are two mud dhabas which mark the turn-off to the Spiti Valley (see p185). You can spend the night here on rock beds in the ***dhabas*** (around Rs175 for dinner, bed and breakfast) or campers can push on to Khoksar, at the base of the descent.

Khoksar (3152m) 72.2/427.8KM

The ***Snowland*** dhaba is friendly although the food is nothing special. The camping field lies behind the police checkpoint. Beyond the bridge at Khoksar the road dips and climbs along the banks of the Chandra Bhaga River and is often rutted and rough until Sissu; some sections may even be washed out.

Keep an eye out for the *mani* wall (a low wall of stones individually inscribed with the Buddhist mantra *om mani padme hum*) which runs alongside the road just after Khoksar. Large shapely *chortens* (domed Buddhist structures) also evoke what lies ahead.

Sissu (3086m) 87.2/412.8KM

Poplars and willows line the road as you approach Sissu and peas, potatoes, barley and buckwheat grow in terraced fields etched into the valley sides. Near the village an impressive waterfall cascades between two mountain peaks on the far side of the valley and there's even a high-altitude beach. There's a friendly family-run guesthouse here called the ***Triveni*** whose doubles cost Rs500 (att); the best one is upstairs at the rear with fantastic views. They can rustle up some food and serve it on the upstairs balcony with views of the valleys, glaciers and waterfalls opposite. Otherwise there's also the ***Himachal Pradesh Public Works Department* (HPPWD) *Resthouse*** (Rs1000).

After Sissu the road climbs by the river past the village of Khanglas where there's a small rural museum. It then starts a descent to the river before Thandi. A nalah before the hairpins is nicknamed '*pagal* (crazy) *nalah*' as it floods without warning and destroys the road.

Gondla (3223m) A small village with a basic restaurant.

Thandi (2922m) 114.2/385.8KM

Half a kilometre after this tiny village is the confluence of the Chandra and Bhaga Rivers; a little further on are a couple of dhabas before the bridge over the Bhaga river and the final 8km climb to Keylong.

Just before Keylong there is a small monument to the Manali–Leh road builders at the side of the road: 'When you go home, tell them of us. For their tomorrow, we gave our today'.

Keylong (3145m) 122.2/377.8KM

This small dusty market town is the last place to stock up on good food supplies. It's entered by a ceremonial gateway after which the road forks. The lower road leads to the town; the upper road is the highway which thunders and honks past the bus station, market and a couple of grotty guesthouses. On the quieter lower road there's the ***Tashi Delek*** hotel whose doubles cost Rs400–800 or cheap guesthouses

THE CHENAB RIVER

Thandi may be tiny but the Chandra and Bhaga rivers which meet here flow on to become one of the mighty rivers of Punjab. The Chandrabhaga, as it is known in its upper reaches, flows through Himachal Pradesh and Kashmir where it becomes the Chenab and joins the Jhelum, Ravi, Sutlej and Beas Rivers. Together they are the 'Panj Aab' or 'five rivers' which give the Punjab its name.

In recent years the Chenab has become controversial as India has built hydroelectric dams along its length thereby, Pakistan claims, jeopardizing agriculture in Pakistani Punjab. The two countries, both of which suffer from both drought and floods, have signed the Indus Water Treaty but as elsewhere in the Himalaya, water is becoming as important as the territory it flows through.

Manali–Leh, 100–200km

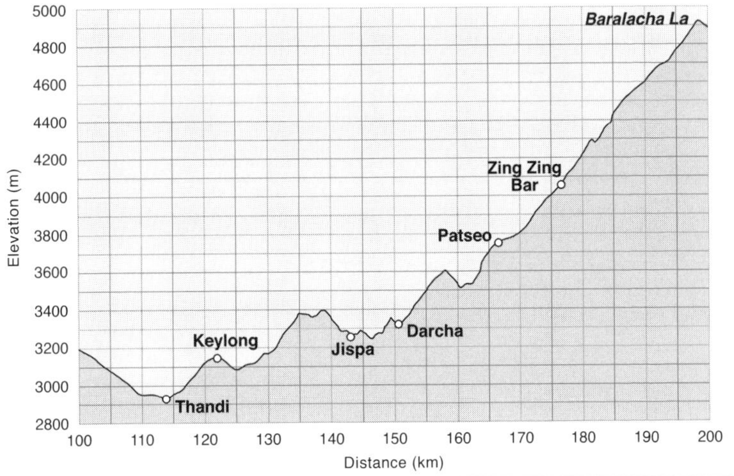

such as the ***Lamayuru*** and the clean ***Gyespa*** whose doubles cost Rs150 (com). The food is better at the Lamayuru. There's an internet café on the lower road near the Lamayuru (Rs30/hr) though the connection is poor.

DAY 3 KEYLONG (3145m) to PATSEO (3751m) 44.5KM

KEYLONG–JISPA 21KM
JISPA–DARCHA 7.5KM
DARCHA–PATSEO 16KM

The valley in which Keylong lies is dotted with small villages, shady poplar and willow trees and rivulets. This is the last permanent habitation until the villages on the far side of Taglang La, over 250km away. Beyond Keylong the road is hacked out of a narrow gorge high above the Bhaga River. It's unmetalled and can become very dusty, especially if the traffic is heavy.

Between the GREF army camp and Gemur there are wonderful views to the glaciers on the southeast side of the valley.

Jispa (3255m) 143.2/356.8KM
The road rises and falls to Jispa, home of the ***Hotel Ibex*** (dbl, Rs1200) and its famous breakfasts. For Rs90 you can eat porridge, toast, eggs, coffee and juice but once you have, it's quite difficult to get going again. Still, the climb to Baralacha La essentially starts from Darcha so this is no time to pass up on calories!

Darcha (3320m) 150.7/349.3KM
Darcha is little more than a string of dhabas clustered by a police checkpoint where you must register. The Jankar River here, meandering on the wide plain, can appear particularly beautiful with swirls of silver backed by the green of the mountains. After crossing the river there's a switchback climb past the turn-off to the Zanskar Valley over the Shingo La pass (signed to Raru), after which the highway unkinks and tracks the Bhaga upstream to Patseo.

Patseo (3751m) 166.7/333.3KM
Hozer's Café is a small parachute tent with beds (Rs150 each) and hot food by a tiny teardrop-shaped lake. There's some flat ground for camping at the far side of the lake and on the lake itself the world's highest pedalo awaits (Rs50 a go). If you're feeling good consider pushing on to Zing Zing Bar which would take 10km off the next day's climb to Baralacha La. Patseo doesn't seem like much but until the 1950s it was the gathering place for traders from Zanskar, Lahaul, Kullu and Ladakh who would meet to barter salt and wool from the uplands for grains and tea from the lowlands.

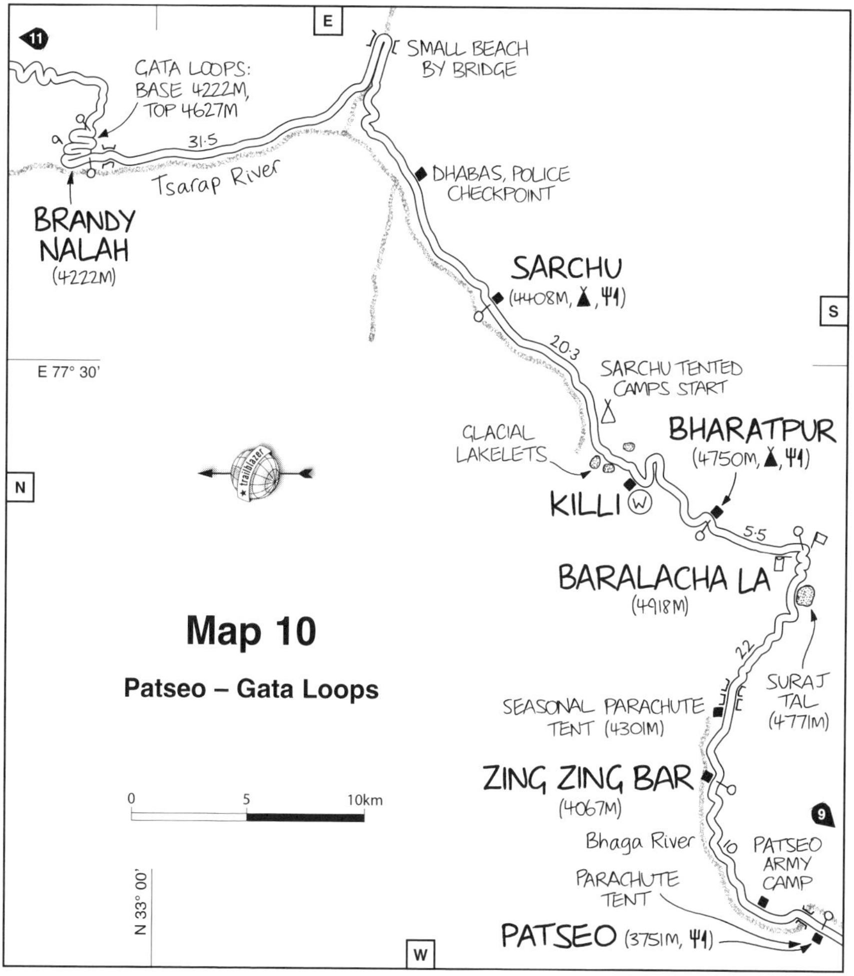

THE GADDIS

A common sight in Lahaul in the summer time are Gaddi shepherds leading enormous flocks of sheep and goats from their village homes in the Chamba Valley to the nutritious grasses of Lahaul and onwards towards Ladakh.

You'll often hear them before you see them: the clatter of hoof on rock as a thousand goats and sheep come skittering down a mountainside, accompanied by the calls and whistles of the shepherds. In their rough, home-spun woollen garb the Gaddis appear as if from another century or even millennium, often with a lamb or kid on their arm or tucked up inside their tunic.

They travel for months to reach Lahaul, as they have done for centuries, for the niru, a blue-green grass which is extremely nutritious and unique to the valley. Christina Noble's book *Over the High Passes* (1987) chronicles a year spent with the Gaddis, at a time when more than 100,000 sheep and goats travelled through Lahaul every year.

DAY 4 PATSEO (3751m) to SARCHU (4408m) over BARALACHA LA (4918m) 57.8KM

PATSEO–ZING ZING BAR 10KM
ZING ZING BAR–BARALACHA LA 22KM
BARALACHA LA–BHARATPUR 5.5KM
BHARATPUR–SARCHU 20.3KM

Just a kilometre from the parachute tent at Patseo is a bridge over the Bhaga River followed by a drive-through army camp where the climb to Baralacha La begins. The road can be rough and the climb steady as it tracks the river for 10km.

Zing Zing Bar (4067m) 176.7/323.3KM

An exotic name for a meagre place. There's a road workers' hut and some level ground to camp on next to the road. It's dirty and glass-littered; solo women and anyone who appreciates scenery would do better to sleep at Patseo.

From Zing Zing Bar the climb continues through a bare, rocky landscape. It's relentless and usually on an atrocious surface. The last chance to filter **water** is at the two bridges 16km from the pass. The pass itself is 1500m beyond the Nissen hut near the emerald lake of Suraj Tal, source of the Bhaga River.

Baralacha La (4918m) 198.7/301.3KM

Brown rocks and the odd patch of snow is not the landscape you'd expect of the Great Himalaya range, but that's exactly what you've just crossed. You are now also 110m higher than the summit of Mont Blanc, Europe's highest mountain. Baralacha La has yet another surprise: it's a three-way pass joining Spiti, Ladakh and Lahaul. The approach from the southeast is an old trail from the beautiful lake of Chandra Tal (see p188) and the Spiti Valley.

The descent from Baralacha La is as rough as the climb but with magical scenery of marbled pink mountains rising from the Yama river set off by swathes of green and glacial lakelets.

Bharatpur (4750m) 204.2/295.8KM

This seasonal parachute tent village is just over 5km below the pass and brews up the usual suspects of chai, Maggi noodles, dahl and rice. The local women do a good line in woolly socks and hats as knitting is a popular pastime while waiting for hungry travellers. Rugs and pillows scattered around tempt weary cyclists to snooze while the food cooks.

After Bharatpur's hairpins you follow the river which shuttles through a gorge until bursting out onto the wide open Sarchu plains. Campers need to draw water from the river by the Kili army camp as there is none on the plains and the tented camps are loath to share theirs.

Sarchu (4408m) 224.7/275.3KM

In the late evening light, Sarchu is stunning: the grass a vivid green, the hoodoos of the canyon picked out by shadow and, best of all the heavenly marriage of tarmac and a tailwind allowing you to relax after the rigours of the pass. There are even small edelweiss-like flowers growing on the verge. The best camping is on the canyon side beyond the tented camps. Each camp has a restaurant, though the food is overpriced as Manali–Leh buses stop here overnight. This is also the border between Himachal Pradesh and Ladakh; finally, you're entering 'the Land of the Lamas'.

THE CALL OF DUTY AND WHY BRIDGES ARE BAD NEWS FOR BATHERS

It's about this time into the ride that you start thinking 'wouldn't it be nice to have a wash?'. So when we spotted a bridge with a handy track down to the river, it seemed the perfect place. I trotted off, soap in hand, while my sister waited. A few minutes later she called, "Have you seen the soldier?", then added, "I think he's seen you!". There he was, above the road, watching intently. We did our best long-distance mime of 'washing' and 'kindly bugger off', but to no avail. "Oh no, madams" he called back, "it is my duty!". And so it was; bridges are vital to the army and so are manned constantly. Lesson learnt!

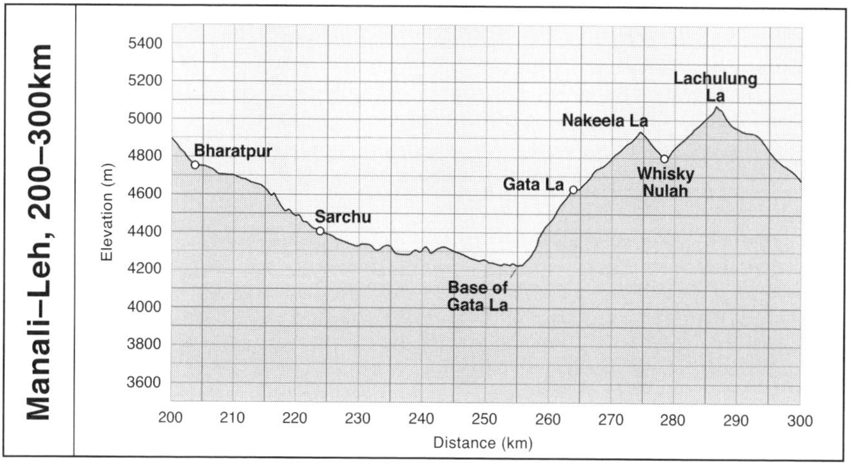

DAY 5 SARCHU (4408m) to WHISKY NALAH (4802m) over Nakeela La (4937m) 55KM

SARCHU–BASE OF GATA LOOPS 31.5KM
BASE OF GATA LOOPS–TOP OF LOOPS 9KM
TOP OF GATA LOOPS–NAKEELA LA 10.5KM
NAKEELA LA–WHISKY NALAH 4KM

How did you sleep last night? Any cyclists who felt the altitude should not climb the Gata Loops today but camp at their base or just kick back in Sarchu. If you do take on the loops note there's no water until Whisky Nalah which is another 400m above: this may not sound like much but it is a critical difference.

If AMS strikes at Whisky Nalah you're in serious trouble because you're stuck between a double pass: 4937m the way you came and 5077m up ahead. Very strong, tentless or supported cyclists have a third option: to ride 85km from Sarchu to Pang over the double pass in one day.

A breakfast of omelette and chapattis infused with Tata fumes can be had at the dhabas after the police checkpoint and bridge 6km from Sarchu. From there to the base of the Gata Loops the road is excellent tarmac and the remaining 25km are quickly done.

En route there is a small detour up the valley of the Tsarap River (which flows on to the Zanskar Valley) as well as tiny high-altitude beaches and the chance for a discreet wash under some bridges, but see box opposite.

Brandy Nalah (4220m) 256.2/243.8KM
This is the level ground at the base of the Gata Loops. Spend the night here if you're unsure you've acclimatized properly.

The Gata Loops

These infamous switchbacks are the Alpe d'Huez of the Manali–Leh Highway. Maybe one day a cyclist will paint numbers on the bends but for now you can enjoy counting all 21 of them down yourself. It's a long hot climb from 4222m up to 4627m so fill up on water beforehand. If you run out there's sometimes some water trickling down the rock face by the natural arch at the top of the loops.

The end of the Gata Loops is not the top of the climb; that's another 10km or so further on at Nakeela La. This last section is often the hardest, especially for legs tired after pedalling over Baralacha La. Try to relax and just take it as it comes.

Nakeela La (4937m) 275.7/224.3KM
A scruffy pass with a short descent to Whisky Nalah.

Whisky Nalah (4802m) 279.7/220.3KM
The best **camping** is next to the stream still high on the valley side, which is the only water supply until the far side of Lachulung La. Tentless cyclists who get

caught out could possibly appeal to the army boys for a bed in the Nissen huts in the dip between the two passes at 4785m, though women travelling solo should probably not. Tata trucks travelling through the night trundle around the hairpins, slinging their headlights across the valley like lighthouse beams.

DAY 6 WHISKY NALAH (4802m) to PANG (4522m) over Lachulung La (5077m) 29KM

WHISKY NALAH–LACHULUNG LA 8KM
LACHULUNG LA–PANG 21KM

In the cold light and air of the morning, you can't help feeling sorry for the poor buggers posted to Whisky Nalah. Sarchu feels like a metropolis in comparison.

Lachulung La (5077m) 287.7/212.3KM If you've been eyeing those hairpins in trepidation the jaunty yellow pass marker is just around the top corner. This is the first 5000m pass so pat yourself on the back if you're still breathing. From here it's downhill all the way to Pang along a bumpy road which skirts a high, grassy pasture then drops through a river gully with a memorial to two army officers who didn't quite make the bend.

Parachute tent and its owner in Pang

Kangla Jot (4760m) The hardy and the dirty might enjoy the rock pools here. Just around the corner is a bridge overlooked by a perfect natural arch carved from the terracotta rock, and beyond that an extraordinary landscape of wind-blasted turrets, spires and flutes.

Pang (4522m) 308.7/191.3KM Once the river widens into a basin and you cross a bridge then Pang is just around the corner. A police checkpoint will ask for passport details and then you're free to explore the delights of Pang's ***parachute tents***. Pang itself is filthy. Rubbish is dumped next to the river and there's a constant ebb and flow of bus and jeep passengers shouting to each other and dropping more rubbish. But the parachute tents are cosiness itself – especially if you're travelling with friends and can secure an entire 'back room' (a bedroom tent joined to the front restaurant tent) for yourselves. All food and drink (within reason) is here: momos, dahl and rice, sabze, chocolate, Godfather beer and army bootleg whisky. Plastic tables and chairs outside make it a happy place to hang out, sip chai and watch the world go by – what there is of it. If you want to wash in privacy ride north past the bridge to the army camp and take the gravel track down to the river (3km round trip).

DAY 7 PANG (4522m) to TSO KAR (4515m) 47KM

PANG–MOREI PLAINS 7.8KM
MOREI PLAINS–TSO KAR TURN-OFF 32.2KM
TSO KAR TURN-OFF–TSO KAR CAMPSITE 7KM

Fill all your water bottles in Pang because there's no water on the Morei Plains; only at Tso Kar (47km) and partway up the climb of Taglang La (58km). After crossing the bridge and passing the army camp, five switchbacks lift you onto the dramatic Morei Plains.

Morei Plains (4655m) 316.7/183.3KM No one could accuse the Manali–Leh Highway of being monotonous and here it transforms itself once again. Fringed by

Manali–Leh, 300–400km

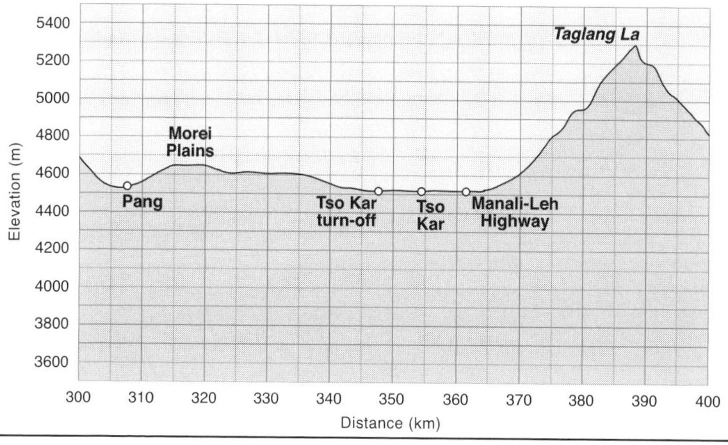

mountains and sliced to the south by a deep canyon, the Morei Plains is a 40-km-long plateau which appears grassy but is in fact peppered with shrubs. Marmots, *pika* (a small furry mammal like a rabbity guinea-pig) and herds of *kyang* (Tibetan wild ass) are frequently seen here. Morei is also the stomping ground of Chang-pa nomads who are scattered on this western corner of the Changthang or Tibetan plateau. The light and scenery here can be dramatic as storms sweep across the sky miles away, plunging the plateau into darkness or flooding it with light while cloud shadows race across it. For a better idea of nomad life turn off towards Tso Kar, one of the many salt lakes sprinkled across the Tibetan plateau.

Tso Kar (4515m) 355.7/144.3KM

From the Highway a sandy 7km jeep

THE NOMADS OF RUPSHU

East of the Manali–Leh Highway lies the region of Rupshu, home to the Chang-pa nomads who raise flocks of yak, sheep and goats. The climate is harsh but the grass is rich and in the past the trading route from Leh to Lhasa passed this way. The nomads have two main villages: Thukje on the shores of Tso Kar, and Korzok on the shores of Tso Moriri. During summer, they live on the move in their yak-hair tents. India's Supreme Court has recently declared 4000 square kilometres of Rupshu a 'wildlife sanctuary' with the consequent restriction on human activity. The Chang-pa have found themselves facing both the loss of their homeland and the extinction of their way of life.

Rupshu is better known as Changthang or the Tibetan Plateau. The average height is 4800m and in winter the temperature plummets to -40°C. The nomads' goats raised in these sub-zero temperatures are famed for their warm underbelly fur, known as pashm. This Persian word (which means 'wool') gives an inkling of how far this valuable commodity travelled: first to Srinagar where the greasy, matted hair balls were untangled and then woven, and then beyond to become delicate shawls known today as pashmina.

Another kind of fabric, shahtoosh, originates from the critically endangered chiru or Tibetan antelope. Shahtoosh is also Persian, and means 'king of wool'. The chiru are not raised, as the pashmina goats are, but are shot in the wild in their thousands. Over twenty chiru are shot and skinned to make a top-quality shawl which even in India can cost over $8500. The perception of shahtoosh on the international market as the 'rarest of the rare' means the shawls reach astronomical prices in the West. For such a reward and with buyers apparently indifferent to or ignorant of shahtoosh's origin, poaching is rife on this border of China and India, hence the designation of the wildlife sanctuary and the loss of the Chang-pa homeland.

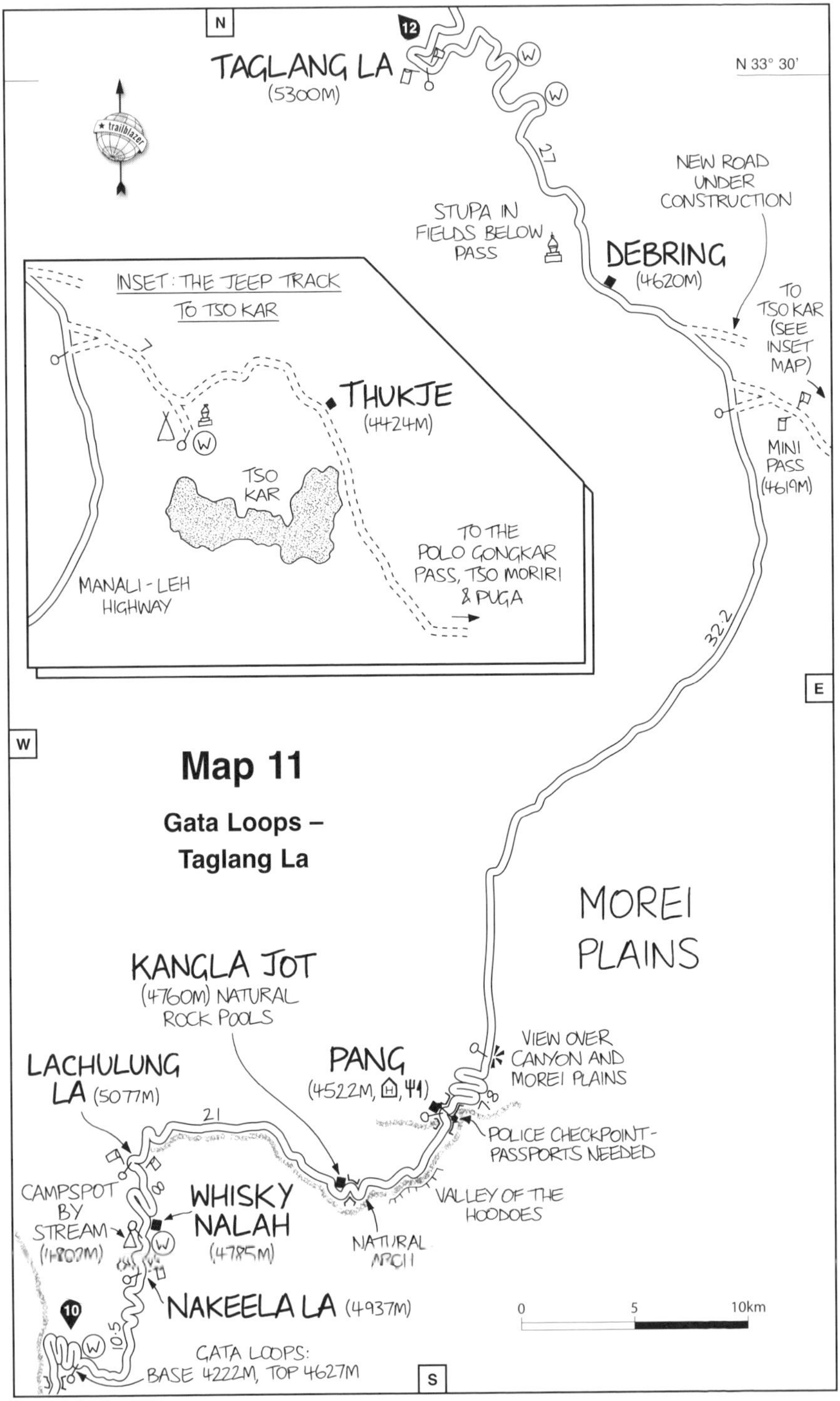

N
TAGLANG LA
(5300M)
N 33° 30'
27
NEW ROAD UNDER CONSTRUCTION
STUPA IN FIELDS BELOW PASS
DEBRING
(4620M)
TO TSO KAR (SEE INSET MAP)
MINI PASS (4619M)
INSET: THE JEEP TRACK TO TSO KAR
THUKJE
(4424M)
TSO KAR
TO THE POLO GONGKAR PASS, TSO MORIRI & PUGA
MANALI-LEH HIGHWAY
32.2
E
W
Map 11
Gata Loops – Taglang La
MOREI PLAINS
KANGLA JOT
(4760M) NATURAL ROCK POOLS
VIEW OVER CANYON AND MOREI PLAINS
LACHULUNG LA (5077M)
PANG
(4522M,
21
POLICE CHECKPOINT - PASSPORTS NEEDED
CAMPSPOT BY STREAM
WHISKY NALAH
VALLEY OF THE HOODOES
NATURAL ARCH
NAKEELA LA (4937M)
0
5
10km
10.5
GATA LOOPS: BASE 4222M, TOP 4627M
S

track leads to the shores of Tso Kar.

The best **camping** is by the chorten with a freshwater stream and gorgeously plush grass; where the track splits approaching Tso Kar take the right (south) fork. If you don't have a tent the left fork leads to the Chang-pa village of Thukje: it looks close from the prayer flags but is still another 10km away over more sandy tracks. You may be able to find shelter here or in the *gompa* (Buddhist monastery) above, though there's no guesthouse or restaurant. During the summer the villagers are on the high pastures and it has an odd feeling: deserted but for various yak parts drying on the roofs.

BRO road workers are building a road between the highway and Tso Moriri lake to the south of Tso Kar but progress is slow because work is only possible for three months each year. For the best view of Tso Kar, take the road to Thukje and

The road to Tso Kar

continue towards the Polo Gongkar pass: beyond the tussocky foreground the sapphire lake shimmers beneath snowy peaks and in the evening the setting sun sets the rocks behind the village aflame.

Beyond Tso Kar is some excellent riding to the village of Puga through a sulphurous valley beloved of the endangered black neck crane.

DAY 8 Tso Kar (4515m) to Lato (4021m) over Taglang La (5300m) 73KM

TSO KAR–HIGHWAY JUNCTION 7KM
HIGHWAY JUNCTION–TAGLANG LA 27KM
TAGLANG LA–LATO 39KM

Back on the Manali–Leh Highway there's usually a tailwind whisking you along the Morei Plains to the base of Taglang La, where a derelict road workers' camp known as **Debring** provides shelter and a water pump if needed. The climb to the pass is steady and on good tarmac; by now you should be well attuned to the altitude. There are two streams to filter water from on the ascent, but no food until Rumtse, 26km after the pass. Look back while you're on the climb and you'll see Tso Kar to the southeast. The road at the top of the pass can be in bad condition, though not as bad as Baralacha La.

Taglang La (5300m) 389.7/110.3KM
At the summit a pass marker cheerfully asks: '*You are passing through second highest pass of the world. Unbelievable is not it?*'

Yes it is and all the more so because you cycled here. The weather is often wild up here but the view of range after range rippling into the distance is magnificent.

Beyond the pass the road curves in a wide sweep along the valley past toppled Tata trucks before descending in switchbacks (or fun shortcuts for mountain bikers) to the powder blue Gya river, which feeds into the Indus some 60km away at Upshi. The poor road surface and strong headwinds rob the descent of the speed you deserve and in bad weather it can be numbingly cold.

The first village is **Rumtse** where there's a police post and ***parachute tents*** dishing out Maggi, chapattis, omelettes

Having a breather at Taglang (Tanglang) La

and chai. As you coast onwards past tiny white-washed villages bounded by kidney-shaped barley fields and chortens the contrast with the remoteness of the last few days is striking.

This is Ladakh proper: prayer wheels, old ladies in traditional dress with woolly socks and sleeveless puffa jackets, teenage boys posing in shades and, unfortunately, little children demanding "one pen, one pen!". You will also feel a difference in the altitude and warmth: Lato lies at an easy 4000m. All this cultivation and village life feels like civilization again so it's strange to realize you're actually twice as high as Manali.

Lato (4021m) 428.7/71.3KM
There are two ***campsites*** in this village, one by the river and the other in a field peering up at two impressive spires of rock. Someone will probably come round to collect a Rs50 camping fee. Anyone without a tent needs to push on to Upshi, another 23km away but all downhill.

DAY 9 LATO (4021m) to THIKSE (3243m) 54KM

LATO–UPSHI 23KM
UPSHI–KARU 10KM
KARU–THIKSE 21KM

From Lato the road funnels you through a fantastical gorge of reds and greens with the strata and fins of rock shooting skywards and green barley swaying by the river. Eventually the multicoloured gorge explodes outwards near the goat farm at Upshi and you emerge blinking in the remarkable light and almost biblical vistas of the Indus Valley.

Upshi (3417m) There's a clump of ***restaurants*** by the junction to Mahe Bridge at Upshi; ask around if you need a bed. If it's summertime, you can ride along the valley in a T-shirt and flip-flops – very different from the passes! From here the road rises and falls along the Indus to Karu and the traffic starts to pick up – mostly military vehicles and tourist jeeps. There may also be a headwind.

Karu (3445m) This ugly military base is also the junction for Hemis monastery (7km and a 300m climb with guesthouses in Hemis village) and the road to Taktok gompa, Wari La and Pangong Tso. There are more ***restaurants*** here. From Karu it's either flat or downhill to Thikse and poplar trees in the villages shade the last section.

Thikse (3243m) Thikse gompa is one of the iconic images of Ladakh and it's also conveniently situated on the Manali–Leh Highway. The view from its rooftop is stupendous. Doubles at the ***Chamba Hotel*** at the monastery cost Rs300 (att) or Rs150 (com) at the sweet ***Kongmanono***

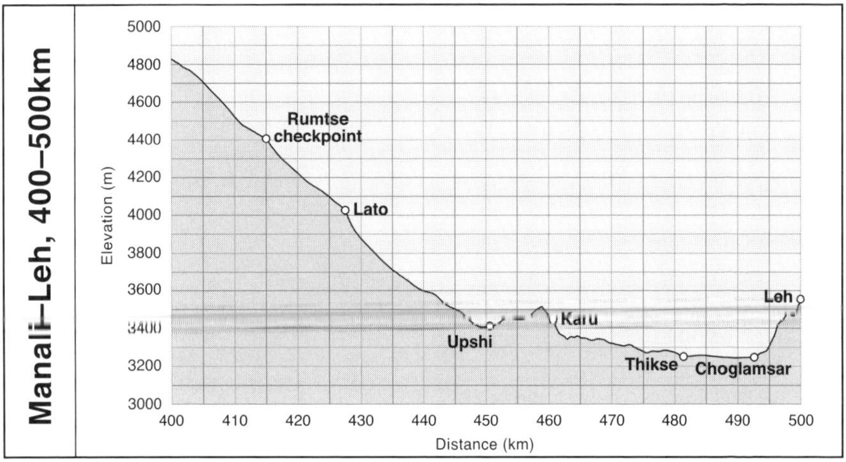

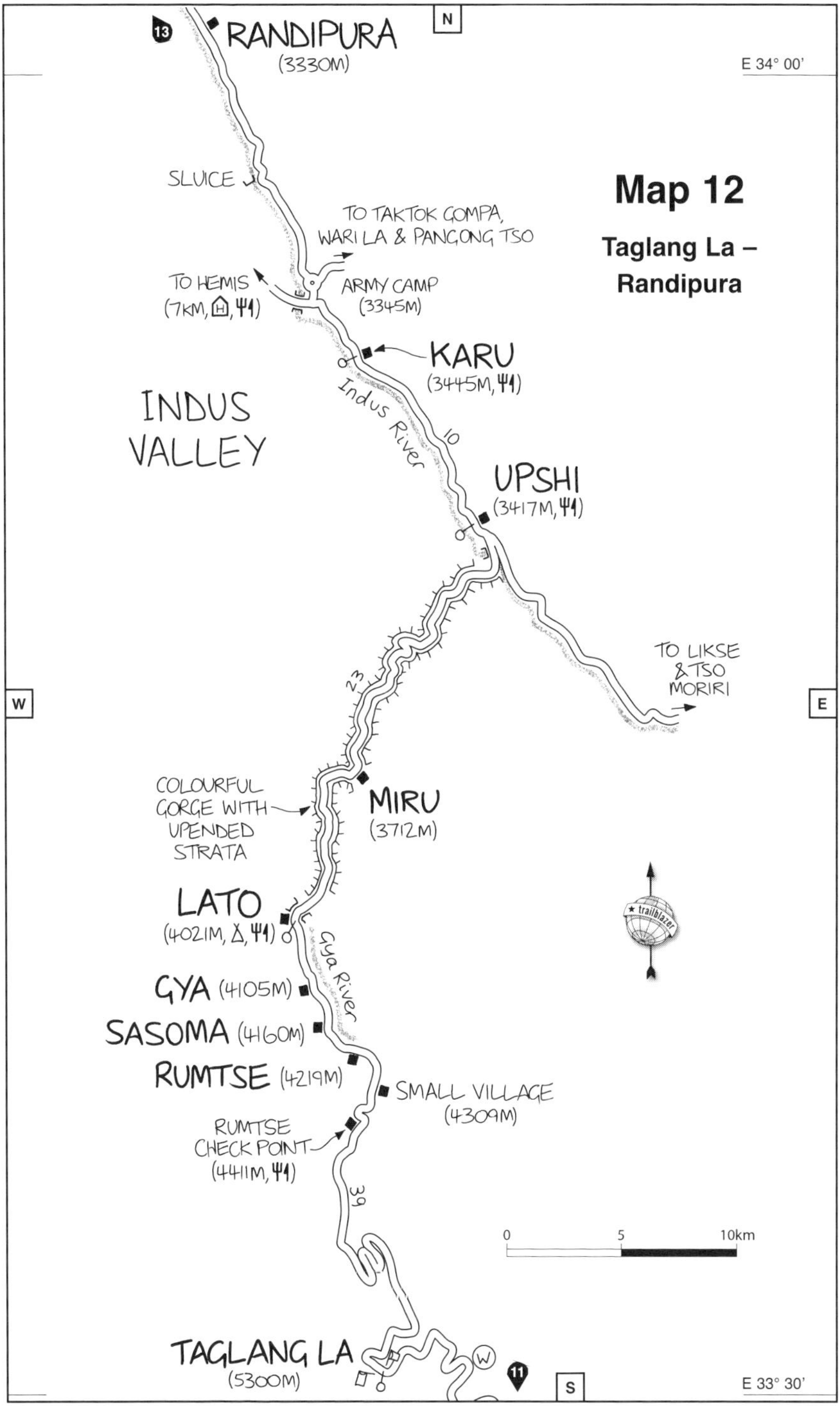
Map 12
Taglang La – Randipura
N
S
W
E
E 34° 00'
E 33° 30'
RANDIPURA
(3330M)
SLUICE
TO TAKTOK GOMPA, WARI LA & PANGONG TSO
TO HEMIS
(7KM,
ARMY CAMP
(3345M)
KARU
(3445M,
INDUS VALLEY
Indus River
10
UPSHI
(3417M,
TO LIKSE & TSO MORIRI
23
COLOURFUL GORGE WITH UPENDED STRATA
MIRU
(3712M)
LATO
(4021M,
Gya River
GYA (4105M)
SASOMA (4160M)
RUMTSE (4219M)
SMALL VILLAGE
(4309M)
RUMTSE CHECK POINT
(4411M,
39
0
5
10km
TAGLANG LA
(5300M)
W
13
11
trailblazer

Guesthouse 100m up the road. The Chamba has a very good *restaurant* with a sunny garden. This is a pleasant place to stay, relax and reflect before the journey is officially over at Leh.

DAY 10 THIKSE (3243m) to LEH (3563m) 18KM

THIKSE–CHOGLAMSAR 11KM
CHOGLAMSAR–LEH ROUNDABOUT 7KM

The final push! The road continues along the Indus River to the busy Tibetan colony of Choglamsar. Just past the ancient palace at Shey and its field of chortens is an enormous rock carving of five Buddhas dated from around the 8th century. These are **Tathagata Buddhas** or Buddhas who have achieved liberation and surpassed being/not-being. While they look contented, their lotus leaves and elephants look a little incongruous.

The Tathagata Buddhas at Shey

Choglamsar (3235m) This Tibetan colony is a tooting mass of trucks, cars and auto rickshaws and from here onwards the traffic is heavy. On the way up the final dusty drag to Leh is 'the highest golf course in the world' (so arid it looks like one large bunker) and the Himank HQ.

Leh (3563m) The large roundabout signals your arrival in Leh; the western road leads to Fort Road and the eastern road leads to Main Bazaar past the hospital and bus station (see map on p150). Many travellers prefer to stay in Leh's outlying villages of Changspa and Sankhar: these are best reached by taking Old Road which leads north from the roundabout and brings you directly into Main Bazaar. The road to the south leads to the airport and then onwards to Srinagar.

LEH (3563m)

The yak trains that once puffed through Leh's dusty lanes may have been replaced by army trucks and tourist jeeps but the capital of Ladakh is still a fascinating destination. After conquering the high mountain passes and camping in the wilds, most bikers are happy to spend a few days relaxing in Leh's garden cafés, strolling around the poplar-lined barley fields and seeing the town's historical sights before exploring further afield.

Leh has a busy tourist scene, and the town is a great base from which to explore the many Buddhist monasteries in the area. It's also easy to reach the Ladakh and Zanskar mountains, and the lakes of Tso Moriri and Pangong Tso towards the border with Tibet.

History

The first European to set eyes on Leh was a Jesuit missionary called Francisco de Azeveda, who turned up in 1631. For centuries Leh was a major staging post of trans-Himalayan trade but the closure of China's borders in the 1950s turned Leh from a cultural entrepôt into a high-altitude cul-de-sac. Until then, the Ladakhi way of life revolved around agriculture and trade. In the last fifty years life has changed radically.

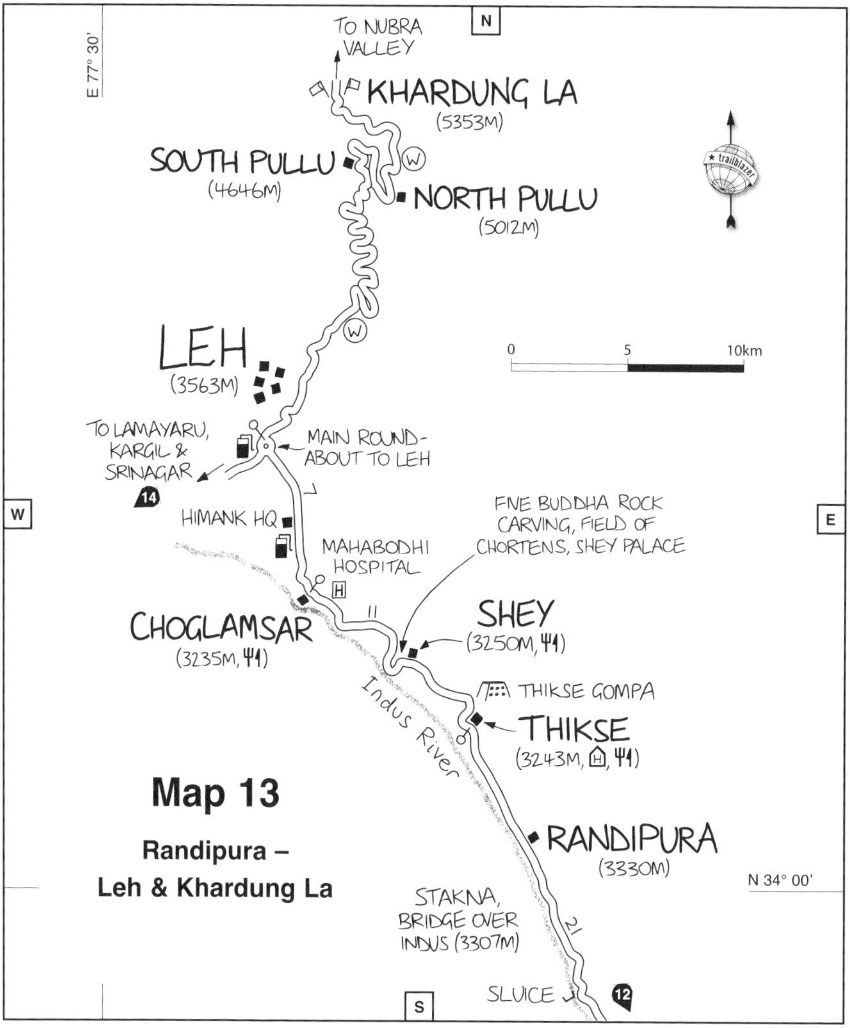

Map 13
Randipura – Leh & Khardung La

The Sino-Indian war in 1962 (see p121) brought an immense military presence to the region which has never dwindled and is periodically buoyed by diplomatic spats with India's other troublesome neighbour, Pakistan. This newly-sensitive border required the construction of the Manali–Leh Highway, the prising open of Ladakh and a fundamental shift of cultural focus – no longer north to Tibet and Central Asia but now south to Hindu India. In 1974 Ladakh was declared open to foreign tourists whose cash now constitutes the bulk of the region's economy.

Arrival and orientation

It's a long, dusty slog up to Leh from the Indus Valley but the lure of a hot shower and a cold beer will make short work of it. If you've flown in from

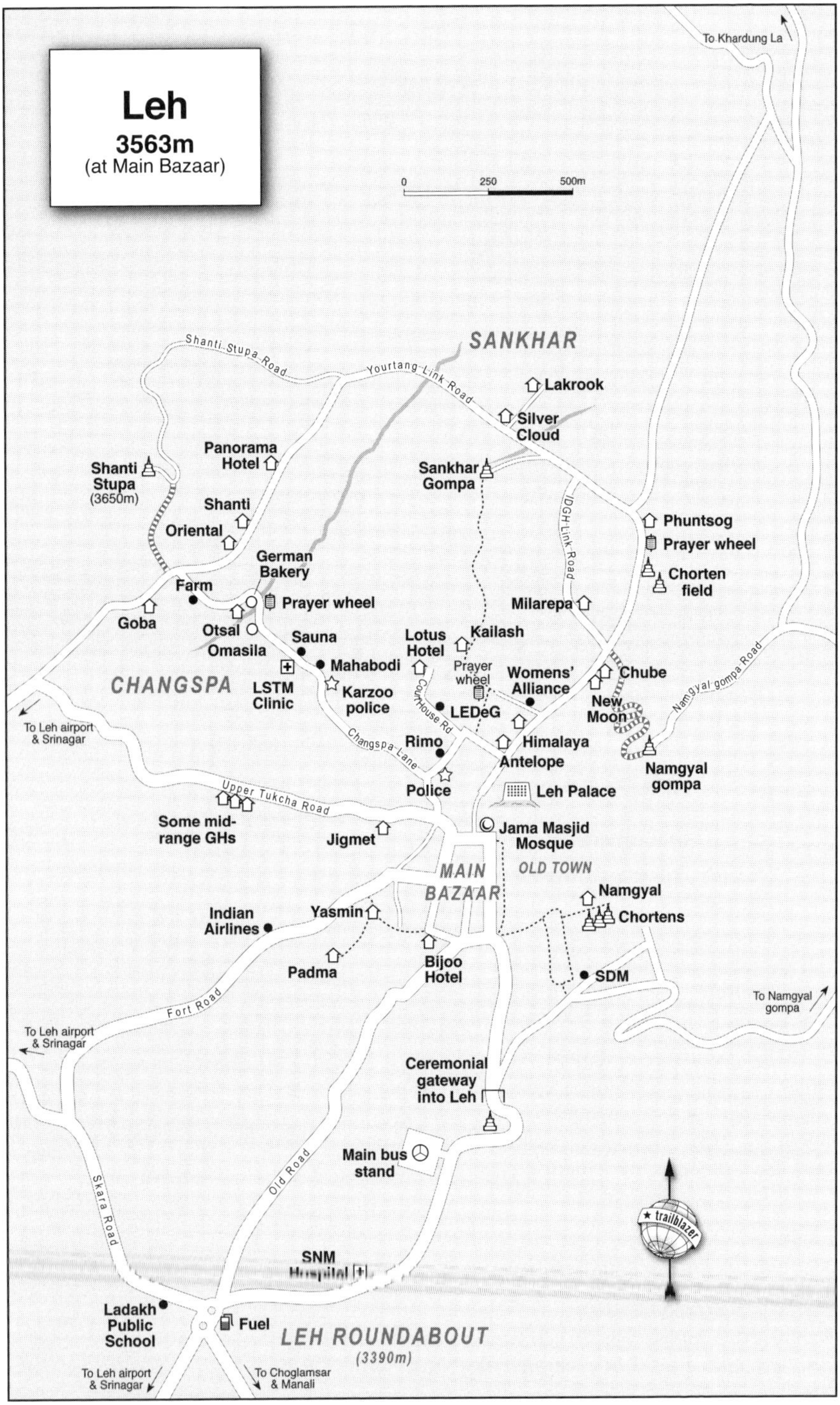
Leh
3563m
(at Main Bazaar)
0 250 500m
To Khardung La
SANKHAR
Shanti Stupa Road
Yourtang Link Road
Lakrook
Silver Cloud
Panorama Hotel
Shanti Stupa (3650m)
Sankhar Gompa
Shanti
Oriental
IDGH Link Road
Phuntsog
Prayer wheel
Chorten field
German Bakery
Farm
Prayer wheel
Milarepa
Goba
Otsal
Omasila
Sauna
Lotus Hotel
Kailash
Mahabodi
Prayer wheel
Womens' Alliance
Chube
Namgyal gompa Road
CHANGSPA
LSTM Clinic
Karzoo police
Court House Rd
LEDeG
New Moon
To Leh airport & Srinagar
Changspa Lane
Rimo
Himalaya
Antelope
Namgyal gompa
Police
Leh Palace
Upper Tukcha Road
Some mid-range GHs
Jigmet
Jama Masjid Mosque
MAIN BAZAAR
OLD TOWN
Namgyal
Indian Airlines
Yasmin
Chortens
Padma
Bijoo Hotel
SDM
Fort Road
To Namgyal gompa
To Leh airport & Srinagar
Ceremonial gateway into Leh
Main bus stand
Old Road
Skara Road
trailblazer
SNM
Ladakh Public School
Fuel
LEH ROUNDABOUT
(3390m)
To Leh airport & Srinagar
To Choglamsar & Manali

Delhi, then the airport is five kilometres southwest of the town. Beware of the altitude – if you're feeling the effects while waiting for your luggage it's better to take a taxi to a guesthouse (Leh Rs105, Changspa Rs136, Sankhar Rs152). If you're pedalling in on the Srinagar road just after the airport is the Tourist Reception Centre (Mon–Sat 10am-4pm; ☎ 01982 252 094).

Where to stay

During the summer many **Ladakhi families** turn their homes into cheap and cheerful guesthouses providing an excellent glimpse of local life and the chance to sample proper, home-cooked Ladakhi food. Nearly all guesthouses have gardens bursting with flowers and vegetables, and are set among barley fields with views over to Stok Kangri. **Mid-range** accommodation means a sit down toilet and hot water which comes from a tap not a bucket. **Top-end** accommodation is mostly poor value for money, with tatty rooms and indifferent staff. Delhi-run hotels will have facilities like a TV and phone; Ladakhi-run ones will concentrate more on traditional furnishings and a friendly atmosphere. **Fort Road** and the **Old Town** in Leh are the most convenient areas to stay if you've got stuff to do in town but howling packs of nocturnal dogs might ruin your sleep.

Changspa is a kilometre-and-a-half out of town and used to be a separate village, but it now has a big budget traveller and Enfield scene. **Sankhar**, a kilometre to the north and set amidst barley fields, is much quieter, though the guesthouses are a little more expensive.

An excellent local initiative is ***Himalayan Homestays*** (💻 www.himalayan-homestays.com) which is run by Rinchen Wangchuk of Snowleopard Conservancy. You'll see plenty of posters advertising it in Leh: half-board in a village costs Rs400 per person or Rs700 for a couple.

Budget ***Oriental*** in Changspa (☎ 01982 253 153) is a very popular guesthouse run by a friendly family in a quiet rural area on the edge of town. It serves filling homemade communal dinners (Rs75) has solar-powered showers and a pleasant outdoor garden. The rooms range from budget for Rs200 (com) to deluxe en suite at Rs750 and all are spotless. There's also an internet café. ***Lakrook Garden*** in Sankhar (☎ 01982 252 987) is a cosy traditional house with new (comfortable) and old (basic) rooms for Rs150-300. You get a sun-filled dining room, a solar-powered hot shower in the enormous flower and vegetable garden and one of the quietest locations in Leh. Tucked beside some huge chortens ***Namgyal*** in the Old Town (☎ 01982 253 307) is a cheap and friendly family guesthouse and an ideal base in town. A new block of rooms has en-suite bathrooms (including hot shower) for Rs300; rooms in the older block are Rs80/100 (downstairs) or Rs150 (upstairs) with common bathroom and hot bucket; there's also a lovely glass room (Rs180).

Ideally situated next to a German bakery ***Otsal*** in Changspa (☎ 01982 252 816), is run by Sonam Tsetan who has mapped every inch of Ladakh and is an invaluable source of information if you'd like to explore off-road. Double rooms are Rs250-300 (com), Rs400 (att). ***Shanti*** in Changspa (☎ 01982 253 084) is a clean, friendly place at the foot of the Shanti Stupa with singles from Rs80–150, doubles Rs200 (common bath) and en-suite doubles for Rs300–350 depending on the view. There are hot showers morning and evening, a communal dinner for Rs55 and a little flower-filled garden to relax in.

Mid-Range ***Padma*** in a lane off Fort Road (☎ 01982 252 630) is another Ladakhi-run guest house with large and sunny rooms (104, 105 and 107 are best) with common bathroom and cold shower for Rs500. Double rooms in the adjoining hotel aren't as good value at Rs2100 but do have powerful hot showers in the en-suite bathrooms and extra touches like reading lights. There's a large flower and vegetable garden with wicker chairs for lounging in and a rooftop terrace with a panoramic view.

Expensive ***Milarepa*** in Chubi (☎ 01982 253 218) is a family-run guesthouse with big doubles for Rs450-550 (com), an immaculately clean tiled bathroom with a hot shower. Their best room (Rs1000) is en-suite, beautifully furnished and has a wooden floor, thangkas on the walls and a window overlooking Stok Kangri. It is the most civilized room in Leh. There's also a traditional family room with low tables and TV for companionable lounging. A three-course dinner is Rs150.

If you're after the full works in a Delhi-run hotel ***Omasila*** in Changspa (☎ 01982 252 119) has a deluxe suite with carpet, TV, phone, soft bed, hot shower and even a sitting room for Rs3200. Double rooms for mere mortals are less spacious but do have access to a sun terrace and large garden. The food here isn't great.

Where to eat

All the guesthouses and hotels can offer a simple breakfast of Ladakhi bread, eggs and tea. For a more substantial (and expensive) start to the day, the seasonal garden cafés whip up a muesli, fruit, curd and honey concoction, while the German bakeries waft enticing smells of chocolate croissants, Danish pastries and cinnamon rolls. If you're interested in local food ask your guesthouse for some *chang* (beer) and *tsampa* (ground roasted barley).

On Fort Rd ***Gesmo*** is a cheap and cheerful have-a-go-at-anything restaurant but serves no alcohol ('officially') while the ***Lamayuru*** nearby is popular with locals and tourists alike for its Rs40 veg *thali* (a plate with separate compartments for an all-you-can-eat meal). The ***Penguin Bakery*** also on Fort Rd is pricey but has a winning combination of garden setting, free newspapers, croissants and filter coffee. Come evening this is a good spot for a beer or three. You'll need to book ahead in summer at the nearby ***Tibetan Kitchen*** as tour groups crowd this small restaurant and garden because they produce the best momos in Leh and have an excellent tandoor.

Fort Rd leads up past the covered vegetable market to the square by Main Bazaar. On the left opposite the square is ***Pumpernickel***, the oldest German bakery and still the cheapest and best; work your way along the shelves of pastries, cakes and croissants for a calorific feast. The bottom shelf of long-life breads and peanut butter cookies is ideal pannier food. Next to the bakery is the popular Pumpernickel restaurant. A little further up the hill is the ***Tibetan Restaurant***, known locally as Tashi's, which is a tiny and friendly restaurant next to the Yak Tail, half-hidden behind a tree. The menu is brief but the dishes are delicious, especially the mixed veg salad and Kashmiri qahwa tea.

In Main Bazaar the ***Golden Dragon*** looks ritzy by night but cheap by day with great food, friendly service and a rooftop terrace overlooking the bright lights of Leh (when there is electricity). Also on Main Bazaar, opposite the

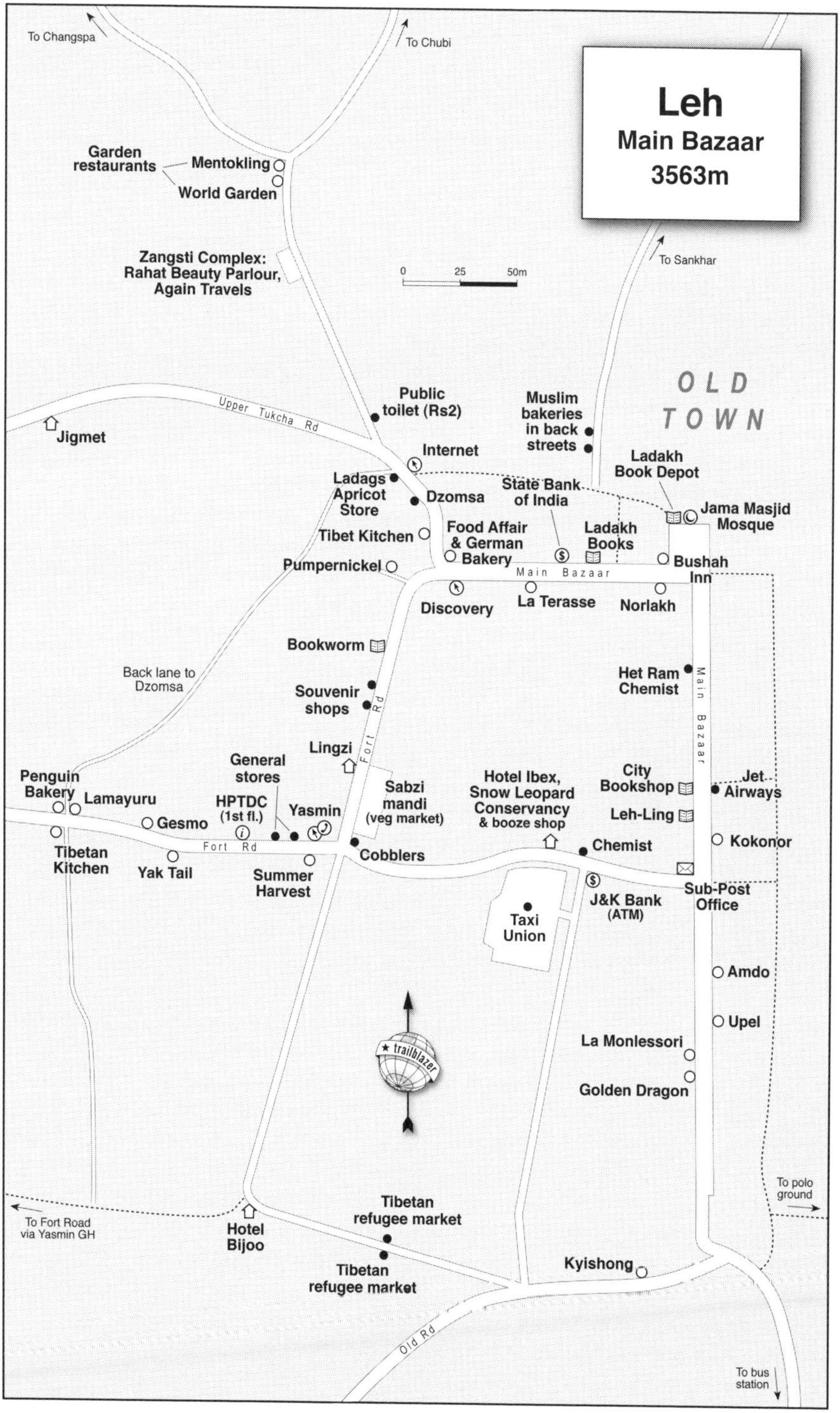
Leh
Main Bazaar
3563m
To Changspa
To Chubi
To Sankhar
Garden restaurants
Mentokling
World Garden
Zangsti Complex: Rahat Beauty Parlour, Again Travels
0 25 50m
OLD TOWN
Upper Tukcha Rd
Jigmet
Public toilet (Rs2)
Muslim bakeries in back streets
Internet
Ladakh Book Depot
Ladags Apricot Store
Dzomsa
State Bank of India
Jama Masjid Mosque
Tibet Kitchen
Food Affair & German Bakery
Ladakh Books
Pumpernickel
Bushah Inn
Main Bazaar
Discovery
La Terasse
Norlakh
Bookworm
Het Ram Chemist
Back lane to Dzomsa
Souvenir shops
Fort Rd
Lingzi
General stores
City Bookshop
Jet Airways
Penguin Bakery
Lamayuru
HPTDC (1st fl.)
Yasmin
Sabzi mandi (veg market)
Hotel Ibex, Snow Leopard Conservancy & booze shop
Leh-Ling
Gesmo
Kokonor
Tibetan Kitchen
Yak Tail
Summer Harvest
Cobblers
Chemist
Sub-Post Office
J&K Bank (ATM)
Taxi Union
Amdo
Upel
La Monlessori
Golden Dragon
trailblazer
To polo ground
To Fort Road via Yasmin GH
Hotel Bijoo
Tibetan refugee market
Tibetan refugee market
Kyishong
Old Rd
To bus station

MANALI-LEH HIGHWAY

Jama Masjid, ***Norlakh*** is one of Leh's older restaurants, serving up a warming breakfast of tsampa porridge with honey and banana or 'beached beans toast and egg'. The mains are a mix of Indian, Chinese and Ladakhi with a rainbow choice of momos including tasty spinach and cheese. Just north of Main Bazaar, towards Changspa, the ***Mentokling*** is a cut above the other garden restaurants with its a wood-fired oven for tasty pizzas.

Moving on

By air Jet Airways (💻 www.jetairways.com), Indian Airlines (💻 http://indian- airlines.nic.in) and Air Deccan (💻 www.flyairdeccan.net) operate routes to Leh, connecting it to Chandigarh, Delhi, Jammu and Srinagar. Flights into and out of Leh are frequently cancelled due to the weather and in peak season (June–Sept) the waiting list for flights has been known to run into the hundreds. Tour groups will always take priority over individual passengers even if you have an international flight connection.

The direct Jet Airways flights from Leh to Delhi are the most over-booked and the most likely to be cancelled. Ways around this are to fly with Indian Airlines instead (their office is on Fort Road) or to fly via Jammu, Chandigarh or Srinagar. You don't have to get off the plane before taking off again for Delhi. Both Jet and Indian Airlines will fly bicycles unboxed, and both have a 30kg luggage allowance. You'll be expected to put your bike and luggage through the security check before queuing up at the check-in counter.

By bus or 4WD If you're intending to fly out but the flights are overbooked and you can't get a seat, a last-minute dash from Leh to Manali is possible albeit unpleasant (22 hours by jeep, dep Leh 2am, arr Manali 12am) and from Manali to Delhi (15 hours; dep Manali 4pm; arr Delhi 7am). It's a total of 53 hours in transit but you're guaranteed to arrive. It's cheapest to negotiate directly with a jeep driver; you'll find them down at Leh's bus stand. Also at the bus stand are the local buses, minibuses and separate booths for the long-distance government and private buses to Kashmir and Himachal Pradesh.

If you're catching a jeep ensure that it's a 4WD Qualis not a Tata Sumo (the ticket price is the same for both). Jeeps can squeeze in up to seven foreigners (double that for locals); the price ranges from Rs1200 to Rs1500 depending on where you sit (front being most expensive).

To Manali The road is 'officially' open (meaning there are road workers on it) from 15 June to 15 September. State government buses only travel while it's officially open – everyone else will try their luck for as long as they can before the passes become snowbound. The road is impassable from late October though vehicles have been stranded between Taglang La and Rohtang La due to heavy snow as early as the first week of October. The most comfortable buses are run by Himachal Tourism (HPTDC) whose office is on Fort Road.

To Srinagar The Srinagar–Leh Highway is open from 15 May to 15 November but this is subject to the weather. Kashmir and the Zoji La receive far heavier snowfall than the drier areas south of Manali. J&K State Road Transport Corporation (J&KSRTC) runs a regular Super Deluxe, A & B class bus service between Srinagar and Leh from the bus stand (☎ 01982 252 085).

RIDES AROUND LEH

Six day ride to Pangong Tso and the Nubra Valley (permit required, see p156)

Start–Finish	Distance	Max	Road conditions
Leh–Tak Tok	47km	3886m	Tarmac
Tak Tok–Tangtse over Chang La*	70km	5328m	Broken road
Tangtse–Pangong Tso–Tangtse	60km	4323m	Broken road
Tangtse–Tak Tok over Chang La	70km	5337m	Broken road
Tak Tok–Khalsar over Wari La	87km	5330m	Sand and rock
Khalsar–Leh via Khardung La*	93km	5353m	Broken road

Six day ride to Tso Moriri and Tso Kar (permit required, see p156)

Start–Finish	Distance	Max	Road conditions
Leh–Likse*	68km	3570m	Tarmac
Likse–Chumatang	70km	4068m	Tarmac
Chumatang–Puga	35km	4447m	Tarmac
Puga–Tso Moriri over Namshang La*	42km	4825m	Sand
Tso Moriri–Puga over Namshang La*	42km	4825m	Sand
Puga–Tso Kar over Polo Gongka	45km	4873m	Sand, track

* Days your Inner Line Permit will be checked.

Services

• **Banks** The State Bank of India is on Main Bazaar (April–Oct: Mon–Fri 10am–4pm, Sat 10am–4pm; Nov–Mar: Mon–Fri 10.30am–4.30pm, Sat 10.30am–1.30pm). The J&K Forex is on Main Bazaar (April–Oct: Mon–Fri 10am–2pm, Sat 10am–noon; Nov–Mar: Mon–Fri 10.30am–2.30pm, Sat 10.30am–12.30pm); its ATM is around the corner, opposite the taxi rank.

• **Bike Hire** Adventures in Zangsti Complex have some clunky town bikes (Rs150/day); Rimo Expeditions opposite the police station have some better Hero Thunderbird MTBs for Rs400/day (Rs300/day if you rent for a week). Check the gears shift properly and inspect the brake pad wear and alignment before leaving.

• **Bike Repair** Moti Market on the road between Main Bazaar and the bus station has a lane of local bike shops. Mechanics here are used to foreigners trailing damaged steeds and will have a bash (literally) at mending derailleurs, etc. Another option is to trawl the cafés and guesthouses for other touring cyclists with bike parts and mechanical skills. For repairing steel frames and damaged trailers there are plenty of welding workshops on Airport Rd just past the General Post Office.

• **Bookshops** Bookworm on Old Fort Road has a good selection of second-hand paperback novels and offers a refund on books returned in good condition. For photographic books about Ladakh and Tibet try Leh-Ling or City Bookshop on Main Bazaar or Ladakh Bookshop on the main square. If you're interested in Buddhism and Vipassana meditation the Mahabodhi Meditation Centre in Changspa has a collection of texts for sale in their first floor library.

• **Chemist** Het Ram Vinay Kumar on Main Bazaar sells antibiotics, ORS sachets, Tampax and other sponge-bag fillers.

• **Dentist** Dr Phuntsok Norboo near the booze shop opposite the taxi stand.

• **Doctor** Dr Tashi Thinles is an excellent allopathic doctor (☎ clinic 01982 255 109; ☎ res 01982 253 143). There's also an English-speaking *amchi* (traditional Tibetan medical doctor) at the LSTM Clinic (mid-June–mid-Sept, daily 7am–8.30pm; mid-Sep–mid-June, Mon–Fri 10am–4pm) on Changspa Road opposite the Mahabodhi Meditation Centre. Payment by donation.

• **Food** For fruit and veg visit Sabze Mandi. There's a smattering of general stores among the handicraft emporiums on Fort Road and Main Bazaar; the best jams are from the Ladags store by Dzomsa and the Pumpernickel Bakery sells long-life bread and cookies.

• **Hospital** The government-run Sonam Norboo Memorial (SNM) Hospital (casualty ☎ 01982 252 360) is chaotic but will do stool tests and treatment is free. Consultations are from 10am-2pm.

• **Internet Access** Wherever you go the connections are excruciatingly slow and expensive (Rs120/hr) but currently the most reliable are ECafé on Fort Road, Julley Net Café on Main Bazaar (first floor, below Golden Dragon) and Discovery Café opposite the State Bank of India.

• **Laundry** If your guesthouse doesn't do laundry, use eco-friendly Dzomsa (daily 8am-8pm; Rs60/kg) on the corner of Old Fort and Main Tukcha roads.

• **Library** The Leh District Library (Mon–Sat 10am–4pm) on Library Road has some dusty books on Ladakh; more appealing is the extensive collection at the Ecology Centre library (Mon–Sat 10am–4pm).

• **Meditation and Yoga** The Mahabodhi Meditation Centre on Changspa Lane runs yoga and meditation sessions during the summer. Visiting teachers will also run classes at their guesthouses (check for their flyers at the bakeries).

• **Permits** Restricted areas such as Nubra Valley (including Khardung La), Tso Moriri, Pangong Tso and Dha Hanu require a **permit**, easily arranged through a travel agent. Hand over your passport by 10am, pay around Rs100 and you'll have the permit by 4pm. Officially you should be in a group of four but if you're not the travel agent will add some imaginary friends to the paperwork.

• **Police** On Changspa Lane; see Leh map p153 (☎ 01982 252 018).

• **Post office** Main Bazaar (Mon–Sat 10am–4.30pm). For sending parcels and for Post Restante use the GPO, 1.5km out on the road to Srinagar (same times).

• **Taxis** There's a pre-paid counter at the airport and union offices at the bus stand and opposite the Hotel Ibex. All taxis carry a comprehensive rate list – ask to see it before agreeing on a price. If you find a driver you like, for a better price deal with him direct rather than through the union.

• **Travel Agencies** If you're interested in trekking, rafting or need to organize a **permit** for visiting restricted areas there's no shortage of travel agencies. We recommend Tsunder at Footprints Himalaya, Raku Complex, Fort Road (☎ 01982 251 799; 💻 www.footprintsindia.com).

THE RIDE TO KHARDUNG LA

No ride from Manali to Leh used to be complete without attempting to conquer the self-proclaimed 'World's Highest Motorable Road', Khardung La (see box below). For cyclists it did seem too good to be true: far from being a remote rough track marooned in some inaccessible border region it is instead a tarmac day's ride from that hub of German bakeries, Leh.

However, if it still appeals or if you want to visit the magnificent Nubra Valley which lies beyond, then firstly you will need an Inner Line Permit (available in a day from travel agents in Leh for about Rs100). The 75km return trip takes about eight hours unloaded (six up, two down) and the road at the top where a small café sells chai has the consistency of muesli. The Nubra Valley is home to the Siachen Glacier, sand dunes and Bactrian camels. On a good day you can see the Karakoram Range, rising to the north-west in Pakistan.

While tourism numbers increase in Ladakh every year, for an Indian soldier this region is the ultimate punishment posting. Riders to Khardung La may meet soldiers on their way to the Siachen Glacier, currently claimed by both India and Pakistan. Since 1984 soldiers have been posted on the glacier and its surrounding ridges, which at over 6000m makes this the highest and coldest battlefield in the world. Actual fighting is sporadic but the politicians in Delhi and Islamabad continue to wrangle despite four out of five fatalities being due to the altitude, weather and terrain. Meanwhile Indian soldiers acclimatize for a week near Leh before enduring a three month tour of duty on Siachen in temperatures as low as -60°C.

THE HIGHEST ROAD IN THE WORLD?

The pass sign at the summit of the Khardung La reads: 'World's Highest Motorable Road, Alt. 18,380 ft' (5602m). Many cyclists have photographed themselves beside this sign as proof that they've bagged the big one. However, this pass was accurately measured in 2005 using GPS and SRTM* data, and the accepted height is now 5359m. The Taglang La on the Manali–Leh highway is 5360m, one metre higher than the Khardung La!

Is the Taglang La the world's highest cyclable road? An unsurfaced track so bad that an unladen mountain bike needs to be pushed to the top surely doesn't count. High altitude roads need regular maintenance or they quickly disintegrate so the situation is always fluid. Another famously high road in southern Bolivia went up to a sulphur mine at about 5900m on the volcano Uturuncu. At one time this was undoubtedly the world's highest road but in 2005 we found that above 5200m much of the ascent was unrideable. The road was blocked to motor vehicles by a landslide at about 5600m and vanished completely at about 5750m, well below the abandoned mine.

Three other "highest road" contenders are the Marsimik Pass (sign 5590m, 5582m by SRTM), about fifty kilometres east of Leh (N34°05′ E78°37′) and two Tibetan passes, the Po Bu La, 5767m (N32°19′ E78°59′) and the Sha Ra La, 5761m (N32°03′ E78°53′). But these are all probably in very poor condition. The Po Bu La road in particular is described as having been destroyed by snow and ice within just a couple of years of its construction in 1997. All three of these roads are close to the disputed border between India and China and are not legally accessible to Western tourists.

Tibet has many passes above 5000m including the Semo La at 5565m (N30°06′ E85°26′), which is known to be cyclable, and the 5578-metre Lo La at (N29°55′ E86°42′). The Lo La is about 150km north of Cho Oyu (the world sixth highest mountain) and was cycled by Dane, Martin Adserballe (🖳 www.adserballe.com) in 2006. Martin's photos show a very convincing road.

Presently (August 2008) the ironically misnamed Lo La has the strongest claim to be the world's highest road and depending on whether the Taglang La or Khardung La is higher, one of these is probably the world's highest bit of tarmac.

Steve Pells

* Shuttle Radar Topography Mission. A very accurate radar survey of the earth carried out from the Space Shuttle in 2000.

4 LEH-SRINAGAR HWY

ROUTE INFORMATION

- **Start / finish** Leh / Srinagar (Jammu & Kashmir, India)
- **Distance** 437km
- **Altitude min / max** 1626m/4105m
- **High passes** Three
- **Suggested duration** Minimum 7 days riding; allow 12 days with flights + acclimatization
- **Road conditions** All tarmac except for sections of Zoji La pass
- **Hazards and dangers** Dangerous in times of military activity: check latest situation (see below)
- **When to go** Mid-May to mid-November
- **Visas** Required for India

Once rivalling Manali–Leh as the classic ride of the Indian Himalaya, the Leh–Srinagar Highway has been cast into shadow by continuing political tensions in Kashmir. The road, which skirts the Line of Control between India and Pakistan, has been the target of Pakistani shelling and crossfire and until 2004 bombs and shootings were common between Drass and Kargil. Srinagar itself is wracked by Pakistani-funded militancy which the oppressive Indian army presence cannot contain. The road is heavily militarized with increasingly frequent police checkpoints as you approach Srinagar. The upside of this is an excellent tarmac surface passing through a stunning landscape of pea-green glacial rivers, crumpled mountainsides the texture of rhino hide and the wonderful *gompas* (monasteries) of Lamayuru, Alchi, Likkir and Basgo. West of the Zoji La the stark Ladakhi landscape softens into the beautiful Vale of Kashmir.

FACTS ABOUT THE REGION

Relations between India and Pakistan are volatile and in times of tension this road should be avoided. Since the 2004 ceasefire shelling and firing on Drass and Kargil has stopped, but **militant activity in Kashmir continues to be unpredictable and brutal**. Foreigners have been targeted and even murdered by militants so keep up with current affairs if you're thinking of riding to Srinagar. Newspapers such as the *Times of India, Indian Express* and *Hindustan Times* all carry stories of unrest in the region. In Leh you can buy copies of the *Kashmiri Times* or talk to the many Kashmiris there who can tell you whether it's safe to travel, though bear in mind that they are keen for tourists to return to Kashmir. So is the Srinagar Tourist Office who euphemistically described its own bombing as 'a fire'. Quite apart from militancy between Leh and

Kargil there is on average one serious accident a day as overloaded trucks topple off the narrow road.

Anyone wishing to explore the little-visited region of Dha Hanu near Kargil will need to organize an Inner Line Permit in Leh (see p156).

History of the road

Until the nineteenth century a rough trade route led from Srinagar to Leh then onwards over the Karakoram into Yarkand (China). From the 1870s, when the British opened a trading office in Leh and negotiated a treaty with the Maharaja of Kashmir which designated the route as being free for commercial travel, this route became known as 'The Treaty Road'. In 1947 after independence the Indian government commissioned the Border Roads Organization (BRO) to build a proper road between Leh and Srinagar, BRO's first ever project, and in 1960 BRO set to work clearing the way at Zoji La. The Leh–Srinagar Highway is now a national highway (NH-1D) and in the near future will be widened to dual carriageway.

Language and religion

English is understood by most people along the highway, as is **Hindi**. Signs from Kargil onwards are in English and Urdu. Up to Mulbekh the predominant religion is **Buddhism**; from Mulbekh onwards it's **Islam**. Kashmiri Muslims are more relaxed than the Shia Muslims of Kargil and the nearby Suru Valley.

PRACTICAL INFORMATION

Which direction?

Most people prefer to start from Leh and celebrate arriving in Srinagar by living it up on a houseboat but in this direction what the highway lacks in ascent it more than makes up for in headwinds. Traffic travels in convoys up Zoji La (see box p173) but bicycles don't count, thankfully, as the set-off time from Minamarg is 4am.

Accommodation, food and money

Camping kit will only slow you down on this ride as **guesthouses** can be found every night along the way and the houseboats in Srinagar make a grand finale to the trip. Beyond Kargil **camping** is not recommended.

This ride is not an easy one for vegetarians or gourmands. Up to Mulbekh the food is **Ladakhi** with dishes such as momos, *thenthuk* (noodle soup in vegetable broth), dahl and rice. Beyond Mulbekh the cuisine has a heavy emphasis on meat, especially mutton. Beyond Kargil there are only a few tea stalls between the towns en route offering Maggi noodles and biscuits. Alcohol is readily bought in Leh but prohibited in Muslim areas: go to expensive hotels if you want a beer.

There are **ATMs** in Leh and Srinagar but no ATM in Kargil where only hotels offer foreign exchange (at a poor rate) so **take enough rupees for the whole ride**. Budget travellers can reckon on spending around $10 per day. See p32 for exchange rate information.

Getting to the ride

For **Leh** see p128. From Delhi, Jammu and Mumbai you can **fly** daily to Srinagar with Indian Airlines (💻 www.indian-airlines.nic.in) and Jet Airways

IS ALL REALLY EQUAL?

From Leh to Srinagar the role of the Indian Army becomes ever less benign. Soldiers in Leh are relaxed if not bored, whereas by Srinagar they're half-hidden by sandbags and barbed wire and always carrying guns. Ladakh is regarded throughout India as a punishment posting and is the butt of many jokes, but once soldiers are here the army does try to ensure parity. Each unit is deliberately comprised of soldiers from all over India and any well-trained soldier will tell you the army's recruitment slogan: "No region, no religion, no caste, no creed – all is equal". Rather like another superpower, India justifies the presence of its army in Kashmir by saying it's trying to win 'hearts and minds'. Amnesty International instead reports 'enforced disappearances' and the apparent impunity of the Indian army in this region has led to widespread resentment.

(www.jetairways.com). Air Deccan (www.airdeccan.com), Spice Jet (www.spicejet.com) and Kingfisher Airlines (www.flykingfisher.com) also fly to Srinagar from various cities including Delhi, Bangalore, Kolkata and Varanasi. From Delhi to Srinagar one-way costs around $90. Luggage allowance for all airlines is 30kg and security at Srinagar airport is strict. A J&K government bus shuttles between the airport and the Tourist Reception Centre (TRC), otherwise a taxi costs around Rs250.

A Jammu & Kashmir State Road Transport Corporation (J&KSRTC) deluxe **bus** takes about 11hrs from Jammu to Srinagar and costs Rs275. An express J&KSRTC bus travels from Connaught Place in Delhi to Srinagar in 26hrs for Rs835, as does an a/c sleeper bus for Rs1500, both are bookable from the J&KSRTC Office, Kanishka Shopping Plaza, Ashok Road, New Delhi. Note that cyclists are not allowed to ride through the 2.5km Jawahar Tunnel on NH1A between Jammu and Srinagar.

Once you're ready to leave Srinagar note that the airport has extremely tight security so allow at least half an hour for vehicle and luggage checks. Cyclists with boxed bikes can prevent them being opened by requesting the 'dog wallah'. The Kashmir **Railway** from Jammu to Srinagar, under construction since 2002 with no expense spared, is currently set to open in 2009.

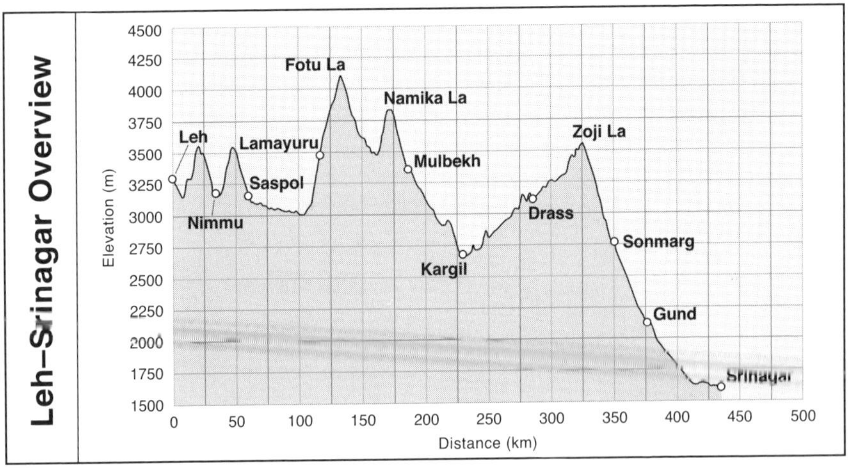

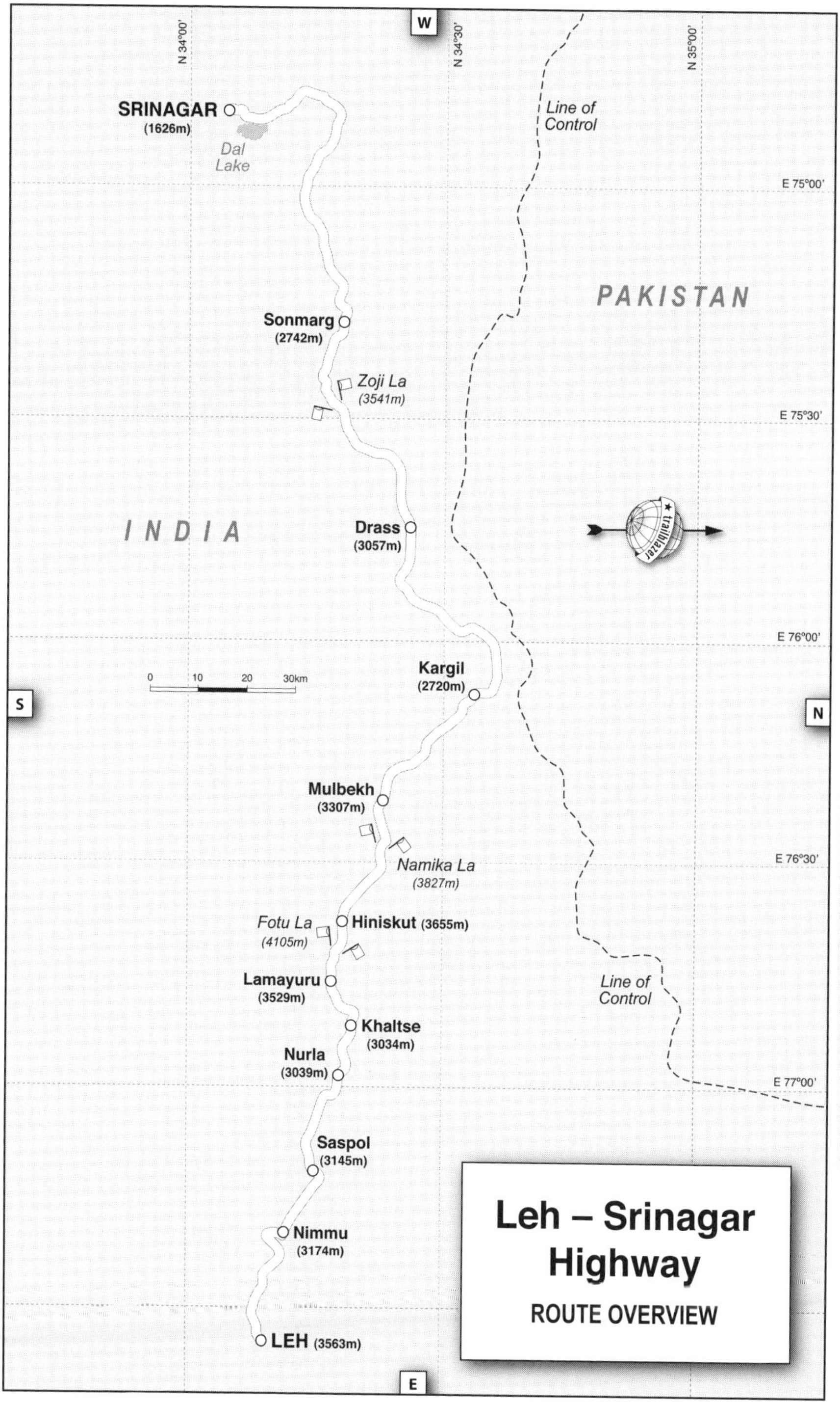

LEH – SRINAGAR

Route guide – Leh to Srinagar

DAY 1 LEH (3563m) to SASPOL (3145m) 61KM

LEH–NIMMU 35KM
NIMMU–BASGO 6.5KM
BASGO–SASPOL 19.5KM

Leh (3563m) 0/437KM
From Leh's petrol station roundabout there's an easy 10km coast past the airport, an army 'Hall of Fame' and endless military outposts, followed by a climb onto a large shoulder of alluvial deposit. The highway here is nothing but a thin ribbon of tarmac surrounded by space and mountain and this section can be hot and shadeless.

Magnetic Hill (3391m) This small stretch is famed for the fact that if a stationary vehicle is left unbraked it will magically roll uphill. Sadly for those on cro-mo bikes it's neither the hill's 'magnetism' or even the gradient performing the feat. The layout of the surrounding land instead produces the optical illusion that what's actually a very slight downhill slope appears to be the opposite.

Just after Magnetic Hill the blue Zanskar River runs into the pea-green Indus. The road is high above the river and near the turn-off to Chilling it's often possible to see rafters bobbing around down below. The mountain flanks are strange hues of grey, green and purple and villages on this stretch come as splashes of green amongst this arid landscape.

Nimmu (3174m) 35/402KM
About 800m beyond the village is the *Lee Gardon* restaurant which serves good Chinese and Indian food outside in the shade. Nimmu village is surrounded by fields of barley and alfalfa and during the late summer harvest villagers totter along the highway under enormous loads of hay for insulating their homes and feeding the livestock during winter.

Basgo (3205m) 41.5/395.5KM
A climb of 7km in three stages starts in Basgo; the first section is past a strangely eroded roadside rock face and the village's ancient fort, then along hairpins behind the ridge and finally up onto the shoulder of an alluvial fan.

If you have energy to spare a link road of about 2.5km leads from the highway up to Basgo fort on its burgundy coloured bluff. Basgo was the capital of Ladakh from 1445 to 1650 and its fort is now under restoration. Although there's nothing to see inside, the view from the roof is great.

Likkir turn-off As the road starts to drop off the plateau there's a turn-off (4.7km) to Likkir. You can't miss Likkir gompa (summer 8am–1pm, 2–6pm) – it's got an enormous gold Buddha sitting on it. As the village is off the highway the simple ***Dolkar Guesthouse*** 200m uphill from the gompa is a peaceful place with an outside toilet and friendly family (B&B Rs150). After the turn-off the highway switchbacks down into a grassy valley, crosses a stream and continues downhill all the way to Saspol.

Saspol (3145m) 61/376KM
The ***Alchi View Guesthouse*** opposite a small general shop charges Rs300 (com) for a sunny triple room. About 800m before the Alchi View is a basic ***no-name restaurant*** next to the State Bank of India branch.

Alchi itself, a small village famous for its gompa and beautiful twelfth-century wall paintings, is 4.5km further on across the Indus. The gompa is open to visitors

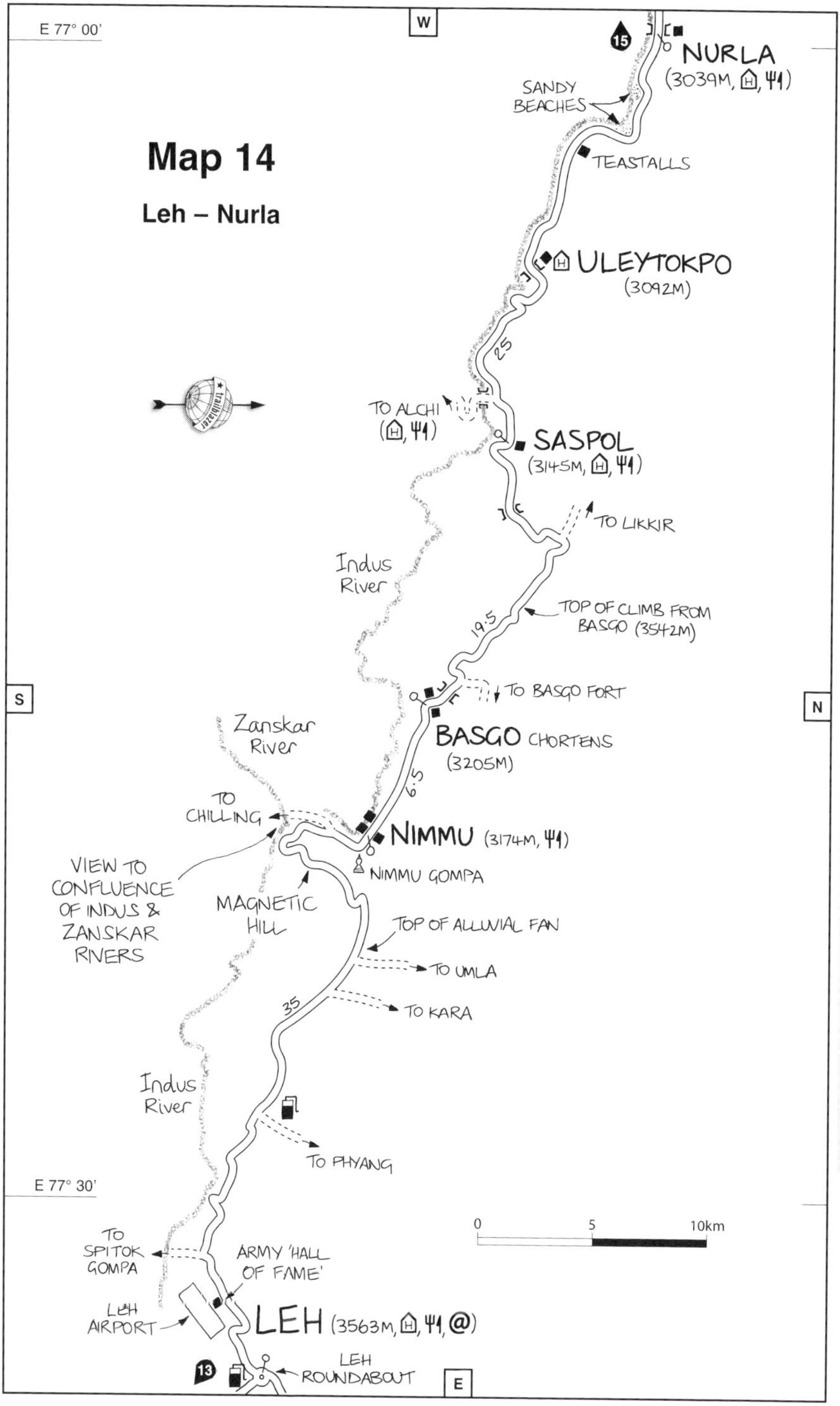
Map 14
Leh – Nurla
E 77° 00'
E 77° 30'
W
S
N
E
NURLA
(3039M, H, ΨΙ)
SANDY BEACHES
TEASTALLS
ULEYTOKPO
(3092M)
25
TO ALCHI
(H, ΨΙ)
SASPOL
(3145M, H, ΨΙ)
TO LIKKIR
Indus River
TOP OF CLIMB FROM BASGO (3542M)
19.5
TO BASGO FORT
BASGO CHORTENS
(3205M)
Zanskar River
6.5
TO CHILLING
NIMMU (3174M, ΨΙ)
NIMMU GOMPA
VIEW TO CONFLUENCE OF INDUS & ZANSKAR RIVERS
MAGNETIC HILL
TOP OF ALLUVIAL FAN
TO UMLA
TO KARA
35
Indus River
TO PHYANG
0
5
10km
TO SPITOK GOMPA
ARMY 'HALL OF FAME'
LEH AIRPORT
LEH (3563M, H, ΨΙ, @)
LEH ROUNDABOUT
15
13

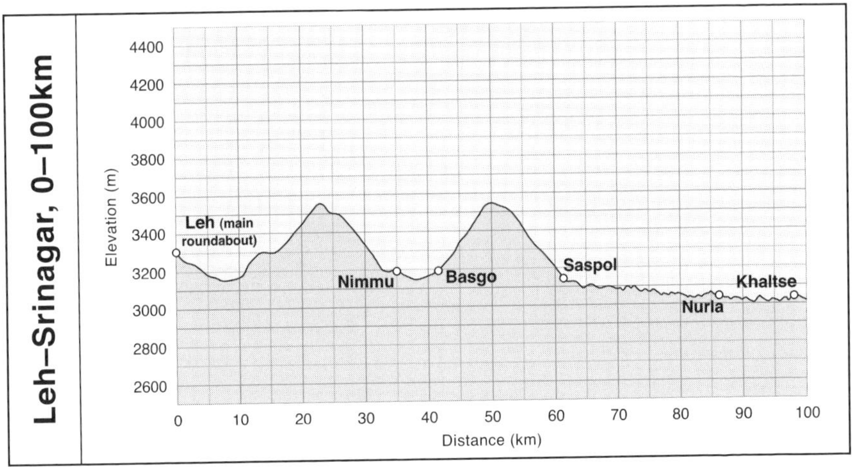

daily from 9am–6pm (Rs25). Alchi has a few guesthouses of its own with restaurants and even a small beach on the Indus (follow the path at the back of the gompa).

DAY 2 SASPOL (3145m) to LAMAYURU (3529m) 57KM

SASPOL–NURLA 25KM
NURLA–KHALTSE 12KM
KHALTSE–LAMAYURU 20KM

From the Alchi bridge the road is a fantastic roller-coaster past multicoloured scree slopes of aubergine and pink rocks alongside the green-blue Indus. Ridges and fins of rock pop out from the hillsides, only occasionally tamed by the poplars and apricot groves of a village. There are a couple of temptingly sandy beaches en route but both have army camps directly above.

Nurla (3039m) 86/351KM
Set besides a roaring tributary, the ***Faryork Restaurant*** is a great place to relax with a Kingfisher beer and watch the Tata trucks rumble past. There are also rooms here for Rs300 (att) as Nurla is the roadhead for the

THE INDUS RIVER

The river from which India and its major religion take their name rises near Lake Mansarovar at the foot of Mt Kailash in Tibet. Along its 2900km length it's fed by the mountain ranges of the Karakoram, Hindu Kush and Himalaya, and thus fortified it flows through Ladakh, Kashmir, Baltistan and through the plains of Pakistan before emptying into the Arabian Sea near Karachi. What we know as the Indus, from the Sanskrit 'Sindh' or 'stream', the Tibetans call 'Sengge Chu' or 'lion river' and the Pathans 'Abasin' or 'father of rivers'.

Archaeological evidence reveals that people lived in the Indus Valley as long ago as 13,000BC. By 3,300BC, while Britain was in the Stone Age, entire cities such as Harappa (in modern-day Pakistan) were starting to flourish. Three thousand years later the troops of Alexander the Great followed the Indus downstream to bring them home at the end of their Indian campaign. Today the Indus is vital for the agriculture and economy of Pakistan, a dependency which Pakistan fears India could exploit despite both countries signing the Indus Water Treaty in 1960. The Karakoram Highway (see p66) follows the river from near Talechi through the high gorges of Indus Kohistan to the Tarbela Dam just north of Islamabad.

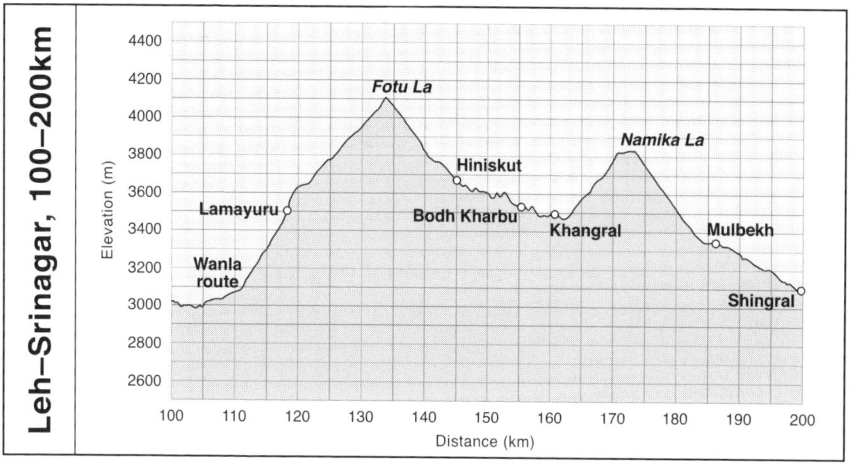

popular Likkir–Temisgang trek. This is a better place to eat at than Khaltse.

Khaltse (3034m) **98/339KM**

This flyblown, dusty army town has a few grubby **restaurants** along its bazaar starting with a cheap samosa place on the left, then on the right a no-name momo joint with a tree growing through the roof, and finally the ***Indus*** restaurant just beyond which sells sweets, cold drinks and *thali* (a plate with separate compartments for an all-you-can-eat meal).

Beyond Khaltse the road forks at a checkpoint. The right-hand fork leads to Dha Hanu – a little-visited region of Dards for which an Inner Line Permit is required. The left fork leads on to Lamayuru and the Indus. The road winds through a small boulder-strewn valley before leaving the Indus (which heads off for Pakistan) and turning south alongside the Wanlah River. The Jalebi Bends (see box below) come into view high above. If the sight of them makes you wince turn left at the T-junction for the shorter (11km), new road to Lamayuru. It's on this lower road that you'll ride through a section of the sandstone 'moonscape' Lamayuru is renowned for, as well as seeing the classic view of Lamayuru gompa on its crag.

Lamayuru (3529m) **118/319KM**

Lamayuru gompa, perched upon its pinnacle, gazes down on a village which is surprisingly undeveloped considering this is one of Ladakh's top tourist destinations. A footpath leads straight up from the chai shops to the gompa, past the village post box and yaks being shooed from their pens to the fields. Full of naughty young monks, the gompa is a timeless warren which comes to life during the morning and evening *pujas* (religious ceremonies).

THE JALEBI BENDS

Turn right at the T-junction for the older, longer (26km) road up to Lamayuru which is nicknamed the Jalebi Bends after an Indian sweet, a deep-fried day-glo orange doodle of syrup-sodden batter. This road to Lamayuru boasts 23 bends across the most extraordinary landscape you can possibly imagine. The initial bends are quite short before looping around to inspect themselves and curling off around the valley to loop themselves even more languorously up another mountain flank. And all the time they look out onto 'The Brain' – a face of creamy sandstone carved by water and wind into whorls and hummocks, rivulets and craters. Most drivers prefer the easier Wanlah route so cyclists tackling the Jalebi Bends can expect a peaceful ride.

The village itself is spread out over the road's switchbacks. The Wanlah road approaches from below past the chai shops and the Jalebi Bends road drops down from above. There are guesthouses throughout the village like the friendly ***Dragon Guesthouse*** near the chai shops which has double rooms for Rs200 (com) but there are cheaper guesthouses higher up the highway such as the ***Shangri La*** which charges Rs150. Next to the monastery the characterless ***Niranjana Hotel***, a recent construction which dwarfs the gompa itself, is only recommended for its hot showers. The concrete rooms are cold and overpriced at Rs100 for a dorm bed and Rs700 (com) for a double.

DAY 3 LAMAYURU (3529m) to MULBEKH (3307m) over Fotu La (4105m) and Namika La (3827m) 68.5KM

LAMAYURU–FOTU LA 15KM
FOTU LA–HINISKUT 12KM
HINISKUT–BODH KHARBU 10KM
BODH KHARBU–KHANGRAL 6KM
KHANGRAL–NAMIKA LA 10KM
NAMIKA LA–MULBEKH 15.5KM

The spectacular 15km climb to Fotu La spirals up through a landscape of rounded hills and rocky spurs. About 10km from Lamayuru a tongue of sediment from green to pink and purple to silver, sticks out towards the road. Adrift in this otherworldly landscape is a lone farm, a tiny patch of green with dry-stone walls, corrals and stacks of hay. The climb takes a couple of hours so take enough water and food as there are no tea stalls on the way.

Fotu La (4105m) 133/304KM

Congratulations! You've climbed the highest pass on the Leh–Srinagar Highway, though if you started from Manali you're probably not even out of breath. The prayer flags will confirm your suspicions; there's a wind and it's not at your back. The ranges visible from the pass are outriders of the Zanskar Range. The descent leads past a beautiful gorge (the start of a seven-day trek to Chilling) into the cultivated valley of the Kanji River.

Hiniskut (3655m) 145/292KM

There's no village at the '0km' sign; the best bet for a Coke and some Maggi (but not mineral water) is the ***tea stall*** a few kilometres along the descent from the pass. During the September harvest the few shops are boarded up as the owners help out in the fields. All through this valley the faces reflect the differing ethnic groups: narrow, hazel-eyed Kashmiris and the broader, high cheekboned Ladakhis. Suddenly 'jullay' feels out of place; it's time to start practising 'salaam aleikum' (peace be with you) and its response, 'wa aleikum salaam' (and also with you).

Bodh Kharbu (3546m) 155/282KM

On the spur three kilometres before Bodh Kharbu a few ***chai shops*** sell Maggi, snacks, biscuits, soft drinks and mineral water – the best option for food in this valley. There's also a general store in the village itself. Already the character of the villages has changed; there are fewer flowers, most homes are bare instead of whitewashed mud-brick, Urdu is scrawled on the walls and signs in English warn against AIDS. Try to ride through this valley during school-time because at other times the children are notorious for chasing bicycles shouting "one pen, one pen" and throwing stones when they don't get one, however amiable you are about it. Here, as in Pakistan, many adults regard begging from foreigners as acceptable so don't look to them for relief but know at least

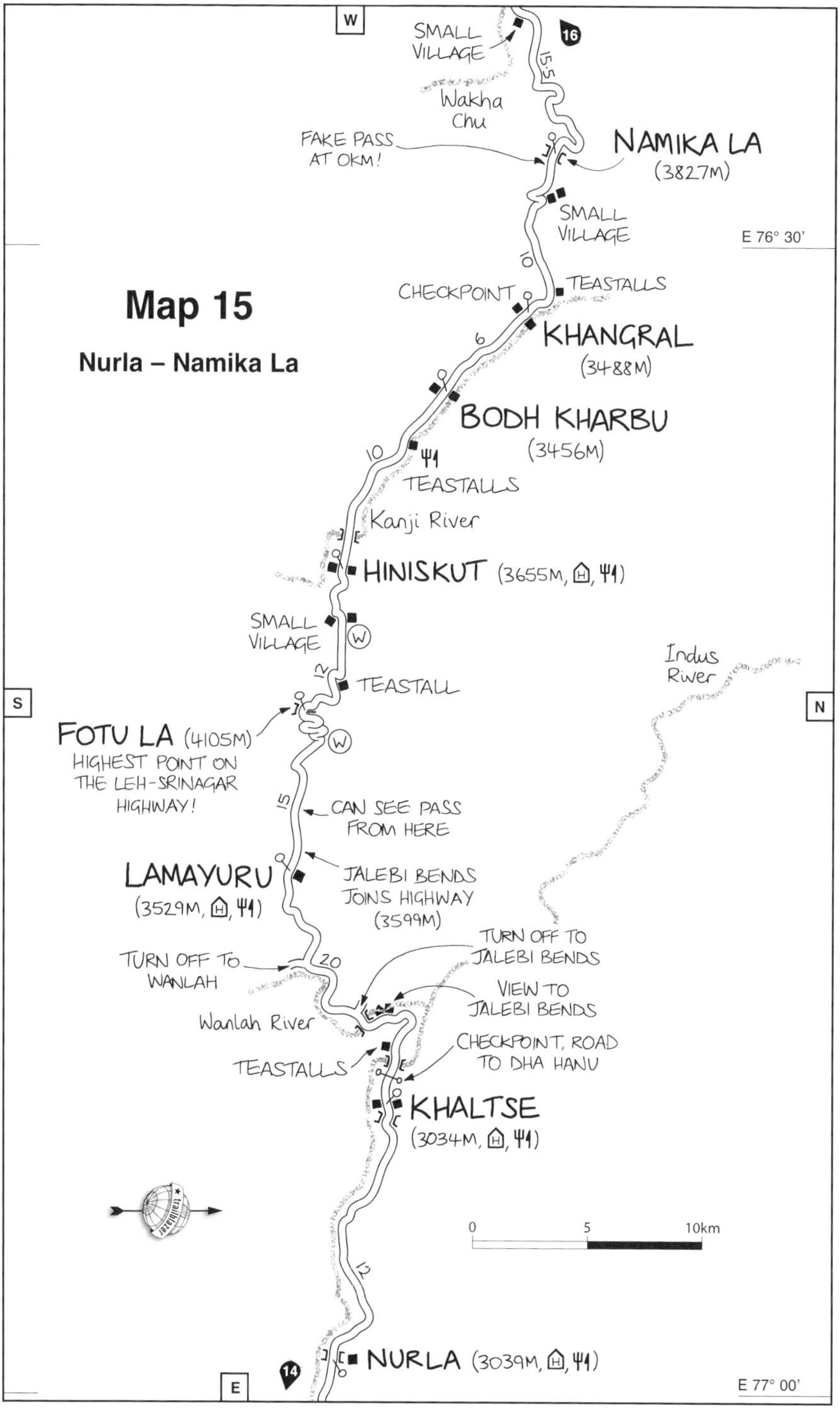

LEH – SRINAGAR

that once singled out the bravado of these mini matadors evaporates.

Khangral (3488m) 161/276KM

Another dusty village with a mosque and a passport checkpoint at the north end. The 10km climb to the pass starts from here, past some tea stalls and one more village.

Namika La (3827m) 171/266KM

The summit is 400m beyond the '0km' sign. The pass takes its name from a nearby rock known as the 'Pillar of the Sky' which must have been eroded long ago by water and wind. The water is long gone but the wind certainly isn't. The landscape all around here comprises rounded hummocks the colour of hide carved by rivulets with a gentle fur of vegetation and behind them the jagged peaks and spires of the Zanskar Range. In the late evening light the slopes turn golden and the dry rivulets are picked out by shadow: it feels as though you are riding among the folds of an ancient elephant. The descent into the Wakha Valley is swooping and fast.

Changing faces: Kashmiri on the left and Ladakhi on the right

Mulbekh (3307m) 186.5/250.5KM

After the mostly Muslim Kanji Valley, Buddhist Mulbekh feels more familiar: whitewashed Ladakhi houses, chattering old ladies in fusty traditional dress, burgundy-clad monks at the general store and the creak and peal of a large prayer wheel. Mulbekh is famous for its eighth-century Maitreya Buddha (Rs10) who stands overlooking the highway with poplar branches swaying around his face.

The ***J&K Tourist Bungalow*** is cheap at Rs100 but there's no running water or food; the ***Paradise Restaurant*** near the Buddha statue has simple rooms above for Rs150 (but check the bathroom isn't padlocked) and an equally simple menu of rice, *rajma* (a side dish made from kidney beans fried in spices and garlic), chapatti and sabze. The restaurant's terrace is a sociable place with a great view of the Wakha Chu River winding through the fields against a backdrop of brown hills topped by rock buttresses. Mulbekh is the last outcrop of Buddhism in Ladakh unless you travel down the Suru Valley from Kargil to Rangdom gompa and onwards to Zanskar. Between Mulbekh and Srinagar the culture is Islamic.

DAY 4 MULBEKH (3307m) to KARGIL (2720m) 40KM

MULBEKH–SHINGRAL 13KM
SHINGRAL–PASHKUM 14KM
PASHKUM–KARGIL 13KM

After yesterday's dry and dusty climbs the ride to Kargil is an effortless descent along the pretty narrow valley of the Wakha Chu. Little rock pools, grass and shady trees make the air feel cool and fresh for the first time in days. A short climb after Pashkum lifts the road out of the Wakha Valley and then sends you rolling downhill again. About 7km before Kargil there's a view south to the 7000-metre Nun Kun Massif in the Suru Valley. From the army camp above Kargil the road descends to cross the Suru River; turn left for the Suru Valley (see box on p170) and right for Kargil where the highway passes the mosque and becomes Main Bazaar. The town itself lies in a bowl with hills rising 10km to the north. Those hills, known as the 'Kargil Heights' are in Pakistan and are the site of the 1999 Kargil War.

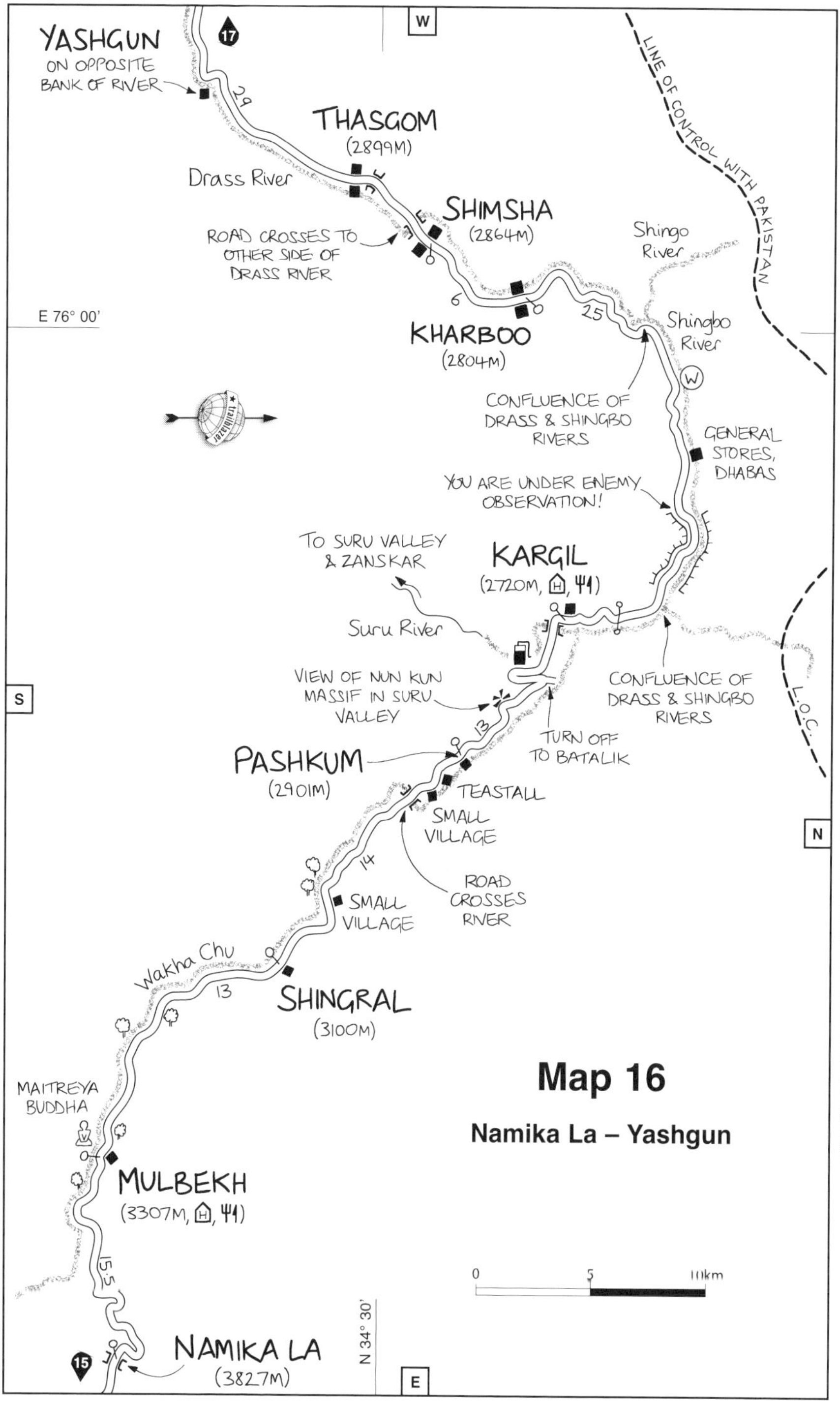

Map 16

Namika La – Yashgun

KARGIL (2720m) 226.5/210.5KM

Many people dislike Kargil and admittedly first impressions aren't favourable. There's a huge military presence, army trucks spewing fumes along Main Bazaar and thousands of flies. Although Kargil is Ladakh's second largest town, it's clearly far poorer than Leh. There are few if any Westerners on the streets and no real tourist facilities. Unlike Manali and Leh there are no German bakeries, no trekking agencies and, ironically, no Kashmiri hawkers trying to sell you a carpet.

Herein lies Kargil's appeal. Anyone who's travelled in Pakistan will recognize something of its culture in Kargil: the few women on the streets wear headscarves and walk in groups while the shop owners sit cross-legged surrounded by gunny sacks, watching the world go past. The minaret's call of the *muezzin* drowns out even the traffic and teenage boys murmur "hibaby hibaby" to passing foreign girls.

In fact, after Partition in 1947 Kargil did become part of Pakistan, and control of the Kargil Heights has shuttled between the two nations ever since. Its location between Leh, Srinagar and Skardu explains the mix of Central Asian faces and topi hats in the bazaar, the gristly mutton dishes on the menus and Tibetan women selling 'Panasoanic' radios and fake watches. A trawl through Kargil's backstreets turns up underpant sellers, flip-flops made from recycled tyres, haberdashers, barbers and severed goats' heads displayed on bookshelves. One of the markets is still called 'Balti bazaar' and now that relations with Pakistan are calming there has even been talk of initiating a bus service between Kargil and Skardu in Baltistan.

Kargil has a hospital on Hospital Road, surprisingly, which leads west of Main Bazaar and is lined with pharmacies. Next to the mosque is a computer

BIKING THE SURU AND ZANSKAR VALLEYS

From Kargil a mostly unsealed road leads for about 220km through the Suru Valley, over the Pensi La (4400m) to Padum, a small town halfway through the Zanskar Trek. The Suru Valley is Shia Muslim and the children have a well-deserved reputation for throwing stones. Many cyclists find themselves racing through this stretch which is a pity because the Nun Kun Massif which towers above Suru is gorgeous. Nun (7135m) and Kun (7077m) are popular mountaineering peaks; short of climbing them the best views are from the Parkachik ridge, a four-hour round trip from Panikhar village.

Trekking through the Zanskar Valley from Padum to Darcha is an excellent overland alternative to riding back down the Manali–Leh Highway. The trek takes between eight and ten days. Since 2003 a jeep track has topped and tailed the trek; a group of four would need a horseman and three horses which costs from Rs250 each per day. By 2010 or so the valley will be prised open to jeeps and trucks which will change this region forever. Zanskaris are keen on the road which will bring the region money and the Indian government likes the year-round alternative to the Manali–Leh Highway, which costs a fortune to maintain and is snowed under for nine months a year. A future of honking Tatas seems a world away from Zanskar now but the descent from the Shingo La pass (5080m) to bridges in mid-construction and a jeep track is a harbinger of Zanskar's future. From Darcha it's an afternoon's ride to Keylong, then a couple of days (120km) back over Rohtang La to Manali.

centre with **internet access**. The State Bank of India on Main Bazaar has no ATM and does not offer foreign exchange; the Siachen and Greenland hotels do but give a poor rate. The Tourist Reception office is near the bus stand.

Where to stay

Crown Guesthouse is by the bus stand and despite its cheery exterior the rooms are noisy, the bathroom filthy and there's no running water. However, it does have the cheapest dorm in town at Rs30 for a space on the floor. Nearby the ***J&K Tourist Reception Centre*** is also noisy but good value at Rs100 (dbl att) plus your own balcony overlooking the river. Down the lane by the taxi stand the ***Siachen*** has plush, carpeted rooms for Rs1200/1500 (sing/dbl att) with clean sheets, TV, reading lights in bed and hot showers (evenings only). This is a quieter place than most as it's set back from the main road and arranged around a courtyard. The manager offers discounts of up to 50% off-season (September onwards) and can also arrange houseboats in Srinagar.

Where to eat

A couple of dhabas between Main Bazaar and the bus stand serve up meaty dishes such as *yakhni*, *goshtaba*, *risti* and *tabak maaz* (all variations of mutton) with deliciously sweet Kashmiri qahwa tea. A ***chai stall*** opposite the ***Naktul*** restaurant in this alley serves up fortifyingly sweet chai with hot Kashmiri bread glistening with melted butter. Down near the mosque a friendly Sikh (you'll see the turban) cooks rice, potato and tomato dishes. Vegetarians should head for the ***Tibetan Kitchen*** on the second floor opposite Shashila Restaurant for its cheap veg momos, thukpa and chowmein. In the Main Bazaar ***Zoji La*** serves Kashmiri food (mutton) and Chinese dishes (noodles, rice) with a few veg options as well as toast and eggs for breakfast.

KASHMIRI DISHES

Kashmir's cuisine is famous for saffron, chillies and the *wazawan*, an epic 36-course wedding feast. Serving meat is the sign of a generous host, with mutton and fish being particularly popular. Vegetarians will find themselves filling up on rice and bread. Here are some common dishes:

Yakhni	Roast mutton with cardamom, ginger, almonds, yoghurt and nutmeg
Goshtaba	Mutton meat balls cooked in yoghurt gravy
Risti	Also mutton meat balls
Tabak maaz	Fried mutton ribs
Vagan	Aubergine (eggplant)
Roganjosh	Lamb seared in *ghee* (butter) and spices with dry Kashmiri chillies and curd
Dum aloo	Potatoes in yoghurt gravy
Nadir	Lotus stem (sold in the floating vegetable market on Dal Lake in Srinagar)
Qahwa or kawa	Green tea flavoured with cardamoms, cinnamon and sugar
Namkeen chai	As in Ladakh, a pinkish tea flavoured with salt, popular with Kashmiris for breakfast

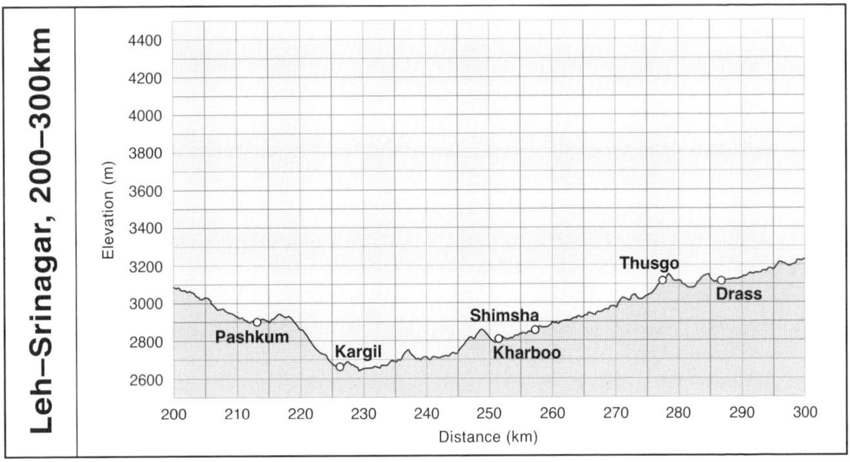

DAY 5 KARGIL (2720m) to DRASS (3057m) 60KM

KARGIL–KHARBOO 25KM
KHARBOO–SHIMSHA 6KM
SHIMSHA–THUSGO 20KM
THUSGO–DRASS 9KM

There's not much roadside food today so cyclists should bring lunch from Kargil. The Highway follows the Suru River downstream past the Silkchey checkpoint until the confluence of the Suru and Drass Rivers. They flow on as the Shingo River into Pakistan just six kilometres to the north while the highway now turns west and climbs upstream along the Drass River. For the next fifteen kilometres the road is walled in by the narrow valley pressed up against the Pakistani border and honeycombed with army bunkers. Frequent signs warn 'You are under enemy observation'. In times of tension you wouldn't want to get a puncture here.

Thusgo (3112m) 277.5/159.5KM
Here are the first dhabas of the day. After the village there's a military cemetery on the right-hand side then a short climb up to Drass.

Drass (3057m) 286.5/150.5KM
This small town claims to be the second coldest town in the world after experiencing temperatures of -60°C (-76°F) in January 1995. The average winter temperature is still mightily cold at -45°C. The record for the coldest town in the world is held by Oymyakon in Far Eastern Russia, for a brain-numbing -71.2°C.

As if the cruel winters weren't enough, Drass hit the international headlines in 1999 when the Pakistanis shelled it. Most of the people who live here are Dards who speak Shina (as in Chilas, see p92) and in the past the men worked as porters over the Zoji La. This region converted to Islam in the 15th century but some Buddhist stone sculptures can still be seen on the highway just before the town.

There's not much to Drass; a few basic ***restaurants*** on the main street and the ***J&K Tourist Bungalow*** where a draughty double room with friendly mice costs Rs100. This town is surprisingly popular with Indian tourists on a 'war tourism' package to nearby Tiger Hill and Tololing Heights, familiar names from the live television coverage of the Kargil War in 1999.

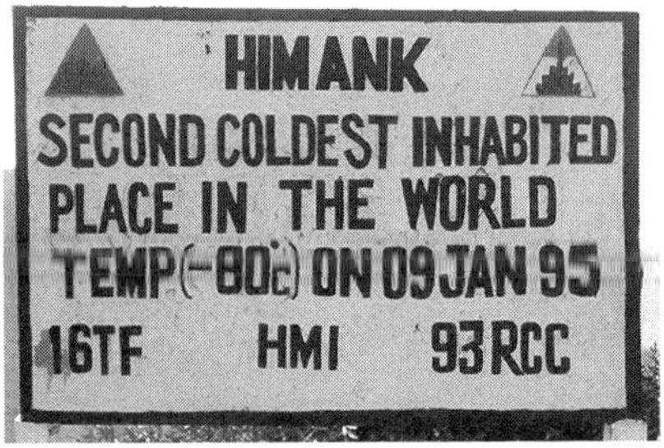

LEH – SRINAGAR

Leh–Srinagar, 300–400km

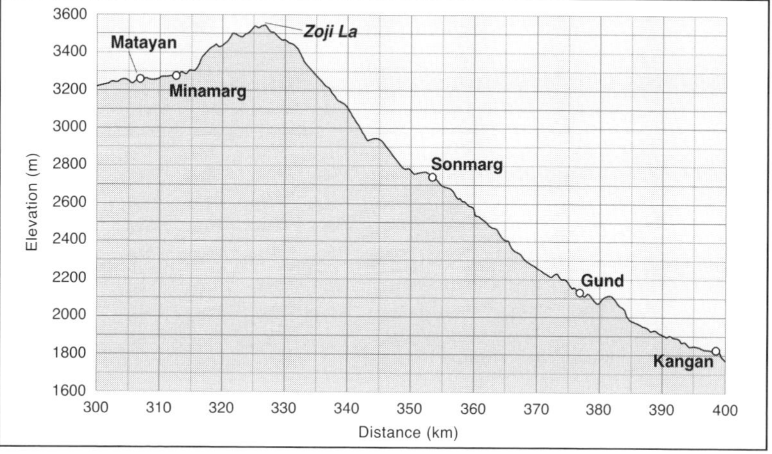

DAY 6 DRASS (3057m) to SONMARG (2742m) over Zoji La (3545m) — 67KM

DRASS–MATAYAN 20KM
MATAYAN–MINAMARG CHECKPOST 6KM
MINAMARG CHECKPOST–ZOJI LA 14KM
ZOJI LA–SONMARG 27KM

Stock up for the climb of Zoji La in Drass as there's no food until Gumry army camp. From Drass the road continues its steady climb alongside the Drass River, past the Kargil Battle School and the army Rock Climbing School.

Machoi (3221m) A small village set hard against the hills. Just after here the road swings south into a large, glacier-scoured valley. Some of the villagers are Brokpas, an Aryan people with surprisingly pale skin and hazel eyes.

Matayan (3260m) 306.5/130.5KM
Both Machoi and Matayan were fought over during the 1948 war to wrest Zoji La back from the Pakistanis. With its broad pastureland braided by the river the valley is picturesque and by late September most of the fields have been harvested and the goats, cows and sheep let loose on stubble. In contrast to this pastoral scene a narrow defile looms ahead, backed by glaciers and 5000m peaks.

At the **Minamarg (3277m)** passport checkpoint the tarmac ends and the climb up Zoji La starts. There's another passport check at Gumry army camp (3487m) with basic ***food stalls*** selling chai and snacks.

Zoji La (3545m) 326.5/110.5KM
Zoji La is the lowest of all the passes which cross the Great Himalaya Range. The Swedish explorer Sven Hedin described it as *"the worst pass I have ever seen, although its altitude did not exceed 11,500 feet"*. In March 1902 it took him four days to cross the pass with a gang of fifty porters. It's as dramatic a crossing as Rohtang La on the Manali–Leh Highway though the road here is even more perilous and in far worse condition. The highway is only open between June and November but locals cross this pass on foot throughout

CONVOYS OVER THE ZOJI LA

The army sends motorized traffic over Zoji La in convoy – check in Kargil but at the time of writing the convoy left Minamarg daily at 4am. Bicycles don't count as convoy traffic so you can safely ignore any well-meaning people who insist that they do and save yourself a horrendously early morning start.

the year, as they have done for centuries. It sits on a broad, grassy saddle with peaks and glaciers on both sides.

Cyclists looking forward to an easy downhill will have to wait because after the pass marker the road dips, becomes cobbled (of all things!) and then climbs briefly again up to 3545m. The far side of the pass is a dizzying zigzag descent into the Sindh Valley past an enormous rock face and shards of rock poking out from beside the road. After possibly weeks of dry, dusty vistas the fir-clad hillsides look odd, but not as odd as the many soldiers attempting to camouflage themselves (in yellow!) by the roadside.

Sonmarg (2742m) 353.5/83.5KM

At the foot of Zoji La lies Sonmarg (or Sonamarg) which means 'meadow of gold'. Until the 1980s it was a popular trekking destination but nowadays the few remaining chalet-type hotels are occupied more by soldiers than by tourists. Sonmarg is a chai stop for the Tatas and buses before the climb proper up Zoji La so the muddy main street is often in a diesel fug, but interesting to people-watch. A common sight is the *pheran*, a full-length gown worn by Kashmiris under which they tuck a *kangri*, a wicker basket of hot coals in dust, to warm themselves on. As one man said, patting his kangri, "it's my winter wife!".

The ***J&K Tourism Bungalow*** sits in a formal garden and has standard rooms for Rs500 (att) or a VIP room for Rs1000 and offers discounts of up to 50% from mid-September onwards. The best of the tea stalls lining the road is ***Nardinder Punjabi Dhaba*** opposite the bus stand, with *rajma* and *alu mutter* bubbling up in cauldrons.

DAY 7 SONMARG to SRINAGAR 83.5KM

SONMARG–GUND 23KM
GUND–KANGAN 22KM
KANGAN–MANGAM 9KM
MANGAM–GANDERBAL 10KM
GANDERBAL–NAGIN LAKE 14KM
NAGIN LAKE–SRINAGAR 5.5KM

The descent from Sonmarg to Srinagar is so fast that even fully loaded cyclists will cover the ground in about four hours. This is just as well since general advice is that **this is not a safe region so don't dawdle and certainly don't camp**. From **Gund** onwards there are dhabas along the wayside as well as fresh fruit vendors. From **Mangam** onwards you can see the broad Vale of Kashmir lying ahead and as the road debouches from the Sindh Valley it heads south directly to the lakes and mosques of Srinagar.

The road from Leh and **Ganderbal** approaches Srinagar from the north past a small piece of Dal Lake to the east then, about 2.5km later, past **Nagin Lake**.

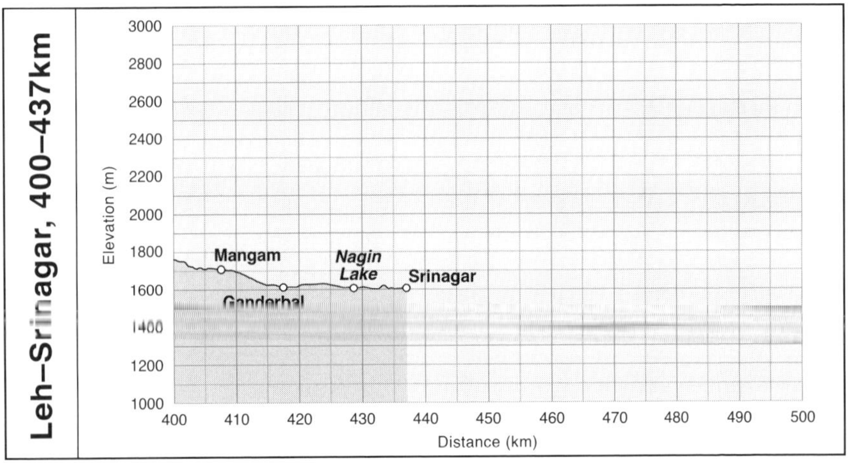

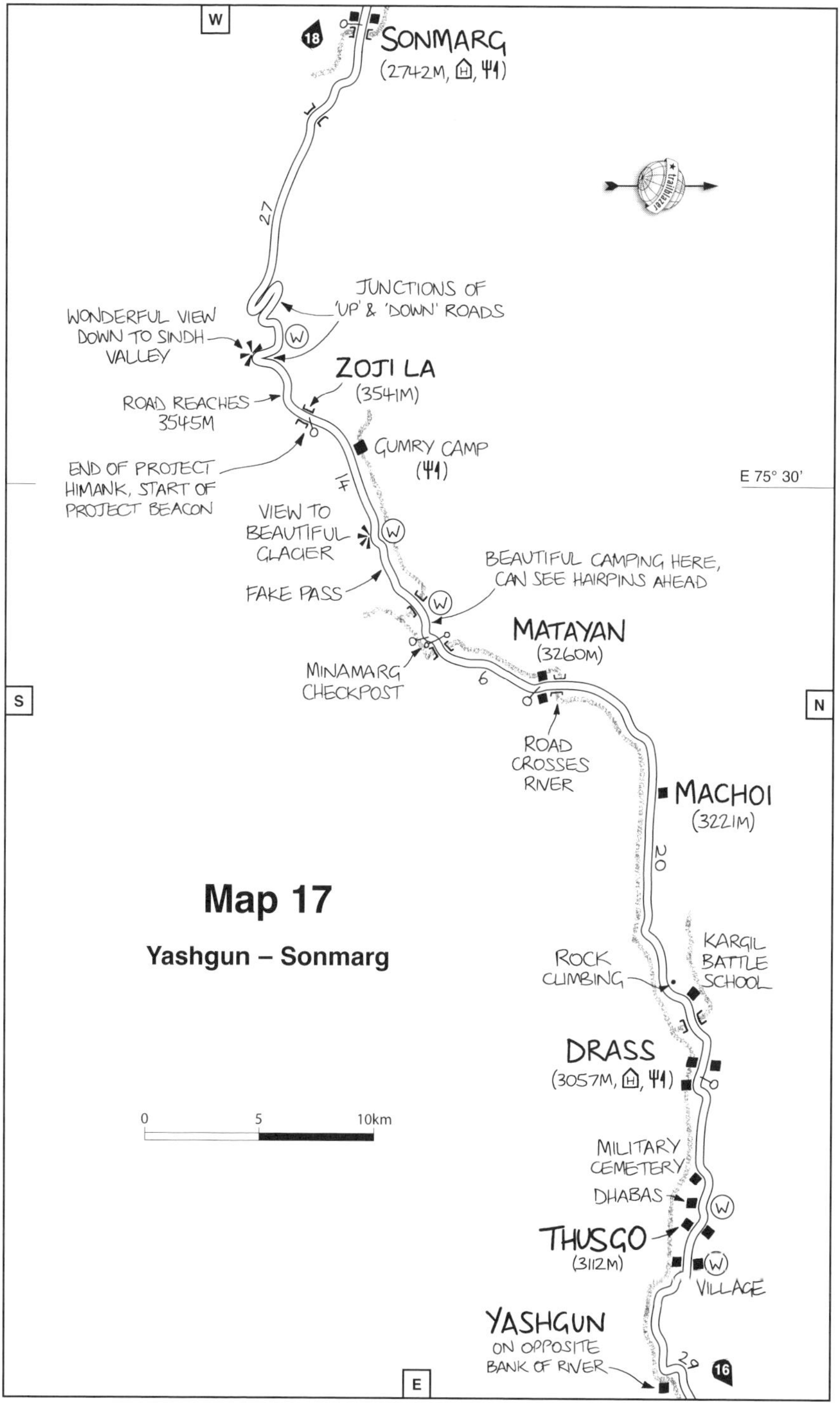
W
SONMARG
(2742M, Ⓗ, Ψ1)
27
JUNCTIONS OF 'UP' & 'DOWN' ROADS
WONDERFUL VIEW DOWN TO SINDH VALLEY
ZOJI LA
(3541M)
ROAD REACHES 3545M
GUMRY CAMP
(Ψ1)
END OF PROJECT HIMANK, START OF PROJECT BEACON
E 75° 30'
VIEW TO BEAUTIFUL GLACIER
BEAUTIFUL CAMPING HERE, CAN SEE HAIRPINS AHEAD
FAKE PASS
MATAYAN
(3260M)
MINAMARG CHECKPOST
6
S
N
ROAD CROSSES RIVER
MACHOI
(3221M)
20
Map 17
Yashgun – Sonmarg
KARGIL BATTLE SCHOOL
ROCK CLIMBING
DRASS
(3057M, Ⓗ, Ψ1)
0
5
10km
MILITARY CEMETERY
DHABAS
THUSGO
(3112M)
VILLAGE
YASHGUN
ON OPPOSITE BANK OF RIVER
29
E

Nagin Lake (1626m) **431.5/5.5KM**
Most foreigners prefer Nagin to Dal Lake as it's quieter and even more beautiful. If you'd like to stay on a houseboat here look out for a small blue sign which points down a lane to the houseboats. If you see a park on your right, you've gone too far.

From Nagin Lake the centre of Srinagar is a further 5.5km down Hazratbal Road (or 15mins by autorickshaw), if you get lost ask for 'Dalgate'.

SRINAGAR (1626m) 437/0KM

Srinagar's soft light and alluring lakes are the perfect balm for the wind-blasted and dusty passes of Ladakh. The Mughals built water gardens and mosques here but it's the experience of staying on a houseboat that truly soothes, especially on quiet Nagin Lake. Entire communities live afloat in this extraordinary city and a *shikhara* (small skiff) ride through their lotus fields lulls you into a dreamy timelessness.

The streets of Srinagar are not so idyllic. Razor wire, sandbag bunkers and machine guns are everywhere as Kashmir is caught in the political crossfire between India and Pakistan. Buildings are still pockmarked by bullets and militants have burned down alcohol shops and bombed the cinemas which distracted the devout from the study of Islam. Check the current security situation before visiting.

History

For the last sixty years Kashmir has been the lit fuse of relations between India and Pakistan and the future of the region remains uncertain. Every Kashmiri you speak to you will say they just want to live a normal life in peace, ideally as an independent state. But neither India nor Pakistan is prepared to concede territory and besides, Pakistan's Northern Areas are now a conduit for lucrative trade with China. Both India and Pakistan want Kashmir in its entirety. When Jinnah's campaign for Pakistan as a separate country for Muslims was adopted and Pakistan was carved out of Hindu India in the Partition of 1947, the Maharajah of Kashmir (himself a Hindu) wavered between joining India or Pakistan, then plumped for India despite his people being predominantly Muslim. Lord Mountbatten recommended a plebiscite at the time to determine where the allegiance of the Kashmiri people lay, which both India and Pakistan agreed to, but which India later reneged on and now says will never happen. The presence of a Muslim majority in Hindu India has always aggrieved Pakistan, which feels that Kashmir should rightly be theirs. The situation at present is that India is prepared to settle for what Kashmiri territory she now possesses by converting the Line of Control into the international border. Pakistan is still demanding a referendum, believing that the people of Kashmir will vote to join Pakistan. And the Kashmiris are still agitating as they have been since 1989 for an independent Kashmir. The international community is prepared to countenance everything except an independent Kashmir which it feels would fuel other separatist states in the region, such as the Sikhs' call for Khalistan in the Punjab.

A lone shikhara on Dal Lake in winter

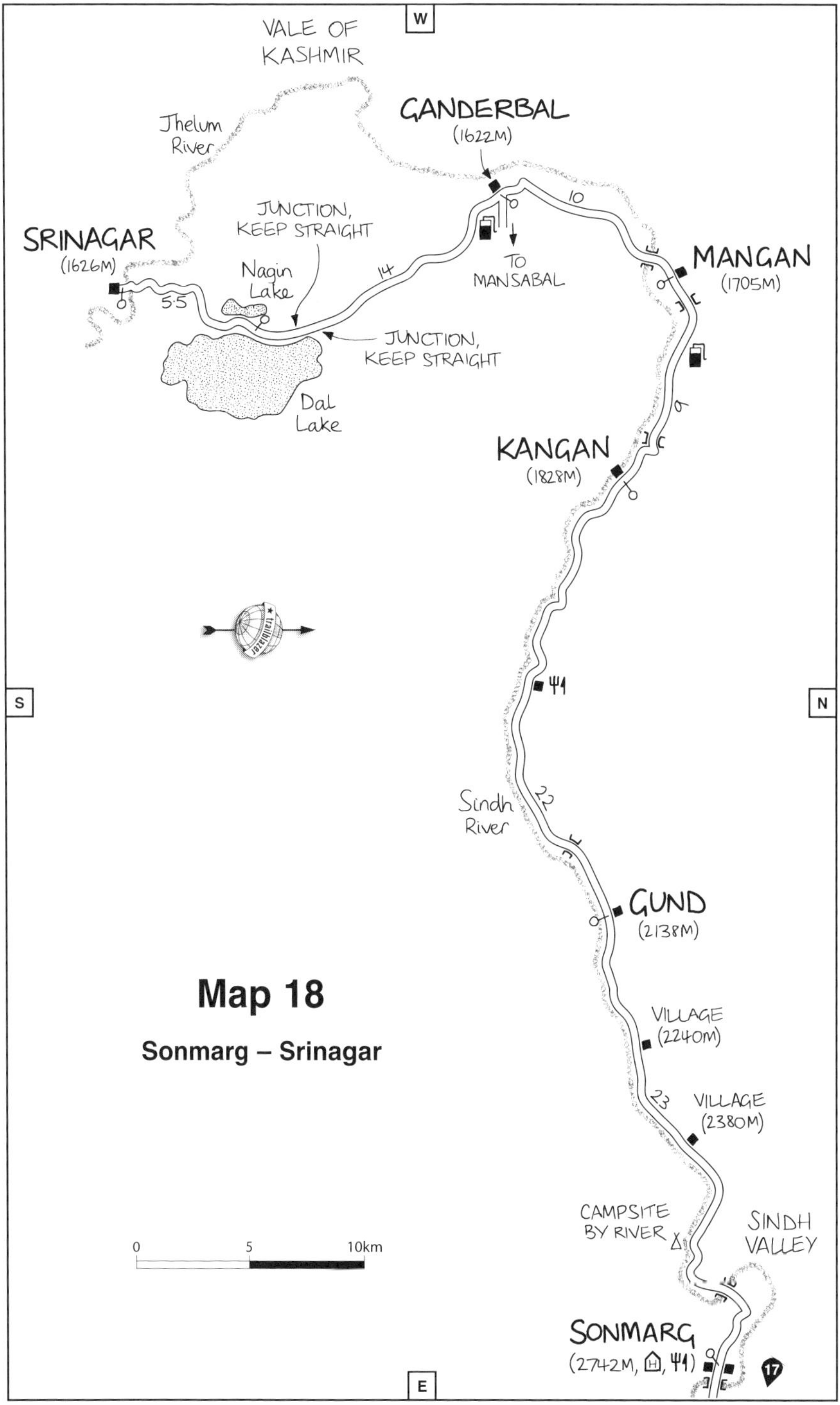
W
VALE OF KASHMIR
Jhelum River
GANDERBAL (1622M)
10
SRINAGAR (1626M)
JUNCTION, KEEP STRAIGHT
14
TO MANSABAL
MANGAN (1705M)
5.5
Nagin Lake
JUNCTION, KEEP STRAIGHT
Dal Lake
9
KANGAN (1828M)
trailblazer
S
N
Sindh River
22
GUND (2138M)
Map 18
Sonmarg – Srinagar
VILLAGE (2240M)
23
VILLAGE (2380M)
CAMPSITE BY RIVER
SINDH VALLEY
0
5
10km
18
SONMARG (2742M, H, ΨΙ)
17
E

Arrival and orientation

Srinagar divides roughly into two halves – the old city around the mosques and Zaina Kadal Bridge and the new city between the Jhelum River and Dalgate with wide avenues such as Residency and MA Rd. Military presence in the new city is ubiquitous but it's the old city which is less safe. The Tourist Reception Centre (TRC) near Dalgate (daily 9am–7pm, during Ramadan 9am–5.30pm, ☎ 01942 452 690/1, 💻 www.jktourism.org) has all the facilities a visitor could need: an ATM, post office counter, houseboat counter, bus stand and taxi rank prices. For getting around auto rickshaws are as common on land as shikharas are on the water.

The State **Bank** of India and its **ATM** are on Residency Road near Ahdoos Hotel; 300m east is a J&K Bank ATM (Maestro only) near its main branch and there are other J&K ATMs on MA Road (next to the Golf Club) and at the TRC. Both banks cash travellers' cheques and change foreign currency.

Sky Biz Cybercafé near the taxi stand at Dal Gate has the quickest **internet connection** for Rs60/hr. For those staying at Nagin Lake there's a tiny internet café where Hazratbal Road curves to the northeast, about 300m north of the lane to the houseboats.

Where to stay

The quintessential Kashmiri experience is to lounge on a deluxe **houseboat**, doing little more than watching the world float past. All but the most expensive of Srinagar's hotels have been taken over by the Indian army so there are few budget places anyway. The Tourist Reception Centre will help you with accommodation and also has a counter dealing with houseboat enquiries, though you'll get a better deal if you approach the houseboats in person.

Ahdoos Hotel (☎ 01904 247 2593, 📠 245 5251) has rooms from Rs1400–1800 plus 10% tax. Its restaurant is known for serving authentic Kashmiri cuisine. The ***Hotel Broadway*** (☎ 01904 245 9001, 💻 www.hotelbroadway.com) facing MA Road is aimed squarely at Indian businessmen with rooms with wi-fi from Rs3500/5500 plus tax. There's also a swimming pool with a poolside bar selling cold beers, two restaurants and a private film theatre – good news since all Srinagar's cinemas have been bombed.

Houseboats

There are more than a thousand houseboats in Srinagar. They are relics of the Raj when Kashmir's Maharajahs prohibited the foreign purchase of land so the ever pragmatic British built houseboats on the water instead. Nowadays the boats possess a faded charm and are an experience not to be missed. Standards vary as you'd expect, with 'Deluxe' at the top, then grading from 'A Class' to 'D Class'. As long as militancy keeps tourists away this is a buyer's market so don't be shy about negotiating a deal – a double en suite room on a deluxe boat with breakfast and filling dinner (Kashmiri dishes and salad) can cost as little as Rs800 per day. As important as the price is the owner: some are hospitality personified, others will alert every salesman in the vicinity to your presence and you'll spend your entire stay fending them off. Most houseboats have between two and five double bedrooms, a large dining room, sitting room and a cushion-spread verandah looking onto the lake. Usually the owner lives next door so if you want to get to know the family or put in some special requests, such as fish or beer, you can. Houseboats lie in three areas of Srinagar:

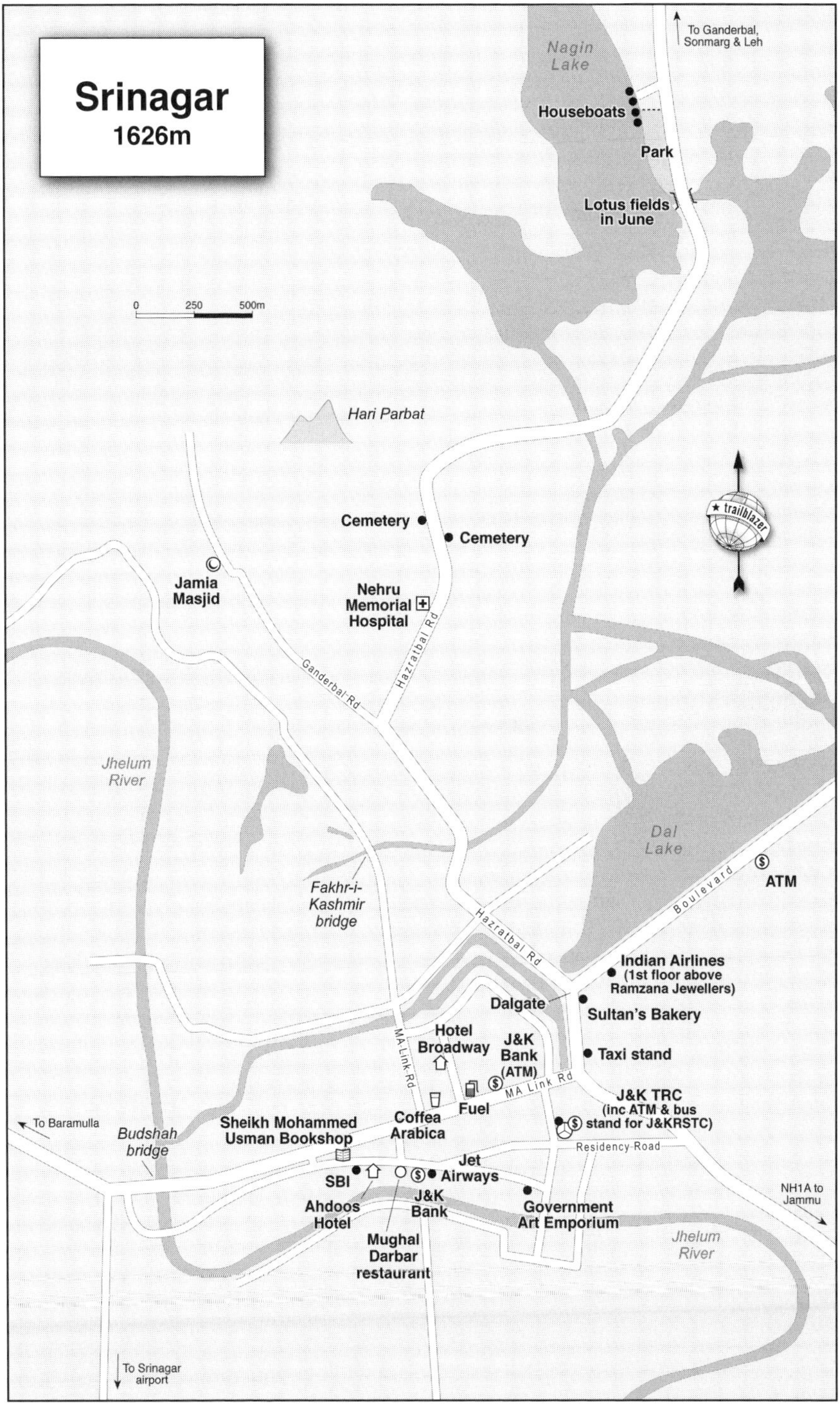
Srinagar
1626m
0
250
500m
To Ganderbal, Sonmarg & Leh
Nagin Lake
Houseboats
Park
Lotus fields in June
Hari Parbat
Cemetery
Cemetery
Jamia Masjid
Nehru Memorial Hospital
Hazratbal Rd
Ganderbal Rd
trailblazer
Jhelum River
Fakhr-i-Kashmir bridge
Dal Lake
Boulevard
ATM
Hazratbal Rd
Indian Airlines (1st floor above Ramzana Jewellers)
Dalgate
Sultan's Bakery
Taxi stand
MA Link Rd
Hotel Broadway
J&K Bank (ATM)
MA Link Rd
Fuel
J&K TRC (inc ATM & bus stand for J&KRSTC)
To Baramulla
Budshah bridge
Sheikh Mohammed Usman Bookshop
Coffea Arabica
Residency Road
Jet Airways
SBI
Ahdoos Hotel
J&K Bank
Mughal Darbar restaurant
Government Art Emporium
NH1A to Jammu
Jhelum River
To Srinagar airport

Dal Lake In the centre of Srinagar so busier and noisier. This is where Indian tourists prefer to stay. Hundreds of shikharas glide about peddling silver, carpets, flowers, chocolate, cigarettes – if you're visible you're fair game for the hard-sell. Houseboats are moored away from land, so you are dependent on shikhara rides to reach shore. Make sure these shikhara rides come free when you negotiate the price for the houseboat.

Nagin Lake 5.5km out of the centre and safer. There are fewer houseboats here and it's far more serene. Houseboats are moored to land at the rear so you're not dependent on shikharas and can ride into town or catch a rickshaw. For a more peaceful journey, Nagin and Dal are interconnected and it's a beautiful one-hour drift by shikhara. Nagin is more popular with foreign than Indian tourists.

Jhelum River In the centre of town, for better and for worse: more convenient, less safe. The houseboats here are mostly 'D-Class' and are moored to land.

Where to eat

Anyone staying on a houseboat will probably eat breakfast and dinner on board. ***Mughal Darbar***, near the J&K ATM and Jet Airways office on Court Road, serves traditional Kashmiri food as does ***Ahdoos Hotel***. ***Coffea Arabica*** is part of the Broadway hotel and serves cappuccino and expressos as well as gooey delights such as chocolate terrine cake. You can order a *sheesha* (hubbly bubbly pipe) for Rs200. As well as baking delicious, sesame-seed sprinkled Kashmiri bread the ***Sultan's Bakery*** also bakes cakes including a Black Forest Gateau.

What to see

Dal Lake Not just a lake but a watery way of life with floating markets, vegetable gardens and villages. The Doongra people live on the lake itself. A one-hour shikhara ride should cost around Rs300.

Old City Many of Srinagar's mosques and handicrafts workshops are tucked into these labyrinthine alleys but it's not so safe and women may feel uncomfortable walking alone.

Jama Masjid Srinagar's largest mosque with 370 wooden pillars and more than 300,000 carpets. Sultan Sikander built the mosque in 1400 but fire has razed it three times since then; its present incarnation is in a very masculine Indo-Saracenic style, almost like a fortress. The pagoda roof looks surprisingly Chinese but is apparently a common element in Kashmiri architecture. A donation of Rs5 is expected.

Shah-i-Hamdam This green wooden mosque with a pagoda-topped roof is much more intimate than the Jama Masjid, though women and non-Muslims cannot enter. Shah-i-Hamdam was a Persian who came to Kashmir in the thirteenth century to preach Islam. Unlike the austere Jama Masjid, this shrine is brightly painted with motifs of flowers and birds.

Services

- **Bike shops** There are basic bike shops at Dalgate and Regal Chowk
- **Book shops** Several along Residency Road including Atlantic Books and Sheikh Mohammed Usman & Sons.
- **Chemists** Plenty in Rainawara around the Nehru Memorial Hospital. Dhar Brothers between the Sultan Bakery and Boulevard sells sanitary towels.
- **Post office and internet** The General Post Office is on the Bund; ISD shops and internet cafés are scattered throughout the town.
- **Taxis** There are seven taxi ranks in Srinagar including one opposite the TRC; all post their rates outside.

SPITI & KINNAUR 5

ROUTE INFORMATION

- **Start / finish** Manali / Shimla (Himachal Pradesh, India)
- **Distance** 651km
- **Altitude min / max** 518m/4695m
- **High passes** Two (Rohtang La and Kunzam La)
- **Suggested duration** 13 cycling days plus a week for exploring side valleys
- **Road conditions** 60% tarmac, very rough between Gramphoo and Losar
- **Hazards and dangers** Floods and landslides after heavy rain
- **When to go** late June to October
- **Visas** Required for India

Unlike many routes in this book, Spiti and Kinnaur are not towns but valleys; the first is Buddhist and closely linked to Ladakh and Tibet, the second is Hindu and runs along the Sutlej River from the border of Tibet to the capital of Himachal Pradesh, Shimla.

Just above Manali, on the north side of the Rohtang La, an unsealed road leads east from Gramphoo. This 'road' to the Spiti Valley climbs north along the Chandra valley past enormous glaciers and a turn-off to the dazzling turquoise lake of Chandra Tal and the 4551-metre Kunzam La. Between Chhatru and Batal the road is in a dire condition but the reward is worth it. The spectacular Spiti Valley (average elevation 4570m) possesses awe-inspiring scenery and fantastical gompas, the most famous of which is the 1000-year-old monastery of Tabo. Spiti was only opened up to foreigners in the 1990s and the sensitive border with Tibet still requires an Inner Line Permit. At Sumdo the valley swings south to its confluence with the Sutlej River as it flows west from its source on Mt Kailash in Tibet. From here the Hindustan–Tibet Road follows the Sutlej westwards as it carves through Hindu Kinnaur, losing altitude from the Tibetan panoramas of Spiti to banana trees, mangoes, monkeys and auto rickshaws before a final climb to Shimla, former summer capital of the British Raj.

This route links to Manali–Leh (see p121) and Leh–Srinagar (see p158) to form a phenomenal 1588-kilometre ride through the Himalaya from Shimla to Srinagar, or vice versa.

FACTS ABOUT THE REGION

Safety and restrictions

Spiti and Kinnaur are both very safe places to travel; any danger comes from natural hazards such as **floods**, **landslides** and the road conditions. Traffic in Spiti is often light or non-existent when the road is blocked; in Kinnaur from Jeori onwards the road is busy and near Shimla chaotic. Kinnaur and Spiti are especially prone to landslides, washed away bridges and monsoon-ravaged roads.

Inner Line Permits are required for travel between Jangi and Sumdo. The application procedure depends on the whim of the official processing them although technically foreigners should be able to get them in Manali, Shimla, Kaza and Recong Peo: the last two are the best places to try. Checkpoints for the permits are at Sumdo, Chango and Jangi.

History of the road

The NH22 national highway is nicknamed the 'Hindustan–Tibet road' but that route, built by the British in the 1800s, took a higher line along the valley. It's fallen into disuse now but can still be trekked so mountain biking could be possible. The British built rest houses along the old Hindustan–Tibet road that now have to be booked in advance – for more details see *Exploring Kinnaur & Spiti in the Trans-Himalaya* (Indus Publishing). The NH22 starts in the Punjabi town of Ambala and ends in Kaurik east of Sumdo on the Tibetan border. Built on the Sutlej's flood plain, the danger of which became apparent in the floods of 2005 (see box p196), the government is considering reinstating the old Hindustan–Tibet road higher up the valley sides.

Language and religion

English is widely understood as is **Hindi**. Local dialects are Spitian (a form of Tibetan) and Kinnauri.

Spiti is mostly **Buddhist** and Kinnaur is mostly **Hindu**, though in places the two religions merge.

PRACTICAL INFORMATION

Which direction?

Both Shimla and Manali are easily reached from Delhi and in **either direction** there are climbs at the beginning and end of the ride. The wind generally blows from the west so riders from Manali to Shimla will at least be on tarmac for the headwinds; those travelling the other way will have the wind as well as an atrocious road surface to contend with.

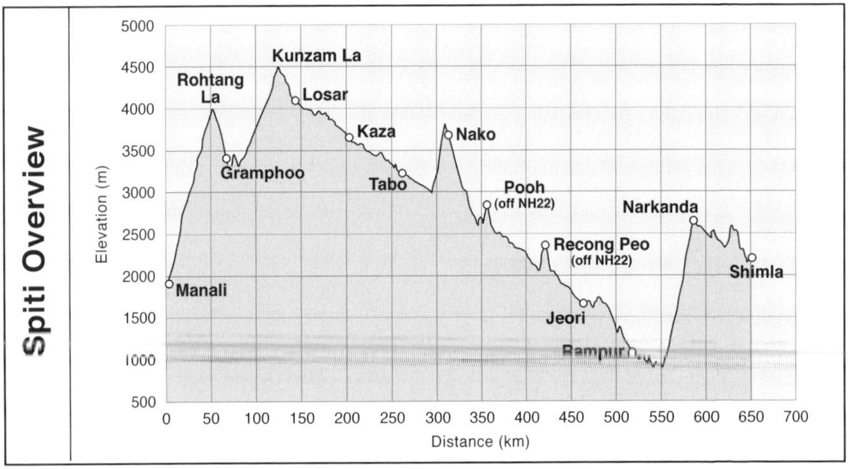

From Delhi some cyclists catch the train to Shimla then cycle east through Kinnaur up into Spiti. Not only does this give you the chance to experience one of India's classic train journeys, it also allows you to build up altitude gently through Kinnaur, before tackling the Kunzum La at the far end of Spiti. The other choice is to catch a bus from Delhi to Manali then do the two big climbs (Rohtang La and Kunzum La) immediately, after which it's downhill all the way until the final climb to Narkanda or, to turn this ride into a loop, Jalori Jot to return to Manali.

Accommodation, food and money

If you are keen on **camping** beautiful sites are easy to find in Spiti but difficult in upper Kinnaur onwards as the valley walls are steep and any flat land is either a village or a field. Between Manali and Losar 'hotels' are very basic rock-built dhabas; otherwise there are expensive government rest houses if

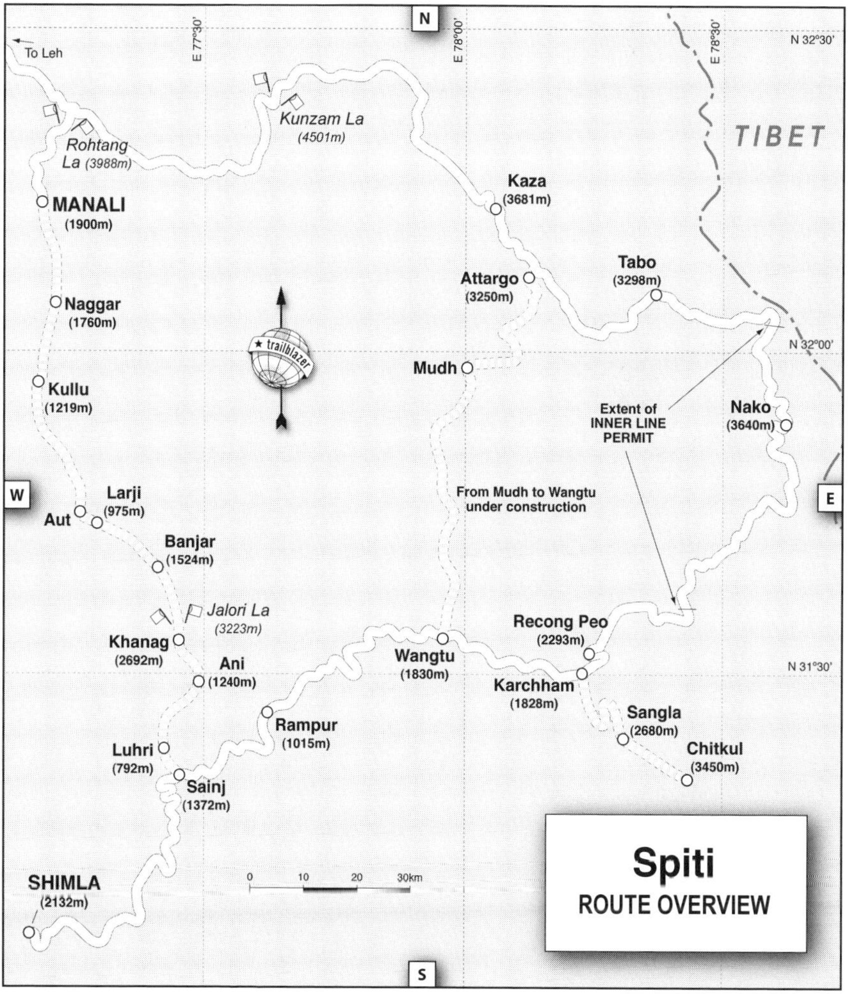

you can find the chowkidar (caretaker). After Losar there are simple guest-houses with common bathrooms for around Rs150 and more fancy options in the towns and touristy villages such as Nako. Spitian towns such as Losar, Kaza and Tabo are on the valley floor; it's the gompas like Ki, Dankhar and Lalung that are a climb to get to. In upper Kinnaur every day finishes with a climb whichever direction you're going in: Nako, Pooh and Recong Peo are anything from 240m to 730m above the highway.

The towns of Kaza and Recong Peo have good food; elsewhere you'll find basic local dishes such as dahl and rice, sabze, *channa* (chickpea) masala and rajma or momos and thenthuk. General stores sell chocolate biscuits and fruit juices.

The **banks** in Manali and Shimla have ATMs and offer foreign exchange. Apart from an ATM at Rampur, there are no other ATMs or foreign exchange en route so be sure to take enough cash (about $10 a day for budget travellers).

Getting to the ride

For getting to **Manali** see p127. **Getting back** from Shimla it's about 370km from Delhi by road. Himachal Pradesh Tourism (HPTDC) runs an a/c **bus** for Rs660. You can check availability online at 💻 www.sugamhimachal.org/hrtctickets and buy tickets at the HPTDC office at the Chanderlok Building, 36 Janpath, New Delhi (☎ 011 2332 5320, 💻 hptdcdelhi@hub.nic.in).

By **rail** Shimla's nearest broad-gauge railhead is 96km away at Kalka, from where the famous 'toy train', a little steam train, chugs bravely through a hundred tunnels and over nearly a thousand bridges up to Shimla. For train details and times see 💻 www.indiagroove.com (the station codes for New Delhi, Kalka and Shimla are NDLS, KLK and SM respectively). Trains leave daily from Delhi to Kalka (four hours); from Kalka to Shimla takes a further five hours.

SIDE TRIPS FROM THE SPITI AND KINNAUR VALLEYS

The following are all recommended detours from the main road through the Spiti and Kinnaur valleys. Some, like Ki and Kibber, are up the valley walls; others up are side valleys such as Pin and Sangla.

From	To	Distance (one-way)
Batal (p185)	Chandra Tal lake (4183m)	13.5km
Kaza (p189)	Ki monastery* (4116m) and Kibber village* (4205m)	7km (Kaza to Ki) 11km (Ki to Kibber)
Attargo (p192)	Pin Valley, Mudh village	approx 38km
Karcham (p201)	Sangla Valley*, Sangla (2680m) and Chitkul (3450m) villages	18km (Karcham to Sangla) 26km (Sangla to Chitkul)

* Distances and altitudes from Nest & Wings' *Tourist Guide Map of Himachal Pradesh*

Route guide – Spiti and Kinnaur

DAY 1 MANALI (1900m) to GRAMPHOO (3245m) 66KM

See Manali–Leh pp134-7 for a full description for Manali to Gramphoo. That chapter ends Day One at Marrhi to aid acclimatization; Spitian cyclists can push on to Gramphoo but should start early as Rohtang is a 51km climb and the weather is capricious. From the top of Rohtang it's easy to see the track to Spiti, threading its way along the Chandra River far below. Though it's no more than a collection of three rock *dhabas* and a cluster of Tatas, Gramphoo is the junction of the Manali–Leh Highway and the road to Spiti over the Kunzam La. It's always a good place to people-watch and the faces at the dhabas here tell the story of the modern Himalaya: Bihari road workers, Nepali cooks, Southern Indian civil servants and everyone on the move. Dinner, bed and breakfast costs around Rs150.

DAY 2 GRAMPHOO (3245m) to BATAL (3915m) 49.2KM

GRAMPHOO–CHHATRU 16.8KM
CHHATRU–CHHOTA DARA 16.7KM
CHHOTA DARA–BATAL 15.7KM

The Spiti road from Gramphoo deteriorates immediately. A cyclist using 700C wheels described it as 'one of the top ten worst roads in the world ... a road so bad that even goats avoid walking on it'. The road is mostly loose rock and nalahs have entirely washed it away in places. There's also the altitude to deal with; pedalling over mud or sand is enjoyable but the steep and/or rocky sections can be exhausting when you're not fully acclimatized. Along the way the character of the valley hardens from the green and grey slopes of Lahaul to a desolate rocky wasteland.

Chhatru (3331m) 83/568.5KM
After rattling over a bridge you get to Chhatru, a base for trekking and mountaineering with a few parachute tents serving chai and snacks and selling woolly socks. Ahead lies the worst section of road; 32km between Chhatru and Batal.

Chhota Dara (3784m) 100/551.5KM
The *Sangke Dhaba* here serves up dahl and grit-flecked rice and has a couple of small rooms (Rs100). The dhaba owner is also the chowkidar of the government rest house here which has large en-suite double rooms with lots of blankets (Rs1000).

Batal (3915m) 115.5/536KM
Situated at the base of the Kunzam La by the banks of the Chandra River, Batal is a

RUMOURS ABOUT THE ROADS

It's quite likely that at some point in Spiti & Kinnaur you'll hear the road ahead is closed. Rumours will abound of landslides, washed-out bridges and other horrors. Sometimes they are true but often a supposedly impassable section can be as banal as a muddy slope too steep for the trucks. Just as distance and time depend on whom you talk to, so do road conditions and the only way to find out is to go and look for yourself.

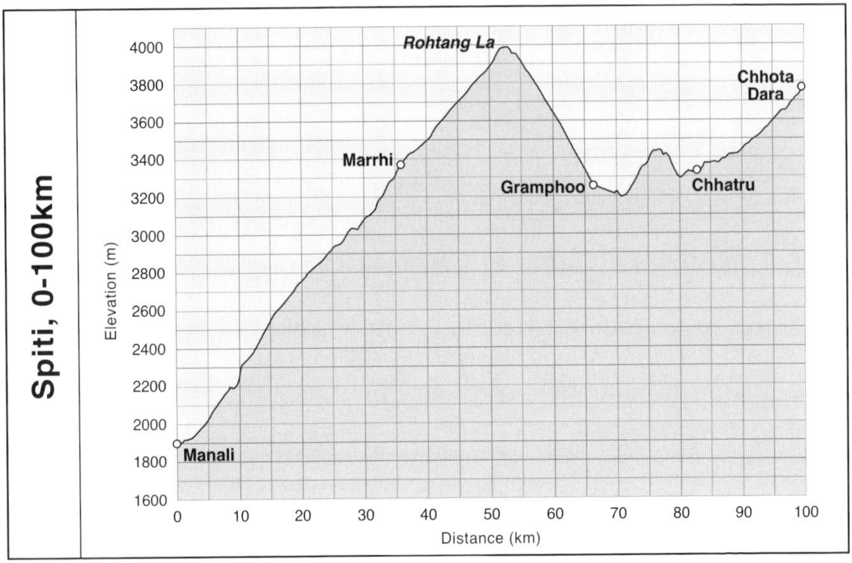

popular truck stop in this bleak and rocky landscape. The *Chandra Dhaba* is a good choice and they've built a small rock cottage opposite (Rs50) for some privacy and distance from the truckers' snores. It's cold at night but the starscapes are spectacular.

DAY 3 BATAL (3915m) to LOSAR (4113m) over Kunzam La (4500m) — 27.3KM

BATAL–CHANDRA TAL TURN-OFF 2.9KM
CHANDRA TAL TURN-OFF–KUNZAM LA 7.6KM
KUNZAM LA–LOSAR 16.8KM

After crossing the Chandra River at Batal the road to Kunzam La starts climbing immediately up a series of twenty hairpins. From the Chandra Tal turn-off (for Chandra Tal see box p188) the climb to Kunzam La continues on packed mud and rock. There's usually a strong tailwind (though it works against you on the switchbacks) and no water so be prepared. The climb is tough until the last kilometre when the pass comes into sight and the gradient lessens.

Kunzam La (4501m) — 126/525.5KM

This is one of the most photogenic passes in the Himalaya and in clear weather the view is worth every metre of the climb. Looking southwest to Lahaul enormous glaciers, cirques and 6000m peaks soar above the Chandra River and on the pass itself are hundreds of prayer flags, a large chorten depicting romping snow lions and a small temple. The road performs a small *kora* (devotional circuit) around them and there's usually a small tea shack near the temple for a celebratory chai.

The descent is a boneshaker over two rivers – one pink, one silver, which give an inkling of Spiti's bizarre and wonderful colour palette. Anyone who's seen the paintings of Nicholas Roerich (see box, p132) will now understand the colours he uses. Felt-like pastures at the base of the pass and a little further along to the east make good camping spots; the road rolls alongside them and the broad Spiti River until Losar.

Losar (4113m) — 143/508.5KM

As you pass under the 'Most welcome to Spiti Valley' ceremonial gateway there's a passport checkpoint. Losar currently has two guesthouses; the *Samsong Guesthouse* proclaims itself 'chep but nice' with doubles from Rs100-200 (com); the airier upstairs rooms with valley

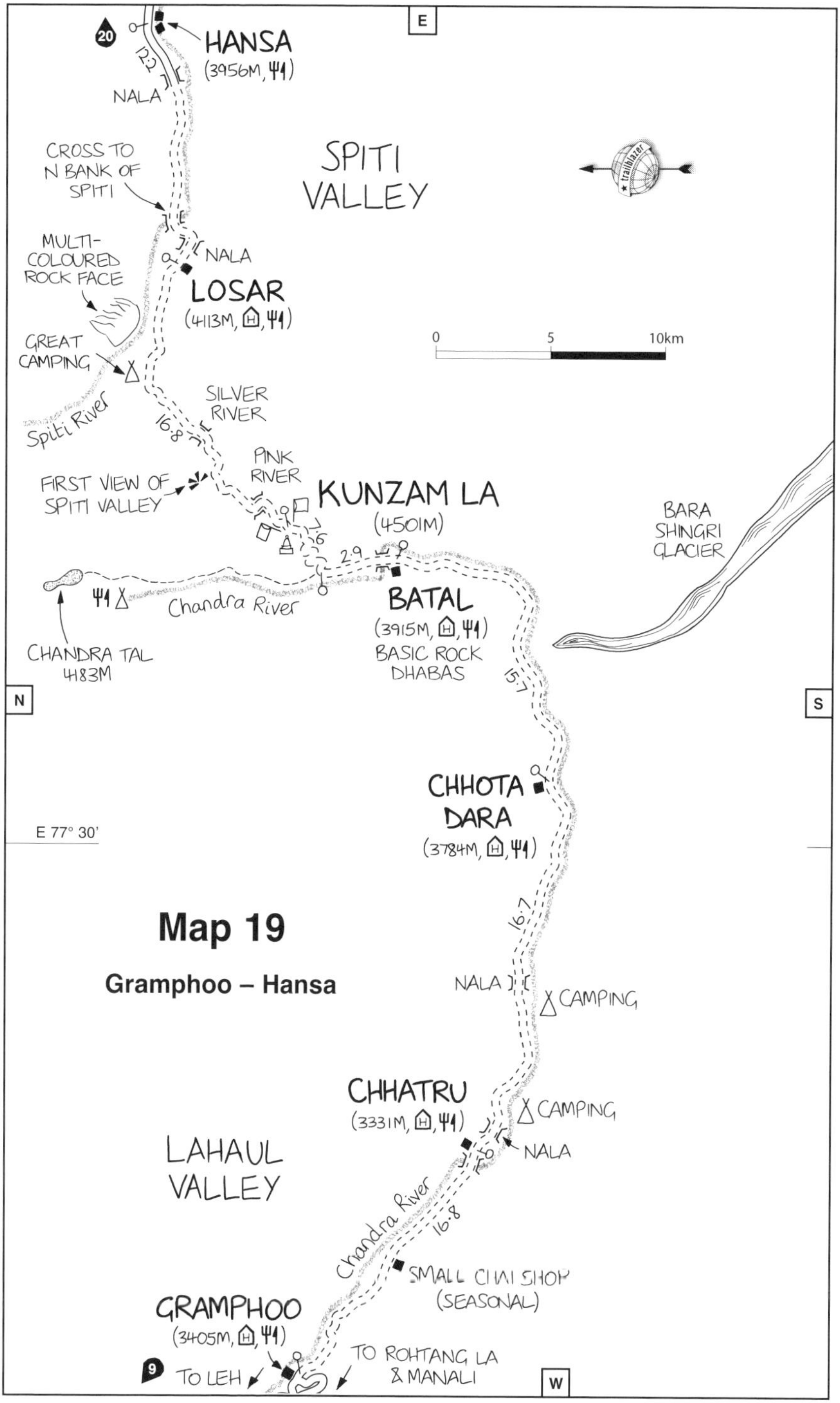

Map 19

Gramphoo – Hansa

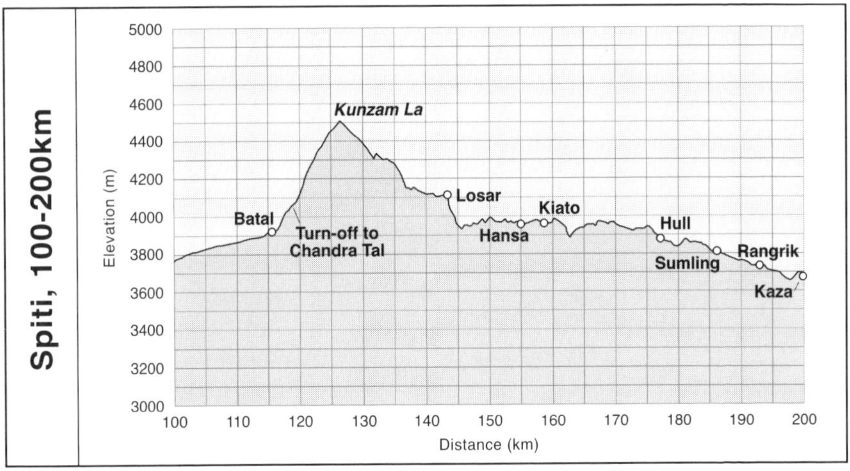

views and TV are the better choice. The restaurant serves chips and 'Spitian beer' or *chang*, a barley beer drunk throughout Tibetan regions. Losar looks much more Tibetan than Kullu; the older houses are whitewashed mud-brick with hay stacked on top and trapezoid window frames. After a tough two days in a godforsaken world of rock and wind, Losar's fields, streams and poplar trees feel very homely.

DAY 4 LOSAR (4113m) to KAZA (3662m) 57.1KM

LOSAR–HANSA 12.2KM
HANSA–KIATO 3.8KM
KIATO–HULL 18.1KM
HULL–SUMLING 9.2KM
SUMLING–RANGRIK 7KM
RANGRIK–NEW KAZA 6.8KM

Take some lunch from Losar because there is no food between Hansa and Rangrik. The road is generally in a good condition and follows the Spiti River along a broad glacial valley, occasionally dropping and climbing steeply to cross a few nalahs.

CHANDRA TAL (4183M)

This turquoise mountain lake is set in a bowl of burgundy and rose hills against a backdrop of peaks to the south. For many bikers it's a highlight of the Spiti route and shouldn't be missed although it lies 13.5km off the main road on a jeep track. Chandra Tal means 'Moon Lake' and Sun Lake its sister is Suraj Tal just below Baralacha La to the north (see p140).

The track to Chandra Tal starts from the third switchback on the steep climb up Kunzam La (2.5km from Batal). It's often in a better condition than the road up the pass though there are still occasional nalahs to be forded. Initially it's fairly flat and clings to the valley walls before heading out over a scree slope. The final section is composed of steep switchbacks after which a final climb and drop brings you to the shores of the lake. Along the way are stunning vistas of glacial valleys, the silver Chandra River below and icy mountain peaks all around. This ride is what Himalayan biking is all about.

Chandra Tal is a wonderful place to take a day off, riding the single track around the lake, swimming in its glacial waters or basking in the sunshine. You could do something useful and acclimatize by walking (or mountain biking if you're confident) along the high trail to Kunzam La. This starts at the stream by the parachute tents that provide food (chai Rs10, mineral water Rs30, dahl and rice Rs40) and bedding (Rs100). A few hardy mountain bikers have explored the trekking trail between Chandra Tal and Suraj Tal but report that it's mostly unrideable.

The villages are small and often off the road and the ride has a desolate feel, especially under low skies and against a headwind.

Hansa (3956m) **155/496.5KM**

This small village has a restaurant (look for the sheep skull wearing a pink woolly hat) but the meat momos (no veg) are lethal for delicate stomachs.

Kiato (3960m) **158.5/493KM**

Another small village but no obvious dhaba. A hilly link road is being built between here and Kibber (see box below) which will be the better route once open. Just after the village there's a butterscotch-coloured moonscape of hoodoos on the west side of the river, just before the road drops in hairpins to cross the Spiti River.

On the south side of the river, the road narrows under an overhang then scrolls over a glacial moraine past wispy trees and fields of peas near Pangmo.

Hull (3883m) **177/474.5KM**

There is a building here signed 'Juley Guesthouse' but it may be locked. After the road drops to a bridge there are views of Ki gompa to the southeast.

Ki gompa as seen on the road to Kibber

Rangrik (3723m) **193/458.5KM**

On the west side of the road is ***Munchies*** dhaba but it's better to keep going to Kaza. After passing the long mani wall and crossing the Spiti again there's an uphill stretch to New Kaza that feels harder than it should. The road north from the Spiti bridge leads up to Ki gompa and Kibber village (see box below).

KAZA (3681m) 200/451.5km

The tin-roofed town of New Kaza is the administrative capital of Spiti and as the Spiti Valley is considered a 'tribal area' by the Indian government, Kaza's special tax-free status has turned it into something of a boomtown. The tourist scene is growing quickly too; in 2003 there were just a few guesthouses and restaurants but by 2006 a German bakery had opened in the small square of Old Kaza and new concrete guesthouses were sprouting up everywhere. The number of restaurants is growing making Kaza a good place for a feed. Although the town lacks charm it's a good hub for visiting nearby gompas such as Ki and Dankhar without having to carry any luggage; just as well considering that all the gompas are perched high above the valley. There's also some excellent single track in the high pastures and valleys around here.

KI GOMPA AND KIBBER VILLAGE

A highly recommended detour from Kaza is the road to Kibber village which passes one of Spiti's most iconic sights: the small gompa of Ki perched upon its rocky hillock. From the bridge over the Spiti between Rangrik and Kaza (see Map 20, p192) there's a climb of 7km to Ki gompa and a further 11km to Kibber. A sign by the bridge claims Kibber's altitude is 4205m thus making it 'the highest inhabited village in the world connected by motorable road and with voting ballot'.

This picturesque and friendly stone-built village is a far better place to spend some days than Kaza, and though it lacks Kaza's facilities there is some fun single track nearby between the villages of Comic, Gete and Tashigang and fossil hunting to be had around here too. You can't miss the ***Norling Guesthouse*** as you enter the village; its doubles cost Rs200 (com) and it serves good food.

The road from Losar enters New Kaza past the hospital and petrol station then veers up a side-valley past Sakya's Abode Hotel to cross the (usually dry) creek which divides Kaza in two. The road unkinks in Old Kaza and passes the Snow Lion Guesthouse and Khaza bakery on the right, from where a dirt track leads steeply downhill past the Mahabudha Guesthouse to Old Kaza's covered bazaar and bus stand. From the east a road brings traffic in at the bottom of Old Kaza past the bus stand and into the bazaar.

Where to stay

If you're staying in Old Kaza, the ***Mahabudha Guesthouse*** is one of the town's old-timers and run by a Tibetan doctor with a small garden, large double rooms (Rs150) and an immaculate shared bathroom with a hot shower. Down by the bus stand, the slightly grungy ***Third Eye Guesthouse*** (Rs250 dbl) has a good restaurant. The ***Phuntsok Palbar*** and the ***Khangre*** are a couple of friendly, family-run guesthouses (Rs150 dbl) on the New Kaza banks of the creek; the nearby ***Mountain Paradise Guesthouse*** (Rs200) has also been recommended. For more comfort a double room costs Rs3000 at the ***Banjara Retreat*** near the large chorten by the petrol station.

Where to eat

For **food**, a solid breakfast of Nutella-smothered brown toast can be had at ***Sachen Kunga*** in the main market, or if it's sunny the outdoor ***Whispering Willow*** make a great veg omelette but can be excruciatingly slow. Later in the day the BYOB ***Yak Café*** in Old Kaza makes some tasty Tibetan dishes such as veg bale (Rs50) and a spicy veg wonton noodle soup. Otherwise the long-standing ***Echi Wan*** near the bazaar has a small terrace for people-watching while you eat, as well as porridge for breakfast. For snacks, the German **bakery** in Old Kaza's market sells cinnamon rolls, croissants and chai. Nearby is an English Wine and Beer shop for bottles of whisky and beer. Many restaurants don't have toilets and at night a torch is handy for negotiating the narrow lanes, especially since there are frequent power cuts.

Services

For the Inner Line Permit (see box on p192) there's a photocopy and passport photo shop in the bazaar in Old Kaza. There is also an **internet café** near the German bakery but its connection is usually broken. The nearby Spiti Holiday Adventure office will change money and travellers' cheques but at a poor rate. There's even a shop in the bazaar that sells 26" **bicycle tyres**. Most of the Chinese goods in Kaza's bazaar are from Delhi, but a few still come the old-fashioned way by horseback over the Tibetan border by Sumdo.

THE RISE OF THE GERMAN BAKERIES

An Indian Himalayan town knows it's firmly on the tourist trail when a German bakery opens in its midst. Already well-established in Manali and Leh, German Bakeries are often little more than a counter selling cinnamon whirls, croissants (plain, chocolate, banana and chocolate), breads and other pastries. No one really knows where the name comes from and today most German bakeries are staffed by Nepalis, but at least it's a more wholesome legacy than the nearby English Wine & Beer Shops!

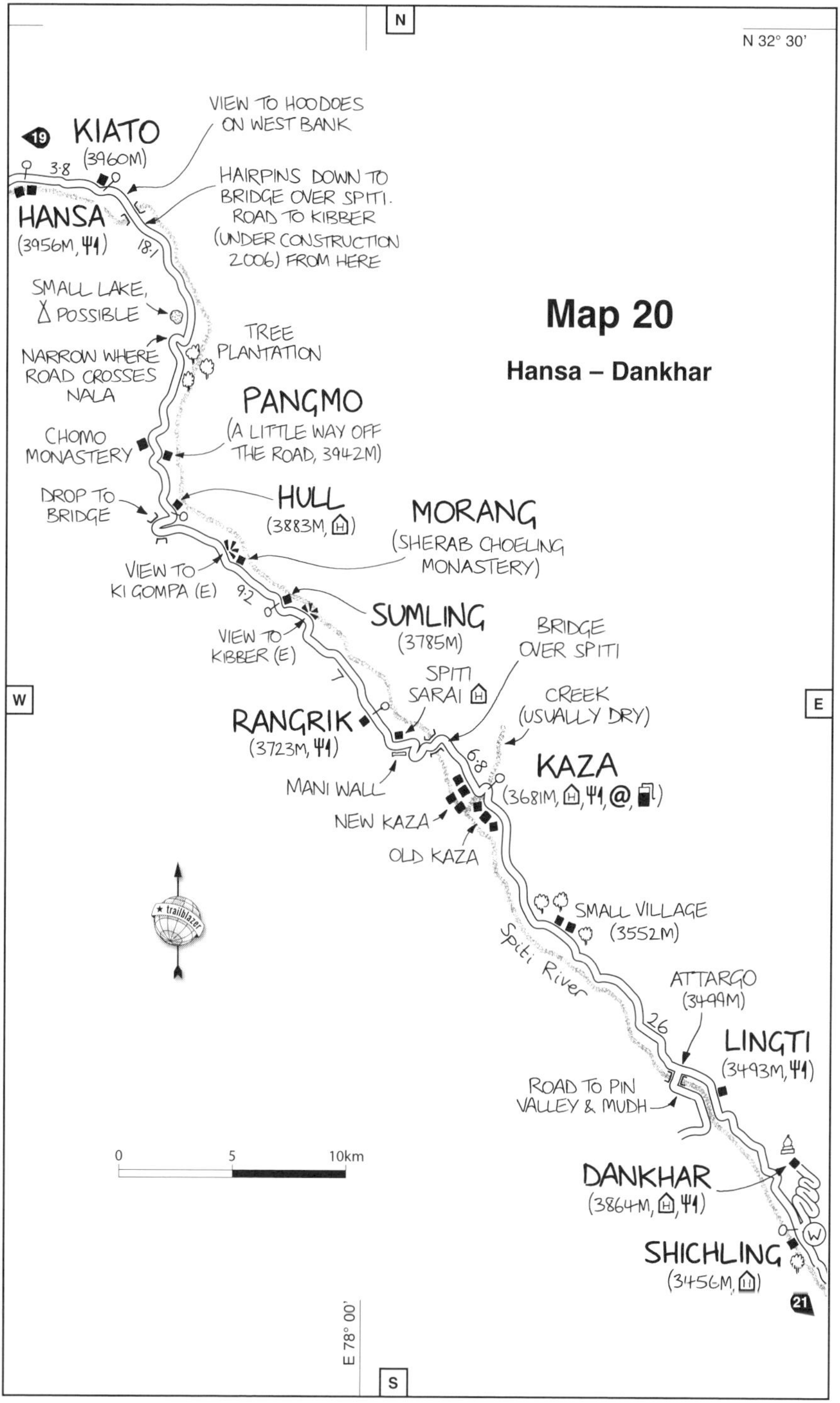

SPITI & KINNAUR

THE INNER LINE PERMIT

Kaza is the last place you can apply for this permit, without which you will not be able to proceed beyond Sumdo, 28km east of Tabo. You can process the paperwork yourself at the Sub-Divisional Magistrate's (SDM) office without using a travel agent; to do so you will need a photocopy of your passport details and Indian visa, two passport photos and your passport. To get there in New Kaza turn downhill at the petrol pump, then right past the Himachal Tourism Tent Camp. The SDM's office (Mon–Sat 10am-5pm, closed Sundays and every other Saturday) is on the first floor of the large unsigned building at the end on the left-hand side. Permits issued in Kaza are valid for a week and you can specify the start date.

Start at Room 2 by asking the clerk for an application form, fill it out then take it to Room 9 where the police will check you against their 'wanted' list, stamp your form then send you back to Room 2. Here the clerk will add it to the pile for the SDM to stamp. Allow two to three hours for this procedure; it is often quite a sociable affair. There are quite a few stipulations on the Inner Line Permit that you can cheerfully ignore (such as not staying overnight) but one thing you must take seriously is the issue of **photography**. Because it's such a sensitive area do not be seen photographing the road, bridges or side valleys. Two cyclists were arrested in 2003 for photographing their bikes on a scenic bridge and ended up in court.

DAY 5 KAZA (3662m) to TABO (3298m) 48.5KM

New Kaza–Attargo 17km
Attargo–Dankhar road 9km
Dankhar road–Poh 13km
Poh–Tabo 9.5km

Unless you plan to visit Dankhar gompa note that there are no restaurants between Kaza and Tabo. The road follows the Spiti River downstream through a broad valley past a small village to **Attargo**. Here the valley narrows and the route to the Pin Valley (signed Kungri gompa 18km) crosses a bridge and continues on the opposite bank. Around here you may see groves of seabuckthorn (see box opposite).

Dankhar turn-off (3442m) 226/425.5km

On a fully loaded bike the tarmac road up to Dankhar is punishingly steep for the first 5km as it zigzags above the main road, climbing 430m in just 8km. Kilometre markers count you down and from 5km the gompa is in sight, sprouting on rocky pinnacles above terraced fields of barley and peas. This was once the official capital of Spiti, and the oldest buildings

Mudh, the village at the head of the Pin Valley

THE PIN VALLEY

This broad glacial valley really shows the dramatic sweep of geology in the Himalaya and its wildness is spectacular. A few years ago the track up to **Mudh** was very rough and rocky but now a road is being constructed through the valley over the Bhabu pass to Wangtu in Kinnaur. The west side of Pin was declared a National Park in 1987 and signs proclaim it as 'Home to the Snow Leopard and Siberian Ibex', but these are rarely seen. It takes a day to cycle from Kaza to Mudh, the uppermost village in the Pin Valley, past Kungri gompa and the villages of Guling and Sangam; basic guesthouses can be found at Sangam and Mudh. Most are farmhouses; animals live on the ground floor and the family above, and lovelorn donkeys bray all night outside the windows.

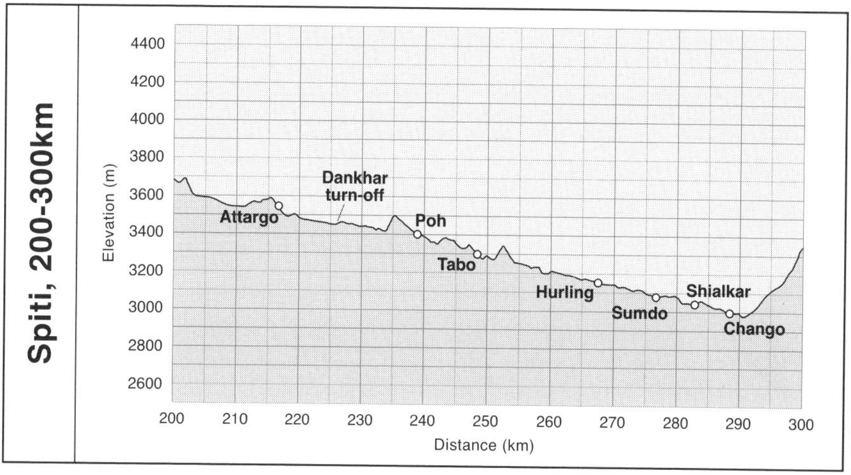

date from the seventh century. Now in ruins, the nearby Nono's palace is rumoured to have a pit dungeon where he incarcerated his enemies.

The views from the gompa are wonderful and for a donation you can stay the night here. Near the newer (yellow) gompa is a small shop and restaurant (rice and dahl, Coke and chai). An hour's walk up from Dankhar there's said to be a small lake which reflects the high peaks and pasture which surround it.

On the main highway after the Dankhar turn-off is the ***Dolma Guesthouse***, in Shichling village. From Shichling the valley narrows again into a gorge with a nasty short climb up to some towers of moraine. The small villages en route do not have restaurants or guesthouses. When the bridge 2km before Tabo was washed away in 2006, a pulley carried people and even motorbikes across the nalah.

Tabo (3298m) 248.5/403KM

After a narrow gorge the Spiti Valley broadens one last time to reveal the world-famous gompa of Tabo. Unlike almost every other gompa in Spiti, this one is not dangling from a cliff-face or perched on a spire but is set very solidly down to earth in the fields, its soft mud

Would you put your pride and joy on this?!

SEABUCKTHORN, THE HIMALAYAN SUPERFOOD

The seabuckthorn shrub grows best in the arid climates of Spiti and Ladakh and its bright orange berries are packed with Vitamin C, E and folic acid. The shrub is thorny, like natural barbed-wire, and in some places is used as fencing. The berries are too bitter to eat raw but can be drunk in a juice called 'Leh Berry' which makes the following claims on its carton: 'Bears clusters of small golden revolutionary berries that have goodness of over 100 nutrients vital for body functions. Seabuckthorn products gainfully consumed since 12th century as per recorded Tibetan Medical History. Monks and horsemen of legendary Genghis Khan extensively used them to improve individual memory, stamina, strength and fitness. Russian cosmonauts used them on Spaceship 'Mir' to combat cosmic radiation and as oxygen supplement'. Whatever next?!

TABO GOMPA

These low adobe buildings may look humble but Tabo gompa is one of the most important ancient Buddhist sites in the world. It's believed that Rinchen Zangpo, better known as the 'Great Translator', founded the gompa in 996AD. The frescoes here were painted by Kashmiri artisans and their rich colours glow in the flickering light of butter lamps. This is a magical place. Puja starts in the new gompa building at 6am in summer with a tea break at half time. Tourists usually take it more seriously than the young monks though it's hard to keep a straight face when the wall clock starts playing 'Twinkle twinkle little star' mid-ceremony.

walls innate to the landscape. Its plain exterior spared it the ravages suffered by Ki and Dankhar gompas in eighteenth-century raids by the Sikhs and Dogras. Today Tabo gompa is marked by a ceremonial gateway next to the main road.

A few guesthouses such as the *Maitreya* (doubles around Rs150; att) are clustered around the gompa. The gompa's monks run the atmospheric ***Millennium Guesthouse*** in the gompa itself for the same price with spotless rooms; the gompa's ***Negi restaurant*** is also good. Those in need of a splurge should head for the ***Tabo Banjara Retreat*** at Rs3000/3300 (att). The Tabo Cybercafé never seems to have a connection and the STD/ISD shop behind the Millennium Guesthouse has an erratic one.

DAY 6 TABO (3298m) to NAKO (3640m) via Malling Slide — 62.8KM

TABO–HURLING 19.4KM
HURLING–SUMDO 8.6KM
SUMDO–SHIALKAR 6.5KM
SHIALKAR–CHANGO 5.9KM
CHANGO–NAKO 22.4KM

Now the high road is open past the Malling slide, there's a long, waterless climb of 850m over the last 23km of the day.

Lari (3320m) This small village has a spivvy ***PWD*** (Public Works Department) ***Resthouse*** where 'tourists are welcome to stay'. After Lari the valley starts to narrow and the Spiti River gathers speed. Apart from occasional plantations of willow and poplar, and the oases of green surrounding the villages the landscape is elemental: just rock and water with occasional waterfalls showering the road. By Sumra, the true right bank of the Spiti now belongs to Kinnaur while the left bank remains in Spiti until Sumdo from where there are views to the distant Leo Purgyal (6791m).

Hurling (3141m) 267.5/384KM
From here until Sumdo the valley constricts into a narrow gorge and the road is blasted out from the rock face with steep drops down to the river. There's a small Hindu shrine to those who have lost their lives here.

Sumdo (3087m) 276.5/375KM
By the bridge is the first (or last, depending on which direction you're riding in) checkpoint for the Inner Line Permit. Your details will be filled out in a ledger giving you enough time to admire the mountains of yellowing paperwork and mottos painted on the walls. A basic dhaba lies opposite in the army compound. Sumdo is only 2km from the Tibetan border and it is here that the Pare Chu river joins the Spiti from the east. Sumdo is the first village in Kinnaur and where the Manali road joins the Kaurik road to become National Highway 22. Despite the grand name, the road gets worse.

Shialkar (3034m) 283/368.5KM
There's a large army camp here and a disproportionate amount of donkeys. Since Sumdo the road has been at river level, now it starts to undulate alongside it, past some meditation caves set in the rock face.

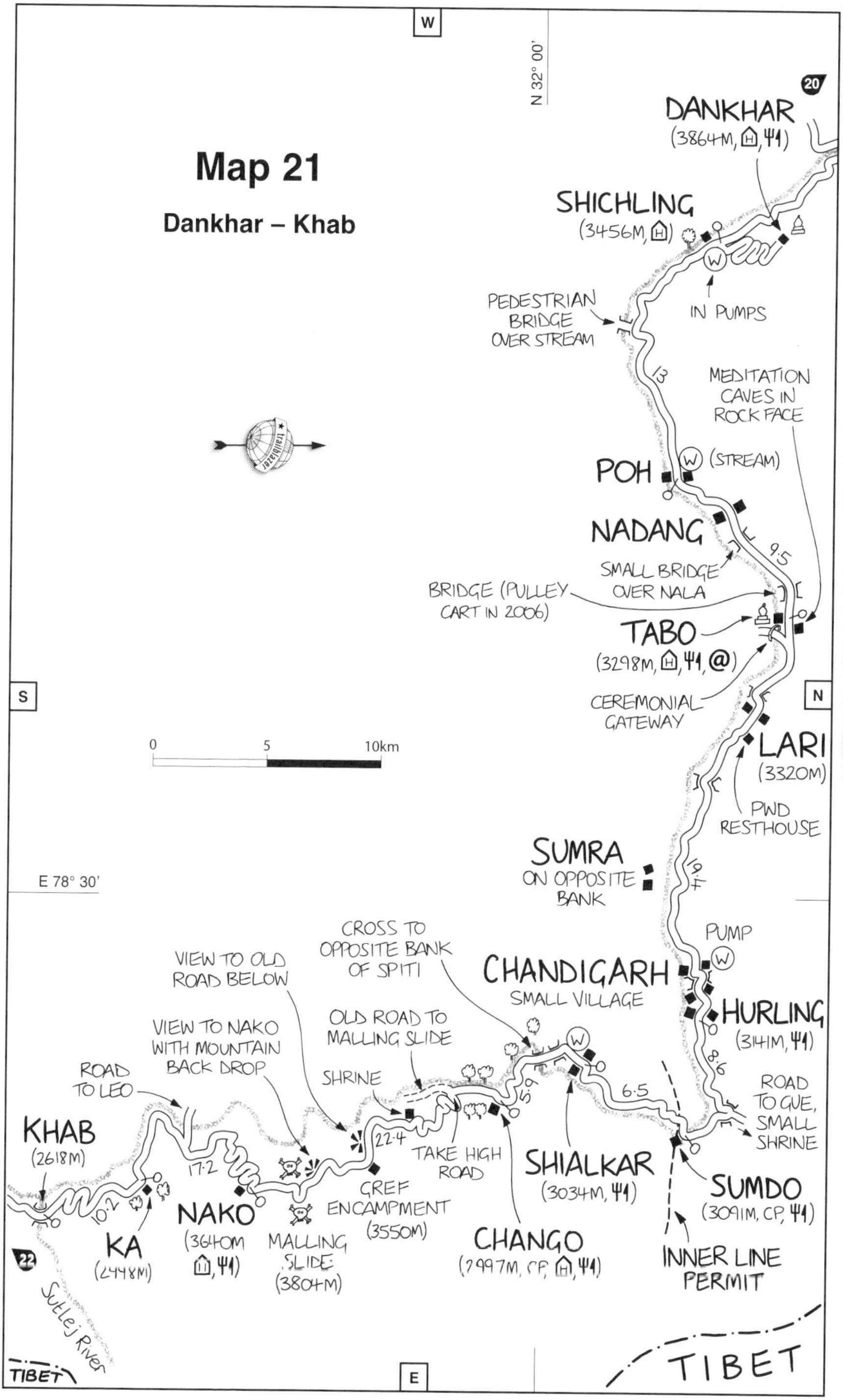
Map 21
Dankhar – Khab
W
N 32° 00'
20
DANKHAR
(3864M, ⌂, ΨΙ)
SHICHLING
(3456M, ⌂)
IN PUMPS
PEDESTRIAN BRIDGE OVER STREAM
13
MEDITATION CAVES IN ROCK FACE
POH
(STREAM)
NADANG
9.5
SMALL BRIDGE OVER NALA
BRIDGE (PULLEY CART IN 2006)
TABO
(3298M, ⌂, ΨΙ, @)
CEREMONIAL GATEWAY
S
N
LARI
(3320M)
PWD RESTHOUSE
0
5
10km
SUMRA
ON OPPOSITE BANK
19.4
E 78° 30'
PUMP
CHANDIGARH
SMALL VILLAGE
HURLING
(3141M, ΨΙ)
8.6
CROSS TO OPPOSITE BANK OF SPITI
VIEW TO OLD ROAD BELOW
VIEW TO NAKO WITH MOUNTAIN BACK DROP
OLD ROAD TO MALLING SLIDE
ROAD TO LEO
SHRINE
5.9
6.5
ROAD TO GUE, SMALL SHRINE
KHAB
(2618M)
17.2
22.4
TAKE HIGH ROAD
10.2
SHIALKAR
(3034M, ΨΙ)
SUMDO
(3091M, CP, ΨΙ)
NAKO
(3640M ⌂, ΨΙ)
GREF ENCAMPMENT
(3550M)
KA
(2448M)
MALLING SLIDE
(3804M)
CHANGO
(2997M, CP, ⌂, ΨΙ)
INNER LINE PERMIT
22
Sutlej River
TIBET
E
TIBET

THE PARE CHU RIVER

In 2005 the Pare Chu was responsible for flooding the entire Sutlej Valley when it burst a dam on the Tibetan side of the border. It's a strange river in that it rises on the slopes of the Parang La (about 15km north of Kibber), flows east into Tibet and then rounds on itself and flows back into India to join the Spiti at Sumdo. The floods in 2005 washed away five bridges and two villages in Kinnaur and rumours circulated that the event was a deliberate act by the Chinese. Since occupying Tibet in the 1950s China now controls the headwaters of many rivers which sustain the Indian subcontinent – a fact which makes the Indian government extremely nervous. Major cities in China such as Beijing are facing a waterless future and, never shy of dramatic measures, the Chinese government is looking to the great rivers and lakes of Tibet to provide the answer. India's suspicion is that the price for eastern China's salvation will be paid for by countries which rely on Tibet's water: India and Bangladesh.

Chango (2997m) 288.5/363KM

Opposite the police checkpost a small dhaba sells basic food and cold drinks before the climb ahead. If the road ahead is blocked there are unloved doubles Rs100 (att) above the dhaba at the ***Himalaya Guesthouse***. A general store selling biscuits is further down the road. The village itself is 2.5km up the side road; a friendly place surrounded by apple, plum and apricot orchards and topped by a gompa.

From Chango the road starts climbing a buttery-yellow ridge in a series of switchbacks; the first kilometre and a half is the steepest. It's a long way up and the top section is the worst: a crossing of the **Malling landslide** (see box below) which is always rough, even if not 'live'. If it is live, take local advice and cross on foot if possible. The road workers will often help but negotiate a price first to avoid any misunderstandings. From the top of the climb the road drops past a Hindu shrine, turns back into tarmac and rolls to Nako village.

Nako (3640m) 311/340.5KM

If Nako had a good restaurant and there were no Inner Line Permit hassles this would be a tempting place to stay for weeks. The village is a higgledy-piggledy jumble of stone-built houses with tiny wooden doors and cow byres all crowded upon each other in earthen lanes, with a gompa to the west and a village pond to the south. Across the valley is an expanse of space and mountain which often gives Nako the feel of soaring among the clouds.

Road workers at the Malling Slide

THE MALLING SLIDE

The whole of this mountainside is unstable, and the Malling nalah is notorious for causing landslides which take out the road for months. Until 2005 the main road used to run along the Spiti River, and crossing the 'Malling slide' on foot could take up to two hours if the slide was unstable or 'live'. Since then the road has been diverted up the mountain to just above Nako and although it's still prone to blockages, the precipitous scramble over them usually takes just twenty minutes. If the road is blocked GREF labourers will help carry your bicycle and panniers (charges range from free to Rs50 per bag). It is no coincidence that the slide area begins from just after the temple.

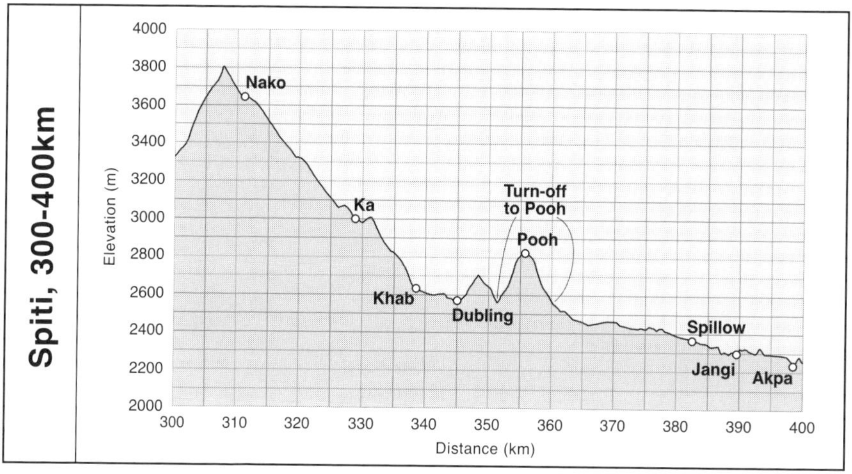

By the village bus stand three guesthouses on the right have similar doubles for around Rs150 (att); the ***Lovon Guesthouse*** has the edge because one of its rooms has a sofa and en-suite bathroom with hot shower. Best of all there are no stairs to carry panniers up and down. All overlook the village, its fields and the mountains beyond. A little more comfort can be had at the ugly concrete ***Reo Purgul*** opposite (doubles Rs400-600; att) while for food the ***Naygo Hotel & Guesthouse*** makes basic Tibetan dishes (chowmein and thukpa) and the Reo Purgul offers equivalent Indian dishes. A general store has intermittent STD/ISD and tourist essentials: woolly socks and chocolate.

DAY 7 NAKO (3640m) to POOH (2811m) 44.2KM

NAKO–KA 17.2KM
KA–KHAB 10.2KM
KHAB–DUBLING 6.7KM
DUBLING–POOH TURN-OFF 5.7KM
POOH TURN-OFF–POOH 4.4KM

Heading south from Nako, fields can be seen scratched into the hills opposite. The Nako road rejoins the NH22 near Yangthang; a clutch of brightly coloured government huts. Near the turn-off to Leo the irrigated valley on the opposite side of the Spiti is the little-visited Hango Valley.

Kazigs (2978m) 'Kazigs start', warns the sign, 'Check brake' as ten switchbacks plunge the highway nearly three hundred metres down to the river.

Ka (2998m) 328.5/323KM
A small oasis of fruit trees and shade amid a burning amphitheatre of bare rock. Somewhere along this stretch of road is a rock saying 'believe it not... Mewar Helipad inaugurated by the IAF on 13th day of March 1991'.

Khab (2618m) 338.5/313KM
Here the Spiti pours into the Sutlej River which flows from the slopes of Mt Kailash to the Arabian Sea near Karachi as the Indus. The Shipki La near Khab was the favoured trading route to Tibet from Hindustan and although a trading post was opened there in 1995 it sees very little traffic. Khab is beetling with armed soldiers but don't miss the awesome face of Reo Purgyal, rising over 3700m to the northeast (no photography though). A paddle of less than 10km up the Sutlej (some chance!) would see you in Tibet. The next big Tibetan town is Tholing whose gompa has Kashmiri frescoes as ancient and important as Tabo's. After

Khab the highway exits the narrow Spiti gorge and near the Namgia turn-off the peaks you can see to the southeast are the Himalaya range.

Dubling (2579m) 345/306.5KM
At the time of research the *Desert Rose* hotel was under construction here, possibly for workers on the *hydel* (hydroelectric) project. Once open it would save the steep climb at the end of the day up to Pooh. There's a small general store with cold drinks just before the bridge over the Spiti.

Pooh turn-off (2571m) 351/300.5KM
Pooh General Store is a cornucopia of all sorts of things you never knew you wanted. The village itself, like most in Kinnaur, is not on the valley floor but a steep 240m above it on a 4.5km link road (signed in Hindi), just past the general store.

Pooh (2811m) 355.5/296KM
Pooh only has one guesthouse, the *Valley View*, which overlooks the village's orchards and the valley but has a rather lonely feel, perhaps due to the Indian salesmen who use it. Doubles with TV (HBO and BBC) and hot bucket shower are overpriced at Rs300 but this is a small matter compared to the flies which are everywhere. The kitchen makes chips and dahl with rice but don't seem particularly bothered and are happy for you to cook your own food. Pooh's small bazaar has ISD shops and general stores.

DAY 8 POOH (2811m) to RECONG PEO (2293m) 65KM

POOH–NH22 4.4KM
NH22–SPILLOW 22.5KM
SPILLOW–JANGI 7.3KM
JANGI–AKPA 8.9KM
AKPA–RECONG PEO TURN-OFF 16.4KM
RECONG PEO TURN-OFF–RECONG PEO 5.5KM

Upper Kinnaur at Pooh is still arid and rocky though it lacks Spiti's immensity and starts feeling much more Indian. The road continues rolling downhill along a bare gorge with the sepia-coloured Sutlej boiling away below. After a while a few stunted shrubs appear as glacier-blue nalahs feed into the valley and the Sutlej tumbles west through interlocking spurs.

Spillow (2360m) 382.5/269KM
Restaurants and general stores line the road but there's no guesthouse here. Both sides of the valley grow trees, the first in days and which against all the odds aren't cultivated. The people are dressed in Indian style: shalwar kameez and gaudy accessories for the girls; the men sometimes wearing the Kinnauri cap: a grey or brown felt hat with a billiard-green front flap edged with an orange and red trim, which will come to be a familiar sight.

Jangi (2294m) 389.5/262KM
This is the last (or first) checkpost for the Inner Line Permit. A small dhaba next door sells dahl and rice for Rs10. The scenery softens somewhat as trees start to cover the hillsides and nalahs rush down from enticing-looking valleys.

Akpa (2231m) 398.5/253KM
Headwinds pick up in the afternoon and by Akpa the highway can be windy and dusty. This is where the floods in 2005 washed away several bridges so the makeshift road can be rough but it leads through pines – the first scent of trees for days. This is the last place to buy snacks before the climb to Recong Peo.

Recong Peo turn-off (1981m) 415/236.5KM
Opposite the GREF camp the road to Recong Peo starts steeply but then settles down into a steady climb through the trees.

Recong Peo / Peo (2293m) 420.5/231KM
Kinnaur's district capital is a noisy clutter of one-up, one-down shops along Main Bazaar selling plastic buckets, cheap clothes and fake watches. But its location sets it apart – balanced on the edge of a hillside, it's dwarfed by the icy Kinner Kailash massif to the south. Prayer flags still flutter here – Recong Peo was the venue for the Dalai Lama's Kalachakra ceremony back in 1992 – but the Tibetan influence so predominant in Spiti is begin-

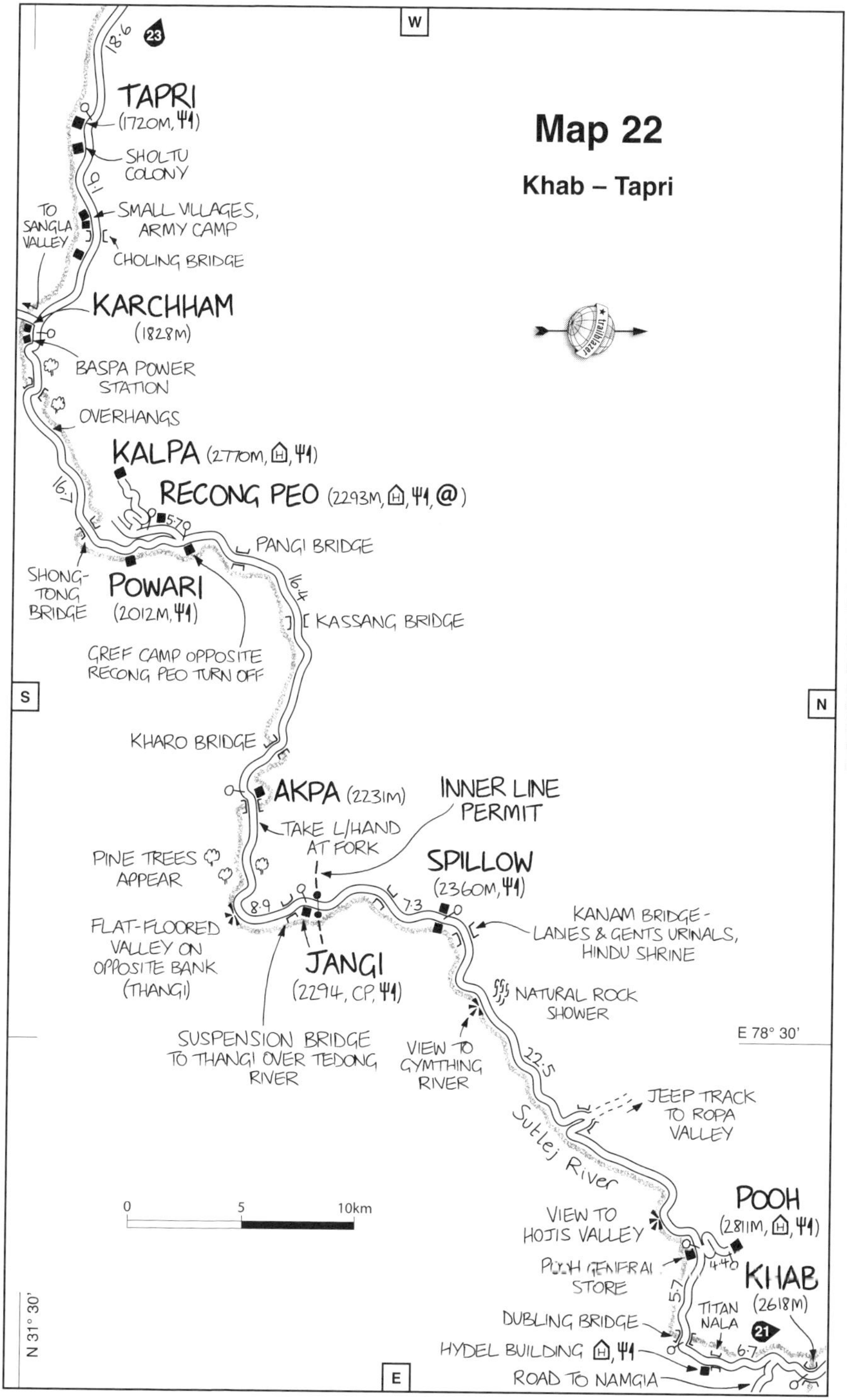

Map 22

Khab – Tapri

SPITI & KINNAUR

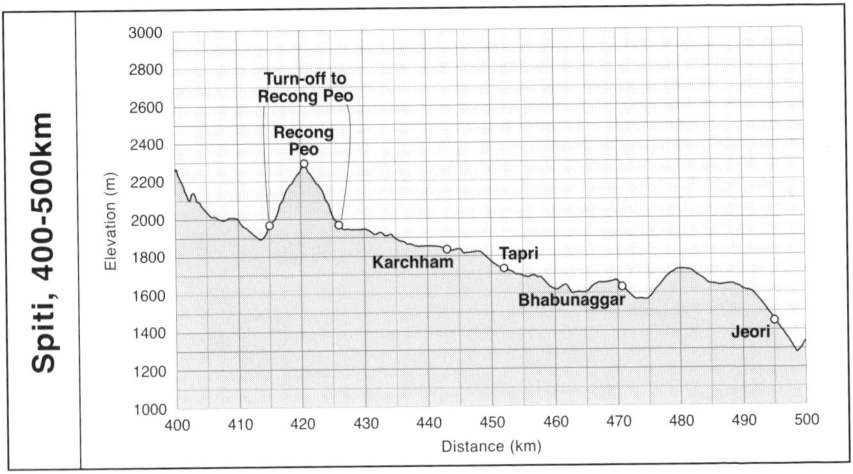

ning to fade and instead the hawk and spit of India returns. The lower town is a sprawl of tin-roofed government buildings followed by a concrete stadium and the Tourist Information Office; Main Bazaar which leads northwest of the chowk is the heart of Peo.

Coming from Spiti, the sight of mangoes, papayas, coconuts, newspapers, phones, an English wine and beer shop and even internet access makes this one-Tata town feel like a metropolis. There's a string of hotels along Main Bazaar, including the tatty ***Snow View*** (Rs200), the overpriced ***Fairyland*** and next door the ***Mayur***, and the clean ***Ridang*** (Rs150-500). The computer shop on the narrow 'first floor' walkway opposite the Ridang rarely has **internet** access; a more reliable place is Raj Internet (Rs60/hr) 2km up the road to Kalpa and 200m past the bus stand. You can reach it on foot by taking the road south of the Little Chef restaurant and climbing the steps to the bus stand. Recong Peo is about par with Kaza for food: the ***Little Chef*** restaurant serves tasty Indian dishes whereas for momos you can either get a dirt-cheap plate (Rs10) in Main Bazaar or visit the awkwardly decorated ***Cafeteria Roof***.

The Punjab National Bank in Recong Peo will have nothing to do with foreign exchange: the nearest ATM is in Rampur. Cozy Medical Centre opposite the Little Chef sells antibiotics and ORS. The hospital is 2km up the road to Kalpa (or you can take a shortcut up the steps to the bus stand); register in room 1 and the pharmacy is in room 11. Diagnosis is free.

KALPA (2770M)

It would be a shame to ride up to Peo but never make it to the village of Kalpa which lies another 500m higher. Riders in a hurry could make an unloaded day trip up to Kalpa, which enjoys even better views of Kinner Kailash and is far prettier than utilitarian Peo. The village is a steep 7.5km ride up from Recong Peo past the jeep stand, Hotel City Heart, the hospital and Raj Internet. Almost at the top of the climb is a junction, turn south (back on yourself) to reach the village. There are several guest-houses, including the ***Apple View***, ***Blue Lotus*** and ***Aucthong*** on the high road among the apple orchards. Anyone who needs to spend a day or two sorting out an Inner Line Permit might prefer the peace and village atmosphere of Kalpa to the bustle and honk of Peo, and surrounding Kalpa are trails to smaller villages such as Ribba and Roghi. This is also the last interesting place on the ride to Shimla for mountain-lovers; from here the road plummets to hot and muggy Jeori and Rampur.

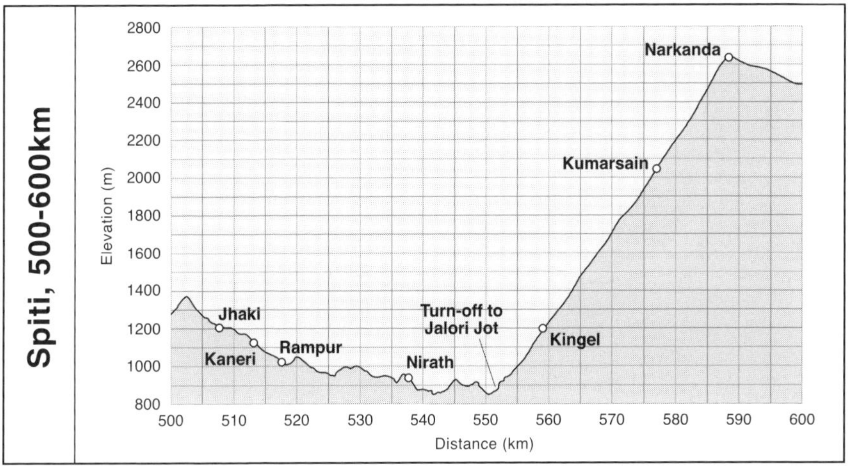

DAY 9 RECONG PEO (2293m) to JEORI (1445m) 74.7KM

RECONG PEO–NH22 5.7KM
NH22–KARCHAM 16.7KM
KARCHAM–TAPRI 9.1KM
TAPRI–BHABUNAGGAR 18.6KM
BHABUNAGGAR–JEORI 24.6KM

From Recong Peo the highway continues downhill past the GREF camp with a couple of dhabas at Powari and pulleys across the Sutlej ferrying villagers and their all-important apple harvests. Chilgoza pines make an appearance around here, you can tell them by their candelabra-like branches. Apparently their pine nuts possess aphrodisiac qualities though peeling them must be fiddly enough to cool anyone's ardour. The road is generally good, teetering under overhangs high above the Sutlej, though there are some rough and dusty patches before Tapri. It's about here that cows start becoming a road hazard.

Karcham (1828m) 443/208.5KM

Just after the chilly spray from the Baspa hydel project is Karcham which marks the turn-off to the Sangla Valley (see box on p202). The valley sides become greener and the river broadens and slows before narrowing into a chute. After the army camp it turns from mellow to monstrous in a few noisy kilometres as the water churns around boulders the size of houses.

Tapri (1720m) 452/199.5KM

This flyblown village has a couple of restaurants, general stores and fruit and veg sellers. From here onwards the valley is greener, warmer and more humid; if you've come from Srinagar this is the first time in weeks you've dropped below 2000m. Just before Wangtu, where the road workers are building a road to Mudh in the Pin Valley (see box p193), the highway gets its first white line painted down the middle.

THE INNER LINE PERMIT

Coming from Shimla, Recong Peo is the last place you can get an Inner Line Permit, without which you will not be able to proceed beyond Jangi, 32km to the east. The Tourist Information Centre (Mon–Sat 10am-5pm, closed every other Saturday) charges Rs150 to process the permit and requires a photocopy of your passport details and Indian visa (but no passport photos). The one restriction is that you must apply in a group of four though this is only for the paperwork and there's no expectation that you will travel together.

THE SANGLA VALLEY

From Karcham a dizzying road climbs up to Sangla, the main town in a valley fabled for being the most beautiful in the Himalaya. Sadly its lower reaches are dominated by the ugly Baspa III hydel project and though there are plenty of guesthouses Sangla itself lacks charm. Beyond Sangla the scenery is far prettier; tented camps along the river banks are surprisingly luxurious and the small village of Chitkul at the far end of the valley has stunning views across its meadows to the Kinner Kailash and Garwhal Himalaya peaks. The village also lies close to the borders of Tibet and Uttaranchal – Tibet is just 30km to the east and Gangotri 60km to the southeast. The gorgeous mountains, friendly villagers, basic family guesthouses and a small tea stall make this a 'sticky place' for travellers. From Karcham (1828m) to Sangla (2650m) is about 17km with a further 25km to Chitkul (3450m).

Bhabunaggar (1615m) 470.5/181KM

There are fruit, veg and soft-drink sellers along the roadside and a line of shops a little above the highway. After the high mountains of Kinner Kailash earlier, the valley near here is glen-like and the shrubs and grasses are flourishing rather than struggling for existence. From here until Jeori some parts of the road are extremely narrow, a mere nick in the rock under beetling overhangs and high above the river. No wonder there are several shrines at the wayside.

Jeori (1445m) 495/156.5KM

The immersion back into 'India' is almost complete: auto rickshaws, tropical plants, Bollywood tunes and cows with no road sense. There is only one hotel in Jeori, the ***Bushahr***; its restaurant has a large bar stocked with flies and whisky which the clientele seem intent on emptying. The fetid doubles downstairs cost Rs200 (att) and have a hot shower if there's electricity. Only the most tired of cyclists would want to stay here rather than Sarahan (see box below).

DAY 10 JEORI (1445m) to RAMPUR (1015m) 22.4KM

JEORI–JHAKRI 12.3KM
JHAKRI–KANERI 5.4KM
KANERI–RAMPUR 4.7KM

Apart from a 3km climb up to a bridge, it's all downhill from Jeori to Rampur and quickly done. The valley widens onto a broad shelf with fields and oxen, and then closes up again. There are no longer views of snowy peaks as in upper Kinnaur; instead monkeys and fruit trees line the road.

Rampur (1015m) 17.5/134KM

Rampur used to be capital of the Himalayan kingdom of Bushahr and is now the commercial and transport hub for Kinnaur. Wedged between the river and valley walls, after the heights you have scaled it's gloomy, hot and humid

JEORI (1445M) – SARAHAN (2160M), 17KM

It's cruel of Kinnaur to finish every day with a climb but Sarahan is far more pleasant than muggy Jeori and its Bhimkhali temple is one of Kinnaur's most attractive sights. A few hotels and guesthouses are clustered around the temple where the *Temple Guesthouse* is the most pleasant and popular place to stay. Marble-floored double rooms with wooden balconies, en-suite bathrooms and hot taps are excellent value at Rs150/200/300 depending on the views. They are arranged around the temple's stone-flagged courtyard which means they are also subject to the temple bell: light sleepers should bring earplugs. To avoid disappointment in high season book in advance by calling ☎ 01782 274 248.

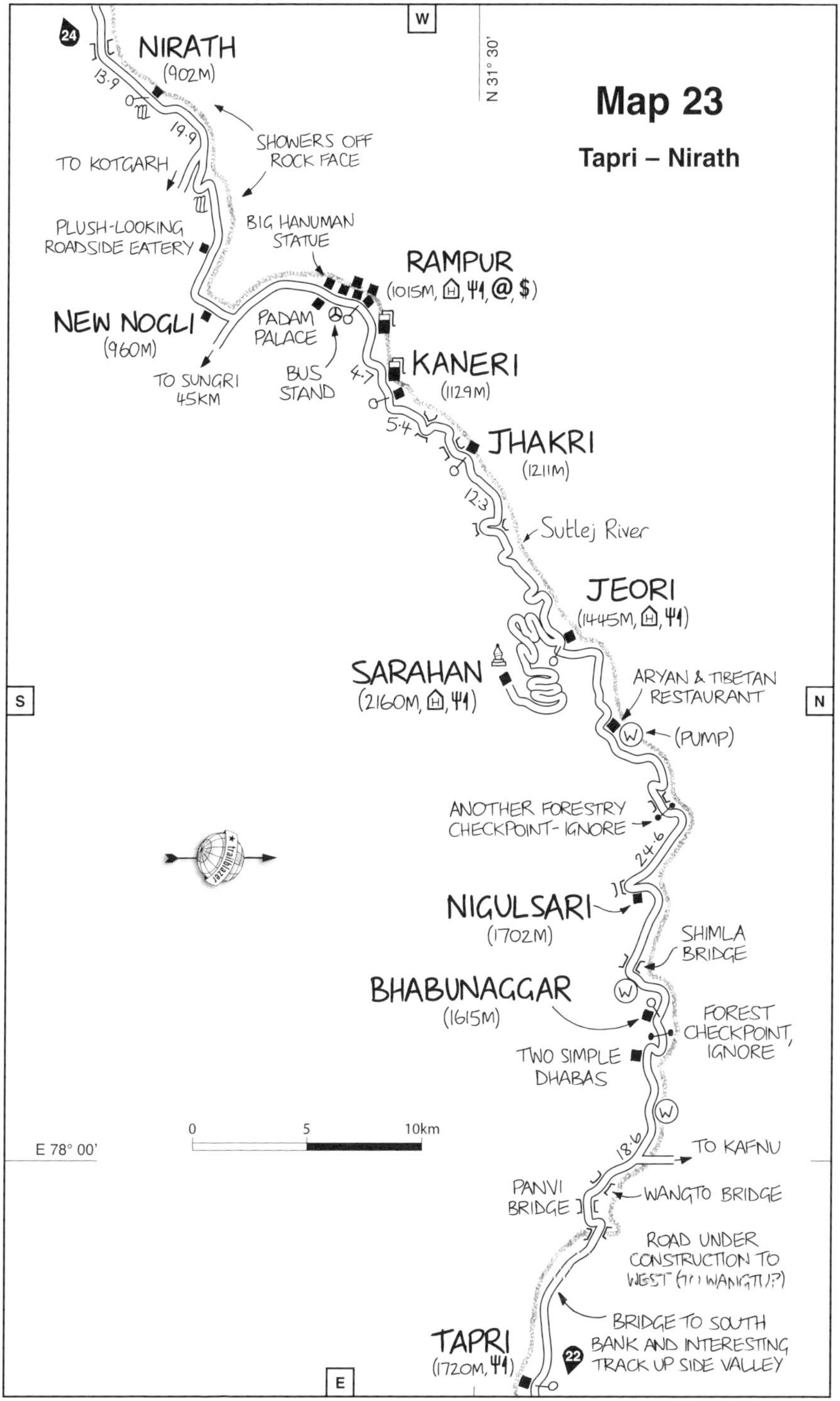
Map 23
Tapri – Nirath
W
N 31° 30'
S
N
E
E 78° 00'
0
5
10km
24
NIRATH
(902M)
13.9
19.9
SHOWERS OFF
ROCK FACE
TO KOTGARH
PLUSH-LOOKING
ROADSIDE EATERY
BIG HANUMAN
STATUE
RAMPUR
(1015M, , , @, $)
NEW NOGLI
(960M)
PADAM
PALACE
TO SUNGRI
45KM
BUS
STAND
4.7
KANERI
(1129M)
5.4
JHAKRI
(1211M)
12.3
Sutlej River
JEORI
(1445M, ,)
SARAHAN
(2160M, ,)
ARYAN & TIBETAN
RESTAURANT
W
(PUMP)
ANOTHER FORESTRY
CHECKPOINT - IGNORE
24.6
NIGULSARI
(1702M)
SHIMLA
BRIDGE
W
BHABUNAGGAR
(1615M)
FOREST
CHECKPOINT,
IGNORE
TWO SIMPLE
DHABAS
W
18.6
TO KAFNU
PANVI
BRIDGE
WANGTO BRIDGE
ROAD UNDER
CONSTRUCTION TO
WEST (TO WANGTU?)
BRIDGE TO SOUTH
BANK AND INTERESTING
TRACK UP SIDE VALLEY
TAPRI
(1720M,)
22
trailblazer

but offers a respite among creature comforts before the huge climb up to Narkanda and Shimla. From the main road the town spills down towards the river across narrow lanes crammed with shops, ranging from old-fashioned wooden hardware stores where the proprietors sit cross-legged among their faded wares, to bright showrooms of electrical goods.

With a bike, keep going down the main road past the bus stand, the Padam Palace and the SBI ATM then take the steep and narrow lane crowded with street stalls on the right just after the police station (if you reach the Highway Home hotel, you've gone too far). You can ride down through the crowded bazaar this way. Keep going over the first junction then turn right at the next. On the left after 250m there's a narrow unsigned lane floored with pink tiles (before the children's playground) which leads to two hotels with rooms overlooking the Sutlej: the plush ***Hotel Bhagwati*** with doubles ranging from Rs165 to Rs385 and just beyond, the ***Amar Jyoti Hotel*** whose doubles cost Rs150 (com).

On foot, a busy set of 122 steps opposite the bus stand twists past shops, dhabas and the poky Rama Guesthouse down to the lanes. An unnamed dhaba on the steps serves *tikki*, deep-fried potato cakes served with channa masala, a splash of curd and a sprinkle of coriander; it's a friendly place and good for watching the extraordinary things like filing cabinets that people carry up and down the stairs on their heads.

DAY 11 RAMPUR (1015m) to NARKANDA (2625m) 70.7KM

RAMPUR–NIRATH 19.9KM
NIRATH–SAINJ 13.9KM
SAINJ–KINGEL 7.7KM
KINGEL–KUMARSAIN 18.1KM
KUMARSAIN–NARKANDA 11.1KM

Today has two parts: an undulating 34km downhill to tropical Sainj, where a road loops back to Manali over Jalori Jot (see box below) followed by a tough climb up to alpine Narkanda. This climb is harder than Rohtang because of the heat and humidity; it's also steeper.

Sainj (835m) 551.5/100KM

This is the lowest point of the ride, where mango and banana trees flourish in the tropical climate, monkeys jeer at the traffic and air is rich with oxygen. That's good because the next 37km to Narkanda are all uphill. If it seems bad at the bottom steel yourself because it gets steeper and rougher higher up. On the plus side the lower section is hot and exposed but higher up the air is cooler and the road runs through shady pine forests. Frequent cold drinks shops offer the chance to rehydrate.

THE ROAD TO MANALI OVER JALORI JOT

From Sainj a tarmac road crosses the Sutlej and climbs past terraces of rice and apple orchards up to the small town of Ani, which has a basic unsigned guesthouse. From Ani onwards the road is prone to landslides and climbs up to the village of Khanag, past a government rest house where Penelope Betjeman (wife of poet John Betjeman and an expert on this region) died; there's a memorial to her in the garden. From Khanag to the pass the road is very steep and rocky.

In clear weather Jalori Jot enjoys wonderful views over the Himalaya, there's also a small temple and a couple of chai shops; watch out for the cook who scours his omelette pan with handfuls of dirt from the road! The south side of the pass is dark and somewhat unfriendly; the villagers have a poor reputation among other Himachalis. The north side feels entirely different: an extremely steep descent to the gorgeous village of Shoja which has a Banjara camp (💻 www.banjaracamps.com) and a couple of enticing wooden guesthouses, then a less severe descent past Banjara and Larji to rejoin Aut and the Kullu Valley on the NH21.

Allow two days to cover the distance from Rampur to Aut. If returning to Manali, there's a quiet road on the true left bank of the Beas between Kullu and Manali.

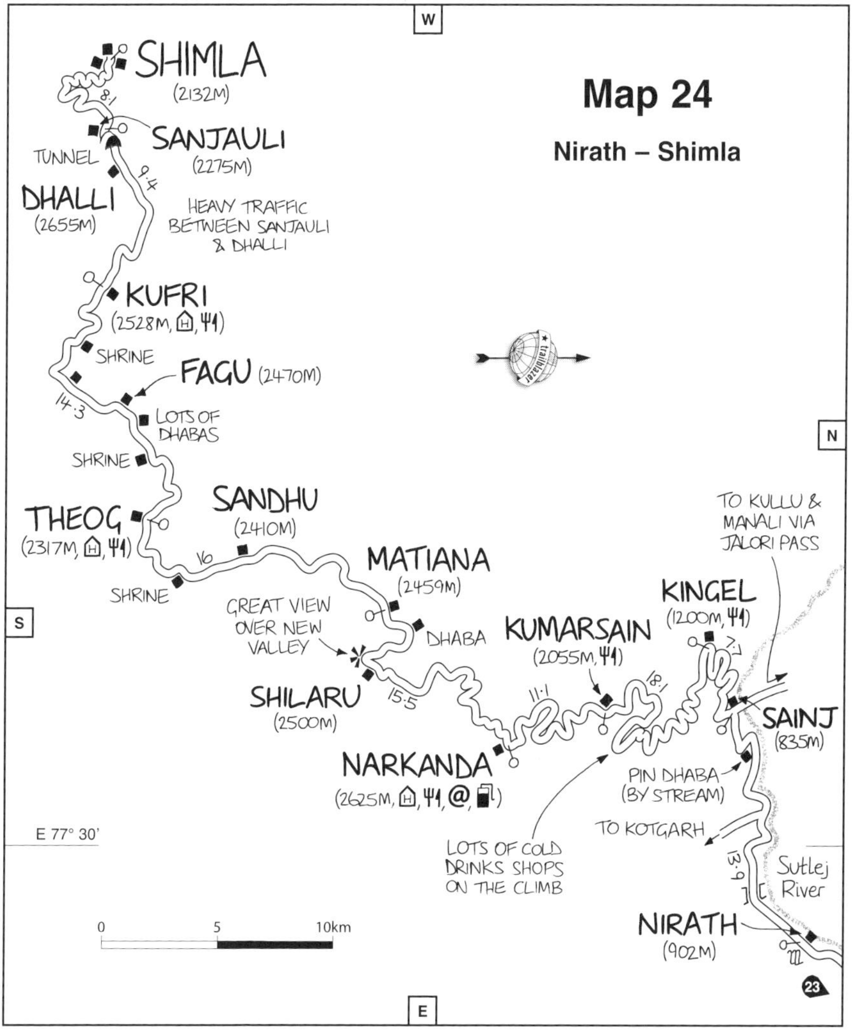

Kingel (1200m) 559/92.5km

There are a few restaurants and cold drinks shops here. After the village the road doubles back on itself so you can see your earlier route along the Sutlej below and reminisce fondly about flat roads. The hillsides are terraced with emerald green paddy fields.

Kumarsain (2055m) 577/74.5km

This is a poor-looking village with a few dhabas. At the fork turn southwest for Narkanda. As the road climbs higher the peaks of the Garwhal Himalaya to the northeast come into view.

Narkanda (2625m) 588.5/63km

The Indian hill town of Narkanda is set among pine-covered slopes with views northeast to a line of snowy peaks. It's a popular place with Indian tourists for trekking and skiing so the accommodation is more expensive than elsewhere: doubles at the ***Hotel Mahayama*** cost Rs650-1000 (att) and the ***HPTDC hotel*** is even more at Rs880–1320.

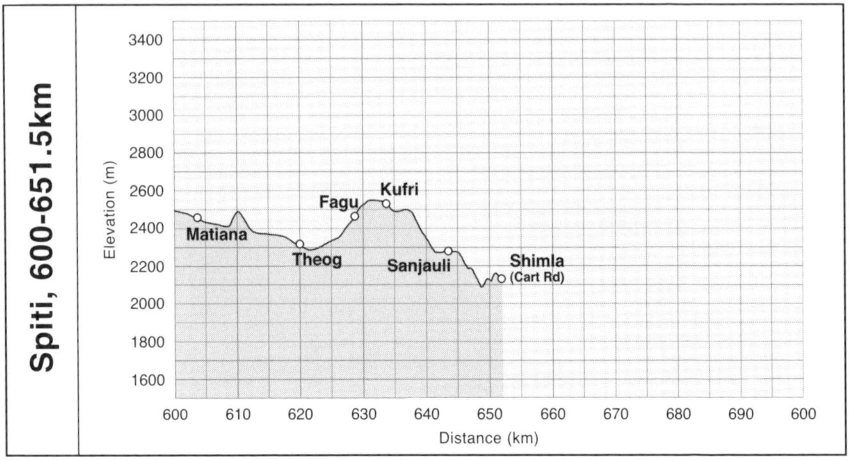

DAY 12 NARKANDA (2625m) to SHIMLA (2132m) 63.5KM

NARKANDA–MATIANA 15.5KM
MATIANA–THEOG 16KM
THEOG–FAGU 9KM
FAGU–KUFRI 5.5KM
KUFRI–DHALLI 8KM
DHALLI–SHIMLA 9.5KM

From Narkanda bus stand the road starts descending gradually along a series of ridges which switch views from valley to valley until Theog. From Dhalli onwards the traffic is unpleasantly busy all the way to Shimla.

Narkanda (2625m) 588.5/63KM

The road travels south out of Narkanda then follows a westerly ridge with views of Hattu Peak (3136m) and precipitous drops down to the Giri River and its tributaries. After yesterday's tough climb this is easy riding with excellent views of the surrounding tropical valleys.

Matiana (2459m) 604/47.5KM

There's a dhaba here and some general stores and a switch in perspective as the road traverses west with views down to the Sutlej.

Theog (2317m) 620/31.5KM

Theog appears at a bend in the road, clinging to a ridge that drops down to the Sutlej river to the north and Giri river to the south. Its bazaar has slightly more hustle than Narkanda's due to its position at the crossroads of the busy fruit-farming valleys of the Giri River. From Theog the traffic increases considerably until Shimla. The road continues through heavily wooded ridge tops with fewer views due to the density of the canopy as it starts the last long climb to Fagu where there are a couple of dhabas.

Fagu (2470m) 628.5/23KM

From Fagu you're on the home stretch to Shimla with more descents than ascents.

Kufri (2528m) 634/17.5KM

Once you reach Kufri the road narrows and you need to keep your wits about you as you jostle with buses and trucks on your way down to Dhalli.

Dhalli (2665m) 642/9.5KM

It's in Dhalli that the road splits to the right, leading through a tunnel which effectively makes up the Shimla bypass. Be careful in the tunnel as it is narrow, unlit and often very wet. Once out of the tunnel you have burrowed through the ridge and are in Sanjauli, on the final run into Shimla. The road bobs and weaves, as does the traffic as both descend into this historic hill

ROAD BLASTING

It's quite likely that at some point along the NH22 or up the side valleys you'll encounter teams dynamiting the road. There's usually somebody with a red rag on a twig to wave you through or keep you back while they're blasting. But it's not an interesting job and so their attention wanders or their eyelids close ... a few cyclists have sailed silently past twig man and then found themselves sprinting through the blast zone. So if you pass a sleeping man with a red rag on a twig ... think twice!

station. Some sections of road are still cobbled and can be quite slippery when wet.

Shimla (2132m) **651.5/0KM**

The Kufri road enters Shimla from the north east and continues along the ridge past Lakhar Bazaar to Scandal Point where it's possible to follow a tangle of alleys directly south to Sabze Mandi where the heart of the town lies. Alternatively you can follow the larger roads of The Western or Eastern Mall which enclose the northerly part of Shimla. To the south of Sabze Mandi lies Cart Road along which you will find various hotels and the bus station to the west of the town.

SHIMLA (2132M)

This famous hill town, former summer capital of the Raj and gateway to the Himalaya is in a state of genteel decay. Traffic is a problem as the town is steep and mostly pedestrianized so the roads that do exist are congested. Europeans expecting some familiarity will be disappointed because modern Shimla is mostly an awkward jumble of tin-roofed buildings scampered over by monkeys.

One of Shimla's notorious monkeys posing with the Himalaya in the background

Arrival and orientation

The main (but longer) road into Shimla from the east is Cart Road, a diesel-belching, pedestrian-squishing, clogged artery which leads past the main bus station, train station and then tunnels under the ridge. This is the route buses take. Most cyclists arrive from the north, past Lakhar Bazaar. From Cart Road narrow lanes and steps scale the hillside up to The Ridge – a much calmer pedestrian thoroughfare with views to both the plains and the Himalaya and glorious sunsets. There's also a lift (8am–9pm, Rs7, bicycles accepted). The Mall which leads down from Scandal Point on the Ridge is lined with restaurants, internet cafés and bookshops. With its ice-cream stands, fast food, promenading couples and pony rides, Shimla has the feel of a bygone British seaside resort, accidentally washed up on a Himalayan hill-top.

Where to stay

Unlike Manali, Shimla doesn't have many hotels in the budget range. The ***Hotel Basant*** is in a noisy but convenient location on Cart Road with lots of steps but the staff are friendly and will help with panniers. Doubles cost Rs350 with TV (att, bucket). The ***HPTDC Hotel Holiday Home*** near the lift on Cart Road is more upmarket than the Basant with deluxe/luxury doubles for Rs1200/2400. Unlike many hotels in Shimla it has 24-hour hot water.

(continued on p209)

Colour section (following pages)

- **1 (Opposite)** National Highway 22 (NH22) enters the Upper Kinnaur Valley (see p198) where overhangs scalp buses and careless drivers plunge into the Sutlej River far below.
- **2** One of the Himalaya's most beautiful mountains: Rakaposhi (7788m) in Nagar, northern Pakistan. This photo was taken from the KKH at Nasirabad (see p100).
- **3 Top**: Be gentle on my curves: the Jalebi Bends (see box p165) on the Leh–Srinagar Highway.
  Bottom left: Local bike shops in the Himalaya, where ingenuity and a hammer go a long way.
  Bottom right: The papers get delivered on foot over a landslide on NH22, Kinnaur.
- **4 Top**: Skewer food restaurant in Shigatse's Food Mall (p266), Tibet.
  Bottom: Riding the Manali Leh Highway, some mud, a friendly Tata, a cheery local woman collecting hay for her animals and in the background the start of the switchbacks up to Marrhi.
- **5** Camping at 4655m on the edge of the Morei Plains, Manali–Leh Highway (see p142).
- **6 (Opposite p209)** 'It feels as though you are riding among the folds of an ancient elephant'... Chrissi freewheels from Namika La into the Wakha Valley, Leh–Srinagar Highway (see p168).

GOODS
TARNUM
TATA

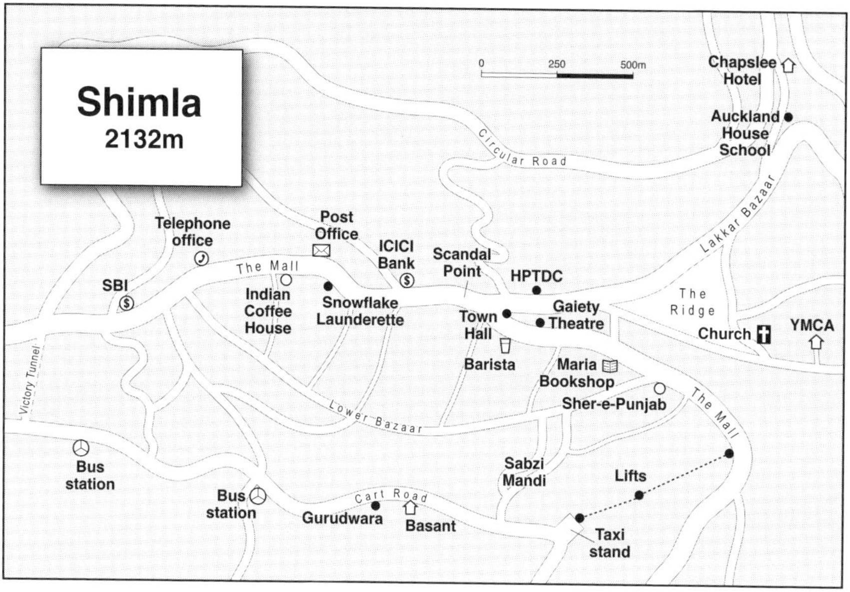

(*Continued from p208*) The ***Chapslee Hotel*** (💻 www.chapslee.com; full-board from Rs9500) is a small heritage hotel packed with antiques and stories, a once-in-a-lifetime place to stay and well-deserved if you are finishing your ride in Shimla.

Where to eat

Apart from the restaurants in ***Clarks*** and ***The Cecil*** (both on The Mall), Shimla's eateries cater to Indian taste buds. A stroll along The Mall will turn up fast food and sweets; for savoury snacks head into the bazaar for street food such as fried potato cakes. The ***Barista*** is a popular Starbucks-style coffee shop on The Mall near Gaiety Theatre with cappuccinos, muffins and brownies while the ***Indian Coffee House's*** faded colonial atmosphere offers a great people-watching spot. The ***New Milap*** is a friendly, diner-style dhaba in Middle Bazaar and ***Sher-e-Punjab*** is a long-established restaurant offering hearty Punjabi fare at the eastern end of The Mall.

Services

- **Banks and post office** ICICI and UTO Banks have ATMs at Scandal Point on The Mall by the post office
- **Bookshops** Maria Brother, Asia Bookhouse and Minerva on The Mall
- **Chemist** Indu Medical on The Mall
- **Internet** Mr Sood's Internet Café below the church on The Mall has the fastest connection (Rs30/hr)
- **Laundry** Snowwhite on The Mall west of the GPO
- **Moving on** HPTDC buses to Delhi can be booked from the booth outside the HPTDC building at Scandal Point.

6 SIKKIM

ROUTE INFORMATION

- **Start / finish** Siliguri (West Bengal) / Shiv Mandir (Sikkim), India
- **Distance** 745km
- **Altitude min / max** 104m/4996m
- **High passes** None. But it is very hilly!
- **Suggested duration** 17 cycling days, three weeks in total
- **Road conditions** 95% potholed tarmac, 5% packed mud
- **Hazards and dangers** Landslides on mountain roads
- **When to go** March – May, October – December. The best views are in November and December; the orchids and rhododendrons are in flower from April to mid-May but haze obscures the views. Avoid mid-May to the end of September as Sikkim's monsoon is torrential
- **Visas** Indian visa required, Inner Line Permit available at state border

Very few bikers make it to the tiny Indian state of Sikkim, preferring instead to range around the mountains of India's western Himalaya. Sikkim certainly is something of a dead end, boxed in as it is between Nepal, Tibet and Bhutan with no border crossings into any of them, but it is extraordinarily varied. For cyclists it's also extraordinarily steep, with gradients of up to 22%.

Half the fun of Sikkim is getting there: the hills of West Bengal are either a taste of the joys to come or a warning of the horrors ahead. From Darjeeling the immense bulk of Kanchenjunga (8585m), Sikkim's highest peak and the world's third highest mountain, floats on the horizon. The few roads that exist in Sikkim pass waterfalls, orchids, gompas and meticulously tended tea estates. They also climb from a jungly 331m at the border to an icy 4996m at Gurudongmar Lake. Views can vary from zero in damp cloud to panoramas of the Himalaya, depending on the season and your luck. As you yoyo up, down and around the hillsides the climate will change too – hot, humid and sweaty in the valleys and cold, rainy and misty (if you're unlucky) on the hilltops. Even Sikkim Tourism describes its state as 'wrapped in mist and clouds'!

Sikkim looks promising on a map, especially now that the Nathu La pass has opened between Sikkim and Tibet, but the situation is quite different on the ground. Independent travel is forbidden east of Gangtok and the border into Tibet at Nathu La is closed to foreigners. To the north of Tong travel is restricted to five days with a guide and jeep; once again independent travel is not allowed. The far north is where the most exciting mountain scenery lies: beyond Gurudongmar Lake the road peters out into a dusty track which is dwarfed by snowy monsters. That leaves Just West Sikkim, which can be toured on a bicycle in five hilly days during which you will glimpse the Himalaya, if you're lucky, in the distance.

FACTS ABOUT THE REGION

Here, where India blurred into Bhutan and Sikkim ... it had always been a messy map... A great amount of warring, betraying, bartering had occurred; between Nepal, England, Tibet, India, Sikkim, Bhutan; Darjeeling stolen from here, Kalimpong plucked from there ... despite the mist charging down like a dragon, dissolving, undoing, making ridiculous the drawing of borders. Kiran Desai, *The Inheritance of Loss*

Sikkim only officially became part of India in 1975 when, supervised by the Indian army, 97.5% of its populace voted to abolish the monarchy and become India's twenty-second state. China, to the north, declared this an 'annexation', allegedly because it saw Sikkim as historically Chinese territory, like Tibet, the Aksai Chin in the trans-Karakoram and Arunachal Pradesh to the east of Bhutan. The stand-off lasted until 2003, when China recognized Sikkim as India's and India in turn recognized Tibet as China's. Sikkim is India's least populated state and many Sikkimese do not consider themselves Indians at all. The most commonly spoken language is Nepali rather than Hindi, and the cultural links with its mountainous neighbours – Nepal, Tibet and Bhutan – are far more apparent than any with India. It's a modern oddity then that Sikkim can now only be reached from India, through the hills of West Bengal.

Despite its miniscule size – just 65km across by 110km from top to bottom – Sikkim is famous for its biodiversity. The state soars from 280m to 8585m with an equally extreme climate range from sub-tropical to tundra. Rare butterflies, unique orchids, snow leopards, red pandas, yaks and figs all thrive here. Flower-spotters will have plenty to distract them: the state is renowned for its 600 species of orchid and 30 species of rhododendron. The state's animal is one that few can resist: the adorable red panda, though you are very unlikely to see one unless you visit the Himalayan Zoo in Darjeeling (see p220). Other interesting animals are yaks and *dzos* (a yak/cow cross), the flighty *kyang* (Tibetan wild ass) and the bharal (Himalayan blue sheep), all of which you are most likely to see in the north. Sikkim is also home to about 500 species of butterfly, and 550 species of bird: nearly half the Indian subcontinent's birdlife.

A typically skittish yak, Yumthang

Sikkim's lushness, except in the icy north, is due to the warm, moisture-laden winds which blow in from the Bay of Bengal. This is a place where clouds possess as physical a presence as people: they pass in groups past windows and wander in through doors.

Until the 1960s, when China closed the border, Sikkim relied on Tibet for trade. Since Sikkim was absorbed by India it has been heavily subsidized by the central government but now that the Nathu La trade route to Tibet has reopened it's hoped that the economy will become more robust. From China's perspective the Nathu La pass enables goods to be imported overland via Kolkata and Siliguri rather than having to make the long sea passage to its eastern seaboard, although the road to the border was so narrow in 2006 that two trucks couldn't pass each other.

Safety and restrictions

An **Inner Line Permit is required** to enter Sikkim; the easiest way to arrange this is at the Sikkim Tourism office at Rangpo (the border of West Bengal and Sikkim) where it takes a couple of minutes and is free. The office is open daily from 7am to 9pm. You'll need to provide a photocopy of the Indian visa and personal details pages of your passport. The permit is for 15 days, and is easily extended in Gangtok (see box p227). You can also obtain the permit at Indian consulates abroad and in Sikkim Tourism Offices in Delhi, Darjeeling, Siliguri and Kolkata. The Inner Line Permit is not valid for the road north beyond Tong, the Goecha La trek north of Yuksom, or the road east from Gangtok to Changu Lake. For these regions you will need a travel agent in Gangtok to arrange a separate permit as part of an organized tour (see p226).

The greatest hazards to foreign bikers are **landslides and traffic** on the roads. Sikkim is otherwise safe though there is still some agitation for a separate Gurkha state known as 'Gorkhaland', especially around Darjeeling and Kalimpong in West Bengal, and along the Nepali border. Tourists are unlikely to be affected by this but should be aware of it.

History of the road

India's Border Roads Organization (BRO) continues the work begun by the British who used Gangtok as a staging post on the journey from the plains up to Tibet, most notoriously when Francis Younghusband set off on his punitive mission to Gyantse in 1904. Sikkim's unstable geology makes its roads prone to landslides: some are so notorious that they even have their own signs. The road to Changu Lake and onwards to Nathu La is an ancient Silk Road feeder, which was closed after the Sino-India war in 1962 and only reopened in 2006. Sikkim's major exports to China are power, medicinal plants, flowers and fruits, which are traded at Dongzinggang bazaar on the other side of the border.

Language, religion and culture

Nepali is the most widely spoken language in Sikkim, followed by **Hindi**, **Lepcha** and **Bhutia**. In rural areas few people speak English.

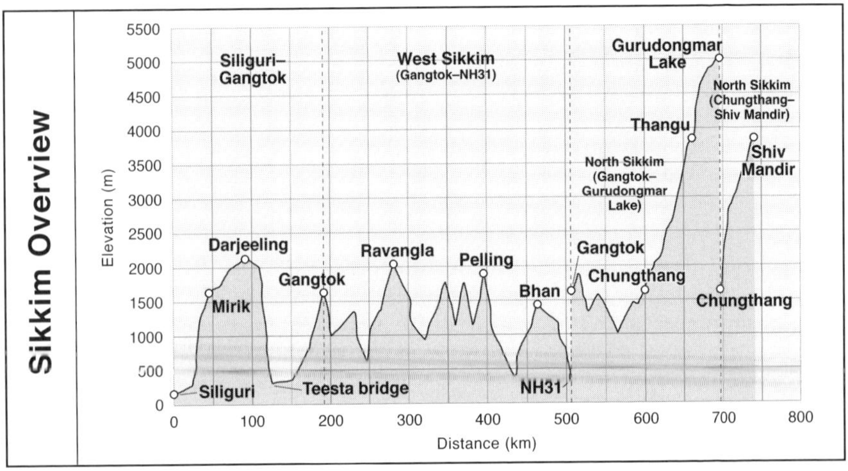

Some 75% of Sikkim's population are **Nepalis**, originally brought here by the British in the nineteenth century to work on the tea estates. The indigenous **Lepchas** and **Bhutias** account for the rest, although with improved transport links, low tax and the opening of the Nathu La trade post an increasing number of entrepreneurial Indians are moving up from the plains.

Although many of the Nepalis are **Hindu**, and just a third of the state's population is **Buddhist**, the Sikkimese celebrate Hindu and Buddhist festivals equally and Sikkim has an overwhelmingly Buddhist feel to it. It's famous for its *gompas* (Buddhist monasteries), especially Rumtek (see box p228), and the landscape is studded with *chortens* (stupas) and draped with prayer flags; another frequent sight along the roads are the slender poles flying long white vertical prayer flags common to the eastern Himalaya. Buddhism arrived in

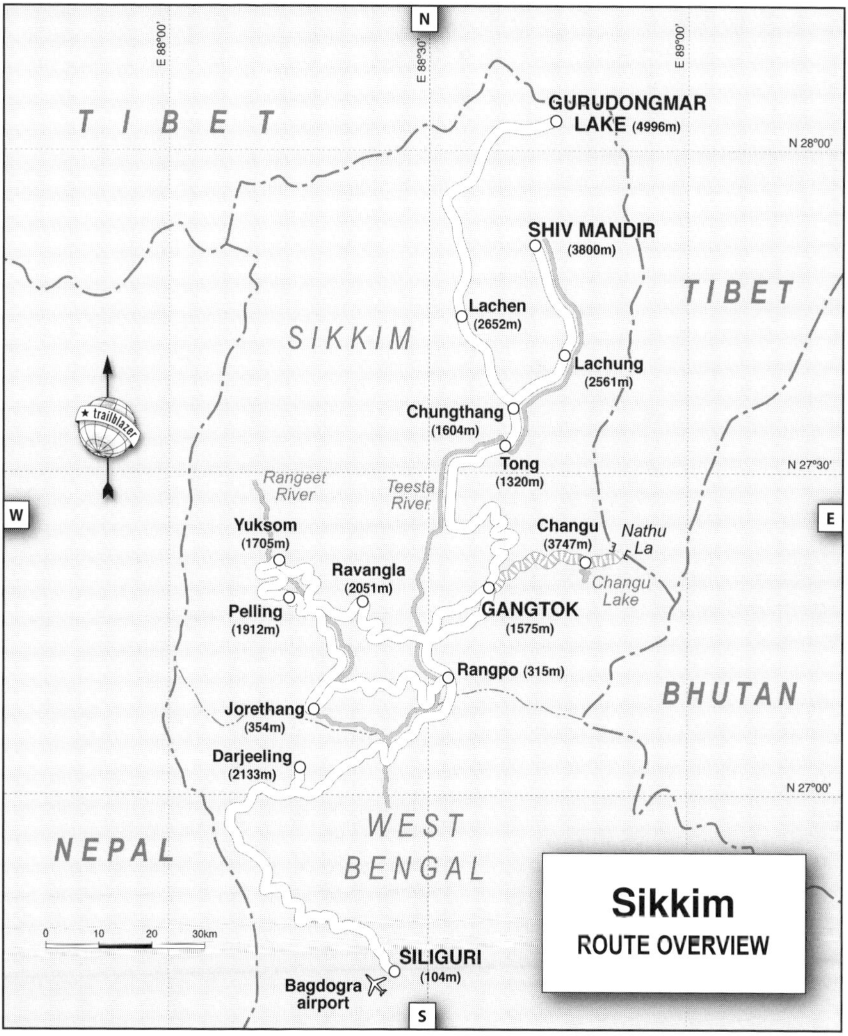

Sikkim in the fourteenth century with a wave of immigrants from Tibet, initially of the Sakya sect and then later, in the seventeenth century, of the Nyingma (Red Hat) sect. Sikkim's oldest inhabitants, the Lepchas, are followers of the animistic **Bon faith** and believe in shamans. Kanchenjunga, the immense mountain massif that dominates northwest Sikkim, is sacred to the Sikkimese who have requested that all expeditions stop five feet short of the summit.

SOME SIMPLE NEPALI PHRASES

Hello	*Namaste/namaskar* (latter is more polite)
How are you?	*Khanu-boyo?* (lit. Have you eaten?)
Fine thanks	*Khai-é* (I have eaten)
Do you speak English?	*Angrayzi bolnoo-hoon-cha?*
Thank you	*Dhan-yabad*
Excuse me (sorry)	*Maf-garnus*
Good/bad	*ramro/naramro*
Cheap/expensive	*susto/mahongo*
Just a minute!	*Ek-chin*!
Brother/sister	*dai/didi* (used to address anyone of your own age)
Good night	*Sooba-ratry*
What's your name?	*Topaiko* (to adult) *timro* (child) *nam ke ho*?
My name is	*Mero nam ..... ho.*
What is this?	*Yo kay ho?*
Where is ....?	*.... kaha cho?*
lodge/hotel	*bhatti*
shop	*possol*
left/right	*baiya/daiya*

straight ahead	*seeda jannus*
steep uphill/downhill	*bhiralo matti/talla*
far away	*tadah*
near	*nadjik*
Please give me.....	*......di-nus*
water	*paani*
cheese	*paneer*
tea	*chiya*
salt	*noon*
coffee	*coffee*
spicy hot	*piro*
milk	*dood*
omelette	*unda*
chillies	*korsani*
no chillies	*korsani chaina*

To ask a question, end the phrase with a rising tone. An affirmative answer is given by restating the question without the rising tone. 'No' is translated as *chaina* (there isn't/aren't any) or *hoi-na* (it isn't/they aren't).

Thanks to *Bryn Thomas*, author of Trailblazer's *Trekking in the Annapurna Region*

PRACTICAL INFORMATION

Equipment

Camping kit is unnecessary but some **means of purifying water** (see p60) is essential, as is **waterproof clothing**. The hills of West Bengal and Sikkim can be wrapped in cloud so dense that visibility diminishes to 50m or so: a **horn** and **lights** are good ways of alerting jeeps and lorries to your presence.

Accommodation

Enough hotels and guesthouses dot Sikkim to make **camping unnecessary** and the hillsides are so steep there are few places to pitch a tent even if you wanted to. Also, a very heavy bicycle will make the climbs even more punishing. Guesthouses usually charge Rs100–300 for a room; at the top end you should get an en-suite bathroom with a hot tap if not a hot shower. There's potential for more luxury in Darjeeling at the older, colonial-style hotels and in Gangtok.

Food and drink

Sikkimese food is a mix of Nepali and Tibetan dishes such as *thukpa* (noodle broth), *chowmein* (noodles) and *momos* (steamed dumplings). The yellowing necklaces you may see older Sikkimese wearing are made from *churpi*, dried yak cheese. In North Sikkim especially yak milk and butter if not meat are eaten daily. Alcohol is extremely cheap in Sikkim (Rs70 for a large bottle of HIT 8% beer) and many places that call themselves 'hotel restaurant bar' are often just a bar. Whisky, rum and brandy are brewed by the army and sold commercially, though alcoholism is now widely recognized as a problem in the state. A local drink to try is *tongba*, boiled water poured over fermented millet which is drunk out of bamboo pipes with a metal straw; it's not for the weak of stomach but comes with free refills. It tastes like *chang* (Tibetan barley beer). Alcohol is not served on full moon days in Sikkim.

Money

Sikkim uses the Indian **rupee**. There are ATMs and foreign exchange for travellers' cheques in Siliguri, Darjeeling and Gangtok. See p32 for exchange rate information.

Rules of the road and repairs

Drive on the left. Where there are chortens, prayer wheels or *mani* walls on the road keep them to your right. **There is a high army presence in Sikkim: give them priority**. Flashing lights mean 'I'm coming through, don't even think about it', rather than 'Please, go ahead'. A truck with its right indicator on might be saying 'overtake me', or just turning right.

Sikkim's smaller towns, such as Jorethang, Namchi, Pelling, Gyalsing, Ravangla, Legship and Mongar all have basic repair shops.

Getting to the ride

By air Sikkim's nearest airport is at Bagdogra (IXB), 15km from Siliguri in West Bengal; daily flights connect to Delhi, Kolkata and Guwahati. Air Deccan (💻 www.flyairdeccan.net), Indian Airlines (💻 www.indian-airlines.nic.in), Jet Airways (💻 www.jetairways.com) and Kingfisher Airlines (💻 www.flykingfisher.com) all run this route. A one-way ticket from Kolkata to Bagdogra starts at $80. The Sikkim Helicopter Service runs daily flights between Bagdogra and Gangtok (Rs1500, 30mins), depending on the weather. They have a stand at Bagdogra airport (as does Sikkim Tourism) but will not carry bicycles.

By road The NH31A covers the 124km between Siliguri and Gangtok but the highway's Tata traffic and diesel fumes make for unpleasant cycling. The longer and quieter road which runs along the Nepali border via Mirik and Darjeeling is far more scenic. Many maps show a hilly road from Nepal into West Bengal just south of Darjeeling at Pasupati but foreigners are only allowed to use Kakarbitta, about 35km west of Siliguri on the plains.

From Siliguri, Sikkim National Transport (SNT) buses run daily from their compound on Hill Cart Road to Gangtok (Rs70, 5hrs), Kalimpong (Rs55, 3hrs) and Darjeeling (Rs45, 3hrs). Bikes travel on the roof. Taxi touts along Hill Cart Rd in Siliguri will want to entice you into their minibuses for the ride to Sikkim; these can be very cramped and charge a full fare (about Rs125) for a bicycle.

By rail Sikkim's nearest train station is New Jalpaiguri (NJP) which lies 6km south of Siliguri and is an important hub for northeast India. Long-distance Delhi–Guwahati trains stop here daily, as do services from Kolkata. The fastest and most comfortable trains are the Rajdhani Express from Delhi (daily, 1534km; 21hrs 30mins; 3AC sleeper Rs1635/$41, 2AC sleeper Rs2205/$55), and the Darjeeling Mail from Kolkata's Sealdah station (daily, 570km; 10hrs 35mins; 3AC sleeper Rs684/$17, 2AC sleeper Rs957/$24).

SILIGURI

This flat and dusty town sits at the feet of the Himalaya. Its main artery, Hill Cart Rd, runs northwest–southeast over the Mahananda River and most hotels and restaurants are along its first kilometre or in the dirt lanes that run parallel. Watch out for traffic speeding the wrong way up the road – a side effect of the central reservation.

Siliguri, NJP (New Jalpaiguri) and Bagdogra form a road, rail and air transport triangle for India's northeast but also for the border towns of Kakarbitta (Nepal) and Phuentsoling (Bhutan). Siliguri also acts as the gateway for Darjeeling, Kalimpong and the mountains of Sikkim. It's West Bengal's second biggest town (though it doesn't feel like it) and a major commercial centre now that trade has officially started at Nathu La. Items (especially electrical) traded unofficially can be found at Hong Kong market in the back roads to the east of Hill Cart Rd.

Where to stay and eat

Siliguri Lodge is set back from the traffic on Hill Cart Rd down a lane; the first floor doubles enjoy a view over the garden. Single rooms are good value at Rs100, doubles cost from Rs150 (common bath) to Rs250 (en-suite). Bicycles can be kept indoors. Just north up the road, ***Khana Khazana*** restaurant with its patio garden is a favourite of both foreign tourists and Indian families who feast on its ice-cream shakes and sundaes (Rs30–60), and it also serves good Indian and Western dishes. A cheaper option is the almost next door ***Sher-e-Punjab***, a dim basement restaurant and bar.

Services

Banks and exchange The State Bank of India on the south side of the Mahananda river bridge has an ATM and changes travellers' cheques.

Information The Sikkim Tourism Office is further south along Hill Cart Rd in the Sikkim National Transport (SNT) compound.

Transport Buses to Gangtok (Rs70, 5hrs) leave daily from the Sikkim National Transport (SNT) compound on Hill Cart Rd.

Route guide – Sikkim

DAY 1 SILIGURI (104m) to MIRIK (1601m) 47KM

SILIGURI–SUKNA 9.2KM
SUKNA–DUDIA 13.8KM
DUDIA–MIRIK 24KM

Today is short but all the more brutal for it with gradients of up to 16%. The riding starts pleasantly but beyond Dudia the road climbs quickly into the hills; cyclists unused to heat and humidity will find this ascent tough. The route mostly runs through tea estates with occasional villages selling *chai* (tea) and biscuits. Carry plenty of water and some energy snacks: with a heavy bike in hot temperatures you will need to drink up to 10 litres to stay hydrated and it will be a marathon effort.

Siliguri (104m) 0/190KM
Follow Hill Cart Rd towards the hills, past the tracks of the Toy Train to Darjeeling. Once beyond the highway the road narrows immediately and the traffic vanishes. Tea estates appear to the left just before the road enters a forest of sal and teak (both hardwoods).

Sukna (170m) 9/181KM
Turn left just after this village (there's a chai shop at the junction, which is signed 'Mirik 44km') and continue west through the army camp with its monkey troupes and 'Live and let live the wildlife' signs. Rejoin the main road at the end of the army camp and head north past a small village.

Gariduhria (223m) There's a one-way system in operation just after Gariduhria; turn left for Mirik.

Dudia (256m) 23/167KM
Here the road points directly into the hills and the gradual tilt of the main street hints at the gradients ahead. The climb proper starts once you've crossed the bridge by the army firing range.

Beyond Dudia the road switchbacks up into the tea estates where brightly dressed women beat the tops of the tea bushes with branches. Every now and then small villages pepper the brilliant

THE DARJEELING HIMALAYAN RAILWAY

A classic journey up into the hills is on Darjeeling's famous toy train, now on UNESCO's World Heritage list. It's not often that bicycles travel faster than trains, especially uphill, but this dinky train chugs at a stately seven kph along its narrow gauge track through tunnels, loops and reverses. Originally the railway was steam but diesel engines are a more common sight nowadays. The daily 2343 Darjeeling Mail from Kolkata Sealdah to New Jalpaiguri (NJP) (dep 2220 arr 0840) connects with the 1D toy train which leaves NJP at 0900 for the hills. According to the timetable it should reach Darjeeling at 1530 but 1800 is more likely. If nine hours on a train sounds too much (unlikely if you spend a lot of time on a saddle), the railway operates two-hour 'joy rides' from Darjeeling to Ghoom and Siliguri to Sukna.

The toy train can be booked at computerized Indian railway stations or online at www.irctc.co.in; first class tickets cost Rs280. For further information (including timetables) see www.dhr.in.

Thanks to *Nick Hill*, author of Trailblazer's *Indian Rail Handbook* green backdrop and after a short while Siliguri and the Mahananda River appear far below on the plains. As the road climbs the temperature falls and Mirik is often shrouded in mist. Just before the town a bypass road turns left – ignore it.

Mirik (1601m) **47/143KM**

This small town is famous locally for its artificial lake, whose serenity is somewhat spoilt by the taxi rank on its shore. Mirik's cool climate and pine-clad hillsides feel a world away from Siliguri, and the surrounding orange groves and cardamom plantations make for fragrant strolls. Away from the taxi stand the only noises are the twittering of woodland creatures, the drums and cymbals of the Buddhist Bokar gompa on its hill and, by night, a cacophony from the town's stray dogs.

The road enters Mirik in an area called Krishnanagar where the homely ***Ratnagiri*** on the left has a range of rooms to suit most budgets; the en-suite double with hot shower, reading lights and TV is good value at Rs300. It also has internet access (Rs45/hr). The Ratnagiri's bamboo-clad restaurant is pleasant as is the garden, but the food is better at the ***Hotel Jagdeet*** a few doors down, which also has a State Bank of India ATM. The friendly ***Lodge Ashirvad***, opposite the post office, is cheaper at Rs150/250 (att); its rooms are spotless but a little musty. Bars selling cheap *tongba* (a local millet-based spirit) can be found in Mirik proper at the other end of the lake; there's a shortcut over the rocks by the lakeshore.

DAY 2 MIRIK (1601m) to DARJEELING (2133m) 43.4KM

MIRIK–PASUPATI 15.5KM
PASUPATI–SIMANA 6.2KM
SIMANA–SUKIA 4.2KM
SUKIA–GHOOM 12.2KM
GHOOM–DARJEELING 5.3KM

Alexandra David-Néel, an extraordinary French explorer (1868-1969), described the forests north of Kalimpong as 'shrouded in the moving fogs, a fantastic army of trees, draped in livid green moss ... warning or threatening the traveller with enigmatic gestures'. This also holds true for these misty hillsides on the border with Nepal. Large tea plantations give way to lichen-wrapped forest and if the clouds close in you'll need to use lights and a horn. She goes on to add: 'the whole country is bathed in occult influences...'and she should know; she was a Buddhist lama.

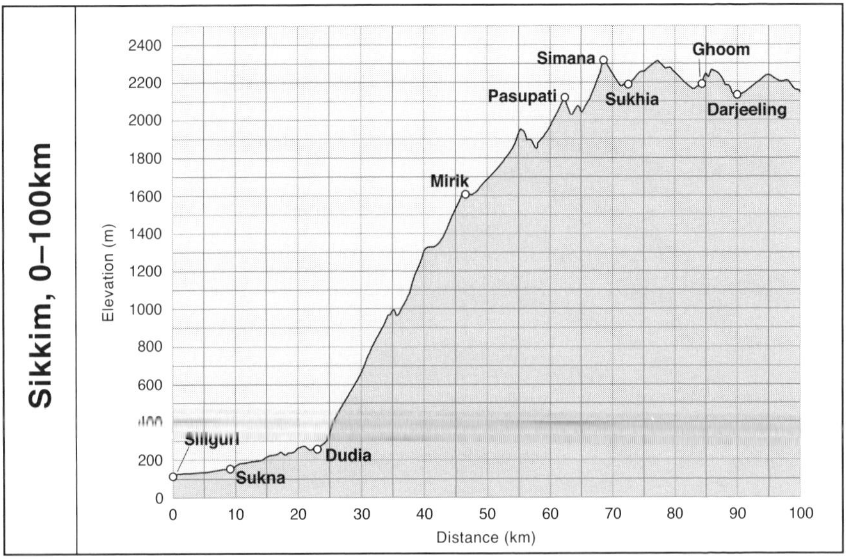

Map 25
Siliguri – Melli

SIKKIM

Mirik (1601m) **47/143km**

Follow the lake road through Mirik bazaar and then, after a brief descent, start climbing through the tea estates of Thurbo and Okayti – suppliers to emporia such as Harrods. These slopes are even steeper than yesterday's and the traffic increases (relatively) as you approach Pasupati.

Pasupati (2115m) **62.5/127.5km**

The border into Nepal here is not open to foreigners. By now the tea plantations have given way to forests of spruce and pine, their floors carpeted with ferns. There are fewer villages with chai shops although houses are dotted every 2–3km.

Simana (2308m) **68.5/121.5km**

The local women have set up some stalls by the road just before this village, selling chai, piping hot veg momos, Nepali cigarettes and chocolate biscuits. They have chosen a fantastic viewpoint: the snowy Kanchenjunga massif rises to the north and green Nepal glitters below; the national border here is very vague! From here the road to Simana village is horribly steep but quickly levels off and even glides down to Sukia. In clear weather there are fantastic views south to the plains as far as Bangladesh.

Sukia (2192m) **72.5/117.5km**

This lively market town has several restaurants – the ***Deorali*** on the left brews big mugs of tea and serves large bowls of warming *chowmein* (noodles) and *thukpa* (noodle broth).

Ghoom (2194m) **84.5/105.5km**

After an enjoyable descent comes a climb up into Ghoom. At the junction by Ghoom railway station the tarmac main road to Darjeeling (Hill Cart Rd) is to the left; for a fun shortcut turn right then, after 700m, left up an improbable-looking track which climbs very steeply at first but then settles down. This is Tenzin Norgay Road, which leads you directly into the heart of Darjeeling via small villages on its quiet eastern flank and past Aloobari gompa.

Darjeeling (2133m) **90/100km**

Tenzin Norgay Road finishes at an off-centre T-junction; turn left for the budget guesthouses on Dr Zakir Hussain Road and right for Chowrasta, the heart of the town. Entering Darjeeling via Hill Cart Rd means finishing with an impossibly steep climb up to the budget hotels on Dr Zakir Hussain Road. Watch out for potholes – the roads here are in bad condition.

DARJEELING

This celebrated hill station spills down both sides of a ridge with spectacular views over its famous tea estates and across to the snowy eastern Himalaya range. Its narrow streets are crammed with a hubbub of dialects and colour: Tibetan matrons in their multicoloured aprons, bandy-legged Nepali hill men and Indian women in flamboyant saris. Much of the architecture they move among dates from the British Raj, though like the roads it has been ravaged by Darjeeling's freezing winters and torrential monsoons. Likewise, the water and electricity supplies are erratic at best. At dusk the smell of corn-on-the-cob and popcorn roasting on braziers fills the streets, at dawn Kanchenjunga often rises clearly in the distance before disappearing once again behind the haze.

The **Himalayan Zoo** (Fri–Wed 8.30am–4.30pm, Rs100) offers the chance to see snow leopards, red pandas and Himalayan black bears up close, although it is distressing to see such wonderful creatures in captivity and, even worse, being taunted by visitors. Next door is the **Himalayan Mountaineering Institute** (Fri–Wed 8.30am–4.30pm, Rs100), which was opened by Nehru in 1954 after Hillary and Norgay's ascent of Everest. Its new museum traces the history of Everest expeditions from 1852 onwards and includes letters from the Dalai Lama, kit from Mallory and Irvine's summit attempt and also the clothing and day-to-day items of local hill people.

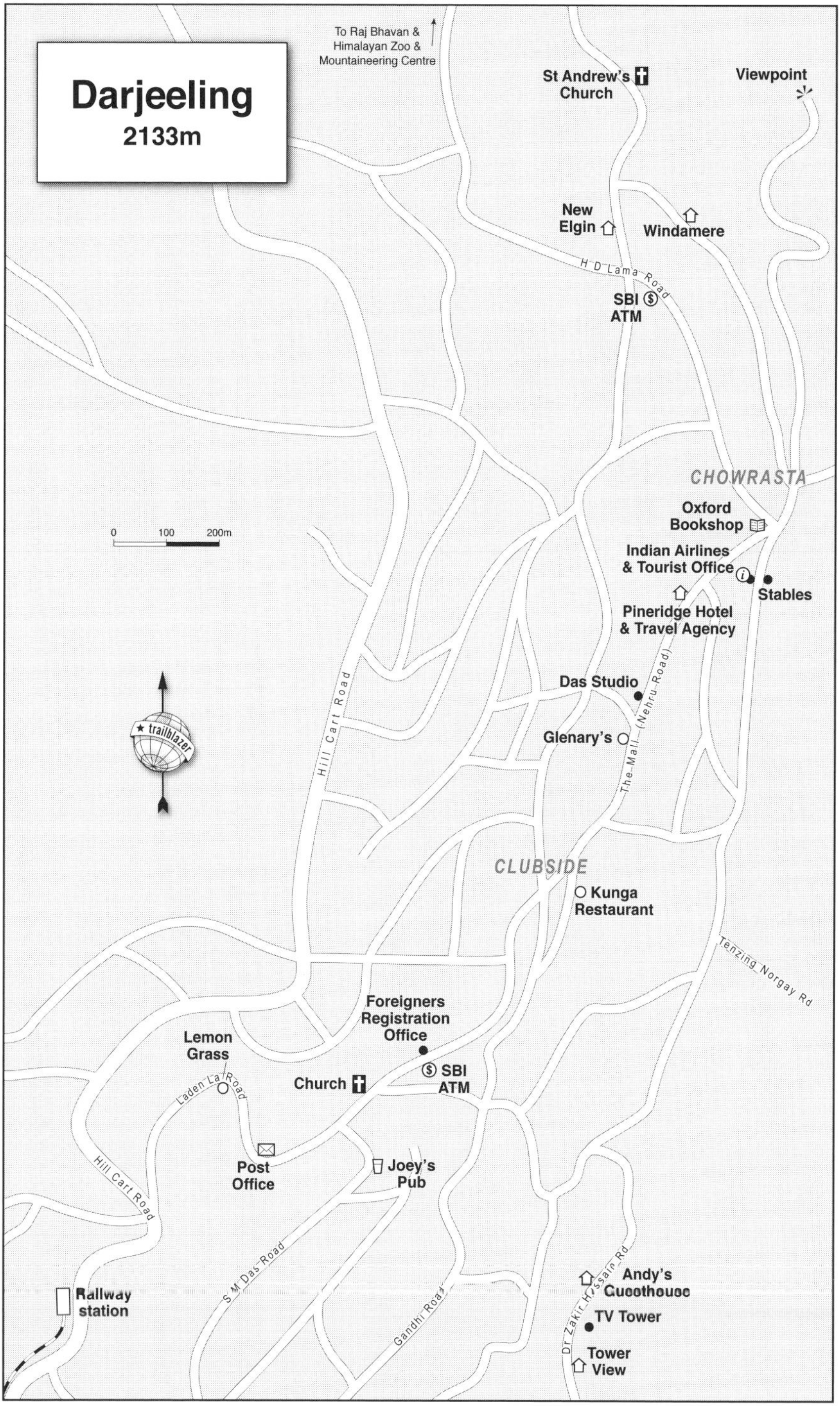
Darjeeling
2133m
To Raj Bhavan & Himalayan Zoo & Mountaineering Centre
St Andrew's Church
Viewpoint
New Elgin
Windamere
H D Lama Road
SBI ATM
CHOWRASTA
Oxford Bookshop
Indian Airlines & Tourist Office
Stables
Pineridge Hotel & Travel Agency
0
100
200m
Das Studio
The Mall (Nehru Road)
Glenary's
Hill Cart Road
trailblazer
CLUBSIDE
Kunga Restaurant
Tenzing Norgay Rd
Foreigners Registration Office
Lemon Grass
Laden La Road
Church
SBI ATM
Post Office
Joey's Pub
Hill Cart Road
S M Das Road
Gandhi Road
Dr Zakir Hussain Rd
Andy's Guesthouse
TV Tower
Tower View
Railway station

SIKKIM

Where to stay

Heritage hotels such as the ***Windamere*** on Observatory Hill and the ***New Elgin*** below Chowrasta offer a slice of history for around $100. Strung along the spine of Darjeeling's ridge is a succession of budget and mid-range hotels. ***Andy's Guesthouse*** (💻 http://andysguesthouse.biz) on Dr Zakir Hussain Rd is the cleanest and best-tended with thriving pot plants and a fantastic panorama from its rooftop terrace but it somehow lacks atmosphere. Doubles cost Rs200/400 (downstairs/upstairs) and have powerful hot showers; advance booking is recommended. Bikes can be carried up the stairs to the guesthouse: Darjeeling is best navigated on foot. Grungier options are the nearby ***Tower View*** and ***Morning Dew*** both of which charge Rs100–200 and sometimes have no running water at all.

Where to eat and drink

The hungry biker will enjoy Darjeeling. ***Kunga's*** Tibetan restaurant on Gandhi Rd opens for a sterling breakfast of butter toast, fried eggs, tea/coffee and a ripe banana for just Rs55, then goes on to produce delicious *thenthuk* (Tibetan noodle soup; Rs45), momos, wonton soup and *bhagthuk* (round handmade noodles) throughout the day. The famous ***Glenary's*** on Nehru Rd also makes a good breakfast of tea (of course), porridge and croissants; bring a paper and relax in the wicker chairs. Brits may be surprised to see a familiar red telephone box in Glenary's bakery, and even more surprised that this one, unlike those at home, still works. Glenary's also has internet access for Rs30/hr. ***Joey's Bar*** on SM Das Rd is the closest thing to nightlife though like everything else it closes at 10pm.

The intriguingly named ***Hot Stimulating Café*** halfway down the path to the Himalayan Mountaineering Institute and the Himalayan Zoo makes great momos and a reviving mug of spicy chai. ***Lemon Grass Restaurant*** on Laden La Road has a romantic evening ambience with candlelit tables, pot plants and good Thai food (chicken tom yam soup, chicken in red Thai curry, papaya salad; Rs50–100); it's just a shame that the staff are glued to the TV.

Services

- **Banks** There's a State Bank of India (SBI) ATM on The Mall.
- **Bookshop** The Oxford Bookshop in Chowrasta is a Darjeeling institution and has shelf upon shelf of books on the Himalaya; they also offer shipping by sea (up to six months) or air (three weeks).
- **Information** There's a counter for the Darjeeling Gorkha Hill Council Tourist Reception Centre on The Mall (Mon–Sat 9am–7pm); if they can't help the main centre is on Jawahar Rd West. Anyone cycling from Darjeeling directly into West Sikkim (ie not via Rangpo) will need to arrange the Inner Line Permit in Darjeeling. It's issued for free but you'll need your passport and a couple of hours. Fill in the permit form at the Office of the District Magistrate (DM) on Hill Cart Rd (Mon–Fri 11am–1pm, 2.30–4pm), get it stamped then take it to the Foreigners' Regional Registration Office on Laden La Rd (daily 9.30am–5pm) where it will receive a second stamp. Take it back to the DM and they'll issue the permit.
- **Post office** The Main Post Office is on Laden La Road.
- **Transport** The Darjeeling Transport Corporation on Laden La Rd runs

shared jeeps twice a day to Gangtok (4hrs, Rs130 per seat). The station for the Darjeeling Himalayan Railway (see box p217) is at the bottom of Hill Cart Rd.

DAY 3 DARJEELING (2133m) to RANGPO (315m) 60.7KM

DARJEELING–GHOOM 6.6KM
GHOOM–LOPCHU 16.9KM
LOPCHU–TEESTA BRIDGE 12.6KM
TEESTA BRIDGE–MELLI 6.6KM
MELLI–RANGPO 18KM

Darjeeling (2133m) 90/100KM

From Darjeeling's Clubside it's a quick drop to Hill Cart Rd which suffers from diesel-belching traffic but does have some points of interest along the way including the Toy Train which crosses and recrosses the road sounding its friendly toot, Batasia Loop (where the Toy Train circles around itself to drop height) and Sakya gompa.

Ghoom (2240m) 96.5/93.5KM

Continue along Hill Cart Rd towards Siliguri but turn left (east) after 700m, just after the Tenzin Norgay Road track, towards Lopchu and Teesta. A few houses line the road but quickly peter out to give a fantastic ride along a tree-clad ridge with views across to Darjeeling's eastern face against the backdrop of Kanchenjunga. This road is a gentle downhill as far as 6th Mile Bazaar so you can relax and survey the tea estates, valleys and Kanchenjunga; after 6th Mile Bazaar the tarmac plunges down to the Teesta River. Watch out for unmarked speed bumps after Lamata.

Lopchu (1612m) 113.5/76.5KM

The road hurtles you down into this village of cheerful turquoise houses; there's a small restaurant and chai stalls on the left opposite the water pump. After the village the road remains very steep and its lumps can throw the bike about. The road crosses a ridge and Kalimpong comes into view scattered along on its own ridge to the east, on the far side of the Teesta River. The road continues its dive to the Teesta, through woods and past ***Triveni View Point*** where the friendly 'Jonny' sells a selection of fruit, local juices (passion fruit, lychee and rhododendron) and drinks cooled in a bucket. It's a good spot to rest and enjoy the breeze off the Teesta and Rangeet rivers whose confluence lies

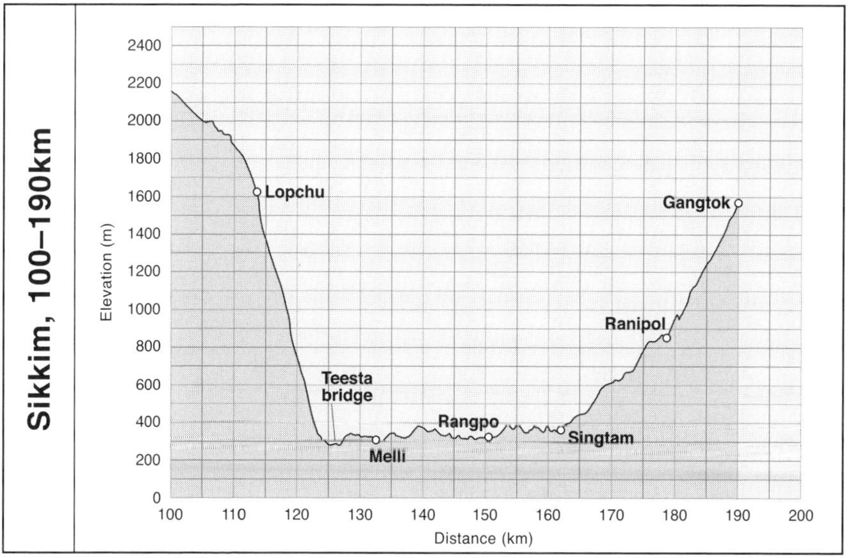

directly below. Locals call it 'Lovers' Meet'. The Rangeet marks West Sikkim's southern boundary and you can see the road from Jorethang skirting its sandy river banks.

Teesta Bridge (287m) **126/64KM**
The difference in climate between chilly Darjeeling and these tropical valleys is striking. From the bridge the road runs alongside the Teesta, past the Kalimpong turn-off, towards Melli. During summer this is a popular stretch of river for white-water rafting.

Melli (302m) **132.5/57.5KM**
The Jorethang road joins NH31A here for the final potholed kilometres to Rangpo, past some small villages. The Teesta River, on whose stony banks people wash their clothes and play cricket, marks the border between West Bengal and South Sikkim.

Rangpo (315m) **150.5/39.5KM**
An ornamental gateway covered in Buddhist motifs welcomes you to Sikkim; the checkpoint is just beyond it. Inner Line Permits are issued by the Tourism Office (daily 7am–9pm) inside the ***Sikkim Tourist Lodge*** on the left; see p212 for required paperwork and other info. All accommodation in Rangpo is relatively overpriced; the Sikkim Tourist Lodge is no worse than any other at Rs400 a room. There are a few restaurants in the bazaar and a UTI Bank ATM. The road quality improves dramatically once in Sikkim but the traffic remains quite heavy and the humid air traps exhaust fumes at the bottom of the valleys.

DAY 4 RANGPO (315m) to GANGTOK (1575m) 39.8KM

RANGPO–SINGTAM 11.6KM
SINGTAM–MARTAM 10.6KM
MARTAM–RANIPOL 6KM
RANIPOL–GANGTOK (MG MARG) 11.6KM

Another long climb today so it's best to leave early while the air is cool.

Rangpo (315m) **150.5/39.5KM**
From Rangpo the highway rolls up and down along the Teesta as far as Singtam, where it branches east to cross the Rongni River. The lower reaches of Sikkim are beautiful with their lush forests, valleys and rivers, but parts are also quite industrial.

Singtam (366m) **162/28KM**
This lively town (see p229) has a busy bazaar on the north bank of the Rongni River. Turn left after the second bridge for restaurants and hotels. The road to Gangtok is to the right and climbs immediately past a hydroelectric plant then pops through the hillside via a small tunnel supported by bamboo scaffolding.

Martam (669m) **172.5/17.5KM**
'Drive skilfully, live funfully!' says the BRO road sign. The GREF (General Reserve Engineering Force) camp just before this small village has a 'wet canteen' which sells an interesting selection of tea, biscuits and underpants. Between Martam and Ranipol the road can be in poor condition.

Ranipol (851m) **178.5/11.5KM**
This roadside town has grown up around the junctions to Gangtok and Pakyong in southeastern Sikkim. 'Hotel Bar Restaurants' line the bazaar but, as elsewhere in Sikkim, it's usually only the bar that's operational. The ***Ajay Hotel*** (drinks only) on the right is friendly and shady.

From Ranipol to Gangtok the climb is steep, hot and increasingly busy. The only respite is around the Rumtek turn-off where the gradient lessens briefly and trees provide shade. Water pipes at the roadside will cool hot heads and there are cold drinks shops every few kilometres. As you approach Sikkim's capital the roads become even busier; the settlement of Deorali now merges into Gangtok's hillside sprawl.

Gangtok (1575m) **0/190KM**
Footbridges over the highway signal your arrival in Gangtok; MG Marg, the main street, starts at the traffic circle on NH31A. Welcome to the capital of Sikkim!

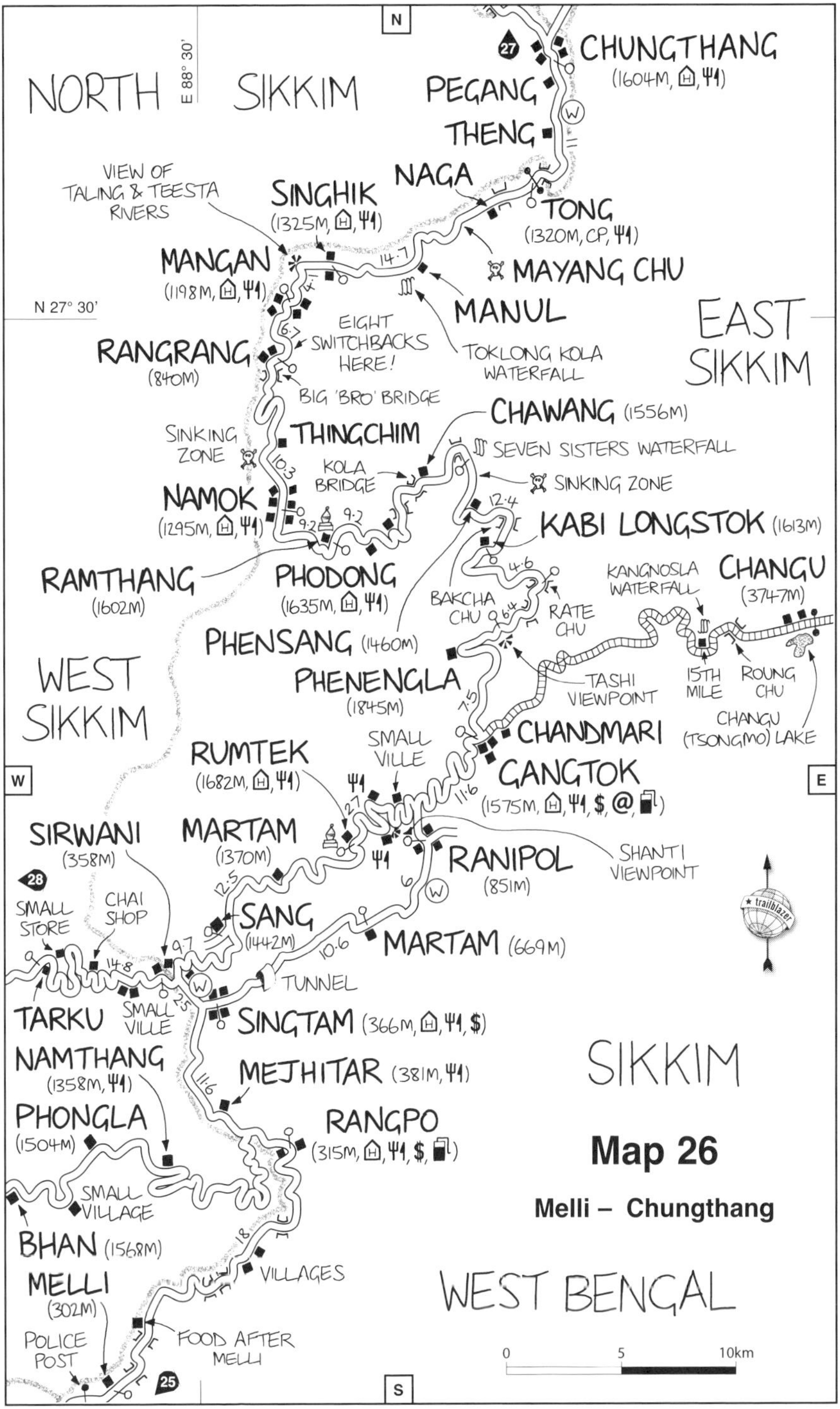

Map 26

Melli – Chungthang

SIKKIM

GANGTOK

This hillside town is a pastel-coloured sprawl of multistorey buildings set amongst prayer flags and wooded hillsides, over which the Kanchenjunga massif rises in clear weather. Development has come quickly here, and the town resounds to the clatter and clang of construction. It's a friendly place, best navigated on foot because the roads are often in bad condition from the rains and because it's so steep, except for MG Marg which is probably the only flat piece of road in all Sikkim.

Where to stay and eat

The ***Modern Central Lodge*** on MG Marg is the most popular budget hotel since its dorm beds cost just Rs50 and doubles Rs250 with en-suite hot shower; the managers (a Sikkimese/Tibetan couple) are well-travelled too. Their restaurant is equally popular with dishes from cheese and tomato toasties to local specialities and all things Indian and Chinese, plus a well-stocked bar. Many of Gangtok's mid-range hotels are poor value for money, but at the top end the ***Hotel Tibet*** on Paljor Stadium Road (doubles from Rs1475) always gets good reviews.

Gangtok's food is enough to keep travellers hanging on for an extra few days and to draw them back after exploring West and North Sikkim. The ***Snowlion*** at Hotel Tibet is usually acknowledged to be the best restaurant in town, though ***Little Italy*** in Deorali (near the bottom of the ropeway) must come a close second amongst pizza-craving Westerners. ***Baker's Café*** on MG Marg makes a good filter coffee and chocolatey treats. Delicious samosas come piping hot from the hole in the wall between Tibet Road and the steep unnamed road opposite Sikkim Tourism on MG Marg.

Services

- **Bank** The SBI ATM is next to Sikkim Tourism on MG Marg.
- **Bookshop** Jain Co near the traffic circle by MG Marg has books on Sikkim and phrasebooks.
- **Hospital and pharmacies** The STNM Hospital is just off NH31A on Paljor Stadium Road. There are a couple of well-stocked chemists on MG Marg who sell ORS sachets and antibiotics.
- **Internet** Internet cafés are dotted around the town and all charge about Rs30/hr: there's one next to the ***Hotel Potala*** on Tibet Road and another on the steps between Kazi and Tibet roads.
- **Post office** Just off NH31A on Paljor Stadium Road, beyond the hospital.
- **Shopping** The Gupta Tea House on MG Marg has almost every provision you could wish for: Nutella, Marmite, Weetabix, Ferrero Rocher, McVities Hob Nobs and even Gouda cheese.
- **Transport** The Sikkim National Transport (SNT) bus depot is on Paljor Stadium Rd; more obvious is the multistorey private bus and shared jeep stand on NH31A as it nears MG Marg which also has more frequent departures. Buses and jeeps travel to Kalimpong (4hrs, about Rs60), Darjeeling (4hrs, about Rs125) and Siliguri (4hrs, about Rs130). Bikes go on the roof and there may be a nominal charge.
- **Travel agents** You will need to use a travel agent in Gangtok if you intend to visit the restricted areas of North Sikkim. A recommended tour operator is

Satish Bardewa of Yak & Yeti Travels (💻 www.yaknyeti.com); he led the first mountain bike expedition up to Gurudongmar Lake and is reliable and courteous. The Yak & Yeti office is in Hotel Superview up NH31A by Zero Point.

INNER LINE PERMIT EXTENSIONS

The 15-day Inner Line Permit can be extended in Gangtok at the Foreigners' Registration Office (FRO) on Kazi Road, down the lane next to the Overseas Bank on the second floor (10am–4pm daily except every second Saturday of the month). It's now possible to extend permits in the district capitals too – Mangan in the North and Geyzing in the West; ask around for the Sub-Divionsal Magistrate's (SDM) Office. Currently you can extend your permit twice at any time during the validity of your permit (ie you don't have to leave it to the last minute), giving you a total of 45 days in Sikkim.

WEST SIKKIM

The weather can make or break a visit to West Sikkim. In clear skies apparently this region is stunning, but if the monsoon rolls in early or lingers too late you'll see nothing but cloud and drizzle. And it gets cold! Almost every day the road plunges from chilly hilltop to sweltering valley floor and claws its way back up again, with occasional respite if it winds along a ridge. The wonderful place names – Poklok, Thingling, Rinchenpong – sound like they are from a fairy tale. It's here that most of Sikkim's *gompas* (Buddhist monasteries) dot the hilltops.

DAY 5 GANGTOK (1575m) to SINGTAM (366m) via Rumtek (1682m) 51.7KM

GANGTOK–RUMTEK 27KM
RUMTEK–SANG 12.5KM
SANG–SIRWANI 9.7KM
SIRWANI–SINGTAM 2.5KM

Keep Left – it's the Right Way to Live
BRO road sign, Rumtek

Gangtok (1575m) 0/314.5KM

It's a 9.5km freewheel from MG Marg back down NH31A to the turn-off to Rumtek, which is marked by an ornamental gateway. This road is far quieter and drops through woods, over a bridge and then climbs through small villages and more woods up to Rumtek, which sits on a ridge surveying the sprawl of Gangtok. This ride only takes a couple of hours.

Rumtek (1682m) 27/287.5KM

If you are interested in Buddhism or prefer Rumtek's peace to Gangtok's bustle the ***Sun Gay Guesthouse*** is 100m inside the gates of the famous Rumtek gompa, down a gated drive. Basic but clean doubles with en-suite hot shower cost Rs150; the same with verandah and stunning views across the valley are Rs200. There's a sunny garden and the food is good. Tea stalls open early by the gompa.

Continuing from Rumtek this small road is threaded along the hillside; there's an initial climb followed by a fantastic swoop with views over to Gangtok and the mighty hills around East Sikkim. It's the quietest road yet – so quiet that goats sleep on it – and passes small rural villages of traditional timber-framed houses painted in cheerful turquoise. These high roads are one of West Sikkim's best features.

Sang (1442m) 39.5/275KM

Follow the tarmac road downhill at the Miniland Public School (signed Sirwani 8km) – the track ahead leads down via Khamdong to a hydel (hydro-electric) plant on the Teesta. A little bit along the track is a chai stall. The tarmac road descends steeply to Sirwani with great

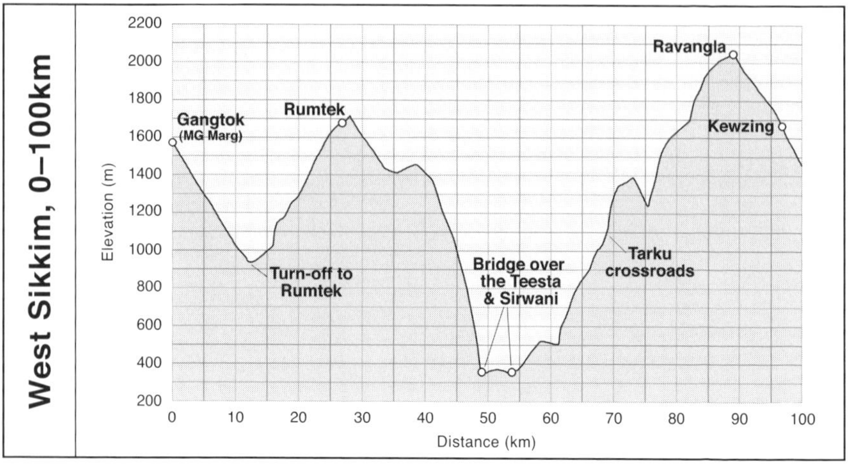

views across rice terraces to the forested hillsides beyond, dropping 1000m in an ear-popping 8km.

Sirwani (358m) **49/265.5KM**
Turn left for Singtam (2.5km) or right to cross the Teesta and begin the climb to Temi ('Timmy') and Ravangla.

Singtam (366m) **51.5/263KM**
This busy bazaar has lots of roadside restaurants and two Indian hotels: the budget ***Carnation*** whose doubles cost Rs100 (com) and the infinitely more luxurious ***Shima*** whose doubles start at Rs500 with TV, balcony and hot shower. There's an SBI ATM near the Carnation.

DAY 6 SINGTAM (366m) to RAVANGLA (2051m) 37.2KM

SINGTAM–SIRWANI 2.5KM
SIRWANI–TARKU CROSSROADS 14.8KM
TARKU CROSSROADS–RAVANGLA 19.9KM

Singtam (366m) **51.5/263KM**
From Singtam bazaar return to Sirwani. Use these few kilometres to warm up your legs for what comes next!

Sirwani (358m) **54/260.5KM**
The climb starts steeply (18%) once you cross the Teesta bridge. Until you gain height the only view is of an the extensive Teesta V hydel project on the river banks. After about 6km there's a simple tea shack at the roadside.

Tarku crossroads (1098m) **69/245.5KM**
From here there are two routes to Ravangla: a series of 18 switchbacks

RUMTEK AND THE TWO KARMAPAS

Rumtek is famous for its Karma Kagyu (Black Hat) Buddhist monastery which has been the home of the *Karmapa* (the head of the Karma Kagyu) since the Chinese destroyed the sect's traditional seat, Tsurphu monastery in central Tibet, during the Cultural Revolution. But when the sixteenth Karmapa died in 1981 two reincarnates emerged to take his place and the rivalry between them is bitter. Rumtek's senior lamas are divided in their support and the dramatic escape of the Dalai Lama's choice, Ogyen Trinley Dorje, from Tibet to India in 2000 has raised the stakes further as the Indian government is still preventing him from reaching Rumtek. The other candidate, Trinlay Thaye Dorje, lives in Kalimpong. Meanwhile Rumtek gompa is patrolled by the Indo-Tibetan Border Police who check passports at the entrance. The two Karmapas have their own websites: www.karmapa.org and www.rumtek.org.

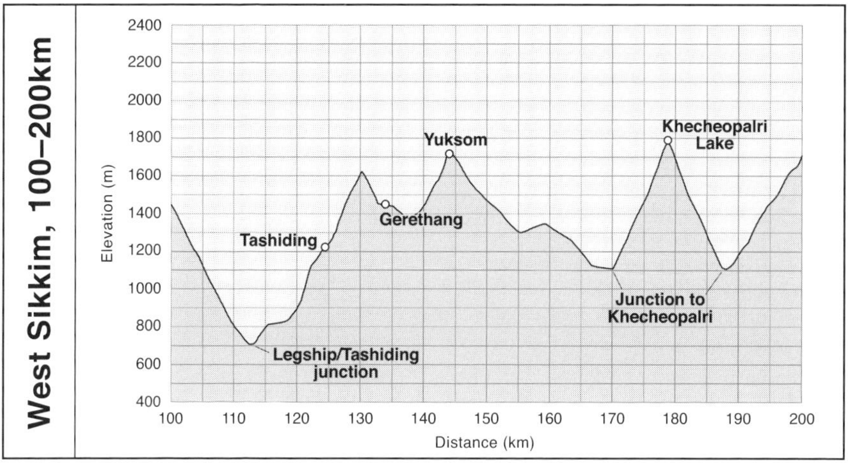

through the emerald-green Temi tea estate to Damthang (signed 17km), after which it's a further 13km to Ravangla (according to two men standing on one of the switch-backs); or a 20km direct route. This second route is a long winding road past small biscuit shops and veg sellers. There are no restaurants. The final stretch climbs up a ridge with great views in clear weather.

Ravangla (2051m) **89/225.5km**
This small town sits at the crossroads of the road to Pelling and the monastery at Ralong, and at the foot of Maenam Hill. The ***Hotel 10Zing*** charges Rs100–300 for a double and their restaurant make a good *gyathuk* (noodles and veg in broth). The few shops (including a pharmacy) are along the stretch of road to Ralong, but the best food is in the hotels. After hot and muggy Singtam, Ravangla can be chilly and damp but if the weather is clear there are some excellent local walks with stunning views; the nearest objective is the top of Maenam Hill which looks across to both Kanchenjunga and the Indian plains.

DAY 7 RAVANGLA (2051m) to YUKSOM (1705m) 55.3km

Ravangla–Kewzing 8km
Kewzing–Tashiding junction 15.4km
Tashiding junction–Tashiding 12km
Tashiding–Gerethang 9.7km
Gerethang–Yuksom turn-off 7.9km
Yuksom turn-off–Yuksom 2.3km

Ravangla (2051m) **89/225.5km**
About 5km from Ravangla is the small Yung Drong Kundras Ling Bon monastery, the only Bon monastery in Sikkim.

Kewzing (1672m) **97/217.5km**
Kewzing has an SBI ATM and basic restaurants. From here the road plunges down the face of the hillside to the Rangeet River.

Tashiding junction (705m) **12.5/202km**
About 2km before Legship is a signed turn-off to Tashiding. The small chai shop just before the turn-off is the best place to fill up with water as there's none on the climb up to Tashiding. The road passes the emerald green Rangeet dam, crosses the river and then after an initially steep climb settles down to wind its way up the hillside to Tashiding, whose gompa is framed by cherry trees and prayer flags.

Tashiding (1222m) **124.5/190km**
Tashiding village has a handful of guest-houses on its one street; the ***Bluebird*** and ***Mt Siniolchu*** charge similar prices (dorm bed Rs40, double com Rs100) but the latter is quieter. The ***New Tashiding Lodge*** has a 3-bed room with common hot shower for Rs200. All serve basic food; ***Pizza World*** at the gompa junction goes one

TASHIDING GOMPA

Little Tashiding gompa is perched on a grassy cone of a hill overlooking the Rathong and Rangeet rivers and is alive with the sound of birdsong and fluttering prayer flags. It's a 30min walk on foot from the road junction by Pizza World; sunrise is a lovely time to visit as the locals make their *kora* (devotional circuit). Unlike the imposing monasteries of Rumtek and Pemayangtse, Tashiding has a very personal feel with its wildflowers, colourful mani walls and friendly resident dogs. The craftsman of the colourful mani wall can be seen at work in his shack halfway around the kora. Amongst the field of chortens is the Thongwa Randol chorten, the holiest in all Sikkim; it's said that the sight of it is so powerful it cleanses all sins.

Visitors are allowed to sleep at the gompa for Rs100 though the dogs do their best to keep them awake.

better with fresh fruit juices and pizzas from Rs50 though be prepared for slow service. There's also a small snack shop at the gompa entrance.

Gerethang (1464m) 134/180.5KM
From Tashiding the road climbs steeply for about 6km onto the spine of a ridge before heading west with views back down onto Tashiding and its little gompa. There are lots of small biscuit shops but the kids can be pesky. Shortly afterwards Pelling and Pemayangtse come into view about 5km to the southwest. There's a friendly chai shop in Gerethang village from where the road drops to Pamrong waterfall; here the road can be quite rough. From Pamrong the road climbs again up to Yuksom, which is 2km up an unpaved road (signed) from the main Pelling road.

Yuksom / Yoksum (1705m) 144/170.5KM
This village is the roadhead for the Dzongri and Goecha La trek and is full of trekkers swapping stories about fantastic guides and stupendous views or porters too drunk to walk and fighting over money. There's a range of accommodation from the basic ***Pemalingpa*** homestays at the top of the village (about Rs100), the ***Yangri Gang*** at the bottom with its pleasant terrace and airy doubles with TV (Rs300 att) and the ***Tashi Gang*** back up by the Pemalingpa (doubles from Rs1350). The best food is at the ***Gupta*** restaurant which also has some basic trekking supplies.

Yuksom's claim to fame is that it was here that the first *chogyal* or King of Sikkim was crowned by three lamas. The original throne still stands in a quiet grove of pine trees near the Tashi Gang hotel.

DAY 8 YUKSOM (1705m) to PELLING (1912m) 60.7KM

YUKSOM–YUKSOM TURN-OFF 2.3KM
YUKSOM TURN-OFF–K'JUNGA FALLS 6.9KM
K'JUNGA FALLS–K'PALRI TURN-OFF 16.8KM
K'PALRI TURN-OFF–K'PALRI LAKE AND BACK 18.2 KM
K'PALRI TURN-OFF–PELLING 16.5KM

Yuksom (1705m) 144/170.5KM
The road is terrible from Yuksom until the suspension bridge, after which it's packed mud until Rimbi powerhouse.

Kanchenjunga Falls (1323m) There are a couple of chai stalls at the bottom of the stairs to a viewing platform for this thunderous waterfall.

Khecheopalri Lake (1794m) 79/135.5KM
Despite being firmly on tourist itineraries Khecheopalri Lake remains peaceful and serene in its forested hollow. It's sacred to the Lepchas, who call it 'Wishing Lake', so a concrete kora path leads around the lake past streams of prayer flags and rows of prayer wheels. Chai shops at the roadhead will rustle up Maggi noodles and even some bedding. They will also look after bikes if you wish to scramble up to Khecheopalri village on the ridge; the steep 20min track starts by the sign forbidding tourists to stay overnight in the monastery complex. Watch out for leeches! The village is a truly beautiful

spot, unspoilt and with fantastic moonlit views to Mt Pandim (6691m).

From the junction of Khecheopalri Lake it's a steady climb to Pelling, with no restaurants but occasional snack shacks such as in Darap bazaar. From Rimbi powerhouse the road to Pelling is tarmac.

Pelling (1912m) 204.5/110KM

Pelling's commanding position on a ridge affords it stunning views of distant Kanchenjunga but this tourist hub of West Sikkim is a victim of its own success. The views are fast disappearing as waves of new construction block out the sunlight and when the mist rolls in the town has a pokey, dark atmosphere. Most of the hotels are on Upper Pelling's ridge; the *Garuda* is down some steps to the right of the traffic circle. It's comfortably designed and should feel great but the staff are apathetic. An internet café down the lane by *Gupta* restaurant charges Rs50/hr.

GIVING AND RECEIVING IN SIKKIM

It's respectful in Sikkim to give things with the right hand, while the left cups the right arm under the elbow. Likewise, it's polite to receive things with both hands.

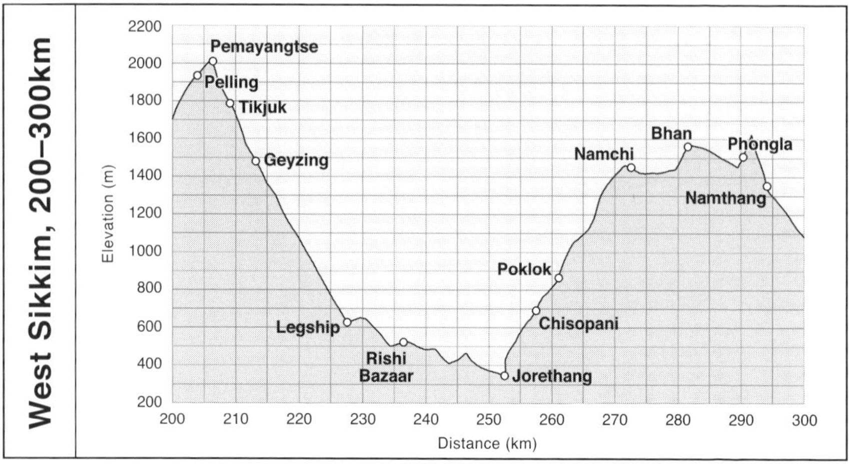

DAY 9 PELLING (1912m) to JORETHANG (354m) 47.8KM

PELLING–PEMAYANGTSE 2KM
PEMAYANGTSE–GEYZING 6.5KM
GEYZING–LEGSHIP 14.4KM
LEGSHIP–RISHI BAZAAR 8.9KM
RISHI BAZAAR–PIPALEY 11.1KM
PIPALEY–JORETHANG 4.9KM

Pelling (1912m) 204.5/110KM
Just 2km from Pelling and 500m up a steep drive lies Pemayangtse monastery, one of West Sikkim's gems. This Nyingma-sect monastery is small and the three-storey main gompa is surrounded by outbuildings with cheery yellow latticework and pot plants. Inside the marble-floored prayer hall are murals and representations of Padmasambhava (the holy man said to have brought Tantric Buddhism to Tibet in the 8th century). Beyond, in clear weather, there should be views over to Kanchenjunga.

After Pemayangtse the road descends through forest, passing a sign to Rabendtse. This is the ruined older capital of Sikkim and can only be reached on foot, down a 2km path. It's currently being restored by the Archaeological Survey of India.

Tikjuk (1796m) Turn left at this little village for the extremely steep 2km shortcut to Geyzing; the 'longcut' is 5km.

Geyzing (1481m) 213/101.5KM
The longcut road from Tikjuk to Legship bypasses Geyzing, the capital of West Sikkim; to reach the bazaar turn left (signed) on one of the hairpins. Past the jeep stand are a couple of cheap hotels in the town square and the *Denkhang* restaurant on Sakyong Road just beyond.

Just after Geyzing follow the signs to 'Gangtok and Siliguri'. Before Legship there are fantastic views east to Ravangla and south down the Rangeet valley towards Jorethang.

Legship (625m) 227.5/87KM
The *Hotel Trishna* at the junction of the Pelling and Ravangla roads serves food and has basic doubles for Rs200. The sombre forests of Pelling have given way to acid green paddy fields. After crossing the Kalek River the road rolls alongside the Rangeet, past trees dripping from gorge walls and luxuriant ferns. The wattle-and-daub houses of Western Sikkim are replaced by woven bamboo and the villages feel poorer.

Jorethang (354m) 252.5/62KM
A large Hindu temple at the roadside signals the approach to Jorethang, which lies on the east bank of the Rangeet River. This small market town can be explored in about 30mins on foot. Despite being busy

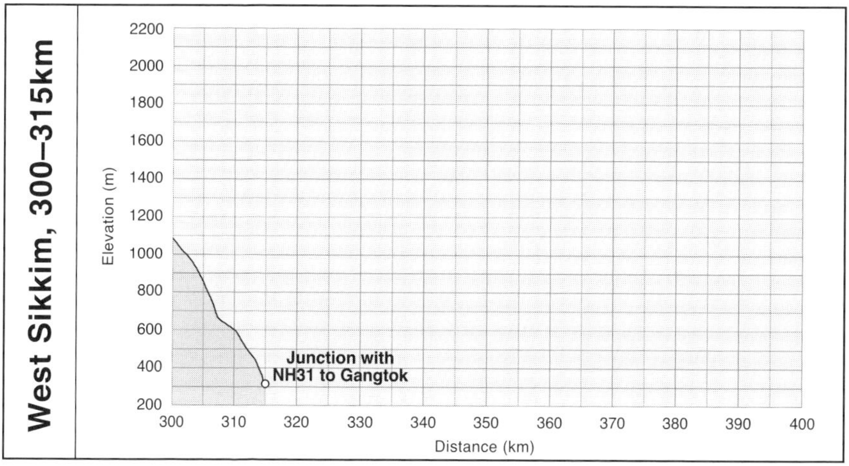

it's surprisingly orderly, for instance it has designated Tata parking. Somehow, after the Buddhist gompas of Tashiding and Pemayangtse, Jorethang feels more Indian again. There are a few hotels, the ***Namgyal*** immediately on the right and the cheaper ***Rangeet View*** opposite; a more comfortable option is the ***Dzongri*** in Street No 3 which has clean, marble-floored rooms with cable TV, fan, balcony and en-suite shower for Rs300. The restaurant is good too. Pharmacies, snack shops and a large fruit and veg market can be found between Street Nos 1 and 2.

DAY 10 JORETHANG (354m) to RAMRING (341m) 62KM

JORETHANG – NAMCHI 19.9KM
NAMCHI – NAMTHANG 22.2KM
NAMTHANG – RAMRING (NH31A) 19.9KM

For an easy day you could follow the main road downstream along the Rangeet to Melli (about 27km). The route described here heads up into the hills again for a final play on West Sikkim's quiet high roads before dropping back to the national highway just north of Rangpo.

Jorethang (354m) 252.5/62KM
The road up to Namchi parallels the Legship road for a while before spiralling upwards through the village of Chisopani. There are a couple of snack shacks but no restaurants.

Namchi (1441m) 272.5km/42KM
Ignore the road that forks downhill when you enter the town, it only goes to the school. At the beginning of the bazaar the ***Hotel Samdruptse*** has a good restaurant and rooms ranging from Rs150/250 (sing/dbl) up to Rs600 (double deluxe). Namchi is famous for its enormous statue of Padmasambhava, which at 42m is the tallest in the world.

The road beyond Namchi rolls up and down, just cresting 1500m, and can be rough in parts. Follow signs to Namthang and Rangpo.

Namthang (1358m) 294.5/20KM
This small bazaar has two hotels, the ***Decorus*** and the ***Tendong***, both of which are really boozers. Still, they have good views over the valley and it's a peaceful place for a drink (if they're not playing rock anthems) before the final fast plunge to Ramring and the NH31A near Rangpo.

Ramring (NH31A; 341m) 314.5/0KM
The NH31A is on the far side of the Teesta Bridge and Rangpo lies only 2km along it to the east. Cyclists who don't fancy repeating the steep climb back up to Gangtok (see profile on p223) should wait for a bus or hitch a lift with a passing Tata.

EAST SIKKIM

The road east of Gangtok to Changu (Tsongmo) Lake and Nathu La is restricted and independent vehicles cannot travel on it. Checkpoints every few kilometres ensure that they don't. If you want to see east Sikkim you must book a one-day jeep tour with a travel agent in Gangtok (see p226 for recommendations).

NORTH SIKKIM

The track now entered the fantastic region near the frontier passes. In the intense silence of these wild majestic solitudes, icy, crystalline, purling brooks chattered gently... Up and up we went, skirting gigantic glaciers, catching occasional glimpses of crossing valleys filled by clouds. And then, without any transition, as we issued from the mists, the Tibetan tableland appeared before us, immense, void and resplendent under the luminous sky of Central Asia.

Alexandra David-Néel, *Magic & Mystery in Tibet* (1965)

Only in the far north of Sikkim does the state feel truly Himalayan, and if you can get as far as Gurudongmar Lake the mountain scenery is truly wild. As with East Sikkim this region is restricted: Gurudongmar Lake only opened up to foreign tourists in 2006 and permits must be arranged in Gangtok for all travel north of Tong; Indian tourists can travel all over without any time restriction. Army traffic can be heavy and takes priority over everything else. Prices for basic items are higher north of Chungthang so stock up in Gangtok. Finally, the people of North Sikkim are a bit rougher around the edges!

DAY 1 GANGTOK (1575m) to PHODONG (1645m) 40.1KM

GANGTOK–TASHI VIEW POINT 7.5KM
TASHI VIEW POINT–RATE CHU BRIDGE 6.4KM
RATE CHU BRIDGE–KABI LONGSTOK 4.6KM
KABI LONGSTOK–SEVEN SISTERS FALLS 12.4KM
SEVEN SISTERS FALLS–PHODONG 9.2KM

Gangtok (1575m) 0/238.5KM
Follow the NH31A up past Zero Point and the Directorate of Handicrafts, through the upper reaches of Gangtok until Tashi View Point, where woods, valleys and waterfalls replace the buildings.

Tashi View Point (1869m) 7.5/231KM
The road that leads east from here is for Changu (Tsongmo) Lake and Nathu La. North of Tashi View Point the road is tarmac but damaged in parts by landslides. Occasional wooden notice boards give the status of the roads as far as Chungthang. A different world opens up: plunging valleys, ridge after ridge fading from green to blue in the distance and the road a thread of silver hundreds of metres below.

Rate Chu Bridge (1637m) 14/224.5KM
Welcome to North Sikkim! So far the scenery is like West Sikkim: deep valleys, powerful rivers and wooded hillsides.

Kabi Longstok (1613m) 18.5/220KM
Sited on the brow of a hill between the Bakcha Chu and Rate Chu rivers, Kabi Longstok is where centuries ago a Bhutia prince swore a pact of blood brotherhood with a Lepcha priest, cementing the bond between the Bhutia and Lepcha people of Sikkim. There's a pillar marking the spot. The road does a fun loop-the-loop around here but is usually in quite a bad condition around Phensang village, a little further on.

Seven Sisters Falls (1626m) 31/207.5KM
There's a chai stall at the bottom of the steps up to a viewing platform, from where the four tiers of the waterfall can be seen.

Phodong (1635m) 40/198.5KM
Phodong's hotels lie 2km beyond the

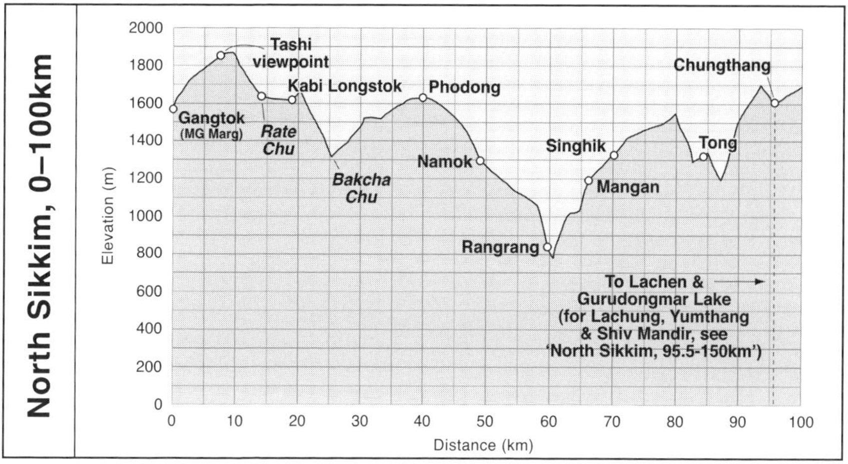

Phodong 0km marker. Rooms at the *Yak & Yeti* are basic and cost Rs200/250 (com). The nearby *Northway* has doubles for Rs150 (com) but is often booked up by Indian tour groups. The no-name building on the left past Yak & Yeti is a simple restaurant with a spare room; the owner Chawang says she rents out beds in it for Rs50. Yak & Yeti has the biggest menu, and beer too.

DAY 2 PHODONG (1635m) to SINGHIK (1325m) 30.3KM

PHODONG–NAMOK 9.2KM
NAMOK–RANGRANG 10.3KM
RANGRANG–MANGAN 6.7KM
MANGAN–SINGHIK 4.1KM

Today starts easily from Phodong as the road is mostly downhill until a BRO (Border Roads Organization) bridge just before Rangrang village, after which there's a switchback climb up to Mangan. Finally there's a feeling of moving into the mountains, of the landscape becoming more immense.

Phodong (1635m) 40/198.5KM

From Phodong the road skirts high above the Dik River before rounding the hillside and turning north, parallel to the thundering Teesta.

Namok (1295m) 49/189.5KM

The roadside *Everest* and *Silver Peak* hotels serve food.

Rangrang (840m) 59.5/179KM

There's a small ***restaurant*** on the left next to M Thapa's shop. The road on the opposite bank of the Teesta leads directly south to Singtam via Dikchu, bypassing Gangtok. Mangan lies at the top of eight switchbacks after this village.

Mangan (1198m) 66/172.5KM

This small town is the capital of North

PHODONG GOMPA

Early risers could walk the kilometre up to Phodong gompa for the morning *puja* (prayers). As at Rumtek, this small, friendly gompa belongs to the Karma Kagyu (Black Hat) sect and a photo of the seventeenth Karmapa takes pride of place on the altar. Snow lions guard the prayer hall's entrance, snarling to the south where the road is visible as far away as Phenengla. Birdsong and the carefully tended gardens outside the monks' cells add to the sense of natural harmony and peace.

Sikkim and its main export is *badi elaichi*, black cardamom. As the sign at the beginning of the town says, 'Welcome to Mangan. Large cardamom capital of the world!'. Foreigners cannot stay longer than five days in Mangan and extensions are only given by the Sub-Divisional Magistrate (SDM) if the roads are blocked by landslides. The ***Mount View*** on the road towards Singhik charges Rs250 for a double room and the best food is served at the ***Himalayan*** restaurant at the junction of the main road and the lower road leading to Namprikdang and Mangan's bazaar.

Singhik (1325m) 70/168.5KM

From Mangan the road keeps climbing but not so steeply up to Singhik, past a viewpoint over the Talung and Teesta rivers. Singhik is a small, friendly village with the homely ***Friendship Guesthouse*** on the left. The owner speaks little English but she feeds her guests handsomely; double rooms cost a non-negotiable Rs250 including all meals. The cosy sitting room and roof terrace look out onto Kanchenjunga's eastern face. The nearby government-run ***Singhik Tourist Lodge*** claims to have the best views in Sikkim but guests have said it's overpriced.

DAYS 3 – 7: FROM SINGHIK INTO NORTH SIKKIM

Just under 26km from Singhik the road forks at Chungthang: west to Gurudongmar Lake along the Lachen Chu valley (see p238), east to Shiv Mandir along the Lachung Chu valley (see p239). Cyclists cannot hope to explore both these roads under the current permit restrictions of four nights and five days. There are therefore two options: either choose one valley and ride up it and back down the same way – I would recommend the Lachen valley to Gurudongmar Lake – or use a combination of the jeep and bike to reach both, as outlined below. Whatever option you go for, your travel agent will have arranged all food and accommodation beyond Singhik.

Day 3	Singhik – Chungthang by bike. Jeep transfer to Lachen
Day 4	Lachen – Thangu – Gurudongmar Lake – Thangu by jeep
Day 5	Thangu – Chungthang by bike. Jeep transfer to Lachung
Day 6	Lachung – Shiv Mandir (above Yumthang) – Lachung by bike
Day 7	Lachung – Chungthang by bike. Chungthang – Gangtok by jeep

DAY 3 SINGHIK (1325m) to CHUNGTHANG (1604m) 25.7KM

SINGHIK–TONG 14.7KM
TONG–CHUNGTHANG 11KM

Singhik (1325m) 70/168.5KM

It's just 3.5km from Singhik to Tokyong Kola, a powerful waterfall which mists passers-by in fine droplets. The road to Chungthang passes various 'trouble spots' such as Mayang Chu; ignore all the roads that lead downhill.

Tong (1320m) 84.5/154KM

Here, just before the road crosses the Teesta, is the police checkpost for North Sikkim permits. There's a snack shack on the far bank at the start of the climb to Pegang, 2km before Chungthang.

Chungthang (1604m) 95.5/143KM

Chungthang is Bhutia for 'flat place' which comes as a surprise because it's wedged between two valleys whose walls close it in, giving it a dark and chilly feel. This oppressiveness is reinforced by the high military presence. Also a surprise is a large *gurudwara* (Sikh temple) up some mossy steps, built to honour Guru Nanak who is thought to have passed through Chungthang on his way to Tibet. Guru Nanak seems to be interchangeable with Padmasambhava here. Opposite the gurudwara a large rock festooned with Buddhist prayer flags bears his footprint, helpfully filled in with yellow paint. The ***Sonam Hotel*** has food and cheapish lodging (dbl Rs250).

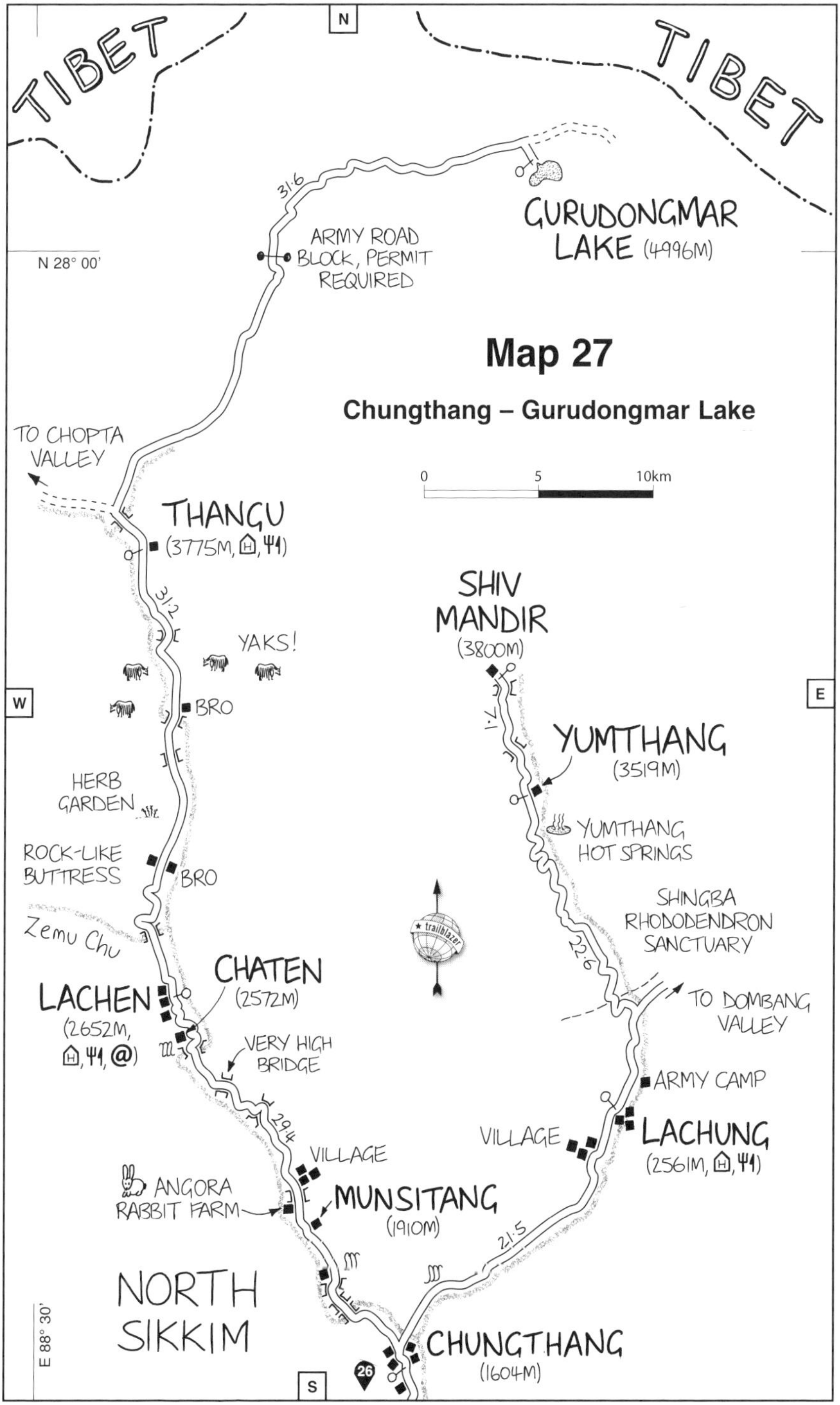
Map 27
Chungthang – Gurudongmar Lake
N
S
W
E
TIBET
TIBET
GURUDONGMAR LAKE (4996M)
31·6
ARMY ROAD BLOCK, PERMIT REQUIRED
N 28° 00'
0
5
10km
TO CHOPTA VALLEY
THANGU (3775M, H, ΨI)
31·2
YAKS!
BRO
HERB GARDEN
ROCK-LIKE BUTTRESS
BRO
Zemu Chu
LACHEN (2652M, H, ΨI, @)
CHATEN (2572M)
VERY HIGH BRIDGE
29·4
VILLAGE
ANGORA RABBIT FARM
MUNSITANG (1910M)
NORTH SIKKIM
E 88° 30'
26
CHUNGTHANG (1604M)
SHIV MANDIR (3800M)
17·1
YUMTHANG (3519M)
YUMTHANG HOT SPRINGS
SHINGBA RHODODENDRON SANCTUARY
22·6
TO DOMBANG VALLEY
ARMY CAMP
VILLAGE
LACHUNG (2561M, H, ΨI)
21·5
trailblazer

At Chungthang the road forks: northwest to Gurudongmar along the Lachen Chu, northeast to Shiv Mandir along the Lachung Chu.

THE LACHEN VALLEY: CHUNGTHANG (1604m) to GURUDONGMAR LAKE (4996m) 92.2KM

The next day I left Lachen, continuing my journey towards the north. Here the scenery, which all along the track lower down had been charming, became simply marvellous. The azalea and rhododendron thickets were still decked with their bright spring garment. A shimmering torrent of blossoms submerged the valley and seemed to be pouring out, on the neighbouring slopes, a resistless flood of purple, yellow, red and pure white waves. Seen from a distance, my porters, whose heads only emerged from the bushes, seemed to be swimming in a sea of flowers... Alexandra David-Néel, *Magic & Mystery in Tibet* (1965)

CHUNGTHANG–LACHEN 29.4KM
LACHEN–THANGU 31.2KM
THANGU–GURUDONGMAR LAKE 31.6KM

Chungthang (1604m) 95/143KM

Beyond Chungthang the road climbs quickly past an army camp towards Munsitang beyond which there is, of all things, an angora rabbit farm, where you can play with the rabbits. The road has been dynamited out of the rock face in places, and grasses and ferns flop off the edges like a fringe. Approaching Chaten the climate changes noticeably; mountains are visible ahead and the trees are mostly juniper. Pretty waterfalls cascade down the valley walls and the road crosses the Lachen Chu on increasingly spectacular bridges.

Lachen (2652m) 125/113.5KM

Perched on the slope of a deep gorge this small town is a mix of traditional wooden houses which look like Swiss chalets in greens and red, and brasher new concrete hotels. Food is hard to find outside the hotels but bars aren't: follow the whiff of whisky to find one. They are mostly male hangouts and cosy, with a traditional hearth, wooden floors, blackened beams, low *chogtse* tables and butter tea in thermoses or *tongba* in its eponymous bamboo mug. Lachen's gompa is the large yellow building topped by a pagoda roof up on the hill – the sounds of puja float across the valley to the waterfalls on the opposite side. There's internet access (Rs20/hr) at the community centre.

Between Lachen and Thangu the road crosses the lively Zemu Chu, which flows from the Zemu Glacier by Green Lake. The road is mostly tarmac but with some rough sections including the last 3km into Thangu.

Thangu (3775m) 156/82.5KM

This small village beyond the army camp is bitterly cold even in summer, which is probably why few Indian tourists stay here and why there are so few hotels. Just beyond the village lies the entrance to the Chopta valley where Tibetan nomads occasionally graze their yaks.

Leave Thangu early if you want to cycle up to Gurudongmar Lake because locals say that the winds are extremely strong after 1pm. The 'Tso Chamo Cold Desert' starts just north of Thangu, inhabited by Himalayan creatures including the snow leopard, Tibetan wolf, kyang (Tibetan wild ass), Himalayan marmot, bharal (blue sheep), pika (a cute rabbity guinea pig) and even the Sikkim snow toad. The green V-shaped valleys which have characterized Sikkim so far become harsher, browner and rounder. All vegetation disappears and the valley looks as if it has only recently been scoured by glaciers. About 16km from Thangu, after the chortens, is an army checkpoint where you

End of the road: up by Gurudongmar Lake

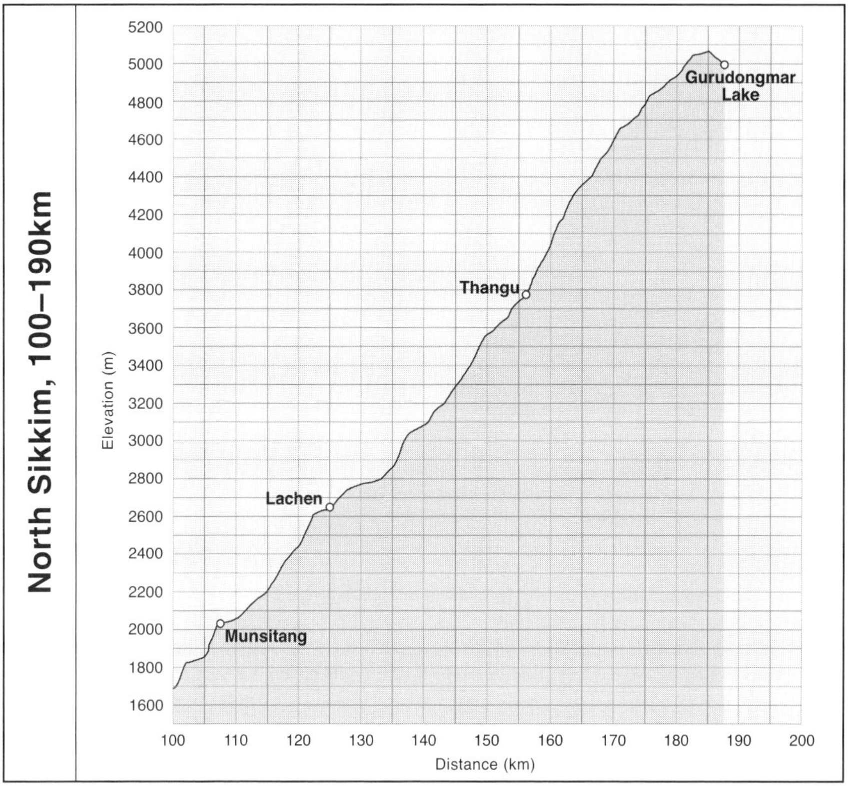

must show a permit to continue. The road turns to track, following a lone telephone line towards Tibet.

Gurudongmar Lake (4996M) 187.5/51KM
The scenery here is the most awesome of all Sikkim, especially towards Kerang. Apart from the army presence, there's nothing here: just indigo skies, muted mountains and glaring white snow on the peaks. What was long ago the Tethys Sea is now the highest plateau on earth. The lake itself is sacred and the source of the Teesta; prayer flags and a kora encircle it. Be warned though, that the landmine signs aren't joking: the mines here date from the Sino-Indian war in 1962. The Indian army hasn't cleared them – only put up signs which sadly yaks can't read.

THE LACHUNG VALLEY: CHUNGTHANG (1604m) via YUMTHANG to SHIV MANDIR (3800m) 51.2KM

CHUNGTHANG–LACHUNG 21.5KM
LACHUNG–YUMTHANG 22.6KM
YUMTHANG–SHIV MANDIR 7.1KM

Chungthang (1604m) 187.5/51KM
Steep hairpins lead away from Chungthang towards Lachung, past the Bhima waterfall. The zigzag road on the opposite side of the valley is to Mt Kiato – it looks tempting but has been banned to all tourists, foreign and Indian, since 2005.

Lachung (2561m) 209/29.5KM
Unlike Lachen, which clings to the sides of its valley, Lachung is spread out on the valley floor beneath a huge waterfall. Tibet lies only 10km to the east and until the Sino-Indian war in 1962 Lachungpas used

to cross the Tangkra La regularly to trade. Now the army controls the area, as far as it's possible to control landscape this wild. The villagers operate a *dzomsa* system of governance, according to which the worst punishments are exile, getting beaten up by the strongest man in the village or having to prostrate the 5km from the village to the gompa. Tourists are not covered by dzomsa – you should take any problems (and there have been reports of theft from tents here) to the police. There are more than 65 hotels in the town but chang bars are indistinguishable from people's houses, and everyone gathers around the hearth as the temperatures outside drop.

North of Lachung there's an immediate climb up hairpins as far the Singhba Nature Reserve. The road rolls through this beautiful landscape of rhododendrons which are in flower in May; there are some water crossings but they are not hard.

Yumthang (3519m) 231.5/7KM

As you approach Yumthang keep an eye out for the hot springs on the right. Yumthang itself is a green pasture alongside the Lachung Chu where a small chai stall makes big business selling chai, *channa* (chickpeas), coffee and biscuits to half-frozen tourists from the plains. In clear weather there are 180° views of the mountains which cradle Yumthang but in bad weather you will be lucky to see the yaks grazing in the mist.

Shiv Mandir (3800m) 238.5/0KM

Foreigners can go no further north than the Indian army igloo but there are gorgeous views down the Yumthang Valley from here. A picnic among the rhododendrons, primula, juniper and pines would be peaceful and a fine epitaph to riding in Sikkim before freewheeling back down to Lachung for some celebratory tongbas.

Colour section (following pages)

● **1 (Opposite)** A selection of northern India's legendary roadsigns. ● **2 Top**: Alpine meadows in the high Himalaya; a fun day spent riding the trail from Chandra Tal (just visible in the background) to Kunzam La near Spiti (see box p188). ● **2 Bottom**: 'Monklets' playing cricket beneath the gaze of some chortens at Lamayuru gompa (see p165). ● **3 Top**: Entering Spiti Valley, a parallel world of vivid colours and indigo skies (see p186). ● **3 Bottom**: Prayer flags snap in the wind around the Namgyal gompa, Leh (see p148). ● **4** On Himalayan shores: Chrissi rides on the edge of Pangong Tso (4323m) on the far side of which lies China (see box p155, p326). ● **5** Monk during puja, Sera monastery, Tibet (see p250). ● **6 (Opposite p241)** Faces of the Himalaya: clockwise from top right: two little boys in Tabo, Spiti; Kashmiri apple-seller; the sisters of my Kyrgyz host, Karakul village; Ladakhi nun, Leh; clerics at Shah-i-Hamdan mosque, Srinagar; a Chinese tourist dresses up in Lhasa.

HIMANK
OVERTAKEN BEWARE
OF UNDERTAKER
III Lives Dangerously
753TF 111RCC
BORDER ROADS ORGANISATION
BE GENTLE
ON MY CURVES
38TF 70RCC
BORDER ROADS ORGANISATION
arling I Like You
t Not So Fast
51
HIMANK
AFTER WHISKY
DRIVING RISKY
BRO
753 TF 111 RCC
BRO
फुल खिले पत्थरमे
GO SLOW
16 TF 93RCC
GREF
BORDER ROADS ORGANISATION
THE JOURNEY OF LIFE
IS LONG AND THE
PATH UNKNOWN
16 81
HIMANK
DON'T GOSSIP
ET HIM DRIVE
PROJECT HIMANK
LOVE NEIGHBOUR
BUT
NOT WHILE DRIVING
HIMANK
YOU LOVE HER
PLEASE
ORCE SPEED
51
BORDER ROADS ORGANISATION
YOU ARE TRAVELLING
ON POTHOLE FREE ROADS
OF 753 BRTF 51 RCC
BRO
WE ALL WISH
YOU A HAPPY
JOURNEY
753TF 111RCC
HIMANK
IVE ON HORSE POWER
OT ON RUM POWER
HIMANK
SAFETY AT ROAD
IS
SAFE TEA AT HOME

FRIENDSHIP HWY 7

ROUTE INFORMATION
- **Start / finish** Lhasa (Tibet) / Kathmandu (Nepal)
- **Distance** 957km (1158km including Everest Base Camp)
- **Altitude min / max** 632m/5251m
- **High passes** Eight
- **Suggested duration** Minimum 13 cycling days (18 including Everest Base Camp), 20/25 days in total
- **Road conditions** 75% excellent tarmac, 25% mud-packed road
- **Hazards and dangers** Altitude sickness in Tibet, traffic in Nepal
- **When to go** September–October
- **Side route** Everest Base Camp (101km, five days there and back)
- **Visas** Required for China and Nepal (see pp28-30)

Starting in Lhasa and finishing in Kathmandu, two of the most exotic-sounding cities in the Himalaya, this long ride rarely drops below 4000m making it the highest route in this book. Along the way are stunning vistas of Himalayan superstars such as Everest (8848m), Cho Oyu (8201m) and Shishapangma (8014m) and the long stretches between towns give you the chance to stay among Tibetans in the villages or to camp alone in the landscape. The ride spans two countries and three cultures: Chinese, Tibetan and Nepalese. Typical scenery includes river valleys with Tibetan villages punctuated by high arid passes with views of Himalayan peaks, as well as occasional Chinese towns and military outposts.

The end of this ride is often billed as the longest descent in the world but cyclists can forget about freewheeling from the final pass all the way to Kathmandu: fierce headwinds, rough roads and sneaky climbs demand pedalling almost all the way. Once in Nepal the road rolls alongside the Bhote Khosi River past lush terraced fields, small villages and water buffalo to the capital, Kathmandu.

FACTS ABOUT THE REGION

Safety

Violent crime against foreigners is extremely rare in Tibet. Far more common is **theft** for which Nyalam and Everest Base Camp have a particularly bad reputation. Don't leave your bike and panniers unattended and keep an eye on kids while riding – many like to hang on to the rear rack and some like to help themselves to whatever is on it.

The Friendship Highway also has a reputation for aggressive begging which is a direct result of tourists handing out pens, money and sweets. Since all tourist jeeps stop in the same places and, during the high season, there are hundreds of tourists passing

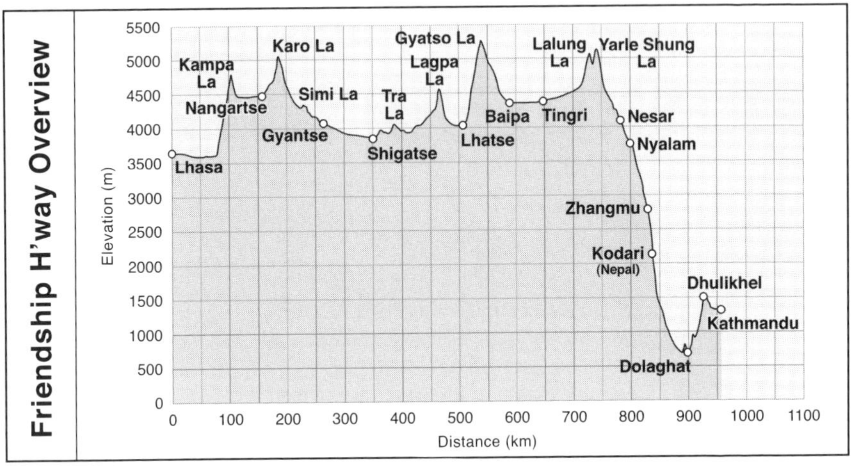

through daily, some local children and adults now expect handouts from foreigners and will pester tourists for them.

The greatest risk posed by the Friendship Highway is **altitude sickness**, and every year cyclists get into serious trouble by underestimating it. See p61 for symptoms and how to manage AMS.

Restrictions

See 'Getting to and from the ride' on p248 for the paperwork required to enter Tibet. As seen in 2008, **Tibet can close without warning**. Once inside, travellers between Shigatse and the border town of Zhangmu should have an Alien's Travel Permit (see below) but police checkposts rarely ask to see them. The side route to Everest Base Camp lies within the Qomolangma National Park for which an entry ticket must be purchased in Baipa (see p272). Note that once in Tibet it's extremely difficult to **extend** a Chinese visa as one of the pieces of paperwork that must be produced is a confirmed flight out of the region; not something a cyclist will have. It's obvious when travelling around Tibet that this is a police state. Whatever your feelings about the Chinese presence in Tibet, don't draw attention from the PSB. Border areas are particularly sensitive. As well as holding a valid Chinese visa (see p28), no foreigner can enter Tibet without a **Tibet Travel Permit**, which is only issued via a travel agent. This piece of paper (which most tourists don't get to see) simply enables you to enter Tibet and travel through its few open areas and so has no expiry date.

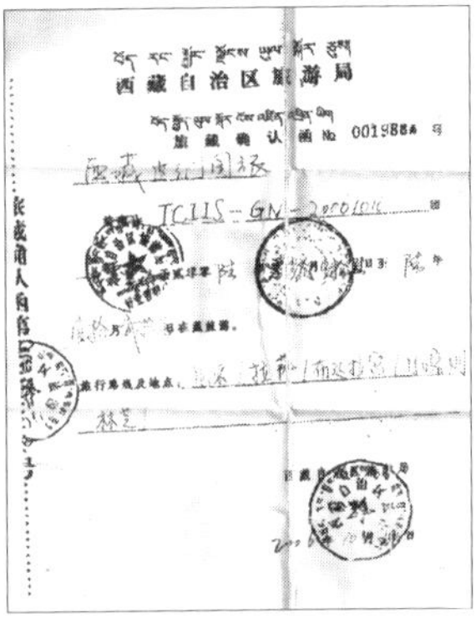

The lesser spotted Tibet Travel Permit

Once outside the Lhasa and Shigatse prefectures (ie open areas) all foreigners should in theory carry an **Aliens' Travel Permit** (ATP) which grants them access to the restricted areas. This is issued by the Public Security Bureau (PSB), but in recent years cyclists have not been asked to show them

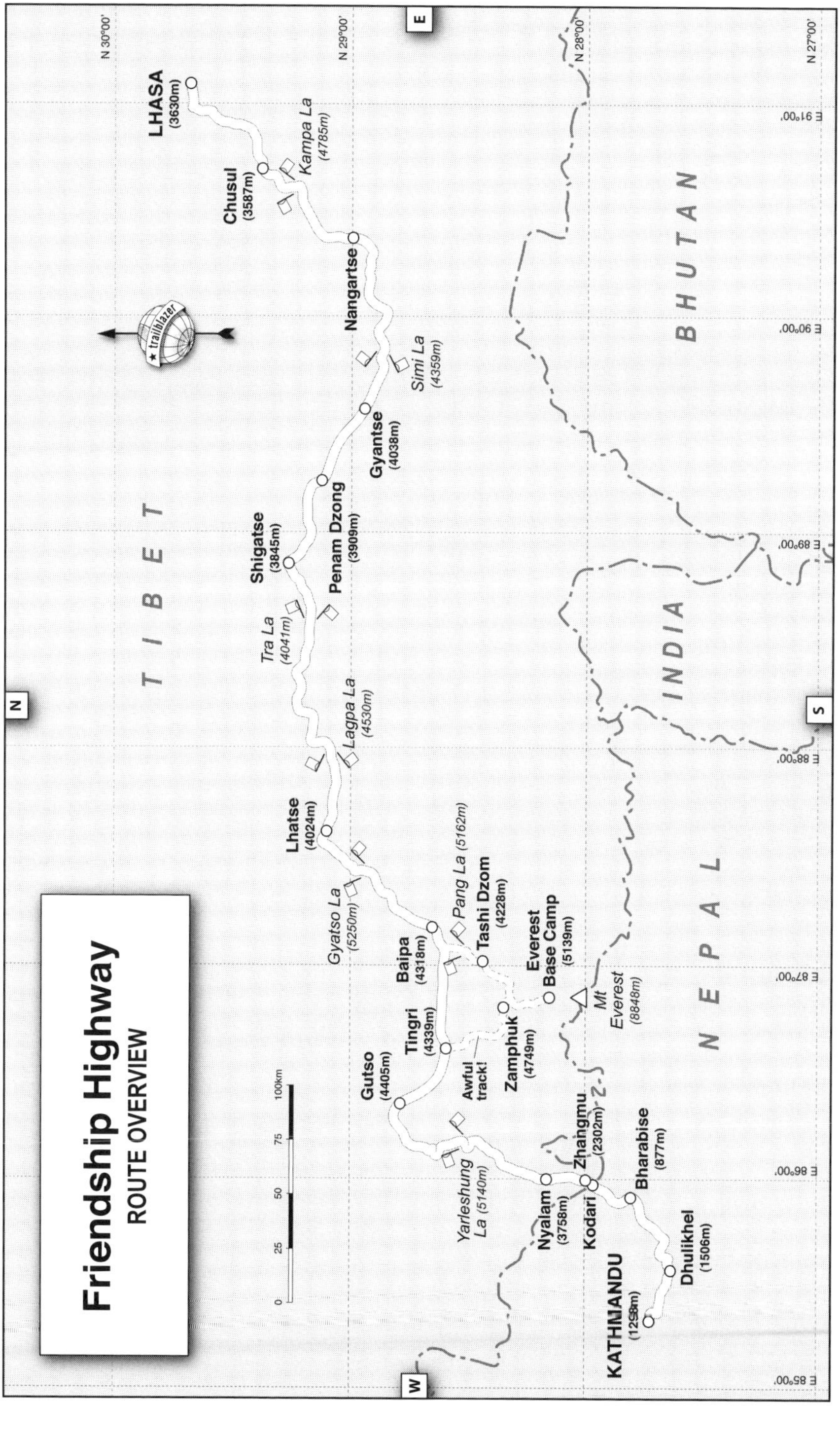

LHASA – KATHMANDU

on the main Friendship Highway, so few people bother getting one in Shigatse.

Visas for Nepal can be bought at the border town of Kodari: a 3-day transit visa is free, otherwise it's $30 for 60 days. You will need a passport photo.

Aliens' Travel Permit (ATP)

History of the road

Most Westerners know the road from Lhasa to Kathmandu as the Friendship Highway but in China the road is known as Highway 318 which runs from Shanghai on China's eastern seaboard to Zhangmu, China's border town with Nepal. Despite being 5372km long, Highway 318 is not the longest highway in China: that honour goes to Highway 010 stretching 5700km from Tongjang on the Russian border to Sanya on Hainan Island in the South China Sea. There's another Friendship Highway in Xinjiang Province, which is better known as the Karakoram Highway (see p66). In Nepal, the section of the Friendship Highway between Kodari and Kathmandu is sometimes referred to as the Arniko Highway. The Friendship Highway was built in the 1950s and 60s, under Chairman Mao's directive to "march while building roads", and was recently upgraded for the torch relay of the 2008 Beijing Olympic Games.

Along its length the Friendship Highway is studded with **kilometre markers**. Chinese road markers follow their own logic: sometimes starting from zero (as at Chaksam Bridge on Day One), sometimes measuring the distances in thousands of kilometres from Shanghai (as out of Lhasa, also on Day One). Since each cycle computer measures distance differently (see box p7), the fixed Chinese markers are used where possible for the route guide although this wasn't possible in places where the Friendship Highway was under construction. Chinese markers are shown every 5km on the maps but on the road itself they appear every kilometre.

Language

The older generations speak only **Tibetan**, but since 1965 Tibetan children have been taught **Mandarin Chinese** from primary school onwards. Only people who deal with tourists will speak some **English**; in Nepal almost everyone does. In Tibet most road signs are in Mandarin, a few are in English; kilometre markers are in Roman numerals. Nepali shares Hindi's Devanagari script and the traditional Hindu greeting of 'namaste' but although the two languages are closely related they are also quite distinct. As some would put it, 'same same but different!'.

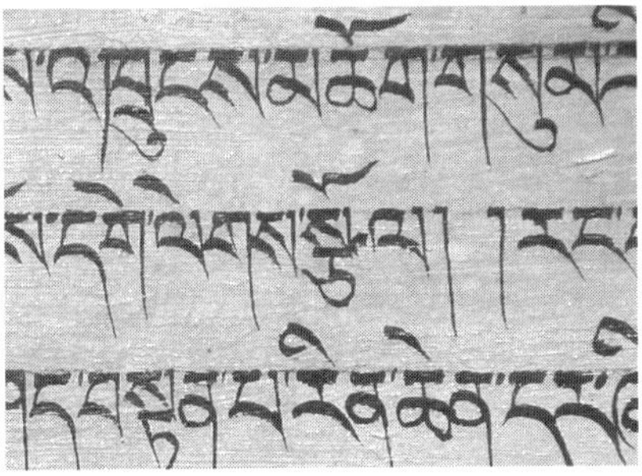
Tibetan script

REACHING PASSES

On reaching a pass religious Tibetans may shout out 'Tso tso tso tso! Lha Gyalo!' (Victory to the Gods!), lob squares of coloured paper printed with mantras up into the air and tie prayer flags to give thanks to the gods for safe passage. Passes are holy and superstition has it that making too much of a ruckus on one will incur bad weather.

Religion

Tibet is the spiritual home of **Buddhism**, but China's Cultural Revolution in the late 1960s saw the destruction of more than 2000 Buddhist monasteries and wide-scale religious persecution. Nothing is quite as it seems in Lhasa and the occupation of Tibet by an officially atheist power has done enormous cultural damage. Recognizing the enormous tourism potential in monks and monasteries, the Chinese have reconstructed many of the more famous monasteries and reopened them to tourists but religious expression remains controlled. Tibet remains a highly sensitive issue for China, as seen by the strong reaction to the 2008 riots prior to the Olympic Games.

It is the custom to move clockwise around Buddhist monasteries, spin prayer wheels clockwise and keep mani walls (walls made of stones chiselled with mantras) to the right. Do the reverse in Bon monasteries (Bon is Tibet's indigenous religion). The Potala Palace, traditional winter seat of the Dalai Lamas, is now a museum run by the Chinese government and monks and nuns throughout Tibet are still periodically 're-educated' to denounce the Dalai Lama. To see Tibetan Buddhism flourishing in the monasteries it's necessary to travel to Ladakh, Sikkim or Bhutan. On a cultural note, when **giving and receiving** in Tibet use both hands to give or take things, and when Tibetans offer you a gift they will sometimes bend forwards and raise it above their heads. Nepal is a mostly Hindu country, though Buddhism is practised by about 10% of the population.

PRACTICAL INFORMATION

Which direction?

Nearly everyone starts in Lhasa. In recent years it's been difficult for independent travellers to cross the border from Nepal into Tibet, and nearly all of those who try are told to join one of the organized and expensive jeep tours from Kathmandu. The few cyclists who manage to talk their way into Tibet are faced with the longest uphill in the world: 155km from a lowly 630m to a head-crushing 5140m on a mud-packed road.

Equipment

There's a general packing list in Part One (see pp34-56). Unless travelling on an organized tour, **it's a good idea to bring camping equipment** to Tibet. This way the days can be planned to put you in the best stead for climbing passes and descending back down to a reasonable sleeping height in daylight.

Anyone cycling in October onwards must be prepared for temperatures below -5°C when coming off the higher passes. The real temperature will be more like -20°C with wind chill factored in. A windproof down jacket with a toggled hood, a down sleeping bag, windproof mittens with a fleecy inner glove and a decent three-season tent will make all the difference between shivery misery and toasty comfort. Balaclavas are useful for keeping the face warm; if the bank robber look doesn't appeal you could try 'the surgeon' and buy one of the dust masks sold cheaply on the streets in Lhasa.

'The surgeon': using dust masks to stay warm

Campers coming from the West should pack some dehydrated food from outdoors shops for those evenings when you feel shattered and just want a comfortingly familiar and hot meal in your sleeping bag with no fuss. At all times of year a good pair of UV-proof sunglasses is essential.

Accommodation

Along the Friendship Highway you can overnight in small towns or use them to eat a hot meal in before camping in the countryside. If you're camping late in the season the bridges and culverts come in very handy, offering protection against the wind while also making you invisible to passing traffic. At other times of the year be absolutely certain a river is dry before pitching the tent under a bridge.

Some people don't bring camping equipment at all to the Friendship Highway, reasoning that doing away with it makes it possible to cover the long distances between towns. This is true for strong cyclists and an itinerary for non-campers could look something like this: Day 1 Dagar; 2 Nangartse; 3 Gyantse; 4 Shigatse; 5 Sakya turn off; 6 Lhatse; 7 Baipa; 8 Tingri; 9 Ritz Guesthouse at Sumdo; 10 Nyalam; 11 Bharabise; 12; Dhulikhel; 13 Kathmandu. Days one, four, eight, nine and from Nyalam onwards will be easy: days five, six, ten and especially seven will be hard.

Snow and sub-zero temperatures in October

The above itinerary is based on where there are guesthouses, but in truth where there are people there will be a bed (for a price). Staying in a home, rather than a hotel or guesthouse, is an opportunity that shouldn't be missed. But in return for the hospitality you must expect to be the entertainment; it's incomprehensibly rude for a guest to want to be alone.

If camping in sub-zero temperatures or lodging with locals don't appeal there are Tibetan guesthouses and the fancier-looking Chinese hotels. Guesthouses usually charge by the bed (Y15-30); Chinese hotels are usually more expensive. The pricier Chinese hotels lure cold and weary cyclists with promises of heating, electricity and hot water. They charge upfront and sometimes fail to deliver.

STOCKING UP FOR THE RIDE

Supermarkets in Lhasa and Shigatse sell dried noodles, instant noodles, packet soups, peanuts and cashews, porridge, tsampa oatmeal, muffins, chocolate bars (Snickers and Dove), tea bags (Lipton's) and milk powder (lactogen), Nescafé sachets with whitener, Coke and loose jasmine tea. Supermarket oddities include yak tendon sweeties and dried waxberries. Wetwipes offer a little luxury when camping in the cold. Plastic containers (similar to Tupperware) are handy for packing extra meals from restaurants. Boiled sweets or throat lozenges will soothe throats which are sore from the cold, dry air.

Food and drink

Traditionally the staple diet of Tibet consists of tsampa, chang and butter tea (tea leaves mixed with salt and butter, pounded together in a cylindrical tube and then brewed). Apart from the tea, you are unlikely to meet people eating this diet along the Friendship Highway unless they are nomads. Cured meat, such a yak leg, is also popular. Much more appetizing are momos, *kothe* (fried momos) and thenthuk. Tibetan bread is disc shaped and palm-sized. Along the Friendship Highway the more modern diet is instant noodles and Lhasa Beer brewed by Carlsberg.

Not only altitude causes headaches...

Many people from Sichuan province in China have moved into Tibet and opened restaurants. The spicy Sichuanese diet of vegetables, noodles and soups is easier to cycle on and has a greater variety. The menus vary too with the English version always costing a few yuan more. Where there aren't menus you can follow the cook into the kitchen and point at what you want. Many cyclists order double portions – one to eat in and one to stow away and eat later. If you don't mind eating just one hot meal a day, you could get away with not carrying a stove and cooking equipment at all.

Whether you eat Tibetan or Chinese food, standards of **hygiene** in Tibet are low and diarrhoea is common so take the usual precautions (see p59).

Money

Tibetan money was replaced in the 1950s by the Chinese Renminbi (RMB), better known as the *yuan* or *kuai* ('kwai'). Its Chinese character is ¥. One yuan (Y1) is divided into 10 *jiao* or *mao*. See p32 for exchange rate information.

DELICACIES OF TIBET

Chinese food is delicious and the Chinese people know no fear when it comes to eating. While some things are lost in translation, others are gained: here are a few morsels you may encounter on your travels:

The palace protects the meat cubelets
Fry the acupuncture needle mushroom
Limp cock's wings
Cookad chickon paws (also called phoenix feet and served cold – very popular in nightclubs!)

The Bank of China in Tibet has branches in both Lhasa and Shigatse which will exchange foreign currency (preferably dollars) as well as travellers' cheques (preferably American Express or Thomas Cook). Bank of China ATMs in Lhasa and Shigatse accept both foreign Visa and Maestro cards.

Rules of the road

Traffic drives on the **right** in China and on the **left** in Nepal; give way to military convoys in both countries.

GETTING TO THE RIDE

China actively discourages independent travel in Tibet and insists that all foreigners arrive from Nepal on an organized tour. Nevertheless entry regulations and fees to Tibet can change without notice. Tibet can only be reached via Nepal or mainland China. There are no border crossings between India or Bhutan and Tibet. Although the Nathu La pass between Sikkim and Tibet has opened for trade independent foreigners cannot cross it. The only international flights into Tibet are from Kathmandu with China Southwest Airlines – tickets are only issued to travel agents, not to individuals and these flights do not operate between November and March. Entering Tibet from mainland China is by far the easiest and cheapest option. However you decide to approach Tibet, to do it legally you will need a **Chinese visa** and a **Tibet permit**.

From China

Most nationalities can enter **Hong Kong** without a visa even though the island has belonged to mainland China since 1994. Once in Hong Kong Chinese visas are issued at the Ministry of Foreign Affairs Visa Office, 5th Floor, China Resources Building, 26 Harbour Road, Wanchai. Hong Kong is also home to the Flying Ball Bicycle Company (💻 www.flyingball.com) in Kowloon at 478 Castle Peak Rd, Cheung Sha Wan (MTR Exit C2), an excellent bike shop.

By air There are flights from Hong Kong direct to Lhasa but they are infrequent and expensive. Travel agents in Hong Kong (even the CITS) take 10 days to process a Tibet permit, whereas on mainland China it can take just 48hrs (see Chengdu, opposite). The best option is to cross to the mainland: Shenzen is only 40mins on the Kowloon Canton Railway (KCR) train. You can then fly from there to Chengdu and on to Lhasa. Don't throw away your boarding card on Chinese **domestic flights** as staff sometimes check it against your luggage tags before allowing you to leave baggage reclaim.

Beijing The cheapest and most reliable way for independent travellers to reach Lhasa – even from Europe – is via Beijing.

- **By air** Flights to Lhasa with Air China are daily and direct (Y2430) and it's easy to buy tickets on arrival in Beijing.
- **By train** The Qinghai–Tibet railway (see box opposite) takes nearly two days to travel the 1142 kilometres from Beijing to Lhasa. The reservations office in Beijing charges Y813 ($116) for a bed in the hard sleeper carriage (six beds, no door into corridor) and Y1262 ($180) for soft sleeper (four beds and a door). There are also reclining seats for the truly hardy. The online travel

THE TIBET TRAIN

In 2006 the Chinese opened the Qinghai–Tibet railway and for the first time rolling stock rumbled over the Tibetan plateau. The 1142-km line cost US$3.7 billion and carried over one million passengers to Tibet in its first six months; an extension to Shigatse in 2010 is expected to bring billions more yuan in tourism revenue.

Once on the train, all the compartments have oxygen outlets, a thermos of hot water and bedding. There are squat and sit-down toilets in each carriage and in the middle of the train is the one restaurant carriage. A ticker board updates passengers on the train's current speed, altitude and the next station while anyone in the restaurant car and soft-sleeper cabins is subject to a piped commentary on the journey (in Chinese and English).

agents 💻 www.chinahighlights.com and 💻 www.chinatripadvisor.com no longer sell tickets for the train; it is much easier and cheaper to buy the train tickets once in China. A recommended travel agent in Beijing is CCTS (☎ 0086 10 8584 6485, 💻 www.cctsbeijing.com), Balizhuang Beili 1#, Chaoyang District, Beijing, 100025. They will require scans of your passport and Chinese visa in order to process the Tibet permit so you can pick it up on arrival in Beijing.

A deluxe tourist train called the Tangula Express will start running from Beijing to Lhasa in September 2008; for more details and fares see 💻 www.tangula.com.cn.

Chengdu Many of the major cities on China's eastern seaboard use Chengdu as a hub to western China. The travel agency at ***Sim's Cozy Guesthouse*** (simscozygh@yahoo.co.jp) can arrange both the flight to Lhasa and the Tibet permit within 1-2 working days. Sim's Cozy Guesthouse is also a pleasant place to stay (Y15/bed in 12-man dorm, up to Y200/dbl with air con, TV, and balcony) while waiting for the permit, and can also give information on cycling to Chengdu's premier tourist attraction: the Panda Breeding and Research Centre which lies just 10km from the city. The hostel is a backpacker favourite and no wonder: the staff are friendly, there's a small garden, bar, a pet pig and even wireless internet.

From Nepal

Chinese policy is fickle but at present it's not possible for independent travellers to get a Chinese visa and Tibet permit in **Kathmandu**. The Chinese embassy will only issue visas to foreigners on package tours. Flights from Kathmandu to Lhasa cost around $300 but again are only issued to travel agents, not to individuals travelling independently.

RIDING IN THE OFF-SEASON

The Tibet off-season starts from late October. Along the Friendship Highway tourist restaurants lie empty and hotels offer up to 50% discounts. Temperatures drop well below freezing at night (even in hotel rooms) and once it gets really cold (November onwards), most basic hotels turn off the mains water entirely and supply a hot thermos and enamel wash bowl. Be prepared for this or you will freeze!

LHASA (3630M)

The capital of Tibet lured early explorers in droves; they found it both fascinating and filthy in equal measure. Nineteenth-century travels through this forbidden kingdom were perilous indeed; Tibetans were notorious for their murderous distrust of foreigners. Encrusted in grime themselves, most explorers reached Lhasa after months of hardship usually spent in the guise and company of Buddhist pilgrims, traders or Chinese medicine men. Once reached, the holy city of Buddhism did not disappoint: the Potala Palace appeared truly extraordinary after the privations of months on the Tibetan plateau, and deep within the warren of filthy streets hundreds of gold Buddhas gleamed in the dim, butter lamp-lit chapels of the Jokhang.

The iconic image of Lhasa:
the Potala Palace

So it comes as a great disappointment that Lhasa is now a modern Chinese city. Indeed, the heavy hand of Beijing could not be more marked. The road to the Potala, residence of Dalai Lamas, is prominently signed 'Beijing Avenue'. Han faces fill the streets; all the beggars are Tibetans. In fact, the Chinese have modernized Lhasa so fast that it now has trendy Shanghai-style cafés in the back streets, wi-fi coffee shops and plenty of brash hotels catering to thousands of Chinese tourists. Karaoke bars, discos and department stores line soulless concrete avenues.

The pace of change from medieval village to 21st century city has transformed everything except the hundreds of pilgrims who still arrive in Lhasa from all over Tibet, prostrating themselves, step by step, around the Jokhang Temple and the Potala. Lhasa's pulse is in the warren of streets around the Jokhang temple, the heart of every Buddhist pilgrimage. A sea of pilgrims and curious tourists ebbs and flows endlessly past stalls laden with slabs of yellowing butter, cheap Chinese goods or bundles of dried yak meat dangling from hooks.

It's a good idea to spend a day or two acclimatizing in Lhasa before setting off. It's easiest to get around on foot or hire a pagoda-topped cycle rickshaw (fix the price before you get on). The Potala and the Jokhang are both must-sees although fluorescent lights, fire hydrants and CCTV cameras have stolen the magic. But generally in Lhasa people-watching is more interesting than sight-seeing and nowhere more so than on the kora procession around the Jokhang: tourists, Chinese businessmen, ruddy-faced Tibetan girls running the stalls or a ferocious-looking Khampa nomad, red thread twisted in his hair and a dagger in his belt, sending a text message. In the next few years Lhasa looks set to change beyond all recognition, with international luxury hotels opening up to cater for the increasing number of tourists arriving by train. If you tire of the town the outlying monasteries of Sera, Drepung and Ganden all make good acclimatization rides.

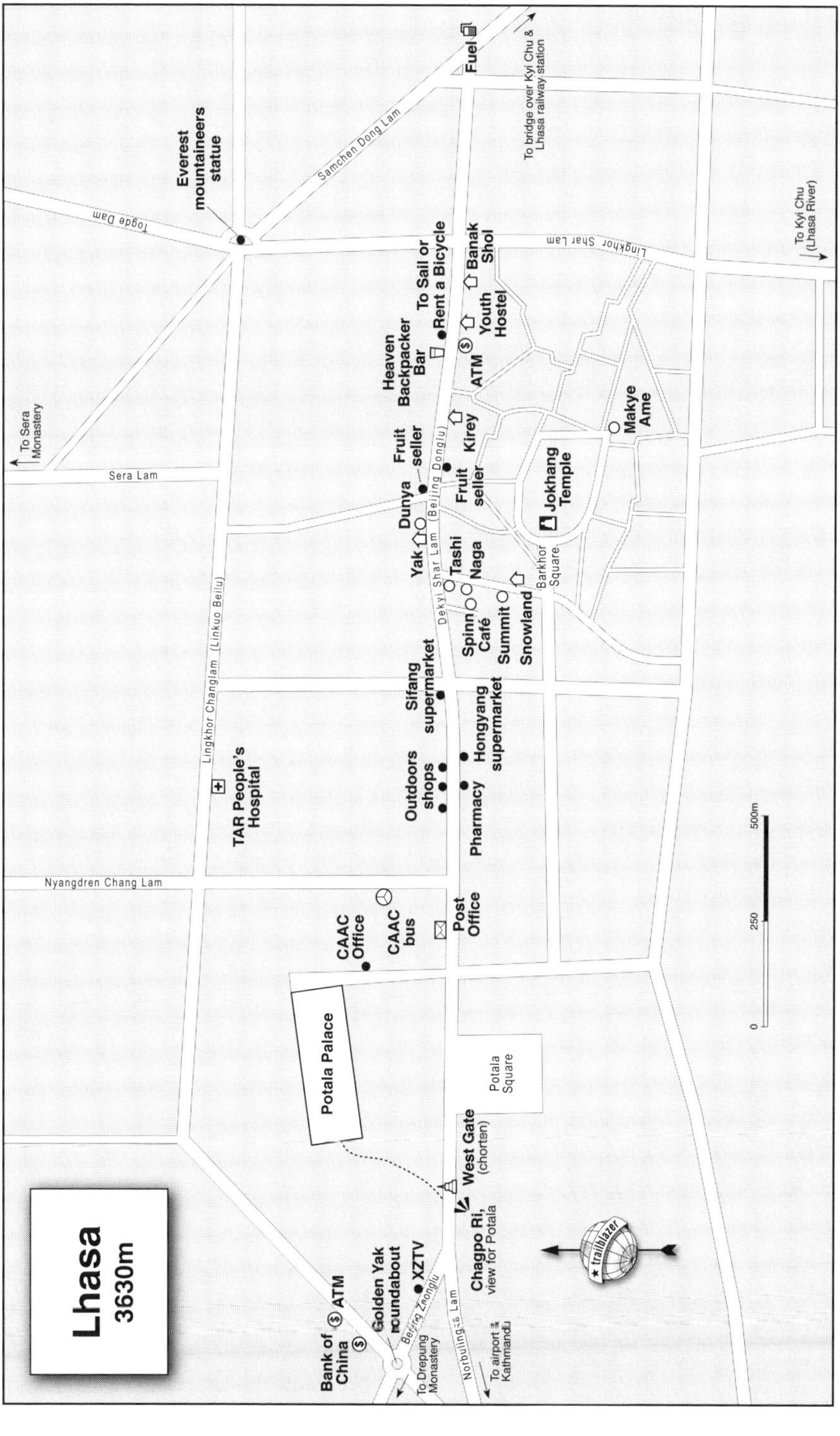
Lhasa
3630m
Everest mountaineers statue
Togde Dam
Samchen Dong Lam
Fuel
To bridge over Kyi Chu & Lhasa railway station
To Sera Monastery
Sera Lam
Lingkhor Changlam (Linkuo Beilu)
Lingkhor Shar Lam
To Kyi Chu (Lhasa River)
To Sail or Rent a Bicycle
Banak Shol
Youth Hostel
ATM
Heaven Backpacker Bar
Kirey
Makye Ame
Fruit seller
Fruit seller
Dunya
Yak
Tashi
Naga
Jokhang Temple
Barkhor Square
Dekyi Shar Lam (Beijing Donglu)
Spinn Café
Summit
Snowland
Sifang supermarket
Hongyang supermarket
Outdoors shops
Pharmacy
TAR People's Hospital
Nyangdren Chang Lam
CAAC Office
CAAC bus
Post Office
Potala Palace
Potala Square
West Gate (chorten)
Chagpo Ri, view for Potala
XZTV
Golden Yak roundabout
Bank of China
ATM
Beijing Zhonglu
Norbulingka Lam
To Drepung Monastery
To airport & Kathmandu
0
250
500m
trailblazer

Arrival and orientation

• **By air** Gongkar airport is about 70km to the southwest of Lhasa. A CAAC (Civil Aviation Administration of China) bus runs on the hour every hour between 7am and 1pm between the airport and the CAAC office in central Lhasa (see map p251); seats cost Y25 and bikes go free. If you'd prefer to head straight to a hotel there are plenty of taxi touts at the airport exit who'll charge Y120 for a small car (the bike box gets stuffed in the boot) or Y180 for a minibus.

• **By train** Lhasa train station lies 12km to the southwest of the city on the opposite bank of the Kyi Chu. Plenty of taxis wait outside.

Where to stay

There are no family guesthouses in Lhasa but most **hotels** offer a range of rooms with the cheapest option being a bed in a mixed dorm. The most popular hotels among foreigners are strung along Beijing Donglu. A favourite among tour groups as well as independent travellers is the ***Yak*** which caters for all tastes with dorm beds from Y30 up to colourful and comfy doubles with central heating, Tibetan decor, TV, en suite bathroom and the Chinese hotel staples of kettle, slippers and bathrobe, all for Y380. It's only steps away from the Barkhor, the spiritual heart of Lhasa, and well placed for the supermarkets too. Closer to the Barkhor is the ***Snowlands*** (dorm bed Y25, dbl com Y50, dbl att Y150), further east along Beijing Donglu are the ***Kirey*** (dorm bed Y30, sing/dbl Y70), the good-value and spotless ***YHA*** (dorm bunkbed att Y25, dbl com Y40, dbl att Y120) and, at the far end, the ***Banak Shol*** (dorm bed Y30, sing com Y40, dbl com Y60, dbl att 140/180 for Tibetan/Western style). All the hotels have **internet** (Y5/hr) and are set back from the road with their own courtyards – perfect for putting the bike together – and all have **notice boards** (the one at the Yak is particularly well used).

Where to eat

A cosy home for cyclists is the ***Spinn Café***, which is run by two cycle tourers down an alley off Beijing Donglu between Tashi and the Kyichu Hotel. The café is open all day every day and serves Thai and Cantonese food (reflecting the owners' origins) as well as full English breakfasts and cocktails. They also stock bike parts (see opposite).

The girls who run ***Tashi***, at the corner of Beijing Donglu and the road down to Barkhor, make a lovely mashed potato with veg (Y10), and serve sweet tea in big mugs. Their best-known dish is *bobi* – crêpes filled with tangy cream cheese and steamed veg. This is an unpretentious place, unlike ***Dunya***, next to the Yak hotel, which has a very European atmosphere with matching prices. The alley running north from Dunya has a few trendy bars such as ***Another Place***, ***The Moment*** and ***For You***, where you can watch DVDs on the sofa while munching bar snacks (popcorn and spring rolls) and sinking

A novel way to avoid washing up?

Lhasa beers. Between Tashi and the Barkhor are plenty more restaurants: the ***Naga*** with French dishes, low tables and floor seating which looks best by night and the ***Tengyelink*** which shares a menu with the tired ***Snowland*** restaurant next door.

The ***Mandala*** on the southern side of the circuit around the Jokhang serves up Nepali and Indian dishes such as naan and tandoori chicken.

Street food in Lhasa is fun, such as the fresh curd (yoghurt) sold in wooden pots (Y2.5) near Sifang supermarket on the corner of Beijing Donglu and Senge Beilu. Self-catering is easy from the supermarkets. Deep-fried skewer men appear on the street outside the Yak at dusk, with aubergine, mushrooms, potato, yak meat, chicken and green beans at the ready (Y1 per skewer). The ***Hongyuang*** supermarket on Beijing Donglu has seating outside where you can slurp at a bowl of cheap noodles, or there are numerous hot pot restaurants along the same road. The ***Summit Café*** in the courtyard of the Shang Bala hotel has cappuccinos (Y20), chocolate brownies, internet terminals (Y8/hr) and free wireless internet for laptops – surely the highest imitation Starbucks in the world!

Bike shops

To Sail or Rent a Bicycle opposite the Youth Hostel on Beijing Donglu can fix simple problems like warped wheels, loose headsets and brakes for Y3-5. The ***Heavenly Backpacker Bar*** next door has outside seating so you can drink a beer or tea while you wait.

The Spinn Café (💻 www.spinn.cn/en, see 'Where to eat' opposite) stocks a wide range of good-quality bike parts and accessories such as Shimano XT cassettes, Selle Italia saddles and Kool Stop brake pads at reasonable prices.

Moving on

Getting out of Lhasa is a whole lot easier than getting in. To fly out simply visit the CAAC office (see Lhasa map p251) or just turn up at the airport and buy your flight there. The left-luggage facility at Lhasa airport costs Y10 per day (negotiable) **upfront**. If you don't have the cash, there's an ATM just outside the entrance to the airport.

RIDING FROM LHASA TO KATHMANDU ON A BUDGET

There's such a thriving outdoor gear scene in Lhasa now that you could fly in almost empty-handed and set yourself up for the ride on arrival. This is especially economical if travelling to Tibet from mainland China, where some airports charge freight prices (Y23/kg) to fly bicycle boxes. To Sail or Rent a Bicycle on Beijing Donglu (see above) sells new Giant bikes: a Giant ATX with V-brakes and front suspension costs Y1500 ($195). With a saddle, pedals, pump, rack and panniers from home, the Friendship Highway is there for the taking and if at the end you think 'never again!' you can sell the bicycle if not some of the kit for nearly the original price once in Kathmandu.

A trawl along the outdoors shops on Beijing Donglu will turn up gear from the big-name brands such as North Face, Mountain Hardwear and Arcteryx at knock-down prices. Most are fakes, but some are still good enough. Chinese brands such as Toread are also worth a look. The following are available in Lhasa: tents, sleeping bags, sleeping mats (not Thermarest), multifuel stoves (Primus), down jackets, fleece tops, warm double-layered gloves and even little luxuries like down gloves and booties.

Route guide – Lhasa to Kathmandu

Between Lhasa and Shigatse there are two roads: the **Central route** along the Yarlung Tsangpo (Brahmaputra River) which is a relatively flat, fast and featureless ride, or the much more scenic, longer **Southern Route** (described here) which includes gems such as Yamdrok Tso lake, several passes and the small town of Gyantse with its fortress, monastery and turbulent British history. There's no point in bringing a bike to Tibet and then choosing the Central Route. Leave it to the jeeps and military convoys, of which there are plenty.

Lhasa–Nangartse

The first day of the Friendship Highway is an easy spin on tarmac southwest along the Kyi Chu (Lhasa River) valley to the base of Kampa La: the first and one of the highest passes on the Highway. The climb is quite steep and long but the tarmac is perfect. Once crossed the road dips to Yamdrok Tso then meanders along the lake shore until the Chinese military town of Nangartse. There may be a headwind but think of it as training because there will be more in the days ahead! There are plenty of petrol stations; for **multifuel stoves** get the fuel direct from the pumps as the stuff in watering cans clogs up stoves.

DAY 1 LHASA (3630m) to FOOT OF KAMPA LA (3598m) 83KM

LHASA–CHUSUL 63KM
CHUSUL–DAGAR 8KM
DAGAR–FOOT OF KAMPA LA 12KM

Lhasa (3630m) 0/966KM
Between central Lhasa and the Gongkar airport turnoff the traffic can be heavy but in Lhasa itself there's a segregated bike lane and after that a hard shoulder to ride on. After the airport turnoff it feels like the ride is really beginning: Lhasa falls further behind and ahead lie the passes, lakes and mountains of the ride to Kathmandu.

Navigating out of Lhasa is straightforward – head west past the Potala (0km) and after the chorten at West Gate take the left hand fork (signed Norbulinka Lam). Go straight over the first crossroads and turn left (south) at the T-junction (the entrance to the Norbulinka Palace) onto National Road. At the next junction, turn right (west) onto West Jinzhu Road. Follow this road all the way out of Lhasa (it will change its name a few times), and at about 11km from the Potala turn south at a large junction (unsigned). The road that continues west is to Nam Tso. This southern road is quieter and will take you all the way to Dagar (68km from Lhasa) so now you can relax.

Tibet railway (3651m) The road passes under a railway bridge; the railway west of Lhasa is still under construction but by 2010 it will span China from Beijing to Shigatse and some time after that, go on to Kashgar.

4679km marker (3650m) Just after the bridge over the Tolung Chu there's a 4679km marker and then another within one kilometre for 4650km – a little hiccup on this route that starts from Shanghai.

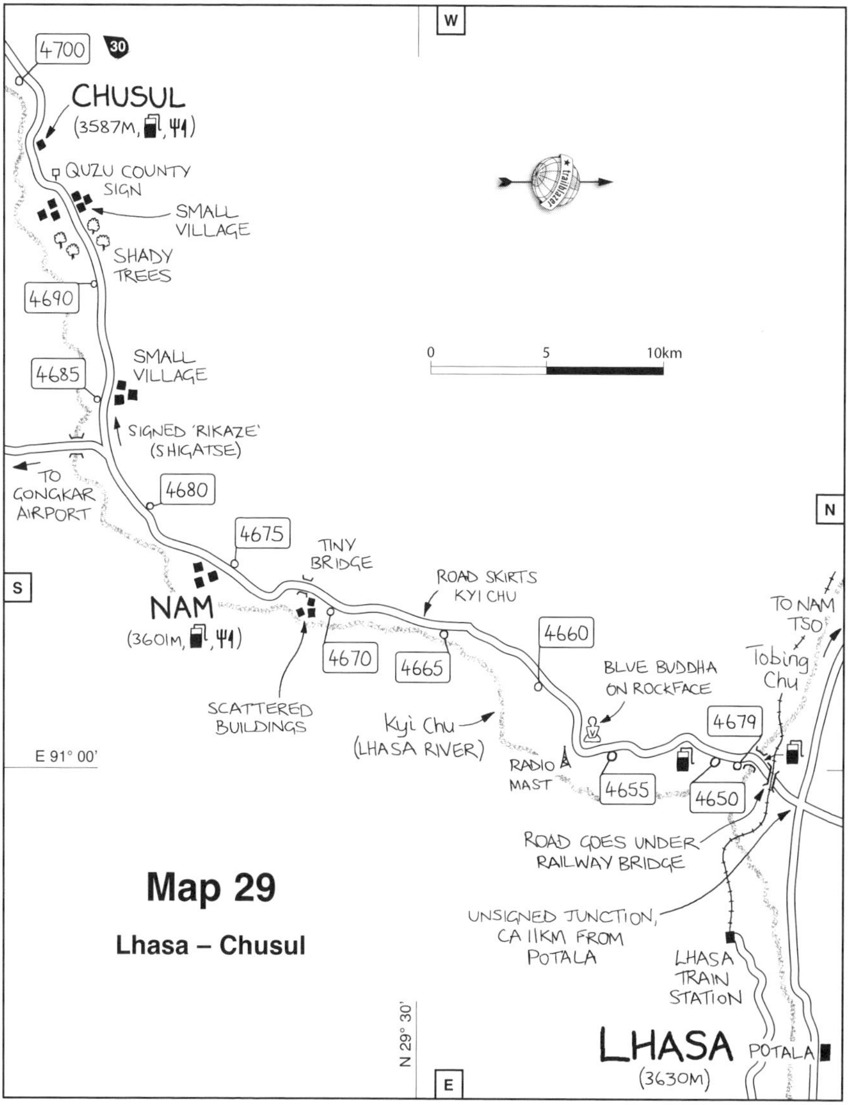

Map 29

Lhasa – Chusul

Blue Buddha (3631m) The Buddha painted on the rock face at 23km is a Medicine Buddha, whose left hand cups a begging bowl in his lap and whose right hand offers a sprig of *arura* (a cure-all in Tibetan and Ayurvedic medicine). It's said meditating on the Medicine Buddha boosts your healing powers and reduces mental and physical suffering – worth practising for those long climbs coming up then!

Nam (3601m) This is a basic village with restaurants on the left hand side behind the door curtains, but better places await in Chusul (see below).

4683km (3591m) Continue along the river bank here; the road south over the Kyi Chu Bridge leads to Gongkar airport.

Chusul (3587m) **63/893.5km**
This Chinese military town after the

Friendship H'way, 0–100km

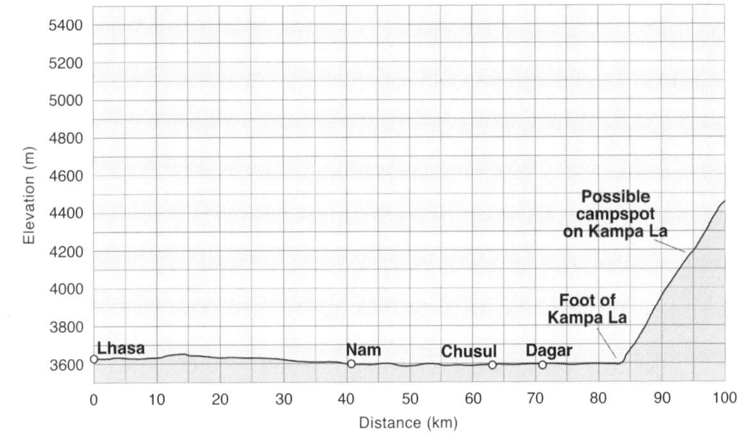

'Quzu County' sign has the best food options for the day – the few restaurants on the east side will cook up whatever you point to in the kitchen (noodles, green pepper, pak choi, raw meat, tomatoes).

Dagar (3588m) 71/885.5km

The Friendship Highway crosses the Kyi Chu here on the Chazam Bridge – a few small shops on the north side sell snacks. The austere concrete buildings and manned watchtower make this a place you won't want to hang around in for long. From the bridge the road veers away from the river and the kilometre markers start at 0km.

Foot of Kampa La (3598m) 83/873.5km

At 11km the road forks with 'Yangze power station' signed to the west: follow the sign and 100m down the road you can drag your bike down among the willows for a peaceful campsite on the banks of the Yarlung Tsangpo River (which later becomes the Brahmaputra).

DAY 2 FOOT OF KAMPA LA (3598m) to NANGARTSE (4460m) over Kampa La (4785m) 79km

Foot of Kampa La–Kampa La 24km
Kampa La–Tamalung 5km
Tamalung–Pede Dzong 20km
Pede Dzong–Nangartse 30km

An early start is needed today to reach Nangartse by late afternoon.

Kampa La (4785m) 107/849.5km

The road up Kampa La is perfect tarmac, but the pass is a consistently steep climb of just under 1200m over 23km. Once past the villages at the base of the pass there's no food and the only water is from two streams (marked on the map on p259) which will need to be purified. If you're unacclimatized, unfit or just hate getting up early about halfway up the pass and directly above the second stream there's a **campsite** (4167m) with views over the road. It's used by shepherds and yak dung collectors so you may need to clear it of broken Lhasa beer bottles before settling in. The pass itself is just after the 35km sign and is marked by prayer flags fluttering over the road, a pit of rubbish, lots of yaks dressed up for tourists (their handlers will demand money for photographs), stray dogs, trinket-sellers and great views over the turquoise expanse of Yamdrok Tso.

The descent off Kampa La is short and sweet. Back on the valley floor you are now above 4000m, and will spend most of the rest of the ride at this altitude or higher.

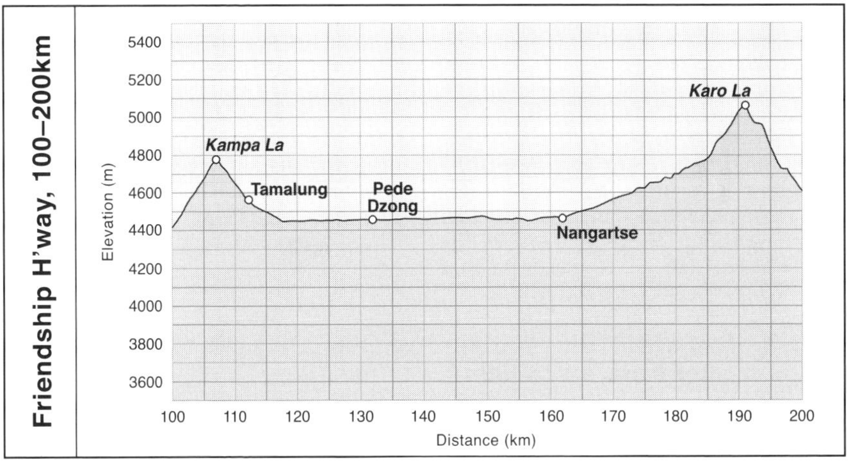

Tamalung (4571m) 112/844.5km

This village about 70m below the main road at the base of the pass is reachable by a dirt road. The nearby hydroelectric plant supplies the Lhasa valley (see box below); the village itself is surrounded by barley fields, with yak-skin coracles and fishing boats moored on the edge of the lake. If you're really shattered, you could find a bed here. Otherwise, it's best to keep pedalling along the shores of Yamdrok Tso towards the fishing village of Pede Dzong at the 59km marker. There are plenty of camping options en route (see map p259). As you circle the lake, the peak of Nojin Kungstang (7190m) swings into view to the southwest – you'll be cycling past this peak tomorrow as you cross Karo La.

Pede Dzong (4456m) 132/824.5km

Another small fishing village. There are two shops opposite each other at the bend to the right; both sell instant noodles (they'll add hot water for you), ancient biscuits and soft drinks.

After Pede Dzong a dirt track leads off at the 67km marker across a dried-up inlet of the lake to a tourist campsite (closed by mid-October) joining the main route on the other side just before the 76km marker, thereby lopping 9km off the ride. Pede Dzong to Nangartse is 26km (taking the shortcut); in early autumn this is very pretty with golden barley in the fields, blue skies and the turquoise lake. But after mid-October the fields are stripped bare and the headwind is biting. After a few villages on the shore which might prematurely get your hopes up, Nangartse finally appears at the 90km marker. A bitter wind whistles through this town of soulless concrete, carrying the martial tunes on the tannoy out into the Tibetan countryside.

YAMDROK TSO

Yamdrok Tso is the third largest lake on the Tibetan plateau, and one of Tibet's sacred lakes. It's easy to see why. This expanse of serene turquoise water reflects perfectly the snowy peaks that surround it. Its peculiar shape has earnt it the nickname of Scorpion Lake, and the scorpion's pincers clutch two more tiny lakes, Gongmo Tso and Jem Tso, just to the east of Nangartse.

In 1984 the Chinese government chose Yamdrok Tso as the site for a massive hydroelectric project despite strong local and international opposition. Yamdrok Tso has no water source except for snow melt, and the greatest fear is that this hydroelectric project, which began operation in 2000, will drain this beautiful lake completely in the next few decades.

Nangartse (4460m) 162/794.5km
At 91km turn right (signed to Nangartse) for the Tibetan quarter, where the *Grain* (Y100/dbl, no electricity, hot buckets) on the corner is a popular place to stay. On the highway itself (signed to Gyantse) there are several cheap Chinese hotels (though they look flash). Doubles at the *Delai* cost Y40 with TV and electricity but a freezing trench toilet block outside. The hotel also has a great **Sichuan restaurant** (fried pak choi and garlic, potatoes, noodles with beef, sweetcorn and green pepper stir fry and Lhasa beer) with an enjoyably mystifying menu. Back in the Tibetan quarter are several more restaurants, a post office and the People's Convenience Supermarket opposite which stocks muffins, pasta, dried fruit, soup stock, chocolate bars, biscuits, yak jerky, soft drinks, wine and beer – but check the expiry dates.

DAY 3 NANGARTSE (4460m) to FOOT OF SIMI LA (4290m) over Karo La (5050m) 66.5km

Nangartse–foot of Karo La 8km
Foot of Karo La–Karo La 21km
Karo La–Ralung 18.5km
Ralung–Lungma 11km
Lungma–foot of Simi La 8km

Two passes, one large and one tiny, lie between Nangartse and Shigatse. The larger of the two, Karo La, is a Himalayan stunner clad in glaciers and whose peaks dominate the skyline. Once crossed, you can relax and enjoy the cycling through quiet valleys to Gyantse. Between Gyantse and Shigatse the road is completely flat.

From Nangartse the road to the pass strikes out at a very gentle climb across the plain. At the fork in the road at 8km bear right (southwest) for Karo La (signed to Gyantse). The road that disappears along the valley to the left (signed to Lhozhag) leads to the Taklung monastery on the southern shores of Yamdrok Tso (17km). After the fork the valley walls close in with a river running alongside the road. There's a small village after 2km where a stream makes a good place to refill water bottles and gaze ahead at the peaks and ice walls of Jetung Chusang (6242m) and Jansang Lhamo (6324m).

Foot of Karo La (5050m) 170/786.5km
As the road climbs alongside the river any glacial headwind you felt in Nangartse will now get funnelled down this valley with increasing force. The climb itself is long and gradual with a kick at around 19km. From the village at the bottom Karo La looks like a large wall of rock but when the road finally turns away from the river at 26km the broad saddle that the pass sits on at 29km comes into view.

Karo La (5050m) 191/765.5km
The non-event of the pass itself – a bare cutting with no prayer flags – is more than compensated for by the fabulous views of Nojin Kungstang (7190m), whose glaciers bristle right next to the road, and the peaks of Jetung Chusang and Jansang Lhamo to the south. The pass itself is exposed and you may want to descend quickly, perhaps to the **restaurant** a kilometre on which has a fantastic view up to Nojin Kungstang and their own mountain of Lhasa beer bottles.

Namru Chu Valley The descent gathers pace through a narrow granite canyon and then spits you out into the Namru Chu valley. This is a wonderful place – spacious with increasingly stunning views of Mt Nojin Kungstang behind you. Yak herds can often be seen in the distance, just specks of shaggy black against the reddish hills. If the sun is shining, it's tempting to lie down on the springy grass and luxuriate in the Tibetness of it all.

Ralung (4475m) 209.5/747km
Very shortly after the bridge over the Nyeru Chu the road passes Ralung on the opposite side of the river, which has a monastery (signed, about 5km south from the road) where you can stay overnight.

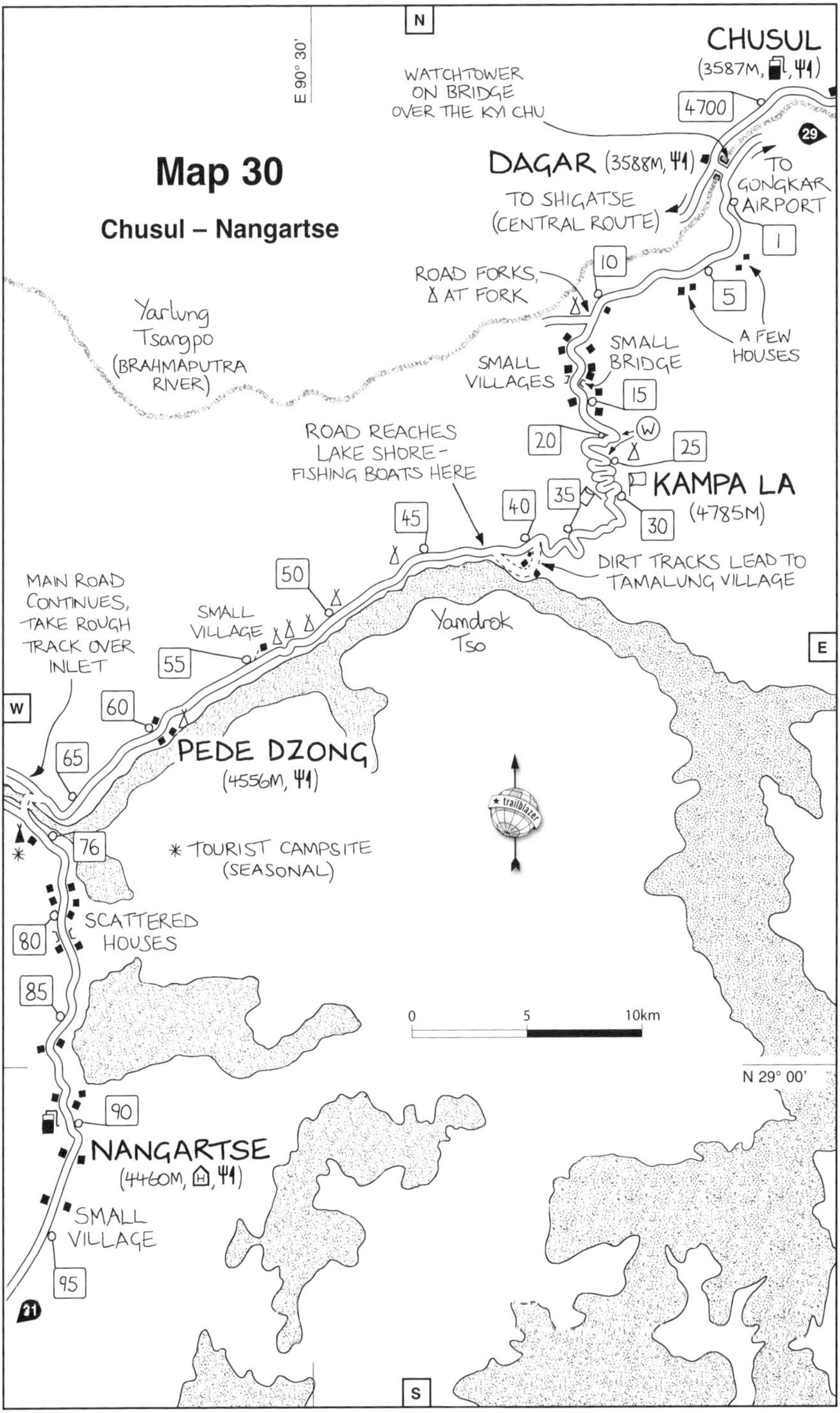
Map 30
Chusul – Nangartse
N
S
E
W
E 90° 30'
N 29° 00'
CHUSUL
(3587M, ⛽, ΨΙ)
4700
WATCHTOWER
ON BRIDGE
OVER THE KYI CHU
DAGAR (3588M, ΨΙ)
TO SHIGATSE
(CENTRAL ROUTE)
TO
GONGKAR
AIRPORT
1
5
10
ROAD FORKS,
AT FORK
A FEW
HOUSES
Yarlung
Tsangpo
(BRAHMAPUTRA
RIVER)
SMALL
VILLAGES
SMALL
BRIDGE
15
20
25
30
35
40
45
50
55
60
65
76
80
85
90
95
ROAD REACHES
LAKE SHORE –
FISHING BOATS HERE
KAMPA LA
(4785M)
DIRT TRACKS LEAD TO
TAMALUNG VILLAGE
MAIN ROAD
CONTINUES,
TAKE ROUGH
TRACK OVER
INLET
SMALL
VILLAGE
Yamdrok
Tso
PEDE DZONG
(4556M, ΨΙ)
TOURIST CAMPSITE
(SEASONAL)
SCATTERED
HOUSES
0
5
10km
NANGARTSE
(4460M, H, ΨΙ)
SMALL
VILLAGE
29
31
trailblazer

Lungma (4339m) **220.5/736KM**
The valley walls close in again as the road swings west then north past a few small villages to Lungma. Set against a backdrop of tiger-striped rocks, Lungma is very small but can offer basic accommodation. You can reach it by cycling to the westernmost end of the houses and then taking the dirt track that turns 180° back up into the village. There's a basic **restaurant** a kilometre later in Shuto (4340m); look for the telephone sign and the billiard table.

Campers might want to continue another 7km along the valley to the shores of a new turquoise lake at the base of Simi La. There are two abandoned villages on the shoreline although Kangwang village, which used to lie at the base of the pass, is now underwater. It's quiet here but carry water filtered from the river before Shuto because the lake itself is silty and disturbingly foamy. If you're very fit you could push on over Simi La to Gyantse today (see Day 4 below).

DAY 4 FOOT OF SIMI LA (4290m) to GYANTSE (4038m) over Simi La (4359m) 37KM

FOOT OF SIMI LA–SIMI LA 5KM
SIMI LA–GYANTSE 32KM

Foot of Simi La (4290m) **228.5/728KM**
From the abandoned villages it's just over 5km to the top of Simi La, now sealed with smooth tarmac. Once over you can relax in the knowledge that you're done with passes until after Shigatse. The reservoir on the other side of the pass is also turquoise, with a picturesque ruin on an island in the middle. The road curls downwards around the lake then climbs to a cleft blasted through the rocks above the dam house on the lake's shore.

Hydel village (4215m) Just around the corner at about 12km is a village built for the Chinese workers on the hydroelectric project; on the right there is the mandatory billiard table outside the shop which sells long expired soft drinks, chocolate wafers and noodles.

After this rather soulless village the scenery picks up. The road stops doodling around the ridges and strikes northwest with purpose towards Gyantse along the Nyang Chu River. This is very pleasant cycling past terraced fields and hills mottled red, purple and cream. By the time the rollers start you can see Gyantse's valley lying ahead, and when you reach the bunch of twigs on a hill to the left, Gyantse *dzong* (fortress) and the red walls surrounding the Kumbum (see p262) are in your sights; it's just 8km to some good food and a proper wash.

Gyantse (4038m) **265.5/691KM**
Plenty of jeep tourists stop off in Gyantse to see the dzong so the town is well set up for accommodation and food. The southern part of the town is Chinese but north and west of the Hero Monument is Tibetan.

As you ride into town towards the dzong you'll pass the ***Gyantse Hotel*** which has the most expensive rooms in town at Y550/dbl. All the other hotels are along Hero Middle Rd in the centre of town – including the ***Wutse*** (Y40 dorm bed, Y200 att dbl), the ***Jian Zhang*** hotel (Y180/200 att sing/dbl, Y160 com dbl, 'time room' (1hr) Y58). Further up at the roundabout, you could try the Y20 bug-filled beds at the ***Hostel of Gyantse Town Furniture Factory*** or the ***Hotel of***

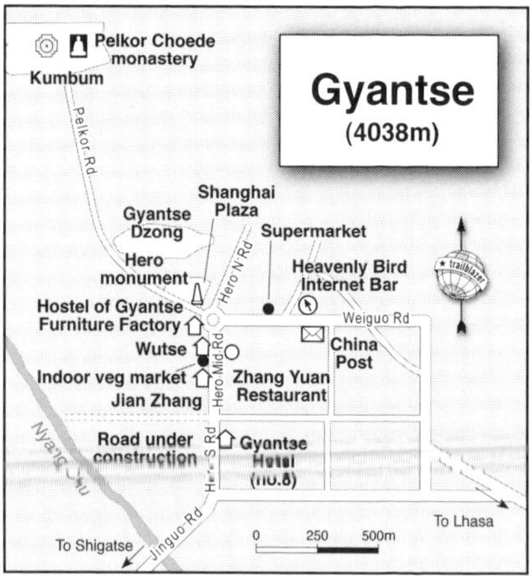

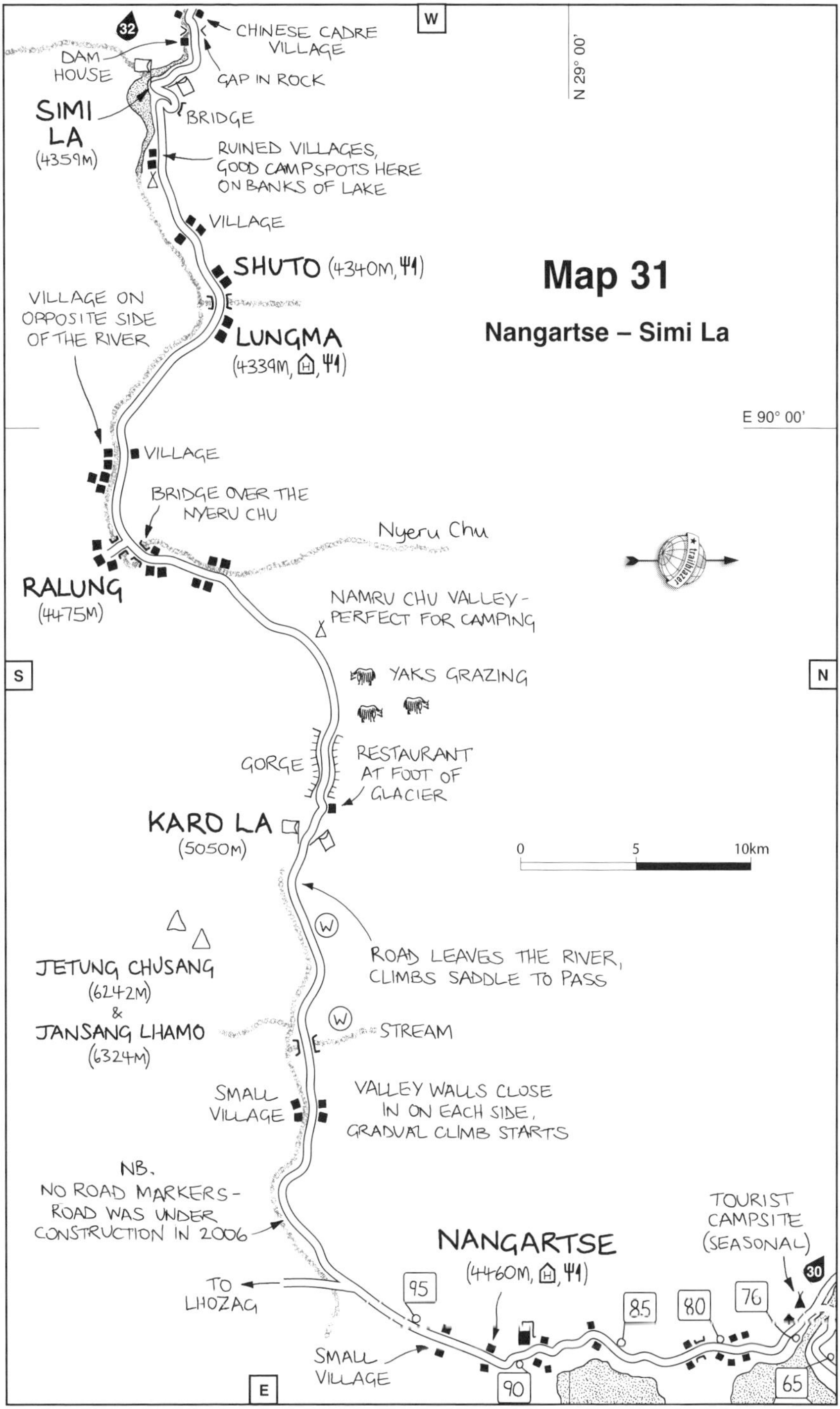
W
32
CHINESE CADRE VILLAGE
DAM HOUSE
GAP IN ROCK
SIMI LA (4359M)
BRIDGE
RUINED VILLAGES, GOOD CAMPSPOTS HERE ON BANKS OF LAKE
N 29° 00'
VILLAGE
SHUTO (4340M, ΨI)
Map 31
Nangartse – Simi La
VILLAGE ON OPPOSITE SIDE OF THE RIVER
LUNGMA (4339M, H, ΨI)
E 90° 00'
VILLAGE
BRIDGE OVER THE NYERU CHU
Nyeru Chu
trailblazer
RALUNG (4475M)
NAMRU CHU VALLEY - PERFECT FOR CAMPING
S
N
YAKS GRAZING
GORGE
RESTAURANT AT FOOT OF GLACIER
KARO LA (5050M)
0
5
10km
W
ROAD LEAVES THE RIVER, CLIMBS SADDLE TO PASS
JETUNG CHUSANG (6242M) & JANSANG LHAMO (6324M)
W
STREAM
SMALL VILLAGE
VALLEY WALLS CLOSE IN ON EACH SIDE, GRADUAL CLIMB STARTS
NB. NO ROAD MARKERS - ROAD WAS UNDER CONSTRUCTION IN 2006
TOURIST CAMPSITE (SEASONAL)
NANGARTSE (4460M, H, ΨI)
30
TO LHOZAG
95
85
80
76
SMALL VILLAGE
90
65
E

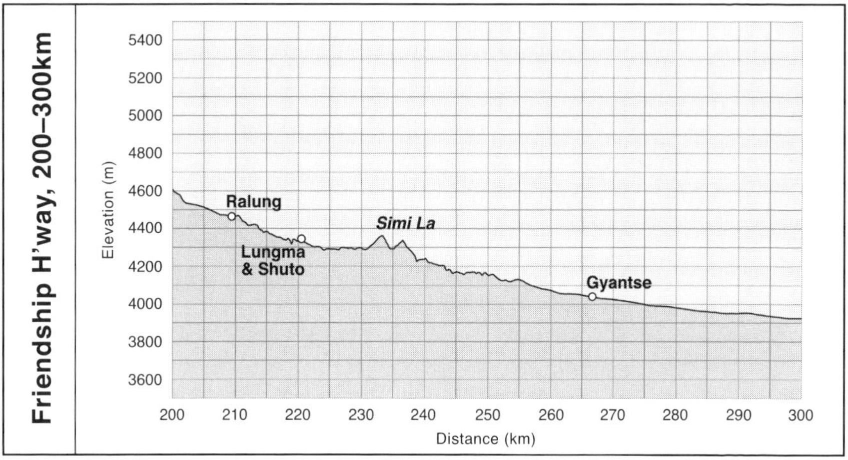

Nationality Clothing Company, though both have been known to turn foreigners away.

Gyantse is a good place for a feed. Along Hero Middle Rd there's an indoor **vegetable market** selling fresh vegetables such as aubergines, carrots, tomatoes, Chinese leaves, tubers, beans and red chillies. Squatting on the side of Hero Middle Rd are the **fruit sellers** with piles of apples, plums and oranges. Almost opposite the Wutse hotel a showman chef from Sichuan has opened the *Zhang Yuan* restaurant with a prominent 'clean food for tourists' sign outside. His dishes are tasty but pricey. This being a Chinese town there is also karaoke (KTV) at the nightclub next to *Tashi* restaurant – look for the Budweiser sign.

The northwest part of Gyantse is dominated by **Gyantse dzong** on its rocky outcrop and the famous **Kumbum** – the largest chorten in Tibet which is said to contain 100,000 images of Buddha. The Kumbum is part of Pelkhor Choede monastery which was razed in the Cultural Revolution. The best views of Gyantse are from the high walls surrounding the monastery, which are also great for a scramble.

DAY 5 GYANTSE (4038m) to SHIGATSE (3845m) 92KM

GYANTSE–PENAM DZONG 43KM
PENAM DZONG–SHIGATSE 49KM

Today is an easy day as the road is mostly flat, perfect tarmac and shaded by trees. After crossing the Nyang Chu River out of Gyantse you're back in rural Tibet and road markers count down from the 90s onwards to 49km, where Penam Dzong is handily situated for a lunch stop.

Gyantse (4038m) 265.5/691KM

Along the way there are great views across the fields to Gyantse dzong and the Kumbum and poking out of hillocks along the road are fort ruins strung with prayer flags. Many of the houses are traditionally Tibetan with the whitewashed walls sometimes tiled with dung cakes and shaded by stands of poplars. Of course, there are army garrisons too and new villages under construction. The pace of life here still seems to be mostly agricultural: pony and traps clop along the road, passed occasionally by a tractor or the odd local cyclist. Dust devils play among the fields. The children, especially the little boys, seem bored and have taken to either collecting 'hellos' from cyclists or throwing stones.

Penam Dzong (0000m) 308.5/618KM

Visible from a few kilometres away, Penam Dzong is an old Tibetan village

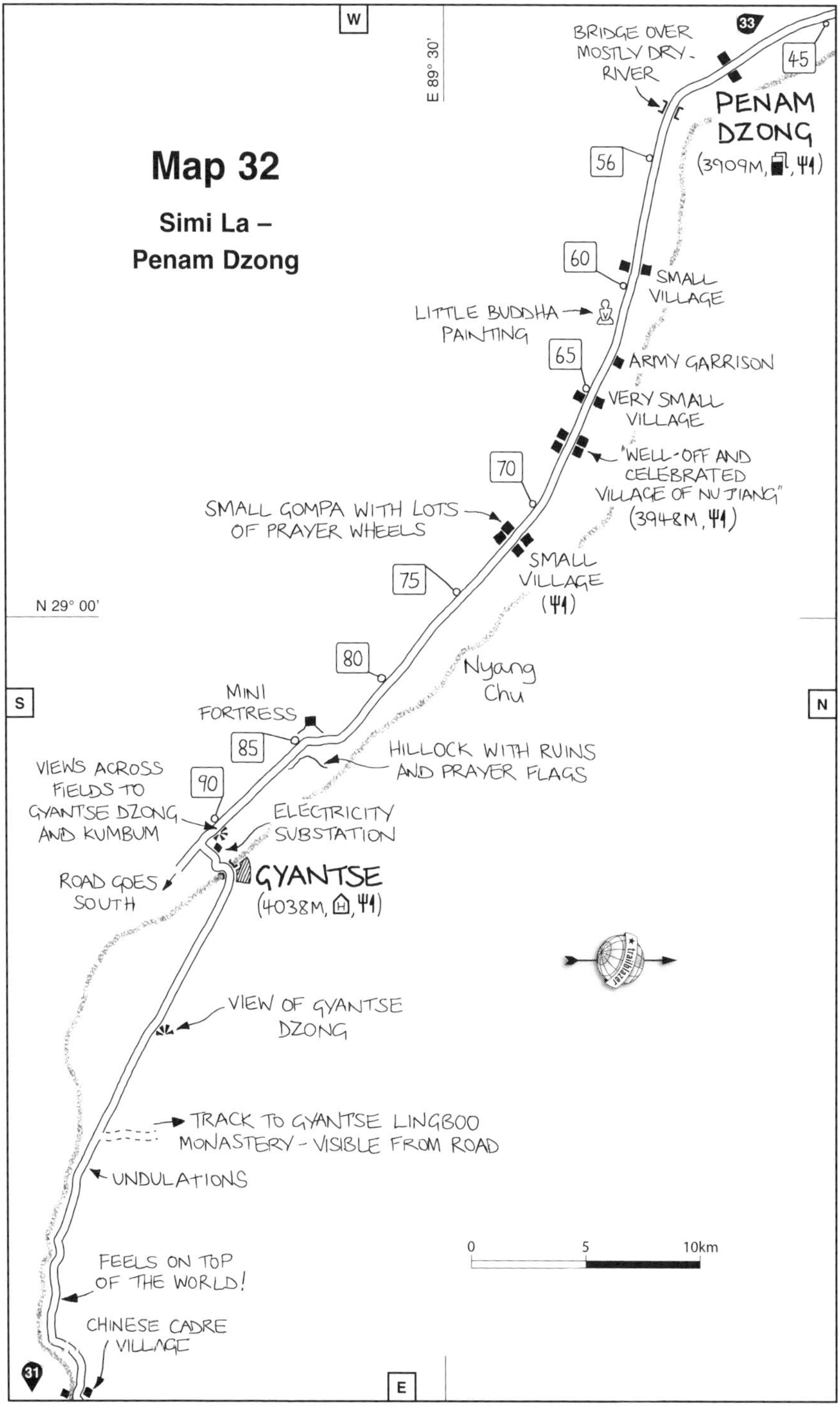
Map 32
Simi La –
Penam Dzong
W
E 89° 30'
N 29° 00'
S
N
E
33
31
BRIDGE OVER MOSTLY DRY RIVER
45
PENAM DZONG
(3909M, ⛽, 🍴)
56
60
SMALL VILLAGE
LITTLE BUDDHA PAINTING
65
ARMY GARRISON
VERY SMALL VILLAGE
"WELL-OFF AND CELEBRATED VILLAGE OF NU JIANG"
(3948M, 🍴)
70
SMALL GOMPA WITH LOTS OF PRAYER WHEELS
SMALL VILLAGE
(🍴)
75
80
Nyang Chu
MINI FORTRESS
85
HILLOCK WITH RUINS AND PRAYER FLAGS
90
VIEWS ACROSS FIELDS TO GYANTSE DZONG AND KUMBUM
ELECTRICITY SUBSTATION
ROAD GOES SOUTH
GYANTSE
(4038M, Ⓗ, 🍴)
VIEW OF GYANTSE DZONG
TRACK TO GYANTSE LINGBOO MONASTERY - VISIBLE FROM ROAD
UNDULATIONS
FEELS ON TOP OF THE WORLD!
CHINESE CADRE VILLAGE
0
5
10km
trailblazer

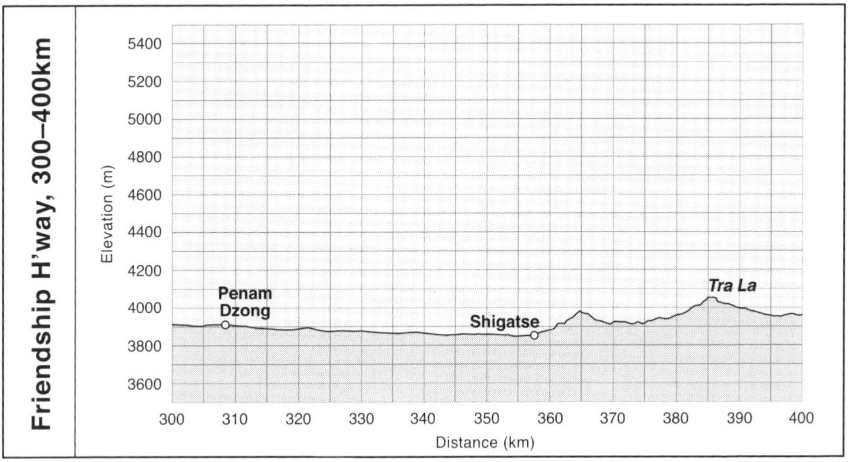

with a modern Chinese town strung out along the highway. Near the China Post there are some cheap restaurants on both sides of the road, near the pool tables.

After lunch, the scenery remains the same until the 15km marker at which point the road swings around a hill topped by chortens where the thangka wall of Shigatse's Tashilunpo monastery comes into view, backed by snowy mountains.

Shigatse (3845m) 357.5/599KM

The highway turns into dual carriageway and enters Shigatse from the south, past a shopping complex, auto workshops and a military compound; ignore the 'Tourist Reporting Point'. Continue straight at the first crossroads of Za De Rd; soon afterwards the Bank of China appears on the right followed by the ***Shigatse Hotel*** at which point you know you're in Shigatse proper – time for a rest day!

GO ON, SPIT IT OUT

In the run-up to the Beijing Olympic Games, the Chinese government initiated a campaign to instil Western manners among the Chinese, the highlights of which were 'Queuing Day' (held monthly to practise lining-up) and the Green Woodpecker Project, whose volunteers roamed the streets intercepting hawkers and spitters with a well-timed tissue.

For the Chinese, spitting is a healthy thing and as natural as the lengthy and deeply-pleasurable nasal foreplay of sucking up all the phlegm from the sinuses, pooling it in the back of the throat and then projecting it at speed and with some aplomb onto the street. The snot blast – where one nostril is pressed shut to better blow the contents out of the other – is another favourite (and also a handy trick on a bike). But both are now in jeopardy for not only are they offensive to the Olympic's foreign guests, they are also now recognised as a major health hazard in a country still in the shadow of SARS. However, Tibet lies a long way from Beijing and the snot blast lives on, especially in Shigatse!

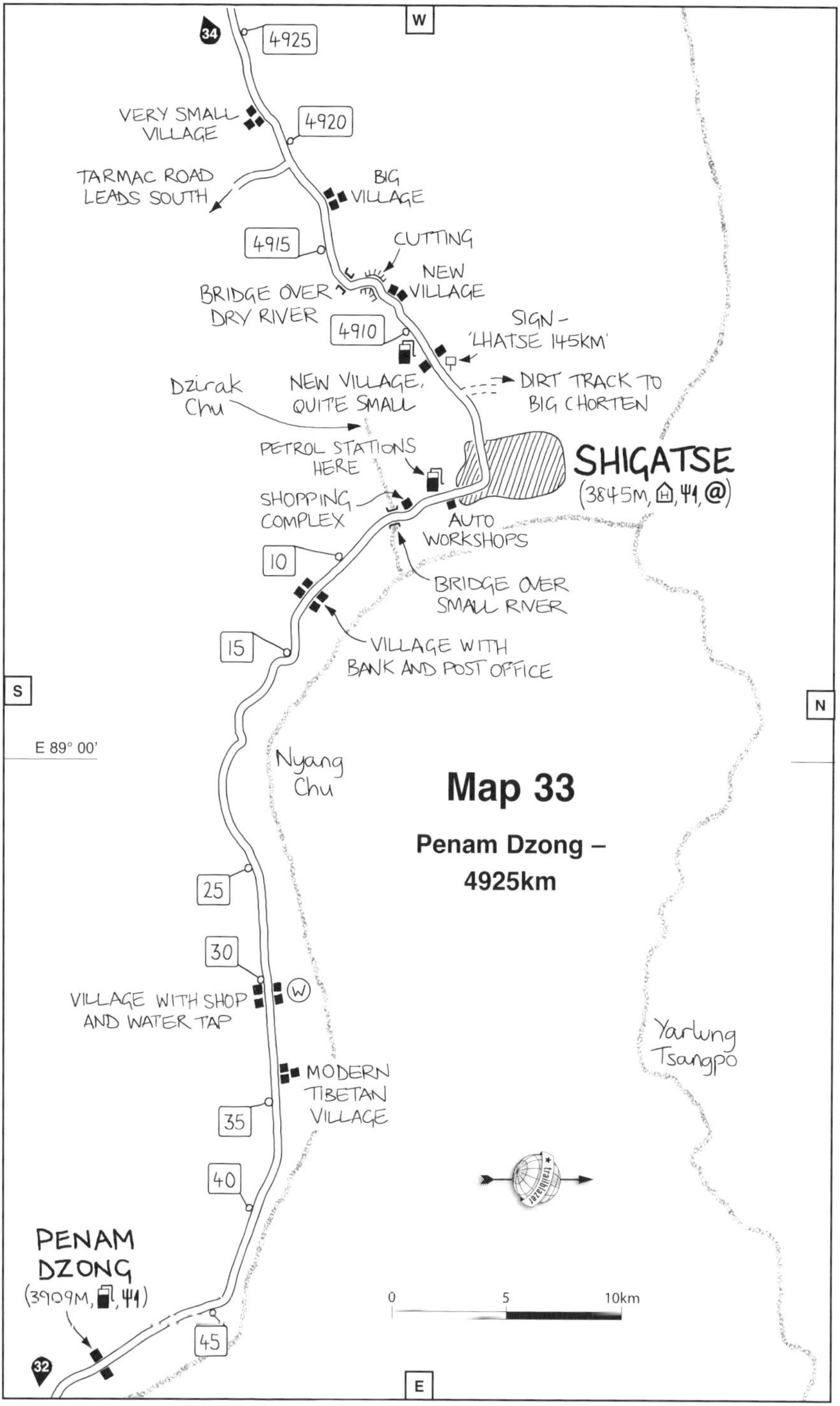

Map 33

Penam Dzong – 4925km

SHIGATSE

Shigatse (also Xigaze or Rìkazé on maps) is the second largest town in Tibet and has everything needed for a day off the bike: a friendly guesthouse, sights to visit, a large supermarket and internet cafés with fast connections. The only thing missing seems to be somewhere good to eat. Shigatse is a mini Chinese city and one which will probably mushroom beyond recognition when the railway arrives in 2010. The roads are broad and lined with white tiled buildings plated in the ubiquitous blue glass.

Officially Shigatse is a different prefecture to Lhasa and an Alien's Travel Permit (ATP) is required to travel onwards from here to Nepal. Since 2005 no one seems to be checking for these permits though most cyclists still buy one from the PSB for peace of mind. Since 2006 the PSB have redirected travellers to the travel agency at Tenzin Guesthouse where the ATP costs Y100 with an extra Y50 for a bike. You should list all the towns you intend to visit and, as it makes no difference to the price, add possibles too such as Sakya and Everest Base Camp. Check the price with other travellers as some people have been overcharged. Don't worry about what day you arrive in Shigatse – although the PSB only issue permits on weekdays, somehow the Tenzin Guesthouse can turn around a permit over the weekend. Getting around Shigatse is easy on foot. Other modes of transport are bicycle rickshaw (Y2-3) and taxi (flat rate in town Y10).

Bronze of a foreign touring cyclist and nomad, Shigatse

For **hotels** there are two choices: either a basic and cheap Tibetan-run place such as ***Tenzin Guesthouse*** (see map opposite) or a more expensive Chinese-run hotel with luxuries such as heating, electricity or a hot bath, like the ***Shigatse Shandong***. An unsuccessful combination is a Chinese hotel with Tibetan staff such as the ***Shigatse Hotel*** (Y300-450/dbl). This used to be the splash-out option but rude staff and bad food have put off all but tour groups. However, there is a fast internet café (Y5/hr) in the lobby downstairs.

Shigatse is where most travellers get diarrhoea. The best food in town (and this is relative) is a small Sichuanese restaurant called ***Tianfu***, near the Tenzin Guesthouse. The most unappetizing place is the ***Shigatse Food Mall*** – a street full of skewer food which is slimy underfoot with the gore of butchered carcasses and where men blowtorch the hair off animal skulls. The hotel and guesthouse restaurants are generally only good for a Lhasa beer or two.

DAY 6 SHIGATSE (3845m) to FOOT OF LAGPA LA (4262m) 100KM

SHIGATSE–TRA LA 28KM
TRA LA–JI-DING 27KM
JI-DING–FOOT OF LAGPA LA 45KM

The next couple of days' cycling lack passes and snowy peaks to gaze at but the road is good tarmac. The scenery switches between narrow river valleys and more open valley floors but there are no major settlements – in fact, this region of Tibet feels the poorest yet. It's often hot through this section until you reach Lagpa La (also known as Tso La).

Out of Shigatse you can either take the road that runs past Tashilunpo southwest or, if you stayed in the south of Lhatse, turn west at Za De Rd. After a small climb followed by a quick descent through a cutting, the road climbs slowly once again to Tra La (4041m) at road marker 4932km. This pass is really the baby of the Friendship Highway at just under a kilometre. From Tra La the descent is flattish, speeding through an industrial valley of gravel-crunching machines and poor-looking villages until swinging northwest just before 4955km and crossing the Sha Chu river into Ji-ding at 4960km. There's no water between Shigatse and Ji-ding so make sure you leave with enough.

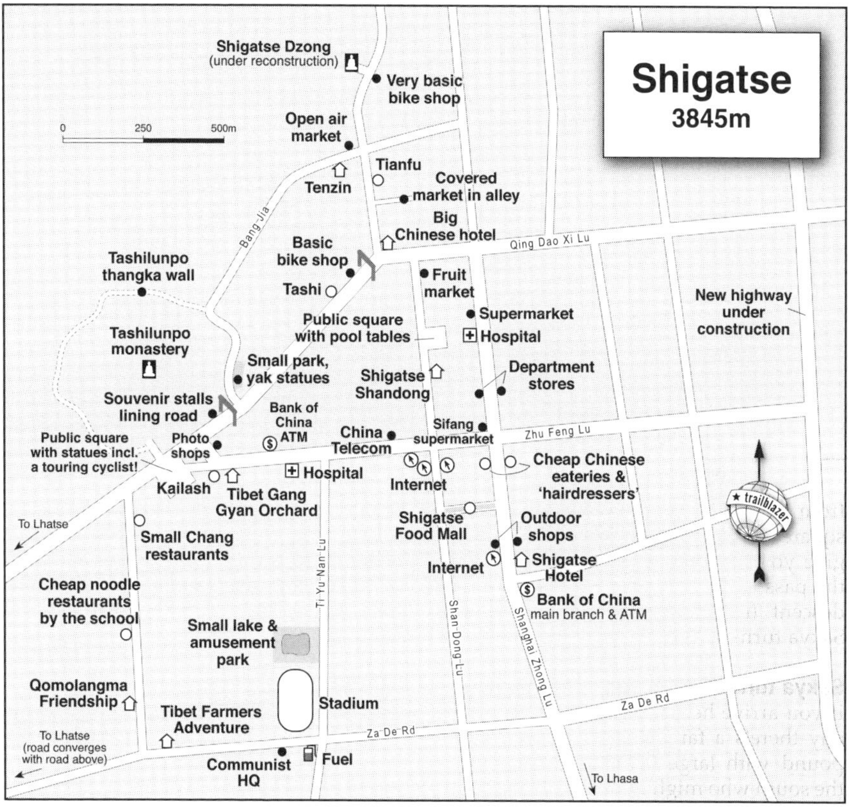

Ji-Ding (3910m) **412.5/544KM**
Here there are a few restaurants and pool tables strung out along the road. The road then rises gradually, ricocheting along a dry river valley with a few tributaries trickling over reddish rocks. From the compound at 4993km onwards you're in a wider valley – there's a small river for water and a few possible camping sites. Trees by the compound offer shelter and privacy or you could push on past the 5000km commemoration marker to the best camping sites which are dotted around the 5005km point. Lagpa La is visible from these but there's still a short warm-up for the legs before it.

DAY 7 FOOT OF LAGPA LA (4262m) to LHATSE (4024m) over Lagpa La (4530m) 50KM

FOOT OF LAGPA LA–LAGPA LA 10KM
LAGPA LA–SAKYA TURN-OFF 14KM
SAKYA TURN-OFF–LHATSE 26KM

Foot of Lagpa La (4262m) 457.5/499KM
From the 5005km marker the climb to Lagpa La (4529m) is less than 10km. Across the valley floor a long drag starts over a dry bridge towards Jungbe village just after 5010km, looping behind the village, crossing a filthy little stream and pulling up those last few steep kilometres.

Lagpa La (4530m) **467.5/489KM**
The pass itself is the best decorated yet, festooned with prayer flags and carpeted in the small paper squares of mantras that Tibetans throw whenever they cross a pass. There are a couple of young boys who seem to live up here, making a living

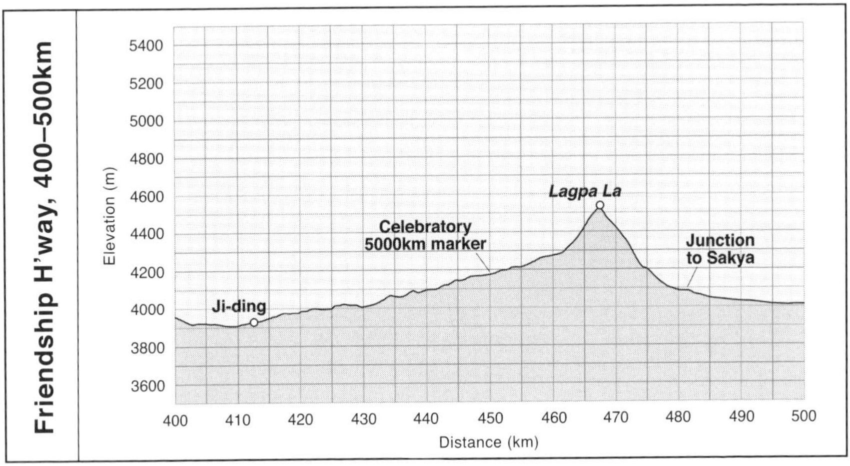

from selling the prayer flags and paper squares – they're good fun and may well give you a round of applause. Just after the pass is the 5014km marker and a fast descent (headwinds permitting) to the Sakya turn-off at 5028km.

Sakya turn-off (4089m) 481.5/475KM

If you arrive here towards the end of the day there's a family in the yellow compound with large Chinese characters to the south who might let you camp for free in their courtyard. This is a better option than taking one of their rooms where at Y2 (15p) you really get what you pay for.

From Sakya to Lhatse is only 26km along a flattish valley floor. There are hot springs just before Lhatse at 5041km on the right, where you can see the rivulets steaming. However, the nearby furniture factory and villagers squatting in the fields might put you off having a splash about. At the petrol station a kilometre before Lhatse the road forks – turn left for the town.

LHATSE

When you reach the sign proclaiming Lhatse as 'the home of Duixie Dance', then you know you've arrived in this exposed little outpost. Lhatse is just a string of hotels and restaurants, scoured by bitter winds and trundled through by Dong Feng trucks. All the same, it's a good place for a hot meal, internet access and buying provisions for the big days ahead. Slower cyclists should consider stocking up in Lhatse and then cycling

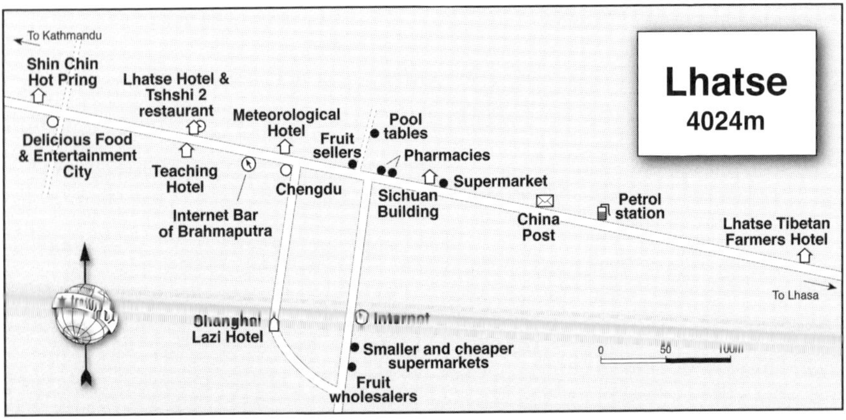

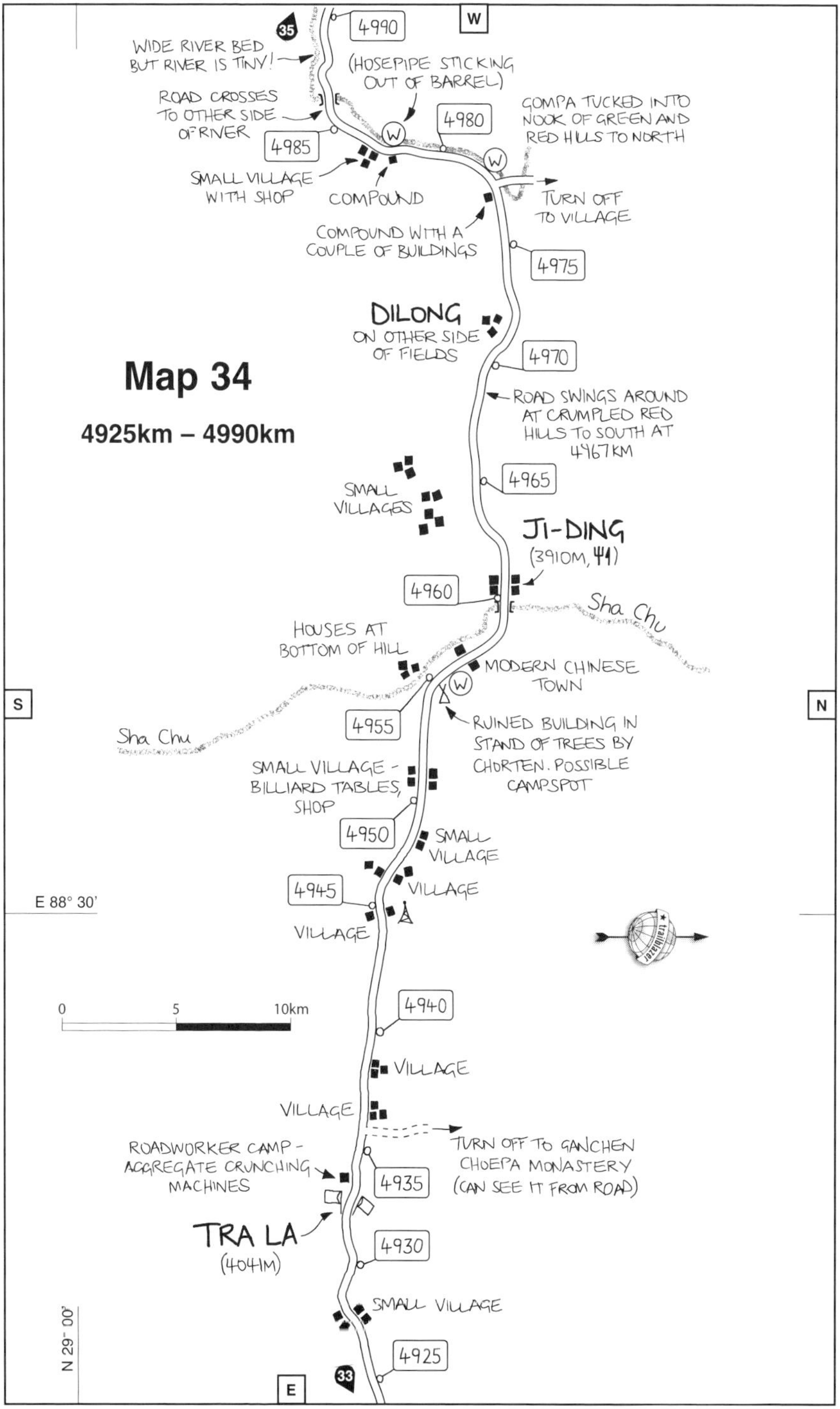

Map 34
4925km – 4990km
35
4990
W
WIDE RIVER BED BUT RIVER IS TINY!
(HOSEPIPE STICKING OUT OF BARREL)
ROAD CROSSES TO OTHER SIDE OF RIVER
4980
GOMPA TUCKED INTO NOOK OF GREEN AND RED HILLS TO NORTH
4985
SMALL VILLAGE WITH SHOP
COMPOUND
TURN OFF TO VILLAGE
COMPOUND WITH A COUPLE OF BUILDINGS
4975
DILONG
ON OTHER SIDE OF FIELDS
4970
ROAD SWINGS AROUND AT CRUMPLED RED HILLS TO SOUTH AT 4967KM
4965
SMALL VILLAGES
JI-DING
(3910M)
4960
Sha Chu
HOUSES AT BOTTOM OF HILL
MODERN CHINESE TOWN
S
N
4955
Sha Chu
RUINED BUILDING IN STAND OF TREES BY CHORTEN. POSSIBLE CAMPSPOT
SMALL VILLAGE - BILLIARD TABLES, SHOP
4950
SMALL VILLAGE
4945
VILLAGE
E 88° 30'
VILLAGE
0
5
10km
4940
VILLAGE
VILLAGE
TURN OFF TO GANCHEN CHOEPA MONASTERY (CAN SEE IT FROM ROAD)
ROADWORKER CAMP - AGGREGATE CRUNCHING MACHINES
4935
TRA LA
(4041M)
4930
SMALL VILLAGE
N 29° 00'
4925
33
E

another 12km (280m ascent) to camp for the night closer to the base of Gyatso La.

If you decide to stay, the cheapest rooms are at the ***Tibetan Farmers Adventure Hotel*** (Y25/45 sing/dbl), which is first on the right as you come in from Lhasa. Set around a small courtyard, the place feels quite homely with cheerful flowerpots and friendly staff, though the toilets are encrusted. The ***Lhatse Hotel*** (Y25 dorm, Y120-125 sing/dbl) is where most of the group tours stay but the staff are indifferent and the rooms grubby. Its restaurant, one of the interminable Tashi look-a-likes, is better skipped in favour of the tasty ***Chengdu*** restaurant on the opposite side of the street, which backs onto the plushest accommodation option in town: the ***Shanghai Hotel Lazi***. Set in its own plaza, the double rooms here are Y250 with heating, TV, hot baths and 24hr electricity. If you're cycling in sub-zero daytime temperatures the luxury of sticking the thermostat up to a tropical temperature, relaxing in a hot bath, washing all your clothes and lounging in a T-shirt is sheer bliss. And, unusually for a Chinese hotel in Tibet, the staff are friendly. Nearby, on the small road running south by the Shanghai Hotel Lazi is the simple but tasty ***Welcome Presence*** restaurant. Clustered around it is a fruit-seller's shop (peaches, plums, oranges, apples, kiwis and bananas), an internet café (Y4/hr) and a supermarket with fair prices – unlike the one on the main drag which is a rip-off despite its intriguing collection of snacks, PRC army uniforms, tools, earflap furry hats, whisky and swords.

DAY 8 LHATSE (4024m) to BAIPA (4318m) over Gyatso La (5250m) 81KM

LHATSE–GYATSO LA 31KM
GYATSO LA–BAIPA 50KM

An early start is needed today because Gyatso La is a big climb with strong headwinds and the possibility of a very cold descent. Furthermore, the road stays high on the other side, not dropping below 4800m for another 23km beyond the pass, so you'll need to clear it early to ensure you sleep at a good altitude. If you set off from Lhatse late in the day consider spreading the ride to Baipa over two days, enjoying a leisurely day today and camping before the pass.

Lhatse (4024m) 507.5/449KM
Rolling out of Lhatse the road passes a tiny gompa lined with prayer wheels and heads along a flat shallow valley northwest until a police barrier (dropped for cyclists) at the fork with the road to Mt

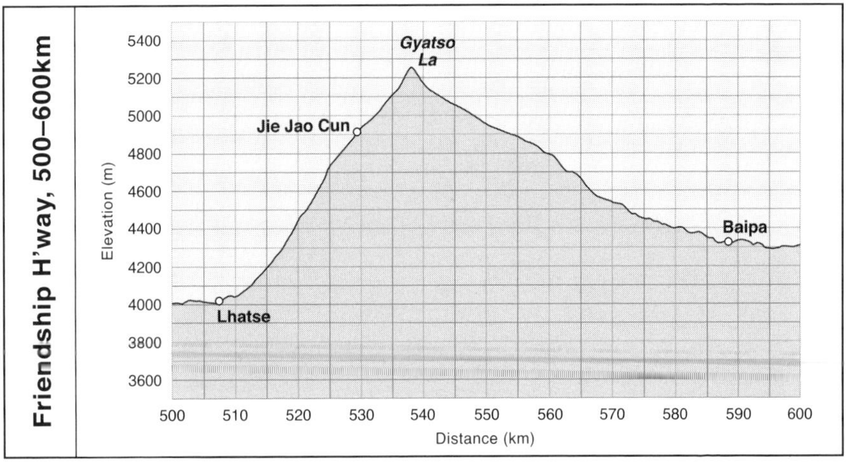

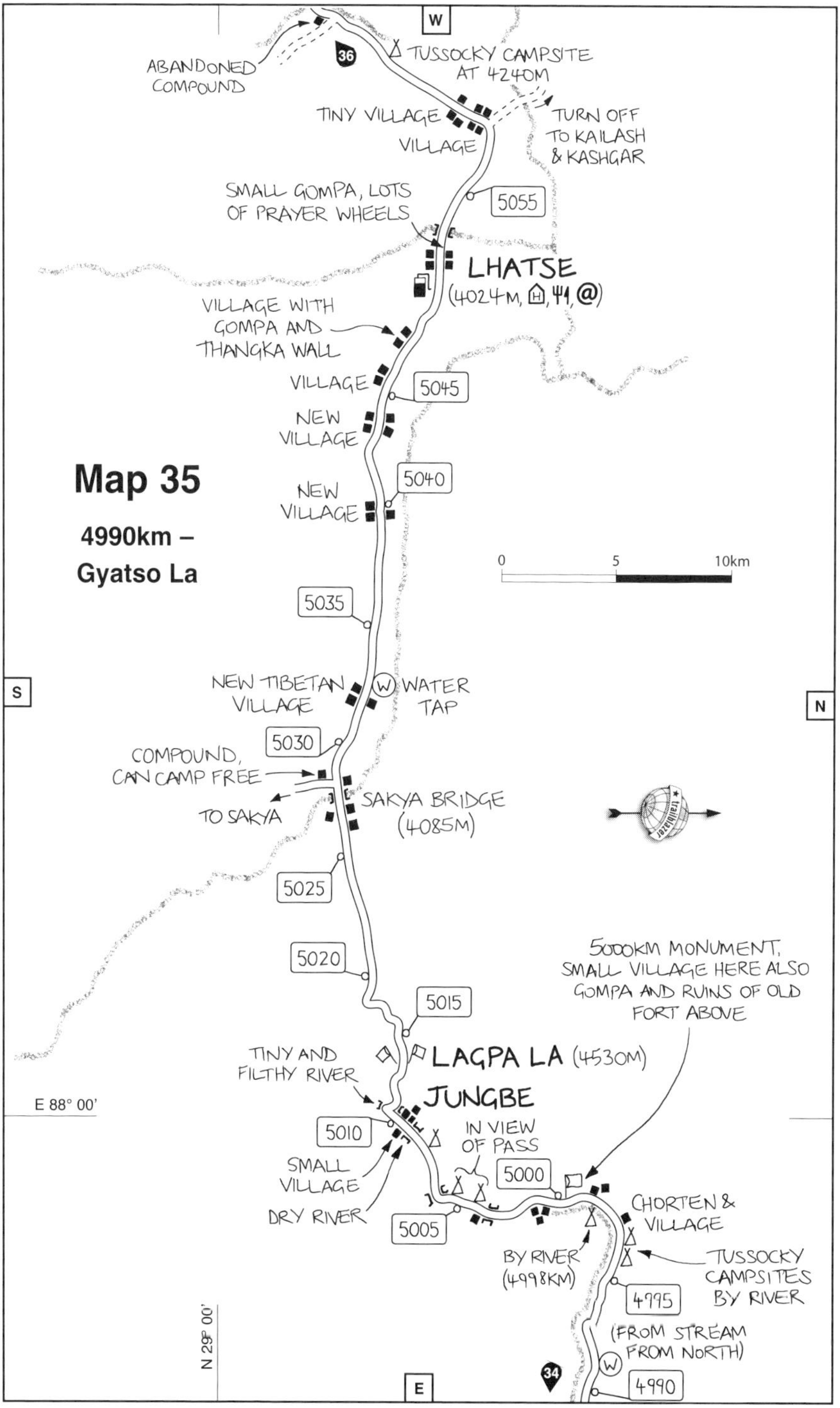
W
ABANDONED COMPOUND
36
TUSSOCKY CAMPSITE AT 4240M
TINY VILLAGE
VILLAGE
TURN OFF TO KAILASH & KASHGAR
SMALL GOMPA, LOTS OF PRAYER WHEELS
5055
LHATSE
(4024M, H, ΨΙ, @)
VILLAGE WITH GOMPA AND THANGKA WALL
VILLAGE
5045
NEW VILLAGE
5040
NEW VILLAGE
Map 35
4990km –
Gyatso La
0
5
10km
5035
NEW TIBETAN VILLAGE
W
WATER TAP
S
N
5030
COMPOUND, CAN CAMP FREE
TO SAKYA
SAKYA BRIDGE (4085M)
trailblazer
5025
5020
5015
LAGPA LA (4530M)
TINY AND FILTHY RIVER
JUNGBE
5000KM MONUMENT, SMALL VILLAGE HERE ALSO GOMPA AND RUINS OF OLD FORT ABOVE
E 88° 00'
5010
IN VIEW OF PASS
SMALL VILLAGE
DRY RIVER
5000
5005
CHORTEN & VILLAGE
BY RIVER (4998KM)
TUSSOCKY CAMPSITES BY RIVER
4995
(FROM STREAM FROM NORTH)
N 29° 00'
W
34
E
4990

Kailash. The Kailash road (see p321) is the dirt track to the west and it's hard to turn your wheels south to Kathmandu and the 1200m ascent that lurks around the corner. Realizing that Kailash is another 800km away should make it easier though. The small village at the junction is only 5.7km from Lhatse – if you started from Lagpa La it's better to push on and camp further up.

Past the junction the road runs alongside a small stream with fields, goats and sheep grazing and brown valley walls. The pass is out of sight, but the valley starts to narrow ominously. It should be sheltered but if there's a wind it's funnelled against you with increasing force the higher you climb. We rode up Gyatso La in early November and ended up wearing thermals, down jackets, woolly hats and full-descent gloves on the final 15km of the climb. For those who skipped Lhatse there's some nice camping on the tussocky grass east of the road at about 4240m, 6km from the Kailash junction. There are more campsites further up but they are increasingly exposed and cold.

Jie Jiao Cun (4905m) The Chinese compound at 4914m should be avoided – it's filthy and the family squatting there demand a ridiculous sum if you ask to camp. Much better is the tiny Tibetan village of Jie Jiao Cun up a track on the small hill opposite, whose villagers might let you camp for the night in the sheep corral. It's pretty dirty but the dry stone walls offer excellent protection against the wind. From these two last settlements, the climb is steep with no more protection and only grazing yaks for entertainment until the pass. The last water available is from the bridge over to the Chinese compound.

Gyatso La (5250m) 538.5/418km
The pass is extremely exposed and in cold weather the temperature can easily drop to -20°C with wind chill. The wind horses are really galloping on the prayer flags tied to the 'Qomolangma National Nature Preserve' sign, and white ceremonial *kutuks* (scarves) whip about in the wind. The elevation profile shows a downhill but in a strong headwind it really won't feel like one – after about 200m of freewheeling the gradient levels off and it's necessary to pedal hard to move and stay warm. The compounds offer shelter but they are still high at over 4800m.

On the south side of the pass a new tarmac road is under construction on the west side of the river which will make an enormous difference to the amount of time it takes to descend to a warmer altitude. Until it's opened the descent is slow and hard work as it's peppered with steep little climbs over rocks covered in ankle-high sand. When the road finally swings south along the Lolo Chu, the Bum Chu valley comes into view. Now it's in your sights the descent is enjoyable: warm, with a ridge topped by ruins and pocked with meditation caves to the west and campsites shaded by trees along the river.

Baipa (4318m) 588.5/368km
This little village is well-used to foreign tourists as it's here that anyone wishing to visit Everest Base Camp has to buy the Qomolangma National Park entrance ticket (Y65, ask for a 10-day pass) at the Qomolangma Service Centre on the opposite side of the Lolo Chu.

There are at least eight hotels strung out between the start of Baipa and the petrol station, most of which are clustered around the turn-off to Shekar (aka New Tingri), which is another 7km away but many people use the names interchangeably. The friendliest and best-value of them is the ***Mt Everest Home Inn*** at Y60 for a double room big enough for two bikes with TV, electric blankets on the beds, hot thermoses, washbowls and even little tumblers complete with toothbrush, comb and toothpaste. Slightly smaller rooms are Y50, and in season they also have hot showers in the toilet block. This is much better value than the basic Y100 rooms (toilet block outside) at the ***Qomolangma Service Centre***, which is cast into cold shadow for most of the day, and the overpriced Y300 rooms at the ***Qomolangma Hotel***, aka Shanghai Mt Everest Hotel, a few hundred metres down the road to Shekar. Back on the main street, there's good food at the ***Chengdu*** restaurant opposite Mt Everest Home Inn; the cosy ***Garkyi*** restaurant does a set breakfast with a decent pancake and little shops sell Nepali goods

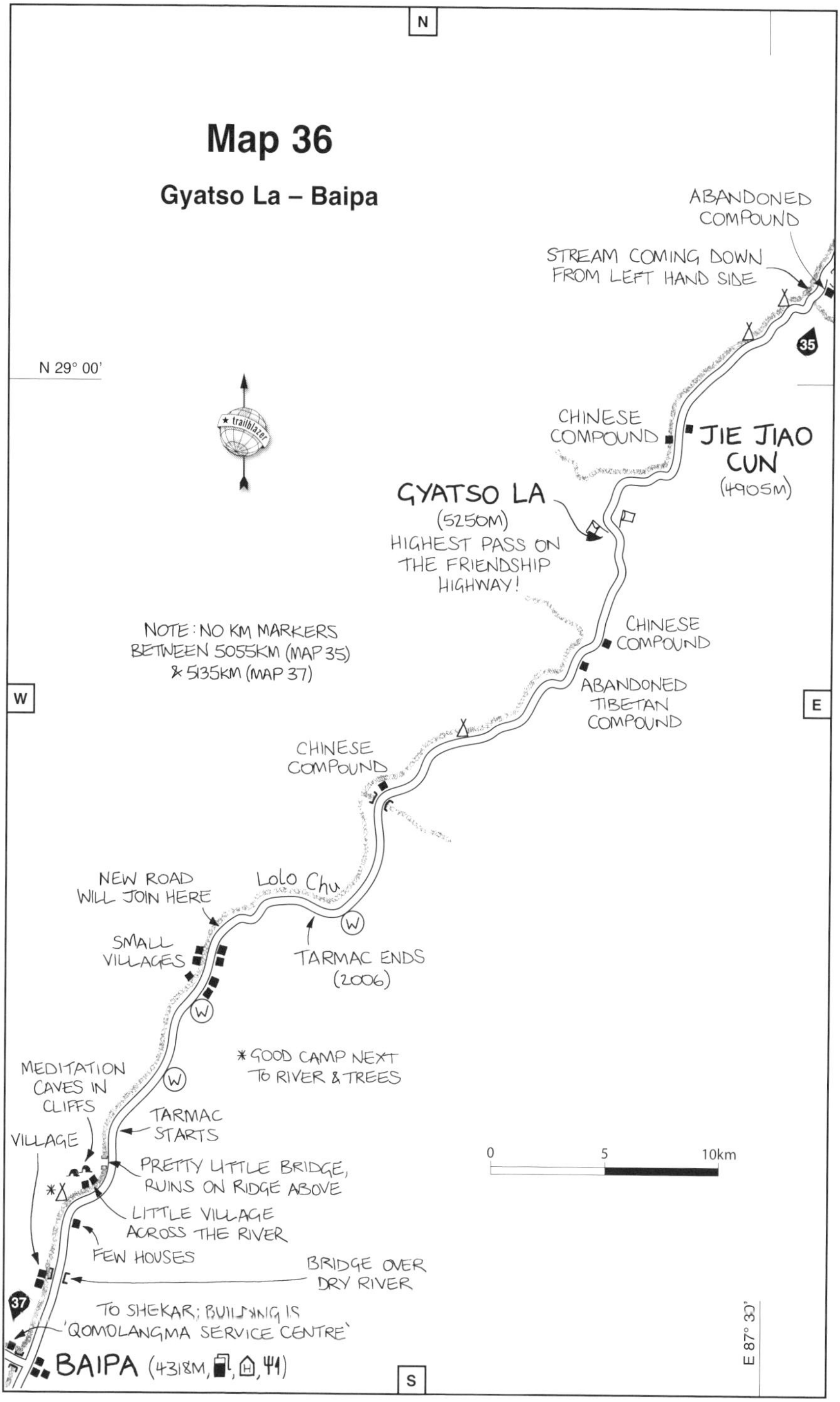
N
Map 36
Gyatso La – Baipa
ABANDONED COMPOUND
STREAM COMING DOWN FROM LEFT HAND SIDE
35
N 29° 00'
trailblazer
CHINESE COMPOUND
JIE JIAO CUN (4905M)
GYATSO LA (5250M) HIGHEST PASS ON THE FRIENDSHIP HIGHWAY!
NOTE: NO KM MARKERS BETWEEN 5055KM (MAP 35) & 5135KM (MAP 37)
CHINESE COMPOUND
ABANDONED TIBETAN COMPOUND
W
E
CHINESE COMPOUND
NEW ROAD WILL JOIN HERE
Lolo Chu
W
TARMAC ENDS (2006)
SMALL VILLAGES
W
* GOOD CAMP NEXT TO RIVER & TREES
W
MEDITATION CAVES IN CLIFFS
TARMAC STARTS
VILLAGE
0 5 10km
PRETTY LITTLE BRIDGE, RUINS ON RIDGE ABOVE
LITTLE VILLAGE ACROSS THE RIVER
FEW HOUSES
BRIDGE OVER DRY RIVER
37
TO SHEKAR; BUILDING IS 'QOMOLANGMA SERVICE CENTRE'
BAIPA (4318M, , ,)
E 87° 30'
S

such as small cartons of Frooti mango juice.

There's not much to do in Baipa apart from watch the traffic go by – mostly tractors, donkeys and ponies and traps. An odd feature of this town is the number of people keen to sell fossils; petrified souvenirs of the Tethys Sea.

DAY 9 BAIPA (4318m) to TINGRI (4339m) 60KM

BAIPA–EVEREST TURN-OFF 12KM
EVEREST TURN-OFF–TINGRI 48KM

Today is an easy day as long as you're aiming for Tingri. If you have Everest on your mind, your legs have got Pang La to look forward to (see pp276-7 for Everest Base Camp). Whichever way you go, carry enough food for lunch and snacks as well as enough water as there's not much of either on the road.

Baipa (4318m) 588.5/368KM

South of Baipa there are views up to Shekar Dzong just after the 5135km marker, after which the road crosses the Lolo Chu, passes some large sand dunes and at 6km reaches a police checkpoint at the bridge over the Bum Chu. You will be asked to show your passport (but not the ATP) and then waved on.

As you approach the 'Way to Mt Everest' turn-off, the hairpins up Pang La come into view to the south but for those staying on the highway, this range of hills mostly obscures the Himalayan peaks lying behind. Instead, the Tsipri range to the north raises its quills like a disgruntled porcupine and straight ahead rises a large sand dune.

Tingri Plains (4440m) Apart from a few small villages and rock towers, there's very little along the road which may be why the children get so over-excited when they spot cyclists. The river doesn't often run close to the road, but the green Tingri plains between the two are a pleasant spot for a picnic and a bask in the sun. The colour scheme today is what you'd imagine of Tibet: the green-yellow Tingri plains, brown hills, snow to the southwest, and an indigo sky. Once the final hill is rounded, the Mahalangur Himal range suddenly starts unscrolling far to the south – first Cho Oyu (8201m), then Gyanchung Ka (7952m) and finally Mt Everest (8848m) – a wonderful moment of grandeur before arriving in the tourist-pestering capital of Tingri.

Tingri (4339m)

The old village of Tingri is huddled to the south of the highway, but you'll only see it if you arrive on the track from Everest Base Camp. A string of hotels and restaurants on the highway itself starts at the 5193km marker. Tingri is an example of tourism gone wrong – where tourists keen to hand out money/pens/food have created a culture of expectation, dependency and resentment. The children and adults here are a little too used to well-meaning Westerners and have become persistent beggars.

All the accommodation options in Tingri are variations on basic: damp bare rooms set around a central courtyard. The friendliest and cheapest is the ***Himalayan Hotel*** at Y25 a bed, with spectacularly garish wallpaper and a hot shower (Y10). The ***Lhasa Hotel Restaurant*** is cosy and makes the best food in town, though that isn't saying much. If you decide to give Tingri a miss there are two basic supermarkets just after the open market at the western edge of town, where you can stock up before moving further up the valley.

Mt Everest from Rongbuk

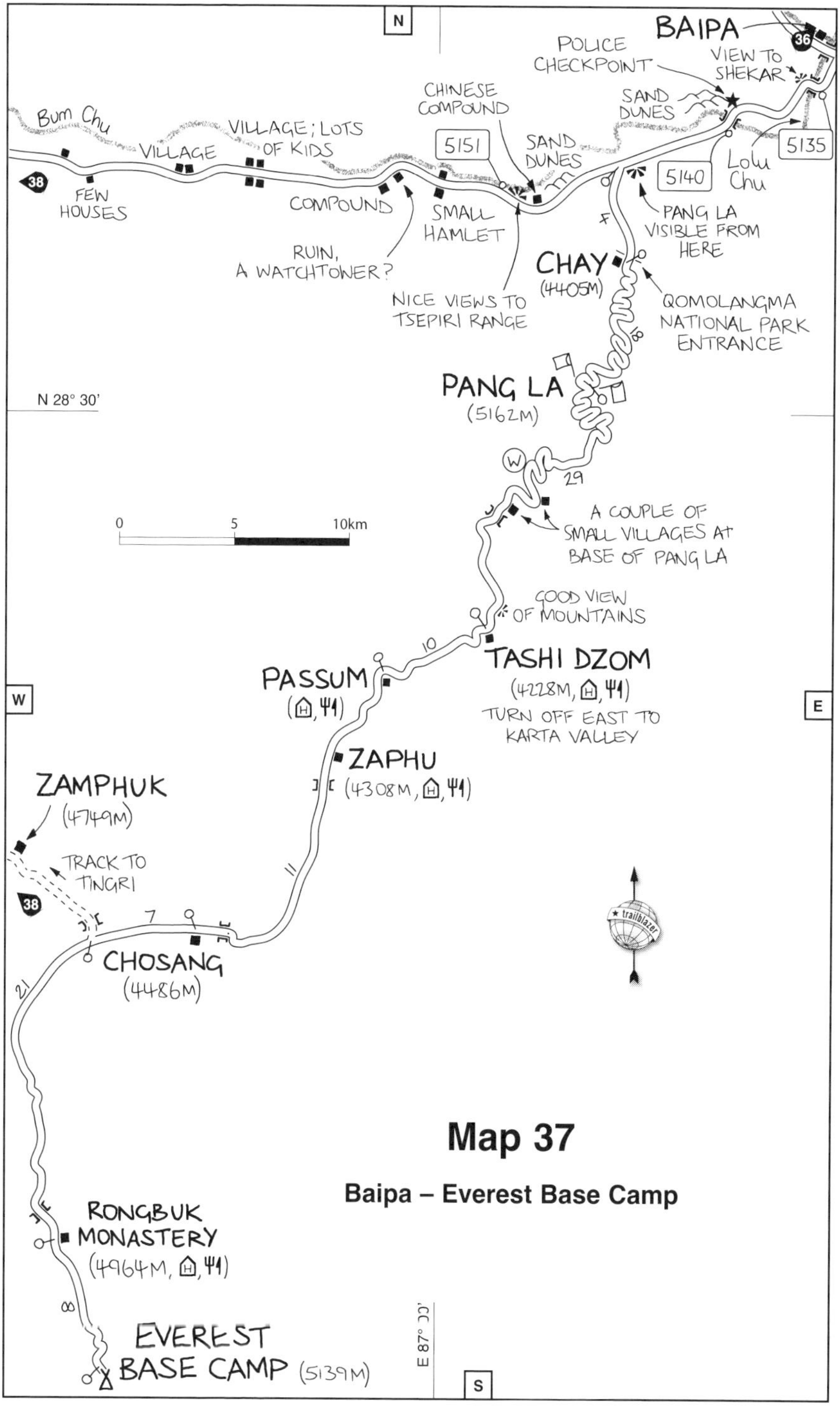

Map 37

Baipa – Everest Base Camp

THE SIDE TRIP TO EVEREST BASE CAMP

FRIENDSHIP HIGHWAY–CHAY 4KM
CHAY–PANG LA 18KM
PANG LA–TASHI DZOM 29KM
TASHI DZOM–PASSUM 10KM
PASSUM–CHOSANG (CHU DZOM) 11KM
CHU DZOM–RONGBUK MONASTERY 21KM
RONGBUK MONASTERY–EBC 8KM

The ride to Everest Base Camp (EBC) is absolutely spectacular and well worth the effort even at this late stage in the ride. It takes most people two and a half days from the Friendship Highway to reach Base Camp which has awesome views up to Everest's North Face. The road used to be notorious for its corrugations and deep sand but is now smooth tarmac, thanks to the pre-Olympic torch relay up Mt Everest in 2008.

From Shekar it's 12km to the Everest Base Camp turn-off, where the little village of Chay is already visible. A checkpost at Chay will inspect your passport and Qomolangma Nature Preserve ticket and then leave you to climb the switchbacks to Pang La which should take between two and three hours. Try to reach the top in the morning for the best views of the Himalaya as by mid-afternoon the range is swathed in clouds.

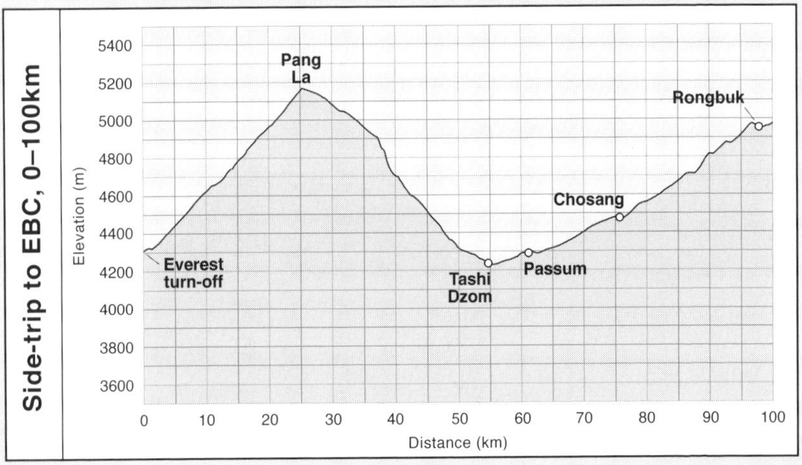

MT EVEREST

The mountain we now know as Everest was first mapped by the Chinese in 1719 and appeared in the Qing Dynasty's Atlas of the Whole Imperial Territory under its Tibetan name, Qomolangma. During the 1800s when the British were conducting the Great Trigonometrical Survey of India, a survey from Darjeeling in 1847 raised the possibility that Peak XV, as it was then known, was the highest mountain in the world. Five years later Radhanath Sikdar, a 39-year old Bengali mathematician at the Survey of India in Dehra Dun, confirmed it to be so at a calculated 8839m / 29,000ft.

Now that the highest mountain had been found, it needed a name. Of course, it was already named by those who lived by it: Devgiri, Deodhunga or Devadurga in Sanskrit (meaning 'Holy Mountain') and Qomolangma in Tibetan ('Mother of the Universe'). But in a paper presented to the Royal Geographical Society in 1856 the Surveyor General of India, Colonel Andrew Waugh, proposed naming Peak XV after his predecessor in office, Colonel Sir George Everest. As both Tibet and Nepal were closed at the time to foreigners, his proposal for 'Mont [sic] Everest' (pronounced Eve-rest) was carried – despite opposition from Everest himself, who pointed out that his name couldn't be written in Hindi or Persian let alone pronounced in them, and

From the top of the pass there's a gentle and enjoyable downhill to the valley floor. After some small villages as the base of the pass the next big village is Tashi Dzom which has good food and is the best place to stay. The other villages further on, such as Passum and Chosang (also called Chu Dzom), offer only basic accommodation and food and the hot valley can make the cycling hard work. However, from Chosang it's just 21km up to Rongbuk (also called Rongphu) and, if you feel up to it, Everest Base Camp 8km further on. Rongbuk's prayer flags are weighed down with chains, which speaks volumes about the winds which blast down this valley.

For the return journey, you can either ride back the way you came, hitch a lift with a jeep tour or take the very rough track via Zamphuk direct to Tingri (see map p279). It's a beautiful ride but steep and gravelly in places, technical and tough on both you and your bike. On the approach to Tingri, home in on Tingri Dzong on the small hill to the south of the town and eventually a small sandy path will appear – this is a shortcut and will bring you out in the middle of the town.

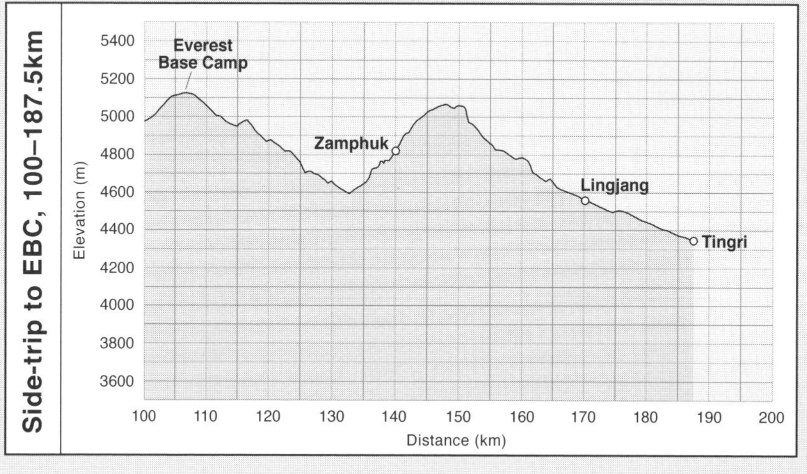

from a Mr B. H. Hodgson of Darjeeling who wrote that '*the mountain in question does not lack a native and ascertained name; the name is Deodhunga*'. Only in the 1960s did the Nepali government assign their own name to the peak; eschewing the existing Sanskrit, Tibetan and English names, they called it 'Sagarmatha' ('Head of the Sky').

Powers have sought to stamp their authority on Mt Everest ever since: the Chinese do not accept the name of Mt Everest, preferring Qomolangma, and the Americans, the British and the Chinese all have their own versions of the height: 8850m, 8848m and 8844m respectively. The ultimate achievement was to conquer the peak, and the race to climb Everest was finally won by Sir Edmund Hillary and Tenzin Norgay in 1953. The Chinese carried the Olympic flame up Mt Everest to inaugurate the Beijing 2008 Olympics, and the Nepali government intend to use the mountain on its banknotes to replace images of its King.

Finally, Mt Everest is only the highest mountain on earth if you start counting from sea-level. The all-out biggest mountain is Mauna Kea in Hawaii which is 10,203m/33,474ft tall but its first 6000m lie beneath the waves of the Pacific.

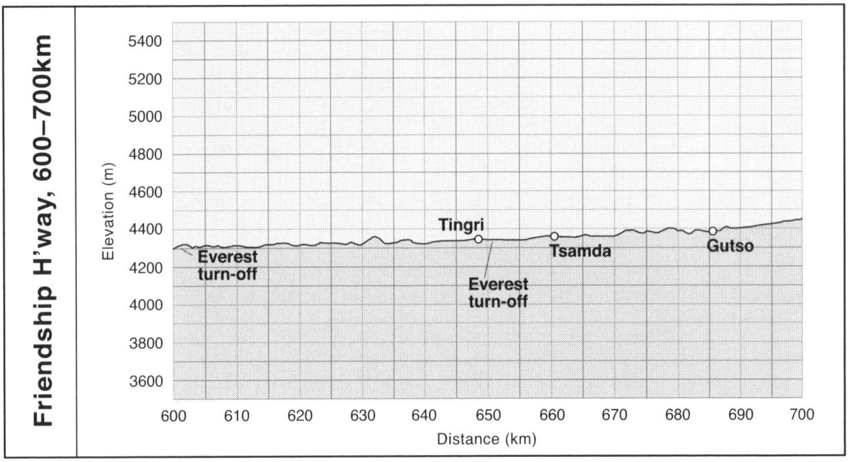

DAY 10 TINGRI (4339m) to FOOT OF LALUNG LA (4561m) 66KM

TINGRI–TSAMDA 12KM
TSAMDA–GUTSO 25KM
GUTSO–RITZ GUESTHOUSE 21KM
RITZ GUESTHOUSE–FOOT OF LALUNG LA 8KM

After Tingri are more fantastic views across to Everest, before the Friendship Highway strikes north – away from Kathmandu! – in a large horseshoe. Maybe one day some very lightly loaded mountain bikers will attempt a shortcut across the Tong La which lies between Tingri and Yarle – I don't think this has been tried yet.

This section on mud-packed road is flattish until the climb up to the double pass of Lalung La and Yarle Shung La – the last passes in Tibet. They are high and are renowned for dust and headwinds which you must battle against as you drop off the last pass and undulate towards Nyalam. There's not much in the way of food, drink and accommodation in this section so stock up in Tingri, but the scenery is stunning with the first really big mountains of the trip (if you didn't visit Everest Base Camp) and especially fantastic views across to Mt Shishapangma (8014m). In 2006 the tar-mac finished in Tingri, and from there to the border was all mud-packed road.

Tingri (4339m) 648.5/308KM
West of Tingri, the Friendship Highway has even better views of Mt Everest before Tsamda, where it heads into a small gorge which swings northwest.

Tsamda (4356m) 660.5/356KM
If the sign to '*Tsamda Hot Spring Hotel* 7km' at the bridge tempted you when you arrived in Tingri, you should know that the hotel is not 7km but 12km further on. In season the doubles (Y150, bargain hard) have steaming private baths sunk into the floor – not so out of season, where the private tubs are dry and the big tub in the courtyard is filled with naked nomad families who party into the small hours before falling asleep under the stars, wrapped up in their sheepskins. The restaurant is as overpriced as the rooms, but they make the best chips in Tibet.

If you decided against spending the night in Tingri between kilometre markers 5205 and 5210 there are some good camping spots between the gorge walls and the river. At the Nyalam Tourist Area sign this gorge opens out into a valley with distant views of snowy peaks such as Mt Tsangla (6386m) to the northwest. There are a lot of ruined forts through this section – remnants of Nepali incursions into Tibet – and some scattered villages, the largest of which is Gutso.

Gutso (4405m) 685.5/271KM
Gutso is about halfway to the pass from

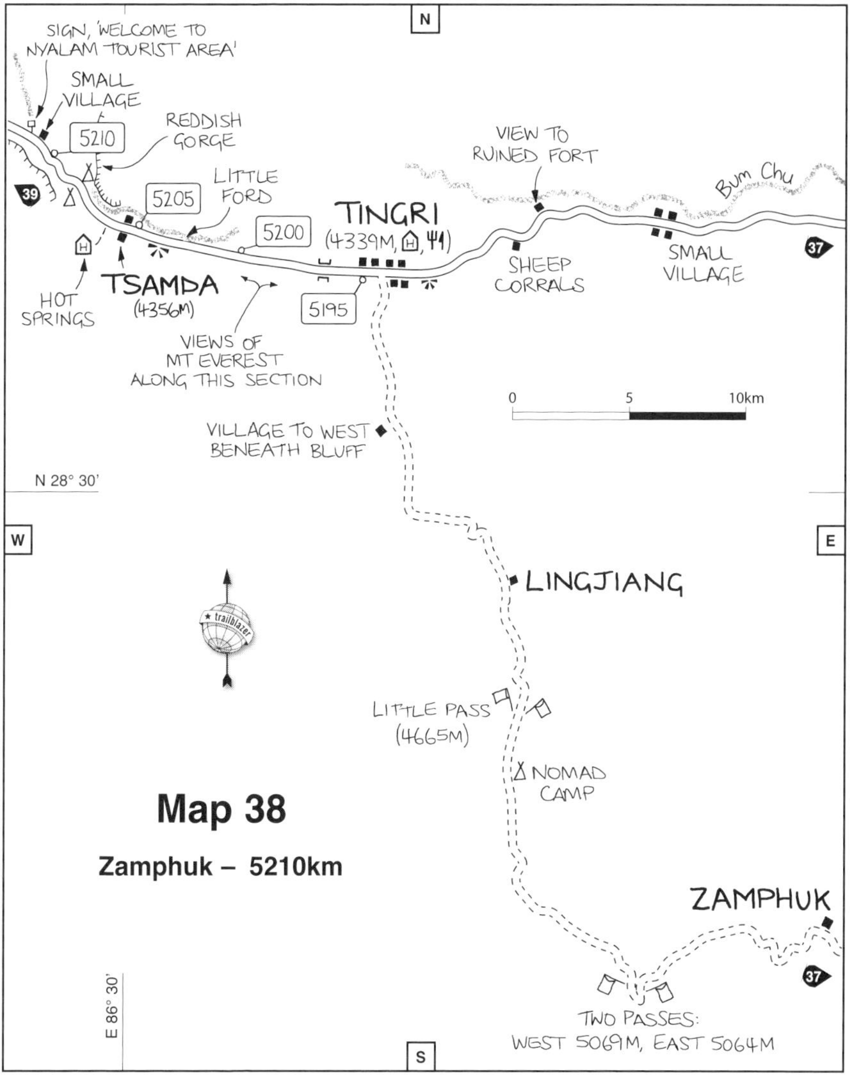

Tingri, and has a small shop and a large military compound with a hospital.

As the road follows the Men Chu River and curves to the west and then south, it starts a long, slow climb into a headwind, passing small villages dotted along the river banks, ruined forts and even two meditation caves plugged into a rock face opposite the 5253km marker.

Sumo (4523m) 706.5/250KM

The *Ritz Guesthouse* on the outskirts of Sumo village is the only place to stay before Lalung La, and it has a cosy restaurant with hot food (rice, potatoes, dahl) and damp cold rooms for Y15.

To have a chance of reaching Nyalam the next day it's better to camp at the base of the pass, 8km further on. The camping is very exposed although in autumn you could camp under the bridge at 5262km for protection against the bitter wind. From the bridge campsite there's water from the Men Chu, a view to the pass and the snowy peak of Mt Shishapangma in the distance.

Friendship H'way, 700–800km

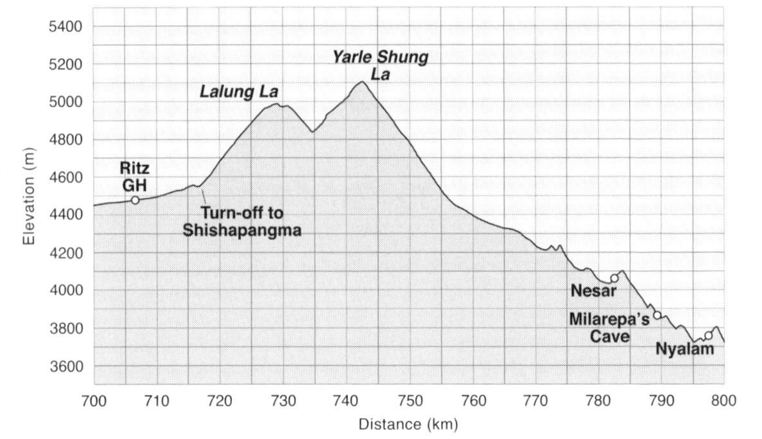

DAY 11 FOOT OF LALUNG LA (4561m) to NYALAM (3758m) over Lalung La (5025m) and Yarle Shung La (5140m) 83KM

FOOT OF LALUNG LA–LALUNG LA 15KM
LALUNG LA–YARLE SHUNG LA 13KM (5KM DOWN, 8KM UP)
YARLE SHUNG LA–NESAR 40KM
NESAR–NYALAM 15KM

Foot of Lalung La (4561m) 714.5/242KM
On paper once you've crossed the passes this is an easy day. The reality is very different. After the junction to Shishapangma (Xixiabangma) at 5265km, lazy switchbacks curl up from the Men Chu valley floor to a shallow tabletop, where the road runs dead straight past Lalung La, plonked in the middle and marked by a few bedraggled prayer flags, yak skulls and cairns.

Lalung La (5205m) 729.5/227KM
At the pass the mountain almost dead ahead to the southeast is Labuche Kang (7367m), part of the little-known Labuche Himal range on the Nepal–Tibet border, and the peak to the southwest, across the field of cairns, is Shishapangma. Almost immediately after the pass, there's another small rise then the road drops off this little plateau (watch out for deep sand on the hairpins) to a bridge over the Lalung Chu.

Lalung Chu (4875m) Just beyond the bridge is a Chinese army compound and a very basic Tibetan restaurant which sells instant noodles, Lhasa beer, raw yak leg and ancient Jin Bao (a Chinese sports drink). There are rooms here if you need to stop. From the bridge it's a long, straight 8km drag up to Yarle Shung La, the final pass! It's not steep but the roaring headwinds make it hard work.

Yarle Shung La (5140m) 742.5/214KM
The reward is a wonderful 180° spread of icy peaks from the Labuche Himal range

SHISHAPANGMA – THE BABY GIANT

Shishapangma (Xixiabangma in Chinese) is the smallest of the 8000m mountains at 8014m, and the fourteenth highest mountain in the world. It's the only 8000-metre peak to lie entirely inside Chinese territory (all the others are either in Nepal or Pakistan) and the last one to be summited. No one really knows what its name means: 'crest above the grassy plains' or 'Sherpa woman' in Tibetan, or 'place of the holy man' in its Sanskrit name, *Gosainthan*.

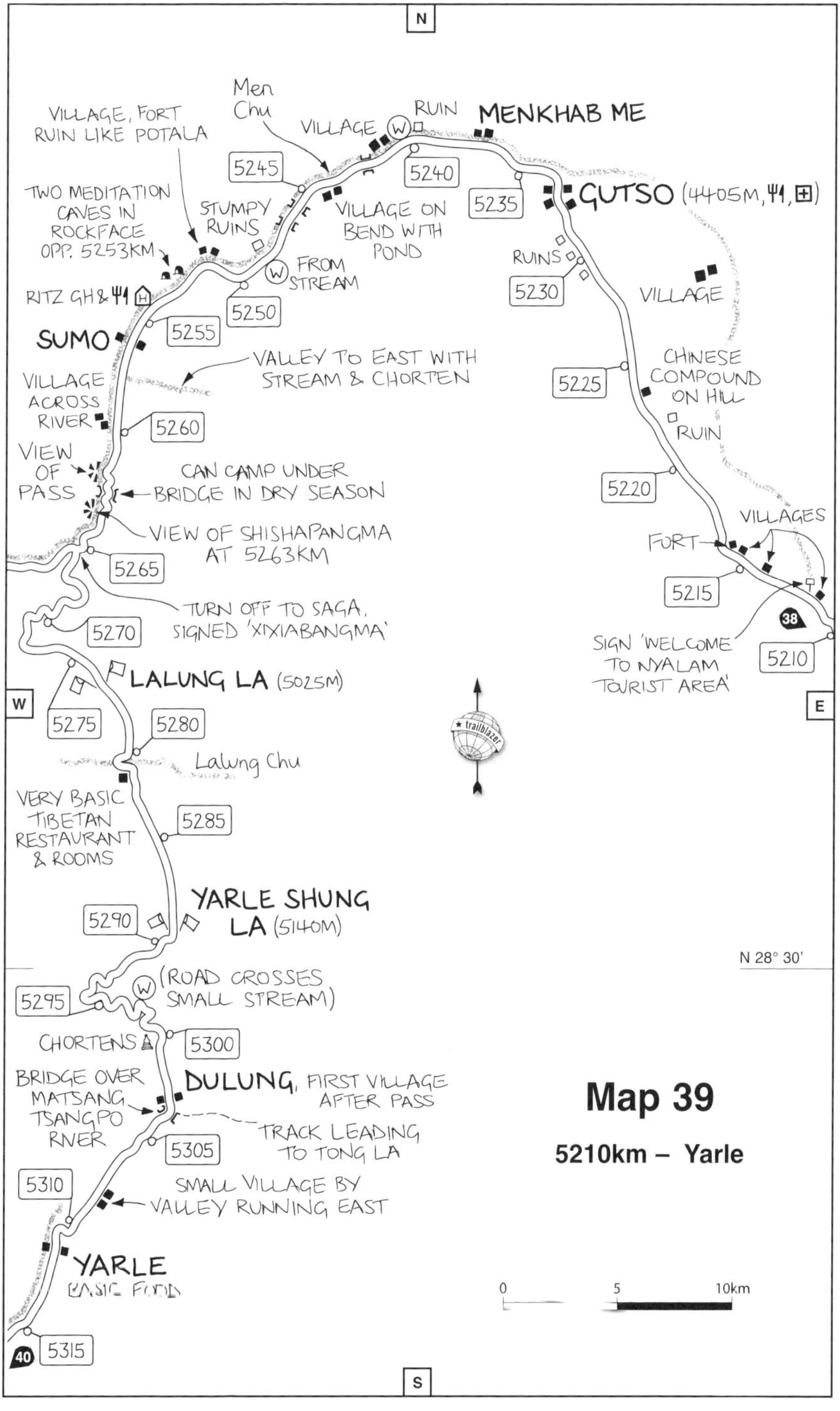

Map 39

5210km – Yarle

in the east to the Langtang Himal in the west, and on the pass itself a magnificent spread of prayer flags and even prayer wheels for a celebratory spin. From here, at 5140m, and after weeks of cycling above 4000m, the road is about to plunge more than 4500m to 632m in Nepal; the longest descent in the world! But nobody talks about the headwinds. They are about to make the longest descent in the world feel even longer, because you are going to have to pedal. And although the road to Nepal is a descent overall, any cyclist will tell you that there's a lot of up for something that's meant to be going down.

But for the meantime, the first part of the descent is perfect – a brakes-off, flat-out swoop past streams and chortens and the first small villages of Dulung and Lasi. For the second part, by about Yarle village, you may well feel as if you're in a wind tunnel. From here the road rises and falls alongside the Po Chu river but as the valley is still narrow there are few places to camp. The road is sandy with little kicks that are surprisingly steep. Somehow these relentless little climbs and descents are harder than the steady effort required for the passes, but that's probably because you'd be expecting to be free-wheeling down the world's longest downhill.

There are a number of small villages along this valley where you could find shelter and food if the light is fading – a good campsite if you're not going to make Nyalam is on the banks of the river at 5331km, just after Nesar. Otherwise you could push on to the little village at Milarepa's Cave (5334km), which should have a guesthouse. From here it's just a few more kilometres to Nyalam, although the landslide-prone road is rough in some sections. Finally, at the prayer flags the road turns a corner and Nyalam pops into view. It's an ugly, Chinese-clone town but at this point you probably won't care. Good food awaits, as well as a hot shower, internet and, tomorrow, the descent to Nepal.

Nyalam (3758m) 782.5/174KM

Barely longer than 500m, Nyalam is yet another military town which is bitterly cold and has a well-deserved reputation for theft. On the plus side, the ***Hotel Kailash*** has sunny rooms (triple room Y30 per bed or double room with electric blankets Y50 per bed) and a large upstairs restaurant which is run by a gentleman from Kathmandu. He imports lots of food from Nepal so the menu is the best in weeks and there are bootleg DVDs to watch too. Opposite the Kailash is 'The Delightfully Fresh Bathroom' bathing house, where an individual cubicle with a warming lamp and hot power shower costs Y10. There's even a hairdryer for when you eventually emerge. Also nearby are a few **internet** cafés (Y5/hr), a small bakery for hot steamed buns (Y0.5) and some Sichuanese restaurants such as the ***Chengdu***.

DAY 12 NYALAM (3758m) to BHARABISE (877m) 68KM

NYALAM–ZHANGMU 33KM
ZHANGMU–KODARI (F'SHIP BRIDGE) 8KM
KODARI–BHARABISE 27KM

From Nyalam, which teeters on the edge of the Tibetan plateau, there's just a 2km climb before the massive descent to Nepal starts. But like the headwinds of yesterday, the rough road robs you of a carefree descent.

Once the border is crossed at the chaotic Friendship Bridge, the road continues descending though it's plagued by landslides which can make it hard-going and, as usual, it rises and falls alongside the river which takes away any real feeling of descent. The harsh sun, icy winds and isolation of Tibet mellow into sunshine and Nepali village life – girls washing their hair, piglets snuffling around, strutting chickens and cows staking their claim on the road.

Tarmac reappears for the first time since Tingri at the small town of Bharabise, and from there on there are only two more climbs before Kathmandu: a tiny one after the village of Chehere, and a longer one from Dolaghat up to

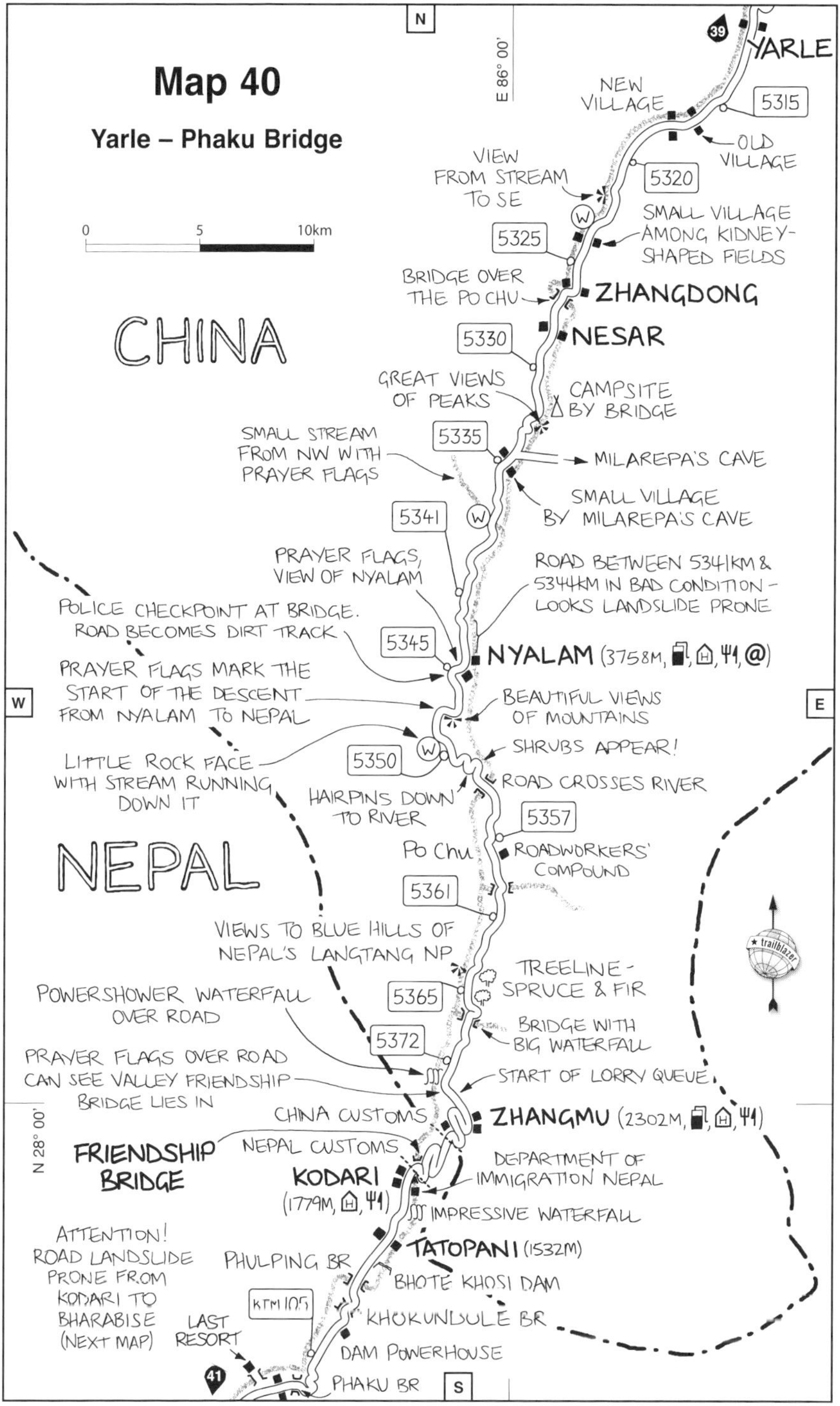

Map 40

Yarle – Phaku Bridge

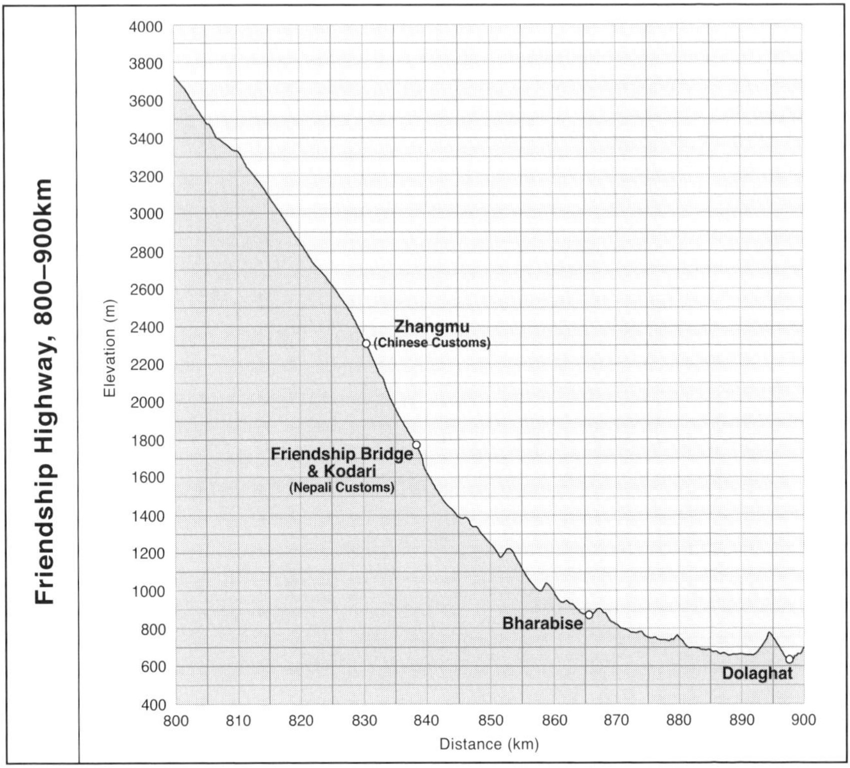

Dhulikhel. The final day into Kathmandu is very short, with heavy traffic from Suryavinyaka onwards.

Nyalam (3758m) 782.5/174KM

Just 2km after Nyalam is a bend with prayer flags and fantastic views across to a crown of icy peaks. This is it! From here it is, really, all downhill. The road is in a bad condition, so riders on rigid bikes will get a pasting, but twisting down into the gorge of the Po Chu and the feeling of dropping off the Tibetan plateau into tropical Nepal is just extraordinary. First appear shrubs, then trees, then waterfalls and grasses, while the temperature soars from the sub-zero icicle chill at Nyalam to a balmy tropical heat, with birdsong and lush greenery. The air tastes delicious (unless a truck is passing), and so thick and rich you feel you can drink it. Savour the solitude of the last few kilometres before Zhangmu and the Friendship Bridge because once you enter Nepal, life speeds up considerably.

Zhangmu (2320m) 830.5/126KM

The Chinese border town with Nepal (also known as Dram) has got an enjoyably Wild West feeling to it and there are plenty of hotels and restaurants should you need to spend a night here. It's set out on a series of hairpins spilling 300m down the valley, with miles of parked trucks snaking down the road and the Chinese customs post at the bottom. Fill out the departure card, have your temperature taken at the quarantine post and then wheel your bike through customs. Money-changers will surround you offering Nepalese rupees – you'll get a better deal here than on the Nepali side. After this, you're in no-man's land for 8km – so which side of the road do you ride on? Wherever you can – this section of road is awful – muddy, steep and rocky.

Kodari (1779m) 838.5/118KM

Welcome to Nepal! Once there's space start riding on the left. The Friendship Bridge was built by the Chinese and opened in 1965, then again in 1984 after getting washed away. It's usually a Tata lorry jam and where there isn't a lorry there's a pavement vendor or twenty. The culture shock on entering Nepal can be quite extreme – suddenly there are people and vehicles everywhere. Also, time has just gone back 2hrs and 15mins. After the bridge is the village of Kodari with twigs holding down roofs of corrugated iron. The building on the left after the bridge is the Nepalese customs and immigration, where 60-day single-entry tourist visas cost $30. Check the exchange rate if paying in a different currency – the officials like to make a little pocket money on the side. A few restaurants serve up the national Nepali dish of *dahl baht* (rice and lentils), and prices after Tibet will seem unbelievably cheap.

There are always jeep drivers here keen to drive tourists to Kathmandu; buses go regularly too but take much longer. A bicycle is probably the most comfortable way to travel because the road deteriorates even more and remains landslide-prone from here until Bharabise. If the bumpy ride down from Nyalam has really been a bone-shaker then the hot springs at Tatopani village just after Kodari will soak those tired limbs. There are cheap hotels (Rs150-200) nearby.

From Kodari onwards you will see signs to ***The Last Resort***, tempting you with 'lassi', 'fresh fruit juice' and 'beer!'. This place is an adventure camp just before Bharabise, located on the other side of the Bhote Khosi River. To get there means carrying your bike up on to the suspension bridge that the resort uses as its bungee point (you can see the cage as you pass). If you fancy a few days of relaxing, rafting and generally chilling out in a very Western atmosphere this is a good place to do it. There are safari-style tents ($40) set amidst jungle, above the roar of the river and the chirp of cicadas. Others may find it altogether too Westernized, with staff by turns indifferent or predatory.

Bharabise (877m) 865.5/91KM

From The Last Resort bungee bridge it's just 7km (albeit up and down) to the small town of Bharabise, which has several cheap hotels, guesthouses and restaurants along the road. This is where the tarmac reappears, and now it's less than 100km to Kathmandu.

DAY 13 BHARABISE (877m) to KATHMANDU (1302m) 91KM

BHARABISE–DOLAGHAT 32KM
DOLAGHAT–DHULIKHEL 27KM
DHULIKHEL–KATHMANDU 32KM

Today's ride is through lush and tropical scenery, alongside the Bhote Khosi River. There are cold drinks shops and restaurants throughout so you don't need to carry much in the way of supplies. From Bharabise the road is easy to Chehere, after which there's a small 2km climb alongside the banks of the Bhote Khosi. The ensuing 2km descent to Dolaghat is a glorious swooper with great visibility – if only all the descents in the last few days were like that.

Dolaghat (638m) 897.5/59KM

This small town is clustered around the bridge where the ***Fish Kitchen*** restaurant makes tasty fried whitebait, though you'll need to eat platefuls to power you up the 900m climb you now have to make to Dhulikhel. But don't worry, you'll be able to do it, no matter how tired you feel. All that high-altitude training is about to pay off!

The climb is not a steady one and anyone who is not desperate to reach Kathmandu today might feel that the gorgeous views of the Himalaya from Dhulikhel are worth spending an evening enjoying before heading into the rush and buzz of Nepal's capital city.

Dhulikhel (1502m) 924.5/32KM

There are a couple of musty cheap guesthouses on the road such as the ***Mount View*** which charges Rs200 for a double (att) but if you can afford to splash out then the ***High View Resort*** boasts really excellent views of the mountains and is peaceful with friendly staff. Rooms cost $31/65 (standard/deluxe), the only

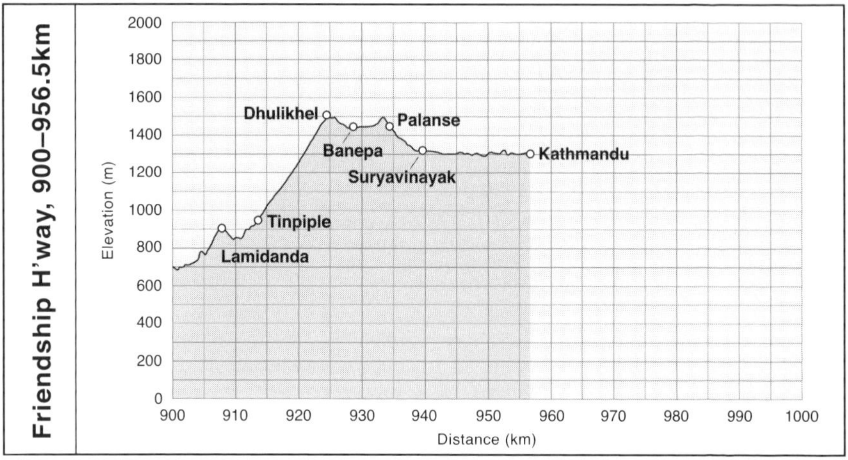

downside is the access – the hotel is up a flight of stairs.

From Dhulikhel, the road drops then climbs once again past Kathmandu University to a ceremonial gateway just before Palanse, at which point the Kathmandu Valley opens up below you. The finish is so close now! Kilometre markers count you down, but keep your head in the heavy traffic. After weeks at high altitude, the smog and pollution of Kathmandu is quite unpleasant. The airport is a great landmark – continue on the highway past the main entrance then at the next junction turn west over the Bagmati River into Kathmandu proper.

Kathmandu (1298m) 956.5/0km

The last few kilometres into Thamel, the famous tourist area of Kathmandu, will be frustrating as there's no clear route but ask around for 'Kathmandu Guest House' and 'Thamel' and everyone will do their best to help. Ride defensively – bikes have no status on Nepali roads. Finally, when the traffic clogs to a standstill and you've seen more Western faces than Nepali, you know you've arrived in Thamel. Time for some of that famous Kathmandu chocolate cake and a cold beer!

KATHMANDU (1298m)

Rather than suffering the stifling heat of the plains like Rawalpindi and Delhi, or being ringed by snow-dusted hills like Lhasa, Kathmandu lies in the rural Kathmandu Valley and faces a chain of Himalayan peaks whose slopes are permanently snow-clad. This mountain promise and the cooler elevation make it a pleasant place to stay; it's no wonder that many expats have made Kathmandu their home. But by no means is it idyllic: gridlocked traffic, pollution, haphazard development and overcrowding are overwhelmingly the first impression and it takes a bit of time to winkle out the time-forgotten corners. Anyone arriving from Tibet will probably have only one thing on their mind: **food**. Kathmandu's reputation for the best travellers' food in the subcontinent is entirely deserved and it's possible to eat in a different restaurant every night for a month and still not get bored. The cooks in Thamel, Kathmandu's tourist district, are well-used to feeding ravenous trekkers and mountaineers and can more than handle the cyclists' diet of breakfast, lunch, second lunch, tea and supper.

As well as good food there's a variety of **accommodation** from dirt-cheap (literally) to luxury and all the facilities a traveller could want. When city life

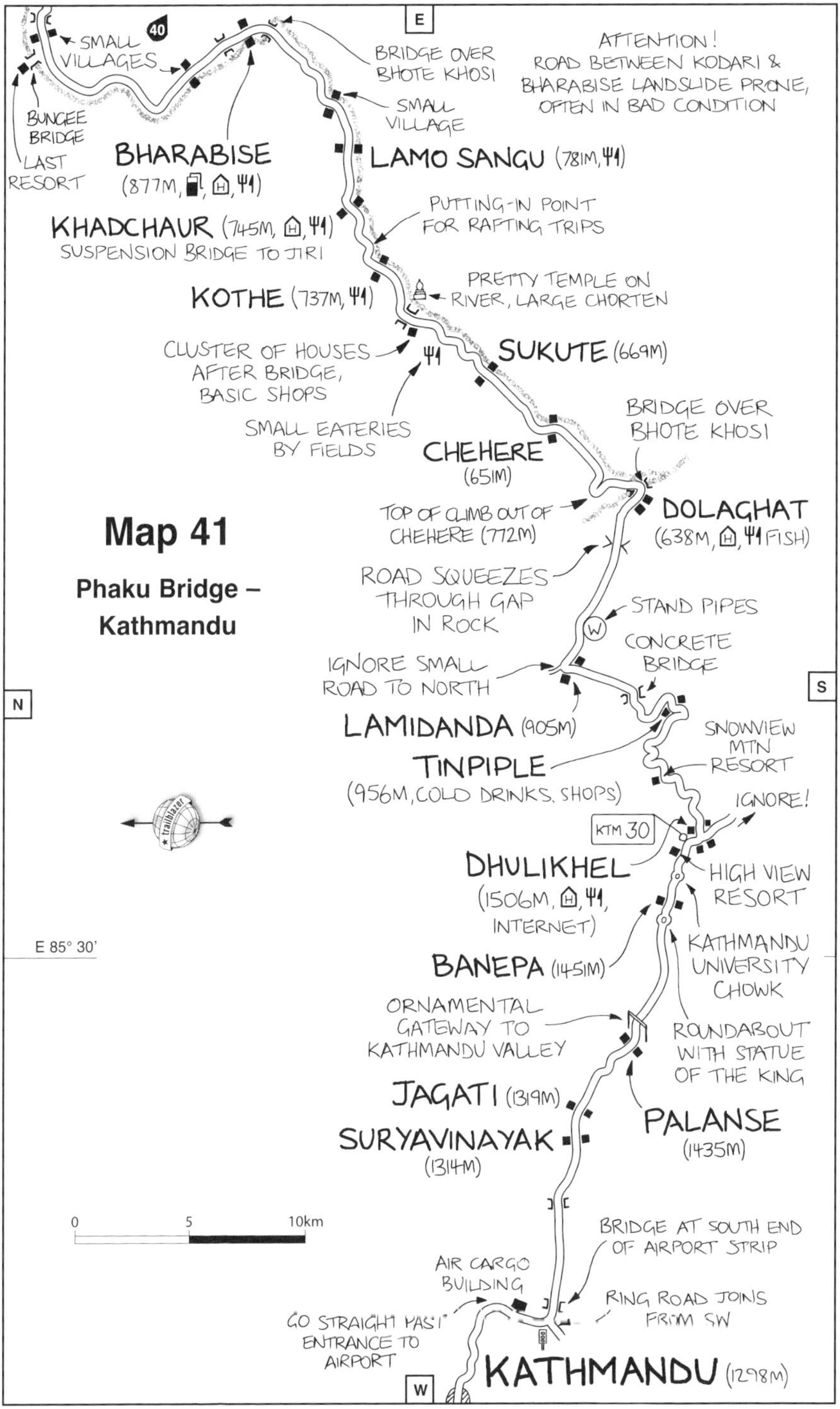

Map 41
Phaku Bridge – Kathmandu
E
N
S
W
40
SMALL VILLAGES
BUNGEE BRIDGE
LAST RESORT
BHARABISE (877M, , ,)
BRIDGE OVER BHOTE KHOSI
SMALL VILLAGE
ATTENTION! ROAD BETWEEN KODARI & BHARABISE LANDSLIDE PRONE, OFTEN IN BAD CONDITION
LAMO SANGU (781M,)
KHADCHAUR (745M, ,)
SUSPENSION BRIDGE TO JIRI
PUTTING-IN POINT FOR RAFTING TRIPS
KOTHE (737M,)
PRETTY TEMPLE ON RIVER, LARGE CHORTEN
CLUSTER OF HOUSES AFTER BRIDGE, BASIC SHOPS
SUKUTE (669M)
SMALL EATERIES BY FIELDS
CHEHERE (651M)
BRIDGE OVER BHOTE KHOSI
TOP OF CLIMB OUT OF CHEHERE (772M)
DOLAGHAT (638M, , FISH)
ROAD SQUEEZES THROUGH GAP IN ROCK
STAND PIPES
CONCRETE BRIDGE
IGNORE SMALL ROAD TO NORTH
LAMIDANDA (905M)
TINPIPLE (956M, COLD DRINKS, SHOPS)
SNOWVIEW MTN RESORT
IGNORE!
KTM 30
DHULIKHEL (1506M, , , INTERNET)
HIGH VIEW RESORT
BANEPA (1451M)
KATHMANDU UNIVERSITY CHOWK
ORNAMENTAL GATEWAY TO KATHMANDU VALLEY
ROUNDABOUT WITH STATUE OF THE KING
JAGATI (1319M)
SURYAVINAYAK (1314M)
PALANSE (1435M)
E 85° 30'
0
5
10km
BRIDGE AT SOUTH END OF AIRPORT STRIP
AIR CARGO BUILDING
RING ROAD JOINS FROM SW
GO STRAIGHT PAST ENTRANCE TO AIRPORT
KATHMANDU (1298M)

gets too much, the Kathmandu Valley and rural Nepal are less than an hour's ride away. Thamel has no pavements and the bleating motorbikes, cars and rickshaws which charge through its lanes fairly squash tourists into the numerous pirate CD shops or up against trundling handcarts loaded with rainbows of fruit. A constant soundtrack is the murmur of 'Hash hash smoking' and the querying 'tiger balm?'. Computers, mobiles, fax – it's all 21st century until you pass a quiet ghat or tiny roadside shrine garlanded with marigold flowers and lounged around by cows.

Peak tourist season in Kathmandu is from September to November, when the narrow streets of Thamel fill with trekkers. The monsoon has retreated south leaving the skies a freshly washed blue (pollution permitting), the temperature mild and the days clear and sunny.

Arrival

Tribhuvan International Airport is a Rs200 pre-paid taxi ride to the east of Thamel (Rs150 if you haggle). ATMs are dotted throughout Thamel; the ATM at Kathmandu Guest House takes all cards.

Where to stay

Thamel has hundreds of guesthouses to suit every budget some of which are institutions such as the ***Kathmandu Guest House***, which started the whole Thamel scene back in the 1970s and stole the show from Freak St. The narrow lanes and bottlenecked traffic make it a noisy area: don't even bother inspecting street side rooms. The best deals can be found by asking rickshaw drivers or hotel touts if there are any hotels which have only just opened – usually the managers are only too pleased to have guests and so will offer an extremely favourable rate. In recent years the prices have hit rock-bottom as Maoist troubles reduced tourism to a trickle. The better hotels (usually the ones that quote in dollars) will charge VAT but not include it in the room quote: to get the true price add another 13%.

Around the Kathmandu Guest House are hundreds of guesthouses. The cheapest is ***Pheasant Lodge***, tucked behind the noisy pubs. Central Thamel's most popular hotels, such as the ***Pilgrim's Guest House*** and ***Down Town*** have tired rooms but are cheap and in the thick of the action. Towards the north end of Panakjol are four quieter guesthouses with pleasant gardens: just before the road forks take the small track on the left with a sign to the 'Kathmandu Garden House'. The prices may start high but are negotiable if they're not full. Tucked at the end of a lane, ***Samsara*** (💻 www.samsararesort.com) has to be one of the quietest hotels in Thamel. It's pricier, but the large double rooms with wooden floors, sofas and en suite bathrooms (such as #406 at $54) are extremely civilized.

Where to eat

For the hungry biker, Kathmandu is foodie heaven. And for the icing on the cake, all the bakeries sell their surplus strudels, croissants and cinnamon swirls at half-price in the evenings.

Breakfast in Kathmandu is busiest at the ***Pumpernickel Bakery*** which is self-service but easily overwhelmed. Coffee fiends might prefer the ***Northfield Café***, where unlimited filter coffee is Rs45. The most potent coffee is at the pricier ***New Orleans*** where it's best combined with a fruit smoothie, poached

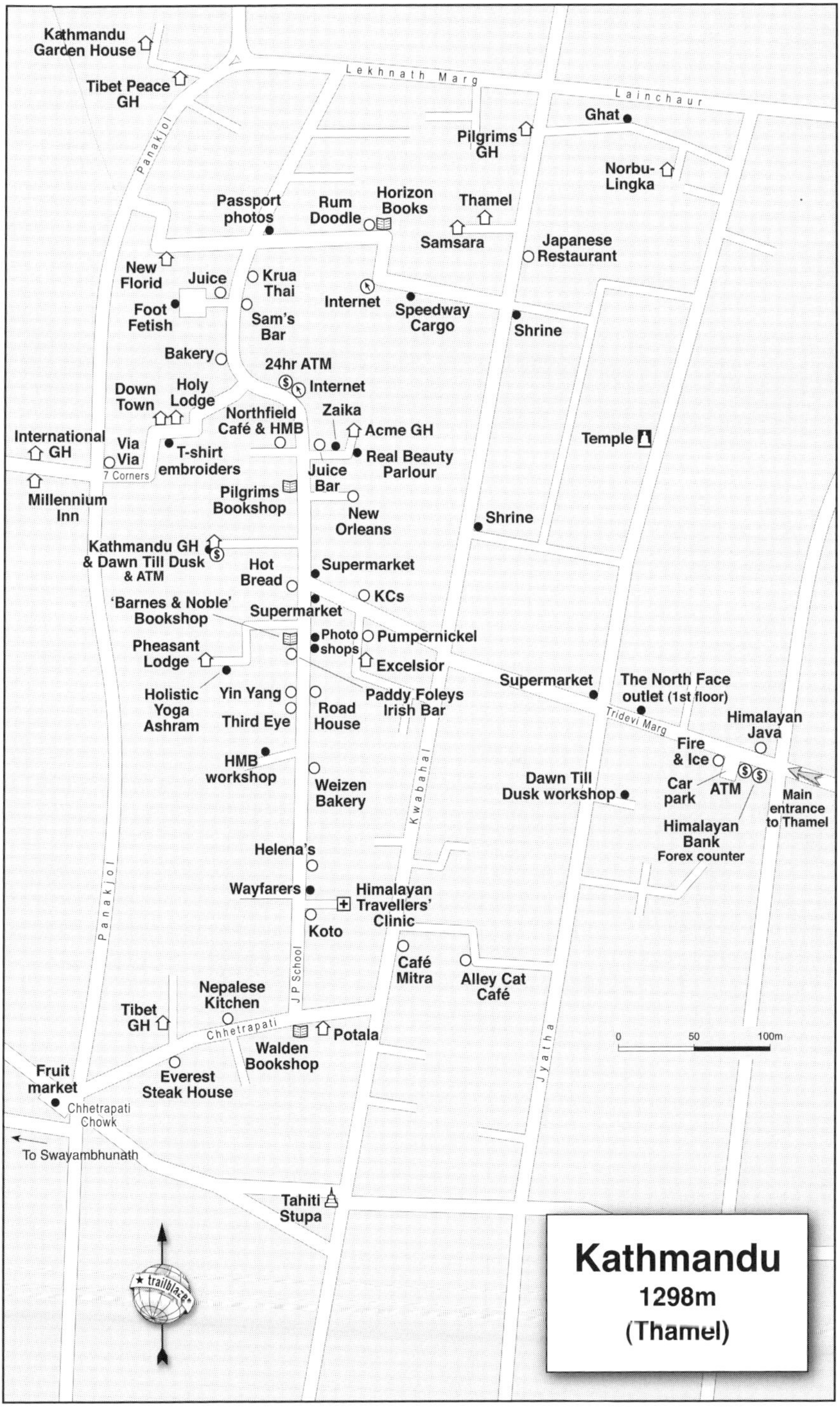

LHASA – KATHMANDU

eggs, potatoes and toast and then slowly digested in the sunshine while reading the *Kathmandu Post*.

Lunch, dinner and everything else in between are really a case of wandering around and seeing what catches your eye. However, some places really stand out: ***Fire & Ice*** does the best pizza in the Himalaya. Apparently the Italian owner has imported her very own furnace, which explains why this place is packed every day with a mix of tourists, well-off locals and ex-pats. Prices vary from a margherita at Rs240 to Rs350 for buff steak with coriander and chilli. Other dishes include pasta such as spaghetti al pesto Rs220 and ice cream (Rs100), and a deliciously refreshing iced tea. This is a place to fantasize about while on the road.

The rooftop at ***Helena's*** is a long way up, but it's worth it if you want to eat delicious chocolate cake with a view. The steak specials (around Rs300) are also good.

As well as serving the best breakfast in Kathmandu, ***New Orleans*** keeps going till the early hours with innovative food, a good buzz and live music in the evenings. Close by, and at the cheap end of the budget spectrum, ***Zaika*** has good Nepali food and is a cheerful place at all hours, since a handy serving hatch doles out baguettes around the clock. A Kathmandu institution is the ***Rum Doodle***, which is famous for its collection of Everest summiteers' signatures and collection of large cut-out Yeti footprints which are plastered all over the walls. It's a group tour haunt, but has a pleasant roof-top terrace and does good steaks (Rs 360). You can eat here free for life, once you've climbed Everest.

Shopping

Kathmandu is a great place to pick up second-hand expedition equipment or get your own designs manufactured. If you're coming through Kathmandu en route to Lhasa, get your kit here and also stock up in the supermarkets for chocolate and muesli.

Alpine Trekking Store in Jyatha manufactures trekking and mountaineering equipment and can get stuff made up too. The Pilgrims Book House situated on the main drag in Thamel is a paradise for bookworms with thousands of books and hundreds of maps. Here is where you'll find all the books on Tibet that you can't find in China as well as the 'On this Spot: Lhasa' map (Rs300, see p54) and shelves upon shelves of history, travel literature, folklore, politics and even cooking. There's a particular focus on the Himalaya, with sumptuous photographic books and just to seal the deal they accept Visa and will airmail the books home. Snapper Photo (91 Tourist Marg) covers all things photographic.

Bars and nightlife

There's no better place to restore your iron levels than ***Paddy Foleys Irish Bar*** where pints of Guinness sell for Rs550 and there are live sporting events on TV. You could be in any fake-Irish pub in the world here. Once restored, ***Sam's Bar*** just up the road is something of a traveller hub due to its good music with wicker chairs outside and a small bar inside. Nearby ***Full Moon*** is a tiny upstairs bar with live music and a mixed crowd of locals and tourists. To finish a big night of drinking in zero style head to the ***Fire Club*** – think disco balls and White Russians. Most spots in Thamel close by 3am – if you still want more wake up a rickshaw driver.

Bike shops

Dawn till Dusk (daily 9.30am–7.30pm) is the best bike shop in the Himalaya. Their office is in the Kathmandu Guest House but it's best to visit the workshop on Jyatha. The staff are extremely experienced Nepali mountain bikers who run tours throughout the Himalaya (💻 www.nepalbiking.com). The workshops stocks comprehensive spare parts from 26" tyres to 700C and even 20-inchers for BOB trailers, Presta and Schrader inner tubes, 7, 8, 9 speed chains, genuine Shimano parts, plus all the accessories such as bottle cages, lights and clothing (including SPD cleats and shoes). A full service for the bike costs Rs700 (tourists) or Rs450 ('adventure people'), they can also do re-spraying jobs and sell new Trek bikes if all is lost. If needed, they can make 'local panniers' based on the classic Ortlieb design but not waterproof.

Himalayan Mountain Bikes will buy second hand bikes, stock bike parts (but not as many as Dawn Till Dusk) and service bikes: Rs1500 for a full service or Rs800 for a general service.

Dawn till Dusk bike shop staff ride every morning and will happily take 'adventure people' (ie cycle tourers) along with them. Himalayan Mountain Bikes do the same, but charge $25 for the privilege.

BOXING THE BIKE FOR AIRLINES

The bike shops in Kathmandu are well-used to cyclists needing bike boxes for the flight home and have started to charge whatever they think they can get away with for flimsy wisps of cardboard. It's better to leave Thamel and ask at shops that sell large electrical items like fridges and TVs for a box: chances are that it will be better quality and they may well give it you for free.

Things to do

Kathmandu's distinctive **architecture** of pale bricks, dark carved hardwood and roof tiles is of Newari origin, and dates mostly from the 17th and 18th centuries. One of the foremost Newari architects was Arniko and it's in his honour that the road from Kodari to Kathmandu is sometimes referred to as the 'Arniko Highway'. The most famous examples of Newari architecture are the pagoda temples of Pashupatinath and Durbar Square and the stupas of Baudhanath and Swayambhunath. Nepalis say that the pagoda style originated with the Newaris in Kathmandu from where it travelled to Lhasa in Tibet and onwards to China. The town of Bhaktapur, back on the Arniko Highway, has been extensively restored over the last few years and is now a showcase of traditional Newari architecture: there's a small charge to enter, but with a small number of guesthouses and no touts, it's a much more peaceful place to stay than Thamel.

A few Nepalese airlines such as Buddha Air (💻 www.buddhaair.com), Yeti Airlines (💻 www.yetiairlines.com) and Cosmic Air (💻 www.cosmicair.com) offer the '**Flight to Mountain**' for around $110 which, despite the name, is a 45min round-trip flight in a tiny turbo-prop plane along the Himalayan peaks past Mt Everest and towards Kanchenjunga. The 6.30am departure is often delayed by ground fog for hours, or even cancelled altogether in poor weather. Buddha Air has the best service: a window seat for each passenger (get a seat on the left as you enter the plane), a route map detailing all the peaks, time up in the cockpit with the captain and at the end a cheesy certificate.

Foot Fetish (10am-10pm) offers reflexology foot **massage** at Rs500/1hr and Thai body massage at Rs600/1hr. Real Beauty down the same alley as Zaika and the Acme Guesthouse, will wax legs, underarms and such like places. As in India, women should be wary of massages done by men.

Moving on

Few airlines fly direct from Kathmandu to Europe. Most break the journey using a hub in Western Europe (eg Vienna for Austrian Airlines, 💻 www.aua.com) or the Middle East, or in India (Delhi or Kolkata). For the Kathmandu–Delhi leg, many Asian airlines offer cheap flights such as the Indian budget airlines Jet Air (💻 www.jetairways.com) and Air Sahara (💻 www.airsahara.net) or Bhutan's national carrier, Druk Air (💻 www.drukair.com.bt), which flies between Delhi and Kathmandu en route to Paro and has an extremely generous luggage allowance at 40kg (35kg hold, 5kg hand) and special deals eg Kathmandu to Delhi for $70.

Kathmandu's airport staff have a bad reputation; see that your bike is properly tagged and goes airside before you do. There's a tourism fee plus departure tax of Rs1695 (Rs1356 for India and SAARC countries) which must be paid at the marked counter in Nepali rupees before you check in.

AIR FREIGHT

If excess luggage is a worry, consider air freighting your possessions home – this will work out much cheaper than charges at airports. For example, Speedway Cargo in Thamel (see map p289) charge $125 for 20kg (including packaging) to fly to the UK, and you can specify the dates your belongings travel. Once home, the airport will give you between three and five days to come and pick up your belongings – though they'll charge a handling fee of £40.

BHUTAN 8

ROUTE INFORMATION

- **Start / finish** Paro / Samdrup Jongkhar
- **Distance** 804km
- **Altitude min / max** 183m/3743m
- **High passes** Ten – nearly one a day!
- **Suggested duration** Minimum 11 cycling days, two weeks in total
- **Road conditions** 100% tarmac
- **Hazards and dangers** None in Bhutan; some political tension in Assam
- **When to go** March–May, September–December. The best views are in November and early December
- **Visas** Required; **independent travel is not allowed in Bhutan**

For most people the cost of visiting Bhutan is prohibitive. This tiny mountain kingdom only admitted its first foreign tourists in 1974 and since then the tourism policy has been cautious. The number of visitors is in effect regulated by price. It costs $200 per day to visit Bhutan ($165 in the monsoon season), a charge which cannot be avoided unless you work in Bhutan or are a guest of the government. However, the $200 does not just pay for you to be in the country, it's an all-inclusive package (see box p299).

So is it worth it? Yes, if your expectations are realistic. Bhutan is the last surviving Himalayan kingdom but don't expect big mountains here. Its few roads don't wind among the Himalaya but along the successive valleys, ridges and passes to the south. It's also a developing country which only ranks 134th in global wealth leagues and although a few luxury hotels have opened up most accommodation is simple. In the east, where there are few hotels, that accommodation may even be a tent. Some Westerners find Bhutanese food unappealing and monotonous but if you're already in Asia the Bhutanese diet will seem nutritious, tasty and, best of all, plentiful. Many people visit Bhutan as a 'last destination' in Asia, once they have already seen Nepal, Sikkim and Tibet. This is the only way to fully appreciate how different it is from its rapidly industrialized neighbours India and China, and also from budget traveller destinations such as Nepal.

After all those caveats, Bhutan is a fantastic place to visit. In comparison to its Himalayan neighbours it's clean, the people are friendly, and its landscape is gorgeously unspoilt. Ever since the King began using 'Gross National Happiness' as a quality-of-life indicator in 1972, Bhutan has placed as much value on its unique culture and pristine environment as on economic growth – a progressive and holistic concept which developed countries are only now starting to appreciate. The Bhutanese are immeasurably proud

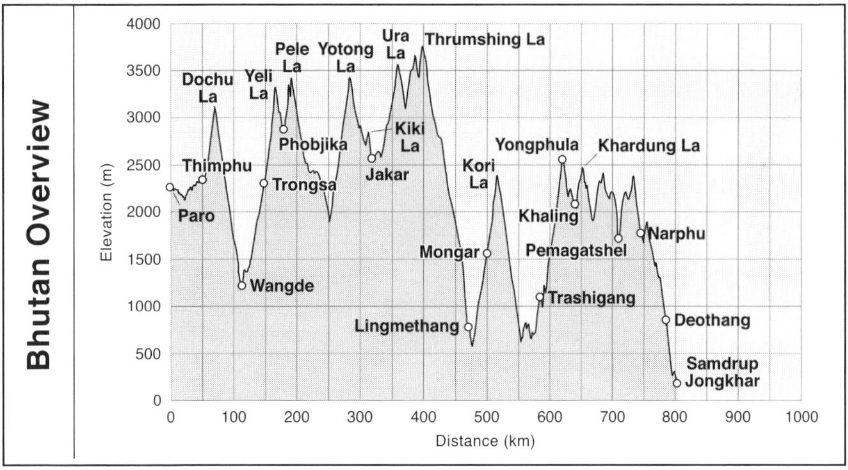

of their country and their king and though Bhutan is still poor there is free healthcare and education for all. There is none of the oppression of Tibet, none of the tourist-gouging of Kathmandu and none of the hassle of India. Bhutan's landscape of deep river valleys, snowy peaks and southern jungle is often seen through a veil of hazy sunshine which half obscures and half illuminates: the overall effect is timeless and dream-like.

Bhutanese roads are famously wiggly. The entire west–east highway is tarmac and mostly single-lane. There is very little traffic once past Punakha and the riding is dramatic as you rise and plunge from high passes dominated by *chortens* (Buddhist stupas) to the warmth of the valleys; en route a hot mug of tea and a fiery plate of *ema datse* (cheesy chillies) can always be found. The road elevation varies from flattish around Paro and Thimphu to high passes in the centre and tropical valleys as low as 600m in the east. The final day's riding dives from Bhutan's blue hills around Pemagatshel through tropical jungle onto the hazy plains of India at just 183m.

The weather in Bhutan is often cloudy; early winter is the best time for clear skies though the passes are cold. From December until February passes on the west–east highway may be snowbound.

FACTS ABOUT THE REGION

When we look at the developed world, we wonder whether there is in fact an advancement in terms of civilization, or whether there has been a decivilization. Because civilization has to do with the development of the human individual, the mind, the finer aspects of humanity; and I think those are lost.

Jigme Thinley, Home and Cultural Affairs Minister, Bhutan

The Bhutanese call their country 'Druk Yul', the Land of the Thunder Dragon. This tiny kingdom is pressed hard up against the Himalaya and clouds rolling in from the Bay of Bengal swathe its many peaks and valleys and bring the rumbling thunderstorms which give the country its poetic name. Bhutan is also pressed between the two massive territories of China and India, whose absorption of Himalayan near-neighbours Tibet and Sikkim have been a wake-up call to the perils of isolation (Tibet) and ethnic dilution (Sikkim); both

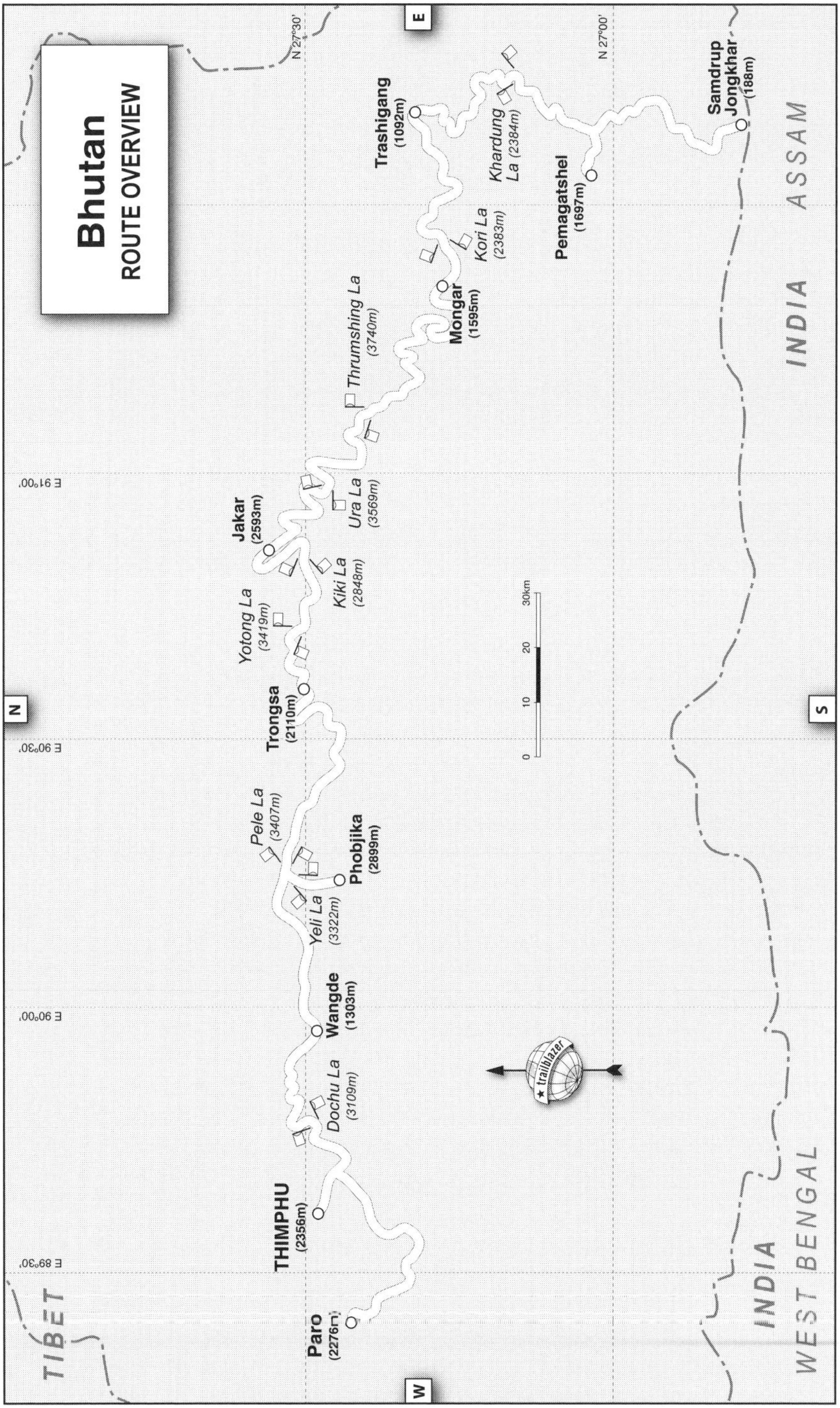
Bhutan
ROUTE OVERVIEW
TIBET
Paro
(2276m)
THIMPHU
(2356m)
Dochu La
(3109m)
Wangde
(1303m)
Yeli La
(3322m)
Phobjika
(2899m)
Pele La
(3407m)
Trongsa
(2110m)
Yotong La
(3419m)
Kiki La
(2848m)
Jakar
(2593m)
Ura La
(3569m)
Thrumshing La
(3740m)
Mongar
(1595m)
Kori La
(2383m)
Trashigang
(1092m)
Khardung
La (2384m)
Pemagatshel
(1697m)
Samdrup
Jongkhar
(188m)
INDIA
WEST BENGAL
INDIA
ASSAM
E 89°30'
E 90°00'
E 90°30'
E 91°00'
N 27°30'
N 27°00'
N
E
S
W
0
10
20
30km
trailblazer

Sikkim and Nepal have also lost their kings. That leaves Bhutan as the only remaining Himalayan kingdom, and the only country in the world whose official religion is Mahayana (Tantric) Buddhism.

Bhutan has a tiny population of just over 672,500 and has to date been an absolute monarchy, factors which have made it possible to implement radical policies such as the drive for Gross National Happiness (GNH). Bhutan's politicians must consider the impact of every new policy not only on GDP but also on GNH, whose pillars are economic self-reliance, a pristine environment, preservation and promotion of Bhutanese culture and good governance as a democracy. On this final point, Bhutan's king is voluntarily abdicating in 2008 in order to bring democracy to his country: throughout 2007 mock elections were held in the country to familiarize the Bhutanese with the process of voting.

Bhutan was the last country in the world to introduce television which it did in 1999 to mark the King's silver jubilee, with 99 channels including CNN, BBC World, Hindi soaps, MTV and the American WWE wrestling series. The last two were then deemed 'too captivating' and subsequently removed. The internet is uncensored, unlike in China; advertisement hoardings, tobacco and plastic bags are all banned. There was one set of traffic lights installed in Thimphu but it only lasted a few days; the policeman who choreographs the traffic so elegantly was reinstated by popular request.

The economy is based mainly on agriculture and forestry as much of Bhutan is given over to subsistence farming and animal husbandry. Hydropower and tourism are the main revenue earners. Western Bhutan, in particular the Paro Valley, is far more affluent than eastern Bhutan, and you will notice the disparity in everything from education to architecture as you traverse the country. There is very little manufacturing; strong ties with India provide both financial assistance and migrant labour, most visibly road workers. There is some political co-operation too: in 2003 the Bhutanese and Indian armies combined forces to oust Assamese ULFA rebels from camps in Bhutan's dense southern jungles.

Bhutan has been criticized internationally for its treatment of the **Lhotshampa people**, descendants of nineteenth-century Nepali immigrants who settled mostly in southern Bhutan. When the 1988 census showed that Bhutan's population was 48 per cent Buddhist and 45 per cent Nepali, the government introduced radical policies to protect the country's traditional Buddhist culture and redefine eligibility requirements for Bhutanese citizenship. Over 100,000 Lhotshampas were rendered stateless as a result of these policies and since the 1990s they have been housed in UN refugee camps in Nepal. When pressed, Bhutanese politicians point to the situation of neighbouring Sikkim which, though ethnically Bhutia and Lepcha, became inundated by Nepalis brought in by the British to work on the tea plantations in the nineteenth century. Nowadays not only is Nepali the dominant language in Sikkim but in 1975 the former kingdom lost its autonomy and become the 22nd state of India. The fate of Tibet, once a Buddhist theocracy and now a Chinese military zone, is seen as equally pertinent.

Travel in Bhutan is particularly exciting at the moment because 2008 sees the coronation of a new king, the hundredth anniversary of the Wangchuk dynasty and the first ever parliamentary elections. Many Bhutanese speak English and are keen to share their history with foreign visitors.

Safety

The only safety issues in Bhutan are on its Indian borders. Phuentsoling (the border town with West Bengal) was bombed in December 2006 and again in May 2007 by a faction called the Bhutan Tiger Force, the militant wing of the Bhutan Communist Party which has sprung up in Nepal's pro-Maoist refugee camps. India's northeast is heavily militarized because of local separatist militants such as the United Liberation Front of Assam (ULFA) and the Bodos (who are fighting for a separate state for the Bodo tribe); the state of Assam is unsafe, especially its capital Guwahati. In Bhutan proper you only need take care on the mountain roads as they are curvy with steep drop offs.

The only Western embassies currently operating in Bhutan are those of Holland and Denmark; if you need consular assistance contact your country's embassy in India (see Appendix A for details).

Restrictions

Visitors to Bhutan must either be guests of the government or tourists on a package tour: free independent travel is not allowed. Individual travel is allowed, it's just more expensive (see box p299). All tourists must apply for visas through an approved travel agent; once the travel agent has received payment in dollars they will process your visa and arrange flights if necessary. Allow at least three weeks for this.

History of the road

Until 1962 there were no roads at all in Bhutan, only footpaths and mule tracks. After China's 'liberation' of Tibet in 1959 Bhutan immediately initiated an ambitious road-building programme. The first road connected Thimphu with Phuentsoling, on India's West Bengal border. Since then Project Dantak, a subdivision of India's Border Roads Organization, has laid more than 1600km of tarmac from west to east Bhutan. Over 700 Dantak labourers have lost their lives building Bhutan's roads; there's a memorial to them at Deothang, near Samdrup Jongkhar.

Language

Dzongkha, or the 'language of the dzongs' is the official language of Bhutan. Its script is Tibetan, but Dzongkha and Tibetan speakers cannot understand one another. **Nepali** is spoken in southern Bhutan and Sharchop in the east. Along the way are all sorts of local dialects, many of which are unintelligible to outsiders. All schools teach **English** and in towns such as Thimphu and Paro you will find many fluent English speakers.

Religion

The official religion of Bhutan is **Mahayana Buddhism**, better known as Tantric Buddhism, whose iconography is often sexually explicit. Symbols of the Buddhist faith are found throughout the country, from roadside chortens to prayer wheels, mani walls and thickets of tall prayer flags lining the roads and crowning the passes. Religious festivals, known as *tsechus*, punctuate the calendar and are now major tourist attractions.

Culture

Bhutan is taking extraordinary measures to preserve its culture. Buddhism and the King are key to Bhutanese society and symbols of both are everywhere. Bhutanese society is liberal although as elsewhere in Asia being affectionate in public is not the done thing. There is now a gap between generations and between those in the city and those in rural areas: those who have grown up in an isolated Buddhist kingdom and those who are growing up with the tempting Western lifestyle as seen on satellite TV and the internet.

Buddhism in 21st-century Bhutan

Archery is the national passion and serious players will spend thousands of dollars on foreign compound bows. These always look incongruous in the hands of a Bhutanese gent wearing Argyll socks and a traditional *gho* (knee-length robe) as his friends hop around him hooting bawdy songs to put him off his aim. The targets, often seen by the roadsides, are white stone markers 120–150m apart with the target picked out in concentric circles of green, red and yellow. The national vice is *doma*, areca nut folded into a betel leaf with a smear of lime paste and chewed as a digestive. It's like *paan* in India and causes the same gory bloodstained teeth among regular users.

Areca nuts for sale at Paro market

PRACTICAL INFORMATION

Tour operators

Adventure tourism comes a distant second to cultural tourism in Bhutan but there are a few local travel agents who offer bike tours. Don't expect as slick an operation as in the West. There will certainly be a back-up vehicle but it will neither signal junctions nor follow you every kilometre of the way so don't rely on it; better to carry a small rucksack or handlebar bag with water, snacks and warm/waterproof clothing. Expect to sleep and eat breakfast and dinner in hotels in west and central Bhutan; on the road you will probably be provided with a picnic lunch and in east Bhutan you may be camping. Restaurants and general stores are listed in the route guide text in case you get peckish. A few Western-led operations and Kinley Tshering of Himalayan Adventure in Thimphu have ridden across Bhutan; most tour operators have no experience of cycling long distances so take their distances and route descriptions with a pinch of salt. See 🖳 www.tourism.gov.bt for a list of tour operators.

Note that although it's necessary to use a tour operator to visit Bhutan that doesn't mean that you have to travel as part of a tour group. Solo travel is possible, just more expensive (see box opposite); best value is to travel in a group

BHUTAN PRICING GUIDE

Bhutan is famous for its astronomical pricing policy. A lesser-known fact about the $200 daily fee is that $65 of it funds Bhutan's free health and education systems. Below are the rates charged by the government in 2008 for package tours:

Number of people	**Daily rates per person** in peak season (Aug–June)	**Daily rates per person** in monsoon season (July, Aug)
1	$240	$205
2	$230	$195
3+	$200	$165

Included in the daily rate is all food, accommodation, transfers, an English-speaking guide and all entry fees to museums and *dzongs* (religious fortresses).

of four. Travelling as a four and dealing directly with a Bhutanese travel agent often works out cheaper than joining a tour package in the West. You also get to choose who you spend your holiday with!

Which direction?
The tour will always start from Paro/Thimphu. Foreigners cannot currently enter Bhutan at Samdrup Jongkhar in the east, though they can exit there.

Equipment
The travel agent should provide a mechanic for every trip but it's always good to be able to fix minor problems (eg a flat tyre, loose bolts etc) yourself so bring along a **multitool** and **puncture-repair kit**. Passes can be wet and cold on the descents so carry warm and **waterproof clothing** in a day pack along with **energy snacks** (nuts, glucose biscuits and chocolate can be bought in general stores).

Accommodation
This will be arranged by the travel agent and can vary from standard hotels – and even the occasional luxury five-star – to cosy guesthouses and tents in eastern Bhutan where there is little tourist infrastructure.

Food and drink
The Bhutanese will often tell you how much they love eating. A favourite story is of the time Indira Gandhi visited the Himalayan kingdom. She was astonished by the prodigious appetite of the Bhutanese and observed that whereas India existed on 'a roti and a dhoti [sarong]', the Bhutanese simply ate their economy. This is a story told with pride!

The star of Bhutanese cuisine is the **chilli**; the hotter the better. No wonder, when the world's hottest chilli, the Bhut Jolokia or Raja Mircha (King of Chillies) comes from neighbouring Assam. Most Bhutanese meals combine a saucy dish or two with a large serving of rice, either polished white rice or the nuttier red rice from Paro. The two favourite dishes are both vegetarian: *ema datse* (chilli and cheese) and *kewa datse* (potato and cheese). *Datse* is a soft white cheese particular to Bhutan; you'll see it in roundels at the side of the road. Popular meat dishes include *kewa phagshu* (pork rind with potatoes) and *tshoem* (buttered beef chuck with oyster mushrooms).

If you're on an organized tour your breakfast and dinner will usually be a hotel buffet; lunch will usually be at a local restaurant or a picnic. As for

TEA TIME

Tea-lovers will feel very at home in Bhutan where comfortingly big mugs of tea are drunk all day long. Ceremonially, tea is drunk in wooden bowls carved from the burls of maple trees, a speciality of the Trashi Yangtse district. In daily life Bhutanese drink mugs of either *ngaja* (sweet tea) or *suja* (butter tea). Hot water with a tea bag on the side and a couple of lumps of sugar is 'tea'; 'readymade tea' is more like Indian *chai* (but without the spices) where all the ingredients are brewed up together. Many roadside restaurants keep a thermos of ngaja for cold and thirsty customers in a hurry.

snacks on the road, biscuits are easily bought: Parle G glucose biscuits work well for cyclists. Big mugs of tea, whether milky (*ngaja*) or salty butter (*suja*), are also readily available. You'll often see fruit-sellers at the roadside, sitting by a blanket covered in anything from tangerines to sugar cane to cheese. Check with your tour operator if the backup vehicle will carry snacks and water; some don't.

Alcohol is readily available across Bhutan, though Tuesday is 'dry day' throughout the country. A popular beer is HIT which is brewed in Sikkim and super strong (8%). Discerning palates might prefer Red Panda, a wheat beer brewed by the Swiss farm in Bumthang.

Money

The Bhutanese currency is the ngultrum (Nu). It's linked to the Indian rupee which is also legal tender throughout the country except for the Rs500 and Rs1000 notes (too many counterfeits in circulation). Bhutan currently has no **ATMs** designed to accept foreign cards, and only three in the whole country for Bhutanese cards. Do not rely on paying with credit or debit cards – a few hotels and shops accept Visa but not MasterCard, Cirrus or Maestro. Travellers' cheques can be cashed in Thimphu; in the rest of the country it is best to carry cash. The Bank of Bhutan is the best place for foreign exchange as all hotels charge at least 5% commission.

Communications

There are Public Call Offices (PCO) throughout Bhutan; you'll see the ISD and STD signs everywhere. Bhutan has just one internet server: at present you can access the internet in Paro, Thimphu, Bumthang (at the Swiss Guest House) and Mongar (at the Dzongkha Hotel).

Rules of the road

Drive on the left. Where there are chortens, prayer wheels or *mani* walls (inscribed with mantras) on the road keep them to your right. Traffic is heaviest in the west of Bhutan between Punakha, Thimphu and Paro. The country's infamously curvy mountain roads in the centre and east have very little traffic – because the quickest way from Samdrup Jongkhar to Thimphu is through India. You might read that cycling down the main streets in Thimphu and Paro is not allowed but in practice no one seems to mind.

Getting to the ride

• **By air** Only Bhutan's national airline Druk Air flies into Bhutan (🖳 www.drukair.com.bt); flights connect Paro to Bangkok, Delhi, Kolkata and Kathmandu.

The Kathmandu flight offers a spectacular view of the Himalaya, passing Mt Everest, Lhotse, Makalu and Kanchenjunga; the Friendship Highway and Zhangmu in Tibet are visible from the port side of the plane. The tour operator responsible for your visa will book the flights. Paro is Bhutan's only airport so there is no chance of domestic flights, nor are there direct flights between Paro and the nearest airports in India – Bagdogra in West Bengal and Guwahati in Assam.

- **By road** All overland routes into and out of Bhutan require an Indian visa. Currently foreigners are only allowed to enter Bhutan in the southwest at Phuentsoling, the border town with India in West Bengal. Phuentsoling to Thimphu is 176km. Exit is possible at Samdrup Jongkhar in eastern Bhutan from where it's a short taxi journey to Guwahati, capital of Assam and north-east India's main transport hub. The central southern route exiting at Gelephu is currently closed to foreigners. Transit visas for India are valid for three months from the date of issue and allow 72 hours in the country; proof of onward travel out of India is required. If exiting Bhutan into India a transit visa takes two working days to issue in Thimphu and costs $10.
- **By rail** There are no railways in Bhutan.

PARO

Bhutan's only airport is just to the south of Paro so for many visitors this town is their first impression of Bhutan. Anyone who has steeled themselves for haggling with commission-driven rickshaw wallahs, or who is expecting a diesel-soaked industrial city, persistent touts or even just a crowd of staring eyeballs can relax. Paro is peaceful. The town is set in a wooded valley alongside the Paro Chu river and the air is clean, even on its one main street. With advertising hoardings banned, the tiny shops use hand-painted wooden placards even for the most modern of commodities such as sim cards and internet cafés. All the architecture is in traditional style (even the airport) and you will see many people wearing the Bhutanese national dress: the *gho* (a knee-length robe) for men and the *kira* (an ankle-length dress) for women. A market is held every Sunday selling the famous local red rice as well as knives, vegetables, meat and brand-name rip-offs like Hortn Face jackets smuggled on horseback from China. At the southern edge of Paro is the archery ground, which is worth visiting if there is a game in progress.

Paro's broad valley is filled with fields, and golden willows flourish on the river banks. The area has some interesting easy rides: 5km up to Paro Dzong from the main bridge and 15km west up the valley on an unpaved road to Drugyal Dzong, past the dramatic Tiger's Nest monastery on a cliff face. From Drugyal Dzong on a clear day the stunning peak of Chomolhari (7314m) is visible far away on the border with Tibet.

Services

- **Banks and exchange** The Bank of Bhutan does not handle foreign exchange; for this you need Thimphu. Shopkeepers along the main street may change Nepali rupees.
- **Internet** There is an internet café ($1/30min) next to the post office in the lane parallel to the main road but to the west.

Route guide – Bhutan

DAY 1 PARO (2276m) to THIMPHU (2356m) 50.8KM

PARO–CHHUZOM 24KM
CHHUZOM–NAMSELING 6.5KM
NAMSELING–KHASTABCHU 5.8KM
KHASTABCHU–THIMPHU 14.5KM

Paro (2276m) 0/804KM

The first day of the ride, from Paro to Thimphu, is the flattest day's riding in all of Bhutan. Enjoy it because from Thimphu onwards the passes begin: the first of many! Phobjika is the last village in western Bhutan before the Pele La, the pass over the Black Mountains into Central Bhutan.

From Paro's archery ground take the small road to the left past the chortens and mani wall (keep these to your right). This is the main road between Bhutan's two major metropolises: a far cry from the frenzy of Delhi or the hubbub of Kathmandu. Once it crosses the Paro Chu the airfield is to your right until Boundey (Bondey) village, beyond which there are some good views back down the valley. Between the Isuna Zam bridge and Chhuzom the road runs along the Paro Chu.

Chhuzom (2122m) 24/780KM

Chhuzom ('Confluence') is the meeting point of the Paro Chu and Thimphu Chu rivers. The roads leading south from here go to Haa and Phuentsoling; the one crossing the Thueen Zam bridge and leading east is to Thimphu.

Between Chhuzom and Namseling the valley is narrow and the road uninteresting; at Khastabchu the side valley of Gidakom opens out on the far side of the Thimphu Chu. After Khastabchu, where there are a couple of restaurants and general shops, the valley widens out and looks decidedly Scottish with blue pines, heather on the hillsides and trout in the river; the only incongruous elements are the prayer flags and an enormous new white chorten. At the roundabout a new 'expressway' leads directly to Thimphu past some new housing units.

Thimphu (2356m) 51/753KM

Bhutan's capital must be one of the most miniature in the world. By royal decree, all buildings must be built in traditional architectural style: the petrol station as you enter the capital is a fine example. The city spills down the hillsides but the main street, Norzin Lam, runs parallel to the river with 'traffic circles' (roundabouts) at either end on which a nattily-dressed policeman performs mesmerizing and traffic-taming tai chi moves. Bhutan's tug-of-war between tradition and modernity is most visible here; it's also where Westerners will find the most creature comforts so stock up before heading east.

Your food and lodging will be arranged for you, as will the sightseeing. A trawl along Norzin Lam will turn up all sorts in the shops: a particular surprise is the range of Thai goods, which arrive on the Druk Air flight from Bangkok. ***Plum's Café*** on the first floor by the southern traffic circle has some great cakes and big mugs of tea.

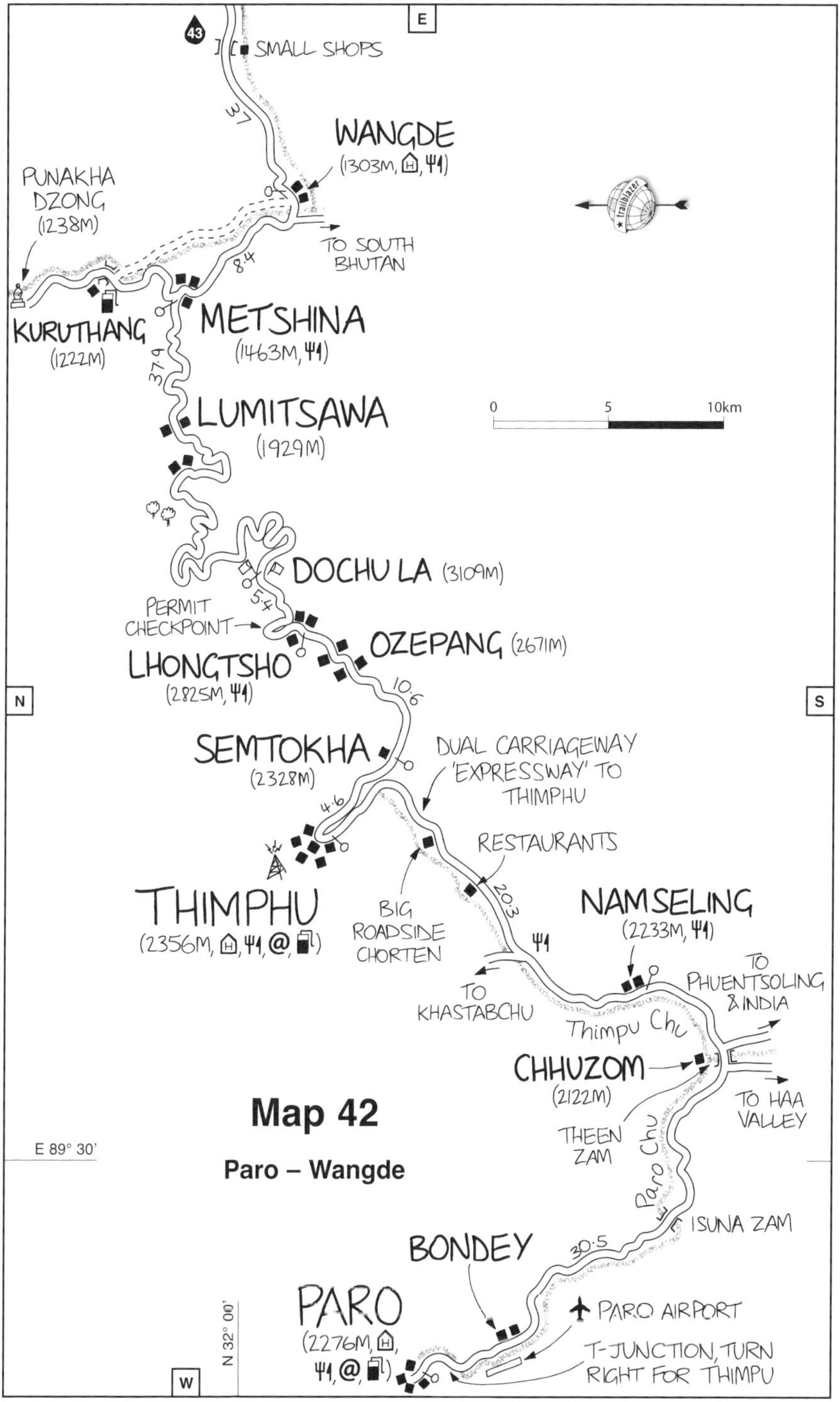

Map 42

Paro – Wangde

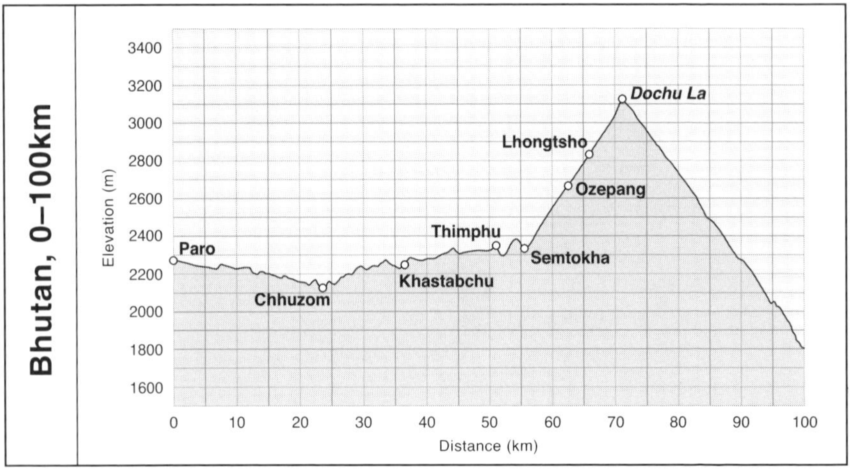

DAY 2 THIMPHU (2356m) to WANGDE (1303m) over Dochu La (3109m) — 66.9KM

THIMPHU (BRIDGE)–SEMTOKHA 4.6KM
SEMTOKHA–LHONGTSHO 10.6KM
LHONGTSHO–DOCHU LA 5.4KM
DOCHU LA–METSHINA 37.9KM
METSHINA–WANGDE 8.4KM

Thimphu (2356m) **51/753KM**
From Thimphu's main bridge take the scenic road to Semtokha on the east bank of the Thimphu Chu, past the helipad and the auspicious Buddhist symbols painted on the road, then start a small climb and descent past the army base to the prayer wheel at Semtokha. The switchback road on the opposite side of the valley will lead to the largest Buddha statue in the world, whose cast is currently (at the time of writing) being built in China. The Buddha has been financed by a Singaporean millionaire and once the cast is complete it will be assembled in situ on this hillside.

Semtokha (2328m) At Semtokha there's a signpost to Trashigang – 546km! At the prayer wheel after the Dantak camp take the high road towards Semtokha Dzong. It starts climbing through groves of pines with great views to the dzong, then past Ozepang village (2671m) and various government agricultural projects.

Lhongtsho (2825m) **66/738KM**
There's a restaurant in Lhongtsho village next to the tall prayer flags, just after the turnip fields to the left. Climb past the checkpost (your driver will need to show your permit), past numerous water-powered prayer wheels, and eventually Dochu La comes into view.

Dochu La (3109m) **71.5/32.5KM**
Watch out for animals on the pass – there are usually some goats with a keen interest in handlebar-bag snacks. Next to the pass is a field of 108 chortens all of which may or may not be visible depending on the weather. The chortens were commissioned by Queen Ashi Dorji Wangmo in 2004 as thanks for the Bhutanese army's rout of the Bodos and ULFA from illegal training camps in the south. On a clear day you can see the eastern range of the Himalaya sprinkled across the horizon; if the clouds are low there will be no views and a very cold descent.

The road twists off the pass through blue pine forest into the pretty Punakha Valley, past a large chorten, a government planting scheme and a few small villages. As the altitude continues to drop the pines and rhododendrons give way to sub-tropical cacti and banana plants.

Bhutan, 100–200km

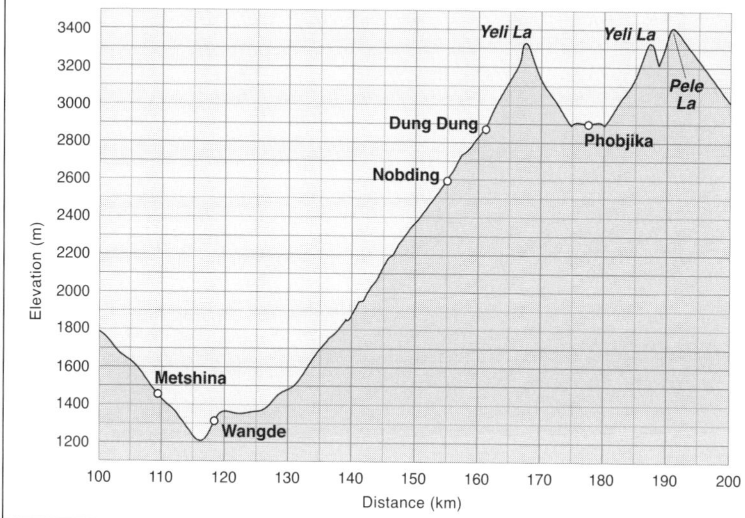

Metshina (1463m) **109.5/694.5KM**

The third village after the pass is Metshina where there's a mini roundabout – turn left here for the road to Punakha Dzong (see box p306) and Khuruthang or continue straight ahead past the restaurants on the left and the market stalls on the right for Wangde (pronounced Wong-dee).

Between Metshina and the turn-off to Wangde there are small beaches down by the river, and a dzong built by Bhutan's favourite rascal and folk hero, Lama Drukpa Kuenlay, better known as the Divine Madman because of his ribald lifestyle and unconventional teachings. Punakha Valley provides most of the sand and raw materials for new construction in Thimphu and the works traffic between the two is the busiest in Bhutan.

The descent continues all the way to the checkpost at the bridge. Cross this bridge for the 2km climb up to Wangde; the road straight ahead for southern Bhutan was closed to foreigners at the time of writing. After about 1km the road forks – right for Wangde, left for Punakha (see box p306).

Wangde (1303m) **118/686KM**

After the hairpin bend you will pass a line of wooden shacks which are Wangde's shops (eventually due to be replaced by modern concrete buildings). The road enters Wangde at the motor stand, where small shops sell snacks for the road.

DAY 3 WANGDE (1303m) to PHOBJIKA (2899m) over Yeli La (3322m) 59.7KM

WANGDE–CHUZOMSA 7.5KM
CHUZOMSA–NOBDING 29.5KM
NOBDING–DUNG DUNG 6.1KM
DUNG DUNG–PHOBJIKA TURN-OFF 5.2KM
PHOBJIKA TURN-OFF-YELI LA 1.4KM
YELI LA–PHOBJIKA 10KM

Wangde (1303m) **118/686KM**

After yesterday's swooping descent today's climb is long with the roughest, steepest part just before the pass; cyclists should expect to spend up to 7hrs in the saddle. The road to Trongsa leads north-east from the shops clustered around Wangde's motor stand. The first ten kilometres until the small village and bridge after Chuzomsa are lovely – a gentle drift through a narrow valley with a young river amongst lots of cherry trees and flowers and very little traffic.

SIDE TRIP: WANGDE TO PUNAKHA DZONG (34KM)

There's an easy day ride from Wangde to Punakha Dzong along the Puna Tsang River, which might be tempting if you've got a spare day and a bike with front suspension as the road on the eastern side of the river is a bit rough. One kilometre out of Wangde on the road to Thimphu there's a tarmac road to the right (unsigned). Take this, enjoy the tarmac while it lasts (which isn't long) and follow the river for about 8.5km until you reach a bridge on your left, which you want to cross to get to the charmless new town of Khuruthang.

From Khuruthang keep heading north for another 4.5km and finally you'll see Punakha Dzong, presiding over the confluence of the Pho and Mo Chu (father and mother) rivers. It's one of the most beautiful dzongs in Bhutan, and for three hundred years it was Bhutan's winter capital. Although Thimphu is now the capital all year round, Thimphu's monks still migrate to Punakha for the coldest months. It used to be that no Bhutanese man could wear woollies under his gho until Thimphu's abbot had moved to Punakha signalling the true onset of winter, but this custom is now mostly ignored.

An unusual feature of Punakha Dzong is the large number of cockerels wandering around. Like all dzongs, Punakha is built for defence – but with particularly good reason as it houses the *rangjung khasapani*, a vertebra of the famous Buddhist saint Tsangpa Gyare, founder of the Drukpa sect of Buddhism, and teacher of Milarepa. This vertebra is Bhutan's most famous relic, though it's originally from Ralung monastery in Tibet. The Tibetans invaded in 1639 to recover it but the Bhutanese repelled the Tibetans and got to keep their backbone – a victory that's celebrated every spring at the Punakha Serda festival.

To get back to Wangde you can either return the way you came, or climb from the petrol station at Khuruthang to the mini roundabout at Metshina and follow the main road from there.

Chuzomsa (1389m) 129.5/674.5KM

Just 4.5km after here the road crosses to the southern bank of the Dang Chu and a photogenic road sign in Dzongka and Roman script marks the start of today's steady uphill. The valley opens out into terraced hills of rice paddy, and ahead the diagonal slopes of the hills fade pleasingly into a hazy blue. Troupes of cows and monkeys saunter along the road and, as time passes, the vegetation changes from the semi-tropical bananas and cacti to marijuana and bamboo. The shop on the bend (see map opposite) sells cold drinks, biscuits and fresh datse – worth buying as the *Phama* hotel at Khelakha or restaurants in Nobding can cook it up for your lunch. On the opposite side of the valley is occasional patchwork pasture, stuck hundreds of metres above the tree line.

Nobding (2593m) 155/649KM

After the Phama hotel the climb steepens slightly to Nobding, a village with plenty of restaurants and a giant signboard showing distances within Bhutan. After Nobding, the road steepens further to Dung Dung.

Dung Dung (2872m) 161/643KM

By this time the warm and sunny morning may well have turned into a chilly and damp late afternoon but a small tea shop on the left and the next section of road will warm you up. The road visible from Dung Dung, winding steadily up the mountain towards Pele La, is the old one; unfortunately it was too prone to landslides and has fallen into disuse. Now there's 'the shortcut' which climbs up the back of the ridge, and it's both steep and rough.

Yeli La (3322m) 167.5/636.5KM

The junction to Phobjika isn't signed but it's the only junction – turn right, back on yourself, and continue to climb, now on a slightly better road, up to the Yeli La. From the pass to the valley floor the road is perfect. The descent starts off in a tight and narrow valley, which broadens slightly to squeeze in some high meadows; from Gangtey monastery the full vista of this wide, glacial valley unfolds before you.

Phobjika (2899m) 177.5/626.5KM

The Phobjika Valley is famous for its

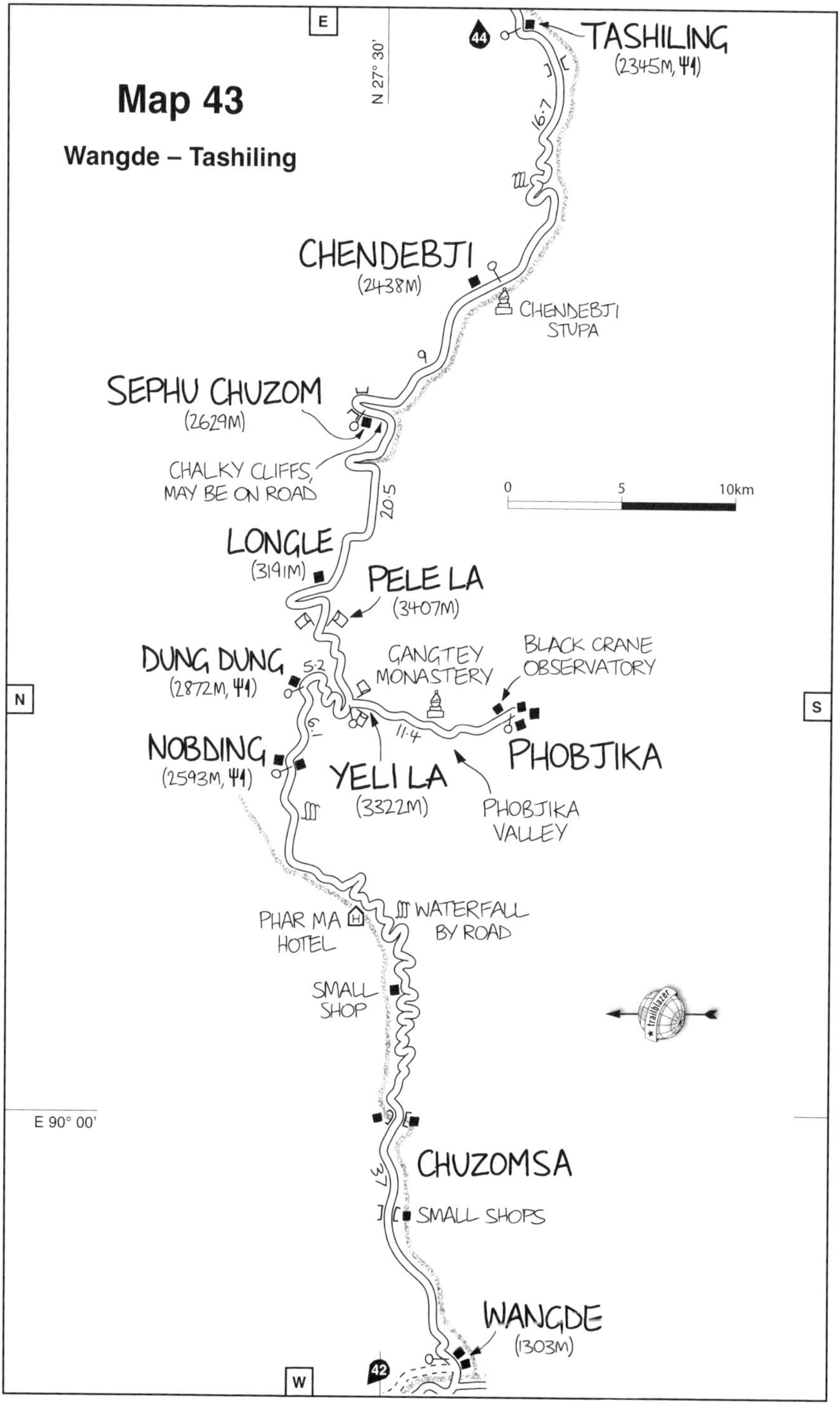
Map 43
Wangde – Tashiling
E
N 27° 30'
44
TASHILING
(2345M, Ψ4)
16.7
CHENDEBJI
(2438M)
CHENDEBJI
STUPA
9
SEPHU CHUZOM
(2629M)
CHALKY CLIFFS,
MAY BE ON ROAD
20.5
0
5
10km
LONGLE
(3191M)
PELE LA
(3407M)
DUNG DUNG
(2872M, Ψ4)
5.2
GANGTEY
MONASTERY
BLACK CRANE
OBSERVATORY
N
S
6.1
11.4
NOBDING
(2593M, Ψ4)
YELI LA
(3322M)
PHOBJIKA
PHOBJIKA
VALLEY
PHAR MA
HOTEL
WATERFALL
BY ROAD
SMALL
SHOP
trailblazer
E 90° 00'
CHUZOMSA
13.7
SMALL SHOPS
WANGDE
(1303M)
42
W

black-necked cranes who arrive from Ladakh and Tibet in early November to spend the winter here. Locals say that on arrival and departure the birds always fly around Gangtey gompa three times – a sort of *kora* (devotional circuit) on the wing. Ornithologists say that this is probably to orientate themselves. Black-necked cranes are elegant birds with a cry that sounds much like a bicycle brake. The best place for viewing them is at the Crane Observation Centre, signed off the road into Phobji village. Its telescopes overlook the marshy valley floor where the cranes love to nibble tubers and insects; there's also plenty of crane-related information and some superb photographs.

DAY 4 PHOBJIKA (2899m) to TRONGSA (2110m) over Pele La (3407m) — 79.6KM

PHOBJIKA–YELI LA 10KM
YELI LA–PELE LA 4.2KM
PELE LA–SEPHU CHUZOM 17.3KM
SEPHU CHUZOM–CHENDEBJI STUPA 9KM
CHENDEBJI STUPA–TASHILING 16.7KM
TASHILING–TRONGSA 22.4KM

Once Pele La is crossed the traffic falls away and after a few days in central Bhutan, Paro and Thimphu suddenly seem like distant metropolises. The region between the Yotong La and Ura La is known as Bumthang and it houses Bhutan's most cherished monasteries. En route is the dramatic dzong of Trongsa, which glowers over the west–east highway.

Phobjika (2899m) 177.5/626.5KM

From Yeli La to Pele La is just another 4.2km and 185m up. Between the two are the best views of the Black Mountains which separate western from central Bhutan; the Pele La is the pass over them.

Pele La (3407m) 191.5/612.5KM

This pass is marked by a large chorten, a juniper burner, strings of prayer flags and quite possibly a herd of yaks or *dzos* (yak/cow hybrid) who are partial to the dwarf bamboo that grows hereabouts. The small white-timbered houses just after the pass are the housing for Bhutan's road workers, what a contrast with India's! The descent is wonderfully fast and winding as far as Sephu Chuzom, past small villages, turnip fields and chalky cliffs.

Sephu Chuzom (2629m) 209/595KM

This is the roadhead for the Snowman trek, a tough 25-day high altitude trek through the remote Lunana region of the Bhutanese Himalaya. *Tsering's Restaurant Cum Bar* at the bridge over the Nikka Chu offers a warming cup of milky tea and some food. There is also an unusual prayer wheel out front with red and blue-faced people: portraits of cyclists going up and down passes?! From Sephu to Chendebji the road rolls gently for 9km.

Chendebji stupa (2425m) 218/586KM

Just beyond the village of Chendebji lies its famous stupa, tucked into a crook of the road by the river against a backdrop of fir trees. Built in the Nepali style, it rises in whitewashed steps to a dome, above which painted eyes gaze in all four directions before tapering off in a stepped cone. Beyond Chendebji the road rises and falls gently along the valley ridge before descending again to Tashiling.

Tashiling (2345m) 234.5/569.5KM

There's small restaurant on the right here. About 5km further on is the first view of the impressive Trongsa Dzong, and 4.5km beyond that, by the chorten, an even better view. By zip line from here, Trongsa is less than one kilometre but by road it's another 13km because of crossing the Mangde Chu (1899m), which entails a final 7km climb up to the town.

Trongsa (2110m) 257/547KM

It's easy to understand the former power of Trongsa, which, thanks to its position, dominated the east–west trade routes in Bhutan. The dzong itself is a cluster of whitewashed tin-roofed buildings with distinctive red bands on the upper storey set amid fir trees with a footpath zigzag-

Bhutan, 200–300km

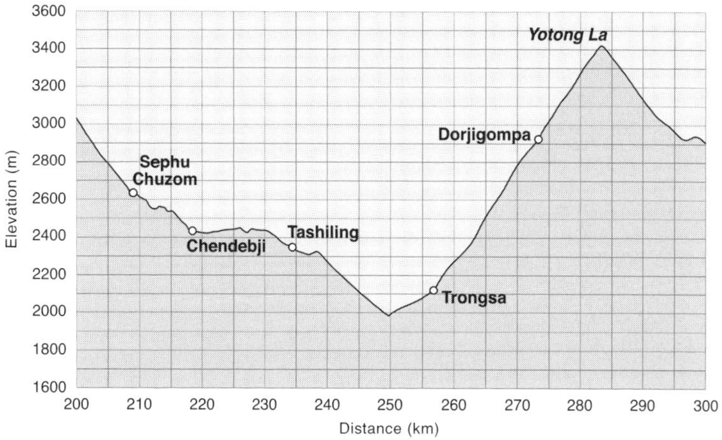

ging down to the river. The town is situated behind the dzong, and tomorrow's road to Jakar winds around the hillside above. Hotels in Trongsa are either situated next to the traffic circle or to the west near the turn-off to the dzong.

DAY 5 TRONGSA (2110m) to JAKAR (2593m) over Yotong La (3419m) and Kiki La (2848m) 63.9KM

TRONGSA–YOTONG LA 26.3KM
YOTONG LA–GAYTSA 11.7KM
GAYTSA–KIKI LA 17KM
KIKI LA–JAKAR 8.9KM

Trongsa (2110m) 257/547KM
The valley that Trongsa glowers over is often steeped in a thick mist early in the morning. If the sun is strong enough the dzong can look spectacular, wrapped in wreaths of cloud shot through with rays of sunlight. If the day is dull there will be no views and you'll be riding inside a chilly cloud for most of the morning. From Trongsa traffic circle the road immediately climbs up to Yotong La. It's a steady ascent on a good surface, with a couple of steepish sections before the tiny village at Dorjigonpa; after that the signs are to the pass itself (14km). There's no food or water (unless you can filter from springs) en route.

Yotong La (3419m) 283.5/520.5KM
There's a small road workers' camp after the pass, after which the landscape changes completely. Red bushes sprout up around the road and Christmassy conifers stretch beyond the broad pastureland and grazing horses.

Chume Valley (2946m – 2758m) This pretty valley is a respite from some long climbing up the pass. The first village is Gaytsa with its small mani wall, fields of potatoes and long fences plaited from bamboo. After Gaytsa and the two bridges are a couple of houses on the left with larger-than-life specimens of Bhutan's favourite fertility symbol, the penis; the second is lovingly detailed. There are general stores at Domkhar, and a local restaurant in Chume on the left. A little further on, the handicrafts store on the right also has a small café.

Kiki La (2848m) 312/492KM
After an enjoyable freewheel from Yotong La, Kiki La is the final kick of the day but it's a tiny pass (150m) and pleasant cycling through pine trees. From the top there's a fun descent to the Bumthang Valley floor, where strong tailwinds usually blow you along the river into Jakar.

Jakar (2593m) 321/483KM
This small town is the centre of the Bumthang Valley, one of Bhutan's most

picturesque regions. General stores, restaurants and barbers are strung out between the traffic circle and the bridge over the Bumthang; apart from the *Swiss Guest House* (see box below) most hotels are up the road towards Jakar Dzong and Khurjey Lakhang.

DAY 6 JAKAR (2593m) to GAYZA CHU (3451m) over Ura La (3569m) 69.5KM

JAKAR–MINI PASS 7.1KM
MINI PASS–TANGSIBI 16.5KM
TANGSIBI–URA LA 12.6KM
URA LA–URA 9.1KM
URA–GAYZA CHU 24.2KM

Beyond Jakar the number of tourists falls dramatically; eastern Bhutan does not boast the impressive dzongs of the west, nor its relative affluence. People are less used to tourists and facilities are more basic. In winter, the passes and descents can be freezing so be sure to carry warm clothes. As you progress east the cold recedes and the roads dip into steamy valleys full of banana trees and monkeys. If you have the time, detours up the side valleys of Lhuentse and Tashi Yangtse are highly recommended.

Jakar (2593m) 321/484KM
Stock up on treats in Jakar because the villages between here and Mongar, two days' ride away, are basic and the route is quite hard.

From Jakar the road leads east and climbs briefly to a mini pass (2563m) above the confluence of the Tang Chu and Bumthang Chu rivers. Ignore the jeep track just after the National Sheep Breeding Centre which leads to the Tang Valley. The highway crosses the little Tang Chu and starts its climb up to the Ura La pass.

Tangsibi (3022m) 344.5/459.5KM
The road carves a wide 'S' above this village, which is surrounded by fields. There's no obvious general store.

Ura La (3569m) 357/447KM
Ura La finally comes into view about 2km after a fake pass. As the sign says, 'Leave not yours! Lets keep our highway clean.' The Ura Valley unfolds below: it's the highest and most remote of Bumthang's valleys and the descent into it can be bitterly cold.

Ura (3220m) The village itself lies in a maze of fields below the ***Arya Zamlha***, a hotel and bar on the right side of the road that may be a very welcome sight. From here there's a further 3km of descent until a small bridge after which the long climb to Thrumshing La, the gateway to eastern Bhutan, starts. It's best to try to reach Gayza Chu today as the next day to Mongar is also long.

Gayza Chu (3451m) 390.5/413.5KM
This small road workers' camp 7.5km before Thrumshing La has a simple restaurant called the ***Kuenphen Hotal*** with two very basic rooms. The family is friendly and most importantly there's a bukhari, whose warmth you might be craving. Larger groups will find space to camp about 200m beyond the restaurant.

THE SWISS GUEST HOUSE, JAKAR

Many places like to call themselves 'The Switzerland of the Himalaya', but Jakar's Swiss Guest House is the real thing. This gem of a place, located on the east bank of the Bumthang Chu and a 2km ride up from Jakar Bridge, is run by the son of Fritz Maurer, a Swiss cheese-maker who came to Bhutan more than thirty years ago. The guesthouse has a cosy restaurant serving Red Panda *weissbeer* (wheat beer) on tap plus roesti, raclette, fondue and homemade bread and cheese. There is also a proper coffee machine and an internet connection. The rooms are just as alpine and cosy; en-suite doubles are wood-panelled and have rugs, a *bukhari* (wood burning stove) and powerful hot showers.

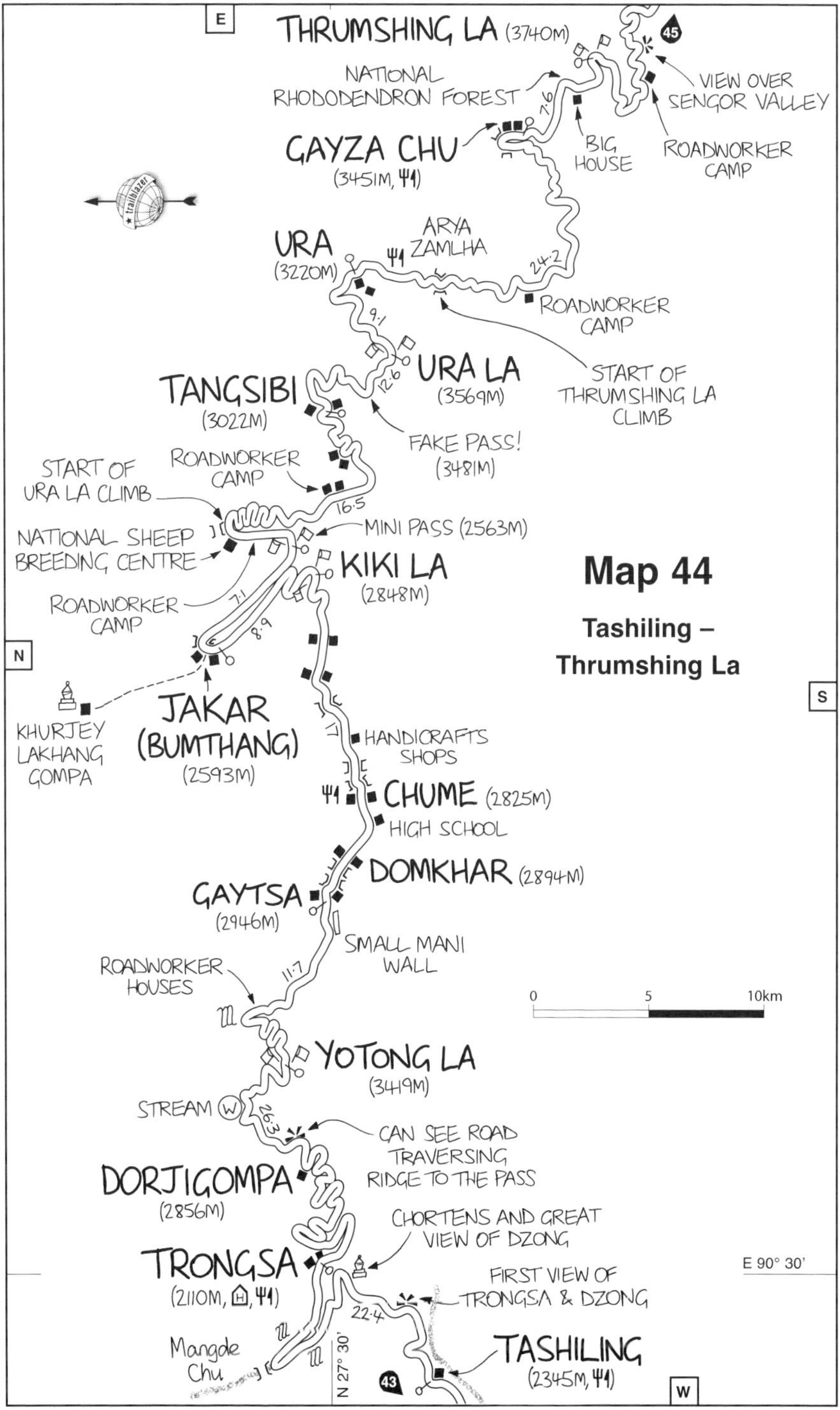
THRUMSHING LA (3740M)
NATIONAL RHODODENDRON FOREST
VIEW OVER SENGOR VALLEY
GAYZA CHU (3451M, Ψ1)
BIG HOUSE
ROADWORKER CAMP
URA (3220M)
ARYA ZAMLHA
ROADWORKER CAMP
URA LA (3569M)
TANGSIBI (3022M)
START OF THRUMSHING LA CLIMB
FAKE PASS! (3481M)
START OF URA LA CLIMB
ROADWORKER CAMP
NATIONAL SHEEP BREEDING CENTRE
MINI PASS (2563M)
KIKI LA (2848M)
ROADWORKER CAMP
Map 44
Tashiling – Thrumshing La
JAKAR (BUMTHANG) (2593M)
KHURJEY LAKHANG GOMPA
HANDICRAFTS SHOPS
CHUME (2825M)
HIGH SCHOOL
DOMKHAR (2894M)
GAYTSA (2946M)
SMALL MANI WALL
ROADWORKER HOUSES
YOTONG LA (3419M)
STREAM
CAN SEE ROAD TRAVERSING RIDGE TO THE PASS
DORJIGOMPA (2856M)
CHORTENS AND GREAT VIEW OF DZONG
TRONGSA (2110M, Ψ1)
FIRST VIEW OF TRONGSA & DZONG
TASHILING (2345M, Ψ1)
Mangde Chu
N 27° 30'
E 90° 30'
0 5 10km
7.6
24.2
9.1
12.6
16.5
7.1
8.9
17.1
11.7
26.3
22.4
45
43
E
N
S
W
trailblazer

BHUTAN

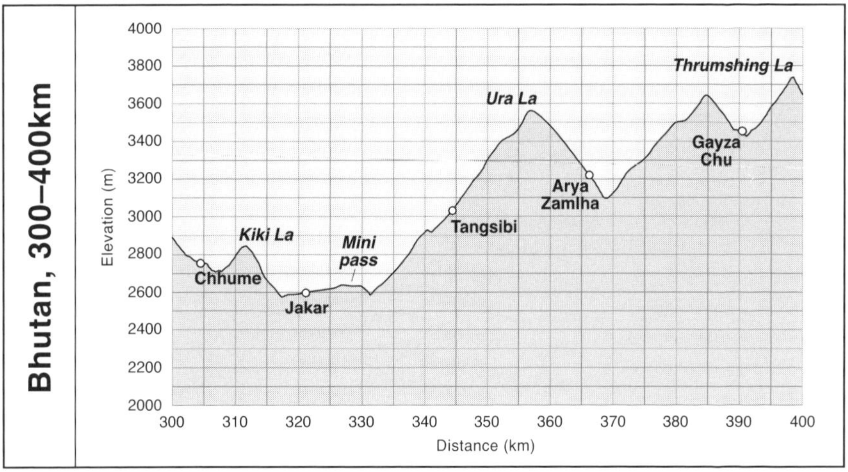

DAY 7 GAYZA CHU (3451m) to MONGAR (1595m) over Thrumshing La (3740m) 109KM

GAYZA CHU–THRUMSHING LA 7.6KM
THRUMSHING LA–SENGOR 17.1KM
SENGOR–NAMNING 20.7KM
NAMNING–YONGKOLA 19.6KM
YONGKOLA–LINGMETHANG 17.3KM
LINGMETHANG–MONGAR 26.7KM

Gayza Chu (3541m) 390.5/413.5KM

From the restaurant it's a steady climb to the top of Thrumshing La. In winter the streams are frozen here and the conifers frosted.

Thrumshing La (3740m) 398/406KM

This is the highest pass on the road and the gateway into eastern Bhutan. After what may have been a couple of long and cold days you are about to descend more than 3000m to hot and steamy Lingmethang, where monkeys frolic. This region is a national rhododendron forest and also a national park, home to red pandas. The descent from Thrumshing La to Sengor isn't steep and is often shrouded in mist.

Sengor (3043m) 415/389KM

There's a general store here and a couple of restaurants. After Sengor the descent continues until another small pass (2749m). Once this is crossed, it's all downhill to Namning. About 8km before Namning (signs count you down) the valley opens up and the hills of eastern Bhutan become visible, although they too will probably be veiled in mist. The side

THE ROAD TO THE EAST

The road between Sengor and Lingmethang is the only horizontal thing in an entirely vertical landscape so it's no surprise that it came at enormous cost. It was constructed during the second king's reign in the 1960s, when Bhutan still had a system of indentured labour (later abolished by the third king). Every family from eastern Bhutan was compelled to send one member to work on the road – which was built by hand and claimed the lives of over 200 workers. The penalty for not working, or failing to pay in kind to the local dzong, was imprisonment. As a result many Bhutanese families fled to India – particularly the northeastern states, Darjeeling and Sikkim – and have never come back. On a more positive note this section of road is reputedly excellent for bird watching.

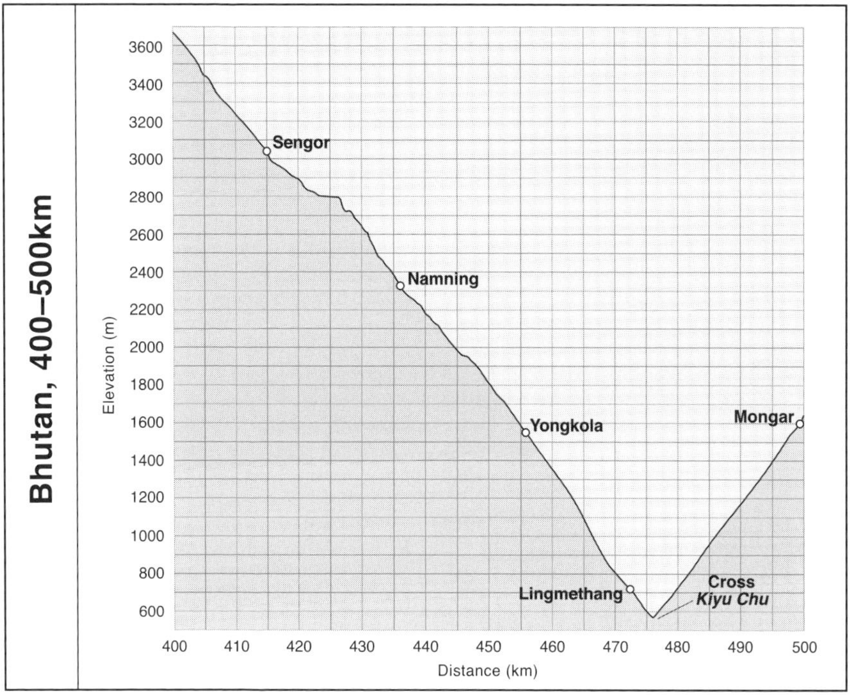

valleys before Namning are steep: no wonder there's a small temple here opposite the spring and shallow rock pool.

Namning (2327m) 436/368KM
There are just a couple of road workers' huts here.

Yongkola (1554m) 455.5/348.5KM
There's a good restaurant on the left just before the village.

Lingmethang (713m) 473/331KM
Welcome to eastern Bhutan! The simple ***Dorjee Hotel Cum Bar*** has en-suite rooms upstairs. The language spoken here is Sharchop, and in Sharchop 'methang' means sister-in-law. Apparently a local custom in eastern Bhutan (and India's northeastern states) is that if a man marries into a family of daughters, not only is he entitled to have sex with his wife, but also any of her younger unmarried sisters.

From Lingmethang the road descends to the bridge over the Karo Chu (568m), from where there's a climb up to Mongar. This will take a couple of hours but the road is often well shaded by pines, with views of the terraced wheat fields rippling down the hillsides. Keep left at the fork by the large prayer wheel: turning right leads to the Kiyu Chu powerplant, one of Bhutan's major hydro projects. The tarmac road to Lhuentse is about halfway through the climb and 16km from Lingmethang, near where there's an 'umbrella' formed by old mustard oil tins.

Mongar (1595m) 499.5/304.5KM
At the time of research, Mongar was a town under construction. The wooden shacks lining its roadsides were being replaced by concrete, albeit with a traditional facade. The shops here are basic in comparison to western Bhutan. If your brake pads need replacing do it tonight because there's a big descent tomorrow. There is one computer with internet access at the ***Dzongkha Hotel***, at the start of the road to Kori La.

DAY 8 MONGAR (1595m) to TRASHIGANG (1092m) via Kori La (2383m) 86.7KM

MONGAR–KORI LA 17.1KM
KORI LA–YADI 18.8KM
YADI–SHERICHU 17.3KM
SHERICHU–CHAZAM 24.2KM
CHAZAM–TRASHIGANG 9.3KM

Mongar (1595m) 499.5/304.5KM
From Mongar the climb to Kori La starts immediately, passing stone quarries and the small village of Kilikhar. A large chorten surrounded by prayer flags makes a good rest stop with views back down to Mongar and, on exceptionally clear days, west to the Sengor–Namning road and north as far as Tibet.

Kori La (2383m) 516.5/287.5KM
You will notice that the distances on the road signs are a little in your favour. The road off the pass is lined with prayer flags as far as the small road worker camps and villages which precede Yadi. This descent doesn't finish until Sherichu 36km away so enjoy!

Yadi (1499m) 535.5/268.5KM
The *Choeden* next to the prayer wheel is a good place to pick up some snacks to enjoy in the sunshine and warmth of Sherichu. Yadi is famous for its 'Loops' – eleven switchbacks which plunge down the hillside from the village towards the Drongmu Chu. There's a great view of them from the ridge just after Yadi; if only all roads were so flatteringly swoopy!

Sherichu (727m) 553/251KM
This roadside viewpoint has some loos (often locked) and picnic tables. The plunge from the pass ends by the bridge just below, at 612m, where there's a small hamlet with a few basic stores. The next section along the Drongmu Chu past the villages of Revidang and Rolong is undulating. After the high passes and some cold nights this section is warm and relaxed.

Chazam (696m) 577/227KM
The 9km climb up to Trashigang starts once you cross the bridge over the Drongmu Chu here. If you continue north instead you will reach Trashi Yangtse – a highly recommended detour as the valley is beautiful. If the climb up to Trashigang is very hot, keep an eye out for the small waterspout on the left 4km after the Immigration Office. The much higher road visible on the ridge above the denuded hillsides is tomorrow's task! From the traffic circle it's just 3km to Trashigang.

Trashigang (1092m) 586.5/217.5KM
As you approach Trashigang (or 'Tashigang') there's a great view of the dzong and its commanding position over the bridge at Chazam. The town itself is tucked into the crease of two valleys and is cold and dark.

DAY 9 TRASHIGANG (1092m) to KHALING (2084m) over Yongphula (2585m) 52.5KM

TRASHIGANG–PAM 5.1KM
PAM–RONGTHUNG 11.3KM
RONGTHUNG–KANGLUNG 4.9KM
KANGLUNG–YONGPHULA 9KM
YONGPHULA–GUM CHU 17KM
GUM CHU–KHALING 5.2KM

Trashigang is as far east as Bhutan's highway goes; from here it turns southwards on its journey to Samdrup Jongkhar and India's plains. In clear weather this section is stunning: deep forested ravines and blue hills that ripple into the horizon until Narphu (161km from Trashigang) when India in all her flatness appears more than 2000m below in the distance. But do not expect a gentle freewheel from Trashigang: the roads keep up the climbs until the final day and they're even steeper over here!

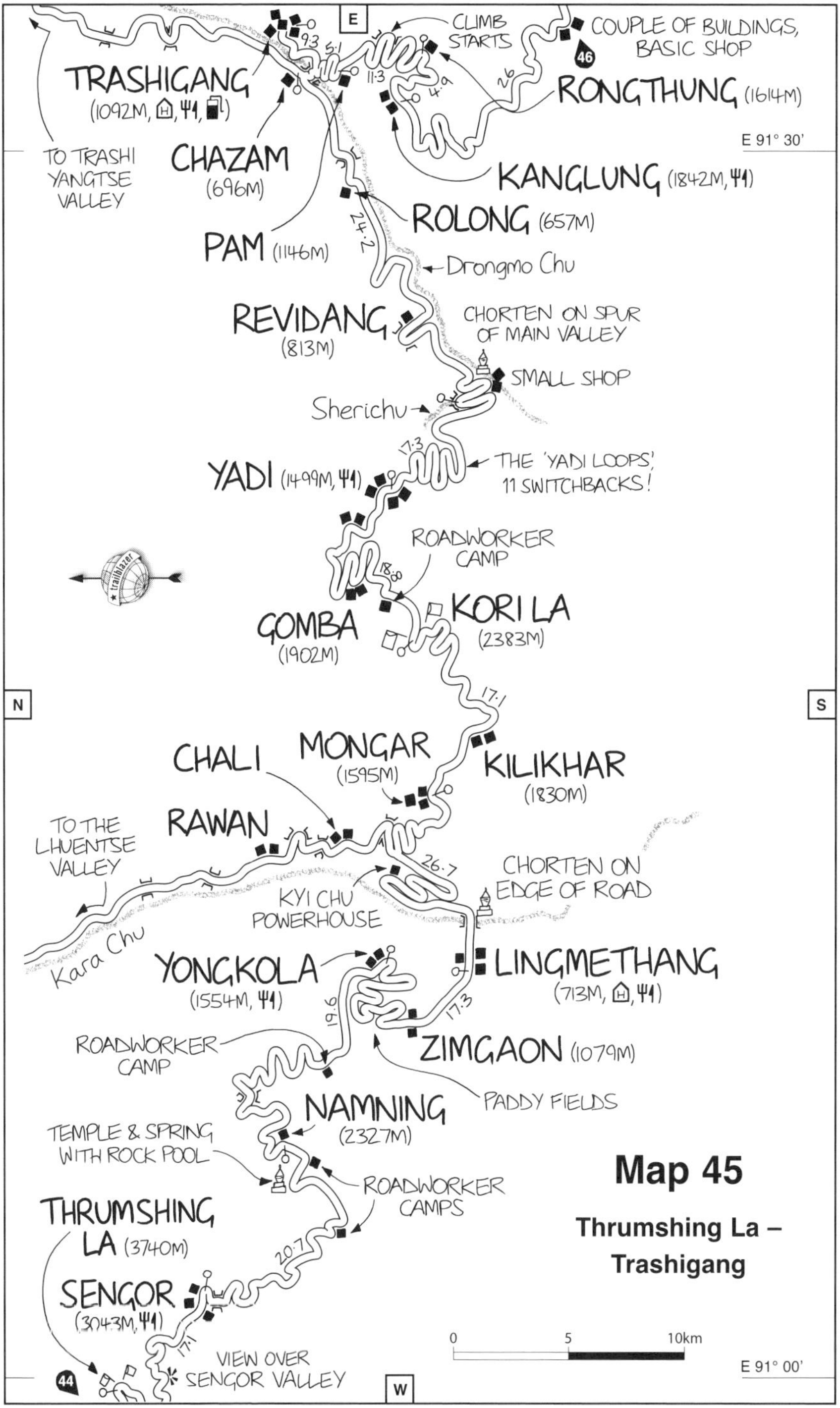

Map 45

Thrumshing La – Trashigang

BHUTAN

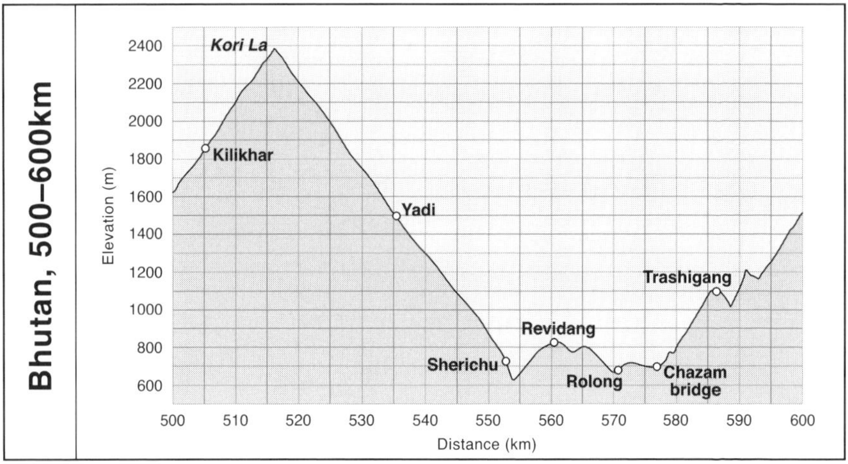

Trashigang (1092m) **586.5/217.5km**
After Trashigang, you can look forward to the pearls of wisdom that are India's Border Roads Organization road signs. Many of the old favourites are here: 'Be Gentle on my Curves' and 'Arrive in Peace, not in Pieces', as well as a new, more macabre one, 'Donate Blood in Hospital, not on Road'. There's about 31km of climbing today.

Pam (1146m) **591.5/212.5km**
The road climbs to Pam then descends to a Bailey bridge, after which it climbs again through lush forest.

Rongthung (1614m) **603/201km**
This pretty village is set amidst rice paddy. There are chortens in people's gardens and studding the rice fields. In late autumn and winter, the harvested hay is kept on platforms in the fields, which gives the impression of lots of mullets on stilts. Climbing the pass there are increasingly good views of the mountains behind Tashi Yangtse, and also a bird's eye view of the last three days' cycling – from the Sherichu Valley to Tashi Yangtse.

Kanglung (1845m) **608/196km**
About halfway up the climb, the small village of Kanglung is good for a quick coffee and some 'donuts' (small dough cannon balls), which can be found at the shed-like restaurant opposite the Sherubtse College gates. The college and Pala's General Store, just 50m before it, feature prominently in Jamie Zeppa's funny and honest memoir of teaching in Bhutan, *Beyond the Sky and the Earth*. Sherubtse College is Bhutan's premier school and the students introduce themselves very politely: 'Good morning, Sir/Madam!' but then can't help collapsing into fits of giggles with their friends.

Beyond Kanglung, there are fantastic views back to Sherichu and a range of peaks above Tashi Yangtse. If you can see those peaks you are looking at Tibet and if you look back along the road the hills on the horizon are in Arunachal Pradesh. There's a fake pass at 2249m – ignore the big tempting chorten with all the flags waving over it.

Yongphula (2375m) **617/187km**
Ignore all the signs to Yongphula too – they count you down to 0km at more chortens but the climb continues for another 5km beyond. The road finally tops out at 2585m while draping itself seductively over a series of south-facing ridges after the army camp. Dantak have erected some novel road signs along the stretch between Yongphula and Gum Chu, giving drivers a crash course (hopefully not literally) in the eight auspicious symbols of Buddhism.

Gum Chu (2217m) **634/170km**
There's a road workers' camp here and a good campsite below the stream.

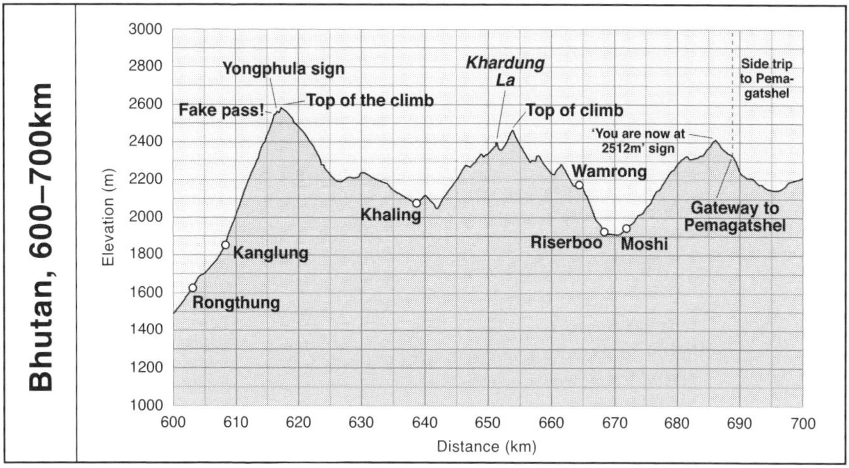

Khaling (2084m) 639/165KM
About 5km downhill from Gum Chu is the little village of Khaling where the *Hotel Sonam* has a couple of basic rooms with a shared bathroom (hot bucket).

DAY 10 KHALING (2084m) to PEMAGATSHEL (1700m) over Khardung La (2452m) 73.4KM

KHALING–KHARDUNG LA 12.9KM
KHARDUNG LA–WAMRONG 12.4KM
WAMRONG–MOSHI 7.8KM
MOSHI–PEMAGATSHEL JUNCTION 16.9KM
PEMAGATSHEL JUNC–PEMAGATSHEL 23.4KM

Khaling (2084m) 639/165KM
The road curls like a horseshoe around Khaling; below in the valley is Bhutan's School for the Blind. A little further on is Bhutan's National Weaving Centre, a definite attraction for anyone interested in textiles (no photos allowed though). After a viewpoint across to yesterday's climb the road twists around into a tiny forested valley with cows grazing and a perfect campsite up above the road on the left.

Khardung La (2384m) 652/152KM
Thankfully this pass is not nearly as high as its namesake in India (see p157). It's marked by an old chorten, prayer flags fluttering above the road and some bamboo road workers' huts. There are great views of the valley to the east, and also of the road's continued climb… this isn't a pass! The surrounding landscape feels quite Swiss – cows, trees, farmsteads and sloping pasture.

About 3km further on the road reaches the top of this particular climb at 2452m and changes course from south to west. There are great views here of the valleys to the south and west, and the road wriggling its way down to Riserboo.

Wamrong (2158m) 664.5/139.5KM
There's a small restaurant and general stores here – worth visiting if you're hungry as there's another long climb coming up in 8km, after Moshi.

Moshi (1913m) 672/132KM
On the climb out of Moshi there are pastoral views of farmsteads and mustard fields, glaring yellow against the green and blue of the hills. The road climbs along the ridge, past a pretty chorten on the right festooned with prayer flags, and then switches between ridge views, topping out at 2407m, where there's a road sign congratulating you on reaching 2512m.

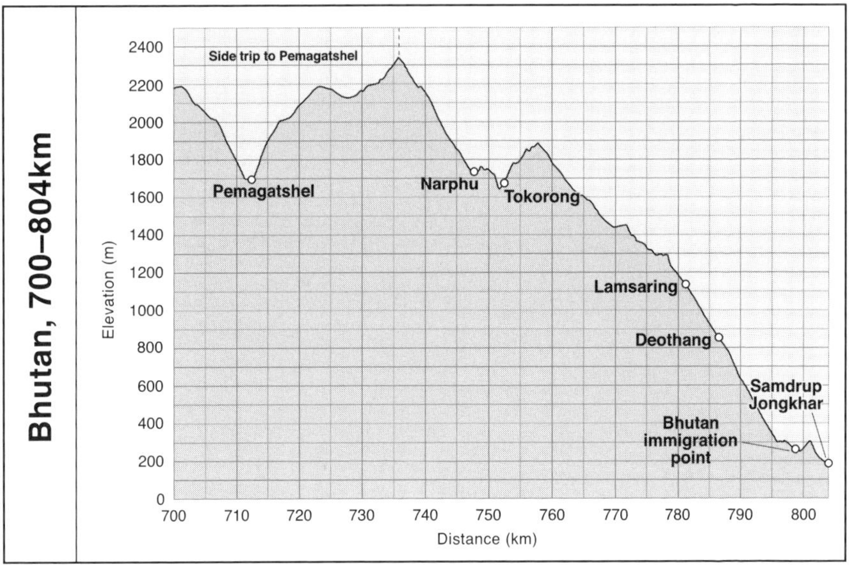

Pemagatshel junction (2340m) 689/115km

The road to Pemagatshel is marked by a large ceremonial gateway adorned with two thunder dragons. From here, the road descends then climbs for a short while to lots of prayer flags before descending again past the police post (they'll ask to see your permit) and into a set of switchbacks. Keep an eye out for Pemagatshel's own ceremonial entrance gate on the left-hand side on a switchback corner – if you miss it you'll end up in the gypsum mines at the bottom of the valley. These mines explain the number of Tatas rumbling up and down the valley.

Pemagatshel (1697m) 712.5/91.5km

Pemagatshel is tiny, just a cluster of shops along the street. There's a couple of restaurants and a dive of a guesthouse; the only other accommodation is at the government guest house (usually reserved for officials, but try your luck) which is at the top of the tarmac road to your left at the bottom of the town.

DAY 11 PEMAGATSHEL (1697m) to SAMDRUP JONGKHAR (188m) 91.4km

Pemagatshel–P'gatshel Junc 23.4km
Pemagatshel Junction–Narphu 11.6km
Narphu–Tokorong 5km
Tokorong–Deothang 34km
Deothang–Samdrup Jongkhar 17.4km

Pemagatshel (1697m) 712.5/91.5km

This is it, the final day. Return to the main highway for the big descent into India.

Standing under the ceremonial gateway at the Pemagatshel turn-off, looking out over Bhutan's endless blue ridges flowing like waves into the distance, it's hard to believe that in just a few hours you will leave the mountains and be standing at near sea-level on India's plains. Between here and there is a really fun 2000m descent which loops through the trees; so it's hard to feel too sad.

Between the junction and Narphu the road switches views from each side of a ridge. Just before Narphu there's a great view down to the village and the particularly bendy stretch of road, even by Bhutanese standards, which leads to it. On a clear day the plains of India stretch away endlessly on the horizon – a saddening sight because these mountain roads are such fun. Up above perches Yongle Gompa. Watch out for the baba

Map 46

Kanglung – Samdrup Jongkhar

(ascetic) at the Shiv Mandir shrine. There are some incongruous urinals opposite.

Narphu (1723m) 747.5/56.5KM

Narphu itself is just eight or so houses long, with a couple of simple shops. Just beyond it is a police checkpoint where your guide will need to show an eastern Bhutan permit.

Tokorong (1675m) 752.5/51.5KM

How rude – a climb! It starts from the ridge covered in prayer flags, just before the simple village of Tokorong, and lasts until just after the big house at Sekpashing, 4.5km away.

After Sekpashing you will fairly fly down the road, except where it's in a bad condition, past the village of Lamsaring (1139m) to the large army camp at Deothang. This bird's eye view of the border topography makes it clear how hard it must be to patrol: jungle covers the hillsides as far as the eye can see.

Deothang (851m) 786.5/17.5KM

After the army camp and its memorial to Dantak labourers be sure to keep going down the switchbacks, and definitely keep going past the Yangdong restaurant, whose food is so hot that it fells even chilli-proof Bhutanese. About 2km further on the ***Sangy View*** restaurant on the right looks like a better choice for lunch. From here it's just under 15km to Samdrup Jongkhar, which will take mere minutes. There's an immigration checkpoint just before the town, where your guide needs to show your Bhutanese permits.

Samdrup Jongkhar (188m) 804/0KM

The guards on the bridge into Samdrup Jongkhar may ask you to push your bike, which is no way to finish such a long journey! The ***TLT Hotel*** is comfortable with a large restaurant and small terrace; it's also set back from the main roads so is a bit quieter. Your travel agent will help arrange your exit from Bhutan to Guwahati, northeast India's main transport hub. The 100km journey takes about two hours by taxi; expect to pay around Rs1500. For safety reasons the car must have Assamese number plates. Samdrup Jongkhar is far easier and safer to navigate than Guwahati so pack your bike here: if you don't have a bike box electrical shops in Samdrup Jongkhar will sell you a large cardboard box for around Rs25 and general stores sell masking tape. No matter what your Indian taxi driver may say, you must get an exit stamp from Bhutan's immigration office which is next to Bhutan Gate. Indian immigration is 10km down the road at Darra: look for the hut on the left signed 'Foreigner Checkpoint'.

GUWAHATI

Because of the various separatist militias in Assam, this polluted and congested city on the banks of the Brahmaputra is filled with barbed wire and armed police. Slogans everywhere illustrate the tension: 'No Bodoland No Rest' versus 'Army is Your Friend. Help Army Curb Insurgency.' However, Guwahati has the best transport links in northeast India with an airport (due to start international flights at the end of 2008) and large railway station with trains to Delhi, Kolkata, Mumbai and even Bangalore. The best trains are the superfast ones: the Rajdhani Express to Delhi (28hrs) or the Saraighat Express to Kolkata (18hrs). While waiting for your connection the ***Hotel Nova*** in Fancy Bazaar has a large restaurant and en-suite rooms (Rs300) with TV which is the only entertainment you'll get as the streets empty at night. Taxis from Fancy Bazaar out to the airport cost Rs350 for the 22km and take about 1hr 30mins.

APPENDICES

Appendix A: Trans-Tibet

The following two routes are included for cyclists wishing to continue across Tibet from **Kashgar** or **Lhasa**. Many thanks to Peter Quaife (💻 www.crazyguyonabike.com/pq) for the Kashgar to Lhasa route description and to Robin Searle and Erika Bird (💻 www.travelblog.org/Bloggers/Banchory-to-the-Bosphorous-by-Bike) for the distances, altitudes and route information for Kashgar to Lhasa and Lhasa to Zhongdian.

THE HIMALAYAN EPIC: KASHGAR TO LHASA

In a world where human influence is difficult to escape and help is just a phone call away, the ride from Kashgar to Lhasa is like stepping back to a time when travel carried real risks. This isn't a prepackaged "adventure" sterilized by the constraints of insurance and health & safety. It's a **long, lonely route** with terrible road conditions, unbridged rivers, sustained high altitude, little in the way of supplies and potential problems with the Chinese authorities. Eastern Tibet has more spectacular scenery and the south has more cultural interest, but this western route is unbeatable if you want remoteness and the sense of a **truly epic journey**. With your back to the road, not only are there no people, there's no evidence that there have ever been people. There aren't many places where you can experience that level of isolation, particularly on a bike. If things go badly wrong you're days, even weeks, from medical help and there's no way of getting a helicopter to airlift you out. The ride is **technically illegal** but for reasons which are hard to fathom, the usual restrictions applying to travel in the region aren't usually enforced against cyclists. This gives you a level of freedom tourists in Land Cruisers accompanied by Chinese minders can only dream about.

The route is exclusively in territory annexed and occupied by China between the 1940s and 1960s. The construction of the road started the Sino-Indian war of 1962 – despite the lack of people this region is at the centre of local power politics. It is manageable though, and every year a trickle of hardy cyclists make it through.

As there are so few navigational decisions to make en route the tables of distances and altitudes on the following pages should suffice. **Passes** are marked in italics, **towns or villages** with food and accommodation are marked in bold, **major towns/cities** are marked in capitals. Alternative place names are also given.

ROUTE INFORMATION

- **Start / finish** Kashgar (Xinjiang) / Lhasa (Tibet)
- **Distance** 3000km with 27,000m of climbing; 3109km if take route from Saga past Shishapangma Base Camp (see p329)
- **Altitude min / max** 1260m (Yarkand) / 5400m (Quishan La, Tibet)
- **Passes** 31 (nine over 5000m)
- **Suggested duration** Reckon on at least 9 weeks riding, 10 weeks including getting visas in Hong Kong (see below) and getting to and from Kashgar & Lhasa
- **Road conditions** The Chinese are laying tarmac on Highway 219 but for the most part it is a dirt or sand road which is often corrugated. Since 2007 road workers have been replacing many of the missing river bridges.
- **When to go** April–October.

July and August is the rainy season which gets more intense as you travel east. The road is rideable during the rains but can get muddy.

Early or late in the season be prepared for intense cold.

- **What to take** Previous experience of riding in remote regions is essential, as is camping kit. Ability to carry 15 litres of water and five days' food. Running big tyres (eg Schwalbe Marathon XR 2.35) half-flat on rough sections works well. All necessary bike spares. The bike (and you!) must be able to endure prolonged bad roads.
- **Visas & permits** A standard Chinese two-month tourist visa will not suffice – British citizens should apply in Hong Kong for a three-month visa. Legally, a permit is required to ride this route, but they are not issued to independent travellers. Usually cyclists are tolerated but it's best to keep a low profile in Kashgar and be aware of the current situation. **The security situation in Tibet can change without warning** so check before you set off. Clampdowns usually follow pro-Tibet protests, but can happen at any time. Most cyclists get away with paying a Y300 fine in Ali and Y50 for a permit but if security is tight you will have to dodge checkpoints at night.
- **Direction** Since 2007 this ride can be ridden in both directions, though most people ride from Kashgar to Lhasa. Riding east–west means more down than up and tackling the toughest section (Ali to Kargilik) later on when you are properly acclimatized and toughened up.
- **Planning** UK–Hong Kong flights can cost as little as £250 if booked well in advance. From Hong Kong it's cheapest to travel to Guangzhou or Shenzen on the Chinese mainland by train, then onwards to Urumchi and Kashgar or Chengdu and Lhasa.

Those travelling overland from Europe to China as part of a longer tour can currently obtain a three-month Chinese visa in Islamabad, Pakistan and Almaty, Kazakhstan, though visa regulations can change at any time.

- **Maps** No map is totally correct for this route and all of them disagree with each other. The best available in the West is the Gecko Himalaya Tibet map (£11.95 from Stanfords). Available locally in Kashgar and Lhasa are road atlases for Chinese truck drivers which give place names in Chinese characters. The best one currently has a dark/black cover with a picture of a steering wheel on it.

Kashgar to Kargilik – across the Taklamakan

Kashgar to Kargilik is **almost completely flat** and skirts the edge of the Taklamakan Desert. It can be done in two days camping at the midpoint (desert, no water) or in three days staying in hotels.

For the most part the route is in desert oases and irrigated farmland, although there are regular stretches of desert with a few sand dunes. Sometimes the snow-capped Karakoram and Kunlun Shan mountains are visible in the distance.

Navigation is simple – just follow Highway 315. Road signs are non-existent for the most part, so finding your way out of Kashgar and Yarkant is a little tricky. Town plans of Kashgar are available at the Seman and Chini Bagh hotels; in Yarkant you'll have to ask around. Kilometre markers confirm when you're on the right road. **Food and drink** is available regularly, the road is excellent and traffic is moderate. The longest stretch with no supplies or water is 53km at the midpoint.

It's wise to **keep a fairly low profile** in Kashgar. There's no need to be paranoid, but don't tell locals about your plans, especially if they work in tourism and don't attempt to apply for a permit – you won't get one and you'll only draw attention to yourself.

KASHGAR TO KARGILIK

KM	KM MARKER & PLACE		ALT (M)	REMARKS	TOTAL KM
0	–	**KASHGAR / KASHI**	1310m	Take Highway 315. Tarmac from here to km marker 93 on Hway 219	0
70	–	Yenisgar	1400m	Town, good stores, hotel	70
50	–	Kizer (?)	1310m	Small town, shops. Last water for 50km	120
53	–	Quarak	1310m	Food, water	173
27	–	**YARKANT / YARKAND**	1260m	City: hotels, restaurants, shops, internet. Turn left off Hway 315 to reach it.	200
65	–	**YECHENG / KARGILIK**	1340m	City: hotels, restaurants, shops, internet. Turn off for 219 to Tibet. Last big town until Ali in west Tibet.	265

Kargilik to Ali – crossing the Kunlun Shan, Aksai Chin and entering Tibet

This section is where the adventure really begins. You'll be **travelling illegally**, at **extreme altitudes** on a terrible road with little in the way of supplies. **Strong winds** are the norm. Your reward is an amazing sense of isolation, astonishing desert and mountain scenery, the feeling of being on an epic journey and one of the greatest cycling adventures in the world.

Follow Highway 315 out of town, and look out for the Km0 marker for Highway 219 on the right after around 6km. There's no sign, but the marker is very obvious at a road junction.

The first section crosses the fearsome **Kunlun Shan mountains**, one of the most inhospitable and remote mountain ranges on the planet. It's extremely dry, very high and almost entirely uninhabited. In its 3000km length, only two roads cross it, Highway 219 being one of them.

The next section is the infamous **Aksai Chin plateau**, previously part of India but annexed by China in 1962. Although its altitude is around 5000m, it's mostly flat with rounded hills and snow-capped peaks in the distance and looks like a set from Star Trek. There's almost no water and apart from a couple of army bases, no inhabitation. As you head east and cross at last into **Tibet**, increased rainfall makes life possible and the first impoverished villages and nomad encampments appear. The continued high altitude still means it's cold and inhospitable, and you wonder why people would choose to live here.

The last five days into Ali are altogether more civilized. There are villages every couple of days, the altitude is a little lower and there's even some tarmac. By the time you get to Ali you'll be in desperate need of a wash and a decent meal. It's not a very appealing place, but the luxury more than makes up for it. Ali is on the infant Indus River. From here it flows down into Ladakh in India, then into Pakistan where it's crossed by the Karakoram Highway.

If you're heading east, the **most significant checkpoint** is in Kudi, not far into the Chiragsaldi climb. If you're going to be sent back, this is the most likely place for it to happen. Under normal circumstances your name will be entered into a big ledger and you'll be asked where you're going. Say you're following Highway 219 – this is sensitive border territory and the military don't like you straying far from the road. If you do get turned back, many cyclists have got through by creeping past the checkpoint early in the morning before it gets light – but beware of dogs if you do that. Remember that the military aren't too bothered about the legality of your journey (that's the job of the PSB) but they don't want you anywhere near their operations.

In Ali you're likely to be accosted by the PSB (tourist police) who will fine you (Y300) and sell you a permit (Y50) for the next section. Opinion is divided about whether it's worth doing this – and it's easily avoided if you don't want to spend the money. Although your permit is asked for at checkpoints, many cyclists get through without. It's not an unpleasant experience – they know that Kashgar won't issue permits to individual travellers and seem embarrassed about the fine. You'll be sat down for a nice cup of tea and a chat. Bear in mind though that this situation could easily change – a clamp-down or a change of staff could make Ali a real problem for cyclists.

Altitude sickness is the biggest danger on this stretch. In a short period of time you'll be up to 5000m which is high enough to cause significant problems. Make sure you understand how AMS works, and what to do about it when it happens. At the very least take several easy days on the ascent of the Chiragsaldi Pass which ascends from 2500m to almost 5000m in one brutal slog, ideally sleeping lower than the highest point you reached that day. An **altimeter** is very useful to make sure you get this right – and be ready to turn back if necessary. Bear in mind that even after crossing the first high pass, AMS can catch up with you. After the Khitai Pass, there's no way of losing significant altitude so make sure you're fully acclimatized before then. Many people also find that spending months at high altitude saps energy, making riding tough. Others thrive on it!

Water is another other big issue. There are long stretches where no water is available (bear in mind that many of the lakes are salty) so you need to be able to carry at least 10–15 litres; much more if you want a decent wash. Sometimes you'll be able to scrounge water from truck drivers and the army, but don't count on it.

Finally you'll need to be able to carry **food** – at least five days' supply. The staple is instant noodles, which are neither tasty nor nutritious. You can pep them up a bit by adding extras – the Chinese shrinkwrap all sorts of peculiar vegetables and tofu, you can sometimes find raisins and dried mushrooms, and biscuits are widely available. Army biscuits are the best – they must be the most concentrated form of calories anywhere and are ideal for the hungry cyclist. If you have a strong stomach, you can buy army rations in metal tins or try some of the dubious highly processed meat products most shops sell. On this section **a decent multivitamin is essential** – however hard you try your diet will be terrible.

KARGILIK TO ALI

KM	KM MARKER	PLACE	ALT (M)	REMARKS	TOTAL KM
–	0	**YECHENG / KARGILIK**	1340m	Road forks at end of town, turn right for Highway 219 at KM0 marker. No water for next 61km and end of flat roads!	265
62	62	Village	1890m	Basic shops, small restaurants	327
9	71	Pusa	2120m	Small village, basic shops and restaurants.	336
22	93	End of tarmac	2570m	Now on good dirt road	358
7	100	Akmeqit	2690m	Small Village. Water but no food.	365

KARGILIK TO ALI *(cont'd)*

KM	KM MARKER & PLACE		ALT (M)	REMARKS	TOTAL KM
4	104	Start climbing pass	2700m		369
8	112	*Pass*	3300m		377
14	126	Village	2570m	Army base and village. No shop.	391
5	133	Army camp	2590m	Tarmac starts. Vicious dogs here.	398
27	160	**KUDI**	2970m	Basic shops and restaurants, army camp, roadworker camp. **Checkpoint** at end of village.	425
34	194	Start climbing pass	4030m	Tarmac ends, hairpins start	459
8	206	Old roadworker camp	4300m	Abandoned – good place to camp as is next to river	471
11	217	*Chiragsaldi Pass*	4980m	Steep switchbacks for last few km. Can see K2 if climb above road.	482
24	241	**Mazar**	3800m	Truckstop with small restaurants, shops, dormitory. Turn left up valley for Ali. Road corrugated with lots of gravel	506
51	292	Start climbing pass	4090m	Less gravel on road. Water.	557
17	309	*Xaidulla Pass / Keycha Daban / Kirgizjangal*	4955m	Steep climb. First water after pass at km317. Road gravelly and corrugated	574
15	324	Abandoned roadworker camp	4420m	Water here	589
16	340	Abandoned roadworker camp	3950m	Water here	605
14	354	End of descent	3615m	Lowest point of Karakax He valley. Most maps incorrectly show Xaidulla here.	619
10	364	**Xaidulla / Shahidulla**	3670m	Grim truckstop and army village. Shops, restaurants, dorms. Bad road beyond here.	629
61	425	*Kosbel Pass* (shortcut of river bend)	4290m	Bad downhill with gravel and stones back into Karakax He valley	690
12	437	Kangxiwar	4030m	End of descent, roadworker camp, abandoned village to the right for camping	702
50	487	**Dahongliutan**	4220m	Basic shops and restaurants, dormitory. Road corrugated	752
25	512	Abandoned roadworker camp	4630m	Water. Steep climb from here up to Aksai Chin	777
6	518	Start of the Aksai Chin / Soda Plains	4945m	Road OK, sometimes sandy	783
18	536	Khitai Pass	5190m	Steady uphill climb to pass	801
9	545	Freshwater spring	4930m	Spring in bend of road. Road mostly sandy and corrugated	810
33	578	Tianshuihai	4735m	Army base and river. Road still bad	843
57	635	Start climbing pass	4960m	Road corrugated and sandy with frequent river crossings	900
15	650	Lake	–	Slightly salty, freshwater inflows	915
10	660	Bigger lake	5075m	Road improves, freshwater inflows	925
12	672	*Pass*	5205m	End of Aksai Chin. Road OK but gravelly	937
4	676	**Tielong / Si Ren Gou**	5005m	Truckstop with basic shops and restaurants, dorms	941
14	690	*Satsum La*	5350m	Road OK, drops to beautiful plain	955
13	703	*Small pass*	5190m	Turquoise lake comes into view	968
4	707	Ceremonial archway over road		Road markers every 5km from here	972
5	712	Start climbing pass	5080m	Lungmo Lake	977
3	715	*Small pass*	5170m	Changthang Nature Preserve. Short and steep uphill on bad road	980
5	720	*Pass*	5265m	Sometimes a nomad camp on the pass. Road OK. Tibetan border.	985
11	731	Sumxi	5230m	First Tibetan town with one shop (noodles and beer). Unreliable dorm and tent restaurant, quite grim. Road corrugated	996
10	741	*Quishan La*	5400m	Highest pass of trip. Very bad road on descent. Freshwater spring circa 20km after pass	1006

KARGILIK TO ALI ***(cont'd)***

KM	KM MARKER & PLACE		ALT (M)	REMARKS	TOTAL KM
49	790	Descent finishes at marshy river valley		Scattered houses, road generally bad, river alongside	1055
38	828	**Domar**	4550m	**Checkpoint**. Army camp, restaurants, dorms / hotels, good shops, bakery, petrol, welders. No water between here and Pangong Tso. Road sandy	1093
17	845	*Domar Pass*	4655m	Steady gentle climb up but corrugated road on descent.	1110
50	895	Pangong Tso	4150m	Freshwater river before main lake. Scattered empty nomad houses, road stony. Lake stretches into India and in sunny weather is beautiful camp spot.	1160
23	918	**Village**	4250m	Fish restaurant, big new hotel. Road OK	1183
12	930	Tarmac!	–	Tarmac until 1259km marker (2007). Km markers every km again	1195
3	933	**Rutok Xian**	4350m	Expensive hotel, good shops, restaurants, market. Turn left off highway into town. Next shop 125km away in Ali.	1198
92	1025	*La-me La*	4840m	No water for circa 20km before pass and between pass and Ali	1290
33	1058	**ALI / SHIQUANHE / SENGE KHABAB / GAR / GARTOK**	4300m	Ali is capital of the prefecture with good hotels, a supermarket, ATM, internet and hot showers.	1323

Ali to Saga – past Mt Kailash

Heading east the ride becomes easier. Higher rainfall and lower altitudes means more people live here. Availability of water, supplies, shelter, and restaurants are much more regular. With people of course comes cultural interest, the highlights on this section being the koras around Mt Kailash and Lake Mansarovar.

But don't be lulled into a false sense of security. The road is still terrible, there are some long gaps between villages, and the wind is a constant problem. The rainfall means there are many more **river crossings**, often with no bridges. Water levels tend to be lower early in the morning because glacial runoff is lower at night.

From Ali take the road across the Indus and just keep going. There are no turnings to worry about till you get to the Friendship Highway just before Lhatse. Alternatively you can take the northern route. Cyclists rarely go this way because it's further (by 250km), more remote, and bypasses Mt Kailash and Lake Mansarovar. However, there are fewer rivers to ford and it crosses the Semo La (5565m), generally reckoned to be the highest road in the world, despite what the *Guinness Book of Records* says (see p157). It rejoins Highway 219 7km west of Raga.

From Saga there is also a rough road south (168km) which crosses three passes and joins the Friendship Highway at the base of Lalung La. Choosing this route means you can take in Shishapangma Base Camp en route to the Friendship Highway and Everest Base Camp from Tingri, though it bumps up the total distance to 3109km.

There are a few worthwhile **side trips** on the section from Ali to Lhatse. The first and hardest is a visit to the ancient Guge Kingdom. The turning is on the right just before Namru, a day or so out of Ali. The road is in a much worse state than Highway 219, includes a lot of climbing, and the deep sand makes it unrideable in places. In the rainy season the mud is diabolical. It crosses two 5300m+ passes before descending through spectacular canyons to 3300m and the amazing Guge ruins. Another road returns you to 219 near Bauer. The loop is around 260km and allowing for sightseeing should take around a week. It cuts out an easy but dull 60km of tarmac riding on Highway 219.

Few riders come this way without visiting the truly squalid town of Darchen and doing the 53km kora around **Mt Kailash**. Buddhists believe Kailash is the centre of the universe and Hindus believe it's the home of Shiva. It's also sacred to the Bon, the pre-Buddhist Tibetan religion. For them, walking around the mountain washes away the sins of a lifetime, but don't get too excited, it doesn't apply to non-believers. Still, it's a beautiful walk with a wonderful atmosphere and isn't to be missed. Darchen is visible to the left a few kilometres off 219 not long after Kailash comes into view. Just head towards it on vague tracks. Most Westerners take three days to do the kora, but having cycled here, you'll be much better acclimatised and fitter than everyone else, so two days with an overnight stop in the monastery before the Dolma La is realistic. Tibetans do it in one day. No need for a tent – just warm clothes, some food and waterproofs. A visit to **Darchen** also means you can avoid the most difficult river crossing on the highway. Leave town along the same track you used at the end of the kora. Where the path swings left into a side valley by a village, you should be able to see a footbridge over the river. Cross it then head towards the highway on narrow, easy-to-ride footpaths.

Shortly after Darchen is the other major pilgrimage site in the area, **Lake Mansarovar**. It's the holiest lake in Tibet, is also sacred to Hindus and has a 100km kora which fewer people do. Turn right in the dusty town of Barka and follow the rough track over a pass and down to Chiu village and monastery on the lakeshore. Darchen to Chiu is around 40km and takes half a day. It's an idyllic camp spot with a basic restaurant and shop. You can return to 219 on the kora route, but be aware that the first 15km on the lakeshore is mostly too soft to ride, but the pushing is worth it. As it leaves the shore the ground firms up and it's a wonderful ride back to the highway, which it joins 10km or so before Horqu. **Horqu** is an important supply stop as there is almost nothing along the road until Paryang, over 230km east. For the older and Tibetan part of Horqu head towards the lake as you enter town.

From Horqu the road climbs continuously towards the **Maryum La**, the highest point on the Ali–Lhatse section, crossing one smaller pass and skirting the vast Kongyn Tso salt lake on the way. Herds of *kiang* (Tibetan wild ass) can usually be spotted on the extensive grassland plains around the lake and before the pass. Maryum La also marks the border between Ngari and Shigatse prefectures.

Descending the pass you reach an **army checkpoint** before crossing an enormous grassy plain that stretches east all the way to **Paryang**, a regular stop-off for tourist jeeps running between Lhasa and Kailash. The Himalaya form an ever present and surreal backdrop to the endless grass and sand dunes.

East of Paryang the route re-enters mountains and crosses two small passes before descending to the Tsangpo/Brahmaputra river and emerging to another broad grassy plain and New Zhongba. This is a new Chinese town;

the more charming, but less modern, Old Zhongba and its monastery are further east. Dhaulagiri can be clearly seen to the south from the plains around New Zhongba in clear conditions.

Continuing further east villages become more frequent. East of Niugu the road enters the valley of the Mia Zhu River and passes several impressive ruined fortifications before crossing the river. Soon after this bridge Dargyeling monastery sits above the road on the left. From Dargyeling village there is only one small climb to a pass before the important town of Saga.

ALI TO SAGA

KM	KM MARKER & PLACE	ALT (M)	REMARKS	TOTAL KM
–	1058 **ALI**	4300m		1323
24	1082 *Pass*	4270m	Fast descent off pass	1347
39	1121 Bridge over Gar river	4280m	Water here. Short climb to Namru	1386
10.5	1131.5 Namru	4330m	Old village. Turn off to Zanda, Tholing monastery and Guge Kingdom	1396.5
2	1133.5 **Namru**	4330m	New village with dorm, restaurants, shop	1398.5
7.5	1141 *Small pass*	4730m	Steepish climb	1406
20	1161 Small village	4480m	Teahouse and basic shop	1426
31	1192 Bauer	4575m	Grim army base with basic restaurants, Tibetan teahouses. Another turn off to Zanda at 1190km	1457
9	1201 Small Village	4630m	Last water before pass. Small teahouse/shop.	1466
17	1218 Jerko La	4820m	Road follows river from here to Moincer	1483
25	1243 **MOINCER / MISAR / MENSI**	4340m	Important town. Restaurants, shops, dorms. Turn left to old Tibetan town, expensive Chinese hotels on highway. Sometimes a **checkpoint** before town	1508
16	1259 Tarmac ends	4630m	End of tarmac and road markers in 2007. Road OK from here	1524
27	– *Pass*	4820m	First view of Mt Kailash!	1551
18	– Turn off to Darchen & Kailash kora	4630m	Entry fee on highway into town; short-cut on rough track with river crossing avoids it	1569
6	– **Darchen**	4680m	Restaurants, shops, hotels. Starting point for the pilgrim circuit (53km) of Mt Kailash but is filthy.	1575
23	– **Barka**	4620m	Shops, restaurants, dorms	1598
24	– **HORQU** and Mansarovar Lake	4600m	Shops, restaurant and hotel in old town. Stock up here – next shops are 231km away in Paryang. At junction 20km before pass go straight	
49	– *Pass*	4840m	Bad road – stony, sandy and corrugated until Maryum La	1622
3	– Kongyn Tso	4800m	Lake is salty but feeder rivers are freshwater	1671
18	– End of lake	–	Nomad houses by bridge. Last water before pass is 9km from here	1692
24	1465 *Maryum La*	5225m	Border Ngari / Shigatse (Xigaze) Prefecture	1716
23	1488 **Army checkpoint**	4800m	Usually only a passport check. Fill water bottles at river 1km after checkpoint as no other water before pass. Road very bad	1739
18	1506 *Small pass*	4820m	Road goes from sandy to OK to sandy and corrugated	1757
30	1536 Tea tent by bridge	–	Basic shop too and water from river	1783
49	1585 Village and bridge	4610m	No shops, used to be a checkpoint here. Bad road.	1829
17	1602 **PARYANG**	4600m	Shops, restaurants, hotels – all expensive. Road often very sandy	1846
26	1628 *Soge La*	4780m	Road initially sandy then OK	1869
14	1642 Village	4600m	Tiny shop on left before village. Road bad	1885

ALI TO SAGA *(cont'd)*

KM	KM MARKER & PLACE	ALT (M)	REMARKS	TOTAL KM
7	1649 *Small pass*	4670m	After pass road follows Brahmaputra River to New Zhongba	1891
26	1675 Turn off to **NEW ZHONGBA**	4590m	New Zhongba 5.5km from Hway 219. Big shops, restaurants, hotel but all expensive. internet here	1916
5	1680 Second turn off to New Zhongba		Petrol station at junction and 400m of tarmac!	1922
24	1704 **Old Zhongba**	4580m	Tibetan hotels, small shops, restaurants, gompa. Road mostly corrugated from here to 1835km marker	1937
23	1727 *Sing La*	4925m		1962
8	1735 Village	4580m	No shops, descent ends here	1970
9	1744 Brahmaputra	4550m	Reach Brahmaputra River (Yarlung Tsangpo)	1979
16	1760 **Niugu/Lhaktsang**	4600m	Hotels, restaurants, small shops. Big police station. No water for 16km after town	1997
59	1819 **Dargyeling**	4625m	Village with basic shops, teahouse, dorm	2060
19	1838 *Pass*	4900m	Short climb to pass, road OK from 1835km marker	2123
9	1847 **SAGA**	4515m	Important town. Restaurants, shops, hotels, public showers, internet. **Checkpoint** just beyond town. End of km markers	2088

From Saga there is a **choice of routes**; continuing east along the 219 to join the Friendship Highway near Lhatse (see below), or taking a rough road south via Shishapangma to reach the Friendship Highway just north of the Lalung La (see p330).

SAGA EAST ALONG HIGHWAY 219 TO THE FRIENDSHIP HIGHWAY

KM	KM MARKER	PLACE	ALT (M)	REMARKS	TOTAL KM
44	–	*Pass*	5100m	Road surface improves and climbs up switchbacks to pass	2132
23	–	**Raga**	4933m	Shops, hotel. Tarmac starts here. Northern route from Ali joins just before village	2155
29	–	Village	4852m	Basic restaurant.	2184
20	–	*Thongsa La*	5089m	Tarmac	2204
30	–	Gyedo	4600m	Village with basic tent restaurant on lakeshore	2234
9	–	*Sangsang La*	4930m	Still tarmac	2243
27				Tarmac stops, **checkpoint** sometimes	2270
10	–	Sangsang	4591m	Town with basic hotels, restaurants and shops	2280
10	–	*Tok-yo La*	4804m	Steep climb to pass on OK mud road	2290
8	–	Village	4529m	Restaurant	2298
10	–	*Ka La*	4724m	Hairpins, not too steep	2308
–	–	Ngamring Tso	4400m	First trees since Kudi!	–
–	–	*Pass*	4500m	Good road around the lake including a low pass	–
32	–	Ngamring town turn off	4400m	Town is 6km off highway (left) on downhill tarmac road. Hotels, restaurants, shops	2340
6	–	*Choctse La*	4533m	Good road	2346
27	–	Lang Tso		Lake	2373
29	2140	Friendship Highway	4050m	End of Highway 219! Turn left on Highway 318 for **Lhatse** (see p268) and final 598km to Lhasa.	2402

From Saga south via Shishapangma Base Camp to Friendship Highway

From Saga there is also a rough road south (168km) which crosses three passes and joins the Friendship Highway at the northern base of Lalung La. Choosing this route means you can take in Everest Base Camp more easily en route, but makes the journey from Kashgar to Lhasa 3109km in total. This route also provides a good shortcut for those heading more directly for Nepal, and avoids the sometimes problematic checkpoint east of Saga.

This road is not a major highway and receives much less traffic than Highway 219. For this reason some sections are even worse than what you will have experienced getting here. In addition there are almost no villages or supplies along this route, so it is best to leave Saga well stocked up. The real highlight of this road is that it takes you up close to the mighty Himalayan peaks around the sacred Paiku Lake, including the Gang Benchen range and the Shishapangma massif, the only +8000m peak entirely within Tibet (see p280).

FROM SAGA SOUTH VIA SHISHAPANGMA BASE CAMP TO FRIENDSHIP HIGHWAY

KM	KM MARKER & PLACE		ALT (M)	REMARKS	TOTAL KM
–	0	**SAGA**	4515m	Turn right off Highway 219 in centre of town and follow good dirt road south out of town to the river.	2088
3	3	Bridge	4420m	Bridge over the Yarlung Tsangpo (Brahmaputra)	2091
10	13	Bridge and small village		No shops. Moderate dirt road.	2101
9	22	*Pass*	4760m	Good dirt road, steep uphill last 2 km. Bad surface on downhill.	2110
4	–	**Village**	4535m	Shop and teahouse. Snacks only.	2114
9	33.5	*Pass*	4840m	Steep climb from village to pass on narrow, rough road.	2123
7	–	Lodu Loney Lake	4700m	Lowest point after pass; salt lake. Road often very sandy. Sometimes nomad tents but often all streams here totally dry.	2130
13	51	Stream/river crossing		Gentle uphill on bad, sandy road from lake to here. First reliable water since the last village.	2143
11	60	Road repair station		Occupied in 2007. Water. OK dirt road, but with sandy parts.	2154
3	63	Turn off to Zhangmu and Highway 318	4860m	Turn left for Zhangmu on new shortcut road up small pass (ahead for Kiryong and older route to Psiku lake). OK road, sandy parts.	2157
??	–	Reach valley and re-join old road, which crosses *pass* further to the south. Cross small pass on new dirt road before descending into valley. We didn't take this new shortcut but advise you to, it is a shorter and better road than the old, longer, rougher tracks that cross the ridge further to the south			2165?
12	–	Psiku/Paiku Lake	4605m	Probably salt lake; water in inflow rivers fresh. Amazing views to Gang Benchen range and Shishapangma. Moderate dirt/gravel road down valley to lake, sandy road around lake.	2177
8	–	**Tibetan teahouse / truckstop**	4605m	Dorm rooms, beer & instant noodles. River crossings here. The road from here all the way to Highway 318 is very bad: stones, sand, gravel, bad corrugations.	2185
21	–	Top of plain	4750m	Long, gentle climb. Ruins on left and right, small river crossings, very bad road, side tracks maybe better.	2206
12	–	Nature reserve centre near Siling	4645m	Teahouse/dormitory. Only instant noodles. Turn off for Shishapangma Base Camp but no view of mountain from here.	2218
21	–	River crossing	4690m	Bridge 200-300m upstream of road. Stupa and prayer flags on road 1km later.	2239
11	5266	Friendship Highway (318)	4550m	Reach Highway 318 near km5266 (see p280). Small village but no shops. Turn right to climb the Lalung La for Nepal, left for Lhasa.	2250

THE TEA ROAD: LHASA TO ZHONGDIAN

This **hard but beautiful ride** follows an ancient trade route which ran through the heart of eastern Tibet from Lhasa to the town of Zhongdian in China's Yunnan province. Tea, salt and sugar were carried to Lhasa from as far away as South East Asia along this twisting route which crosses what must be some of the steepest terrain on the planet, whilst horses and other animals were traded in return. Today it is a spectacular highway which crosses a succession of high passes and some of Asia's largest rivers – the Salween, Mekong and Yangtze – as they tumble off the Tibetan plateau through some of the world's deepest canyons. The ride ends in Zhongdian, now a modern Chinese city although historically a major Tibetan trading town on the frontier with China. Culturally it is still very Tibetan, with the Gamden Sumtseling gompa and a re-furbished Tibetan old town. To promote tourism the government officially changed the name from Zhongdian to Xangelila (usually translated into English as "Shangri-La") in 2001; since then ever-increasing numbers of tourists are visiting this open Tibetan outpost. It makes for a good place to relax at the end of the ride, or before heading further south, and downhill, into Yunnan.

This ride is **physically demanding** as there are few flat sections and several climbs of 1500-2000m or more, with equally large descents. It's essential to be aware of **AMS** (see p61) and to be well-acclimatized before tackling the higher passes. The landscape varies between alpine tundra on the passes and sub-tropical rainforest in the lowest valleys while higher precipitation levels make this the greenest and most naturally diverse region of Tibet, with some amazing wildlife. It is also one of the most populated parts of Tibet but whilst there are certainly more towns and villages than in the west, it still feels like an enormous, empty landscape. Eastern Tibet, or Kham, is home to the Khampa tribe and was the hotbed of resistance against the Chinese for many decades. It is common for cyclists to meet parties of pilgrims walking the road to Lhasa, or even Mount Kailash, some of whom perform prostrations with every step.

The route is **technically illegal** and most cyclists choose to ride through certain towns or checkpoints at night, although this may not always be necessary (see 'Permits' p322). Whilst the majority make it through without any problems, most years a small number are caught and fined. **Checkpoints** often move or change from year to year, as will the attitude of the authorities – for example the entire region clamped down after the Tibetan riots in 2008. Check online for news and up-to-date information from other cyclists before setting off.

Large sections of the route are now surfaced but there are still a few significant sections that are not and cyclists should be prepared for rough conditions, particularly on some of the highest passes. Food is not a problem and frequent streams and rivers mean it is not usually necessary to carry more than three litres of water when cycling. It's also easy to always camp near water, though be sure you have some means of purifying it. There are relatively frequent towns and villages and no really major stretches without settlements so it is not usually necessary to carry large quantities of food – one or two day's worth is sufficient. It's possible to go lighter but then this becomes a trade off between carrying supplies and making potentially risky shopping trips. Noodles are available in even the most basic shops; a better range of supplies (including porridge) can be found in the larger towns. Most of the settlements on this route have some form of accommodation so in theory it should be possible to do this ride without needing to camp or cook. However, without a permit your presence is illegal so minimize the time you spend in larger villages and towns (especially ones with a police presence). Don't stay in hotels and guesthouses as their owners are required to register you with the Public Security Bureau (PSB) and be quick when buying supplies or having lunch in a restaurant.

ROUTE INFORMATION

- **Start / finish** Lhasa (Tibet) / Zhongdian (Yunnan)
- **Distance** 1609km
- **Altitude min / max** 1950m (Dragon Barrier gorge) / 5008m (Dungd La)
- **High passes** 14 (two over 5000m), including one double and one triple pass.
- **Suggested duration** Most people take 22-26 days to ride this route. Count on a month altogether.
- **Road conditions** Most of Highway 318 between Lhasa and Markham is now surfaced but some sections are still dirt road and often rough. In 2007 Highway 214 from Markham south to the Yunnan border was being widened and prepared for surfacing; on the Yunnan side the road is bad until Meilixueshan.
- **When to go** April–October/November. During the rainy season (June–August) the road is rideable but the unsurfaced sections can get muddy and the risk of landslides is much higher. Early or late in the season be prepared for intense cold and potential snow and ice on the higher passes.
- **Direction** This ride can be ridden in both directions and the distance climbed is roughly 16,000m either way. Many people ride into Tibet from Zhongdian then continue to Nepal as part of a longer tour. Alternatively it can be ridden west–east as described here, either starting in Lhasa or as a continuation of the Kashgar–Lhasa route (see p321) to make a complete trans-Tibet tour.
- **Visas and permits** A standard Chinese two-month tourist visa is sufficient to ride this route as a stand-alone tour. Both Lhasa and Zhongdian have airports. Lhasa is also on China's rail network, but currently the nearest railway to Zhongdian is in Dali, about 300km to the south. A three-month visa is required (see p28) to combine this route with the Friendship Highway or Kashgar–Lhasa. It may also be possible to extend your visa from inside Tibet using postal-service visa agencies such as 💻 www.visainchina.com.

  An 'All Tibet Permit' is required to enter Tibet and these are not issued to independent travellers. However, a flight or train ticket into Tibet will include a permit (shop around as prices change). However, its name is misleading because it only allows access to open areas of Tibet. For restricted areas (such as most of this ride) you also require an Alien Travel Permit (ATP), which is also not issued to independent travellers. It may also be possible to arrange an ATP for a group riding with a jeep and guide. Independent cyclists ride without this permit (ie illegally), dodging checkpoints where necessary.

  Those who get caught without an ATP are arrested, fined and/or sent back (or forward) to the nearest unrestricted area. Most get away with paying a fine of Y500-1000 ($70-140) but if you cannot pay it your bicycle and other property may be taken in forfeit. Recovering confiscated belongings from Chinese authorities usually requires consular assistance. Check the security situation before you set off; clampdowns are certain after pro-Tibet demonstrations but can happen at any time.
- **What to take** Previous experience of riding in remote regions is essential, as is camping kit. Running big tyres (eg Schwalbe Marathon XR 2.35) half-flat on rough sections works well. The bike (and you!) must be able to endure prolonged bad roads – bring spare parts.
- **Maps** No map is totally correct for this route and all of them disagree with each other. The best available in the West is the Gecko *Himalaya Tibet* map (£11.95 from Stanfords), though its coverage ends at Benzilan. Both Reise-KnowHow and Gizi also make good Tibet maps. Available locally in Zhongdian and Lhasa are road atlases for Chinese truck drivers which give place names in Chinese characters. The best one has a dark/black cover with a picture of a steering wheel on it.

As there are so few navigational decisions to make en route the table of distances and altitudes on pp334-8 should suffice.

Passes are marked in italics, towns or villages with food and accommodation are marked in bold, major towns/cities are marked in capitals. Alternative place names are also given. Altitudes are approximate and incomplete but give a reasonable impression of the height differences between the passes and valleys. Information on checkpoints and police posts is from 2007 but please note these change all the time.

Lhasa to Markham

From Lhasa, Highway 318 travels east for 1200 kilometres to Markham, a major Tibetan trading town where the highway splits. From Markham, Highway 318 continues east into the hills of Sichuan; Highway 214 turns south to follow the Mekong River into Yunnan to Zhongdian.

Leaving Lhasa the road is paved for the first 500km as it follows the Yarlung Tsangpo River upstream through a broad valley between barren hills. Beyond Meldro Gonkar the road begins a long climb towards the first pass, the **Mi La**, the top of which forms a boundary between central Tibet and the greener lands of Kham to the east. Following the Mi La is a long descent into the valley of the Nyang Chu, a major tributary of the Tsangpo/Brahmaputra, and as you descend more and more forest begins to appear. At the end of the valley lies the sprawling Chinese town of **Bayi**, a major military base whose PSB is notorious for arresting cyclists. There is no longer any real checkpoint here but many people still choose to ride around Bayi and the next town, Nyingchi, under the cover of darkness.

Immediately beyond Nyingchi another long climb begins, this time up to the **Sekye La**. From the summit of this pass there are spectacular views in clear weather to Namche Barwa (7782m); between this mountain and its 7000m+ neighbours lies the deepest gorge in the world, whose invisible depths hold the Brahmaputra River. From the Sekye La the highway drops to below 2000m in **'Dragon Barrier' gorge**, another tributary of the Tsangpo and itself allegedly the third deepest gorge in the world. A fantastic dirt road clings to tiny ledges on the gorge's vertical walls; this is the lowest point of the route and it lies in the sub-tropical rainforest zone, complete with leeches and mosquitoes in the wet summer months.

From the truck-stop town of **Tangme**, which has a notorious checkpoint, you climb over 2600m up to the next pass beyond Rawu. **Bomi**, another big military town on the way up this valley, is also best passed through swiftly. This entire section is prone to **landslides**, especially in the wetter summer months. The beautiful alpine Zhongmu Lake lies on the tree-line, just before Rawu.

Crossing the **Dokha La** takes you out of the Brahmaputra river system; from here there is another long descent, this time down into dry, barren, treeless country around the Nujiang/Salween River. From here to Markham the route is an unrelenting succession of monster climbs up and out of one river valley, only to plunge immediately back down into the next. From the Salween river the road climbs nearly 2000m in only 40km up to the Gama La on a section of unsurfaced, dusty road known as the "**72 switchbacks**". At Bomda turn right to stay on the 318 and follow a high river valley downstream to the

Chinese town of Dzogong, another place to be careful of the PSB. Leaving Dzogong the tarmac finally ends for good as you begin the climb to the highest pass on this route, the Dungd La. The road descends from here to a small village before climbing another, smaller pass (where the road clings to cliff ledges with some enormous drop-offs) before descending steeply down to the Lancang/Mekong river at Juka bridge. After crossing this river the road yet again begins immediately to climb another enormous pass, this time the double Lao La pass that takes you out of the Mekong valley to the Tibetan city of Markham.

LHASA TO MARKHAM

KM	KM MARKER & PLACE	ALT (M)	REMARKS	TOTAL KM
–	4635 Central **LHASA**	3630m	Road is tarmac and flat. Frequent towns and villages until Meldro Gongkar	0
72	4563 **MELDRO GONGKAR**	3800m	Large town, many shops, police.	72
54	4509 **Rutok**	4380m	Hot springs, shops, teahouses, guesthouses. No Police here in 2007. Road already climbing towards pass.	126
25	4484 *Mi La*	5013m	Water most of the way up the pass, long climb.	151
28	4457-56 **Shungdor**	4300m	Truck-stop/village with restaurants, guesthouses and shops. Small police station at western end by km 4457.	179
3	4454 Army Checkpoint		Wooden watchtowers. No barrier in 2007, cyclists generally not stopped.	182
34	4420 **Syangboteng**		Shops, restaurants. No police in 2007.	216
17	4403 **Jinda**		Small town with shops, restaurants and a small PSB station. In 2007 a bigger police station seemed under construction.	233
43	4360 **KONGBO GYAMDA**	3400m	Highway 318 bypasses the town which lies on the north side of the river. Petrol and shop on main road 2km before town, also some shops on bypass. The town is large and has an active PSB; cyclists were arrested here in 2007.	276
48	4312 **Namtse Tsampa**		Small town with shops, restaurants, hotel, internet and PSB.	324
20	4292 **Bepa**		Shops, guesthouse, restaurants. Small police station.	344
49	4243 Good camp		Last trees for hidden camp before Bayi.	393
8	4235 **BAYI** (start of town)	3000m	Big Chinese city whose PSB is notorious for arresting cyclists. Most people pass Bayi & Nyingchi in the dark, but some cycle safely around Bayi bypass in daytime. Bear to left for bypass road.	401
5	– End of town			406
16	4214 **NYINGCHI**	3000m	Short climb and descent again before the town. PSB & history of arrests here. The barrier at the end of town (km4214) is usually up.	422
4	4210 Small village with power plant		Road climbs uphill immediately after Nyingchi.	426
3	4207 Good camp		Near prayer flags and pilgrim paths in forest above road. Last good camp before the pass (or before Nyingchi/Bayi if coming other way)	429
24	4183 *Sekye La*	4620m	Steep climb from Nyingchi. View to Namche Barwa peak from summit.	453
25	4158 **LUNANG**	3300m	Shops, hotels, restaurants. Police Station.	478
29	4129 **Tongyuk Bridge**	2700m	Small village, basic shops. No Police in 2007.	507
17	4112 Asphalt and kilometre markers end.		Valley descends into rainforest zone. End of tarmac road from Lhasa, dirt road generally good in dry season, but muddy during rains.	524

LHASA TO MARKHAM *(cont'd)*

KM	KM MARKER & PLACE	ALT (M)	REMARKS	TOTAL KM
10	– **Trulung**	2000m	Small village of wooden huts in rainforest. Small shops, restaurants and guesthouse. No Police in 2007.	534
2	– Rong Chu valley	1950m	Lowest elevation of the route. Climb from here along the narrow gorge on an amazing twisting dirt road.	536
14	– Bridge		Army checks here sometimes, usually no problems for cyclists.	550
1	4086/4098 Start of asphalt again		Kilometre markers reappear. Should start at 4086 but instead first is 4098.	551
1	4097 **TANGME/ TONGMAI**	2100m	There's a big police station and **checkpoint** at the entrance to this town. Some cyclists were arrested and/or sent back from here in 2007. Town is small with shops, hotels etc. There's an army base after town.	552
3	4094 Camping site		Flat hidden areas in forest on river side of road. Leeches in rainy season.	555
8	4090-4086		No asphalt for these 4km in 2007 Good dirt road for 4km through landslide damage.	563
6	4080		Start to climb out of the rainforest zone.	569
13	4067 **Small village**		Basic food shops and no police.	582
29	4042-4038 **Series of villages in wider part of valley**		Some small shops and no police.	611
14	4024 Bridge		Small food shops next to bridge.	625
15	4009-4006 **BOMI**	2750m	Big town, good shops and supplies. Also big PSB office & lots of army.	640
23	3986 Small Village		Power station and small shop	663
21	3965 **Small town**		Shops. Police station with barrier but usually no problems here.	684
18	3947 Good camp		Flat places near river in otherwise steep valley.	702
6	3941 Army base		Barrier across road, usually no problems here.	708
9	3932 Army base		Some shops (sometimes closed) by road. No barrier here.	717
1	3931 End of tarmac		Corrugated dirt road for next 33km up narrow gorge with lots of landslides.	718
33	3898 Start of tarmac		Good tarmac begins again.	751
2	3893 Zhongmu lake	3900m	Reaching lake at top of gorge.	753
6	3887 **Small village**		Guesthouse, no shop.	759
6	3881-80 **RAWU/ RAWOK**	3900m	Shops, restaurants, hotels. Police **checkpoint** at start of town. Army base in town. The climb to Dokha La is fairly gentle.	765
19	3862 *Dokha La*	4618m	Broad, flat topped pass.	784
24	3828 Village with food shops		Long downhill after pass.	808
38	3790 **BAXOI**	3200m	Big town, good shops, market, internet etc. Big PSB office here & army bases too.	846
15	– Tarmac ends		Start of dirt road in dry desert-like gorge. Surface generally good though some stones. Kilometre markers erratic and/or inaccurate.	861
12	– Nujiang/Salween bridge	2700m	Cross Salween River on bridge with unavoidable army **checkpoint**, usually no problems.	873
1	– Ruins		Burnt-out shell of building (previous hotel/restaurant) above river.	874
2	– Start of climb away from Salween River		Start of "72 Switchbacks". Huge climb on dirt road, generally OK but surface can be very loose on hairpin turns.	876
10	– **Small village**		At least three kiosks/snack shops; very basic food only.	886

LHASA TO MARKHAM *(cont'd)*

KM	KM MARKER & PLACE		ALT (M)	REMARKS	TOTAL KM
10	–	Small village		No obvious shops.	896
18	3712	Tarmac and kilometre markers start again just below summit of pass.			914
3	3709	*Gama La*	4618m	Summit of pass.	917
13	3696	**BOMDA**	4000m	At junction turn right to stay on Highway 318. Left bears north towards Amdo and Cham. Police checkpoint as enter town on Highway 318. Town has shops and restaurants. From here road is flat along Yu Chu river to Dzogong.	930
41	3655	**Village**		Basic shops, restaurants and guesthouse. Also small police station by bridge.	971
22	3633	**Village**		Big gompa, shops and police barrier in village.	993
45	3588	**DZOGONG/ ZUOGONG**	3800m	Big town with food shops, restaurants, hotels and PSB. Police **checkpoint** and barrier at end of town.	1038
9	3579	Tarmac & regular kilometre markers end. Begin climb to pass on dirt road;		surface generally decent but worsens near top of pass.	1047
23	3556	*Dungd La*	5008m	Highest pass on east Tibet route. Decent dirt road follows river from Dungd La.	1070
38	*3518*	**Deng Ba village**	3600m	Good camping before village. Village has a basic shop and an overpriced Chinese guesthouse.	1108
15	3503	*Jyo La*	4000m	Crest of small pass over to Mekong valley.	1123
25	3478	**Chuka/Juka Bridge**	2800m	Village and bridge over the Mekong River. Shops and hotel in the square with police barrier. Truck-stops by army base at end of town after bridge.	1148
37	3441	*Lao La*	4338m	Big climb up to double pass with some shops in villages en route. Decent dirt road over the pass then isolated patches of tarmac on descent. Tarmac starts properly about 2km before Markham.	1185
12	3429	**MARKHAM / MANGKAM**	4000m	At junction turn right (south) for the town centre, Zhongdian and Yunnan on Highway 214, keep straight (east) for Highway 318 to Sichuan. **Former checkpoint** just before junction but it appeared disused in 2007. Big **checkpoint** on Sichuan road as leave town.	1197
2	–	**MARKHAM TOWN CENTRE**		Big Tibetan town with shops, market, hotels, restaurants. Also PSB and police.	1199

Markham to Zhongdian

Leaving Markham Highway 214 follows a long, high valley south before climbing another pass that returns you to the Mekong River. A huge descent follows with stunning views across the bottomless canyon below to the forests, glaciers and snow peaks beyond.

Yenjing is home to some famous salt pools and the most isolated church in China. Shortly after Yenjing lies the political border of Yunnan and the Tibet Autonomous Region (TAR), although this part of northern Yunnan is predominantly Tibetan.

The first section of road on the Yunnan side is truly awful, but tracks the **Mekong River** along the bottom of the gorge. Beyond Foshan and after re-crossing the river you are officially back in an open area. Before you reach the comforts of Deqin there is still another long climb back out of the Mekong valley, over the **Meilixueshan pass** and tourist resort of the same name, which has amazing views across to Kawagebo Peak, the highest peak in Yunnan and a holy Buddhist mountain which has its own kora route.

From **Deqin** the route crosses the high triple Yak La pass before dropping to 2000m again to meet the **Yangtze River** at Benzilan, where you can at last warm up. Don't get too used to it though – after crossing the Yangtze there is one last, long, steep 1500m climb back into the pine forests and over the last pass to Zhongdian.

On arrival in **Zhongdian** the majority of guesthouses are found in the 'old town' which is at the southern end of the city – the far end as you cycle in. The main market is in the centre of the modern Chinese-built city, whilst Gamden Sumtseling gompa lies only a few miles out of town. For those not wishing to end their ride here there is a choice of routes south towards Lijiang and Dali, one of which takes you through Tiger Leaping Gorge on the Yangtze river.

MARKHAM TO ZHONGDIAN

KM	KM MARKER & PLACE		ALT (M)	REMARKS	TOTAL KM
–	–	**MARKHAM TOWN CENTRE**	4000m	See 'Markham town centre' opposite. In 2007 Highway 214 was under construction all the way from Markham to the Yunnan border.	1199
3	–	Outskirts of town		In 2007 bad dirt roads led south out of town to the new Highway 214 which was little better.	1202
22	–	**Village**		Small shops, teahouses. Bad dirt road follows the river valley south.	1224
25	–	Start ascent	3600m	Climbing out of valley above river.	1249
15	–	*Pass*	4400m	Amazing view to ranges west of Mekong River.	1264
38	–	Junction, back in Mekong Valley	2600m	Long downhill, lots of road construction work. At junction do not descend to river, follow valley.	1302
6	–	**Small Village**		**Former checkpoint** (barrier) appeared disused in 2007.	1308
3	–	**YENJING**	2600m	Shops, restaurants, hotels. Sharp right turn into town centre. PSB here but in 2007 no sign of **former checkpoints** on main road.	1311
7	1760	**TIBET–YUNNAN** border		Arch/gate over road. New road ends at border.	1319
9	1769	**Small village**		Small shop. Bad mud road after border.	1328
13	1782	**Small village**		Two shops, one restaurant, one guesthouse. No PSB.	1341
16	1798	**FOSHAN**		Small town with shops, restaurants and a hotel. PSB and a barrier (usually up) marking the **end of restricted/closed area.**	1357
3	*1801*	Bridge		Road crosses to west side of Mekong. Kilometre stones erratic on this section. Dirt road improves.	1360
12	*1813*	Bridge back to east bank of Mekong		Old road camp/barracks on east side with small truck-stop kiosk. Police post and barrier but usually no problems.	1372
12	1825	**Small village**	2000m	Two shops, a guestroom in the pharmacy/clinic and a road camp. Not much food here.	1384
1	1826	Begin ascent		Road turns into small side valley and starts long climb out of Mekong valley.	1385
9	1835	**Truck stop**		Small shops, teahouse/restaurant.	1394
1	1836	Tarmac starts		Take uphill fork at junction.	1395
18	1852	***Meilixueshan***	3500m	Tourist resort on top of pass with hotels, bars, restaurants and small shops.	1413
11	1863	**DEQIN**	3300m	Big town with hotels, restaurants, internet, shops and market. Steep climb from here to viewpoint.	1424

MARKHAM TO ZHONGDIAN *(cont'd)*

KM	KM MARKER & PLACE	ALT (M)	REMARKS	TOTAL KM
8	1871 Viewpoint & stupas		Short downhill before long climb to pass.	1432
20	1891 Asphalt ends.		Cobblestones start, not too bad, continuing over triple Yak La pass.	1452
7	1898 *Yak La (First pass)*	4300m	First summit	1459
3	1901 Low point	4100m	Lowest point between passes.	1462
4	1905 *Second Pass*	4350m	Second summit.	1466
4	1909 Low point	4100m	Lowest point between passes.	1470
3	1912 *Third pass*	4270m	Third summit. Long downhill from here.	1473
8	1933 Tarmac starts		Road in good condition from here all the way to Zhongdian.	1494
12	1945 **Village**		Small shops.	1506
22	1967 **BENZILAN**	2100m	Hotels, shops, restaurants. Join Yangtze river.	1528
12	1979 Bridge	2000m	Cross Yangtze river	1540
3	1982 **Village**		Small shops, restaurant. Start of climb to last pass.	1543
28	2010 **Village**		Small shops, restaurant.	1571
7	2017 **Nixi**		Small shops, cafés.	1579
7	2024 Nixi Ski Resort		Ski resort just below pass.	1586
3	2027 *Pass*	3560m	Short descent to high plateau.	1589
20	2047 **ZHONGDIAN / XANGELILA**	3250m	"Shangri-La" – big city with hotels, shops, restaurants and internet.	1609

Appendix B: Motorcycling in northern India

While the routes in this book were researched and written for cyclists, all this information can also be used by those who'd prefer an engine to do the hard work. Distances, altitudes, petrol stations and water sources are marked up on the maps; cumulative distances in the text should help motorcyclists plan their journeys independently of the days suggested for cyclists.

In northern India there are probably as many foreigners travelling on motorcycles as there are on bicycles. Usually cyclists and motorbikers don't mix, but up in the mountains there is often a sense of camaraderie between two-wheelers (as they are quaintly called in India) for taking on the challenge of riding through such a landscape, rather than getting on the bus. Nor is motorcycling the easy option: classic bikes such as the Enfield (see below) are as capricious, and stubborn, as yaks. Ask them to ford rivers and climb 5000m passes with you on their back and it is certain that you'll be spending some time at the side of the road, coaxing them to continue. But like many things in India, that is all part of the experience. The reward is the feeling of a leaky British classic beating a steady tattoo under you – the icy wind in your hair as you stare at an unreal horizon, or of a ribbon of tarmac curling through the alpine Himalayan forests, climbing higher and higher through impossibly high passes shrouded in mist and cloud to suddenly emerge into a cold, yellow, mountain lunarscape flecked by turquoise lakes and fluttering prayer flags. Your ancient single-cylinder motorcycle sends ibex skittering down the slopes with its unmistakable flat bark. You push down on the handlebar and the bike dives to clip the apex of an onrushing left hander. Bedding down in the berm created by heavy military trucks, the bike powers out, scattering shale as you flick it over for the right hander looming ahead. It just goes on and on and on. The Himalayan country. Life is suddenly perfect. But don't just dream it! It's time to break the bank and bid adieu to a boring job, grab that AGV helmet, book cheap tickets to India and head out to the Himalaya for a life-changing motorcycling adventure!

CHOOSING A BIKE

The Enfield

The Enfield Bullet 500, the favoured machine for this adventure, seems to appeal greatly to both Indian and foreign bikers. Normally Indians are seen astride new Bullet models in the Himalaya and foreigners aboard heavily loaded, more vintage examples. It's not that Indians are richer, they just plan to spend several years riding the same steed. When viewed over a long period of ownership it is better to stack the odds in one's favour as far as possible, and a new Enfield is the best insurance. The latest version of this old warhorse is the Bullet Machismo 500 complete with 5-speed tranny, electronic ignition, disc brake up front and the gear lever on the left (correct!) side. Die-hard Enfielders sneer at the upgrades like the front discs, but they have proved more than useful in saving riders from the eager hands of the grim reaper. An older, second-hand traditional Bullet 500 can fit the bill for a Himalayan tour if properly prepared and somewhat understood, though a 30-day relationship with one of the older Bullets is drama enough for most.

The Enfield's problem is its power to weight ratio. Its heft gives the illusion that it can carry a rider, a pillion and the entire material belongings of a hippy commune. It cannot. The engine, producing all of 17 KW at 5600 rpm, will definitely pack up when overloaded halfway up a remote mountain pass and will stubbornly resist restarting. Enfields break down and need to leak oil to fulfil their karmic existence. Earlier models bled themselves to death when not attended to instantly, but the later upgrades seem to manage their haemophilia better. Overheating seems to be the most common problem. Strangely the Enfield's unreliability is its lure. In a technically perfect world this marque stands out and stubbornly refuses to be tamed.

To be a rider on a heavily laden Enfield with a pillion is entertaining. Small bumps on a climbing road leave the front wheel so un-weighted that steering is reduced to a lottery. Hairpin bends up the Gata Loops to Nakeela La, the third pass on the way to Leh, are steered in instalments as and when both front wheel and wind settle sufficiently to allow steering traction. To ride pillion on an Enfield is to embrace gluteus maximus hell. The thin rear part of the seat is both hard and unfriendly, its design intrinsically cruel. Reject this option at the start and learn to ride your own bike.

At over $2800 new (Rs110,000), the second-hand option (Rs45,000–55,000) is definitely more popular with the foreign adventure holiday crowd. Careful preparation, a single rider and light luggage (10kg or less) is the key to a successful foray into the Himalaya.

Japanese machines

The alternative to the Enfield 'experience' is to go Japanese. Indian motorcycles almost exclusively have Japanese collaborations and as the big four are well represented one is spoilt for choice. However, their offerings are limited to tiny bore bikes. Modern-looking, with all the trappings of larger machines, they have it all: disc brakes, digital twin spark, fuel injection, space age everything – but no horse power. From this selection only three bikes stand out for a Himalayan tour: the Hero Honda Karizma (225cc), the Bajaj Pulsar DTS Fi (220cc) and the TVS RTR 160.

A clever advertising campaign has unfortunately made the Bajaj Avenger DTSi the chosen mount of several urban cowboys, seduced by images of this powerless chopper clone blazing through Ladakh to a pulsing soundtrack and the strapline 'Feel Like God'. Nicknamed the Indian 'Hardly' Davidson for its fat rear tyre and low ground clearance, this bike is often out of its depth well before the first Tibetan monastery looms onto the horizon. That said, almost any Japanese bike will do this trip and not miss a beat. But once weighed down with luggage, riders look like Don Quixotes astride anaemic, spindly legged donkeys – not really an image you want to cherish as you age, reminiscing over dog-eared photos of your adventure.

350cc or 500cc?

Due to the low atmospheric pressure in the mountains all carburetted engines experience a drastic cut in power as they climb. More horsepower is better. The 500cc has more horsepower than the 350cc while the weight remains roughly the same. More relevant, the 500cc produces more power at a lower rpm and given the twisty dirt roads of the Himalayas that's exactly where one needs it.

With second-hand reconditioned machines it is difficult to tell whether a 350cc has been converted to a 500cc by replacement of both block and head or if it was originally assembled at the factory as a 500cc. Most bikes available are an aftermarket upgrade. If done well there should be no problem. However, the local parts market provides spares at half the price of the originals and that is incentive enough for the rebuilder to opt for the cheaper versions. The first signs of a bad rebuild are leakages (normally wiped clean 10 minutes before you show up for delivery) and overheating even in normal riding conditions. Also listen for tappet chatter that signals a bad tune up and a rough feel during gear changes. Grinding sounds indicate a worn timing chain or cheap engine bearings. Remember to test the front brake in case it is the older drum unit. If it doesn't work don't try to get it fixed – opt for the disc option.

WHERE TO BUY / RENT MOTORBIKES

Before paying for or accepting a rental machine – RIDE IT! Make sure it seems all right. This is an intuitive thing and unfortunately no hard and fast rules exist except that machines that ride straight with hands off the bars, and that feel right and sound good normally behave well.

Delhi

The best bet is to buy/rent the bike in Delhi. At least there is a choice of machines spread over a few rebuilders. Lalli Singh (see p350) has the best reputation and his machines tend to stay together better than most. As everyone has to fly into Delhi it is better to do the biking part of the journey from here upward. Buying from Delhi will also ensure that you can resell in Delhi without hassles. Normally the supplier will give you a buy-back deal (but see below). If you pick up a bargain from another state, selling it in Delhi at the journey's end will entail extensive formalities (ie hassle), as the bike will have an out-of-state number.

Reconditioned bikes from Lalli Singh or Madaan Motors in Karol Bagh will normally have a larger petrol tank (very useful for the Manali–Leh Highway), separate seats for rider and pillion and a pannier frame made of metal tubing. Luggage can be fitted into this frame. It looks robust and although it will soon develop resonance cracks it is a leg saver during slow-speed crashes as it prevents the bike from biting your trapped ankle. During negotiations try and source these goodies for free.

• **Buy back** This is a murky affair at best and each biker has to navigate the shoals on their own. It helps to have some sort of **commitment in writing** (even if just on the back of a business card) **before buying the bike**.

Manali

Those looking to escape the heat by rushing to the mountains can pick up a bike in Manali from Anu (☎ +91 9816 163 378). Anu has a fair number of Classic 500cc Bullets. Not particularly enamoured with the high failure rate of the cdi units on the newer bullets he sticks to the old contact breaker point fired Enfields. Daily rentals for Manali and around are in the region of Rs400 for the 350cc and Rs500 for the 500cc; to ride to Leh expect to pay Rs600 a day. Anu keeps about €300–400 as deposit. All damages will be charged extra on return of the machine. Outright purchase of his machines will range from Rs 45,000 to Rs70,000 depending on the machine's vintage. The older beasts are late 1995–99 whereas the newer offerings are early 2001–04. Buy back can be negotiated. Bike trips for groups are also arranged.

Leh

One can contact several travel agencies who rent out Japanese 100cc machines for the day for Rs350–550 depending on how new the bike is. Fuel is your responsibility. Enfields are few and far between and unreliable.

Japanese machines are ideal for cloverleaf tours to the Nubra Valley and Pangong Tso as they give better fuel mileage and so a greater range for exploration. As there is no fuel outside Leh one needs to plan cloverleaf tours with care. The Pumpernickel Bakery (see p152) in Leh bazaar, run by a Sikh with a Dali moustache, has a notice board where everything from bikes to mules are traded. If you plan to buy a bike from a foreign tourist who is flying back to Delhi, make sure you get the paperwork that bridges the ownership between the Delhi seller, the foreign tourist and you.

Srinagar

This is a bad idea. There are almost no Bullets available in the region owing to legislation restricting sale of 350+cc bikes in this part of Jammu & Kashmir for security reasons.

LEGALITIES AND PAPERWORK

Necessary paperwork

• **Registration Certificate of the motorcycle** If you bought the bike it's a good idea to carry the letter of sale, or if you are renting then a letter of authorization to use the machine signed by the registered owner.

BASIC MOTORCYCLE MECHANICS

All second-hand dealers will show you basic survival procedures if you're willing to learn from a grease monkey no older than 12 years and no heavier than 17kg. At the very least you should be confident you can do the following:

- Remove front and rear wheels to fix a flat
- Remove and refit the carburettor in case it is full of water instead of fuel
- Remove the spark plug in case the cylinder is flooded
- Tension the chain
- Start the bike and be proficient in Enfield foreplay before that first kick!
- Replace headlight bulbs
- Bribe a policeman for helmet-free travel.

THE RAID DE HIMALAYA

Set in the Western Indian Himalaya, the Raid de Himalaya is Asia's toughest and the world's highest Rally Raid, recognized by both the Federation Internationale Motocyclisme (FIM) and the Federation Internationale Automobile (FiA). Set at the onset of winter and with freakish weather conditions almost guaranteed, the Raid runs the gauntlet of treacherous mountain roads in Kinnaur, Lahaul and Spiti, Ladakh and Kashmir over about 10 days.

The Himalayan Motorsport Association is the architect of this event; their website, which underplays the risk involved completely, is www.raid-de-himalaya.com. Despite the jovial approach, the event is run by a committed and experienced team and uses modern communications, medical back-up facilities and army support.

Entries to the Raid open in May every year and the entry fee becomes more expensive as one nears the flag off date, normally in early October. The event is open to cars, motorcycles, quads and trucks and is run as per the International Raid regulations for all the above categories. Both teams and individuals are welcomed.

- **Certificate of Insurance**
- **Driving Licence** An International Driving Permit is good though your driving licence will do.
- **Pollution under Control Certificate** These are available at various pumps for a small fee. Make sure you get one which is valid for six months and if possible has a picture of your bike on it. They do it with webcams now.

Importing and exporting bikes

Legally, buying a bike in India and riding it out of the country is now almost impossible. The only option is to break it down into unrecognizable parts and ship them home as free business samples, then spend the better part of your life aligning holes that have mysteriously drifted apart. Apart from Nepal and Bhutan, all other countries bordering India are hostile and will immediately impound an Indian-registered motorcycle. Furthermore, carnets for Pakistan, Bangladesh and China are not really issued. Headhunters in Arunachal will probably get you before you can enter Burma!

Enfield sporadically appoints dealers in countries like Turkey but the UK and the US are better places to source a suitable steed. For a ridiculous solution to the export problem, buy an Enfield in the west and then ride it to India and back! UK dealerships are listed at www.royal-enfield.com/dealers.htm and US Dealers at www.enfieldmotorcycles.com/locator/dealers/usa/ start.

If issued in India, a carnet de passage will require you to place in bond an amount of money several times the price of the motorcycle and this will be stamped on your passport as well. This money is refundable only when the vehicle returns to India within a stipulated time. Should it fail to return within that time, you lose the deposit. Carnets in India are only issued to Indian citizens so that pretty much is that.

Similarly, bikers reaching India on a carnet de passage cannot sell their bikes here as they will lose their bond deposit and be tracked down by the police of their country. Crashed bikes must be shipped back home irrespective of the extent of damage so claiming a total loss is strictly a no-no. Trying on a story about your bike being stolen or sinking (!) with customs officials won't get you very far: they've heard it all before.

SUGGESTED ROUTES

The roads that link Kinnaur, Lahaul and Spiti in Himachal Pradesh to Ladakh in Jammu and Kashmir are very fragile ribbons that connect an otherwise untrammelled Himalaya. Sometimes tarmac, mostly broken gravel, they are easily breached by landslide and avalanche and for half the year lie buried under glaciers, denying access to all but the snow leopard and ibex. For the other half, they reveal a paradise that is unimaginable. Fantastic rock formations, rushing cataracts and a cold moonscape set under an azure sky that will be the backdrop to your motorcycle adventure.

You will have to plan the trip well, for though this is a land of stark beauty there is very little infrastructure along the route, and to break down can be disastrous. The sign at Tandi petrol pump on the Manali–Leh Highway which informs you that the next fuel pump is 365km away may not seem that intimidating. But at high altitude fuel averages halve and Manali to Leh takes a minimum of two whole days. Knowing your mount and planning the details will bring success. Assuming, incorrectly, the presence of civilization, will not.

The following tours are detailed earlier in this book (apart from the ride up from Delhi):

The Grand Tour (20 riding days)

Day 1 Delhi–Shimla
Day 2 Shimla–Rampur–Sarahan
Day 3 Sarahan–Sangla
Day 4 Sangla–Chitkul–Nako
Day 5 Nako–Tabo
Day 6 Tabo–Dhankar–Attargo–Pin Valley–Attargo–Kaza
Day 7 Kaza–Komic–Losar
Day 8 Losar–Gramphoo–Manali
Day 9 Manali (rest day)
Day 10 Manali–Jispa
Day 11 Jispa–Leh
Day 12 Leh (Permits)
Day 13 Leh–Nubra
Day 14 Nubra–Leh
Day 15 Leh–Pangong Tso–Leh
Day 16 Leh–Korzok (Tso Moriri)
Day 17 Korzok–Pang
Day 18 Pang–Manali
Day 19 Manali
Day 20 Manali–Delhi

The Short Tour (12 riding days)

Ride from Delhi to Manali (two days) and then join the Grand Tour at Day 10.

You could do the Grand Tour if you have a month to hand, or the Short Tour if you have around a fortnight. Either way you would pick up the motorcycle on arrival in Delhi, brave the Grand Trunk Road as far north as Ambala and then fork right for Chandigarh on NH22. For Manali take the road from Chandigarh via Bilaspur and Kullu. Delhi to Manali can be done in one very long day but if it is your first day it might be advisable to break the journey en route.

For Shimla you will need to negotiate the traffic snarls at Pinjore and Kalka. From Parwanoo, the entrance to Himachal Pradesh, the tarmac curves deliciously all the way to Shimla. Delhi to Shimla is about 367km and can be done in one long day of between nine and eleven hours. Between Narkanda and Rampur you could take the old Hindustan–Tibet Road via Baghi, Khadrala and Sungri which joins NH22 at New Nogli.

Cloverleaf Tours

For motorcyclists astride Indian machines, whether the small but efficient Japanese offerings or the larger but whimsical Enfield, rest is crucial for both man and machine. On these recuperative days it is good to be able to do 'half-day Cloverleaf tours' that bring you back to base after a short blast. The Pin Valley in Spiti and the Sangla Valley in Kinnaur (for both see the box on p184) are pleasant diversions. From Leh there are two out-and-back routes which make good three-day tours, the first to Pangong Tso via Karu, Chang La and Tangtse and the second to Khardung La and the Nubra Valley via Khardung La and Hundar. For both these routes see the box on p155.

All alone or in a group?

Riding alone in a strange country with little or no signage can be a surreal experience. If you travel alone there are no conferences, no agreeing reluctantly to another's plan. As long as things are going fine you may even feel like God! However, if you break down there is no one watching out for you. You are not likely to be scalped by marauding nomads but luggage, spares and equipment suddenly becomes fair game when left abandoned by the roadside as you walk towards help. If you fall and are trapped under the bike you will lie there until someone chances upon you. Working knowledge of a simple motorcycle engine and loads of native cunning are invaluable when travelling alone.

Sensibly the odds are in your favour if you travel in small groups of two and three rather than go it alone. Firstly, if your group has the same model of motorcycle the spares inventory per bike is halved at least. And you only need one team member to know the basics of motorcycle resuscitation. Secondly, the pitfalls that accompany a motorcycle trip rarely hit all members of the convoy at the same time, except food poisoning. The strongest band of merry Enfielders is therefore the one with diverse eating habits. At such high altitudes it's a good idea to have someone riding as a sweeper, just in case you fall prey to a sudden attack of mountain or Enfield sickness.

Unless your motorcycling mates are people you planned this with from back home and have done many trips with, fifth-day syndrome will cut in with certainty. By the time you have spent five days riding 250 kms every day with each other, you will have somehow focused on all the irritating aspects of your companions' riding, eating, sleeping and refueling habits and will be ready to cut the umbilical cord and go it alone. Don't. Instead, plan to do a cloverleaf tour on your own for half a day and return to the main event as a team member after some 'alone time' visiting monasteries and riding at a leisurely pace! The syndrome may cut in a bit earlier or a bit later but it will cut in. All you need to do is to rest yourself when it does – not endanger your life by cutting away from the group.

Finally, if you're dreaming of riding a motorbike in northern India but aren't quite ready to take the plunge consider an **organized tour**. Suzie Lumsden's Blazing Trails (💻 www.blazingtrailstours.com) comes highly recommended; they run 14-day tours in Spiti and Ladakh on 500cc Enfields from £2254.

NECESSARY KIT

• **Helmets** The use of helmets in India is compulsory in all states. However, even though cops may not take notice in Ladakh, they will certainly question your duelling with death in the big cities. Helmets in Delhi are best bought in Karol Bagh. Wear a helmet – it saves lives and keeps hypothermia at bay!

• **Clothing** Bear in mind that between mid-June and late October (when these roads are open), the temperatures in the Himalaya can vary from 25°C (77°F) in the day to -15°C (5°F) at night or with windchill. You need to bring proper riding gear as it is not available in India. Think Enduro boots rather than motocross or street and plan for it to be cold. Enduro boots let you walk far further than full-on motocross ones. A good helmet, full gloves and insulated trousers are perfect for a Himalayan adventure. If you haven't brought any gear jackets, gloves and tank bags can be had from Adventure 18 in Delhi (call Mohit on ☎ +91 9810 043 029). If you are an extra large person you probably will not get stuff to fit you in India. If you are riding pillion bring along a gel pad for the seat.

• **Maps and GPS** For riding out of Delhi Eicher publishes the most comprehensive maps in India these days. Available at any good bookshop they are fairly easy to read and mostly accurate.

For motorcycle use a GPS can be handy for making tracks and saving them for either passing them on to other bikers or using them to backtrack to base turn by turn.

Garmin Nuvi GPS units and the like are not very useful in India; Garmin's GPSMap series is better, of which the 76csx is the best. If the GPS unit is not preloaded with a Pacific Basemap you will need to load the India map from Garmin's Mapsource Worldmap CD, although there is no software available for the Indian Himalaya. For GPS tracks of the Himalayan region contact Himalayan Motorsport at 💻 info@raid-de-himalaya.com. Use a RAM handlebar mount for easy fit and removal. GPS units are more expensive in India then in Europe or the US but if you want to buy one call Sumit Sabharwal on ☎ +91 9811 184 437.

TECHNICAL TALK

Some pointers

• **Jetting** This is critical on the Enfield. Lean jetting in the hot plains will get the machine running hot and rich jetting in the Himalaya will have it choking on its own vomit. A chronic misfire preventing acceleration beyond 3000 rpm is a sure sign of rich jetting. It might be a good idea to get the lean jets put in at Manali and the rich ones back once the journey nears the plains again. The

ROAD ETIQUETTE

Once you are used to driving on the left of the road things will seem friendlier. Blowing the horn in India is not a rude gesture. It is a celebration of life. Make sure your horn works perfectly or else you might be left out of the celebration. Pedestrians may see you coming and still not change course. On impact they will blame you for not blowing the horn to warn them. Having seen your bike bearing down means nothing. In India unless the horn has been sounded needlessly long then a fair warning has not been given!

If you feel all the larger vehicles are out to kill you – you're right! Take evasive action, blow the horn and flash lights at the slightest doubts. When a vehicle flashes the right indicator light he may be asking you to overtake or he may be indicating a right turn. If he drifts to the left, while doing this, be sure he is going to swing across your nose for a killer right turn. If he carries on straight he probably wants you to go by. The end result will always be blamed on your kismet so be careful.

Enfield Club at the turn-off to Vashist near Manali might know what to do. Buy the lean jet in Delhi and keep it in a cool dry place.

As you cannot increase airflow into a carburettor you can change only the fuel air ratio. Reduce the jet sizes in the carburettor as you climb, so that the fuel/air ratio remains the same when the oxygen levels drop. Another good idea is to fit a high volume air filter element like those made by K&N. These filters allow more air to pass through than the stock filter. However, the K&N filters are fully exposed and if you drop your bike in a stream they will suck in water resulting in instant hydrostatic lock. The cure is to not try restarting but to remove the plug and then pump the kickstarter till all the water has geysered out. Reinsert the plug and pray that you didn't bend the conrod. Kick viciously to find out. K&N Filters can be bought at 💻 www.planetdsg.com.

• **Overheating** This is the number one cause of Enfield breakdown. Cooling the older Enfields along the way should be done by filling one's mouth with water and spitting it out over the overheated fins! Splashing the old cast iron blocks sometimes causes them to crack. Water crossings on overheated bikes should be attempted after a preliminary cooling for the same reason using the same method. Don't put muddy stream water into your mouth, use bottled water! The resulting steam can get into the plug lead leaving condensation that might cause a misfire till it dries up. Relax. It will.

• **Cush Rubbers** Ensure that the cush rubbers in the rear drum are new and original. Carry a spare set. Ever since the front discs have been introduced heat build up in the rear drum, which destroyed the cush rubbers earlier, has been reduced dramatically. However the Manali–Leh Highway is replete with long descents.

• **Chain stuff** A new chain (Rolon) is a must. Try to understand how to tension it. Carry spare chain locks and get the one fitted painted a bright yellow so that it is easy to locate in fading light. If you are riding an older Enfield you may have to open the chain before you can remove the tyre to fix a flat.

• **Inner tubes** A useful rally tip is to fit two tubes in each tyre. How? Firstly make a hole in the metal wheel rim for the second tube nozzle, directly opposite the first one. Install both tubes side by side. Inflate one tube, leave the other deflated. Paint the nozzle of the inflated tube bright yellow. When you

USEFUL WEBSITES

Enfield dealers

www.royalenfield.com Gives info on everything Enfield, from the latest models to prices and also various first-hand experiences of other riders.

Tales from the saddle

http://indiamotorcycle.googlepages.com Well-written account of a 32-year-old woman's solo Enfield journey in India.

www.thebrightstuff.com/indiaoverview Articles and photos from two years of riding in the Indian Himalaya

Information and resources

www.horizonsunlimited.com Encyclopaedic site which is the online bible for all motorbike adventurers.

www.indiamike.com Online travel forum with a thread for motorbike touring in India

www.60kph.com Indian motorcycle touring forum

www.adventure-motorcycling.com Website of Trailblazer's *Adventure Motorcycling Handbook*, the classic guide for motorbikers planning The Big Trip.

have a puncture try and locate the cause (usually a nail or glass) and remove it. Now inflate the other tube (unpainted nozzle) to continue without having to do the repair on the road. Flat fixers do work so carry at least one with you.

Once you have removed the nail and injected flat fixer foam into the tube don't wait around but drive off immediately. Centrifugal force will push the sealant into the leak and seal it. After about 3km stop to check. If necessary correct the pressure with a foot pump. If the tyre is ripped a flat fixer is useless so save it for another day.

• **Stands** Always keep the centre stand fitted even if you use the side stand. It is invaluable when a flat is to be fixed, plus it will scrape the asphalt even on mild turns, sending up sparks that will delight onlookers endlessly. Keep spare springs for the centre stand.

• **Fasteners** Try and get nylock nuts for as many of the bolts as possible. This will give you some more holiday time and reduce the daily tightening routine to a few minutes.

• **Fuel** Indian bikes, whether Japanese or Enfields, will run on any grade of petrol. Though the Japanese crotch rockets are equipped with fuel meters, the Enfield refuses to let one of its "favorite surprises" be spoilt by any such techno wizardry. It is very important to work out the mileage achieved to avoid unpleasant news. Understand which is the fuel tap 'reserve' position. Always ride with the tap in the 'main' position so that when the bike sputters to a halt you still have some left in reserve. When in doubt peering into the dark tank is the only way to work out what is left. Try not to use that wonderfully etched Zippo lighter for illumination. Carry spare fuel in two five-litre plastic jerry cans; these should fit into the Enfield luggage racks. Refuel frequently. Ask about the distance to the next pump.

On the Manali–Leh Highway the Enfield biker needs to tank up at Tandi (oversize tanks can carry up to 17 litres) and then carry some spare in the two jerrycans. The spare is necessary in case blocked roads force you to return the same way, and if one leaks you won't lose all the petrol. Japanese bikes give better averages but have smaller tanks so a bit of mental arithmetic is in order. Leaving the fuel tap open on Enfields during stops is a bad idea. Carburettors overflow and the Ladakhi desert swallows up precious fuel.

"WHY DON'T YOU GET A PROPER BIKE?"

Enfields have a reputation for being sluggish and unreliable. I was blissfully unaware of this when a Dutchman invited me to buy one and join him on his travels around India. He lured me with his tales of the open road, omitting details like days spent in workshops doing maintenance. Seven years and 67,000 kilometres later, I've long since lost the Dutchman but kept my 500cc Bullet, travelling through twenty countries home to the UK. Whilst I agree that they are not built for speedy travel, the reputation of these faithful working examples of early British motorcycle design is undeserved. It's time to redress the balance!

On Independence in 1947, the Indian Army chose the Royal Enfield as the most efficient means of reaching all parts of the country from the arid, hot south to the snow-covered Himalaya. Eventually, they bought the whole factory from England, took it to India and Enfields have changed little since. This robust motorcycle with its impressive torque and basic single cylinder 4-stroke engine is capable of going just about anywhere barring serious avalanches and water deeper than my mid-thigh (I am 5'2"). I've shouted at my bike only once, when I threatened to leave it permanently at the roadside in Java – but it was my own incompetence that caused the outburst.

With no initial mechanical knowledge, I have now learned how to do basic maintenance and repairs thanks to other people's advice and the two workshop manuals I carry as bedside reading. I've made a gasket out of car radiator hose and replaced a burnt-out stator with a vacuum cleaner nozzle wound round with metres of copper wire. If a job is beyond me often people go out of their way to help, often refusing payment, and can be endlessly resourceful and inventive – a welder in Pakistan made a gearbox spring from scrap metal which he measured by eye, trimmed, tempered and fitted; an engineer in Malaysia crafted me a new spring for my kick-starter. An upside-down Yamaha front brake lever still serves as my clutch lever.

I carried many spare parts in the beginning because you never know what's going to need replacing; but short of carrying an entire spare Enfield with you, you have to be selective. In Australia my spare parts bag was stolen so I decided to replace just the bare essentials which are: two inner tubes, puncture repair outfit, oil filter, cables, fuses, spark plugs, condenser, regulator/rectifier, bulbs, chain links, front brake link rod and front fork lug caps. Cable ties are useful and duck tape is essential! But if a vital part can't be mended, bought locally or made from bits of scrap, Enfield dealers will send spares anywhere in the world.

Sceptical bikers look at my Enfield and say, "Why don't you get a proper bike?" This was from some bike travellers who had been stuck for weeks in Islamabad's campsite waiting for a sealed unit to arrive from Europe. Later we met a man on a 'proper' motorbike complete with heated handlebar and jacket retracing his route down from the top of the Karakoram Highway near the border with China. "You'll never get up there!" he said, but we made it through the snow and ice to enjoy the spectacular views and a cup of tea with the border guards. Although my bike is sturdy, it is not heavy and can nip down little side streets as well as leaping smartly up and around mountain roads. In Mexico I left my companions on their Harleys slowly rounding the bends as I rode fluidly and ecstatically round the curves. They caught me up on the straight bits though!

Even after all these miles, I still never know if my bike is going to start with one or twenty-one kicks on the kickstarter. It can be temperamental. I've spent far more than it is worth shipping it around the world and bringing it home but I love it.

So to all those who laugh at my Enfield, I say… " Why don't YOU get a proper bike!"

Jacqui Furneaux, UK

Keeping the peace: daily routines

• **Clean it** Have you noticed how a clean bike rides better than a dirty, oil-smeared, one? Keep your bike clean and, whenever you can, get it washed out. India is littered with car washes that will hose down the entire machine for Rs 50. Compressed air blasts may be required to blow the moisture out of the plug wires and the contact points to restart so make sure your chosen bike wash has the necessary air mover.

- **Oil check** Check the engine oil by unscrewing the oil filler cap; it has an in-built dip stick.
- **Chain service** Lightly oil the chain frequently, especially if you hear a sibilant hiss when coasting downhill.
- **Brakes** Adjust the rear brakes when they need to be stood upon to bring about decent retardation.
- **Punctures** Change the tubes if they have had more than two punctures and plug the nozzles with valve caps so they don't clog with mud.

Recommended garages and mechanics in northern India

Delhi

- **Lalli Singh, Inder Motors**, 1740-A/55 (basement) Hari Singh Nalwa St, Karol Bagh, ☎ 011 2572 8579, 💻 www.lallisingh.com.
- **Soni Motors**, 1737-B/56 Hari Singh Nalwa St, Karol Bagh, ☎ 011 4154 8958, 💻 www.sonimotors.com.
- **Madaan Motors**, 1737/53 Naiwala St, Karol Bagh, ☎ 011 2573 5801, 💻 www.madaanmotors.com

Manali

- **The Enfield Club**, at the turn-off to Vashist, ☎ 01902 254 090.
- **Satyarth Bikes**, opposite the Circuit House, New Manali, ☎ 01902 175 131.

Shimla

- **Motoworld**, Navbahar, Shimla, ☎ 0177 2842917.

Vijay Parma,
President of the Himalayan Motorsport Association

Appendix C: Embassies

PAKISTAN

British High Commission
Diplomatic Enclave
Ramna 5
PO Box 1122
Islamabad
☎ +92-51-201-2000
🖹 +92-51-282-4728
💻 www.britishhighcommission.gov.uk/pakistan

United States Embassy
Diplomatic Enclave
Ramna 5
Islamabad
☎ +92-51-208-0000
🖹 +92-51-282-2632
💻 http://islamabad.usembassy.gov

Canadian Embassy
Diplomatic Enclave
Sector G-5
GPO Box 1042
Islamabad
☎ +92-51-227-91-00
🖹 +92-51-227-91-10
💻 www.islamabad.gc.ca

Australian Embassy
Constitution Ave and Ispahani Rd
Diplomatic Enclave No. 1
Sector G-5/4
PO Box 1046
Islamabad
☎ +92-51-282-4345
🖹 +92-51-282-0112
💻 consular.islm@dfat.gov.au

New Zealand Consulate-General
10B/II 4th Zamzama Street
DHA Phase V
Karachi 75500
☎ +92 21 565 6993 / ☎ +92 21 565 6994
🖹 +92 21 565 6995
💻 nzcgpk@gmail.com

CHINA

British Embassy
11 Guang Hua Lu
Jian Guo Men Wai
Beijing 100600
☎ +86 10 5192 4000
💻 www.uk.cn

US Embassy
2 Xiu Shui Dong Jie
Beijing 100600
☎ +86-10-6532-3431 6532-3831
after-hours ☎ +86-10-6532-1910
🖹 +86-10-6532-4153
💻 http://beijing.usembassy-china.org.cn

Canadian Embassy
19 Dongzhimenwai Dajie
Chao Yang District
Beijing 100600
☎ +86-10-6532-3536
🖹 +86-6532-5544
💻 www.beijing.gc.ca

Australian Embassy
21 Dongzhimenwai Dajie
Sanlitun
Beijing 100600
☎ +86-10-6532-2331
🖹 +86-10-6532-4605
💻 www.china.embassy.gov.au

New Zealand Embassy
Ritan Dongerjie No. 1
Chao Yang District
Beijing 100600
China
☎ +86 10 6532 2731
🖹 +86 10 6532 4317
💻 nzemb@eastnet.com.cn
💻 www.nzembassy.com click on 'China'

INDIA

British High Commission
Chanakyapuri
New Delhi 110021
☎ +91-11-2687-2161
🖹 +91-11-2687-2882
💻 www.britishhighcommission.gov.uk/india
💻 postmaster.NewDelhi@fco.gov.uk

US Embassy
Shantipath
Chanakyapuri
110021 New Delhi
☎ +91-11-2419-8000
🖹 +91-11-2419-0017
💻 http://newdelhi.usembassy.gov

Canadian High Commission
7/8 Shantipath
PO Box 5207
Chanakyapuri
New Delhi 110021
☎ +91-11-5178-2000
🖹 +91-11-5178-2020
💻 delhi.consular@international.gc.ca
💻 www.dfait-maeci.gc.ca/New-delhi

Australian Embassy
Australian Compound
No 1/50 G Shantipath
Chanakyapuri
New Delhi
☎ +91-11-5139-9900
🖹 +91-11-2687-2228

New Zealand High Commission
Sir Edmund Hillary Marg
Chanakyapuri
New Delhi 110 021
☎ +91-11-2688 3170
🖹 +91-11-2688 3165
💻 nzhc@ndf.vsnl.net.in
💻 www.nzembassy.com click on 'India'

For all other nationalities see embassy details in India

NEPAL

British Embassy
Lainchaur
PO Box 106
Kathmandu
☎+977-1-441-0583/1281/4588/1590
🖹 +977-1-441-1789
💻 britemb@wlink.com.np
💻 www.britishembassy.gov.uk/nepal

U.S. Embassy
Pani Pokhari
Kathmandu
☎ +977-1-441-1179
🖹 +977-1-444-4981
💻 http://nepal.usembassy.gov

Canadian Embassy
PO Box 4574
Lazimpat
Kathmandu
☎ +977-1-4415-193/389/391/861 4426-885 4425-669
🖹 +977-1-4410-422
💻 cco@canadanepal.org
💻 www.cconepal.org.np

Australian Embassy
Siraj Niwas Compound
500 metres north of Narayan Ghopal Chowk
Bansbari
Kathmandu
☎ +977-1-437-1678
🖹 +977-1-437-1533

New Zealand
See New Zealand High Commission India

BHUTAN

Canadian Consulate
PO Box 201
Thimphu
☎ +975-2-322-109
🖹 +975-2-332-614
💻 canada@druknet.bt

Appendix D: Emergency medical facilities

PAKISTAN

Shifa International Hospital
Sector H-8/4,
Islamabad
☎ +92 (0)51 460 3666
💻 www.shifa.com.pk

CHINA

Beijing United Family Hospital and Clinics
#2 Jiang Tai Lu
Chaoyang District
Beijing 100016
☎ +86 (0)10 6433 3960
Emergency Hotline ☎ +86 (0)10 6433 2345
💻 www.bjunited.com.cn

INDIA

Indraprastha Apollo Hospital
Sarita Vihar,
Delhi-Mathura Road
☎ +91 (0)11 2692 5858 or 5801
💻 www.apollohospdelhi.com

East-West Rescue
24 hour response throughout India, Pakistan and Nepal. Offers medical assistance (by road, by air), hospitalization and repatriation, also liaises with insurance companies.
☎ +91 (0)11 2469 9229 or 2469 0429
💻 www.eastwestrescue.com

NEPAL

CIWEC Clinic
Yak and Yeti Road,
Durbar Marg,
PO Box 12895,
Kathmandu.
☎ +977 (0)1 422 8531 or 424 1732
💻 www.ciwec-clinic.com
Visa and MasterCard accepted

Nepal International Clinic
GPO Box 3596,
Laldurbar,
Kathmandu
☎ +977 (0)1 443 4642 / 443 5357
💻 www.nepalinternationalclinic.com
Visa, MasterCard and American Express accepted

BHUTAN

There is only a referral hospital in Thimphu. Evacuate to Delhi, Kathmandu or Bangkok.

Glossary

AP / MAP / CP / EP	Pricing plan used in some Indian hotels: American Plan (bed plus breakfast, lunch and dinner), Modified American Plan (bed plus breakfast and either lunch or dinner), Continental Plan (bed and breakfast) and European Plan (bed only)
Att	(hotel room) with attached bathroom
Bailey bridge	Truss bridge
Bhagthuk (Tibetan)	Noodle soup
BRO	Border Roads Organization
Cantonment	Military camp
Caravanserai (Persian)	Roadside inn with a large entrance lead into an open courtyard surrounded by stalls or rooms to lodge travellers and their animals
Channa (Hindi)	Chickpea
Chang (Tibetan)	Tibetan version of beer, brewed from barley
Chapatti / chapathi (Hindi)	Flat pancake-like bread
Charpoy (Hindi)	Simple bed made of ropes knotted together on a wooden frame
Chillum (Hindi)	Hash pipe
Chogtse (Tibetan)	Low Tibetan table
Chorten (Tibetan)	Domed structure (stupa) on a square base built to commemorate relics of a Buddhist lama; often topped by a conical spire and crescent moon
Chowk (Hindi and Urdu)	Place where roads meet / intersection
Chowkidar (Hindi)	Caretaker
Chowmein (Mandarin)	Noodle dish
Chu (Tibetan)	River
Com	(hotel room) with common bathroom (not attached)
Crore (Hindi & Urdu)	Numerical unit meaning 10,000,000 (ten million, or one hundreds *lakhs*)
Dahl (Hindi)	Lentils; *dahl baht* is rice and lentils
Dhaba (Hindi)	Roadside restaurant (often basic) in Pakistan and India
Dzong (Tibetan)	Religious fortress
FIT	Travel agent speak for Foreign Independent Traveller ie foreign tourist not on package tour
FWO	Frontier Works Organization
Gali	Pass or defile
Ghat (Hindi, Nepali)	Steps down to a bathing / washing place
Gompa (Tibetan)	Buddhist monastery
GREF	General Reserve Engineering Force
Gulab jamun (Hindi)	Dough balls fried in boiling rosewater-infused oil and served with syrup
Hoodoo	Spire of rock
HPTDC	Himachal Pradesh Tourism Development Corporation
Hydel (Hinglish)	Hydroelectric
STD/ISD (Pakistan, India, Nepal, Bhutan)	Subscriber Trunk Dialling / International Subcriber Dialling; STD works for local and national calls, ISD for international calls
Jawan (Punjabi)	Soldier in the Indian army
Jot (Himachali)	Pass

Kora (Tibetan)	Act of walking around a holy site or object, usually done by pilgrims as an act of devotion
La (Tibetan)	Mountain pass
Lakh (Hindi)	Numerical unit meaning 100,000; a hundred lakhs make a *crore*
Lama (Tibetan)	A senior Buddhist monk
Lassi (Hindi)	Yoghurt and water frothed up and served sweet or salty
Laghman (Uighur)	Noodles in a sauce of onion, garlic, green pepper, beef, tomato and courgette
Mani (Tibetan) wall	Wall built of stones inscribed with holy mantras
Metalled / unmetalled	Tarmac / not tarmac
Momo (Tibetan)	Steamed dumpling
Moraine	Sediment deposited at the side of a glacier
NAPWD (Pakistan)	Northern Areas Public Works Department
NATCO (Pakistan)	Northern Areas Transport Corporation
Nalah / nullah / nala (Hindi)	Tributary stream
Nono (Spitian)	Local ruler
ORS	Oral rehydration salts
PTDC	Pakistan Tourism Development Corporation
Puja (Sankrit)	Religious ceremony (Hindu or Buddhist)
Rajma (Hindi)	Vegetarian dish of kidney beans cooked in spices and garlic
Rasmallai (Hindi)	Paneer balls in milk flavoured with sugar, pistachios and saffron
Sabze / sabzi / sabji (Hindi)	Vegetables fried in oil and spices
Shikhara (Kashmiri)	Skiff boat
Spur	Small ridge that projects sharply from the side of a mountain
Stupa (Indo-Aryan)	See *chorten*
Tata	India's largest commercial vehicle and automobile manufacturer, best known for its trucks
TDCP	Tourism Development Corporation of Punjab
Thali (Hindi)	A plate (often tin) with separate compartments for an all-you-can-eat meal usually comprising rice, dahl, sabze, pickle, curd and chapatti; common in India
Thangka (Tibetan)	Religious painting on scrolled canvas
Thenthuk (Tibetan)	Noodle soup in vegetable broth
Thukpa (Tibetan)	Broth of fresh diced vegetables and noodles
Tongba (Sikkimese)	Millet-based alcoholic beverage
Tsampa (Tibetan)	Ground roast barley; a staple food in remoter parts of Tibet
Tso (Tibetan)	Lake
Wallah (Hindi)	A man who provides a service, eg the chai wallah is the man who sells tea

INDEX

Abbreviations: (**B**) Bhutan; (**In**) India; (**N**) Nepal; (**P**) Pakistan; (**T**) Tibet; (**X**) Xinjiang; (**Y**) Yunnan. (**FH**) Friendship Highway; (**KKH**) Karakoram Highway; (**KtoL**) Kashgar to Lhasa; (**LtoZ**) Lhasa to Zhongdian; (**LSH**) Leh-Srinagar Highway; (**MLH**) Manali-Leh Highway; (**S&K**) Spiti & Kinnaur

Town plan key

- Café/Bar
- Post Office
- Internet
- Museum/gallery
- Fuel
- Bus station
- Where to stay
- Campsite
- Where to eat
- Bank/ATM
- Tourist Information
- Library/bookshop
- Buddhist temple
- Stupa
- Hospital
- Railway station
- Park
- Other

Route map key

- Hotel/ guesthouse
- Camping spot
- Buildings
- Fuel
- Road
- Track
- Bridge
- Pass
- Lake
- River
- Tented accommodation
- Place to eat
- Internet
- Drinking water
- Waterfall
- Viewpoint

TRAILBLAZER

OTHER GUIDES FROM TRAILBLAZER – see p368 for full list

Tibet Overland – a route and planning guide
Kym McConnell, 224pp, 16pp colour maps
ISBN 978-1-873756-41-6, *1st edition,* £12.99
Featuring 16pp of full colour mapping based on satellite photographs, this is a guide for mountain bikers and other road users in Tibet. Includes detailed information on over 9000km of overland routes across the world's highest and largest plateau. Includes Lhasa-Kathmandu route and the route to Everest North Base Camp.
'...a wealth of advice...' ***HH The Dalai Lama***

Adventure Cycle-Touring Handbook – a route & planning guide
Stephen Lord, 320pp, 28 colour & 100 B&W photos
ISBN 978 1 873756 89 8, *1st edition,* £13.99
For anyone planning (or dreaming) about taking a bicycle on a long-distance adventure. This comprehensive manual will make that dream a reality whether it's cycling in Tibet or pedalling from Patagonia to Alaska. Part 1 covers Practicalities; Part 2 includes Route outlines; and Part 3 has Tales from the Saddle.*'The definitive guide to how, where, why and what to do on a cycle expedition'* ***Adventure Travel***

The Silk Roads – a route & planning guide
Paul Wilson, 384pp, 50 maps, 40 colour photos
ISBN 978-1-905864-00-3, *2nd edition,* £13.99
The Silk Road was never a single thread but an intricate web of trade routes linking Asia and Europe. This guide follows all the routes with sections on Turkey, Syria, Iran, Turkmenistan, Uzbekistan, Kyrgyzstan, Kazakhstan, Pakistan and China.

Trekking in Ladakh
Charlie Loram, 288pp, 75 maps, 24 colour photos
ISBN 978-1-873756-75-1, *3rd edition,* £12.99
Fully revised and extended 3rd edition of Charlie Loram's practical guide. Includes 75 detailed walking maps, guides to Leh, Manali and Delhi plus information on getting to Ladakh.
'Extensive...and well researched'. ***Climber Magazine***
'Were it not for this book we might still be blundering about...'
The Independent on Sunday

Adventure Motorcycling Handbook
Chris Scott, 288 pp, 28 colour, 100 B&W photos
ISBN 978-1-873756-80-5, *5th edition,* £12.99
Every red-blooded motor-cyclist dreams of making the Big Trip – this book shows you how. Top ten overland machines, choosing a destination, bike preparation, documentation and shipping, route outlines. Plus – ten first-hand accounts of epic biking adventures worldwide.
'The first thing we did was buy the Adventure Motorcycling Handbook*'*
Ewan McGregor, *The Long Way Round*

Trekking in the Annapurna Region
Bryn Thomas, 288pp, 55 maps, 28 colour photos
ISBN 978-1-873756-68-3, *4th edition,* £11.99
The most popular walking region in the Himalaya. Includes route guides, Kathmandu and Pokhara city guides and getting to Nepal. *'Good guides read like a novel and have you packing in no time. Two from Trailblazer Publications which fall into this category are* 'Trekking in the Annapurna Region' *and* 'Silk Route by Rail' '. ***Today***

TRAILBLAZER

OTHER GUIDES FROM TRAILBLAZER – see p368 for full list

Indian Rail Handbook **due Oct 2008**
Nick Hill & Royston Ellis, 256pp, 80 maps, 30 colour photos
ISBN 978-1-873756-87-4, *1st edition,* £13.99
India has the most comprehensive railway network in the world, with almost all tourist attractions accessible by rail. For most visitors travel by train is the preferred means of transport, the ideal way to see the country. Fully-indexed **rail atlas** of 80 maps showing **all 7326 railway stations**. Suggested itineraries, special trains, how to book tickets, railway history and timetables. Foreword by Mark Tully.

Trans-Siberian Handbook
Bryn Thomas, 480pp, 55 maps, 32 colour photos
ISBN 978-1-873756-94-2, *7th edition,* £13.99
First edition short-listed for the **Thomas Cook Guidebook Awards**. Seventh edition of the most popular guide to the world's longest rail journey. How to arrange a trip, plus a km-by-km guide to the routes. Updated and expanded to include extra information on travelling independently in Russia. New mapping. *'Definitive guide'* **Condé Nast**

Tour du Mont Blanc
Jim Manthorpe, 224pp, 60 maps, 30 colour photos
ISBN 978-1-905864-12-6, *1st edition,* £11.99
At 4807m (15,771ft), Mont Blanc is the highest mountain in western Europe, and one of the most famous mountains in the world. The trail (105 miles, 168km) that circumnavigates the massif, passing through France, Italy and Switzerland, is the most popular long distance walk in Europe. Includes Chamonix and Courmayeur guides.

The Walker's Haute Route – Mt Blanc to the Matterhorn
Alexander Stewart 256pp, 60 maps, 30 colour photos
ISBN 978-1-905864-08-9, *1st edition*, £12.99
From Mont Blanc to the Matterhorn, Chamonix to Zermatt, the 180km walkers' Haute Route traverses one of the finest stretches of the Pennine Alps (the range between Valais in Switzerland and Piedmont and Aosta Valley in Italy). Includes Chamonix and Zermatt guides.

Corsica Trekking – GR20
David Abram, 208pp, 32 maps, 30 colour photos
ISBN 978-1-873756-98-0, *1st edition,* £11.99
Slicing diagonally across Corsica's jagged spine, the legendary red-and-white waymarks of the GR20 guide trekkers across a succession of snow-streaked passes, Alpine meadows, massive boulder fields and forests of pine and oak. Physically demanding from start to finish, it's a superlative 170km, two-week trek. Includes guides to gateway towns: Ajaccio, Bastia, Calvi, Corte & Porte-Vecchio. '*Indispensible*'. ***The Independent*** '*Excellent guide*'. ***The Sunday Times***

New Zealand – The Great Walks
Alexander Stewart, 272pp, 60 maps, 40 colour photos
ISBN 978-1-905864-11-9, *2nd edition,* £12.99 **due Dec 2008**
New Zealand is a wilderness paradise of incredibly beautiful landscapes. There is no better way to experience it than on one of the nine designated Great Walks, the country's premier walking tracks which provide outstanding hiking opportunities for people at all levels of fitness. Also includes guides to Auckland, Wellington, National Park Village, Taumaranui, Nelson, Queenstown, Te Anau and Oban.